Industrial Sociology

McGRAW-HILL SERIES IN SOCIOLOGY

RICHARD T. LaPIERE, *Consulting Editor*

SANFORD DORNBUSCH, *Associate Consulting Editor*

Baber—MARRIAGE AND THE FAMILY

Bergel—URBAN SOCIOLOGY

Blalock—SOCIAL STATISTICS

Bowman—MARRIAGE FOR MODERNS

Davie—NEGROES IN AMERICAN SOCIETY

Dornbusch and Schmid—A PRIMER OF SOCIAL STATISTICS

Freedman, Whelpton, and Campbell—FAMILY PLANNING, STERILITY, AND POPULATION GROWTH

Gittler—SOCIAL DYNAMICS

Goode and Hatt—METHODS IN SOCIAL RESEARCH

House—THE DEVELOPMENT OF SOCIOLOGY

LaPiere—A THEORY OF SOCIAL CONTROL

LaPiere—COLLECTIVE BEHAVIOR

Lemert—SOCIAL PATHOLOGY

Queen and Carpenter—THE AMERICAN CITY

Schneider—INDUSTRIAL SOCIOLOGY

Tappan—CONTEMPORARY CORRECTION

Tappan—CRIME, JUSTICE AND CORRECTION

Tappan—JUVENILE DELINQUENCY

Thompson—POPULATION PROBLEMS

Walter—RACE AND CULTURE RELATIONS

INDUSTRIAL SOCIOLOGY

The Social Relations of Industry and the Community

EUGENE V. SCHNEIDER

Department of Sociology and Anthropology, Bryn Mawr College

McGRAW-HILL BOOK COMPANY, INC.

New York   Toronto   London

1957

INDUSTRIAL SOCIOLOGY

IV

Preface

This book has been written with two aims in mind. The first aim is to describe the social structure of modern large-scale industry and its relations to society. Social structure and societal relations are conceived as being in a state of flux, having developed out of previous forms and changing into new forms. The analysis, therefore, deals not only with the present form of industry, but with its past; it deals also with some of the dynamic forces to which industry is subject. The second aim, not unrelated to the first, is to systematize a large body of existing research in the field of industrial sociology and other disciplines within one framework, in a sense to codify these separate pieces of research and to bring them into meaningful relation to one another.

In order to accomplish both these aims, *Industrial Sociology* is cast within the framework of a body of social theory. This social theory is essentially designed to provide a dynamic analysis of social systems, using particularly the concepts of role, structure, generalized goals, and strain. Industry is analyzed in terms of these concepts as a special type of social system. Furthermore, by viewing industry as a system, it is possible to locate separate pieces of research in an orderly and systematic manner. For instance, this book attempts to bring together, within the theoretical framework, separate studies of managerial motivation, trade-union structure, worker productivity, motives for union activity, and so on.

Where research does not exist, or exists only in fragmentary form, the author has taken the liberty of speculation, always within the theoretical framework of the book. Undoubtedly, there are certain dangers in such procedure. But it should be pointed out that in speculating from the basis of the systematically known into the unknown, we are following good scientific practice. The author would, of course, readily acknowledge that such speculation must be quickly checked against fact. In areas where research is particularly sparse—especially in the area of the relationship between industry and society—he has attempted, in a preliminary way, to fill at least a few gaps on the basis of available data gathered for other purposes. It goes without saying that more directed, more precise, research is needed in these areas.

A word should be said about the point of view from which *Industrial Sociology* is written. There is no gainsaying the fact that by using a theoretical approach to our material, we are imposing a certain selectivity on our data. We will look for certain *types* of roles, seek certain *types* of strains, and be alerted to certain *types* of reactions to strain. To say that all investigations of social data (or of any kind of data) are necessarily selective, is truistic. But the question still remains what kind of selectivity our theoretical scheme is imposing on us. Particularly is this question important in respect to any possible bias toward the material with which we shall be dealing. Industry, perhaps more than some other human organizations, is marked by divergence of interest, and by conflict. Is our theoretical scheme such as to cause us to favor the interests or the concerns, immediate or long-term, of one group or another in industry? This question is not merely a hypothetical one; charges have been raised that industrial sociology as presently constituted is management-oriented, that, in fact, it is a managerial sociology.

The most precise answer, even if not a satisfactory one, that can be given to this question is that the selectivity that results from the use of our theoretical scheme is the same as that which results from the use of this theory in any area of society. That is to say, our theoretical scheme is pitched in such a way as to select out those elements of a social organization which are functioning to maintain the organization, but which *may* also be functioning latently to disrupt it. This is an approach to social phenomena which has proved useful in analyzing the sources of social persistence and social change in other areas. In itself, this approach is not biased toward any element in society or within a social organization. It is, as Robert K. Merton has said of functional theory in general, inherently neutral; it has no ax to grind, no cause to uphold. It can be used equally by whoever would have knowledge of social phenomena.

This is not to say, of course, that this type of selectivity may not violate the expectations of some individuals or groups in or out of industry. The theory used here is, as we have said, a *dynamic* one; that is, it deals not only with persistence and structure, but also with conflict and change. There may be those who are so bound up with the present order of things, or who long so strongly for a presumed past Utopian order, that they wish to close their eyes to these dynamic elements, and by shutting them out of sight, somehow wish them out of existence. For instance, some people might wish to deny that the roots of unionism are to be found in the normal social processes of industry, or that the present structure of trade unionism contains elements of instability. Those who hold to this type of "unenlightened conservatism" will find any theory which even admits of the possibility of change unacceptable, perhaps even frightening. But here, of course, the bias is in those who take this point of view, not in the nature of social science.

The author would like to acknowledge certain debts which are not sufficiently stressed in the body of the text. A heavy burden of debt is owed to his teachers at Harvard University, particularly professors Talcott Parsons, Arthur K. Davis, and Oscar Handlin. He would also like to acknowledge his debt to two former colleagues at the University of Wisconsin, Howard Becker and John Useem. None of the foregoing can, of course, be held responsible for any mistakes he has made in this book. Finally, he would like to thank his colleague, Frederica de Laguna, for her forbearance and patience while this book was being written.

Eugene V. Schneider

Contents

Contents

CHAPTER 1

Introduction

This book deals with the industrial institutions of the United States. The term *industrial institutions* is taken here to mean mainly manufacturing, but it will be used in a wider sense to refer also to transportation, to the production of raw materials, and to the disposal of manufactured goods. In all cases, interest will be centered on the large-scale organization, where, in fact, a large and increasing percentage of American production is concentrated.

The Problem. Industrial institutions form just one part of our large and complex society. Yet social scientists often label it an "industrial society." This title reflects the fact that industrialism is by far our most important mode of production, just as guild production or slave production have predominated in other times and in other cultures. By calling our society "industrial," social scientists also imply that in innumerable direct and indirect ways industrialism places its stamp on our culture as a whole; that it shapes men's lives, molds our institutions, and in the long run helps shape the values, ideals, and goals of society as a whole.

Industry provides livelihoods for millions of Americans, though on a widely varying scale. It requires managers, engineers, foremen, lathe tenders, truck drivers, locomotive engineers, salesmen, psychologists, and ditchdiggers. In a heavily industrialized country, a large part of the working force makes its living within industry. Directly dependent on them are millions of others: parents, wives, husbands, children. Furthermore, a host of Americans are indirectly dependent on industry for livelihood; this host includes the merchant in the industrial city, the possessor of bonds and collector of dividends, or the farmer who supplies raw materials to the factories. The economic fate of these people is just as surely tied to industry as that of the workingman or the business executive.

Furthermore, industrial institutions have changed the mode and standard of life of most Americans. The floods of goods pouring from our

1

factories have radically altered the physical environment of many homes, changed the nature of our political institutions, had profound effects on recreation, altered the dress of multitudes, even changed the nature of morality. To name just one typical industrial product, the automobile alone has had incalculable effects on the lives of almost all Americans, whether through provision of a cheap means of transportation to a distant job, through changes in the patterns of courtship, or by altering the meaning of recreation. Myriads of other industrial products have had similar, if less drastic, effects on our social life.

Industry has had direct and indirect influence, sometimes of a drastic nature, on other institutions in society. For instance, it has both directly and indirectly molded the shape of the American family. American families have felt the effects of industrial prosperity or depression. More directly, the demands of nightwork, the absence from home of mothers working in industry, industrial employment for adolescents, all these factors have helped to shape the structure of what is designated as the working-class family. Similarly, industry has helped to shape the nature of social stratification; thus it has created a large "working class" in all industrial societies. A large section of the middle class is composed of office workers, skilled shop workers, engineers, and others employed in industry. Industry has also had strong influence on the political institutions of America. To name just one influence, politics in the United States is strongly influenced by industrial pressure groups; organized management and organized labor are the best example of such groups. Political campaigns in the United States are often waged around industrial issues; for instance, labor laws or tariff laws. Politicians appeal to groups which are industrially based in whole or in part; thus, they try to influence the "labor" vote, the "business" vote, the "white-collar" vote. Further analysis would show how industry influences other institutions: education, religion, recreation, the armed services.

There can be no doubt that industry has considerable effect on the personalities found in American society. By virtue of playing industrial roles, men and women must adopt the values and goals of those roles. Thus a drive for maximum profit, or for maximum efficiency, or for maximum rationality, becomes a part of the personalities of men and women in industry. As a part of the personality, these goals and values channel effort and thought, hopes and fears, ambitions, love and hostility. In another sense, industry provides an environment which helps mold the personality or which forms conditions to which the personality must react. Thus the industrial workingman works within an environment of specialization, routinization, and mechanization, which in many ways affects his innermost thoughts and attitudes. Indirectly, industry affects personality in so far as it helps shape the form of the family and other agencies of personality formation. By helping determine the relationship of husbands to wives, of parents to children, and of children to each other, industry is helping to determine the types of personalities which will emerge from childhood.

The cultural product of man—his art, philosophy, music, painting, and science—also reflect the nature of our industrial institutions. For instance, modern man tends to view nature as rational, impersonal, and governed by inexorable laws. This view of nature finds expression in science, in philosophy, even in the arts. Veblen has suggested that this view is related to the rational, impersonal, inexorable nature of modern machine production.[1] In the Middle Ages, nature was looked on quite differently; it was considered as controlled by animate forces such as gods, spirits, or devils, in precisely the same way as a guild craftsman might control and shape raw materials with the use of his tools.

On a less high-flown plane, there can be no doubt that industry is a vitally important factor in forming the complex social problems of our time. Controversial social movements such as the union movement, with all its significance for American life, have been the direct result of industrialism. The strikes and lockouts which have accompanied trade unionism have been complex social issues in themselves and have given rise to other social problems. Industrialism has contributed heavily to economic cycles, and the social problems raised by these cycles can hardly be overestimated. Industrialism has given rise to cutthroat competition and white-collar crime; it has helped foster an often tendentious system of advertising. It has, furthermore, created great social problems concerning the relationship of man to machine, of industry to society.

Thus, industry is like the center of a web whose strands reach out to embrace almost every aspect of society, culture, and personality. Whoever would understand the nature of modern society must first understand the nature of its industrial institutions. Common-sense knowledge of so vast and intricate an institution cannot be trusted; such knowledge is necessarily limited and is often distorted by bias or interest. It is the aim of this book to study systematically one particular aspect of industry, which may be labeled preliminarily the "social aspect of industry," and the effects of industry as a whole on some sections of society. In order to understand the framework within which industry will be studied, it will be necessary to say something about the development of an industrial sociology.

The Rise of Industrial Sociology. The appearance of the sociologist as a student of industry is quite recent, and it must be understood as the result of several converging factors.

[1] Thorstein Veblen, *The Instinct of Workmanship,* The Macmillan Company, New York, 1914, pp. 303–304.

In the first place, the rise of industrial sociology is to be attributed to a growing interest of both industry and society in the social factor in production. The realization has been steadily growing that industrialism creates and is dependent on the social cooperation of hordes of men, that industry is itself a vast social organization and is composed of a myriad of lesser social organizations. In an industry as large and as complex as that existing in the United States today, this social factor cannot be taken for granted; there must be systematic knowledge of industrial social organization and of the problems in human relations arising from that social organization.

In the second place, the rise of industrial sociology has been the result of certain developments within sociology itself. In one sense its scope has changed greatly in recent years. Traditional sociology was concerned either with a few special "social problems" or with vast historical and even philosophical questions. Thus it concentrated, on the one hand, on such areas as the family and marriage, juvenile delinquency, crime, penology, prostitution, or suicide. On the other hand it was concerned with sweeping questions about the inner nature of society, its origins and its destiny. Great "systems of sociology" were created; some of these "systems" attempted to relate all social phenomena to some underlying principle or force, whether economics, sex, or cycles.

Modern sociology has moved away from both these extremes. It has altered its fields of investigation to include new types of social groups and social relationships. This development has rested on the realization that human beings act in social groups, large or small, formal or informal, tightly knit or loosely organized. The sociologist today may investigate the organization of a community, morale in the armed forces, or the structure of the medical profession. His interests may range from the corner gang to the community as a whole, from the executive board meeting to informal groups among workingmen; he may study the entire structure of an industry.

As sociology has altered its sphere of investigation, it has developed new methods of research. This has meant the development both of new techniques of investigation and of new types of theories. Sociological research uses highly refined questionnaires and schedules in its investigations. It applies to its data complicated scaling techniques; it relies heavily on statistics. Of late there has been an increasing tendency to apply nonstatistical mathematics to social data. The search for new techniques is a constant, and seemingly increasingly fruitful, one.

Sociological theory tends to concentrate on problems of limited scope. Within these areas it seeks for limited answers; e.g., sociological theory may be concerned with the relationship of certain types of personalities to certain types of groups, it may be concerned with the process of decision making, or it may describe the influence of social classes on human action. One sociologist has called these theories the "theories of the middle range."[2]

These developments explain why sociologists have become interested in industrial problems, but the student may, nevertheless, ask what new contributions sociology can make to the study of industry. This question is especially pertinent because extensive investigations of social factors in industry have been carried out by economists, industrial psychologists, industrial engineers, and many other types of experts. In addition, many industries maintain large personnel departments which deal with the practical problems of social relationships, and which have evolved a considerable body of practical and theoretical knowledge in the field. Before we can define the special contributions of industrial sociology, it will be necessary to say something about the basic difference between sociology and other social sciences.

Broadly speaking, there are two types of social science.[3] First, there are social sciences which deal with a special area of social life. Political science, for instance, is interested in the structure and sources of authority in society. Economics is concerned with the rational production and exchange of goods in the market place. Psychology, on the other hand, is an example of a generalizing social science. Psychology deals with the formation and reactions of the human personality in general. Psychological principles apply to human behavior in *all* spheres of life; political, economic, familial, etc. Sociology is *both* a generalizing and a specializing social science, and it makes contributions to the study of industry in both its aspects.

In so far as sociology is a specializing science, it concentrates on certain types of data which other social sciences either ignore or treat as peripheral to their main interests. For instance, the existence of informal groups among workingmen has long been known to the economist or to the industrial engineer. However, to these experts, the informal group has been merely an irregularity, an aberration, or a triviality, depending on the circumstances. To the sociologist, on the other hand, the informal group is a central object of interest; he has long dealt with its exact counterparts in the clique or the gang. As another example, the soci-

---

[2] See the discussion by Robert K. Merton in *Essays in Sociological Theory: Pure and Applied* by Talcott Parsons, Free Press, Glencoe, Ill., 1949, p. 14. Incidentally, the present author does not maintain that these latest developments in sociology are necessarily improvements, or that modern sociology is universally superior to traditional sociology. Certainly there are already signs that the overspecialization of modern sociology has had certain unfavorable results; e.g., an overconcern with the trivial, a failure to understand the significance of facts, and a worship of facts for their own sake.

[3] Pitirim A. Sorokin, *Society, Culture, and Personality*, Harper & Brothers, New York, 1947, pp. 6–18.

ologist studies the formal social structure of industry as a variant of a type of organization called *bureaucracy*. The sociologist has known and studied bureaucracies in other cultures. There are many other areas of similar interest to the sociologist in industry, which are analogous to areas with which the sociologist has had experience; for instance, a board meeting is a type of small social group, conflict between management and labor is a type of social conflict. It should be noted that the sociologist can bring to the study of social life in industry the same methods of research and the same theoretical insights with which he has worked in the community.

As a generalizing science, sociology aims at quite other goals. Here it is concerned not with this or that social group but with the properties of groups in general. Thus as a generalist, the sociologist studies roles and statuses, values, motivations, social attitudes; he seeks for laws of social processes, laws of the development and change of social groups.[4] These general interests cut across the fields of other experts, such as personnel managers, economists, or labor historians, all of whom deal with the resultants of group action but not with the group action itself. Thus the sociologist may consider industrial conflict, morale, productivity, or union organization *as examples of social processes*. To take another example, the sociologist as a generalist deals with the various types of action which are found in all sorts of social situations; thus, he recognizes the existence of rational action, affective action, tradition-directed action, or action motivated by idealistic reasons. For instance, the sociologist might point out that a great deal of the action which occurs in industry is not rational action at all by the usual definition. The manager, worker, foreman, or engineer is capable of acting toward his fellow men because he seeks their approbation, because he fears them, hates them, or loves them. Furthermore, it is not at all clear that what is rational for management is rational for the worker, e.g., in regard to what constitutes a fair wage.

Thus, as a generalizing science, sociology cuts across other social sciences; it forms a parallel discipline to industrial psychology. Just as industrial psychology concentrates on the individual in industry, so sociology deals with the social factors in industry.

The Scope and Plan of this Book. The scope of this book has been determined partially in relationship to the special contributions which it is believed industrial sociology can make to the study of industry. In accordance with the generalizing aspect of sociology, industrial organization will be analyzed as a particular type of social institution. This will involve a study of the structure, roles, strains, values, and other component parts and processes of an industrial organization. It will also involve

---

[4] These concepts are more fully discussed in the next chapter.

a study of the relationships between that organization and the personalities of its members. Finally, it will be necessary to discuss the relationships between industry and other institutions in society. On the other hand, the analysis will also show the influence of the special findings of sociology; thus there will be found in this work discussions of specific forms of groups and other types of social organizations. Although the point of view of this book is sociological, no attempt will be made to maintain hard and fast lines between sociology and other disciplines concerned with industry. Throughout this work will be found contributions from industrial psychology, from the literature of industrial management, from history, from economics, and from other fields as well.

The plan of this book is as follows. In the next chapter, there will be a discussion of the major theoretical concepts of sociology which are employed in this book. Although these concepts reflect a certain interpretation of sociology, it is believed that they will prove acceptable to those whose background and training as sociologists have been in other directions. At any rate, the author has attempted for the most part to employ such concepts as have received a rather wide acceptance; these concepts, furthermore, have been drawn from varying sources. This does not mean that the author favors an eclectic approach to his subject; on the contrary, a certain point of view toward the material is maintained throughout this book. It does mean, however, that there has been a definite attempt to avoid dogmatism; concepts are used in this book only when they serve to throw light on problems in industry.

Further in Part 1, there is a brief discussion of the rise of modern industry, from its beginnings in England at the close of the Middle Ages, to its more recent development in the United States. This section is intended to provide an historical perspective to the area of our interest. It is hoped that an appreciation of the history of industry will demonstrate to the student the dynamic nature of industry. Furthermore, history has a special value in that it provides the material for comparisons of the various stages of development in industry.

Part 2 of this book will be concerned with the social structure of industry. The method of analysis here is to center attention on the relationship between personality and social roles. Individual chapters are devoted to the roles of management and the worker. The role of the engineer, the white-collar worker, the foreman, and the research man are considered more briefly. Along with the discussion of role and personality other elements of industrial organization, such as authority, lines of communication, and status, are discussed. A considerable amount of attention is devoted to the strains which arise in the plant at various levels; there are special sections on managerial failure, industrial fatigue, boredom, and other types of strains. The aim of Part 2 is to provide an over-all picture of the social organization of industry, of the relationship of its several parts, and of the strains which arise within that organization.

Part 3 is concerned with the labor movement. This movement is often thought of as a unique phenomenon, something quite outside of industry, something essentially economic or political in nature. But it will be the position of this book that from one point of view the trade union is an integral part of modern industry. Certainly some sort of trade-union movement, formal or informal, conservative or radical, with a limited philosophy or a universal one, seems inevitably to arise, soon or late, in industrial societies. Furthermore, the trade-union movement has had profound countereffects on industry. Trade unionism not only has important economic effects on industry but also induces important changes in the social structure of the factory.

In Part 3 there is a discussion of some of the major forms of relationships between management and labor in the United States. Here the discussion will center on the two major modes of adjustment provided in our society today: industrial conflict, and collective bargaining. The scope of the discussion extends from the local relationships between foremen and shop stewards, on the one hand, to industry-wide bargaining and conflict, on the other.

Part 4 deals with some of the manifold relationships between industry and society. The selection here has been necessarily arbitrary, but in general most attention has been paid to those areas of society which bear some rather direct relationship to industry. Besides a general chapter on the nature of industrial communities, there are special chapters on the relationship of social class to industry, of the family to industry, of politics to industry, of minority groups to industry. A final chapter discusses industry and social change and seeks to suggest several alternative directions in which industry may develop in the future.

PART ONE

Social Theory and Productive Systems

CHAPTER 2

Industry and Sociological Theory

We have described the aim of this book as the analysis of the social structure of industry. This means that we shall cull out some data from all those available and ignore others. But in what terms shall we make our selection? To answer this question it is necessary to describe the frame of reference in which this book is set. We shall now, therefore, discuss briefly those concepts, sociological and nonsociological, which we shall be using in this work.

Role. Perhaps the single most important concept that we shall employ is that of *role*. By "role"—a term borrowed from drama—is meant the part that an individual plays as a result of occupying some position or *status* in life.[1] Thus by virtue of the fact that a male is born into a family he plays the role of a son. Similarly, human beings, as the result of occupying other statuses, play such roles as father, mother, factory worker, manager, friend, and soldier. All these are separate and well-defined roles. Of course, no one individual can play all the roles in a society. There are far too many of them, and some are incompatible with each other, for instance, the roles of mother and father. But every human being plays many roles. Thus a man may be a factory worker, a father, a son, a brother, a member of a church, a steward in a trade union, and so on.

What makes the role of such importance is the fact that it largely determines how human beings will act in certain areas. For instance, the role of father demands certain duties, affords certain privileges, and determines certain relationships to others. Similarly, the role of factory worker implies certain duties and certain rewards, certain relationships to management and its representatives, and other relationships to fellow workers. We may say, then, that roles are *structured* or *patterned* in definite ways to specify duties, rewards, punishments, and even attitudes and beliefs. This is not to say that roles determine all human

---

[1] Ralph Linton, *The Study of Man,* Appleton-Century-Crofts, Inc., New York, 1936, pp. 113–114.

action; much action is not role-patterned at all, while even role-patterned action admits of much variation, depending on the role played and the personality of the role player.

While roles determine the general direction of action, yet it is important to realize that no two individuals play the same roles in exactly the same way. Individuals *do* differ as fathers, managers, workers; and the situations which they face are never exactly the same. One father must relate himself to a wife with one type of personality and to children with other types of personalities; for another father the situation may be completely different. Similarly, the personality which one man brings to the role of factory worker and the way in which he plays his role may differ radically from the personality of fellow workers and *their* ways of playing roles.

This leads us to an important point: the difference between individual personality and role. The role, of course, is real only as a consequence of human action. But any role represents merely one aspect, and perhaps a limited aspect, of human action. The personality, on the other hand, is made up of all the attitudes toward, ideas of, beliefs in, and knowledge about the environment with which the living organism must interact.[2] The roles which the individual must play may modify his personality, mold it, even become a part of it; but the personality is always something more than any one role or even than any combination of roles.

The roles which individuals play are, then, in some sense independent of, external to, individual personalities. The individual finds that if he does not conform to the role and its expectations he will be punished, and if he does conform he will be rewarded. For instance, one of the expectations of the manager's role is that he be successful in maximizing profits and in cutting costs; this is the way people in this status are expected to act. If the manager succeeds in his role—e.g., by maximizing profits—then he will be rewarded in terms of financial power or increased prestige, or in other ways; if he fails he will be punished, perhaps by removal from the role. In the latter case some one else will be found to fill the role. At all events, the role has a life, a sort of existence, apart from the personalities who fill it at any one time.

How can roles exist apart from the individuals who play them? Generally speaking, the answer may be found in the fact that some roles are a part of the culture of a given society. By a culture we mean "that complex whole which includes knowledge, belief, art, morals, law, custom and other capabilities and habits acquired by man in a society."[3] Culture is our social heritage; it consists, on one hand, of the habits and ideas, and, on the other, of all the material objects—machines, buildings,

---

[2] Talcott Parsons, *The Social System*, Free Press, Glencoe, Ill., 1951, p. 17.
[3] E. B. Tylor, *Primitive Culture*, Brentano's, New York, 1924, p. 1.

tools—which have descended from the past. Thus the role of factory manager, or the role of shopworker, are parts of our culture, of our social heritage. These roles, like the culture as a whole, are older than any individual now alive, and they will, in all probability, outlast any living person.

But culture not only determines what roles exist in a society; it also provides certain norms or values by which roles are to be played. By a value is meant a "criterion or standard for selection among the alternatives of orientation" to action.[4] Values determine the definitions of "good" workers or "bad" workers, "good" managers or "bad" managers, "good" engineers or "bad" engineers. A value is always accompanied by some emotional charge; people feel emotionally that some way of acting is right, some way wrong. Consequently some individuals are adjudged "good" or "moral" or "admirable"; others are adjudged "immoral" or "bad" or "despicable." Feelings of anger, hostility, love, or admiration may accompany these judgments. Values differ from society to society, depending on the culture. Thus there is one set of values respecting the family, sex, or work in a primitive society like Samoa,[5] and there is quite a different set of values for family, sex, and work in our own. For instance the need to maximize profits or wages, the need to work hard, reflect values peculiar to our own and closely related societies; such values are found only rarely in other parts of the world. Even *within* societies there may be found somewhat differing cultural contexts, and therefore somewhat different values. Although America is a single culture, the subcultures of management and labor are sufficiently diverse so that these two groups possess somewhat different values toward each other's roles. As we shall see, these differing values greatly affect relationships between management and labor in many areas.

Roles, in turn, can, at times, strongly influence values, and even create them. Each generation not only inherits culture but helps create it. The ways in which roles must be played, as well as the ways in which they relate to each other, are strongly influenced by the physical and social environment. This means that it may be necessary to create certain values in order to play a role at all. This may be seen in the case of family members who must, if the family is to survive, learn values of cooperation and compatibility. Similarly, the facts that the worker is concerned with automatic machinery which he does not control, that he is relatively powerless as an individual, that opportunities for leaving his role are scarce, necessitate the creation of certain values favoring collective

[4] Parsons, *op. cit.*, p. 12.
[5] See Margaret Mead, *Coming of Age in Samoa*, The New American Library of World Literature, Inc., New York, 1928. It is possible that Mead's view of Samoan society is one-sided, but her major point remains valid.

action, equality, loyalty to fellow workers, and so on. It will be a major
task of this book to see how values, as well as action, are determined by
role playing. Here it is necessary to emphasize the fact that the relationship between roles and values is an interdependent one; roles create
or influence values, values modify roles.

Role and Personality. Although role and personality are distinct, they
are at the same time related to each other. How are personalities motivated to play certain roles? For instance, how is it that individuals are
motivated to play roles in industry, and to play them well or ill as the
case may be? Or, to put it another way, what satisfactions or rewards
or inducements can the role afford to individuals so that they consent
to fill the role? Much hinges on the answers to these questions, for they
involve the over-all relationship of individuals and industry, the morale
of industry, and perhaps also the strength of industry in the society.

In general, it would seem that individuals are induced to play roles,
and to play them well, in one of two ways. Either the individual is made
to "want" to play a certain role by making the role and its values a part
of the personality; or he is brought to play the role because of certain
pressures put on him, rewards or punishments. In either case, the process
of "role taking" is a process of learning; it is not something innate in
the individual, as it is innate in the ant or the bee to play certain roles
in heap or hive. In fact, it seems certain that any normal person can
learn to play any role for which he is biologically suited. Undoubtedly
different roles make varying demands on intelligence, strength, emotions;
but there is little reason to think that any roles, except a very few, make
insuperable demands in any of these ways. Therefore there is equally
little reason to suppose that innate biological capacity determines who
will become a manager, who a foreman, and who will "remain" a factory
worker. This is not to say that the worker and the manager are necessarily equally endowed; rather it would seem that any difference which
exists between them is very likely to have been acquired through a
process of learning to take roles, beginning with the process of internal-
izing roles.

If, as has been pointed out, almost anyone can learn to play any role,
then it must follow that human nature is flexible to a very wide degree;
that there is very little of "essential" human nature which we inherit as
we inherit our bodily frame and eye color. In fact there is little reason
to suppose that the human infant is born with more than rudimentary
sets of drives, which are related to the basic needs of metabolism, reproduction, movement, and relaxation. But except for these elementary
drives, all other components of the personality—values, attitudes, and
tastes—are the result of cultural conditioning. Even the answers to such
basic needs as hunger are strongly conditioned culturally. *What* the in-

fant will learn to want to eat, *how* he will eat it, and how many times a day—all these are almost certainly determined by the culture. There is hardly any evidence to suggest that there are in human beings any of the more elaborate "instincts" about which there has been speculation from time to time; for instance, an instinct to lead or an instinct to follow, a predatory instinct, or an instinct of workmanship. In fact, it seems very doubtful whether there are any role-playing instincts at all. This is not to say that some individuals may not have strong drives to lead, or strong needs to follow, etc. It is to say, however, that such needs or tendencies to play certain roles are learned. All this is not merely a matter of conjecture; anthropological literature strikingly demonstrates the amazing flexibility and adaptability of the human organism, the varying róles that it can be taught to play.[6]

It seems certain now that the process of learning to play roles begins very early. Leaving out the possibility of prenatal learning and of learning in infancy, it can be said with some surety that the process of role taking begins when the child first begins to react to other people in a conscious way; that is, when he comes to understand the meaning of his own act to others, when he can see himself as others see him, when he becomes aware of himself.[7] Perhaps the first role which the infant learns to take is in relationship to his parents; he learns that there are some standards which he is expected to meet, some forms of behavior he is expected to follow. From these beginnings, the child broadens his capacity to take roles and to learn the values involved in the roles.[8] In the game, the child must learn to play complex roles, intimately related to the roles of all the other players. Thus in a game of baseball the child must not only learn the role appropriate to his position on the team, but he must learn the expectations of all the members of the team to his role and to each other's roles. Similarly, the child learns to play roles in school, and later, when he assumes the statuses of adulthood, in the occupational world and in marriage. To a varying extent these roles and their values are *internalized* in the personality; that is, they become a part of the personality. Certainly role taking is one of the major processes in the formation of adult personality.

Although the ability to learn roles continues throughout life, there is considerable evidence to suggest that the earliest roles (and values) that

---

[6] The interested student may wish to consult the following: George Peter Murdock, *Our Primitive Contemporaries,* The Macmillan Company, New York, 1934; Clyde Kluckhohn, *Mirror for Man,* McGraw-Hill Book Company, Inc., New York, 1949, chaps. I, II, VIII; William J. Herskovits, *Man and His Works,* Alfred A. Knopf, Inc., New York, 1949, chaps. 33–36; Ruth Benedict, *Patterns of Culture,* Penguin Books, Inc., New York, 1934.

[7] See George Herbert Mead, *Mind, Self, and Society,* University of Chicago Press, Chicago, 1934, pp. 144–152. Copyright, 1934, by The University of Chicago.

[8] *Ibid.,* pp. 152–164.

are learned are of especial importance. The roles which are learned and internalized early seem to be of exceptional strength and durability in the personality. Furthermore, this early learning is likely to influence strongly the way in which roles are played in later life. Thus the child's attitude toward his parents may, in later life, influence attitudes toward authority figures, such as foremen. But while early learning is undoubtedly of importance in determining attitudes toward later roles, it by no means follows[9] that individuals cannot overcome or at least modify early training, although this may be difficult. Thus even a person bred in a nonurban, nonindustrial society may learn the factory worker's role. Furthermore, practically every adult must learn to play some roles for which he has not been prepared by early training, for instance, in the army or in the occupational world.

Let us sum up what has been said thus far about role. Three aspects of the role concept have been discussed. First, we have tried to show that roles channel human action in certain directions. The individual who occupies a certain status must act in a certain way, within certain limits. Secondly, we discussed briefly the relationships between values and roles. We attempted, thirdly, to show that role playing is learned and that in some cases roles may become a part of the personality. We shall now examine those cases where role and personality are separate. When such a separation exists, individuals must be somehow motivated to play roles.

Generalized Goals and Role Playing. Many sorts of motives, drives, or goals have been thought, at some time or other, to explain all man's actions in society. It has been held that man is essentially an economic animal, or a sexual one, or a religious one; that he is moved only by self-interest, or by altruism, or by a desire for power, or by anxiety in the face of a threatening world. Thus the orthodox Freudian considers religion as a distorted form of a basically sexual urge,[10] the Nietzschean considers love as a manifestation of the drive to power. Actually there is little evidence to support any of these monocausal theories. Comparative studies of many different types of society, ranging from the most complex to the most primitive, reveal that man may act in society through a wide variety of motives. He may act through narrow economic motives; but he may also act through anger, grief, love, or a desire for recognition. In fact, whatever motives have driven men to act in any sphere at all

---

[9] The reason for this note of caution is that some psychologists have tended to explain *all* adult action as a result of early socialization. Thus if the worker is hostile to his foreman this is explained as a transference of hatred from the father of the worker to the foreman. Actually, as we shall see, there are plenty of frustrations in the role of the worker which could account for the hatred toward the foreman.

[10] Sigmund Freud, *The Future of an Illusion,* translated by W. D. Robson-Scott, Hogarth Press, Ltd., London, 1928.

may drive him to act in social situations. To list all these motives in all their variations and modulations would be an almost hopeless task. Instead we shall follow another tack.

In examining the roles which exist in any society, it will be found that there is "built into" each role, so to speak, rewards for those who play the roles and play them properly, and sanctions for those who fail in either respect. These rewards are compatible with a very wide range of human motives. Sometimes the rewards are means for fulfilling some other motive; sometimes the rewards directly fulfill the motive. These "built-in" rewards we shall, following Parsons, call "generalized goals."[11] What makes this approach to the problem seem promising is that by concentrating on the generalized goals provided by roles, the problem of motivation in role playing is greatly simplified. Thus, it seems possible to speak of as few as four major categories of generalized goals, some or all of which are provided by the roles men are expected to play, and which act as magnets to attract and hold men to these roles.

1. The instrumental goal. One of the generalized goals provided by roles is the opportunity to attain other ends. For instance, a man will play the role of student in order to be able to fill later the role of businessman or professional. Prisoners play their roles in order to avoid additional punishment. Especially in occupational roles, the goal sought is often pecuniary; the role provides means to achieve a certain standard of living. Thus many factory workers play their roles not for any intrinsic satisfaction they might derive from them, but in order to be able to fulfill other goals outside the factory. In this case, the higher the wage the more meaningful is the role to the worker. In all such instances, the real wants of the individual are not being met within the role but outside it. In one sense the instrumental goal acts as a form of coercion; the actor *must* play a certain role if other wants are to be achieved.

2. Recognition. A second major generalized goal, provided by some roles, is the opportunity for recognition. By recognition is meant here a feeling of being respected, "looked up to," valued by other *significant* human beings. The italicized word in the last sentence is important. Undoubtedly, there are some people who can develop a feeling of self-esteem without reference to the opinions of others. Such people are, however, rare. For most people recognition involves attracting the favorable attention of people who are highly regarded in the situation. The type of significant "other" varies widely from group to group; it may be one's "boss," one's wife, or one's friends whose good opinion is desired. It should be noted that the converse also holds here; many individuals are strongly motivated by the fear of losing recognition. As we

[11] Talcott Parsons, *Essays in Sociological Theory: Pure and Applied*, Free Press, Glencoe, Ill., 1949, pp. 37–39.

shall see, the amount of recognition that the playing of a given role affords is crucial in determining the morale of those who are playing the role.

The desire for recognition not only may motivate the individual to play a role, but it may motivate him to attempt to acquire a status of a higher order, that is, one having more prestige, honor, or privilege. Such action is usually designated *status striving*. It should be noted that such striving is an important motive in our type of society. In contrast, in many nonindustrial (and less dynamic) societies, statuses are not open to the ambitious to the extent that they are in our society, and status striving is comparatively unimportant. Even within our own society, as we shall see, status striving is limited to certain sections of the population.

3. *Security*. Another generalized goal which may be attained through role playing is security. Roles may offer economic, social, or psychological security. For instance, the role of teacher may offer economic security; the role of an army officer may offer economic and psychological security. In bureaucracies, security may be attached to higher roles or may be acquired with seniority. In all the cases mentioned here, security is offered as a reward for playing a role or as an inducement for striving to higher roles.

There is another way in which security may operate as a general inducement to role playing. Here the goal is essentially a negative one. The individual may be constrained to play a role through fear, timidity, anxiety, or desire to avoid the strange and unexpected. This negative goal will motivate individuals who are cautious, conservative, concerned above all with making secure or guaranteeing a stake in the role. As we shall see, this negative aspect of security is of great importance in a complex, industrial society where livelihood and advancement depend on the demands of the market or the impersonal judgment of superiors.

4. *Response*. A fourth type of generalized goal is the opportunity which certain roles afford to form satisfying social relationships in which the individual feels reasonably certain of the continuing favorable responses of people important to him.[12] This generalized goal we shall label *response*. It should be noted that the goal of response implies the need not only to receive affection but also to give it. The importance of the response goal, in family relationships, for example, will be immediately apparent. But what is not so apparent is that the goal of response may assume important dimensions precisely in a social organization like that of a factory which is marked by anonymity, impersonality, and the absence of many close, well-knit groups.

[12] See W. I. Thomas, *The Unadjusted Girl*, Little, Brown & Company, Boston, 1923, p. 17.

It often happens, however, that the recognition, security, and response which a high-ranking role affords may come to be symbolized in a high salary—high, at least, relative to other salaries in the same general area. In cases like this it may seem that the pecuniary return is the motivating goal, whereas in actuality other goals are of decisive importance. For instance, the salary of a Supreme Court justice is higher than that of other justices; nevertheless it would probably be a mistake to assume that it is the financial reward which motivates men to seek seats on the Supreme Court. Rather the goals of recognition and response are probably more important in this case. Similar cases will often be found among high-ranking industrial roles. This is not to say, of course, that financial goals are always symbols for other goals, as some have assumed —that behind the expressed desire for a raise in wages, for instance, is a desire for more security or response. It is always necessary to distinguish between those cases where the financial reward is an instrumental goal and those where it acts as a symbol for other ends.

The four generalized goals mentioned here are not, of course, the *only* goals which roles may offer. For instance, W. I. Thomas, who pioneered in this field, spoke of "opportunity for new experience" as a generalized goal.[13] In certain cases satisfaction may result from the role itself; for instance, the teacher may derive pleasure from the process of instruction, the artist from the process of creation. But the four goals listed above are more commonly found to motivate role playing; thus manager, foreman, workers, and technicians alike may be seeking response and security in their roles. In the second place, each role offers varying means for achieving the four generalized goals. In some cases these means may be contradictory. For instance, the factory manager may seek for security in his role by maximizing production, but the worker may seek security by limiting production.

Roles differ sharply in the extent to which they offer these generalized goals as rewards to those who play the roles and play them well. For instance, the role of the successful manager affords, as we shall see, security, response, and recognition; it also affords high financial return not only as a symbol of these other goals but also as a means for achieving a high standard of living and high status in the community. On the other hand, certain roles may be filled only for instrumental reasons. In general, it seems safe to say that the more goals a role can fulfill, the more eagerly will the role be sought after and the more avidly will it be played. Where a role can, at the same time, both provide these generalized goals and yet be internalized as a portion of the personality, there is an optimum motivation for role playing. But it is doubtful

[13] *Ibid.*, pp. 4–12.

whether such roles exist in industry to any extent; perhaps they are found most frequently in families or in other intimate groups.

The Social System. In this book we shall not be considering roles or personalities in general but, rather, a series of interrelated roles and personalities clustering around a process of production. These interrelated roles are not distributed in a random fashion; they are related to each other in definite patterns. That is, they constitute a social system.

Social systems may differ from each other in several ways. The social system may be of the most varied sort or extent; it may be limited to a group of workingmen at a bench, or it may include the entire factory, or the society as a whole. Furthermore, it may unite people who are playing similar roles (as in the case of a friendship group in the factory), or it may unite individuals who play roles as diverse as that of manager and floorsweeper. The social system may involve only direct face-to-face relationships, or it may bind together individuals who will never see each other.[14] There are many other ways, too numerous to mention here, in which social systems vary.

The social system should be clearly distinguished from the social group. A *social group* is one form of a social system, marked by a specially high rate of interaction between members, who are set off by sharply defined interests and sentiments from other individuals.[15] We shall see that the factory is always a more or less well developed social system, but it is usually only the small-scale factory which approximates a social group. On the other hand, within any factory will be found many small groups, embedded in the larger social system, yet distinct from other parts of the social system.

Many ways of interpreting the social system exist, but in this book we will use what has been called the structural-functional theory.[16] This approach is closely related to theories used in biology and psychology. The biologist begins with the structure of the healthy organism. He then proceeds to study how the various parts of the body function to maintain this organism; e.g., how the heart supplies blood to the body, how the blood carries oxygen to the tissues and removes waste material. The sociologist uses much the same type of theory in analyzing the

[14] This distinction is sometimes expressed as the difference between "primary" groups and "secondary" groups. See Charles H. Cooley, *Social Organization*, Charles Scribner's Sons, New York, 1924, chap. II. Cooley did not use the term "secondary group."

[15] Robin M. Williams, *Modern American Society*, Alfred A. Knopf, Inc., New York, 1951, p. 446.

[16] For a detailed discussion of the structural-functional approach, see Parsons, *Essays in Sociological Theory: Pure and Applied*, pp. 17ff, and Parsons, *The Social System*, pp. 19–21. See also Robert K. Merton, *Social Theory and Social Structure*, Free Press, Glencoe, Ill., 1949, chap. I; Marion J. Levy, Jr., *The Structure of Society*, Princeton University Press, Princeton, N.J., 1952.

social system. His point of reference is the ongoing, "healthy" social system. He then proceeds to show how various parts of the system function to maintain the system as a whole. It is very important, however, not to make the mistake of considering society as a direct analogy of the body; that is, it is not valid to think of the society as possessing a nervous system, a circulatory system, or a brain. Rather, the connection between biology and sociology in this case lies in the fact that they are using the same *type* of theory.

The Functional Prerequisites of a Social System. The structural-functional approach is essentially a means of analysis which relates the various roles, groups, institutions, and personalities in a social system to the needs of the social system as a whole. These needs are often called the *functional prerequisites*[17] of a social system. What are the needs of a social system? No simple answer can be given, because social systems differ widely in their nature. For instance, a group of workingmen has one set of functional prerequisites, while a large-scale society has another set. Since this book will deal with social systems of many different types and sizes, the following analysis is necessarily couched in general terms.

One major prerequisite for a social system is the accomplishment of the major purpose of the system in such a way that conflict which might disable it is avoided. In other words, a prerequisite for a social system is the maintenance of order as an organization goes about its business. This, of course, does not mean that any one type of arrangement is necessary in an industrial organization. A wide variety of role structures might enable an industry to achieve its goals with a minimum of friction. On the other hand, this variety is not limitless; industrial conditions impose certain limits on the types and relationships of industrial roles. Furthermore, some particular role structures are bound to be more effective in certain situations than others.

The social system, furthermore, must secure itself from encroachment from the outside or from threats arising from the intended or unintended consequences of the actions of members of the organization.[18] In the case of an industry, threats may rise from rival firms, from the government, or from the hostility of employees to the organization or to each other.

Another prerequisite for the social system is the motivation of human actors within the organization. The social system must "secure adequate participation of a sufficient proportion of these actors in the social sys-

[17] See D. F. Aberle, A. K. Cohen, A. K. Davis, M. J. Levy, Jr., and F. X. Sutton, "The Functional Prerequisites of a Society," *Ethics*, vol. 60, no. 2, pp. 100–111, 1950.

[18] See Philip Selznick, "Foundations of the Theory of Organization," *American Sociological Review*, vol. 13, no. 1, p. 29, 1948.

tem, that is [it must] motivate them adequately to the performances which are necessary if the social system in question is to persist or develop."[19] There are two aspects of this problem, the positive and negative. On the negative side, the individual must be prevented from disrupting the orderly functioning of the social system. Such disruptive behavior may not be consciously intended by the actor involved, but whatever the motive, the disruptive behavior must be controlled if the social system is to exist. On the positive side, the social system must, as we have seen, channel human action in such a way as to ensure adequate playing of roles. When roles and human motivation diverge, severe strains are set up in the social system.

A fourth prerequisite for the maintenance of a social system is adequate communication between its members. If an organization is to function, there must be some means of getting orders from those heading it to those whose business it is to carry out the orders. Furthermore, the orders must come down in such a form that those who receive them recognize their legitimacy and authenticity and are prepared to obey them; that is, the communication must bear the stamp of authority and legitimate decision.[20] At the same time, information must flow from the bottom and intermediary positions in the organization up to the top levels. Without valid information about the organization, no leadership can hope to issue workable orders for any length of time. Yet the maintenance of continual communication upward is one of the most difficult of all organizational tasks, and the fate of many an organization has been sealed because top leadership incorrectly estimated the state of morale or the efficiency of the organization.

Finally, it would seem to be a prerequisite for the maintenance of a social system that its members hold in common certain beliefs, definitions, and values. It is of particular importance for the stability of an organization that its members share a common belief in the high value of the social system, in its purpose and performance, and in the roles to be played within it. Unless such a consensus can be reached, the unity of the social system is seriously threatened, because individual interests may take precedence over organizational goals. Even if the social system does not disintegrate immediately, its efficiency may be seriously impaired. For instance, when groups of workingmen cease to believe in organization values or even define those values as hostile to themselves, the stability of the organization is threatened. Such a condition is often a prelude to industrial conflict and perhaps a temporary disintegration of the social system.

[19] Parsons, *The Social System*, p. 29.
[20] Chester I. Barnard, *The Functions of the Executive*, Harvard University Press, Cambridge, Mass., 1945, pp. 165–171.

To sum up, there are certain universal prerequisites for the existence and stability of a social system; e.g., the maintenance of order, the motivation of actors within the system, communication between the actors; a consensus in beliefs, values, and definitions; and protection from the encroachment of external forces. These are the *most general* prerequisites for social systems; every social system, of whatever nature, must somehow provide for them. But each individual social system has additional prerequisites, which are peculiar to it. For instance, a list of prerequisites for a large-scale society would include, besides those already mentioned, the provision for sexual relationships, reproduction, the socialization of children, education, and many others besides. The prerequisites for the maintenance of an industrial social system include the maintenance of solvency and an efficient system of production.

How does the small-scale social system meet these prerequisites? To put it differently, how does a system function to maintain itself? What we shall be seeking to determine first is the structure of small-scale social systems. Since such systems vary, even within the field of industry, what we say here must not be taken to be a final description of such social structures, but rather an outline of those structural elements which are found in all or almost all small social systems. Of course, in any specific system there will be additional structural elements.

Many approaches to this aspect of the study of social systems are possible, but we shall follow that of Parsons, who has said, "The fundamental focus for the analysis of the [social] system . . . concerns the ways in which roles within it are differentiated, and, in turn, these differentiated roles are integrated together, that is 'mesh' to form a functioning system."[21] That is, from our point of view, it is some arrangement or "structure" of roles which functions to meet the prerequisites of a social system.

The Structure of Social Systems. Just as there are general prerequisites which are found in all social systems and prerequisites which are peculiar to individual social systems, so there are some structural arrangements which are universal and some which are found only in certain social systems. Furthermore, the student must avoid the easy assumption that, because certain prerequisites must be met in all social systems, the same type of structural arrangements will be found in all social systems. On the contrary, a wide variety of such structural arrangements can fulfill the same prerequisite. For instance, the prerequisite of the maintenance of order may be met through the use of a sys-

[21] Talcott Parsons, *The Social System*, Free Press, Glencoe, Ill., 1951, p. 114. By permission. However, we are not following exactly Parsons' ideas of the ways in which roles are structured.

tem of force, through a system of persuasion, or through some combination of these.

One of the most important features of any social system is the way in which the necessary work is divided among the roles, that is, the division of labor. For instance, in some social systems roles may be differentiated according to the capabilities of its members. Thus, in a peasant family everyone above the level of infancy is assigned a role to perform; roles are differentiated on the basis of physical strength, sex, age, marital status, and so on. Or roles may be differentiated by the criterion of effectiveness for the achievement of the over-all aim of the organization. In this latter case, individuals are "fitted in," so to speak, to the roles. It is this latter type of differentiation of role which is almost always found in the industrial social system, though instances of the former type are not entirely unknown.

The differentiation of roles, or division of labor, is of great functional importance for the social system. A proper division of labor is necessary for the attainment of the aims of a given system; in fact, the industrial system is particularly dependent on a very fine division of labor. The maintenance of order and the absence of friction are also dependent on the creation of sharply defined roles. It should be noted, incidentally, that the division of labor which actually exists in a social system may not coincide with what, for instance, is pictured on an organizational chart. As we shall see, informal roles may have important functions for the maintenance of a given system.

A second important feature of every social system is its authority structure. Roles are differentiated in terms of the amount of power or authority assigned to them. Each system assigns great amounts of authority to certain roles and much less or none to others. In the family it may be the father's role which possesses authority; in the plant, that of management. In all cases, the authority structure is shored up by various devices which are designed to make that authority binding on other individuals in the social system. For instance, positions of high authority may be invested with the right to use force in order to enforce their authority.

The functional value of the authority structure for the social system is quite clear. The authority structure sanctions and enforces the division of labor, thereby maintaining order and avoiding friction within the system. The authority structure may mobilize the power of a social system to meet threats from the outside. The authority structure may, finally, serve as a means of communication through which decisions, orders, as well as vital information may be conveyed to other sections.

Thirdly, in every social system there is found a prestige or status structure, which has important functions for the system. These structures take the form of scales along which the roles are distributed. Thus great prestige may be attached to certain roles, while little or none may be attached to others; indeed, certain roles possess a negative prestige, and cast dishonor on those who play them. It is also important to note that social honor or prestige is conferred on the player of a role in relation to the way in which the role is played. However, although prestige structures are found in all social systems, the actual criteria by which roles are assigned certain amounts of prestige differ widely from one system to another. In an army or a factory, the prestige of roles is closely related to the authority structure. In a corner gang prestige may be assigned to roles on the basis of loyalty to the gang, sexual prowess, or pugilistic ability.

Prestige structures often have high functional value for social systems. The prestige structure may operate as a means of motivating individuals to play the proper roles and to play them well, thereby contributing to the stability of the system. The prestige structure may also shore up the authority system by conferring on positions of high authority great amounts of prestige and by legitimizing the decisions of high authority. Furthermore, by conferring great amounts of honor on certain roles— for instance, the role of president of a firm—the prestige structure strengthens belief in the values which those roles symbolize.

A fourth important structural feature of all social systems is the way in which the satisfactions or rewards that the system produces are distributed among roles. These satisfactions or rewards vary greatly. In some cases, the rewards are concrete, e.g., economic goods, or money; in others, the rewards are more intangible. In many social systems, both types of rewards are operative. The criteria by which these products are distributed among roles vary widely. They are often, but not always, distributed according to prestige. They may be distributed according to skill, type of occupation, or seniority. Sometimes, satisfactions are distributed on the basis of tradition. But never is the distribution of rewards a random matter; it always proceeds on the basis of a definite scheme, which gives to certain roles more rewards than to others.

Here again, functional value is very high. Motivation of individuals to accept the aims and values of the organization, to fill roles properly, to protect the organization against encroachments, all depend in large part on the effectiveness with which the system of distribution of rewards function. Nor does this involve merely the creation of an effective system of monetary reward. That the distribution system may be extremely complex will appear when we come to regard industry as a system for creating and distributing rewards of all types.

Undoubtedly, still other structural elements with high functional value will be found in any particular social system. But the structures listed

here—division of labor, authority, prestige, and reward distribution—
are found in all social systems with which this author is acquainted. Any
analysis of a social system which does not deal with these general structural elements would necessarily be incomplete. In our analysis, for instance, we shall deal with these universal elements as well as others peculiar to the social systems of industries.

Social Disorganization. An analysis of the social system cannot be
confined to the methods by which it maintains itself; it is also of great
importance to investigate its breakdown. Historically, the breakdowns
of social systems, like the breakdowns of personalities, have been so
spectacular that attention has usually been drawn to this area first. As
long as a social system continues to function it is taken for granted. The
fact that a factory completes twenty-four hours of normal undisturbed
production generally goes unnoticed. Newspaper headlines are reserved
for a financial crisis or a strike. However, from our point of view, in
order to understand breakdowns, it has been necessary to consider first
the social system which is functioning normally.

The disorganization of social systems may arise from one of several
sources. One important source, to which we shall pay much attention
in this book, lies in the failure of individuals in a social system to meet
the demands of roles. The failure of the personality to "mesh" with the
social system may come about as a result of some inadequacy in the
personality, such as mental deficiency or unbalance. Or the failure may
result from the inability of the social system to provide means for the
fulfillment of certain human goals within the approved channels. For instance, a social system which fails to provide opportunity to all or some
of its members to achieve security, or recognition, or response, or
means for achieving other ends, is subject to more or less violent strain.
This is the situation which Durkheim called "anomy."[22] It does not always follow that disintegration will result from such strains. Other channels of action may be open to the individuals who cannot fulfill their
goals within the social system; these individuals may engage in ideological self-delusion, daydreaming, scapegoating, or may retreat into apathy.
But when there is a state of anomy, the possibility always exists that entirely new channels of action will be sought. In such cases the disintegration of the social system may follow, or a new system may spring
up alongside or within the old. For instance, the slum boy who finds it
impossible within home or school to get recognition or response, to feel
security, or to derive pleasurable new experience, may create or join a
gang which provides roles through which these basic human expectations can be fulfilled. As we shall see, sometimes new roles are created

[22] This concept is most fully developed in *Suicide*, by Emile Durkheim (no
translator noted), Free Press, Glencoe, Ill., p. 258.

in this way within the factory. On occasion the newly formed roles may become so stable as to form an alternative or latent social system within the old system.[23] At times such latent role structures may be directed by values contrary to the values of the plant. Under certain circumstances, these latent social systems may lead to the disintegration of the parent system, or at least to its modification.

Another source of strain in a social system may be role conflict. Role conflict occurs when one individual must play mutually incompatible roles. For instance, the role of foreman may be incompatible with the role of friend. The foreman, as a foreman, may have to make certain demands on the workingman which he would never make as a friend. Under these circumstances there is a distinct strain either to evade the role, or to redefine it, or to create new, more compatible roles.

Disorganization may also arise from the discrepancy between the demands of roles and biological capacity. For instance, the emotionally and intellectually mature adolescent who is not permitted to play adult roles may seek to create alternative roles, some of which are harmful to existing social systems. Similar strains may result in an industrial organization where workers are assigned to jobs above or below their mental capacity. In either case there is a tendency to evade established role patterns and/or to create new ones which more nearly meet the demands of the personality.

Social systems may also disintegrate, or at least lose their effectiveness, as a result of some fault in their structure. The division of labor may become obsolete in the face of new needs. A prestige structure may lead to envy, invidious comparison, and destructive conflict. Channels of communication and authority may be blocked. The reward system may fail in a variety of ways. In all these cases the functional prerequisites of the social system may not be met, and as a result the system may not be able to function. Examples of complete breakdown due to structural defects are rare, but there can be no doubt that such structural defects may at least decrease the effectiveness of an organization.

Finally, the social system may disintegrate not through internal defects but simply because it cannot cope with the environment. In the case of industry, competitors may be too numerous and too efficient, a union too powerful and hostile, governmental demands too high. In all these cases the profitability of the industry may vanish, and along with that the reason for its being.

In this book our main concern will be with that type of disintegration, or loss of effectiveness, dependent on a discrepancy between role

---

[23] A recent study shows how new roles are created by delinquent youth from various classes in society; this process is not unlike that which we shall trace in this book. See Albert K. Cohen, *Delinquent Boys*, Free Press, Glencoe, Ill., 1955.

and personality. Other types of disorganization will be largely treated in so far as they are related to the failure of personality and role to "mesh." This choice has been dictated not by a conviction that these other types and sources of disintegration are unimportant, but rather by the direction of interest as well as the theoretical framework of this book.

CHAPTER 3

Types of Productive Systems

In the last chapter the general nature of social systems was discussed. In this chapter we shall discuss certain general characteristics of social systems in the productive process. Then we shall describe a few specific systems found in productive processes. Our treatment here will necessarily be highly selective, both because of the immense scope of the data[1] and because of the special area of interest of this book.

Types of Social Relationships in the Process of Production. In order to understand the development of social relationships in our modern industrial system, it is necessary to distinguish between two types of relationships into which men enter during the course of production. These relationships tend to develop in separate though related paths. The first type, which is by far the more enduring and stable, may be called the *formal social relations of production;* the second type, *social relationships at work.*

The formal social relationships of production result from the socially defined rights of individuals to have access to the means of making a living, and to a share in the results of the productive process. Thus in a primitive society based on agriculture, the right to till fertile land and to share in the products of agriculture is dependent on membership in a certain family. The formal social relations of production in such a society coincide with the social relationships of the family. This means, for instance, that the head of the family has the same type of obligation toward, and expectations from, subordinate family members in the economic sphere as he has in other spheres. As we shall see, the guild system, the putting-out system, and the factory system, each similarly specify the terms under which individuals may enter the productive process and the rights to a share in its results. As a result there are certain types of formal social relationships peculiar to each system.

By social relations at work, on the other hand, is meant those social

[1] The bibliography for this chapter, which appears at the end of the book, will serve to introduce the reader to the field of economic history.

relationships into which men enter by virtue of their association in a cooperative process of production. Thus, to take the same example used in the last paragraph, in an agricultural society men may find it necessary to work in pairs, in teams, or in groups; families as a whole may cooperate with each other at certain times of the year, such as harvest time. These social relations at work are apt to be determined most directly by the technology and division of labor of a particular productive process. For instance, where tools are used in the productive process, men form one type of social relationship; where machines are used, other types of social relationships are formed. As compared with the formal relations, the social relations are more often of a direct or "primary" character, involving face-to-face contacts.

These two types of relationships are connected to each other in a variety of ways. First, the formal social relationships of production and social relationships at work may involve the same or different individuals, depending on the nature of the productive system. Thus in a simple agricultural society the two types of social relationships are almost always combined; not only is one obligated to work *for* one's father, but one generally works *with* one's father in the productive process. On the other hand, in the industrial system, particularly in its later phases, the formal social relations of production are rarely combined with social relations at work. As we shall see, the workingman may never know or meet the people for whom he works. This split has had profound effects on our industrial system, and indeed on our society as a whole.

Secondly, although a given type of formal social relationship in the productive process *tends* to create a given set of social relationships in the work situation, actually the two often vary independently. For instance, under the formal social relationships of industrialism men have formed the most varied types of social relationships with their fellow workers. The social relationships between the men in a steel mill are very different from those between the men on an assembly line; yet all these workers are subject to the same set of formal social relationships of production. Conversely, it may also happen that, although the formal social relations of production change, the social relationships at work do *not* change, or at least not immediately. As we shall see, this occurred to some extent in the switch-over from the guild system to the factory system.

Thirdly, as a rule the formal social relations of production change much less rapidly and frequently than social relationships at work. Perhaps only four or five different types of formal social relationships have existed in history. Social relationships at work, on the other hand, have been extremely variable, based as they are mainly on technological conditions which are subject to frequent variation. It is also important to note that, while changes in the formal social relations of production have been accompanied by vast changes in society, changes in the social relations of work have usually affected only the workers involved and those dependent on them. However, one type of relationship should not be studied to the exclusion of the other; both of them must be considered in an analysis of industry.

The Guild System. One type of productive system which has flourished in many times and places is the guild system. In Europe the guild system probably reached its climax in the thirteenth century, when it was strongly entrenched in all branches of industry;[2] however, some guilds survived into the nineteenth century, and even today traces of this system remain.[3] The term *guild* is usually taken to mean an organization of the workers in a special craft;[4] thus in the Middle Ages there were guilds of carpenters, weavers, goldsmiths, ironmongers, etc. What distinguishes a guild from like organizations, such as craft unions, is that a guild includes *all* the members of a given vocation, employers and employed alike.

The guild had two principal aims which contrast sharply with the aims of our own industrial system. First, the guild tried to preserve equality, at least among the masters of the craft.[5] To this end the guild above all tried to prevent the growth of unduly wealthy masters. Thus technological change was strictly prohibited, lest some masters be able to produce more and at less cost than other masters.[6] For the same reason techniques were minutely regulated, even to the specification of the tools that could be employed, the number of apprentices and journeymen that each master might employ, and the level of wages and hours. Access to raw material was also controlled. The craft or town bought the raw material and sold it to the masters, thereby preventing wealthier masters from securing a monopoly of raw materials. Finally, masters were forbidden to work for others as journeymen lest the integrity of the class of masters as a whole be threatened.

The second aim of the guild system was to maintain its economic position in society. To this end several practices were adopted. In order to maintain employment the guilds decreed that work must take the longest possible course. Work was not divided among guild members on the basis of technical specialization. For instance, the guild clothing worker

[2] William J. Ashley, *An Introduction to English Economic History and Theory,* Longmans, Green & Co., Inc., New York, 1925, vol. I, p. 76.

[3] For instance, in the building trades; thus one speaks of apprentice, journeymen, or master plumbers.

[4] Max Weber, *General Economic History,* translated by Frank H. Knight, Free Press, Glencoe, Ill., 1950, p. 136.

[5] *Ibid.,* p. 138.

[6] Henri Pirenne, "Guilds, European," in *Encyclopedia of the Social Sciences,* The Macmillan Company, New York, 1936, vol. 7, pp. 208–214.

did not specialize on a particular process such as spinning, weaving, or dyeing; rather one worker would be engaged solely in the manufacture of coats, another in the manufacture of hose, and so on.[7] The result was more work to go around. In order to bar cutthroat competition,[8] prices were regulated and the sale of goods made by outsiders was prohibited. In order to control competition, the guilds strove to make membership in the guilds compulsory. They also strove to gain a monopoly of their crafts in a given area, but they were successful only in certain places. Thus the famous guild regulation of the manufacture, quality, and price of products was designed not only for the common good, as is often supposed, but also for the realistic interests of the guild members, particularly the masters.

The relative success of the guilds in enforcing these practices was the outcome of existing economic, social, and political conditions.[9] The guilds produced for a limited, stable, and therefore predictable market; for this reason prices and methods of manufacture could be controlled, while quality had to be guaranteed. Furthermore, the fact that the guilds produced mainly the necessities of life, rather than luxuries, also tended to increase the stability of the system, since the demand for the necessities varied comparatively little. Again, since skill and stable connections to a body of consumers were more important than capital in determining the success of a guild, it was unlikely that one guild or master could easily grow wealthy at the expense of another. Finally, the guilds received considerable help from medieval town governments in enforcing guild regulations.

Turning now to the internal social structure of the guilds, the most important formal social relationships existed among three classes of members: masters, apprentices, and journeymen.

The *masters* were, in one sense, the managers or controllers of the guild system. Their relations to the productive process, however, differed widely from those of the modern industrial manager or owner. The guild master, it is true, "owned" a shop, and he may even have had hired workers. However, the master did not necessarily own the tools which his subordinates used, these often being the property of the individual workers. Furthermore, the guild master worked in the shop alongside other workers; he neither managed nor administered in the modern sense of the term. Ideally, the master was the most skilled workingman in the shop; the term "masterpiece" remains as a tribute to his skill. Theoretically, at least, the master had achieved his position not by investing

[7] Weber, *op. cit.*, p. 139.

[8] E. Lipson, *The Economic History of England,* The Macmillan Company, New York, 1929, p. 301.

[9] The discussion of this paragraph is based on Ashley, *op. cit.*, pp. 92–95.

capital, or by appointment, but by moving up a ladder of skill and through seniority. As a result of all these factors, his relations to his workers, particularly the apprentices, differed widely from the relation of the modern industrial manager to his hired hands.

The *apprentice* was usually a young worker who was "bound over" to serve a master for a period ranging from three to seven years. The relation between master and apprentice involved certain definite rights and obligations on the part of both. The primary obligation of the master was to train the apprentice in the skills of the craft so that he could some day qualify as a journeyman or a master. In addition the master usually agreed to provide the apprentice "bed and board" and the other necessities of life; sometimes schooling was provided and even a small salary. The master had the right to discipline him, and in general was responsible for his good conduct, much as if the relationship were that of father to son. On his side, the apprentice owed certain duties to his master: obedience, self-control, loyalty, honesty, good conduct. In some cases he could not even marry without the consent of the master. However, he had the right to leave his master if he could prove that the conditions of the apprenticeship were not being met. In general, the "bond between master and apprentice was of the closest description; the master stood in *loco parentis* to the apprentice, who . . . associated with him in the workshop and the home in terms of the most personal intimacy."[10]

When an apprentice finished his term of service, he became a *journeyman*. A journeyman was a fully qualified worker who for some reason did not or could not become a master, and who secured his livelihood by working at wages for a master. Sometimes the journeyman was compelled to work for a period for the master to whom he had been apprenticed, but in other places the journeyman had to "wander" for a period of time gaining experience with different masters.[10a] The journeyman's aim remained, however, to succeed a master or to open his own shop. Ideally the journeyman stage was the bridge between the highest and lowest rungs of the occupational ladder.

The formal relations of production were enforced by the guild itself. In many guilds an assembly which, theoretically, was composed of all the men in the guild, met annually, drew up regulations, and appointed officials to administer them. These officials, often called *wardens,* usually held office for a year and were given power to dispense judgement and to punish wrongdoers. In this way disputes between apprentices, journey-

---

[10] Lipson, *op. cit.,* p. 282.
[10a] It should be noted that the term *journeyman* is not derived from the English word *journey,* but from the French word *journée;* that is, a journeyman was a worker who worked and was paid by the *day.*

men, and masters were adjusted within the framework of the formal organization. Ideally the formal productive relations of the guild system were similar to the social relationships of a family, and whatever disputes arose were settled by the normal "family" processes of authority and compromise.

However, the reality of the guild system is only partially reflected by this idyllic picture, which incidentally has awakened so much nostalgia among those who are disturbed by strife within the modern industrial system. Actually, there were numerous areas of disharmony in the guilds. To judge by the number of advertisements of runaway apprentices, the lot of the latter must often have been a harsh one. In addition, the occupational ladder often tended to become sealed off at the top. Mastership became difficult or impossible to achieve; in fact, the position often became hereditary. Journeymen were prevented from becoming masters in a number of ways; the term of apprenticeship was extended, high fees were demanded from the would-be master, an expensive and technically difficult "masterpiece" as proof of competence was required, and so on.[11]

By the seventeenth century, the journeyman was almost everywhere a permanent wageworker. A symptom of his position was the formation of journeymen's societies, which were very much like trade unions in their economic and social demands. Strikes began to be used as a weapon against the masters; a printers' strike actually lasted for more than thirty years! Thus, alongside the formal relations of production of the guild system, there appeared relations of quite another type, perhaps best described as a "small capitalism."[12]

It is harder, on the other hand, to generalize about the social relations at work in the guild system. The social relations of work depend, as we have seen, primarily on the division of labor and on the type of technology. Within the guild system there were many different crafts, each with a distinct division of labor and technology. Nevertheless, certain generalizations may be made. In the first place, in the guild system labor was divided on the basis of the total product rather than on the basis of individual steps in the process of production. Consequently, there were relatively few types of jobs; where one might expect to find two or three thousand separate guilds, actually only about two hundred existed. In the second place, the technology of the guild system was predominantly handicraft. Although machinery was by no means unknown, it was the tool upon which the productive system was based. As a result of these two factors, labor in the guild was relatively unspecialized, unroutinized, unstandardized and unmechanized.

[11] Henri Hauser, "Journeymen's Societies," in *Encyclopedia of the Social Sciences,* vol. 8, pp. 424–427.

[12] Weber, *op. cit.*, p. 143.

The guild worker was not a part of an intricate social process such as one finds in a modern factory. The social relations at work in the guilds were not based directly on the productive process so much as they were based on the structure and values of the guild organization. For instance, it seems reasonable to suppose that status within the guild was based on the caliber of the work performed, on faithfulness to guild regulations, and perhaps on official position held within the guild. Similarly other types of social relations at work—for instance, authority relations—must likewise have been based directly on the formal social structure of the guild. Furthermore, guild workers were not strangers to one another, as industrial workers today often are; they were permanent members of small enduring organizations. They often lived together on a single street or in the same quarter of town.

To sum up, the social relations at work in the guild system resembled those of a small well-knit community. These relationships were of primary nature; that is, each worker interacted in a myriad of face-to-face relationships with other workers who were well known to him. In the guild system it was impossible for men to treat each other expediently, as means to other ends, as commodities. Rather social interaction was governed by a rigid social structure and by sharply defined values which guaranteed certain rights to all and exacted certain duties from all.

The Decline of the Guild System. By the sixteenth century the guild system was showing signs of decay. No exact date, however, can be assigned as the fall of the guilds; they continued to exist side by side with other systems of production for many centuries. Only gradually did they lose importance, while their ultimate dissolution did not occur until long after the final triumph of industrialism.

There were various factors operating to weaken the guild system:

1. The harmony of the system was gradually destroyed by increasing difficulty in attaining the rank of master. The result was the formation of a class of journeymen fundamentally opposed to the masters. The bitter strife which followed led to the intervention of town authorities in guild affairs and the weakening of guild autonomy and power.

2. The very strength of the guilds and their monopoly in certain areas of manufacturing aroused the hostility of other groups in society. Eventually these hostile groups were able to use the state to strike at the guilds. The state forced the reduction of initiation fees, curbed the power of the wardens, placed the guilds under the courts.

3. In the course of time, wealth accumulated in the hands of certain masters. In some cases this capital was used to employ workers and to engage in manufacturing for profit outside the guild system. In other cases, wealthy masters gained full control of the guilds and excluded other guild members from voting in the assembly, thus rendering them politically powerless. The masters thereby gained control over tech-

niques, tools, quality of products, and traditional guild practices. Since those who now controlled the guilds were interested in producing as cheaply and as quickly as possible, one of the major supports for the stability of the guild system was lost.

4. As wealth accumulated in the hands of certain masters, some craft guilds were transformed into merchant guilds. Two opposite processes then resulted, both of them equally destructive of the guild system. In some cases the merchant guild absorbed the craft guilds, with consequent loss of independence of the latter. In other cases the guilds split up into relatively small and weak guilds, which were no match for the powerful merchants. In either case, production came to be reorganized as small-shop capitalistic industry.

5. As the market for manufactured goods, particularly overseas, widened gradually, the guilds became dependent on the exporting merchants. The exporters possessed the necessary capital to finance the process of manufacturing for a foreign market, which involved a long interval between production and final sale. Furthermore, only the exporters had the necessary knowledge of trade operations and marketing in a foreign country. Thus the guilds were reduced to the position of manufacturing not for a market but for an entrepreneur.

6. Beginning with the sixteenth century, widening horizons and increasing trade led to a demand for new products. The manufacture of these products often necessitated expensive imported raw materials, entailing increased costs which the guilds could not bear. Here again was an opportunity for the man of capital who could carry the costs of the productive process and also wait for a return on his investment. Thus the guild workers became, in effect, employees of a merchant entrepreneur.

Thus through a combination of external social, political, and economic factors, as well as through its own internal weakness, the guild system gradually decayed. But to understand what gave the death blow to the system, we must concentrate our attention hereafter on the new man, the man who possessed capital, the "capitalist."

The Putting-out System. The merchant-capitalist, then, gradually extended his power over the guilds. At the same time, however, he found the guild system inadequate or too costly to meet his needs for commodities. While domestic and foreign markets were expanding, while the new national governments were continually increasing demands for military products, the guild system persisted in its traditional techniques, in maintaining wages and quality, and in limiting the numbers of workers in a given craft.

Under these circumstances, the merchant-capitalist had two courses of action, either of which led to revolutionary consequences. Using his power over the guilds, he could, in the manner described above, transform the craftsmen into wageworkers; or he could attempt to find workers outside the guild system entirely.

When the capitalist sought for alternative sources of labor he naturally turned to the countryside. It is true that traditionally the countryside was organized along feudal lines and so was closed to capitalist penetration. However, certain economic and demographic changes had greatly altered this situation. As a result of these changes surplus labor appeared. Other peasants, caught in an economic squeeze between rising prices and low incomes, were eager to find additional employment. It is true that this labor was unskilled in the industrial arts, but the introduction of new simplified techniques decreased the need for skill. Furthermore, with the rise of new industries without traditions of skilled guild labor, the labor of the peasants could not suffer by comparison.

The new system of production which arose in the countryside is known as the *putting-out system*, sometimes the *domestic system*.[13] This system appeared as early as the thirteenth century in the English woolen industry, but its greatest development was between the middle of the fifteenth and the middle of the eighteenth century; thus it existed side by side with both the guild system and the factory system.[14]

The worker in the putting-out system usually owned his tools; at all events this was true while machines or tools were simple and inexpensive, perhaps a loom or two. Sometimes, however, the merchant supplied tools to the worker, and in this case "the worker was entirely separated from the means of production."[15] Whether or not the merchant-entrepreneur owned the tools of production, he almost always supplied the raw material and owned completely the finished product.[16]

In the putting-out system the formal relations of production departed sharply from those of the guild. The only classes in the putting-out system were workers or entire families of workers, on the one hand, and merchant-entrepreneurs, on the other. The worker was related to the entrepreneur solely through a *cash nexus;* that is, the worker received wages from the entrepreneur while the entrepreneur received the completed product from the worker. Unlike the journeyman or apprentice, the worker of the putting-out system was not bound to a master by guildlike regulations. The sole obligations of the merchant and the worker to each other were contractual.

As time went on, the formal relations of production became increasingly capitalistic in nature. From the point of view of the merchant,

---

[13] Edwin F. Gay, "Putting-out System," in *Encyclopedia of the Social Sciences*, vol. 13, pp. 7–11.

[14] Nor is it completely dead even today in certain areas.

[15] Weber, *op. cit.*, p. 159.

[16] Ashley, *op. cit.*, vol. I, part II, p. 220.

the putting-out system was hopelessly inefficient. It was extremely difficult to supervise the labor of scattered workers, and there was great loss through waste and embezzlement. Furthermore, the labor supply was uncertain and shifting. Under these circumstances, the merchant tried to control the worker in several ways. One device was to keep the peasant firmly bound in a chain of debt. Another was to deprive him of ownership of the tools of production. In the latter case the worker was forced to rent the tools from the merchant and was reduced, in effect, to a completely dependent employee.

While the formal relations of production were gradually moving toward a capitalistic form, the social relations of work resembled those of the guild system or the peasant family. Many of the guild terms were used in the putting-out system: "master," "journeyman," and "apprentice." Work was often conducted in the old guild shop; however, as time went on there was a tendency for the worker to rent a machine in the employer's own workshop. In this latter case the worker was not bound by factory discipline or factory legislation. More often work was performed at home, and usually the productive process became a family affair. For instance, in the house of a weaver each member of the family had a special task; the wife and daughter, perhaps, did the spinning, the children carded the wool, while the father worked at the loom.[17] These social relations at work of the putting-out system tended to be identical with the social relations of the peasant family.

As in the case of the guild system, a good deal of nostalgia has been expended on the putting-out system. An idealized picture has been drawn of the patriarch of the family, helped by his sturdy son and industrious wife and daughters, maintaining economic independence, half farmer and half worker. Actually, the putting-out system was often the product of economic desperation and, in turn, produced further economic deprivation. The place of work was frequently an unhealthy cottage, with little sunshine or air; the main and sometimes only room served as kitchen and workshop. Furthermore, the putting-out system often led to the merciless exploitation of women and children. This was true alike in the seventeenth century and at the turn of the century among the garment workers of the lower East Side of New York.

From the point of view of the entrepreneur, the social relations of work in the putting-out system had serious defects. Much waste was caused by entrusting material to scattered, careless workers, whose main values were bound up with other systems of production and who could not be adequately supervised. In addition the system involved much carriage back and forth of materials going through various stages in the

[17] Paul Mantoux, *The Industrial Revolution in the Eighteenth Century*, Harcourt, Brace and Company, Inc., New York, 1928, p. 58.

productive process, with a consequent waste of time. Still further, this productive system imposed great obstacles to the division of labor and the introduction of new machinery. Thus it was almost impossible for the entrepreneur to cut costs or to increase production. As the demand for goods continued to grow and as the call for better quality was heard, the merchant-capitalist began to cast about for better systems of production. By the time this happened the formal relations of the guild system had been completely shattered; it was now necessary only to revolutionize the social relations at work.

The Factory System. The entrepreneur attempted to extend his control over production in several ways. The most successful in the long run was to separate the place of work from the household, and to bring the workers together in a central place—under one roof, if possible. In other words, what the entrepreneur tried to do was to reconstitute the old shop industry of the guild, but on a different basis. Shop production was very old; it had existed in ancient Rome, indeed even in ancient Egypt. The guild system, as we have seen, developed shop production to a high plane. But the new shop production differed from all others in one respect; the means of production were completely in the hands of the entrepreneur, who had invested capital in tools, plant, raw materials, and labor. This new type of shop production we may call a *factory;* that is, "a factory is a shop industry with free labor and fixed capital."[18] The only thing lacking to turn this type of shop into a modern factory was large-scale machinery and mechanical power.[19]

Causes and Conditions of the Rise of the Factory System. The factory system of production was destined to sweep almost all before it; it was due to a combination of economic causes and of favorable external conditions, which enabled it to overcome severe obstacles, first in England, and then elsewhere. The "causes" and "conditions" of the rise of the factory system, as well as the actual story of that rise, form some of the most complicated pages of economic history. There is much debate among economic historians as to which factors were important in the rise of the factory system, and as to the order of their importance. In what follows, certain generally recognized causes and conditions are listed, not necessarily in order of importance.

As early as the sixteenth century an increasingly large and stable market for manufactured goods began to develop with the growth of purchasing power among certain groups and with the development of a money economy.[20] It is significant that the factory first appeared to

[18] Weber, *op. cit.,* p. 163.
[19] Note that it was the factory system which created the conditions for the use of machinery and mechanical power, and not vice versa.
[20] Weber, *op. cit.,* pp. 163–164.

supply the constantly growing and dependable demands of the national state for coins, uniforms, and gunpowder. A second market developed among the wealthy classes for luxuries: porcelain, glass, soap, silk, velvet. Later markets developed among the not-so-wealthy for imitations, of these goods. Still later, the factory system spread and captured other markets, again partly as a result of increasing and reliable demand.

In general, satisfaction of a growing, dependable market implied the need for a dependable, efficient system of production. This the factory system succeeded in furnishing. By bringing workers together under one roof, the entrepreneur could institute a rigid discipline for the first time over the system of production. By depriving the workers of ownership in the means of production, the entrepreneur forced the worker into complete economic dependence. As a result of both these factors, the quantity, quality, and uniformity of work could, for the first time, be guaranteed.

Once this system was established it offered unheard-of opportunities for further increases in efficiency, productivity, and therefore, profit. Labor could be divided and subdivided in the interests of efficiency. The use of central sources of power, such as water or wind, became economically and technologically feasible. Still further, production became a calculable process; budgets and plans could be used to cut costs in a hundred ways.[21] The profitability and dependability of the factory system in turn made it more and more attractive as an area of relatively safe investment. All these factors enabled the factory to squeeze out the guilds and the putting-out establishments in one field after another.

The fact that the guild system was decaying internally and losing power externally was another factor in the rise of industrialism. The breakup of the guild system, with its monopoly on skills, markets, and labor, offered opportunities to the factory system in every one of these areas. Of course, once the new industrial system was well established, it furthered the decay of the guilds.

Another necessary condition for the growth of industrialism was the destruction of the social relationships of feudalism. Especially was this true of the relationships between the peasant and the lord and between the peasant and his land, for these feudal relations inhibited the conversion of the rural population into a working force mobile enough to meet the changing demands of industry and without recourse to means of livelihood outside the factory. From its earliest days the factory system was the enemy of feudalism.

Here again conditions in Western Europe, particularly England,

[21] Max Weber, *The Theory of Social and Economic Organization,* translated by A. M. Henderson and Talcott Parsons, Oxford University Press, New York, 1947, p. 247.

favored the cause of industrialism. In England the breakup of feudal relations was already well advanced. Indeed, by the sixteenth century so many peasants had been evicted from the land that it was necessary to pass laws for relief of the poor. In Continental Europe, feudalism lasted somewhat longer, but it began to decay after the sixteenth or seventeenth century, and rural unemployment appeared on the Continent also.

Still another necessary condition for the establishment of the new industrial system was the creation of large amounts of capital, available for investment. This condition was realized, generally speaking, after the sixteenth or seventeenth century. Although there is disagreement as to the causes of the appearance of this new capital, it is certain that the voyages of discovery, which opened new routes to the Orient and revealed new worlds in the West, played a large part. The discoveries opened new, lucrative markets, while the mines of Peru and Mexico poured a stream of precious metals into European trade and industry.[22] Nor should one overlook the extent to which the discoveries stimulated the imagination and inventiveness of men, causing them to seek new fields in which to invest their new-found wealth.

Favorable political conditions also played a role in the development of the factory system. The legal position of early industry was very insecure, especially in the face of guild hostility. As a result, industry turned to the state for protection. The state was ready to grant this protection for a variety of reasons: to ensure the manufacturer of necessary military provisions, to provide employment for a population which could no longer find work in the guilds, and to increase tax revenues. In turn, as industry grew in power it lent support to the state, and the alliance between these two forces was cemented.

It is possible that even these causes and conditions would not have been sufficient to ensure the triumph of the industrial system, were it not for the existence of a climate of opinion favorable to capitalistic industry.[23] The factory system was the outcome and embodiment of a rational view of life. The factory system was based on a rational technique of production, rational accounting, rational budgeting, rational rules of operation. By way of contrast, the guild system was governed by tradition, by adherence to old techniques, to a customary pace of work, and to a certain standard of living. Furthermore, traditionalism was often

---

[22] John Lawrence Hammond, "Factory System," in *Encyclopedia of the Social Sciences,* vol. 6, pp. 51–54.

[23] This discussion is based on the work of Max Weber. See Weber's *General Economic History,* chap. XXX; and his *The Protestant Ethic and the Spirit of Capitalism,* translated by Talcott Parsons, George Allen & Unwin, Ltd., London, 1930. See also R. H. Tawney, *Religion and the Rise of Capitalism,* Harcourt, Brace and Company, Inc., New York, 1926.

backed by magical and religious beliefs. Capitalistic industry demanded a rational man, self-controlled and disciplined.

It is startling to find, then, that just prior to the appearance of the factory system and throughout the early years of its development, a religious movement developed which was essentially antimagical and which demanded a rational way of life as the road to salvation. This religious movement was the Protestant Reformation. Note that it was *not* that Protestantism approved of capitalism; on the contrary, like many other religions, it was generally opposed to money-making. But Protestantism, especially its stricter branches such as Calvinism, *did* demand rigid attention to the everyday affairs of life, and devoted, rational labor in a vocation. If wealth were gained thereby, it was to be interpreted as a sign of success in pursuing the work of the Lord. The result was, as Weber says, that "the entrepreneur had a fabulously clear conscience—and also industrious workers."[24] Thus Protestantism created a rational climate in which industrialism could flourish.

All these causes and conditions, and undoubtedly many more besides, operated jointly to favor the rise of the factory system. No unicausal theory can account for such a profound overturn in the affairs of mankind.

The Formal Relations of Production in the Factory System. With the development of the factory system, there appeared the two great economic groupings with which we are familiar under the names of capitalist and labor, or management and worker. The formal relations which existed between these groups were essentially *market relations;* that is, employers and workers approached each other as buyers and sellers, with the matter at sale being the labor of the workers. As in every market, action was oriented to "advantage in exchange on the basis of self-interest."[25] No "particularistic" ties existed between the entrepreneur and the worker; ties such as had existed between slaveowner and slave, between lord and peasant, or between master and apprentice. Let us look more closely at these new partners in production.

The Entrepreneur. The entrepreneur or manager was, in the first place, distinguished from both the guild master and the merchant-capitalist of the putting-out system by the fact that he owned—or, as Weber puts it, "appropriated"—all the physical means of production: land, buildings, machinery, tools, raw materials. To the entrepreneur these had become property, which could be disposed of as he wished; his rights in them were practically unlimited. The goods which were produced by the factory also belonged solely to the entrepreneur, to be used either for personal needs, for speculation, or for sale.

[24] Weber, *General Economic History,* p. 367.
[25] Weber, *The Theory of Social and Economic Organization,* pp. 212–213. The discussion of this section is based on Weber's work.

In the second place, in order to carry out the process of production, the entrepreneur, unlike the feudal lord, bought or "hired" labor. In the ideal case, which was often the actual case in the early days of the factory system, this labor was bought at a price set by the laws of supply and demand; that is, the amount of labor being offered for sale and the needs of the entrepreneur jointly determined the level of wages. The responsibilities of the entrepreneur to the worker were ended once the wages had been paid; the entrepreneur was responsible neither for the conduct of the workers apart from working hours nor for their maintenance in the absence of work. Thus the new entrepreneur combined the advantages of ownership of the means of production on the one hand and a lack of responsibility for the human element in the productive process on the other.

Thirdly, the supreme purpose of the entrepreneur in "appropriating" the means of production and in "hiring" workers was the creation of profit. By profit making, in the broadest sense, we mean activity which is aimed at attaining "power of control over goods."[26] When defined this way it can be seen that the search for profit is a well-nigh universal human endeavor; profit may be gained through trade, speculation, extension of credit, financing of wars, exploitation of colonies, or tax "farming," to name just a few. However, the distinctive features of the new type of profit making were that (1) it was sought through a *productive* enterprise; (2) it was a continuous rational process, in which at least a part of the proceeds from the sale of goods might be used to create new opportunities for profit; and (3) profit was sought for its own sake, rather than as a means to something else (e.g., the purchase of land). In the factory system the *maximization of profit* was desired. This specific kind of profit making has dominated the factory system and has gone far toward determining its history and special characteristics.

It will be evident that the position of the entrepreneur in the market was a strong one. Owning the means of production, free from immediate economic need, without personal ties to the worker, the entrepreneur could afford to bargain long and shrewdly with his workers. Indeed, the great economic power of management is one of the dominant themes of industrial history.

Although management and the worker were sharply severed in theory, this sharp division did not necessarily develop immediately. Frequently the early entrepreneur was also the chief foreman of the works, the designer, the tool builder, and on occasion one of the workers.[27] The social separation of management and the worker occurred only at a later stage of industrial development.

[26] *Ibid.,* p. 191.
[27] Thorstein Veblen, *Absentee Ownership and Business Enterprise,* B. W. Huebsch, New York, 1923, p. 103.

The Worker. The factory system created a special type of worker, a type which had appeared in history before, but never on so large a scale. The most distinctive feature of the new worker was that he was formally free from compulsory ties to lord or master, that he owed no man servitude or labor. At the same time his "freedom" included an absence of rights to support by his employer, or of rights to work. Positively, his freedom meant that he could offer his services to any man, at any type of work, unlike the caste member, for instance, who can work only within his caste and at a hereditarily determined task.

The worker established formal relations with his employer not by virtue of being born into a family, as in the case of a serf, or by being "bound over" as in the case of an apprentice, but through the medium of the market. But where the employer entered the market in the hope of gaining profit, the motives of the worker were quite different; the major motive was usually dire economic need. Economic need was made all the more pressing by the fact that the worker had no recourse to livelihood except through the factory; only rarely did he till a piece of ground, or hope to compete through his own enterprise with the fast, efficient production of the factory.

Furthermore, the entrepreneur's "appropriation" of the means of production held a special meaning for the worker. Above all, it increased his economic dependence on the employer, who now controlled access to the tools by which the worker made his living. In addition, since the entrepreneur consented to the use of these tools only when there was a prospect of profit, the worker became even more dependent on the economic activity and whims of the entrepreneur.

These formal relations of production were impersonal and universalistic to an extraordinary degree; workers and employers were bound to each other only through a cash nexus. No longer was the worker paid in kind or provided with board; he earned wages, which were calculated on a basis of time at work or productivity.

These factors operated to lessen the power of the worker in his formal relations to his employer. "Freed" of rights to support in times of slack work, forced to find work in a market in which labor was usually plentiful and unorganized while employers were few and cohesive, cut off from ownership of the tools of production, and therefore dependent on a job for existence, the worker was rarely a match for the employer.

Social Relations at Work. The new social relations at work created by the factory system are difficult to describe in general terms. These relations varied greatly from case to case. However, there were certain forces at work in the factory system which tended to mold the social relations at work into a more or less unified form. Perhaps the most important of these forces was the rationalization process to which the new industrial technique was subjected. *Rationalization* meant the organization of production according to the canons of logic and efficiency. In the factory this was reflected above all in two processes: refinement in the division of labor, and increasing mechanization. Let us look at these processes and their effect on work relations in greater detail.

Specialization of work contributed to the efficiency of the factory in several ways. By dividing labor into minute tasks, work was greatly simplified, thereby permitting the workers quickly to become proficient at their job. Furthermore, production became a continuous process; costly delays while work was carted from place to place were eliminated.[28] Again, as work became less demanding of the worker's energy, the rate of production was stepped up. However, even apart from the demands of efficiency, the increasing size of the industrial enterprise by itself necessitated an increasing division of labor, both because of the great numbers of new tasks in industry and because the solidarity of large-scale enterprise depended in part on the coordination of diverse tasks.[29]

The specific form of the division of labor varied from one factory to another, as well as within factories. In some factories labor was divided into special tasks. For instance, in the manufacture of carriages the labor was divided among locksmiths, painters, and carpenters. In other factories a single task was divided into several minute parts. For instance, the task of manufacturing a pin was divided into eighteen distinct steps. In other cases the worker was restricted to one type of product; a leather worker, for example, might specialize in making a certain type of pocketbook.[30] Thus, in the factory labor might be divided so that separate tasks were performed independently but simultaneously, independently but successively, or in a coordinated system of production resembling the interaction of a symphony orchestra.[31] The specific form of the division of labor was determined in particular cases by such factors as the type of product being made, the nature of the raw material used, and the type of machine employed.

In general, division of labor helped in various ways to determine the social relations of work. Specialization, for instance, helped to create the specific roles which individuals played within the factory. Common

[28] Adam Smith, *The Wealth of Nations,* Modern Library, Inc., New York, 1937, pp. 8–9.
[29] This is the thesis of Emile Durkheim. See his *The Division of Labor in Society,* translated by George Simpson, Free Press, Glencoe, Ill., 1947.
[30] Carl Bücher, *Industrial Evolution,* Henry Holt and Company, Inc., New York, 1901, pp. 284–290.
[31] Weber, *The Theory of Social and Economic Organization,* pp. 226–227.

labor was separated from management, the worker from the technical specialist, the clerical worker from the bench worker. Specialization also helped determine the ways in which these roles were related; thus, production might be carried on in pairs, in groups, or in isolation. Furthermore, the division of labor helped to differentiate jobs on the basis of honor or status, skill, or the type of work done, and thereby still further determined certain aspects of relations between roles. Finally, specialization played a large part in the formation of informal work groups, whose importance is now coming to be widely recognized.

The division of labor also played a part in creating certain strains in the social relations at work. For instance, it will be shown in Chapter 8 that as the division of labor tended to standardize, routinize, automize, and simplify the work process, the worker suffered certain deleterious consequences. As a result, there appeared among workers certain attitudes toward management, toward fellow workers, and toward work itself which caused great strains in the industrial system.

No less important in creating the social relations of work in the factory was the process of mechanization. The machine was a device which directly performed some industrial task, without direct human intervention. Man "tended," "fed," "operated," or "ran" the machine, but it was the loom which wove the cloth, the press which embossed the leather, the locomotive which pulled the train. Sometimes man supplied the energy to run the machine, but more often some other agency was used: animal, wind, water, steam, and later electricity and atomic energy.

The machine took a firm grip on industry in England in the last half of the eighteenth century. It appeared first in the textile industry and then spread to other industries. This was the so-called Industrial Revolution. Actually the machine had existed in some form for thousands of years, and in Europe the first great wave of mechanical development had occurred as early as the tenth century.[32] However, it was in the England of the late eighteenth century that there appeared for the first time the necessary conditions for a really large-scale mechanical development.

These favorable conditions may be grouped into several categories. First, mechanization was strongly favored by the same factors which had led to increasing rationalization of production through the division of labor, that is, the expansion of domestic and foreign markets, the demands of growing military machines, and the drive to cheapen costs in order to increase profits or gain new markets. Mechanization greatly increased the efficiency and effectiveness of industry. The machine raised output levels, often improving the quality and durability of the goods in

[32] For a history of machinery, see Lewis Mumford, *Technics and Civilization*, Harcourt, Brace and Company, Inc., New York, 1934, chaps. I–V.

the process. Furthermore the machine cut costs by displacing labor, by replacing skilled workers by unskilled workers (at first, often women and children), and, initially, by lengthening the workday. At the same time the increased profitability of industry as well as improved commercial and financial conditions resulted in the accumulation of large amounts of capital available for further investment in mechanization.

Technological and scientific advances in eighteenth-century England supplied the necessary conditions for mechanical development. Techniques for the working of metal had been so refined that the construction of complicated machinery became possible. Similarly, tools had been developed to the point where the accurate work necessary for machine production could be done. In the realm of science, knowledge of such aspects of nature as the physical and chemical properties of gases or the laws of mechanics had reached a stage of development at which this knowledge could be applied to the solution of technological problems.

Another factor favoring the development of mechanization was the refinement in the division of labor, which has already been mentioned. As tasks were broken down into ever more refined and yet simple tasks, the technological problems of converting handicraft into machine production became simplified. It was, for instance, virtually impossible to mechanize the manufacture of clothing while one worker performed every aspect of the manufacturing process. However, when labor was divided so that one worker was concerned with spinning the cloth, another with weaving, another with dyeing, another with sewing, and so on, machines could be invented to perform each single process.

With the development of "new" industries which were not hampered by guild restrictions or restrictive legislation, the introduction of machinery on a large scale became possible. This was true, for instance, in the cotton industry. The spirit of the age itself favored the development of mechanization. The eighteenth century was marked by concern with the world and a desire to master it. There was consequently a great interest, among other things, in invention, which received the sanction of the state through the passage of patent laws.

In attempting to assess the influence of the machine on the social relations of work, one must take into account the very great variety of machines that appeared. For instance, it made a great difference to the worker whether the machine was fully automatic or only partially so, whether it was a mobile machine (like a locomotive) or a stationary machine, whether it needed "tending" or "operating." In many cases, the "flow of work" from machine to machine was one decisive factor in arranging the social relations of work.[33] The work flow determined with

[33] See Lewis Corey, "Machines and Tools: Modern," in *Encyclopedia of the Social Sciences,* vol. 10, pp. 21–26.

whom a worker would have social contacts and the form and duration of such contacts. In general the more automatic and stationary the machine, the fewer the social contacts. The very noise and clatter of machine industry tended further to inhibit social interaction.

The machine altered social relations at work in other ways; for instance, with the machine process there tended to appear one class of workers who operated the machines, and another class which supervised the operation. As time went on both categories became still further divided; supervisors according to their degree of authority and responsibility, and workers into the skilled, semiskilled, and unskilled; into "heavy" workers or "light" workers. These new divisions, and many others, led to new types of social relations, new power relations, new forms of communication, new informal relationships.

Like the division of labor, the machine also had certain effects on the psychology of the men engaged in the productive process. The machine tended to reduce the worker to an appendage of itself, destroying the need for skill in the process. The machine standardized and routinized work, making it repetitious to the nth degree. As a result the worker became exposed to the danger of monotony and boredom. He was often dominated by a sense of the meaninglessness of work, by a lack of interest in his job. Furthermore, the machine caused a profound feeling of insecurity in the worker; it directly threatened his livelihood, or indirectly served as a weapon in the hands of management. The early factory workingman, who was accustomed to the more secure, more leisurely, and less rationalized work of the guild system or the putting-out system, at first bitterly resented the discipline and insecurity caused by the machine. The early riots against machinery, during the course of which whole factories were destroyed, was an expression of this resentment. At the same time, for the entrepreneur, the engineer, or the technician, the machine meant increasing freedom from restrictions on production, widening horizons and soaring ambitions, which were to lead to the enormous expansion of the machine industry in the nineteenth and twentieth centuries.

Spread of the Factory System. Large-scale industrialism spread from these beginnings in two directions. Externally, it spread from one nation to another. From England, the factory system jumped to the countries of Western and Northern Europe and then to the United States. The industrialization of Russia began under the czarist regime and was greatly expanded by the Communists. Japan also industrialized its economy, and today other Asiatic countries are trying to follow her example. Even in those areas in which the factory has not thus far appeared on a large scale, there is reason to believe that the future, perhaps the near future, will witness large-scale industrialization. It is apparent that we are in the midst of an historical movement which is far from its end.

Industrialism also expanded internally, conquering one field after another. Of particular importance was its spread, in the nineteenth century, to the manufacture of capital goods, such as iron and steel.[34] This process is by no means complete even today; for instance, agriculture is as yet industrialized only in certain areas. There is every reason to believe that industrialism will continue to expand until it embraces almost all the production of industrialized nations.

This chapter has presented a brief account of three systems of production, of the social relations in each system, and of the development of one system into another. We shall now turn to the growth and development of the industrial system in one specific case—that of the United States.

[34] G. D. H. Cole, "Industrialism," in *ibid.*, vol. 8, p. 21.

The Development of Industry in the United States

The American Environment. The development of industry in the United States was carried out under special conditions not duplicated anywhere else in the world. In England and other European countries, feudalism and the guilds had greatly hampered the growth of industrialism. In America feudalism was unknown, except perhaps in the South. In England, and later in Europe, the labor force had been recruited from the countryside, among dispossessed peasants, or from unemployed artisans, bound by tradition and loyalty to other systems of production. America, a land with no peasantry and no rural surplus, was forced to *create* a labor force through the immigration of diverse peoples from many nations. Furthermore, unlike Europe, America knew nothing of an ancient aristocracy or church; she had no traditions of ambitious kings or jealous lords. She suffered comparatively little from civil wars or foreign invasions. Here, then, was a land without traditions, without deeply entrenched classes; a land without a mass of apathetic peasants, bound by a millenium-old tradition. Here was a land where capital, enterprise, and energy could be expended in novel ways, where new techniques could be tried, where new paths could be blazed.

Physical and climatic conditions were also favorable to the growth of industry. The soil of America was rich and, over vast areas, well watered. Underneath the soil lay huge deposits of raw materials, particularly those very minerals necessary for industry: iron ore, coal, limestone, oil. Communications were good; broad, navigable rivers cut through the Eastern mountains, and great inland lakes connected the major deposits of iron and coal. Distances from other countries and within the country were, it is true, vast; but they were overcome in time by ship, by train, and by road. These distances, it should be remembered, helped give American industry the peace and tranquillity needed for growth.

Although a land without traditions, American life and conditions soon created a specifically "American spirit," a spirit which was to play an important role in the development of American industry. Confronted by a seemingly limitless frontier[1] and unending resources, cut off from European feudalism and European tradition, Americans quickly came to value the individual over the state, ambition over apathy, the new over the old, and hard work over leisure.[2] This spirit was expressed in and reinforced by the prevailing Protestantism, which, as we have seen, preached a concern with the things of this world, single-minded devotion to the task at hand, and a drive for success as a measure of God's favor. Thus, American industry was nourished from the beginning by a hard-driving, self-sacrificing, individualistic, optimistic, energetic, and even ruthless people.

However, it must not be thought that, because conditions in America were potentially favorable to the growth of industry, therefore this industry quickly sprang to a position of world leadership. On the contrary, American industrial development for a long time lagged behind that of Europe. Some of the "favorable" factors mentioned above at first posed great barriers to industrial development. The frontier, at the same time that it was helping to create the American spirit, acted as a huge drain, absorbing surplus population, making the price of factory labor dear. For what farmer or farmer's son would work in an Eastern factory while land, cheap and fertile, lay to the West? Until the beginning of mass immigration, American industry was hampered by the absence of a fully urbanized mass of cheap labor. Similarly, the vast distance from Europe, a favorable factor in one way, also meant separation from markets and from the center of technical and scientific knowledge. Internally, distance meant an unending struggle to connect scattered settlements, to build roads, dig canals, and find means to cross great rivers and high mountains. Even the tranquillity of American life was not an unmixed blessing, for industrial growth has always been closely connected with war. And finally, one must not forget that for half its history America was a colonial realm, subject to the greatest industrial nation on earth, a nation which jealously guarded its own prerogatives and advantages.

The purpose of this chapter will be to trace out the development of industry in the United States from the point of view of this book: that is, primarily, the social relations of production. Our story will carry us from the household industry of colonial times to the era of large-scale production. But, as we shall see, no matter how great the changes

---

[1] For a discussion of the influence of the frontier in American history, see the classic work of Frederick Jackson Turner, *The Frontier in American History*, chap. I, "The Significance of the Frontier in American History," Henry Holt and Company, Inc., New York, 1920.

[2] See Harold J. Laski, *The American Democracy*, The Viking Press, Inc., New York, 1949, chaps. I and II.

in American productive systems, the special factors noted here are always operating to some degree, giving to American industry its peculiar stamp.

American Industry to 1789. The early development of American industry bears little resemblance to the development of industry elsewhere. Many of the stages of economic development through which other countries passed were skipped entirely. America never developed more than the rudiments of a guild system.[3] Nor did a putting-out system ever achieve more than a local importance, except perhaps in a few industries. In truth, much early American production was of an even more primitive variety. Some early production consisted of handiwork, carried on by artisans operating individually in their own shops or in their homes. The major share of early production took place within families which were primarily engaged in agriculture. Home industry, producing mainly for direct family consumption, but sometimes for a particular customer, or even for general sale, was to be the dominant mode of production for many years.

The goods produced under these simple productive systems were of a simple "homespun" quality and necessarily limited variety. For more complicated industrial products the colonies relied on England. English goods were relatively cheap, well made, and usually plentiful; the products of the most advanced factories and technology of the time. Against this sort of competition colonial manufacture could make small headway, especially as British merchants knew how to defend their trade in the halls of Parliament.

What there was of colonial industry tended to flourish only at certain times and under special conditions. For instance, when wars cut off the colonies from the motherland, or when, for whatever reason, the cost of British goods soared above the pocketbooks of the colonists, or when the colonists sought to strike back at the British through economic boycott, native industry got its chance; indeed, colonial governments often subsidized the fledgling industries at such times.[4] Another factor favoring the growth of some domestic industries was the costliness of shipping to inland points. This difficulty so increased the cost of imported goods that some centers of manufacture grew up away from the seaports. By the end of the colonial period there were at least rudimentary industries in the fields of textiles, fishing products, lumber products, whaling products, shipbuilding, ironware, printed goods, and mining. But very little of this industry was organized on a true factory basis. The textile in-

---

[3] Victor S. Clark, *History of Manufactures in the United States*, Carnegie Institution of Washington, Washington, D.C., 1916, vol. I, p. 113.

[4] Fred Albert Shannon, *America's Economic Growth*, The Macmillan Company, New York, 1940, p. 81.

dustry alone showed much advance in that direction in pre-Revolutionary times.[5]

In spite of these local gains, American industry was very slow in developing. There were several reasons for this lack of development. High labor costs, poor transportation, uncertain and shifting markets, and a lack of native capital, an unstable currency, lack of credit institutions, an unskilled labor force and a backward technology, all contributed to the stagnation of American industry. But over and above these factors loomed the unshakable hostility of the British manufacturing and commercial classes. A stern watch was maintained by the British government lest the colonists succeed in building up an industry which would undermine the privileged position of British manufacture in the colonies, and perhaps even compete with the British in the West Indies.[6] The British policy toward its American colonies was aimed at using the colonies as a market for goods manufactured in British factories, and as a source of raw materials for British industry.

The Revolution, which was itself partly the result of British economic policy, had varying effects on the development of industry. On the favorable side were the new and unheard-of demands which the war made on native industry for military supplies. At the same time, British manufactures were cut off by war. As a result there was a double demand on American industry. This demand was partially met because of a sudden availability of capital formerly invested in commerce. However, the Revolution also had an unfavorable effect on the colonial industries. British and loyalist capital fled from the land. Among the loyalist émigrés were some of the most technically competent workers. The labor that remained was relatively unskilled and scarce. Finally the war itself destroyed many small workshops, mills, and forges, which the colonies could ill afford to lose.

Victory for the Americans resulted in no dramatic upsurge of native industry. Growth of industry remained slow, in the face of continued British competition. It is significant that manufacturers were enthusiastic supporters of the Constitution and looked forward to economic gains when that document should become the law of the land.[7] Above all what they hoped to gain was protection from the competition of the older, more technologically advanced nations of Europe, particularly the British.

American Industry: 1789–1860. The hopes of the American manufacturers were not to find immediate realization. In spite of Hamilton's

[5] Clark, *op. cit.*, pp. 188ff.

[6] Louis M. Hacker, *The Triumph of American Capitalism*, Simon and Schuster, Inc., New York, 1940, pp. 140ff.

[7] Charles A. Beard, *An Economic Interpretation of the Constitution of the United States*, The Macmillan Company, New York, 1923, pp. 40ff.

report in 1791, calling for the development of American industry, Congress was slow to pass the needed legislation, such as a tariff high enough to protect native industry. Nor was native capital eager to plunge into workshop and mill. British industry, although deprived of its position of privilege by the Revolution, remained superior to American industry in terms of technology, productive power, the cheapness of its labor, the quality of its products, and, in some cases, in its access to cheap raw materials.[8] Under these circumstances American capital was attracted to overseas trade, to toll roads and canals, or to land speculation in the West. The typical capitalist of this era was not a manufacturer but a merchant or an investor.

Nevertheless, manufacture, even if it could not rival commerce in importance, continued to grow. Conflict with England, culminating in the War of 1812, eliminated competition from that quarter for a time, and gave American industry a golden, if limited, opportunity. The years of agrarian dominance which followed, typified by the Jacksonian regime, slowed this growth but did not put a stop to it. After 1820, investment in industry doubled in each decade until the Civil War. The decade of the 1850s particularly witnessed a phenomenal growth in manufactures. Capital was supplied by a prosperous agriculture which had resulted in numerous small accumulations of capital. It was the function of the corporation, which first appeared on a large scale at this time, to tap and concentrate these small accumulations. It was at about this time that a flood of immigrants began pouring in from Europe. Some of them, like the Irish fleeing the famine of 1848, were ready to work at low wages. Others, like some of the refugees from the 1848 revolts, came bearing capital. The discovery of gold in California enabled American industry to import the machinery it needed. And everywhere, and at all times, American industry kept expanding, up every mountainside and along every valley, multiplying constantly the needs for the products of manufacture.

Accompanying this growth was a constant development in technology. This era witnessed the introduction of many inventions, both native and foreign. Automatic machinery, powered by steam or stream, spread to new industries; the textile industry, as usual, was the leader. Perhaps of equal importance for industry, though indirectly, was the application of steam power to land and sea transportation.

In terms of social organization, American industry was, until the 1850s, predominantly a household, cottage, and mill industry, all these forms existing together. Although the formal relations of production were even at this early time primarily of a capitalist nature, the workingman was not an industrial worker in our sense of the term. Rather,

[8] Clark, *op. cit.*, p. 243.

he (or she) was usually an agriculturist, or a temporary employee, working in order to supplement income or, like the female textile workers of New England, in order to save money for marriage. It was only after 1850 that there began to appear on the American scene the true type of factory. This type of organization relied on a permanent working force paid in cash and with no other means of livelihood. Furthermore, in the factory labor was highly specialized and organized by departments. Buying and selling was systematized, and in general, "commercial, technical and operative elements . . . were brought together in accordance with an intelligent plan."[9]

By the 1850s the American scene was beginning unmistakably to reflect the growing power of the manufacturer and the dominance of the factory. The mercantilist with his inherited wealth, his ships, land deeds, stocks and bonds, was fading into the shadows cast by the artisans' and farmers' sons who were creating the new industries.[10] But not all was plain sailing for the new industrialist; squarely across his path was a determined adversary, the Southern planter and slaveholder. This adversary, furthermore, largely dominated the Federal government and the armed forces. The interests and values of factory and plantation conflicted at many points. Where the manufacturer needed a high tariff as protection for his industry, immigrant labor, improvements in the means of transportation, and a sound currency, the Southern planter wanted a low tariff so that he might buy cheaply in the market where he sold his cotton, "cheap" money, an end to the flood of immigrants swelling the ranks of the North, an end to all other measures which hastened the growth of industry and threatened his power.[11]

The Growth of American Industry after 1860. The Civil War was fought over a variety of issues: slavery, states' rights versus Federal rights, and the indissolubility of the Union. It also settled the conflict between planter and manufacturer. With secession and the outbreak of the Civil War, control of government passed out of the hands of Southern legislators and their Northern allies. In their place came a new group representing a coalition of Northeastern manufacturers and independent, Middle Western farmers.

This new alliance wasted no time in enacting a program to provide for the growth of industry and the enrichment of its owners. Even dur-

[9] *Ibid.*, p. 450.

[10] While some mercantilist capital went into industry, by and large American industry was not created by merchants. The reasons include the absence of large capital accumulations among merchants, deficiencies in the type of talents needed for industry, and a tradition of luxurious living which absorbed capital. See Hacker, *op. cit.*, p. 322.

[11] Charles A. Beard and Mary R. Beard, *The Rise of American Civilization*, The Macmillan Company, New York, 1928, vol. I, pp. 614–615.

ing the Civil War the tariff was boosted upward to a level which afforded secure protection from foreign competition. Between 1857 and 1864 the average level of tariff rates rose from about 19 per cent to 47 per cent.[12]

Protection from domestic taxation was offered American industry. Even during the Civil War profits were not taxed drastically, while the moderate income tax of those days did not long survive the peace. The Civil War was financed almost entirely by bond issues, which were sold at terms greatly benefiting the investor.[13]

Generous appropriations were made for the internal improvements which were necessary if industry and commerce were to flourish. A Pacific railway was chartered, and large areas of public land as well as a Federal loan were granted to its builders. By this stroke, the market area for American industrial goods was enormously enlarged. The new government at Washington took pains also to satisfy the demands of Middle Western farmers through a Homestead Act. Measures were taken to ensure a supply of cheap labor through the encouragement of immigration.

Finally, the triumphant industrial interests were given constitutional protection from unruly legislatures, state or Federal, which might be dominated by antibusiness forces. This protection was embodied in the famous clause of the Fourteenth Amendment, which forbade any legislative body in the United States to deprive a person of "life, liberty or property" without due process of law. Since a corporation was defined as a person, this meant, in effect, that the United States Supreme Court had the power to invalidate any act of legislation which sought to impose special restrictions, such as high taxes, on corporations. As interpreted by succeeding generations of conservative Supreme Court justices, the "due-process" clause ensured industry for all practical purposes from the threat of any effective sort of hostile government intervention.

The enactment of this political program created the condition for a veritable explosion of American industry in the latter half of the nineteenth century. As the immigrants streamed into the country after the Civil War, the domestic market grew enormously. At the same time, the exploitation of the Western lands, which was made possible through improvements in communication, provided huge stocks of relatively cheap food for the expanding population. Surpluses of food were ex-

[12] This trend toward protectionism was to continue throughout the nineteenth century (except for the ineffective bill of 1894) until America virtually became an exclusive market for American industry. *Ibid.*, vol. II, p. 108.

[13] At the same time the government took pains to found a national banking system, which ensured a "sound" currency and taxed "cheap" money out of existence. *Ibid.*, p. 107.

changed abroad for raw materials, and semiprocessed goods were used to meet the interest charges on foreign borrowings.[14]

The resulting growth of manufactures in the United States between 1860 and 1900 was fantastic. In 1860 products of American factories were valued at over 1,800 million dollars. By 1870 this figure had doubled, by 1880 it was three times as large, and by 1890 it was five times as large. Between 1860 and 1880, the production of pig iron increased by almost five times, while the production of steel increased by 155 times. In 1860, America had been the world's fourth most important industrial power; by 1894 it had surpassed all other countries in industry. In fact, in that year America produced more than the British Isles and Germany combined.[15]

Although the over-all growth of American industry was most impressive, its progress was uneven. It grew in spurts of intense activity, interspersed with periods of stagnation and retrenchment. Boom and bust alternated. The Civil War had created insatiable demands for provisions of all sorts and had acted as a great spur to industry. Between 1865 and 1868, however, with the cessation of war orders, the economy turned downward. The period of 1868–1873 was a boom period based primarily on railroad construction. In 1873 a long period of depression began as the age of railroad building came to an end, large surplus stocks of agricultural goods accumulated, and European sources of credit dried up. Production dropped, prices fell sharply, unemployment became widespread, immigration dropped off. There was widespread vagrancy and serious labor conflicts. Recovery did not come before 1879. In that year the renewal of railroad construction and the modernization of existing railroads brought a boom to heavy industry. European crop failures led to improving agricultural conditions and a corresponding increase in purchasing power. Except for the short depression of 1883, American industry remained prosperous until 1893. In that year there was another sharp panic, not as prolonged as the panic of 1873. By the 1890s, American industry had grown so huge that each downward economic shift produced its millions of unemployed and affected millions more adversely.

Part cause and part effect of this rapid increase in production was an equally rapid technological development. Industry after industry became mechanized, in whole or in part. The iron (and later the steel) and machine-shop industries led the way, and others hastened to follow as soon as technical and economic conditions would permit. Steam, manu-

[14] Hacker, *op. cit.*, pp. 401–402. The new communication system also linked the great ranges of high-grade iron ore, the vast stores of lumber, and the extensive oil fields to the factories and linked the factories to their markets.

[15] Arthur Meier Schlesinger, *Political and Social History of the United States, 1829–1925*, The Macmillan Company, New York, 1925, pp. 280–281.

factured by burning coal, became the universal source of power. As a result there were sharp increases in productivity. Between 1865 and 1886, productivity per worker increased 50 to 70 per cent in the manufacture of agricultural implements, 80 per cent in the manufacture of boots and shoes, 65 per cent in the production of carriages, 40 per cent in the production of machines, and 50 per cent in silk manufactures.[16] As productivity increased, the price of manufactured goods steadily decreased.

Another measure of the technological development was the increasing number of inventions. Prior to 1860 a total of less than 36,000 patents had been granted by the Patent Office. In the forty years from 1860 to 1900 the total granted was 640,000.[17] This period saw basic inventions in the use of electricity, the invention of the air brake, the development of practical automobiles, new types of agricultural equipment, the introduction of typewriting machines, the appearance of the telephone; it witnessed the development of photography, linotyping, motion pictures, great advances in aeronautics, and so on. Invention ceased to be solely a matter of chance discoveries or the tinkering of practical men; it came to be more and more a matter of the systematic application of science to the technological problems of industry.

Leading this vast industrial development was a singular group of men. By and large these men were not the scions of the old illustrious mercantile families of the seaports, or the sons of the landed esquires of Virginia or the Hudson River Valley. An overwhelming number of them were "new men." Some of them sprang from humble families and mediocre, or worse, surroundings. Carnegie was the son of poor Scottish immigrants; Rockefeller was born in a backwoods community in New York State. Many of the new industrialists came from the ranks of the middle class and brought to industry a shrewd knowledge of trading and bookkeeping and enterprise, but little capital or culture. Only a few, like Morgan, were the products of families of considerable wealth and refinement.

Many of these men came from strict Calvinistic households, where they were early taught the values of hard work, self-denial, thrift, and prudence; they quickly learned that success was a sign of the Lord's favor and that the poor were poor because they deserved no better. Others bore the mark of the lawlessness and violence of the frontier, or the aggressiveness and lack of sentimentality of the immigrant.[18] When these traits were combined the result was a rational, shrewd, individual-

---

[16] Louis M. Hacker, *The Triumph of American Capitalism,* Simon and Schuster, Inc., New York, 1940, p. 402. By permission.

[17] Schlesinger, *op. cit.,* p. 280.

[18] Matthew Josephson, *The Robber Barons,* Harcourt, Brace and Company, Inc., New York, 1934, pp. 20–22.

istic, frugal, adaptable, aggressive, and self-confident man. The result also was a dangerous opponent and a doubtful ally, adept at struggle, hard-bitten, and callous.

That this is a fair description of the early "captains of industry" no one who studies their characters can doubt. But we can only speculate about the exact nature of the motives which drove these men. Certainly, the view of the muckrakers that greed was the sole motive is too simple. Greed there may have been, but perhaps a desire for achievement, a desire to shape and control the environment, a desire for self-expression were no less important in their make-up.[19]

Whatever the motives driving the creators of our industry, it is certain that as a class they knew what they wanted, and they let nothing stop them. The business tactics employed in this period were sometimes dishonest, sometimes unethical, often ruthless. Railroad-rate discrimination, espionage, the employment of bogus independent companies, price slashing to annihilate rival companies were frequently used tactics. Nor should the reprehensible part played by these men in the political life of the nation be glossed over.[20] Perhaps this type of business tactic was the exception, not the rule. Nevertheless, there is justification for comparing some of these men to the robber barons of medievalism. Of course, it is interesting to speculate as to whether, in some larger historical sense, these tactics were justified because they helped create the greatest industrial nation on earth. On the other hand, it is legitimate to ask whether such an industry might have been created more efficiently without such tactics. These are questions for which satisfactory answers are not likely to be found.

It is important to note that the dynamism of the "robber baron" resulted not only in the expansion of industry but also in the growth of monopoly. The formation of huge monopolies or trusts began within a very few years after the Civil War. In the process, large firms combined and small industries were swallowed up. The reason for the success of the monopolies was a simple one: they proved more efficient and profitable in many ways than small industries. The monopoly could afford to install expensive machinery, to employ highly trained managers, to reduce waste in numerous ways, to purchase supplies in large quantities and at a relatively low cost. It could, through its control of the market, eliminate some of the cost of salesmanship and marketing. Because of the volume of its business, the monopoly could get certain advantages from other firms, for instance, reduced freight rates. It could put to use the by-products of manufacture.

[19] Allan Nevins, *John D. Rockefeller*, Charles Scribner's Sons, New York, 1940, vol. I, p. 711.
[20] *Ibid.*, pp. 707–708.

Furthermore, the monopoly possessed another distinct advantage over the small firm. Because it had large financial resources, it was in a position to influence political parties, elections, and legislatures. Using this influence, monopolies secured favorable tariffs, land grants (as in the case of the railroads), control over sources of raw materials, and, from the states, generous corporate charters. From the courts the monopolies secured protection from undue interference by legislatures.

Large-scale industry and monopoly found an almost perfect means of social organization in the corporate bureaucracy.[21] Once organized in a corporate form, the large-scale enterprise could tap the financial power of an unlimited number of individuals through sales of shares, sometimes in small lots. Furthermore, the shareholders were liable for the debts and possible failure of the business only to the extent that they were invested in it; that is, the corporation minimized risk. Under these circumstances, the corporation had no difficulty in accumulating vast amounts of capital.

The corporation was peculiarly suited to the needs of large-scale industry in other ways also. For instance, it was blessed with an existence independent of the lives of its individual members; managers and shareholders might come and go, but the corporation remained. Therefore, under the corporate form, large-scale planning for the future was possible in a way which could never have occurred in a partnership.[22]

The growth of monopolies was all the more remarkable because it occurred in the face of bitter opposition. In the years after the Civil War, wave after wave of "antimonopoly" movements swept through the country. "Antimonopoly" as a political and social program found its support in the middle class, among farmers, and in the labor movement—all threatened, though in different ways, by the growing monopolies. The antimonopolistic feeling finally found legislative expression in the Sherman Antitrust Act of 1890, which declared illegal "every contract, combination in the form of trust or otherwise, or conspiracy, in restraint of trade or commerce among the several states, or with foreign nations." However, initially the government made very little attempt to enforce the Act. Furthermore, the Supreme Court quickly interpreted the Act in such a way as in effect to protect the monopoly.

One effect the Sherman Act did have, and that was to speed up the adoption of the corporate form of organization. Trusts dissolved and resumed life as huge corporations, securely entrenched in the generous law of some state. As a result, the Sherman Act had little effect on the

---

[21] See Adolf A. Berle, Jr., and Gardiner C. Means, *The Modern Corporation and Private Property*, The Macmillan Company, New York, 1933.

[22] Schlesinger, *op. cit.*, p. 361. The bureaucratic aspects of the corporation are discussed in Chap. 5 of the present book.

growth of monopoly. In fact, in the ten years after the passage of the Sherman Act more industrial combinations were formed than in the previous thirty years. Between 1860 and 1890 twenty-four combinations had appeared, with a total capital of 436 million dollars; between 1890 and 1900, 157 combinations were organized, with a total capital of 3,150 million dollars. In 1901 the United States Steel Corporation was formed, and this corporation alone was capitalized at more than 1 billion dollars. Within a few years, this giant organization controlled 70 per cent of iron and steel production. Similar monopolistic practices continued to occur in many other fields, industrial, commercial, and financial.[23]

Oddly enough, the growth of monopoly marked the end of the brief reign of the "captain of industry"—indeed, the end of "free enterprise" in its classical sense. Control of industry now passed into the hands of those with large amounts of capital. The investment banker, whose power lay in control of the insurance company, the trust company, the savings bank, and the investment concern, bought control of existing enterprises, drove competing firms out of business, and sent more than one captain of industry into retirement.

The investment banker, as a type, differed in many important ways from the captain of industry. The captain of industry had had a personal interest in the concern. He knew at least some of the workers. Often he had close knowledge of techniques, frequently one which he had invented. To the investment banker, on the other hand, the firm was a far-away and lifeless thing, its employees mere abstractions, and its technology a mystery.

The movement toward monopoly and concentration, the tendency for control of industry to pass into the hands of the investment banker, and the bureaucratization of industry all had certain effects on the social relationships of production. Formal relations of production remained of the capitalistic variety, but they were greatly rigidified. The workingman, who may formerly have worked in close relationship to the owner, became a minute and anonymous part of a vast organization. The impersonal aspects of the capitalistic relationship became greatly accentuated. Capital and labor tended to confront each other not only in theory but in fact as vast impersonal, often hostile, masses, each seeking the most advantageous terms of the other in a market relationship.

Social relationships at work were also greatly changed. The result of increasing size and bureaucratization was an ever greater division of labor and more mechanization. These latter changes led, in turn, to new types of formal or informal associations at work or to associations outside of work, which were of great influence on the social relationships at work.

[23] *Ibid.*, pp. 371–372.

With the growth and concentration of industry, major changes occurred in the social life of the nation. A drift from rural areas to the city set in as industrial jobs opened up. Industry also turned to the masses of Europe for factory labor. Wave after wave of immigration poured into the United States; between 1861 and 1900 over 14 million immigrants arrived, and between 1901 and 1920, an even larger number. These immigrants were largely drawn from Southern and Eastern Europe. Separated from the native Americans by culture, language, and religion, they tended to form homogeneous communities within the cities, close to the factories. In this way were formed the "Little Sicilies," "ghettos," and "hunkytowns."

As a result of these population movements the cities expanded enormously. In 1850 only 15 per cent of the American people lived in cities. By 1900 the figure had risen to almost 40 per cent. In 1950, 58.7 per cent of the American people lived in cities. New York City, which had a population of less than 700,000 in 1850, was by 1900 a metropolis of almost 3½ million people. Chicago expanded from a town of less than 30,000 in 1850 to a metropolis of nearly 1,700,000 by 1900. With this rapid urban growth there appeared many of our familiar social problems: overcrowding, slums, municipal corruption, crime, race and ethnic prejudice.

Concomitant with the development of large-scale industry was the development of an American labor movement.[24] The period between 1865 and 1890 witnessed the rise and collapse of a great industrial union, the Knights of Labor. This was followed by the founding of the much more successful American Federation of Labor. This period also saw bitter labor struggles such as the great railway strikes of 1877, the Homestead strike in 1892, and the Pullman strike of 1894. From the beginning the union movement in the United States faced the bitter opposition of employers, of the courts, the legislatures, as well as an often hostile public. Under these circumstances, growth was slow. By 1900 the AFL had an enrollment of 550,000, which was only 5 per cent of the total American labor force. It is significant that only 17½ per cent of American workers were in unions by 1920, and as late as 1935, less than 10 per cent of them were organized. Even today the figure is less than 35 per cent, the great majority of the working force being outside the union movement entirely.

By the year 1900, then, the foundation of modern American industry had been in the main put down. A huge railroad network had been created, great heavy industries had been built, the major urban-industrial centers had been created and were being rapidly filled by a labor force

[24] A discussion of the history of the American labor movement will be found in Chap. 10.

entirely dependent on industry for livelihood. Impersonal financial control of industry had, in good part, replaced the personal reign of the captain of industry. Industrial concentration was already far advanced. The large-scale bureaucracy had proved to be the most suitable instrument for large-scale production.

The development of American industry since 1900 has been spectacular. Vast new industries have been built: the automobile industry, the television industry, the airplane industry, the industries devoted to the production of atomic energy. Industry enabled America to wage two world wars successfully and to rise to a position of dominance in the world. American industry helped create a unique standard of living. Yet all these accomplishments were based on the industrial developments of the latter portion of the nineteenth century. For this reason it is not too much to say that, of all the revolutions and changes through which America has gone, the most significant for modern times was accomplished by the construction of a great industry between the years 1860 and 1900.

The development of American industry in the twentieth century was no more a straight-line development than it had been in the nineteenth century. Booms and busts continued to exhilarate or depress American industry in a regular succession. The great industrial boom of the 1920s was followed by the abysmal bust of the 1930s, when almost countless millions were thrown out of work, and the national wealth declined by about a third. Industry continued to meet stern opposition from other institutions in society. Since the leaders of industry, rightly or wrongly, were partly held responsible for the Great Depression, Federal government, under the New Deal, moved to regulate (and even forbid) many traditional industrial practices. Furthermore, during the 1930s there appeared in the Congress of Industrial Organizations perhaps the most successful militant, large-scale labor movement in American history. This confederation of unions quickly, and apparently permanently, established itself in some of the most important industries. During and since World War II, industry has largely recovered its prestige, if not its freedom of action, and gone on to attain new heights of expansion and production, in a period of remarkable prosperity.

The Present Structure of American Industry. Let us attempt to picture the structure of American industry today. How large is it? Who owns it? To what extent is it a concentrated industry, to what extent dispersed? We must keep in mind the fact that the picture we shall present is necessarily static, imaging the state of our industry at one historical moment of time. Reality is composed not only of structure but of process, and those forces which have underlain the formation and development of industry, or forces like them, are operating in the present also.

The Size of American Industry. At the present time American industry far overshadows that of any other country, at least in the quantity of goods produced. Soviet Russia is the second most powerful industrial country, yet the United States produces approximately 1.6 times as much coal, 6 times as much petroleum, 3.5 times as much electricity, 2.2 times as much steel, and 2.1 times as much pig iron. In relationship to the entire output of Western Europe (west of the Iron Curtain), America produces almost as much coal, approximately 5.6 times as much petroleum, 2.2 times as much electricity, 1.6 times as much steel, and 1.7 times as much pig iron. As compared to the combined production of Western Europe, the Soviet Union, and all its satellites, American coal production is half as large, but America produces 2.6 times more petroleum, 1.2 times more electricity, 82 per cent as much steel, and 86 per cent as much pig iron. These statistics suggest that the American industrial plant is approximately as large as the rest of the world's put together.

Concentration in the American Economy. This enormous industrial output is the product of a relatively few large-scale organizations. One index of the concentration of production in the United States can be found in numbers of workers employed by various corporations. Considered from this point of view, most corporations in the United States are relatively small. In the 1930s, 25 per cent of all corporations employed only one worker, 3 per cent employed fifty workers or less, and 90 per cent thirty or less. On the other hand, firms which employed 10,000 workers or more accounted for 12 per cent of all jobs in the United States. Yet such large-scale firms made up only $\frac{1}{100}$ of 1 per cent of all firms. In fact, 5 per cent of all firms employed 70 per cent of all workers in this country.[25]

Another index of the concentration of production in this country is the amount of assets held by industrial corporations. There were in the 1930s some thirty industrial and nonindustrial corporations with assets of 1 billion dollars or more. The largest of those corporations, Metropolitan Life Insurance Company and the American Telephone and Telegraph Company, were richer than any one of 38 states. Only New York, Pennsylvania, Ohio, California, Massachusetts, Michigan, New Jersey, Indiana, and Wisconsin possessed more wealth.[26] The 200 largest nonfinancial corporations possessed about 55 per cent of all the assets of

[25] By permission from David Lynch, *The Concentration of Economic Power,* Columbia University Press, New York, 1946, p. 114.
[26] *Ibid.,* pp. 111–113.

nonfinancial corporations. One-tenth of 1 per cent of all corporations earned 50 per cent of all the net profits earned by corporations.[27] In 1935, considering both financial and nonfinancial corporations, 780 corporations controlled about 52 per cent of corporate assets. Of course, such concentration of production varies markedly from field to field; the assets of the metal and metal-products industry are much more concentrated than those of, say, the textile industry.

A third means of measuring the concentration of industry in the United States is through observation of the amounts of production carried on by various firms in several industrial fields. In the 1930s the 45 largest transportation corporations owned 92 per cent of the transportation facilities, and 80 per cent of public-utility facilities were owned by the 40 largest corporations in that field.[28] One firm manufactured all the virgin aluminum produced in the United States, three automobile concerns accounted for 86 per cent of the automobiles manufactured, two firms produced 95 per cent of the plate glass. In only a few areas, such as bakery products or women's clothing, was production diffused over a large number of firms.

Whether the index used be numbers of workers employed, assets of corporations, or amount of production, the only conclusion that can be reached is that American industry is highly concentrated. Writing almost a quarter of a century ago, Berle and Means concluded that the 200 largest corporations (other than banking) controlled about 49 per cent of the corporate wealth, about 38 per cent of all business wealth, and (including banking corporations) 22 per cent of the national wealth.[29] Furthermore, the influence of these giant corporations extended far past their boundaries. Many smaller companies sold to or bought from these huge corporations and consequently were at the mercy of their price policies.

However, the indexes used thus far probably do not tell the full story of concentration in American production. Beginning at a time not long after the Civil War, corporations habitually grouped themselves together in pools, or rings, for purposes of cooperation, of stifling competition, fixing prices, etc.; these were truly the combinations of giants. Today, the major instrument of this type of combination is quite another type of organization—the trade association. The trade association may be defined as a "voluntary non-profit organization of enterprises engaged in a particular type of business."[30] Its development can be traced to the latter part of the nineteenth century. By 1933 there were 7,800 of

[27] Smaller War Plants Corporation, *Economic Concentration and World War II*, Government Printing Office, 1946, p. 55.
[28] *Ibid.*
[29] Berle and Means, *op. cit.*, p. 32.
[30] Lynch, *op. cit.*, p. 95.

these trade associations in this country, 6,000 of them local, the rest national in scope. There were, for instance, associations of industries concerned with metal production, associations of owners of bus lines, and associations of manufacturers connected with the cottonseed industry.

Trade associations have two types of functions. First, they serve as a meeting place for manufacturers in the same or related fields who wish to cooperate with each other by standardizing procedure and products. Such cooperation may entail pooling research, conducting joint advertising campaigns, settling codes of business ethics, interchanging credit information, collecting and distributing statistical information, or planning joint representations to governing bodies.[31] These activities in themselves represent a form of combination. Secondly, the trade association, formed as it is of competitors or supposed competitors, may serve as a very convenient vehicle for minimizing or reducing competition, fixing prices, lobbying against unfavorable laws, and, in some cases, excluding new firms from the field entirely.

Of all the trade associations, the most important is the National Association of Manufacturers (the NAM) which is, in a sense, an association of trade associations. Although the NAM has never possessed a large membership, it has succeeded in establishing a decided influence over perhaps 80 per cent of American manufacturing.[32] One of its major functions is to coordinate the efforts of all business associations—not merely manufacturing associations—in the United States. The NAM has served as the national voice of business, has lobbied for and against legislation, and has devoted great efforts to the task of placing the businessman's and industrialist's version of events before the American public. There can be no doubt that the ability of American industry to act as a unit is greatly enhanced by the activities of this organization.

Ownership of American Industry. The question of the ownership of this vast industry is a complex one. Those who "own" industry may not necessarily "control" it, and those who "control" do not necessarily have to "own." Furthermore, both control and ownership do not necessarily stop at the boundaries of a single industry; many types of cross control, interlocking control, partial control, and in many different degrees, are to be found in industry, and the same is true of ownership.

Formally, any incorporated industry is owned by its stockholders and bondholders. Shares of stock usually include not only the right to dividends but also the right to vote in the selection of the board of directors, which in turn has the right to choose management. From this point of view, much American industry is owned by a very great number of

[31] *Ibid.,* p. 97.
[32] Robert A. Brady, *Business as a System of Power,* Columbia University Press, New York, 1943, p. 203.

small stockholders. The dispersion of the ownership of stock has occurred to the greatest degree among the large industries, and to a considerable extent among medium-sized firms. In general, the larger the
company, the more widely dispersed the ownership of its stock.[33] The
stockholder lists of the largest railroad (the Pennsylvania Railroad), the
largest public utility (the American Telephone and Telegraph Company), and the largest industrial firm (the United States Steel Corporation) show in each case that the principal holder in 1929 owned less
than 1 per cent of the outstanding stock. " . . . Even the aggregate
holdings of the twenty largest stockholders of the Pennsylvania Railroad
amounted in 1929 to only 2.7%, of the Telephone Company to 4.0% and
of the Steel Company to 5.1%. The remainder of the half million Telephone stockholders, the 196,119 stockholders of the Railroad and the
182,585 holders of Steel stock were negligible as individual holders."[34]
Furthermore, this dispersion of ownership seems to be increasing; thus
the American Telephone and Telegraph Company had sixty times more
shareholders in 1931 than in 1901, and in about the same period the
numbers of holders of Pennsylvania Railroad shares increased by eight
times.

However, the dispersion of ownership of American industry is to a
considerable extent illusory. In the first place, while the number of
shareholders is very large, much of the stock is concentrated in a relatively few hands. Thus in the 1930s only 10,000 persons, 0.008 per cent
of the population at that time, owned one-fourth of the stock; 75,000
individuals owned one-half of all corporate stock. Furthermore, only
1,000 individuals received 10.4 per cent of all dividends, while 61,000
persons received half of all dividends paid by stock. To put it another
way, the top 1 per cent of book shareholders owned 60 per cent of all
common stock. Of the 200 largest nonfinancial corporations, the twenty
largest stockholders held more than 50 per cent of the stock in about
fifty corporations.[35]

In the second place, the dispersion of stock does not, by itself, necessarily indicate wide-scale control of industry. It is entirely possible for
de facto control of industry to be separated from ownership; that is,
the actual controllers of an industry may own little or no stock in the
corporation, and in fact, this is what has happened. As industries have
grown larger and as thousands of small stockholders have acquired
shares in corporations, management and ownership have tended to

[33] Berle and Means, *op. cit.,* pp. 47ff.
[34] Adolf A. Berle, Jr., and Gardiner C. Means, *The Modern Corporation and Private
Property,* The Macmillan Company, New York, 1933, pp. 47–48. By permission.
[35] *The Distribution of Ownership in the 200 Largest Nonfinancial Corporations,*
Temporary National Economic Committee Monograph 29, Government Printing
Office, 1940, chap. II.

separate more and more. When the shares of a corporation are thoroughly diffused, it may be possible to locate its controllers only by discovering those individuals who are, in fact, in a position to choose or influence the actions of the board of directors. Since, in the cases we are examining, these people are not majority stockholders, their control must rest on bases other than ownership of stock. Perhaps three major types of such "ownerless" control can be distinguished.[36]

First, a corporation can sometimes be controlled without ownership through the use of certain legal devices. One such device is *pyramiding*, in which one corporation holds a majority of shares in another corporation, and so on. In this way an individual with a relatively small investment in a parent company could ultimately control a corporation worth many times his original investment. Other devices of this sort have been used, although some of them have been declared illegal.

Second, sometimes individuals who own relatively small amounts of the stock of a corporation may, in fact, unchallengedly control the corporation. Such control rests on the fact that many small shareholders are unconcerned about control of the corporation in which they have invested their money and are easily persuaded to surrender the votes to which their stock entitles them to those with substantial minority holdings. By combining minority holdings and proxy votes, one individual or a group of individuals may control a majority of the stocks of any single corporation. The minority stockholder or a combination of minority stockholders will then be able to choose the board of directors of that corporation.

Finally, control may sometimes be achieved without ownership of any stock at all; such control is often called *management control*. Management control occurs, generally, in those companies in which the ownership of stock is most widely diffused. In such a case, the individual stockholder, perhaps the owner of a handful of stocks, will ordinarily surrender his vote to a proxy committee, if indeed he even bothers to do that. Since the proxy committee is selected by management, then it follows that management is in a position to choose the board of directors instead of the directors selecting management. Although management control may seem tenuous, it is, in fact, extraordinarily stable. Because of the apathy of the stockholders, because they are widely scattered geographically, and because they are unorganized socially, revolts against management control are practically unknown.

The data presented thus far indicate that control of our large-scale industries is highly concentrated. Actually this is only a part of the story.

[36] The following discussion is based on Adolf A. Berle, Jr., and Gardiner C. Means, *The Modern Corporation and Private Property,* The Macmillan Company, New York, 1933, pp. 70ff. By permission.

For one thing, the boards of directors of the large corporations tend to overlap.[37] In the year 1935, it was found that, of the 200 largest non-financial corporations and the 50 largest financial corporations, only 25 failed to have at least one director in common with some other corporation; 151 of these corporations shared at least three directors with other corporations. It is significant to note that only 400 men held nearly a third of the 3,544 directorships on the boards of these 250 corporations.

Secondly, the device of pyramiding not only permits minority control but also makes it possible for a relatively few individuals to control a number of corporations. Thus in at least 30 of the 250 corporations noted above, at least 10 per cent of the voting power was derived from stock held by other corporations, directly or indirectly.[38]

In the third place, control may be indirectly concentrated through a common reliance on certain types of organizations, providing special services of a legal, financial, or accounting nature.[39] Particularly strategic in this connection are certain investment houses, which market the securities for corporations which are seeking to raise capital. This business is in itself highly concentrated, with perhaps 5 per cent of the investment houses dominating over 90 per cent of the business in the field.[40] The investment house is in a position to influence almost every corporation it serves, through its access to confidential financial information, through its ability to give financial advice, through the interlocking of its board of directors with the boards of industrial corporations, and in other ways besides. The National Resources Committee found in 1935 that the Morgan First National group was in a position to influence no less than 41 large corporations, including the United States Steel Corporation, American Telephone and Telegraph Company, numerous utilities, 11 major railroad lines, and several other important financial institutions.[41] It is, of course, difficult to measure the extent to which such groupings are true combinations, but it is clear that to some extent they act as coordinated units.

In a somewhat similar manner, certain investment concerns such as banks and insurance companies, which hold large blocks of stocks in various firms, may serve as instruments for the concentration or the coordination of industries.

Concentration in American industry seems to proceed along two axes. First, there is concentration stemming from growth in the size of industries. This type of concentration is motivated from *within* industry, so

[37] Smaller War Plants Corporation, *op. cit.*, pp. 16–17.
[38] *Ibid.*, p. 17.
[39] *Ibid.*
[40] Lynch, *op. cit.*, pp. 127–128.
[41] *Ibid.*

to speak; that is, through a desire for maximization of profit, through the demands of efficiency, through technological change. Second, there is concentration in the sense of concentration of control. Undoubtedly, both types of concentration are related to each other; thus, growth in the physical size of the American industrial plant has been furthered by the concentration of control, while this has, in good measure, been made possible by increase in size of industrial organizations.

Where so many factors are operating to further concentration, it might be expected that American industry would have become by this time one large coordinated unit, owned or controlled by a mere handful of men. This view is too simple. At one time the symbol of Wall Street as the final owner and arbiter of American industry was quite popular. Probably this symbol most nearly approximated reality in the early years of this century. Today, however, it is probably no longer true that the large investment houses (which was what was usually meant when the term "Wall Street" was used) do control the vast industrial corporations of America, whose capital resources are, in many cases, entirely adequate to finance almost any conceivable undertaking. Nor is "Wall Street" a house undivided; it contains a number of diverse and, at times, even conflicting interests. Finally, large and important segments of American industry retain their financial independence and are free of ties to other firms, investment houses, or groupings of industry.

Present Trends in Concentration. It will be noted that almost all the figures quoted in this section of the chapter refer to the decade of the 1930s. Is there reason to assume that the story is different today—that the trend to concentration has been reversed? Unfortunately, no studies comparable to those cited in this section have been made since the thirties. However, there is some information about the development of American industry during World War II. This brings the story up to 1945. Since the period from 1945 to the present has been one of war and intensive preparation for war, it seems reasonable to conclude that at least some of the same trends noted during the war are continuing today.

What happened to American industry during World War II? On the one hand, small business increased its importance in the American economy in an absolute sense; on the other hand, big business gained both relatively and absolutely.[42] For instance, the vast increase in employment between the years 1939 and 1944 was absorbed almost entirely by large firms employing more than 500 workers. To take one specific case, in the ordnance industry, which was virtually nonexistent in 1939 but which by 1944 employed 700,000 workers, almost the entire labor

[42] Smaller War Plants Corporation, *op. cit.*, pp. 21ff.

force was concentrated in the larger firms. The same situation held in the other major war industries: iron and steel, nonferrous metals, machinery, transportation equipment, chemicals, petroleum and coal products, and rubber products. By 1944 the top 2 per cent of manufacturing firms accounted for 62 per cent of total employment.

Basically the reason for this great expansion of large firms was the urgent need for maximum production at maximum speed. The government, which had 200 billion dollars of contracts to allot, quite naturally turned to the giant firms. The large-scale corporations benefited in several ways. In the first place they made substantial profits on war production. Furthermore, throughout the war they received top priorities in the allocation of scarce materials and supplies, with which they raised the technical levels of their plants. In addition, the giant firms received the benefit of much scientific and technological research financed by the government. Again, the government constructed many modern and efficient plants, which ultimately reverted to the industry at nominal cost. Finally, these large corporations were the beneficiaries of extremely favorable tax laws, designed to encourage plant expansion.

War production had the effect of increasing the power of the large firm over the small plant in still another way. The holder of the prime contract had the right to put out work to subcontractors. This meant that the large corporation could determine how much work the subcontractors would receive, and what priorities for materials and supplies they would get.[43]

Thus, although war production resulted in the revival of some small industries and led to the founding of others, its primary effect was to increase the size, efficiency, and economic power of the large plant. War and its demands hastened along the process of concentration.

The trend of concentration since World War II is not easy to discern from the data on hand. During the decade of the fifties, American manufacturing experienced a wave of mergers, though to what extent this has served to increase concentration cannot now be ascertained. On the other hand, the continuing high degree (in an absolute sense) of concentration is not a matter of dispute.[44]

[43] Even so, there was perhaps less subcontracting than is commonly supposed; only about 34 per cent of prime contracts were let out. It is important to note that three-fourths of the work which was let out went to firms having more than 500 employees.

[44] For a detailed analysis of American industry's concentration, see M. A. Adelman, "The Measurement of Industrial Concentration," *The Review of Economics and Statistics*, vol. 23, no. 4, pp. 269–296, 1951. See particularly tables 11, 13, 14. See also George W. Stocking and Myron W. Watkins, *Monopoly and Free Enterprise*, The Twentieth Century Fund, Inc., New York, 1951, chap. 2.

PART TWO

The Social Structure of Industry

CHAPTER 5

The Industrial Bureaucracy

The major steps in the development of American industry have been traced and the major structural features of American industry described. We shall now turn to the internal structure of that industry.

The aim of Part 2 will be to picture the social life of man in industry: the role he plays, the formal and informal social groups to which he belongs, the influence of industrial organization on his personality, and the strains to which he is subjected. The hypothesis is that all these diverse elements of social and psychological life are, in the last analysis, determined by the demands of industrial production, organized along capitalistic lines. The hypothesis will state further that the action of industrial man is not aimless or random; he acts, and to a good part thinks and feels, *organizationally*.

In this chapter some of the broadest features of industrial organization will be discussed. Other chapters in Part 2 will be devoted to an analysis of certain crucial industrial roles. As elsewhere throughout this book, major concern here is with the large-scale industrial plant.

The General Nature of Bureaucracy. An examination of large-scale industry in the United States reveals quite clearly that much of it is organized socially around a certain form. This form most closely resembles the type of organization which social scientists call a *bureaucracy*. The bureaucratic form is found in many areas: in industry, in certain religions, in the state, in the army, in education. Furthermore, bureaucracy has existed in many other times and places; for instance, it reached a high stage of development in ancient China and in ancient Egypt. Industrial organization, then, is one variant of the bureaucratic type. For this reason, it will be necessary to describe the major features of bureaucracy in general before proceeding to an analysis of the industrial bureaucracy in particular.

Great care must be taken in describing a pure or ideal type of bureaucracy, because it is entirely possible that a feature present in one bureaucracy may be absent in another.[1] For instance, in many bureaucracies officials are appointed by higher authority. However, in some bureaucracies officials are elected; in others, they enter their offices through automatic promotion or by taking an examination. The ideal type of bureaucracy which is described below must not be taken as a description of any specific bureaucracy, but rather as a rough outline of certain universal characteristics of all bureaucracies.

In each bureaucracy there is a distinction between the administration, or *hierarchy,* of the bureaucracy on the one hand, and the masses of people who are administered to or governed, the *laity* on the other. For instance, in the Roman Catholic Church there is a sharp distinction between the clergy and the parishioners. In an army there is a distinction between the officer corps and enlisted men. In industry the distinction is between management and workers. In speaking of bureaucracy it is necessary to keep these distinctions in mind because the conditions and rules which apply to the hierarchy rarely apply to the laity.

The hierarchy of a bureaucracy consists of a series of offices, or positions, each of which has more or less carefully specified duties and areas of competence. For each office there is a set of rules, which states in a formal, though often inaccurate, way the obligations of the office, its relations to other offices, and the privileges which belong to it. The office is usually given a name—vice president, general of the army, etc. —and sometimes is surrounded by considerable ritual. These offices may be related to each other in one of two ways. On the one hand, offices may have certain obligations to other offices. For instance, the function of one office may be to supply technical knowledge to other offices. On the other hand, the offices may be (and usually are) arranged along an authority axis, so that any one office is usually superior to some offices and subordinate to others.

Another characteristic of most bureaucratic offices is the considerable specialized knowledge demanded of officials. As a result those who fill the offices usually must have specialized training. Often, this specialized training involves formal education. However, in addition, each office demands certain specific skills which can usually be acquired only through long service in the organization. As a result the amount of specialized knowledge necessary for each office is greatly increased.

The bureaucratic office is rather strongly marked by the great amounts of documents and other written records which are produced at all levels of the hierarchy. In fact, in the advanced bureaucracy great numbers of

[1] For a discussion of this point see Carl J. Friedrich, "Some Observations on Weber's Analysis of Bureaucracy," in Robert K. Merton et al. (ed.) *Reader in Bureaucracy,* Free Press, Glencoe, Ill., 1952, pp. 27–33.

specialists and expensive equipment are necessary just to handle paper work. It is no wonder that to the layman bureaucracy means red tape!

Finally, the bureaucracy is marked by certain types of relations between the office and the official or bureaucrat who fills the office. The office exists and operates continuously, irrespective of what individuals happen to fill it at any time. The office of the papacy, for instance, has existed for centuries. Whatever authority, prestige, or power the incumbent of an office possesses inheres, at least in theory, in the office, not in the individual.[2] Furthermore, the official does not own the facilities— such as desks, laboratory, machines—which he uses; these belong to the office. Usually the official has to tender account of his use of organizational funds and equipment. It is interesting to note that, just as the workingman is separated from the means of production in our society, so the official is separated from ownership of the means of administration.

However, the relationship of the official to his office differs in many striking ways from the relationship of the worker to his job. The office is regarded as imposing certain duties on the official, and the income connected with it is not in the nature of wages paid but of a salary designed to ensure a certain standard of living. In addition, the official is governed by a professional code of loyalty to his organization. It might also be noted that he is appointed to his job for an indefinite period of time, unlike the wage worker who is employed only when there is work. Furthermore, also in contrast to the wageworker, the official of the bureaucracy follows a career and expects, in the normal course of events, to "move up the ladder." That is, a part of the official's expectations is that he will move, step by step, through positions providing ever-increased responsibilities, power, social esteem, and salary. Often the various steps of the ladder are so clearly delineated that an official can know how high he may expect to be in ten or twenty years.

These, then, are the most general characteristics of the bureaucratic office. But why has bureaucracy developed in the sphere of industry? After answering that question, we shall consider the particular type of bureaucracy which appears to be most often associated with industry in the United States.

Causes of the Rise of Industrial Bureaucracy. If bureaucratic organization has triumphed in industry, it is because bureaucracy has met cer-

---

[2] The discussion of this section, particularly of the nature of the hierarchy in a bureaucracy, relies heavily on the classic analysis of Max Weber. See his *From Max Weber: Essays in Sociology*, edited and translated by H. H. Gerth and C. Wright Mills, Oxford University Press, New York, 1946, pp. 196–244; and his *The Theory of Social and Economic Organization*, translated by A. M. Henderson and Talcott Parsons, Oxford University Press, New York, 1947, pp. 329–341.

tain needs inherent in large-scale production. What are these needs, and why have they resulted in bureaucracy?[3]

1. In general, bureaucracy seems to develop in any type of social organization which experiences considerable growth in size, especially if this growth is a long-term trend. The case of industry fulfills this condition for the growth of bureaucracy. Industrial expansion has not been based on a myriad of small establishments but, typically, on gigantic individual units or clusters of giant units. This pattern of growth has resulted, as we have seen, from the demands for efficiency, from the need to use central sources of power, and from the resultant superior profitability of large-scale enterprises. Today, as in the past, existing large-scale units tend to continue to grow in size, and large-scale production continues to invade areas formerly dominated by small-scale production. At least up to the present, this has been a well-nigh irreversible process. Only rarely has the opposite occurred, that is, the breaking up of the large-scale enterprise into small productive units.

As the size of industrial units has increased, the task of administration has increased in something like a geometric progression. The large-scale procurement of raw material, the necessity for hiring and training large numbers of managers, experts, and workers, the need to coordinate the activities of large numbers of men and machines, and the necessity for disposing of a great quantity of finished products—all these pose administrative problems of a vast scope. The solution of these administrative problems demands a corps of trained experts, centralized planning and control, efficient communication between various parts of the organization, discipline, and a complicated system of record keeping. In each of these respects, bureaucracy offers great advantages. It provides for specialized offices and a rigid system of central supervision. It provides means for enforcing discipline. It provides channels of communication, through which information and orders can flow. So great are these advantages that it seems doubtful whether a continuous large-scale industry could have developed, or could continue to exist, except within the bureaucratic framework.

2. The development of specialization in industry (that is, a very fine and increasing division of labor) has increased the need for bureaucracy in our system of production. Undoubtedly, specialization is possible within many different types of social organizations; for example, it occurs in the family. But bureaucracy offers certain advantages for the development of a particularly elaborate system of specialization. One

[3] Weber, *From Max Weber: Essays in Sociology*, pp. 209–211; Marshall E. Dimock, *Bureaucracy and Trusteeship in Large Corporations*, Temporary National Economic Committee Monograph 11, Government Printing Office, 1940, chaps. V and VI; Alvin W. Gouldner, *Patterns of Industrial Bureaucracy*, Free Press, Glencoe, Ill., 1954.

advantage is that bureaucracy creates offices, with carefully defined spheres of operation. Specialization can, so to speak, be hung on the peg of the bureaucratic office.

Furthermore, the sharp separation of the bureaucratic office from all other nonindustrial roles coincides with the needs of industry. Industrial specialization demands single-minded devotion to the task at hand and the sloughing off of other roles during working hours.

Finally, the fact that bureaucratic offices are circumscribed by rules dovetails neatly with the needs of industrial specialization, which depends upon elaborate rules as to the rate, quality, and precision of work.

3. Large-scale industrial production depends on the application of expertness and technical knowledge to the specialized task. This is true as much for the operation of a complex machine as for the conducting of a complicated experiment in a research laboratory or the administering of a managerial office. In fact, the ability to supply special scientific or technological knowledge to a given task is another factor in the superiority of the industrial system over other productive systems. Bureaucracy offers great advantages for the utilization of the expert and of specialized knowledge. For one thing, the bureaucracy, which is itself a rationalized social organization, helps to create the proper attitudes in its members for the application of rational knowledge and techniques. Furthermore, because the bureaucracy is divided into offices and positions which demand the full time and attention of those who fill them, there is the opportunity for becoming really expert at one job. This holds as much for the scientist in the laboratory as for the worker at a press. By way of contrast, we may consider how relatively little expertness could be achieved at any one task by the guild workingman who manufactured an entire suit of clothing. Bureaucracy is the natural habitat of the expert.

4. The development of a mechanized technology in industry has hastened the development of a bureaucratic social organization. Mechanization inevitably increases specialization and therefore, in the manner noted above, the need for bureaucracy. Also, mechanization demands the coordination of human activities; there must be a steady supply of raw materials for the machines, various mechanized tasks must be integrated so that a smooth flow of work is maintained, uniformity in the finished products must be ensured. Such coordination demands not only careful and rational planning but also a rigorous system of discipline, both of which can be best attained under a bureaucratic form of organization. Furthermore, the bureaucracy provides opportunity for the efficient organization of production into departments such as procurement, production, inspection. For instance, successful regulation of the activity of the machine tender, both as to rate and quality of work, demands a

rigid chain of command and discipline. Finally, only bureaucracy seems to be able to match the ever finer division of mechanized tasks with equally finely defined roles; both the machine process and bureaucratic organization seem to be almost infinitely divisible. It is hardly accidental then that the machine age is also the bureaucratic age.

5. The marriage of industry and bureaucracy is also founded on the need of industry for long-range planning, for rational calculation for the future. Industry needs long-range planning in order to meet future orders, in order to have adequate and proper types of raw materials on hand, in order to ensure itself of proper types of labor, in order that machines and plants may not suffer periods of idleness. Long-range planning is also needed in order that research on new products may be undertaken, in order that capital may be accumulated at a proper rate and invested wisely, in order that payrolls may be met. In fact, modern industry is founded on rational planning no less than on the machine technology. But if long-range planning is to be a success, a type of social organization is demanded in which the actions of individuals are controllable and predictable, in which the power of management to control the use of raw materials and machines is unchallenged. A type of organization is needed in which the power of human whim or fancy to disrupt a plan is reduced to a minimum. It will hardly be necessary to point out what advantages bureaucracy offers in this respect.

6. Finally, though by no means of least importance, industry finds in bureaucracy a means for creating and maintaining a continuous and rigid discipline over its personnel at all levels. The need of industry for the coordination of many diverse tasks, the need for fitting human activity to the highly rational and often monotonous routine of the machine, the need for long-range planning—all these demand a close supervision of work, a rigid obedience to rules, and the suppression of many natural human impulses.

These needs bureaucracy can meet in a number of ways. It will be recalled that, in a bureaucracy, the worker as well as the official is separated from ownership of raw materials or machines or other facilities. This means that both worker and official are economically dependent on the bureaucracy, and consequently are necessarily submissive to the demands of the organization. Furthermore, the fact that a bureaucracy assigns certain tasks to certain offices or positions, and surrounds each office or position with rigid rules, means that the quality and quantity of the performance of each worker or official can be determined, and properly rewarded or punished. Finally, the rigid lines of authority in the bureaucracy mean that responsibility for the performance of a task can be definitely located; someone must assume responsibility for deficiencies and failures, or receive credit for successes.

We may say, then, that the bureaucracy more nearly meets the needs of industry than any other type of social organization. The reason for this, as Max Weber said,[4]

has always been its purely technical superiority over any other form of organization. The fully developed bureaucratic mechanism compares with other organizations exactly as does the machine with the tool.

More specifically, Weber found the superiority of the bureaucracy in its[5]—

precision, speed, unambiguity, knowledge of the files, continuity, discretion, unity, strict subordination, reduction of friction and of material and personal costs.

Undoubtedly, there are also social and cultural factors in the spread of bureaucracy in American industry. For instance, the development of mass markets, the development of rapid means of communication, the leveling of social classes have all, in various ways, played a part in the development of bureaucracy. However, the main reasons for the triumph of bureaucracy in industry seem to be inherent in the inner compatibility of bureaucracy and large-scale production.

It would be erroneous to suppose, however, that bureaucracy has failed to meet resistance in industry. In a later section of this chapter, as well as in subsequent chapters, it will be shown that certain areas in industry have eluded the grasp of bureaucracy. For instance, there are certain informal groups in industry whose organization and aims are often diametrically opposed to those of the bureaucracy.

Structural Features of the Industrial Bureaucracy. The variant of bureaucratic social organization which has developed in industry reflects the basic needs and conditions of industry. As a result, industrial bureaucracy is unique, bearing close resemblance to other bureaucracies, but with no exact parallels anywhere. In this section some of its main structural features will be described.

Line and Staff Organization. One major structural feature of the industrial bureaucracy is division into *line* and *staff* organization. Indeed, it is this division which is most often found pictured on managerial organization charts. On such charts, line organization is shown as a series of offices and positions of varied function and authority, tied to a technological process. Each office or position is related to other offices and positions in one of two ways: in terms of carrying on a given task for the organization as a whole or for some part thereof, or in terms of

---

[4] Weber, *From Max Weber: Essays in Sociology,* edited and translated by H. H. Gerth and C. Wright Mills, Oxford University Press, New York, 1946, p. 214, by permission.

[5] *From Max Weber: Essays in Sociology,* p. 214. By permission.

subordination or superordination. For instance, a given worker is shown to interact with other workers in the productive process, and at the same time to receive orders and direction from a foreman.

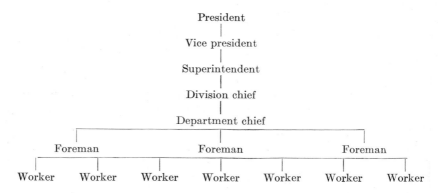

Line organization. This chart is greatly simplified.

Line organization corresponds to certain needs of industrial production. Perhaps the most important of these is the need for rigid discipline. In line organization, authority stems from definite and usually well-recognized sources, whose legitimacy is unquestioned. Orders can be made simple, clear, unambiguous, continuous. The focus of responsibility is clearly fixed, and punishments and rewards can be accurately distributed.

A second advantage of line organization lies in the possibilities it offers for the coordination of the manifold tasks of modern industry. It concentrates authority at the top, in the position marked "president" in our diagram. This top office is given the power to plan for the needs of the entire industry, to make allocations of personnel and raw material. It has the power to plan how the activities of the personnel may best be directed. And it is in a position to get its plans carried out. These two advantages of line organization—there are others—are by themselves sufficient to ensure the permanence of this principle of organization in industry.

Staff, or functional, organization is designed to meet the need of industrial organization for special knowledge or skill. This principle of organization finds expression in, first, the departmentalization of industry; that is, in the division of the industrial process into various specialized fields such as maintenance, research, advertising, personnel, etc. Each of these areas is relatively separate from all others, the chief link between them being their common subordination to high managerial officials. The operation of staff principles in industry may also be seen in the existence of special units designed to provide special knowledge or skills to the line. Units of this type include engineering departments, research laboratories, maintenance departments, legal staffs, public relations units, etc. It will be noted that most of these special units are designed to serve one or two positions on the line organization. Finally, staff principles of organization can be seen in the existence within certain industries of "staff officers," who function as advisers or special assistants to high officials of the line. Staff officers have no place on the line itself. However, in practice they may often operate there. For instance, staff officers may be used on the line to conduct a private investigation for a high official, to make direct contact between a high line officer and a relatively distant portion of the organization, or to fulfill some sort of a special task.

Any large-scale industrial organization is almost certain to represent a mixture of line and staff principles. The actual situation will depend in part on the conditions existing in the industry, in part on the ideology of management. The relative emphasis on line and staff principles of organization has tended to vary from time to time. Following the work of Frederick W. Taylor[6] in the early years of this century, the functional emphasis in industry became very heavy. In the 1920s, however, a reaction against staff principles set in, largely on the grounds that the authority principle had been weakened.[7] Since that time the importance of the line organization has received renewed emphasis, although staff principles have necessarily retained much importance.

The Role Structure of Industrial Bureaucracy. Since the main concern of this section of the book is with the role structure of industry, discussion of this vitally important aspect of the industrial bureaucracy will be confined to a few general remarks. Like all bureaucracies, industrial bureaucracy is marked by a sharp distinction between its hierarchy of officials and its laymen. In industry this hierarchy is usually at present labeled "management," the older term "capitalist" having, in part, become obsolete, and in part, fallen into ideological disfavor. The laymen are the "workers," a title which thus far no one has seen fit to change. In addition there are other industrial roles which cannot be clearly classified either as managerial or worker; for instance, the roles of foreman, certain types of specialists, and office workers.

A very important difference between the industrial hierarchy and laity is that the means of administration and the means of production are, at least in theory, solely in the hands of the hierarchy. This does not mean, as we have seen, that management necessarily has a property right in plant or tools; but it does mean that for all practical purposes

---

[6] For a compilation of the most important works of Frederick W. Taylor, see his *Scientific Management*, Harper & Brothers, New York, 1947.

[7] Albert Lepawsky, *Administration: The Art and Science of Organization and Management*, Alfred A. Knopf, Inc., New York, 1952, pp. 301–302.

management can control their use and disposal. The evolution of this situation has already been traced; suffice it to say here that many technical, economic, and commercial factors have operated to further the process of "expropriation," wherever industry has developed on a large scale.[8] Except where this situation has been modified by union power, the worker has as little property right in the tools with which he works as the soldier has in his weapon, and rather less than the citizen has in public buildings or parks.

There are many other significant differences between the position of management and the position of the workers in the industrial bureaucracy. A few of these differences will be listed here, pending a fuller discussion in the following chapters.

It has been already noted that one of the characteristics of the hierarchy of a bureaucracy is that its members supposedly follow a career. A career implies a reasonable expectation of movement up a ladder, each rung bringing increasing remuneration, power, prestige, and perhaps generality of task. Furthermore, a career normally implies something like tenure; that is, a guarantee of one's position during good behavior and with evidence of competence. This description of the career pattern rather closely fits the situation of managerial officials in industry, although, of course, for any individual official there can be no guarantee as to how far his career will proceed.

On the other hand, the worker cannot be said to have expectations of a career, in this sense. Neither in terms of tenure nor in terms of movement up a recognized ladder can the worker be said to be following a career. The worker's tenure on the job is determined by technical and economic conditions. For the majority of workers, advancement does not mean climbing a ladder of offices, but, rather, movement from one type of job to another *within* the same general role. No one should underestimate the differences in attitude and outlook between workers and management which results from this difference in their roles.

Another important difference between the positions of management and of the worker is the degree of specialization in their roles. It is important here not to confuse professionalization and specialization. The role of management is professionalized, that is, it demands extensive knowledge and performance of a task according to certain codes. The worker's role in industry, by contrast, is usually of a highly specialized nature. His task may be confined to no more than one or two operations in the manufacturing process. Most workers' jobs are semiskilled or unskilled; very few require formalized training, for instance, in an advanced school. Nor could it be said that the worker is bound to his job by a code of performance, or even, in many cases, by a feeling of loyalty

[8] Weber, *Theory of Social and Economic Organization*, pp. 246–248.

to his company.[9] He may be strongly motivated to perform well at his job, but, as we shall see later, these motives are rarely professional ones.

The difference between the professionalized industrial official and the specialized industrial worker is symbolized by the differing modes of remuneration found at each level. Management is paid a salary, which is not so much a reward for a specific amount of work done as it is recognition of rank held and of general usefulness to the company, and a guarantee of a certain standard of living. Workers, on the other hand, are paid in wages; that is, in strict accordance with amount of work done, or of time put in. It is significant that workers expect to be paid for overtime, usually at advanced rates, while this is almost never the case on the managerial level.

Authority System. A third important structural feature of the industrial bureaucracy is the system of authority. A system of authority may be defined as the sum total of means which the industrial bureaucracy employs to ensure that its members will act in accordance with the aims of the organization as a whole. The major function of the system of authority is not to originate or issue commands, but, rather, to guarantee that these commands will be obeyed.[10]

One means by which a bureaucracy seeks to obtain the obedience of its members is the creation of universally recognized and "legitimate" seats of authority and chains of command. "Legitimate" authority exists when those who are subject to this authority feel an *obligation* or a *duty* to comply with its demands. "Legitimate" authority *has the right* to command acquiescence.[11] In the industrial bureaucracy, authority, in this sense of the word, is concentrated in some of the offices, which we may call authoritative offices or positions. It should be noted that the members of a bureaucracy are not bound to obey the incumbent of the office as a person, but only the authority which inheres in the office.[12] In the last analysis, this right to command obedience is based upon the fact that the authoritative position is a fundamental part of the organization. Obedience to a command issuing from a position of authority is a recognition of the legitimacy of the entire organization; while disobedience to an order is a fundamental denial of the legitimacy of the entire organization.

The authority of each office in a bureaucracy is defined by rules which,

---

[9] There are, of course, many exceptions to this point, which will be dealt with later. Even where the worker does have feelings of loyalty to his industry, they are rarely professionally based.

[10] See Chester I. Barnard, *The Functions of the Executive*, Harvard University Press, Cambridge, Mass., 1945, p. 136. Copyright by the President and Fellows of Harvard University.

[11] Individuals may obey commands without thereby recognizing the source of the commands as legitimate; e.g., in armed robbery.

[12] Barnard, *op. cit.*, p. 173.

among other things, carefully delimit the extent of the authority. The rules specify those individuals and offices which are subject to the authority of a particular office. The rules also specify the means of compulsion which each office may use. Offices differ, of course, in the area of their authority and in the sanctions which they may employ. But there are no offices which are not subject to certain rules and limits. Even a top executive cannot violate those rules which have come to be associated with his office. Were this to occur—were, for instance, a top executive to claim authority in certain spheres of life—he would be almost certainly resisted and, in the long run, probably successfully.[13]

If commands are to be recognized as "legitimate," not only must they emanate from certain universally recognized and respected sources, but they must come through certain definite channels of communication, which are also recognized as legitimate. This implies that every individual in the organization must know what the lines of communication are, what his place in the system is, and how to recognize an authentic communication. In practice this has meant that lines of communication must be short, that the entire line of communication must be used for every order (depending on where it originates and to whom it is directed), that lines of communication must not be interrupted while the organization is functioning, and that competent persons must be present at each stage of the line of communication.[14] Only under these conditions will orders, even though they emanate from a "legitimate" source, be considered binding by recipients of the orders. The lines of communication also serve another vital function in the authority system. If the executive, or any other official, is to be able to issue workable orders, there must be accurate and up-to-date information about conditions on the levels where orders are being carried out. Such information, normally, will pass *up* the line of communication. The effectiveness of the authority system of a bureaucracy will be in proportion to the efficiency of the line of communication in this respect.

Thus far the discussion has been about authority which is based on position. However, authority may also be based on certain special qualities in an individual. These special qualities may include superior knowledge, understanding, or intellect. Sometimes the quality is an intangible aspect of personality. This type of authority is called *charismatic*

---

[13] In the industrial bureaucracy, as in most bureaucracies, authority is formally concentrated, in very large measure, in the office of the top executive, usually the president. However, the president usually delegates certain authority, sometimes on a permanent basis, to certain suboffices. Therefore, not every order in an industrial bureaucracy originates in the office of the top executive; actually, only a very minute portion of all orders originates there. However, there is no doubt as to where the ultimate authority lies, and it is this which "legitimizes" the authority of the suboffices.

[14] Barnard, *op. cit.,* pp. 176–181.

authority, and a person endowed with charisma is called a *charismatic leader*.[15]

It might seem, at first glance, that an industrial bureaucracy is so highly dependent on authority of position that it is necessarily inimical to charismatic authority. In part this is true. The charismatically endowed leader may disrupt established lines of communication and cast doubt on the legitimacy of established authority. Historically, charismatic leaders have functioned in precisely this way, particularly among industrial workers. However, charismatic authority may also serve to reinforce authority of position. For instance, the president of a firm may possess certain charismatic qualities. Here the authority of charisma is added to the authority of position. An executive of this type may wield a very strong authority indeed. In fact, it is probable that no really successful industrial leader is without certain charismatic qualities.

It is important to note that no authority system can function unless the recipient of the order or directive consents to obey. In general, obedience can be obtained only under certain conditions. The recipient of the order must understand what he is being told to do. He must have the requisite mental and physical ability to comply with the order. The personal interest of the recipient must not be threatened by the order, e.g., by degradation or humiliation. Furthermore, the order must not flagrantly violate the aims of the organization as the recipient understands them. Within these conditions, according to Barnard, there exists a "zone of indifference" or "acquiescence" within which orders will usually be obeyed. As long as an order lies within a zone of indifference, the recipient's failure to acquiesce will usually meet the disapproval of his fellows, whose own interests may be threatened by disobedience.

On the positive side, individuals will accept positional authority or charismatic leadership for a variety of psychological reasons. They may obey orders because of the training they have received in obedience, both in the community and on the job. They may obey because they are advised to do so, by individuals or institutions that they respect; they may be taught that disobedience is wrong and impious. They may assent to authority because they feel a loyalty to the organization. Obedience, in some cases, may result from the social pressure applied by friends or fellow workers. Again, individuals may be brought to assent, to obey, through the use of incentives, such as bonus systems, higher wages, shorter hours, or social recognition. Finally, they may obey orders through inertia, or custom—because things have always been done in this way, because it is easier to comply than to rebel.[16]

---

[15] Weber, *Theory of Social and Economic Organization*, pp. 358–363.

[16] For a discussion of indirect means of securing assent, see Herbert A. Simon, "Decision-making and Administrative Organization," *Public Administration Review*, vol. 4, no. 1, winter, 1944, pp. 16–25.

In summation, the authority system of the industrial bureaucracy is usually a complex mixture of positional authority and charismatic authority. The successful functioning of this system depends on certain psychological reactions in those subject to the authority. But the surface of this topic has barely been scratched; we have not attempted to describe the possible combinations of the types of authority and conditions listed above. Furthermore, it should be strongly emphasized that the formal authority system is not the only one existent in the plant; there are also informal lines of authority in any industrial bureaucracy.

Status Systems. A fourth important structural feature of the industrial bureaucracy is the system of status. By *status* is meant here the prestige, deference, respect, or social honor which is attached to a given position in the organization. By a *system of status* we mean the tendency of roles to fall into some sort of rank order according to the relative amounts of prestige they possess.

Many different systems of status operate in the industrial organization, some formal and well recognized, some informal. If we consider first the formal status systems, it will be immediately apparent that one aspect of the status system is tied to the system of authority. The more authority a position has, the more prestige is attached to it. Highest prestige resides, of course, in the office of president, while lowest prestige is assigned to members of the working force.

A second system of status, often met within the industrial bureaucracy, is based on the amount of scarce skill or training required in a job. An engineer, with a relatively low position on the authority system, may nevertheless be afforded high amounts of prestige. The same may apply to staff advisers to high officials, though in this case they may also be borrowing prestige from the men whose assistants they are.

Prestige based on authority and prestige based on skill are alike in that they receive formal recognition from the bureaucracy. This formal recognition in the industrial plant most often takes the form of high salaries, titles, or special privileges, such as special hours of work, special offices, private secretaries. Less frequently used in the industrial bureaucracy are such symbols as insignia, ceremonies of initiation, or ritual. The purpose of all these symbols is, of course, to emphasize and to concretize the high prestige of these positions in the organization.

In addition to these formal distinctions, there are numerous status systems which receive no formal recognition, or only semiformal recognition. For instance, there may be semiformal or informal status distinctions between the various departments in a plant. An accounting department may be rated above a personnel department. Positions in these two departments may be rated accordingly, even where positions are formally on the same status level. Another status distinction, very frequently met with in industry, is between the shop and the office.[17] For reasons which are not wholly clear, office work seems universally to be rated above shop work. Furthermore, this distinction receives some semiofficial recognition, e.g., in the differing modes of payment as between office and shop (although hardly in the amount of payment), in the differing dress permitted or required, and in somewhat different hours. A third type of semiformally recognized status may be found in the practice of assigning higher status to senior officeholders; that is, of two occupants of formally equal offices, the senior may be awarded certain symbols of prestige such as higher pay, a bigger desk, or more access to superiors.

Formally or semiformally recognized status systems possess important functions for the industrial organization. The status authority system is of particular importance, since it functions to shore up the authority system.[18] For example, where high status is attached to authoritative positions, there is an additional insurance that orders emanating from those positions will be obeyed. The higher the position from which an order comes, the greater the prestige attached to the order, and the more respect it is likely to command.

All the systems of status which we have discussed are functional in that they may serve as incentives, and very strong ones, to individuals to fulfill their roles effectively or to move upward through the organization. Departments may strive to outdo each other for the sake of prestige. Higher status serves to determine the willingness of office workers to work at relatively low wages. Status striving sometimes may serve to motivate the worker on the bench to excel in speed or quality of work. Certainly the possibility of enhanced status is a strong motive for many specialists. In all these ways, the status system operates to ensure the efficient functioning of the organization.

Again it is important to note that the formal status system of an organization has different implications for industrial hierarchy and for industrial laity. To believe that management and workers respond in the same way to the same status system is to risk the possibility of misunderstanding what actually goes on in industry. For one thing, since the worker occupies the bottom of both the authority-status scale and the skill-status scale, he is fundamentally denied the right to the satisfaction of status within the formal organization. It is to be expected, therefore, that he will resist the formal status system. Furthermore, in so far as the worker resists the formal authority system (and it may be

---

[17] The reasons for this are discussed somewhat more fully in chap. 7.

[18] For a closely reasoned analysis of the functioning of the formal and semiformal status system in a bureaucracy, see Chester I. Barnard, "Functions and Pathologies of Status Systems in Formal Organizations," in William F. Whyte (ed.), *Industry and Society*, McGraw-Hill Book Company, Inc., New York, 1946, pp. 46–83.

necessary for him to do so under certain circumstances) he of course will resist the formal status system; that is, he will deny the formally recognized claims to social honor by certain offices and officials. Similarly, where the engineer or other specialist threatens the skill of the worker, or competes with the worker, it will be found that the formal status system is again denied; specialists may be called, contemptuously, "college wonders." Again, if the worker is, for some reason, resisting management drives to higher production, he will resist the use of status as an incentive, and one of his major means of resistance will be to deny the validity of the status system. The presence of a union in the plant may radically alter the status system for the worker; he may transfer his status striving to the union organization, or he may seek to raise the status of the workers as a whole through union action.

New informal system of status often tend to evolve among workers. The nature and causes of these informal status systems will be discussed in Chapter 9.[19] Suffice to say here that system of status among workers may be based on superior strength, intelligence, or personality. Status may also be based on certain distinctions borrowed from the community, e.g., sex, age, race, ethnic background, religion. Finally status may be assigned on the basis of an individual's ability to maneuver through the social structure of industry, to get advantages for fellow workers, and possibly to circumvent the aims of management.

Sources of Equilibrium in the Industrial Bureaucracy. A fifth important structural feature of an industrial bureaucracy consists of those mechanisms by which the organization maintains itself in a state of equilibrium. However, there is no one aspect of a bureaucracy which may be labeled the "equilibrium system." The authority system, the status system, the arrangement of offices according to line and staff principles, even the separation of the industrial bureaucracy into hierarchy and laity, are designed, in part, to maintain the equilibrium of the organization, to solidify it. These aspects of the bureaucracy are a part of the equilibrium system.

The ability of an industrial plant to achieve equilibrium is also dependent upon its success in integrating individuals with the various features of the social structure described above. Individuals must somehow be motivated to play organizational roles, to play them properly and at the proper time, to abide by the principles of the authority system, to recognize the system of status. Unless these conditions are met, the organization will disintegrate.

In general, men may be induced to cooperate in a number of ways. This aspect of the question is considered theoretically in Chapter 2, and

---

[19] Informal systems of status also appear in the industrial hierarchy, wherever the demands of status cannot be met through the formal organization or where status can be employed as an instrument of advantage.

then in connection with actual roles in Chapters 6 and 9. Here it will suffice to say that the individual's reasons for cooperating may range from an intense personal concern with the well-being of the organiza- *rubbish* tion and identification of its ends with personal ends, on the one hand, to cooperation for purely instrumental reasons, on the other. Lying between these extremes are motives such as loyalty to the organization, a feeling of solidarity with fellow workers, pride of accomplishment, the fear of ridicule.

In general, it would seem that the more individuals are motivated *?* by noninstrumental ends, the more stable the social organization of the *.* plant.[20] The reason is probably that noninstrumental motives spring from deeply rooted portions of the personality. Where an organization can tap the noninstrumental motives of its members, it possesses the strongest possible guarantee of loyalty to the organization. In such a case the individual is, in effect, merging his personality with the organization. This individual need be subjected to no outer pressures to make him conform; he conforms because he is, thereby, fulfilling his personality.

However, where individuals are motivated to conform only for instrumental reasons, the solidarity of the organization is much more tenuous. In such cases, not only is the individual's personality "unabsorbed" by the organization, but his primary loyalties may easily be turned to other organizations or groups. Nor, of course, is this type of personality motivated to perform a task at more than a bare minimum of acceptability.

It is very important to note that in the industrial bureaucracy there is marked difference between the motives which operate in the hierarchy and those which operate in the laity. Although there are numerous exceptions, in general the noninstrumental motives are much more abundant among members of the hierarchy, while economic or instrumental motives predominate among the industrial laity. As will be pointed out in subsequent chapters, the possibilities for achieving power, status, authority, security, *within the industrial organization,* are realistic goals only for the hierarchy. For the laity, on the other hand, the most realistic goal, within the formal organization of the plant, is the pecuniary one. This does not mean that the "noneconomic" goals are not of importance to the worker; on the contrary, they are of great importance, but, as we shall see, their fulfillment must be sought outside the formal organization of industry. For this reason, loyalty to the organization, identification of personal ends with organizational ends, "high morale," "esprit de corps," are much more likely to be characteristics of the hierarchy than of the laity.

[20] See F. J. Roethlisberger, *Management and Morale,* Harvard University Press, Cambridge, Mass., 1946, chaps. IV and X. Copyright by the President and Fellows of Harvard University.

Strains in the Industrial Bureaucracy. The industrial bureaucracy is subject to many types of strains. For one, in so far as industrial organization is bureaucratic, it is subject to certain defects which have long been noted in bureaucracies. These defects include a tendency toward an overrigid adherence to the rules, timidity, refusal to take responsibility, secrecy, "red tape," officiousness, jealousy of other departments or offices, lethargy, inability to change, etc.[21] As compared to other types of bureaucracies, industry seems to come off relatively well in these respects. If this is true, it may be that greater competition and pressure for success in industry may counter some of the tendencies noted above.

Industrial bureaucracy is furthermore perhaps peculiarly subject, as will be shown in detail in later chapters, to the danger of the disorientation of personality systems and social systems. This is true because industrial organization (perhaps much more than most other bureaucracies) is vulnerable to forces which may either drastically change the social organization or cause individuals to withdraw their cooperation. An example of the first would be technological change, which may wreak havoc with established status systems, incentive systems, and authority systems. Similarly, an economic downswing may necessitate layoffs and thus threaten the social structure of the plant. An example of the second force may be found in economic resentment on the part of the workers, which leads first to a slowdown and then to a complete stoppage of work. It seems safe to say that such "unhinging" of personality and organization is only very rarely encountered in an army or in a church bureaucracy.

Many other types of strain occur. Status systems, instead of motivating individuals to succeed, may frustrate them, especially if the status system rigidifies. A communication system may break down because of the incompetence or improper motivation of one human link in the chain. A somewhat different type of strain results from improper organization. For instance, there may be an overemphasis on "staff" organization or, as is sometimes the case, an emphasis on advertising or selling to the detriment of research and production. Certain strains are imposed by the strong drive for success, especially within the hierarchy. This may lead to timeserving, favor currying, even corruption among the lower levels of the hierarchy. On the upper levels it may lead to "white-collar crime" or to unethical conduct of various types.

---

[21] Many other charges against bureaucracy have been made. Two sources are cited here, though many more might be added: Harold J. Laski, "Bureaucracy," in *Encyclopedia of the Social Sciences*, The Macmillan Company, New York, 1933, vol. 3, pp. 70–73; and Marshall E. Dimock, "Bureaucracy Self Examined," in Merton et al., *op. cit.*, pp. 397–406.

The list of such strains might be greatly prolonged, but enough has been said here to indicate in what directions an industrial bureaucracy may break down. It should be noted that these strains arise out of the very nature and structure of industrial bureaucracy.

Nonbureaucratic Elements in Industrial Bureaucracy. The conclusion must not be reached, from what has been said in this chapter, that bureaucratic organization has completely triumphed in every sphere of industry. Some branches of industry have thus far successfully resisted bureaucratization. This has been true in those numerous small industries which do not demand large capital outlays; e.g., in feeder plants which have sprung up on the periphery of large industries, or in industries manufacturing for a local market (for instance, the baking industry). Nor has bureaucracy triumphed in industries where, for various reasons, there has not been a demand for specialization, professionalization, a machine technology, or split-second coordination; for instance, in the building industry.

Furthermore, within all large-scale bureaucracies there are certain nonbureaucratic tendencies. For instance, as will be shown later, informal social groups, informal social relationships, informal chains of command, and informal chains of influence, all of a distinctly nonbureaucratic nature, exist in all large-scale industry. The reasons for the existence of these nonbureaucratic elements are not as yet clear. However, it seems safe to say that one reason lies in the incompatibility of a rational social organization with certain irrational aspects of human nature. Where individuals associate over long periods of time, they are bound to form friendships and antipathies, which have little or nothing to do with the formal organization. Groups will also form on the basis of social backgrounds, interests, or education. These informal groups usually have an amorphous structure, since their major function is performed in the association of individuals; the groups as such have no aim. Informal "expressive" groups of this kind may be found at all levels, and in every type of industry.

In addition, nonbureaucratic relationships and groups may serve rational purposes. Three types of such relationships or groupings may be distinguished: those which function for the interests of the formal organization, those which function outside the formal organization but not specifically against its interests, and those which function directly against organizational interests. The first type performs certain functions which could not be accomplished through the formal organization. For instance, where it may become necessary for an executive to circumvent the normal line of communication for the purpose of issuing a direct command, or for the purpose of securing information about conditions on lower levels, an informal chain of communication may be used. In this case the executive may have contact directly with an individual or individuals who are not directly below him on the chain of command. Again certain types of contacts between members of different departments may be necessary for the purposes of the organization, although such contacts are not provided for in the formal organization. In this case a pattern of "lunching" or other informal types of association may arise. Examples of the functional operation of informal groups might be multiplied. In fact, it is doubtful whether a formal organization could operate at all without these nonbureaucratic types of social relationships.

Nonbureaucratic relationships or groups may also function for non-organizational purposes. For instance, on the level of the hierarchy, such groups may function to circumvent bureaucratic values of professionalization and impersonalization, e.g., by currying the favor of a powerful official, or by excluding individuals of "improper" social, religious, racial background, or by mutual back scratching, exchange of information, and so on. The purpose of this kind of group is not to defeat the aims of the organization but rather to circumvent its rules for personal advantage.

The third type of nonbureaucratic group functions, to greater or lesser degree, in opposition to the aims and rules of the bureaucracy. For instance, informal groups among workers may try to limit production,[22] or to undermine an incentive system. Such groups may deny the status system of the plant and set up a counter status system. The authority system of the plant may be more or less subtly sabotaged by such a group. Actually, however, the antiorganizational group seldom seeks to destroy the bureaucracy. The members of an informal group of working men are usually interested not in complete defeat of management but in the limitation of its power.

These groups and relationships not only operate to limit the power of bureaucracy, but in their internal structure they are essentially non-bureaucratic. Within an informal group there may be a leader, a lieutenant, and followers, but social relationships are of a basically primary character; social contacts are face to face, of long-continuing duration, highly personalized. Roles in the group are relatively unspecialized and are assigned on bases which have little to do with bureaucratic values. Power and status are also distributed within the group on bases which have nothing to do with the values of formal organization. It is highly significant to note that even within a rigid formal organization the individual may actually move, think, and react within a nonbureaucratic group.[23]

The existence of nonbureaucratic elements in the industrial bureauc-

---

[22] A study of this kind of informal group will be found in Chap. 9.

[23] In Chap. 9 we shall discuss in more detail the reasons for the formation of the antiorganizational group.

racy raises large questions. There is evidence that, although antibureaucratic elements may be weak taken alone, as a whole they constitute a formidable power. At times this power may be sufficient to defeat or circumvent management, for instance, through sabotaging a production plan, through use of the slowdown, or through a wildcat strike. But short of this, the informal group without doubt seriously limits the action of management in its day-to-day operations. Since this is the case, it is possible that the overwhelming strength of bureaucracy has been overestimated. In fact, it is possible that the larger and more extensive bureaucracy becomes, the more these nonbureaucratic elements tend to appear. This raises the possibility that industry will evolve in the future not in the direction of more bureaucracy but in that of less.

exactly

The student may well ask: How can industry evolve through a form of organization which seeks to circumvent its most cherished aims and rules? However, it is by no means given that nonbureaucratic elements *must*, in the very nature of things, be antiorganizational. It is entirely conceivable that these nonbureaucratic elements may, under certain circumstances, function for organizational ends. Indeed, cases of this type have already been discussed. It is conceivable that much of the day-to-day operation of industry might be conducted in a nonbureaucratic fashion.

These, of course, are speculative questions. They are put here not because they can be answered at this time but simply to warn the student against an easy acceptance of the belief that, because the present trend toward bureaucracy in industry is strong, it must therefore continue indefinitely. There will be occasion to explore further these nonbureaucratic elements as we turn to an examination of the major roles in industry.

Politics within the bureaucratic structure?
e.g. Director of followers v. Director & followers.

CHAPTER 6

The Executive in the Industrial Bureaucracy

The great importance of the executive has long been recognized, and much attention has been paid to him and to the tasks which he must perform. However, almost all this attention has been in the form of advice as to how to be a good or efficient executive.[1] He has been admonished to be "progressive," to be "forward-looking," to be "flexible," to be "mature," etc.[2] Less attention, however, has been paid to the realistic characteristics of the role which the executive is supposed to play, a role which limits and constrains him, and which he can modify only to a limited degree. The concern of this chapter will be the status and role of the executive in the modern large-scale bureaucracy.

Definition of the Executive Role. By *executive role* is meant here that role in which resides ultimate authority for the administration of the day-to-day affairs, both internal and external, of the industrial bureaucracy. The executive role is charged with "all the work essential to the vitality and endurance of an organization, so far, at least, as it must be accomplished through formal coordination."[3] It should be carefully distinguished from the role of owner. The owner does not today, either in theory or usually in fact, administer the industrial bureaucracy; he is not directly responsible for maintaining the vitality and endurance of an organization. It should be noticed, incidentally, that the modern executive may be an individual or a plurality of individuals, for instance a board of directors.[4]

---

[1] As an example of this type of work, see H. C. Metcalf (ed.) *Business Management as a Profession*, McGraw-Hill Book Company, Inc., New York, 1927. Although we shall offer no rules here about "how to be a good executive," it may be expected that a sociological approach may add to the possibility of efficient executive operations.

[2] See B. M. Selekman, *Labor Relations and Human Relations,* McGraw-Hill Book Company, Inc., New York, 1947.

[3] Chester I. Barnard, *The Functions of the Executive,* Harvard University Press, Cambridge, Mass., 1945, p. 125. Copyright, 1938, by the President and Fellows of Harvard College.

[4] Adolf A. Berle, Jr., and Gardiner C. Means, *The Modern Corporation and Private Property,* The Macmillan Company, New York, 1940, p. 220.

The role of the executive is directly shaped by the nature of the organization whose "vitality and endurance" are being maintained. As we have seen, modern industrialism is marked by a complex machine technology and by a bureaucratic type of social organization. Furthermore, certain conditions in Western civilization and culture have yielded an industrialism which is individually (rather than societally) controlled and is capitalistically oriented. Each of these factors has helped to structure the role of the executive, to give it a characteristic form, which determines to a large extent the action, and even thinking, of those who play this role. These three aspects of the situation of the executive will now be considered in greater detail.

The role of the executive is, in the first place, shaped by the over-all aim of the organization. This over-all aim is the production of profits. It has been shown that all other goals of the industrial organization— even the goal of production—are subordinate to the overriding demand for profit. Since the drive for profit is a central fact of our industrial institutions, it must be a central fact for those men who are charged with their "vitality and endurance."

There has been a certain amount of confusion as to the supreme importance of profit in our industrial system and as a factor shaping the executive role. One school of thought has argued that every organization in society must, from a certain point of view, be "profitable." That is, every organization must show, in the long run, favorable fiscal balances, if the organization is to continue to endure. For instance, a college is not as such a profit-making organization, but it must balance a budget between costs and income. The industrial system is not, therefore, unique, it is argued, in striving for profit; rather such striving is a universal of all human organization and, in a wider sense, of all human effort. There can be no doubt that this argument establishes a fact of great importance in understanding social organization. However, it would appear necessary to note a difference between this use of the term "profit" and its use earlier in the paragraph. It is true that industrial enterprises must be profitable in that they must show favorable pecuniary balances, like other organizations. In addition, however, industrial organization exists for the creation—indeed, the maximization—of profit. The difference may be illustrated by comparing the aims of a college and an industrial plant. The college exists primarily to educate, not to create profit; if a college shows a profit, this reflects a healthy state of its finances, not the attainment of its primary aim. An industrial plant, on the other hand, exists primarily to create profit, and its success or failure is directly proportionate to the amount of profit it attains.

A second school of thought holds that the importance of profit in our industrial institutions has greatly decreased because of the displacement of ownership control by professional management. It is argued that, while owners are dominated solely by the goal of high profit, managers are dominated primarily by the value of high productivity and efficiency.[5] As one author has put it, "salaried managers without direct financial risk in [an] enterprise can scarcely be claimed to be driven by the profit motive."[6] If this were so, there would be profound effects on the role of the industrial executive. It does not seem possible to this author to accept the validity of the argument as a whole, even though there is considerable validity in the facts to which the argument refers.

There seems to be considerable validity to the argument that as industry has grown larger and more complex, "experts" have tended to replace owners, as controllers of industry. This change has been a consequence of the dispersion of ownership, the enormous complexity of modern industrial organization, and the consequent need for "expertness."[7] The type of individual who owned and managed a business directly, and who was in business directly for profit, has tended to be replaced by an individual whose primary aim is to fulfill successfully a certain role, that of manager. In this latter case, the attainment of profit becomes a part of the role obligation of the hired manager or executive. It might be said that the "creation of profit" is what the manager is hired for. Therefore, the replacement of the owner by a hired manager does not affect the over-all organizational aim. The confusion seems to stem from a failure to distinguish personal motivation from organizational aims. The executive may be motivated by a desire for a large salary, personal glory, or a lust for power; it makes no difference as far as the organizational aim, the creation of profit, is concerned. The success of even the hired manager is measured still in terms of the amount of profit attained.

If profit is the primary aim of the manager's role, the means by which this aim may be achieved is manipulation of a system of production. The system of production itself is made up of two major parts, technology and social organization, and each helps to shape the executive's role.

The industrial executive administers vastly complicated technological processes, which in turn are closely linked to mechanization and to science. Each technological process imposes certain limits on the executive's role, positively determining certain functions and negatively circumscribing his freedom of action. For instance, the executive of an industry which is based on assembly-line production must be necessarily concerned with problems of coordination and conservation of energy

[5] See James M. Burnham, *The Managerial Revolution*, The John Day Company, Inc., New York, 1941.

[6] Wilbert E. Moore, *Industrial Relations and the Social Order*, rev. ed., The Macmillan Company, New York, 1951, p. 59.

[7] See Berle and Means, *op. cit.*, chap. V.

and motion. At the same time, the state of advancement of the technological process limits what the executive can do in the commercial field, the commitments that he can make. Furthermore, a technological system tends to develop according to the values of engineering or science, that is, the values of logic and efficiency. The executive must guide and limit this logic of development, reconciling it with the need for profitability.

The other means which are at the disposal of the executive, the bureaucratic social structure of modern industry, also play an important part in structuring or limiting the role which the executive plays. It was shown in Chapter 5 that a bureaucracy is essentially a hierarchy of specialized offices, with power inhering in the office rather than in the man, and with a definite "chain of command" uniting the offices.[8] The fact that the executive heads such an organization imposes certain administrative functions on him. At the same time, bureaucratic organization limits the freedom of action of the executive. For instance, an industrial executive may employ certain types of punishments and rewards and must forgo the use of other types. He must rely on the chain of command existing in his organization, and so on.

Bureaucracy adds a unique dimension to the role of the executive, a dimension which would not be present if production were carried out under some other form of social organization. Just like technology, bureaucracy helps shape the functions of the executive and his relations to the outside world; it helps determine the form of executive thinking and the strains to which the executive role is exposed.

The profit motive, the technological process, and bureaucratic organization are the dominating factors in the shaping or structuring of the executive role. If the nature and implications of executive action are to be understood, it is necessary to remember that such action may have its source in, or be related to, each or all of these three areas. It is seldom possible, certainly, to understand executive policy, thinking, or programs without realizing the many-sidedness of the situation in which the executive operates.

Furthermore, the executive is operating in a dynamic situation. Not only are all aspects of his role constantly changing, but often they are changing at different rates. Technology may change faster than social organization, conceptions of profit may lag behind technological potentialities, and so on. As the situation changes, the role of the executive must inevitably adjust to the change. The discussion which follows sets forth a relatively static analysis of the executive's role, which should not be allowed to obscure the dynamic nature of the role.

[8] Weber, Max, *From Max Weber: Essays in Sociology,* edited and translated by H. H. Gerth and C. W. Mills, Oxford University Press, New York, 1946, pp. 106ff.

The Functions of the Executive. The fact that the executive operates within an industrial bureaucratic organization which is oriented to the attainment of profit does not tell us what specific functions he must perform or how he performs them. It will be the aim of this section to investigate the content of the executive's role.

This problem may be looked at from two points of view. From the point of view of the executive himself, the job often consists of a myriad of small tasks; that is, he is constantly shifting attention from "production to sales, to finance, to merchandising, to personnel, to public relations, and so on in an interminable but ever varying sequence."[9] The task of listing the specific types of executive action is almost impossible, because of the extremely generalized nature of the role. Furthermore, the tasks which occupy executive attention may vary from time to time, from order to order. The executive is also faced with special problems which are constantly arising in the plant.

For these reasons it is more useful to look at the executive role from a functional point of view.[10] The fundamental problem is: Given the nature of the situation which the executive faces, what things must he do if the organization is to attain its aims and to endure? From this point of view, there would seem to be three general types of executive functions: (1) setting the general policy of the organization, (2) establishing proper relations between the industrial plant and important external forces, (3) guiding or directing the internal organization of the plant.

The Formulation of Policy. The executive must formulate two major types of policy. He must, on the one hand, set the purposes and objectives of the plant as a whole. In general, the basic aim of any industrial plant is set *for* the executive by the culture. This aim, as we have seen, is the production of profits through the manufacture and sale of a product or services. But the executive must decide which products are to be manufactured and in what quantity and at what time. On the other hand, he must determine how the end shall be attained, what efforts shall be devoted to its attainment, and how the effort shall be apportioned among members of the organization.

In general, executive policy making is oriented to several considerations. Three such considerations will be discussed below. This does not

[9] Melvin T. Copeland, *The Executive at Work,* Harvard University Press, Cambridge, Mass., 1952, p. 84. Copyright by the President and Fellows of Harvard University.

[10] The following discussion of the functions of the executive leans heavily on, and is used by permission from, Chester I. Barnard, *The Functions of the Executive,* Harvard University Press, Cambridge, Mass., 1945, particularly chap. XV. For other interesting discussions of the functions of the executive in the modern large-scale plant, see T. N. Whitehead, *Leadership in a Free Society,* Harvard University Press, Cambridge, Mass., 1936; and Marshall Edward Dimock, *The Executive in Action,* Harper & Brothers, New York, 1945.

mean, of course, that each executive must constantly, every day, face all these problems; however, when policy decisions must be made, it seems safe to say that some of these factors must be taken into account.

First, the executive must consider a wide variety of factors which are related to the market and which are usually termed "economic" in nature. He must estimate the market potentialities of the type, quality, and quantity of goods he is planning to manufacture. This, in turn, involves an estimate or guess as to the future state of the market. In addition, the executive must take into account the action of actual or potential competitors, for such competition may greatly affect his own ability to enter the market, or the time at which he wishes to make his entrance. Furthermore, the executive's estimate of the market situation and of competition may necessitate a decision as to the merchandising and advertising of the product in question. Crosscutting all these considerations is the further consideration of the economic state of the plant. How much capital is available for manufacturing and selling the products? How much capital, including liquid capital and fixed plant, shall be allotted to one product and how much to other products?

In an individualistically oriented society such as our own, where national economic decisions are made through the operation of an impersonal market, the making of policy decisions such as these is necessarily a crucial function of the executive. Should he make a mistake—should he, for instance, incorrectly estimate the future of the market—the consequences for his organization might be very serious. Yet the situation in which the executive works is one of much uncertainty; ill-understood laws of supply and demand, changes in fashion and taste, the impact of domestic or foreign events, might invalidate a policy decision which was correct at the time it was made. It is no wonder, then, that some of the most difficult tasks of policy making concern the making of "economic" decisions.

Secondly, the executive must orient his policy making to the internal state of his plant. He must take into account, for instance, the availability and caliber of the working force. Thus, it is one thing to decide to switch over to manufacture of a complex military object with a working force which has had long and continued experience at fine lathe work; it is something else again to attempt such a switch-over with a working force which has been newly recruited from a rural area. Similarly, the availability of labor must be taken into account, at least in prosperous times, in policy making. The situation is even more acute, perhaps, in relation to technical specialists and lower-level administrators; especially in wartime, there is a dearth, in many industries, of certain types of engineers, and the supply of good lower-level administrators never seems to be plentiful, good times or bad. The executive must also consider the nature of the technology at his disposal; its state of obsolescence, its utility in manufacturing various types of products, the possibilities of upkeep or replacement. And, finally, the executive must always consider the type of social organization, formal and informal, that he is heading; the state of its efficiency, its adaptability to various purposes.

Finally, management must take into account the extraordinarily dynamic situation in which industry exists when it seeks to formulate policy. This dynamic situation has already been described in this and previous chapters, and it will be necessary here only to recall certain aspects of the situation. The technology of many, if not most, industries is inherently in a state of flux and change. In some cases new technological processes may make completely obsolescent an entire system of production; in other cases, the changes may be slow and cumulative but very great in their over-all effects. At all events, management must make sure that it will not be left behind in the apparently endless process of technological progress, because such progress invariably involves lowered costs, not to mention the possibility of producing entirely new types of goods. The executive who neglects technological innovation is therefore risking disaster; the disappearance of countless enterprises because of their inability or unwillingness to meet a new technological condition is sufficient proof for this point.[11]

The same situation prevails, if not so dramatically, in respect to social organization. Here too the executive must formulate policy in regard to a changing situation which is constantly advancing new and more efficient social techniques and social technicians to the industrial front.

Not less important for the executive is the necessity for orienting policy making to the dynamic situation outside the plant. The executive must operate in a dynamic social and political environment. This environment may, at any time, throw up new forces which greatly affect industry. Examples of such events include the emergence of the CIO in the 1930s, the appearance of masses of governmental legislation, or the outbreak of a war. Here too the price of survival is adaptability in policy making by the executive. Shall reserves be accumulated? Does a new law necessitate a change in existing practices? What is the meaning of the new labor union that has entered the plant? It is questions like these that the executive must consider when he formulates objectives or decides on the distributing of effort.

The Establishment of Relations with External Forces. A second major function of the executive is to relate his organization to the external world; in a sense, that is, he must formulate a foreign policy for his

[11] For a general discussion of the need for executive adaptations, see Copeland, *op. cit.*, chap. VI, "Survival in a Changing World."

enterprise. He must, in the first instance, relate his firm to other firms. He must decide whether to attempt an all-out war of competition or to negotiate a tacit truce. Again, the executive must relate his firm to the government. Here he must decide on interpretations of (often unclear) government directives. He must decide on whether to make appeals from some government decisions. Furthermore, the executive may have to relate his firm to a labor union, either present or in the offing. He must adopt some policy toward labor. Is the labor union to be fought? Is it to be accepted? Should the attempt be made to integrate the labor union into the structure of the plant? Or should its role be strictly de-limited? In this connection one important executive function may be the negotiation and signing of a labor contract. Finally, the executive must, whether consciously or unconsciously, relate his firm to the public at large. In the case of the large-scale plant this may involve wide-ranging advertising campaigns for good will. It may involve working through the National Association of Manufacturers. In the case of the smaller plant, the contacts between the firm and the public may be handled on a much less formal basis.

In a later chapter the relations between industry and various aspects of the local community and the nation will be considered in greater detail. Attention will be paid to the exact nature of the decisions which the executive may be called upon to make in relation to the community.

Administering or Directing the Operation of the Plant. The third major function of the executive is the administration of the internal affairs of the plant. It is in his capacity as an administrator that the executive is a familiar figure to most people; he is the man who "gets things done," who "runs things." The action verbs reveal the popular dynamic image of the executive as doer and performer. Yet, as we have already seen, the executive is not only a man of action but a strategist and a diplomat. The popular image is therefore wrong, at least as concerns two of the three major functions of the executive. It is strange to note, then, that the relationship of the executive to the plant, even as an administrator, is much more complex than is usually supposed. He is perhaps more an initiator than a doer, more a passive observer of events than an administrator of them. In fact, to some extent a successful executive is one who is able to adapt to a trend of events over which he may have but little control.

The administrative aspects of the executive role are shaped by the nature of complex organization. It is obvious that a complex social organization, comprising perhaps thousands of workers, sometimes widely scattered geographically, cannot be controlled or administered directly by any one executive, no matter how energetic or well supplied with assistants. The job is simply too big. Furthermore, the technological processes of modern industry are usually too complex for even the most highly trained executive to administer directly. Under these circumstances, executive operation comes to be a matter of ensuring coordination and of securing cooperation rather than one of leadership, as that term is popularly understood. The executive role becomes the focal point toward which flows information from all sections of the plant, and from which go out those directives and orders designed to ensure the continuing harmony of the plant as a whole. In other words, the executive role may be thought of as a communication center through which information, reports, directives, requests, etc., are transmitted from one part of the plant to other parts. As an administrator the executive is concerned with ensuring the balance of the functioning organization, and with restoring those parts of the organization which have ceased to function.

More specifically, executive administration of the large-scale industrial plant may be reduced to three essential subfunctions: (1) setting up the organization of the plant, (2) securing proper personnel, and (3) securing essential services.

SETTING UP THE ORGANIZATION OF THE PLANT. Although the administrator may be a passive observer of, and a focal point of communications in, a largely self-operating and self-controlled organization, nevertheless it is this administrator who sets the organization in motion, who provides it with its initial direction of movement. The executive, on the one hand, initiates action by determining the aim and major line of strategy of the organization as a whole. On the other hand, he initiates action for the plant by determining the scheme of social relationships within which individuals will interact. This he does by setting up the social organization of the plant, determining what positions will be subordinate and what superordinate, in which directions authority will flow, and how communication will be maintained. Thus, although the executive may be physically incapable of controlling more than a tiny fraction of the total number of human actions undertaken in a plant, he has, by setting up the scheme of organization, overwhelmingly determined the *general* direction of action, as well as some of the most important social relationships that can be formed in the plant. Additional proof of this is seen in the fact that, once the organization has been set up as a functioning unit, the executive can best exercise direct control by changing the entire social organization of the plant, or some part of it.

It has been shown that the demands of modern industrial production have led to the predominance of the bureaucratic form of social organization, particularly in large-scale industry. Thus, in one sense, the type of social organization which the executive sets up is predetermined.

However, *within* the general bureaucratic framework, there is room for a great deal of flexibility. Different types of industry necessitate differing schemes of social organization. For instance, the social organization necessary for a railroad differs from that necessary for a steel plant. It is the function of the executive to determine the most efficient scheme of social organization for each type of industry in the light of existing conditions, internal and external.

One condition to which the scheme of organization must be constantly adapted is that of the demands of technology. This means adaptation not only to an existing technology but also to technological changes. These changes may vary from entire new systems of production, necessitating completely new schemes of social organization, to small routine changes necessitating only local adjustments in the social scheme. Although it is the former type of change which presents most dramatically the need for a revision of the social organization, the cumulative effect of small changes may necessitate a reorganization no less drastic. The function of the executive is to adapt social organization to such changes so that the general direction of action and the major social relationships within the plant are continually adjusted to changing technological conditions.

Another condition to which the scheme of organization must be continually adapted is the type of personnel which are available to fill organizational posts. For instance, on the upper levels of the industrial bureaucracy, the organization may have to be adapted to the scarcity of properly qualified persons for positions of great responsibility or skill. Even the need to replace a single highly skilled individual may necessitate a drastic reshuffling of such organizational features as division of labor, responsibilities, and titles. On the lower level of the bureaucracy examples of this adaptive process may be found where the nature of a working force changes, e.g., during a war period. For instance, let us suppose that one working force is strongly imbued with a work ethic which dictates a consistently high standard of performance, promptness, a minimum of absences as well as a long tradition of union organization, while another group of workers has directly opposite characteristics. Under these circumstances, the social organization which is suitable for one working force may be totally unsuitable for the other.

Finally, the executive must continually adapt the social organization of his plant to changing forces in the external environment. Some of these "community" forces have been previously mentioned, e.g., competition, public opinion, the state, and the union organization. Competition, for instance, may gradually change the basic aim of an industry. Union organization may necessitate the sharing of power and control in the plant. Public opinion may radically affect the nature and mood of the working force, or the freedom of action granted to industry. In these cases, as in others, the executive may have to change the general directions of men's actions and the social relationships of production. And this can be accomplished primarily by remolding the form of the social organization.

SECURING THE PROPER TYPE OF PERSONNEL. An industrial social organization is a complex system of roles. However, the most perfectly organized industry from the standpoint of roles and role structure remains a lifeless abstraction until the roles are filled with flesh-and-blood people. But if roles are to be activated they must be played by people with certain technical skills, capacities, attitudes, motives, even personalities. Filling the industrial role with the proper type of personnel is the function of the executive as an administrator. It is an extremely important function because the executive is peculiarly dependent on personnel, over whom he has only indirect control. At the same time it is a difficult function because the executive must secure personnel to fill roles as diverse as the chemist, the benchworker, the engineer, the salesman, the foreman, and the junior executive. Ability to secure and hold the proper type of personnel very frequently is the major difference between success and failure for the executive.

From the point of view of the executive, personnel should possess two general characteristics. They must have the proper technical skills for the performance of the job at hand. This does not necessarily mean that the executive must, in all cases, secure personnel who are already trained in precisely those techniques required in a given role. But it does mean that there must be at least a minimum of skilled workers or officials who can be placed in key spots in the industrial organization. It may also mean that personnel who are brought within the plant must have at least certain basic skills, such as literacy, mechanical (or other) aptitudes, or merely a general acquaintance with the culture of an industrial civilization. Certainly experience in such backward agricultural countries as the Soviet Union (at least at the time of the revolution) and China today has shown the difficulty of using personnel from peasant cultures in modern industry.

An adequate personnel, from the point of view of the administrator, should also be marked by a certain set of attitudes toward work and toward the organization as a whole.[12] Personnel must be loyal; that is, they must identify themselves emotionally with the organization and, to some degree, make its ends and values their own. They must have a feeling of responsibility toward the organization, so that necessary tasks will be carried out and standards maintained, even in the absence of direct supervision. Finally, personnel must be marked by a capacity to be

[12] Barnard, *op. cit.*, p. 221.

dominated by the organization. For practical purposes this means that they must be prepared to sacrifice personal interests and even values to the demands of organization. This, of course, is the ideal, not a description of the actual personnel situation of any specific industry. However, the executive can function as an administrator only with a personnel which *at least to some degree* approaches the ideal.

It should be noted that informal relationships and groupings within the plant influence the definition of an "adequate" personnel for each industrial organization. For the informal group, adequacy of personnel may refer primarily to personal traits such as manners, speech, personal appearance, education, experience, age, sex, race, nationality, or faith. If the executive is striving to maintain the balance of his organization, he must consider the informal definition of adequacy as a factor in the situation. On the other hand, it is quite possible that, at some point, the organizational definition of adequacy will clash with the informal definition. In this case the executive must decide which definition of adequacy is of most value to the firm.

SECURING ESSENTIAL SERVICES. The problems of securing proper personnel and of securing essential services from such personnel are quite distinct. Obviously, the executive cannot hope to secure essential services if he does not have proper personnel. But the reverse does not hold; even with entirely adequate personnel the problem of eliciting services remains. The third major function of the executive as an administrator, then, is to motivate individuals to perform adequately within the roles to which they are assigned.

In general, there are two interrelated methods which executives use to motivate individuals to perform roles adequately: the method of incentives, and the method of persuasion.[13] When the executive uses the method of incentives he will attempt to increase the satisfaction and decrease the dissatisfaction to be obtained from the environment of work. The use of monetary incentives is considered by most executives (and by most union men) as the most important means of increasing role satisfaction. Bonus plans, group-rate plans, and piecework plans are further developments of this incentive. In addition, the executive may hold out incentives such as security, pleasant physical conditions of work, congenial social relations, opportunities to obtain power, in order to elicit essential services and to maintain standards.

The executive may also attempt to increase satisfactions in role playing by holding out the possibility of acquiring prestige or status. In this case, he functions through his ability to afford or withhold opportunities for individuals to increase personal distinction through role play-

[13] *Ibid.*, chap. XI, The following discussion represents an adaptation of Barnard's scheme.

ing.[14] In turn this may involve the manipulation of certain physical objects which take on a symbolic value. For instance, increased remuneration may serve as a symbolic recognition of high status, the relative amount of remuneration being more important than the absolute amount. The executive may also manipulate such symbols of status as titles, freedom of movement, shortened hours, secretarial help, or the size and location of a desk, or ability to wear a "white collar" on the job.

When the executive uses the method of persuasion, he is attempting to convince individuals of the necessity of accepting the organization's incentives.[15] Three major types of persuasion may be used.

First, he may use coercion or threats. In the industrial bureaucracy this involves the use of demotion, the withholding of promotion, and, in extreme cases, discharge. It is generally thought today that the effectiveness of coercion as a means of persuasion is limited, since the industrial organization is largely self-controlling. In general, the coercive power of executives would seem to be greatest where employees are unorganized and in times when a surplus of workers exists, as in a depression. Secondly, the executive may use propaganda in an attempt to persuade men that it is in their interest to fill roles and perform them adequately, that the incentives that the plant offers are worthwhile and desirable. For instance, he may attempt to convince workingmen that they benefit from increased productivity or that it would be desirable to adopt a piecework plan. Thirdly, the executive may attempt to instill in personnel certain attitudes of loyalty to the plant, of a feeling of responsibility in relation to work. He may attempt to inculcate such attitudes through exhortation, education, precept, or, at least at certain times, appeals to such general goals as patriotism. This method is the most difficult, because it seeks to enter and influence deep-lying aspects of the personality. At the same time, it is, when successful, the most effective.

The executive usually uses a mixture of methods in eliciting essential services. Monetary rewards may be used in motivating the shopworker, but junior executives and office help may be most strongly motivated by a desire for status. Persuasion through propaganda or force may reinforce an attempt to increase role satisfaction. The function of the executive as an administrator is to discover the proper types and balance of incentives and persuasion in order to motivate men in the proper directions, and at a minimal cost to the organization as a whole.

The "Dimensions" of the Executive Role. In the preceding discussion, it was shown how the functions the executive must perform for the or-

[14] See Chester I. Barnard, "Functions and Pathology of Status Systems in Formal Organizations," in William F. Whyte (ed.), *Industry and Society*, McGraw-Hill Book Company, Inc., New York, 1946, pp. 46–83.
[15] Barnard, *The Functions of the Executive*, p. 149.

ganization as a whole are shaped by the nature of industrial organization. In this section, attention will be turned to the way in which industrial organization shapes the characteristic structure, or the dimensions, of the executive role. Three structural aspects of the executive role are of interest: (1) how access to the role is attained, (2) the limits of the role, and (3) the norms and values governing the role.

How Access to the Executive Role Is Attained. One striking characteristic of the executive role is that it must be *achieved*. It will be recalled that an *achieved* role was defined in Chapter 2 as one requiring "special qualities" and filled by "competition and individual effort." This was contrasted with *ascribed* roles which "are assigned to individuals without reference to their innate differences or abilities."[16] Roles may be ascribed on the basis of such factors as age, sex, kinship, or social position. The role of the industrial executive is far too specialized and far too demanding of certain rare skills and aptitudes to be ascribed. Ability and performance must inevitably be used as the major criteria for selection to the executive's role.

Ideally, then, selection for the executive's role may be made from the entire population, without regard to ascription of any kind. However, although there are numerous examples in American industry of the "office-boy-to-president" type of career, the ideal form of selection for the executive's role is greatly modified in practice. There is good evidence, for instance, to show that social origin plays an important part in the selection of executives. It is true, of course, that a comparatively large number of executives have risen from disadvantaged socioeconomic classes. Nevertheless, the fact remains that a much larger number of them have come from relatively advantaged groups, particularly business groups. This appears to have been true even in the nineteenth century, precisely the time of greatest opportunity. At that time fully two-thirds of the business elite were drawn from the three upper classes of society.[17] Similarly, to a less measurable extent, other factors, such as kinship, sex, religion, race, and nationality, have determined selection for the executive role.

The Limits of the Executive Role. A second characteristic of the executive role is its relative flexibility. That is, the executive role is both extensible and diffuse.

---

[16] These quotations are from Ralph Linton, *The Study of Man*, Appleton-Century-Crofts, Inc., New York, 1936, p. 115.

[17] C. Wright Mills, "The American Business Elite: A Collective Portrait," *The Journal of Economic History*, vol. V, supplement V, p. 42, December, 1945. Two other important studies of business leadership should be consulted: F. W. Tanssig and C. S. Joslyn, *American Business Leaders*, The Macmillan Company, New York, 1932; and W. Lloyd Warner and James C. Abeggeln, *Occupational Mobility*, University of Minnesota Press, Minneapolis, 1955. The discussion of the social origins of business leaders is treated in greater detail in chap. 18.

An *extensible* role may be defined as one whose limits can be stretched or contracted according to the personality of the role player or the exigencies of the circumstances. As we have seen, the role of the executive is circumscribed in certain directions, e.g., by the need to maximize profit, by the demands of a machine technology, by the social organization of the plant, and by external forces such as the union. However, within these limits, the role is extensible in many directions. The executive may "shoot for the sky" in an attempt to increase the size, efficiency, or influence of his organization. Furthermore, he may vary the duties associated with the role; one executive may concern himself directly with the specific tasks of administration, another may concentrate on strategy, a third on external affairs. As one writer has put it: "The job of company president varies with the personality of the man who holds it, and . . . as a corollary . . . his bigness or smallness, as the case may be is reflected in the personality of the corporation."[18] It is instructive to compare the executive role in this respect with a relatively nonextensible role, such as the operation of an automatic press or the tending of an automatic loom.

By a *diffuse* role is meant a role concerned with a multiplicity of tasks and necessitating a variety of skills. A diffuse role is best compared with a *specific* role, such as that of an office clerk. In this latter case, the role player is concerned with a definite task, and only a few precise skills are used. The executive, on the other hand, must perform a multitude of tasks: policy formation, formulation of strategy, and administration. The skills needed in the performance of this role—handling men, negotiation, decision, compromise—are of an equally diffuse and imprecise nature. These are generalized skills which can be employed in a wide variety of situations, rather than a specific skill needed for a definite job.

Norms and Values Governing the Executive Role. The situation of the executive in the industrial bureaucracy determines certain norms and values which are characteristic of executive roles. Perhaps the most important values which govern the action of industrial executives are marked by universalism and emotional neutrality.

By *universalistic* values are meant here those which govern the relations between the role and the environment in terms of some general impersonal standard. For instance, a teacher is governed in his relationships to his students by certain values respecting performance, intellect, and aptitudes, which are meant to apply to all students regardless of any other considerations. By *particularistic* values, on the other hand, is meant those which directly relate the player of a role to some definite person or persons. The role of a son is particularistic, since it is

[18] J. Elliot Janney, "Company Presidents Look at Themselves," *Harvard Business Review*, vol. 30, no. 3, p. 59, May-June, 1952.

directly related to particular parents, not to people in general, or even parents in general.

Ideally the executive role is governed by universalistic values of various kinds. The executive is governed in his relationships to others by certain impersonal external codes; e.g., Federal laws, or the union contract. This may mean that he must provide certain conditions of work for *all* employees; that the working day of *all* personnel, or a class thereof, can be only of a certain length; that *all* workers must be hired irrespective of race or ethnic background and promoted according to ability or seniority. The executive role is also governed by an impersonal code of loyalty to the general purpose and methods of the organization. In this connection, all judgments of, or actions toward, others must be undertaken in light of specific organizational ends. Considerations of race, sex, age, kinship, or friendship are irrelevant. The only relevant standards are the competence of subordinates and their ability to contribute to the aims of the organization. Another universalistic standard which governs executive action is suggested by the phrase, used by Barnard, "the good of the organization as a whole."[19] This is perhaps the widest of all the general standards, and it involves executive judgment of others as total personalities capable of helping or hindering the "vitality and endurance" of the organization. In fact, certain judgments which would be labeled particularistic from one point of view are clearly universalistic by this standard. Thus executives may refuse to hire Negroes if they think that the stability of their organization would be threatened thereby.[20]

The executive role is also characterized in its relationship to other roles by emotional neutrality. Speaking in the ideal sense, it is only the organizational aspects of people's personalities with which the executive must concern himself. That is, he is concerned with personnel only in so far as they function in the division of labor or in a chain of command. This is not to say that his role is free of affective elements. He regularly interacts, on a face-to-face basis, with a small group of people and it seems safe to say that he must judge *these* subordinates in emotional terms to some degree. In addition, it is probably true that emotional elements enter the relationships between the executive and masses of subordinates with whom there is no direct contact. For instance, it is clear that the executive and workingman may react to each other in terms of fear, love, hate, aversion, sympathy, etc. For this reason it is impossible to characterize the executive role

[19] Barnard, *The Functions of the Executive*, p. 273.
[20] Whether such executive action does not violate the universalistic standards of the society as a whole is another question. The point here, however, is to understand the organizational basis of executive action.

as clearly neutralistic in spite of the demands of industrial bureaucracy for this value.

Personality and Role. Three major aspects of the executive role have been considered: the relation of the role to the culture of industrialism, the functions of the role for the organization as a whole, and the dimensions or structural characteristics of the role itself. We shall now discuss the relationships between the executive role and personality. Two interrelated problems confront us here, though time will permit the consideration of only the first in some detail. The first problem concerns the way in which individuals are motivated to play the executive role. The second question concerns the types of personalities best suited to play the executive role. The first problem is essentially sociological and social psychological; the second is primarily a psychological problem.

The Structurally Generalized Goals of the Executive Role. It has already been pointed out that all roles in society are made concrete— brought to life, so to speak—by flesh-and-blood human beings; in one sense it might be said that society is made a reality by human beings playing roles. But how are human beings made to play roles? How are they persuaded or forced to play roles properly, to play them in one way rather than in another? How can diverse and unique human personalities be motivated to conform to the demands of society and social organization? More specifically, what motivates individuals to attempt to achieve executive roles and to meet the harsh demands of the executive position? Why has the executive position served as a model to so many who had little or no chance of ever achieving the role?

It has been suggested in Chapter 2 that the answer to such questions must be sought, at least in part, in the inducements which are "built into" the roles themselves. These inducements have been called *generalized goals.* They are generalized in the sense that they meet the needs of a variety of different types of personalities, with diverse motives. What are the generalized goals of the executive role? To answer this question, a number of studies of executive motivation have been examined. Many different types of generalized goals came to light in this survey, but when boiled down almost all of them seemed to fit in one of these categories.

1. Remuneration. One of the most striking features of the executive's role is the unusually large monetary reward attached to it. In fact, the manager of the successful large-scale industrial enterprise is often one of the most richly rewarded men in American society. In 1940, when industry had barely shaken off the effects of the depression, executive salaries ranged from $15,000 to over $200,000 a year;[21] in the large

[21] *Fortune,* "The 30,000 Managers," vol. 21, no. 2, p. 58, February, 1940.

corporation, $60,000 a year could be considered a minimum executive salary.[22] In that same year, 1,000 major officers and 600 lesser executives of large plants were receiving $50,000 or more per year.[23] However, these figures do not provide the full measure of financial reward. The job of the executive is, on the whole, exceptionally secure. Very few executives lost their jobs during even the worst of the depression, and it is a startling fact that executive salaries never fell very far.[24] It is reasonable to expect that jobs offering such great financial inducements would attract extremely able men and that these men would be motivated to an exceptional degree to seek success in their roles.

It is important to realize that to the executive remuneration on this princely scale does not mean the same thing as a wage to the workingman. To the workingman the wage is a means to a living. For the executive, financial reward may be a symbol of social prestige and social class position. The executive who drives himself to success in his role is creating the means by which certain community goals can be achieved. The financial reward is also a symbol of the executive role itself, its power, its dignity, its freedom. In this connection, it is not the absolute amount of financial reward that is important as a generalized goal; it is the superiority of executive remuneration relative to all other roles in the plant. The $15,000-a-year salary of the owner of the small plant symbolizes this superiority as much as the $200,000-a-year salary of the executive of the large corporation. The meaning of the symbol is the same in both cases: the executive role is the top.

2. *Accomplishment.* Perhaps no role in society affords more of a sense of accomplishment, of doing vital things, than the executive's role. The pragmatic bent of our society, its emphasis on the creation of material values, its admiration for large-scale effort reinforces this sense of accomplishment. Nor does the executive have to rely on the reaches of history or the slow understanding of men's minds for proofs of achievement. Tangible proofs of accomplishment surround him; there is the superior salary, the deference of subordinates, the long gleaming factory buildings, the profit record, the title of president itself.

3. *Status.* Closely related to accomplishment and remuneration as generalized goals is the goal of status, taken here in the sense of prestige or esteem. Status may be attained in many areas of life, but occupation is probably the most important source of status, since an individual in our society is judged primarily by his occupational role and his performance within it. If occupations were arranged on a status scale, the role of the large-scale corporation executive would be at or very near

22 *Ibid.,* p. 106.
23 *Ibid.*
24 *Ibid.,* p. 108.

the top. In fact, our society gives the successful, large-scale corporation executive roughly the same degree of status that other societies accorded royalty, knighthood, or the church.

The high status of the executive is symbolized in many ways. Within the plant it is represented by his title, his salary, the attitude of his subordinates, the size of his office, the leisure to which he is entitled. Outside the plant the executive's status is symbolized by his high standard of living, the weight attached to his words, the high position to which he may be called in the government. The strength of status as a generalized goal is further enhanced by the fact that the executive is selected from a group of highly competitive equals and then elevated far above them in prestige.

4. *Power.* A recent discussion of the executive asks why the boss worked.[25] And it answers, in part, that he loved working—that he gained a sense of power from his work. Power—the ability to control the action and even the minds of other men, the ability to initiate vast undertakings, the ability to overcome obstacles and opponents—inheres in the executive role as surely as it does in the role of political leader or general. Like these latter two, the executive is the head of a (sometimes vast) bureaucratic organization, in which all lines of authority finally converge in himself. This point, discussed in Chapter 5, will bear repetition here. Business organization is essentially nondemocratic; authority does not flow from the bottom up to chosen leaders or representatives. It flows from the top down to special delegates, who owe their authority to the executive, the only source of authority in the industrial organization. The power of the executive, except in so far as it is limited by the operation of external factors and by the nature of industrial bureaucracy, is absolute. This is not to say, of course, that power is equally attractive to all men, or to all executives; it does, however, state a fact about the nature of the executive role.

5. *Freedom.* Another general goal which is "built into" the role of executive is the relatively great freedom or autonomy which the role offers. Objectively, the executive is free in that he is not tied to a machine, a desk, or a room. His movements are, within the limits set by the demands of business, determined by himself. His working hours are not of the rigid 9-to-5 variety; they may be much longer, but at any rate they are self-determined. Subjectively, although the executive may be almost crushed by the weight of work and responsibility, he is free in the sense that he makes final decisions and is subjected to no one else's orders. At the same time, he can direct, control, and mold the men under him. He decides men's fate; the distance they can and will go in the organization, the amount of rewards they will be permitted to have.

[25] *Fortune,* "What Makes the Boss Work?" vol. 37, no. 4, p. 105, April, 1948.

The executive achieves what many men dream about, but fewer and fewer attain in our society: objective and spiritual freedom from control by other human beings.

Thus at least five generalized goals—goals which many people in our society ardently desire—may be achieved within the executive role. Some executives may be motivated more by one aim than by another; some may be motivated by a combination of goals. But probably very few of them would deny that at least some of these goals have been instrumental in driving them toward the executive role and executive achievement.

The Personality of the Successful Executive. Attention has been focused in this chapter on the social side of the executive role; the relation of its aims, functions, dimensions, and generalized goals to industrial organization. But there is another, equally important, side to this picture; namely, the individuals who play this role, the individual differences between them, and the varying motives of their diverse personalities. Other disciplines, such as industrial psychology and industrial management, have focused on the individual side of role playing. It is beyond the scope of this book to try even to review the literature in these fields. Here little more can be done than to suggest certain broad features of the personality system of the executive which are necessary if the demands of the role are to be met.

In general, the executive must possess strong self-discipline if the role is to be first attained and then successfully filled. In the course of achieving the role, the executive must show himself capable of accepting authority without resentment and of subordinating immediate goals to the demands of the career. As an executive he must constantly keep himself under control, emotionally and intellectually. Furthermore, the typical successful executive must possess unusual ambition, a relentless drive to get ahead, to "achieve," to be successful. In the pursuit of his goals he must be hyperactive, superbly energetic, stopping at no obstacles. Failure must represent the ultimate calamity, to be avoided at all costs. Ruthlessness may well be an asset to him; he must be able to drive not only himself but his subordinates. His decisions may be made "on the spot" or after long deliberation, but he must stick to them and carry them through at all costs. His self-confidence must be without qualm.

Yet, at the same time, the executive must be extremely skillful in handling people. He must be able to adjust to varying types of personalities, to understand their motives, attitudes, beliefs, values, and symbols. He must be able to organize and direct the activities of others. This means that he must be superbly skillful at directing human action; yet he must also be skillful at compromise, knowing when and what to yield. He must know how to make diverse personalities work together; in fact, he must know how to harness diversities in personalities to the aims of the organization. And not least, he must be able to understand himself, to know what his true motives are, to take into account both his effect on others and his reaction to others.[26]

It is beyond the scope of this book to investigate the deeper-lying aspects of executive personality, those traits which could be revealed only by psychoanalysis. However, it may be noted that the sort of person who is successful at the executive role is one who typically has broken strong emotional ties of a sort which would hamper his career. This means that in our culture he has, typically, broken away from dependence on the mother image.[27] The father as an image of authority, on the other hand, remains much admired. In a sense, the executive may be striving to emulate a father, either a real one or an idealized one. It is by no means impossible that the paternalistic trends in American industry—which have been intermittently strong—reflect this attraction to the father image.

Finally, the executive must possess intelligence, foresight, and insight of a very high order. Technical competence, although the pride of many executives, is much less important than these generalized attributes. The demands of the executive roles are so ill defined, so subject to shifting external forces, that specific skills may be as great a handicap as a too rigid personality. The extensibility of the role strengthens the need of high general capacities. It is the creative, inventive, adaptive personality who succeeds at the executive role.[28]

Strains in the Executive Role. Practically all roles in our society impose some sort of strain on those who play them. In Chapter 2 it was shown that strains arise as a result of disorientation between the personality and role. A strain always arouses tension in the personality. This tension may be directed at the self, that is, the personality may be changed by, or adapted to, the role. Or it may be directed against the environment, in which case an attempt is made to change or control the role, realistically or symbolically. In the executive role, strain may arise in several ways, of which three seem to be the most important.

1. Strains may arise from a disorientation between the personality and *the types of skill* demanded in the executive role. The official in the industrial bureaucracy has usually been trained for certain specific tasks. If this official then is elevated to the executive role, this may mean, on the one hand, that the new executive is too inflexible for the role; he

---

[26] Janney, *op. cit.*, p. 61.

[27] *Fortune,* "The Tests of Management," (quoting Burleigh Gardner and William E. Henry of Social Research, Inc.), July, 1950, pp. 92ff.

[28] *Fortune,* "The 30,000 Managers," vol. 21, no. 2, p. 58, February, 1940.

may be unable to change from a concentration on specialized work to the diffuse tasks of the executive, such as planning or administration. On the other hand, he may be unable to make the shift from certain social skills, such as obedience, competition and striving which have been acquired as a subordinate, to the executive skills of decision and command. In the first case, the executive will fail because of his inability to see the woods for the trees; in the second case, because he is unable to offer leadership.

2. A similar type of strain arises from disorientation between the personality system and the *generalized goals* of the executive role. Here again the discrepancy may be noted in the case of the newly made executive, who has received his training in a subordinate role. In this case, where one of the generalized goals of the executive role is superior status, the executive may remain emotionally bound up with certain informal relations to former coworkers. Where the executive role offers great amounts of freedom, the executive may have strong needs for dependency on others. Where the executive roles offers power as a generalized goal, the executive may have a strong subconscious desire for a nonresponsible, subordinate role. It is no wonder that many new executives complain of loneliness—of being treated as an office, rather than as a person.[29] Old friendships cannot be maintained.[30] Former peers become deferential, perhaps even subtly hostile; the new executive now suddenly finds himself the object of the fear, secrecy, and ambition which formerly motivated his own actions in relation to his superiors.

3. Strain also arises from the conditions in which the executive operates. Bureaucratic organization, it will be recalled, concentrates authority and power in the executive role. This means that the executive is solely responsible for decisions, which in some cases will affect the well-being of the entire organization. This in itself would be sufficient to cause major strain; responsibility is not an easy load to bear even for the personalities who achieve executive success. But what makes the matter worse is the uncertain situation in which the executive operates.[31] Whether he must make a decision in regard to the marketing of a certain type of product, enunciate a labor policy, create a bonus system, or adopt a certain position in relation to a competitor, he rarely can operate with an adequate knowledge of the facts. For instance, in marketing a

[29] *Fortune,* "The Tests of Management," July, 1950, p. 107.

[30] This is very often true for the executive's family as well. His wife, for instance, will find it very difficult to retain the friendships she formed when her husband was on the way up. See two articles by William H. Whyte, Jr., "The Wives of Management," *Fortune,* October, 1951, and "The Corporation and the Wife," *Fortune,* November, 1951.

[31] The author is indebted, in this discussion, to lectures delivered by Talcott Parsons at Harvard University, 1946–1947.

new product, the executive has no way of foreseeing sudden shifts in demands or tastes. He can only guess whether a new product should be released for sale or be kept in the laboratory for another five years of development and perfection.[32] In this case, he must take responsibility for a decision without knowledge of what conditions will be at the time the decision takes effect. There is reason to believe that this situation is quite general in the executive role. Almost every decision is a gamble in the face of uncertainty and imperfect knowledge.

Underlying and surrounding the uncertainty and heavy responsibility of the executive role is the ever-present possibility, however remote, of failure and of dismissal from office. It will hardly be necessary to point out what the executive loses by failure. Not only may he lose his lofty standard of living, or his high status, or the power that goes with office, but there is little likelihood that he can easily shift to another executive position of comparable status. He is not in the position of the unskilled or semiskilled workingman, to whom one job is much like another. There may be only one opportunity per lifetime for each executive. Furthermore, considering the intense ambition of most men who get to be executives, and the intense competitiveness in the struggle to achieve the role, the possibility of failure must be particularly frightening to them. Certainly it seems difficult to explain the behavior of some executives if one does not understand the nature of this fear of failure.

The tensions created by the uncertain and dangerous position in which the executive operates may find expression in several diverse ways. For instance, strain may create in the executive large amounts of diffuse anxiety, frustration, and free-floating aggression. These emotions may then be released against the environment in a nonrational way, or they may be turned against the self. In the former case, the executive may discover or create certain scapegoats who are then made the object of the emotional affect. He may blame his troubles on "that Man in the White House," "labor agitators," "unfair, sly competitors," and so on. Since this is essentially a magical reaction, the possibility of realistically meeting the demands of the role is further decreased. If the emotional affect is turned against the self, some sort of psychosomatic symptom or disease may well appear. It is not only in popular folklore but in actuality that executives suffer from nervous breakdowns, peptic ulcers, and coronary disease. These diseases are undoubtedly related to fundamental discrepancies between role and personality.

In addition to scapegoating and the psychosomatic symptoms, there is still another possible reaction to strain—a reaction which may have grave consequences not only for the executive, but for the society as a whole. The executive may attempt to meet the strains in his role by con-

[32] Peter F. Drucker, "The Function of Profits," *Fortune,* March, 1949, p. 111.

trolling or changing the environment. He may attempt to influence public opinion, to lobby for certain political programs, or to maneuver against competitors. These actions may be entirely legal and proper. However, it seems to be unfortunately true that in some cases industrial executives have tried to control the environment in unethical and even illegal ways. This reaction may be seen in the high incidence of what has been called "white-collar crime,"[33] e.g., the defrauding of the government of tax returns, the delivery of inadequate products to the armed forces even in wartime, the tendency to evade legislation safeguarding standards of work in industry, and illegal methods of opposition to labor unions, including the use of open violence and terrorism. If the dishonest or semidishonest advertising campaigns which many industries sponsor —or give tacit consent to—are not criminal, they are close to the borders of the unethical.

Two types of deleterious consequences flow from the criminal or unethical practices of industrial executives. The executive may evolve a sort of dual or schizophrenic personality. His business activities are governed by values diametrically opposed to other value systems. He may, therefore, try to compartmentalize his personality; he will evolve a business self, a family self, a religious self. If the executive is unable to reconcile the conflicts between the values, the result may be, on the one hand, certain nonrational reactions. That is, the guilt and anxiety may be either converted into some sort of psychosomatic symptom (in the manner described above) or projected onto scapegoats. The "labor-hating" executive may very well be displacing his feeling of guilt about unfair labor practices onto the victims of those practices; this type of executive may, for instance, accuse labor of the very things of which he himself is guilty. On the other hand, the executive may suppress one set of values—e.g., social values—in order to engage in "smart" business practice. In this case he is protecting himself against feelings of guilt, but at the price of detaching himself and his industrial organization from the values of society as a whole.

The second deleterious consequence of illegal or unethical executive practice is the harm done to the relation between society and industry. There can be no doubt that grave material damage is wrought on society by some business practice; inferior products are manufactured, cutthroat competition is practiced, misleading advertising causes people to spend money unwisely, in some cases the lives and well-being of employees are endangered. Furthermore, society suffers spiritually when public confidence in one of its most highly respected and admired groups is destroyed. This lack of confidence is inevitably extended to the whole

[33] See Edwin H. Sutherland, *White Collar Crime*, The Dryden Press, Inc., New York, 1949.

business community, which becomes identified in the public mind with dishonesty and social irresponsibility. The result is that the organic interrelationship between society and its industrial institution is severed, and in its place arises a relationship of mutual distrust. It is no wonder that society reacts to this situation by attempting to control industry; e.g., the government may pass laws regulating working conditions, business practice, advertising claims, or the quality of products. Business executives may inveigh against government "interference," but such interference is inevitable when an institution as vital as industry becomes detached from the rest of society.

Summary. The role of the industrial executive has been analyzed in its relationship to the culture of industrialism and to the personality of executives. It has been shown that the executive role is shaped by its culturally given aim, the production of profits; and by the culturally defined means, technology and bureaucracy. It was then shown how industrial organization imposed certain functions on the executive role. The dimensions or the structure of the executive role were related to the needs of large-scale industry. Further, an attempt was made to show how the executive role is related to personality. The key point of connection between the role and personality was found in the structurally generalized goal, which functioned to channel and focus diverse personalities and motives within the executive role. Finally, it was shown how strain might arise between the personality and the role, and how this strain might be released in harmful or beneficial directions. Thus the executive role was seen to be a sort of mold, which shaped all types of individuals who might attempt to play the role.

CHAPTER 7

"Minor" Roles: The Specialist, the Office Worker, the Foreman

Before proceeding to an examination of the industrial laity (the factory workers), we shall briefly consider several "minor" industrial roles, which cannot be satisfactorily considered either as managerial or worker roles. The roles to be considered are those of the specialist, the foreman, and the office worker. Each of these roles differs significantly from both managerial and worker roles in relation to content, structure, and the types of strains to which it is subjected.

THE ROLE OF THE SPECIALIST

The specialist's role may be defined as one oriented to the application of many types of scarce and hard-to-acquire information or skill to the process of production. It has been shown that the application of technological skill and scientific knowledge to production has always been one of the characteristics of the industrial system. However, in modern industry the role of the specialist has assumed a position of ever-increasing importance. This modern upsurge of the specialist is the result of several factors. The continuing technological revolution has greatly increased the complexity of the productive process and, along with this, the need for engineers of all kinds. The increasing involvement of science in production has greatly increased the need for research specialists. The increasing size and complexity of industrial bureaucracies has heightened the need for experts in social organization and the handling of personnel. Finally, the complexity of the relationships between modern industry and many areas of society has created the need for experts in "foreign relations," e.g., the lawyer, the advertising man, or the public-relations counselor.

The increased importance of specialists is reflected in their increasing numerical importance in industry as well as in the growing facilities allotted to them. At the end of World War II, 75 research laboratories, employing more than 100 specialists, were maintained by industries. By 1950 there were almost 150 large research laboratories in the United States.[1] In 1948 the Bell Telephone Laboratories employed 6,100 employees, of whom 2,400 were basic scientists and engineers.[2]

Specialists may be found in many different positions in the industrial bureaucracy. The specialist may be the lone assistant of an executive or other high official. He may work as a member of a small group of experts, or be a member of a relatively large department. In general, however, he is rarely located in the line organization. However, whether specialists have power to issue orders to the line, or whether their role is strictly advisory, depends on individual plant policy and sometimes on the accidents of personality. It should be noted that where they are responsible to highly placed line officials, they may have great informal power over the line organization or some section of it.

Functions of Specialists. Specialists in industry perform an increasingly great number of functions. In the past, the industrial plant employed only a few types of experts, mainly engineers. Today, however, not only engineers but also geologists, lawyers, economists, and psychologists may be found in the industrial plant.[3] These experts may be classified in the following categories according to the functions they perform in the plant.[4]

1. One group of specialists is concerned primarily with maintaining the productive process itself. These specialists, usually known as engineers, are concerned with such areas as machine design, safety, maintenance, efficiency. They constitute the most numerous type of specialists, and were, in fact, the first type to appear in the plant.

2. A second type of specialist is concerned with administration and with plant organization. His function is to bring the plant organization into line with the demands of production. He may be concerned, for instance, with finding the proper proportion of line and staff organization in a particular plant.

---

[1] Peter F. Drucker, "Management and the Professional Employee," *Harvard Business Review*, vol. 30, no. 3, p. 84, May-June, 1952.

[2] *Fortune*, "The Scientists," October, 1948, p. 108. It should be noted that this recent upsurge of the specialist in industry is only a part of a general increase in the numbers of salaried professionals in the United States. Taken as a whole, the proportion of salaried professionals in the working force has increased from 1 to 6 per cent in the last two generations; in that same period professionals increased from 4 per cent of the middle classes to 14 per cent of the middle classes. See C. Wright Mills, *White Collar*, Oxford University Press, New York, 1951, p. 113. The composition of the middle classes is discussed in chap. 16 of the present book, "Industry and Social Stratification."

[3] Drucker, *op. cit.*, p. 84.

[4] Our discussion here draws heavily from the excellent description of the specialists' function provided by Wilbert E. Moore. See his *Industrial Relations and the Social Order*, rev. ed., The Macmillan Company, New York, 1951, pp. 129–132.

3. Another group of specialists is concerned with the human material of the plant. These specialists include personnel men, physicians, nurses, and social workers. Their functions are extremely varied; for instance, personnel men may be responsible for hiring, for assignment to jobs or for reassignments, for the determination of aptitudes, for the formulation and application of incentive systems, for the operation of savings and insurance plans.

4. Some specialists are concerned with the enormously complicated commercial and financial aspects of industry. These include cost accountants, bookkeepers, treasurers.

5. Other specialists usually have no professional titles as such, but their function is definitely of a specialist nature. These are the special assistants to high executive officials. Their duties may include gathering information from the external world or from the plant, and the preparation of programs or orders for the consideration of the executive. The special skills which these experts employ may range from intimate knowledge of a technical or administrative process to a diffuse knowledge of public relations or to a knack for handling people.

6. Still another group of specialists, found usually only in the largest corporations, are not immediately concerned with technology or administration at all. These specialists, rather, deal in basic research, which may or may not have ultimate practical use. They are also concerned with inventions, or with the search for new products. Chemists, physicists, geologists, biochemists, are to be found in this group.

7. Finally, there are those specialists who are concerned with the "foreign relations"[5] of the industrial plant, particularly with the relationships of the plant to the community. Advertising men, market analysts, designers, may be concerned with the public as customers.[6] Lawyers and other legal consultants handle the relationships between industry and government. Other specialists may handle the problem of negotiations with the union and the implementation of the contract. Public-relations departments may be concerned to present the industry in the best possible light to the general public.

Structure of the Specialist's Role. Although specialists perform all these diverse functions within the industrial bureaucracy, certain regularities or patterns may be detected in the structure of their roles.

1. In spite of the diversity in technical content and function, many specialists operate in similar social environments within the plant. Regularities in this area arise from the needs and interests of the professional

---

[5] This term is used by Moore, *ibid.*, p. 131.

[6] Or the firm may hire outside specialists to do these jobs. In recent years industry has come to depend more and more on the advertising agency, the market-analysis firm, etc., to perform some of these functions.

role. For instance, in order to apply special skills or to conduct research, the specialist must be able to establish certain types of social relationships with others. The specialist role may directly necessitate social relationships with assistants; it may be necessary to provide the specialist with fellow specialists with whom he can exchange ideas. These characteristics of the specialist role are not peculiar to industry; they arise out of the nature of the specialist's work.

2. Another set of patterns governs the relationships of the specialist's role to other roles. These relationships reflect the difficulty of integrating the specialist role with other parts of the bureaucracy, particularly with the line organization. This problem arises from the almost natural resistance of line organizations to advice and counsel from the staff. The problem is all the more difficult because the expert is rarely given direct authority over the line. Under these circumstances, the specialist may attempt to inculcate attitudes in the line organization respecting the necessity or advisability of accepting expert advice. He may stress his special training and his professional standing. He may also stress professional values, e.g., disinterestedness and impersonality.[7]

However, there is good evidence to indicate that the specialist may have difficulty in securing acceptance by the line, except perhaps in those cases where he is close to a top line official and can thus wield indirect power.[8] Under these circumstances, certain informal patterns for securing acceptance by the line tend to evolve. For instance, informal relationships of friendship between experts and powerful members of the line may serve as a channel for bringing staff ideas to the line. Sometimes patterns of accommodation arise between line and staff officials; for instance, experts may habitually overlook line errors, or hold back technical inventions, or even surrender a portion of their organizational funds, in order to secure acceptance for certain ideas. These patterns are often also used for nonorganizational ends;[9] e.g., to secure the transfer of an expert to a more desirable line position. It seems doubtful if staff organizations could function at all except through such informal practices.

3. A third set of patterns governs the relationship between the specialist and management. From the point of view of management, the specialist must be motivated to operate as an expert and yet be controlled within the limits of organizational aims and purposes. Motivation of the specialist to enter the organization and to act efficiently within it

---

[7] For a discussion of the patterns surrounding professionalized roles, see Talcott Parsons, "The Professions and Social Structure," in *Essays in Sociological Theory: Pure and Applied*, Free Press, Glencoe, Ill., 1949, pp. 185–199.

[8] Melville Dalton, "Conflicts between Staff and Line Managers," *American Sociological Review,* vol. 15, no. 3, pp. 342–351, 1950.

[9] *Ibid.*, pp. 348–350.

as a specialist is, today, usually accomplished by offering relatively high salaries.[10] The superior financial resources of industry, as compared, say, to those of colleges and universities, has made it possible to attract increasing numbers of talented individuals in this way. The specialist may also be attracted by the facilities, such as up-to-date laboratories, that industry can provide. For some specialists, the chance for relatively high status, and the opportunity for close identification with management, perhaps for eventual entrance into the ranks of management, may serve as a motivating force.

Control of the specialist is another matter. As we have seen, he brings to his role certain attitudes and values derived from professional traditions. If these attitudes and values are not controlled they may be, potentially, sources of strain in the plant. For instance, the expert's value of efficiency, or his desire to see his ideas for a new product accepted, may lead him into a struggle for power with members of the line organization. Furthermore, his values and the values of management may clash, for instance, over the question of maximum production versus maximum profit. In both these cases, management finds it necessary to limit the power of the expert. In order to control the expert, it is often necessary to subordinate him formally to line officials. Informal methods of control may also be used. Ridicule may be an effective weapon against the specialist. Ideas, inventions, or innovations which threaten the interests or values of other sections of the bureaucracy may be quietly sabotaged. It is important to note that, in spite of the expectations of those who have held that the future belonged to the expert, the patterns described here usually result in the rather complete subordination of the expert within the industrial bureaucracy.[11]

4. It has already been pointed out that the expert brings to his role certain attitudes and values which arise from the cultural tradition within which he has been trained. This cultural tradition may be that of science, in the case of the research expert. It may be that of technological achievement in the case of the engineer. It may be a humanistic bias in the case of the lawyer or the personnel man. However, in all cases, the expert owes at least formal loyalty to a set of values which are external to the plant, and which may be in conflict with organization values. For instance, if the research man acts in relation to norms of "truth" or of "knowledge for its own sake," he inevitably adjusts his relations to others in the plant in terms of these universalistic and affectively neutral values.

5. Another set of patterns in the specialist's role reflects the "in-

[10] "The Scientists," pp. 108–109.
[11] See, for instance, Thorstein Veblen, *The Engineers and the Price System,* The Viking Press, Inc., New York, 1933, particularly chaps. III and IV.

terests" of the experts. These interests include, of course, maximization of financial return, power, status, and privileges. In addition, the expert has an interest in maintaining the values of the cultural traditions in which he has been trained, in safeguarding the professional status of the expert, and in consolidating and advancing the power of the staff organization in the plant. In order to attain and safeguard these interests, the expert strives to pattern his role in such a way as to emphasize the value of his service and the high skill needed in his field. Accordingly, he may try to maintain secrecy as to methods and results of his operations. Exclusion of outsiders is practiced also, sometimes through the use of a professional jargon unintelligible to any except specialists.

The interests of the specialist are also safeguarded by certain ideologies—or, if one prefers, "mythologies"—which are designed to prove the necessity for accepting the specialist's claims in industry. One element of this ideology is to be found in the "logic" of efficiency which the specialist uses as a guide to, and judge of, action in the plant. According to this mode of thought, all the acts of all the members of the organization as well as all innovations are to be judged solely as they contribute to the productive capacity of the plant. By this criterion everyone else in industry would, of course, be judged by the specialist. At the same time this ideology is useful to the expert in that it releases him from the consequences of his innovations, no matter whose interests are injured by these innovations.[12]

To sum up, the role of the specialist in industry is structured by the needs of the industry, by the nature of the specialist's field, by the professional code of the field, by the tenuous position of the specialist in the industrial bureaucracy, and by the need to safeguard the interests of the specialists under these disadvantageous conditions.

Strains in the Specialist's Role. Numerous strains arise in the specialist's role. Some of these strains are common to other bureaucratic roles; some of them are peculiar to the specialist. Of the latter, the most important seem to arise from the difference in the values and outlook of the specialist on the one hand, and other sections of the bureaucracy, on the other hand.

One important strain arises from the difference in outlook between top management and the specialist. By and large the specialist rarely has much understanding of the problems of business, nor does top manage-

[12] It has been noted that reference to a professional ethic or a "logic" is a common way for the expert to absolve himself of responsibility for technological unemployment or other harmful results of inventions or innovations. See Robert K. Merton, *Social Theory and Social Structure*, Free Press, Glencoe, Ill., 1949, pp. 323–324.

ment readily sympathize with the specialist's outlook. As Veblen has put it[13]—

with the continued growth of specialization the experts have necessarily had more and more to say in the affairs of industry; but always their findings as to what work is to be done and what ways and means are to be employed in production have had to wait on the findings of the business managers as to what will be expedient for the purpose of commercial gain.

The result has rarely been overt strife; probably more often the specialist has had to reconcile himself to defeat and dissatisfaction. This situation has not been helped by the frequent failure of management to reward hard research labor for which no practical use can be found.[14]

A constant source of strain and irritation is found in the relationships between staff and line. There is an understandable tendency on the part of line organization to interpret staff advice as threatening or degrading to itself. The line fears that it will be "shown up" to management by staff advice, that it will lose power to the staff; often the line regards the staff as a managerial club held over its head.[15] The staff, on its side, must have its ideas accepted by the line if it is to make an impression on management and justify its existence in the plant.[16] Line opposition to staff proposals is thus often a desperate matter to the expert.

Other sources of line-staff friction are to be found in the differing work habits of line and staff personnel. The line is oriented to discipline and coordination; the staff, to individual effort and to perfection in the job. Nor does the staff take kindly to the strict subordinate-superordinate relationships of the line.[17]

The fact that the staff organization constitutes an alternate line of communication to top management, lying outside the jurisdiction of the line organization, may also lead to friction. The line may suspect staff personnel of feeding information to management. Staff may suspect the line of withholding information and of covering up mistakes.

Another source of strain springs from the differing social characteristics, backgrounds, and training of staff and line personnel. Staff personnel are usually younger than their counterparts on the line; they have usually begun higher, and they have advanced further than a man on the line could in the same time span. The line may attribute this rapid

[13] Thorstein Veblen, *The Engineers and the Price System*, The Viking Press, Inc., New York, 1933, p. 60. By permission.
[14] Drucker, *op. cit.*, p. 85.
[15] Dalton, *op. cit.*, p. 348.
[16] A good account of line-staff strain of this type is to be found in Burleigh R. Gardner, *Human Relations in Industry*, Richard D. Irwin, Inc., Homewood, Ill., 1945, pp. 75–78.
[17] Another good account of line-staff strain is provided by Drucker, *op. cit.*

advancement to the higher social class background of staff personnel, to superior education, rather than to superior knowledge or competence. Whether this charge is true or not, there can be little doubt that existing differences in social class and education make for divergences in the outlooks and expectations of staff and line personnel.

The staff may also, on occasion, find itself in conflict with the workers in the plant. Friction here may arise as the result of staff desires to hire, fire, upgrade, and downgrade in terms of its own logic; that is, the logic of efficient production. Trouble may also arise as a result of the incompatibility between the specialist's desire to run production according to norms of efficiency, on the one hand, and the aims and values of the workers, on the other. This situation is exacerbated by the fact that the background, training, and outlook of the specialist rarely fits him to understand the worker's mentality, and the reverse is certainly true.

The strains which have been described here are sufficient to make the specialist's role a difficult one. This may explain the rather high turnover rates of specialists, particularly those who are at the beginnings of their career. The average young specialist coming out of college, trained usually only in his specialty, is rarely prepared for what he will encounter in the plant. Instead of benighted workers and foremen waiting eagerly for his expert knowledge, he finds hostility, evasion, and sometimes overt opposition. He may find that he has to fight hard and make all sorts of compromises in order to get an idea accepted, and even then he may fail. He may also find that his feelings of identification with management are, at this stage of his career, somewhat illusory. Furthermore, our young specialist is usually an ambitious, restless individual, thoroughly imbued with a desire for success. Yet he may be surprised to find that while his starting salary is relatively high, advancement is slow, particularly because staff organization has relatively few rungs in its organizational ladder. He may also find recognition for his talent and education slow in coming or, in fact, entirely absent. Thus, while the specialist's role has many real rewards, it is by no means devoid of struggle, disappointment, and the possibility of failure.

THE ROLE OF THE OFFICE WORKER

The role of the office worker is difficult to classify as either of the staff or line organization. In one sense, as we shall see, it much more closely resembles the role of the factory worker than any other role. However, many office workers, and perhaps to some extent management also, tend to consider this role a part, if a humble one, of the hierarchy. It will be of great interest to us to trace the causes for this split between objective situation and subjective definition.

The Development of the Modern Office. In order to analyze the office worker's role, it is necessary, first, to say something about the development of the modern business office. The modern office has been an outgrowth of large-scale industry. In the days when industry was conducted on a relatively small scale, before the development of industrial bureaucracy, offices were correspondingly small. Office employees were few in number, highly trained, relatively well educated as compared to shop workers, and in close personal contact with management. The private secretary was, perhaps, the most important worker in the old-fashioned office. The private secretary, almost always a woman, was in close personal contact with the "boss"; she took his dictation, arranged his schedule for the day, and performed a myriad of other tasks. Even lesser office workers, such as stenographers, had a sort of personal contact with members of management which few shop workers ever experienced.

It is, perhaps, not correct to say that this type of office is now entirely obsolete. But as industry has grown larger and more complex, certain strong forces have operated to produce radical changes in the nature of the office. For one thing, there has been a very great increase in the amount of paper work in modern industry. The very increase in the size of industry has meant that the actions of more human beings must be recorded, more pay records must be kept, more orders for raw material must be placed, more correspondence with customers must be conducted. As the industrial process has become more complex, there have been more firms to deal with, subcontractors to engage, negotiations about patents. The amount of paper work in industry was enormously increased during both world wars as a result of greatly increased production and government controls. During the 1930s, the New Deal and the rise of unionism had much the same effects. Such New Deal measures as unemployment insurance, social security laws, and corporation tax laws—to name only a few—necessitated vast amounts of paper work in industry. With unionism came the union contract, usually specifying in minute and written detail the multifarious obligations and rights of management and labor.[18]

Under these circumstances the number of office employees necessarily increased very greatly. Between 1909 and 1927 the number of salaried employees of all types nearly doubled.[19] Between 1940 and 1954 the number of white-collar employees of all types increased by 67 per cent, while the number of manual workers increased by only 26 per cent. Office-machine operators increased by 138 per cent, telephone operators

[18] Mills, *op. cit.* See particularly chaps. 9 and 11.
[19] See Lewis Corey, *The Crisis of the Middle-Class,* Crown Publishers, Inc., New York, 1935, p. 142. Of course many nonindustrial organizations helped to absorb this increased number of office workers. For instance, the insurance companies employed great numbers of office workers during this period.

by 79 per cent.[20] As the size of the office increased, costs increased. Payrolls increased, more space was occupied, new facilities and equipment had to be purchased. This increased cost led management to apply the methods of rationalization to office work. These methods are, today, changing the nature of the office. We shall consider these measures briefly.

One tendency is to concentrate the numerous offices which tend to develop at many levels of the plant. A central office provides for the efficient performance of work and safeguards against duplication. This has made it possible for management to hire fewer new office workers even in the face of great increases in the amount of paper work.

A second result of rationalization has been the mechanization of office work. In the traditional office, typewriters and adding machines were the only really widely used machines. Starting with World War I, hundreds of different types of machines, designed to do a very wide variety of tasks, began to make their appearance in the office. However, the industrial revolution in the office did not really begin in earnest until World War II. The enormously increased work loads of wartime, the shortages of office workers and their steadily rising wages, made mechanization imperative. As Mills put it, today "we are still only in the beginning of the office machine age. . . . Today the machine investment per industrial worker varies from $19,375 in the chemical industry to $2,659 in textiles, the average per office worker is not more than $1,000."[21]

Changes in the Role of the Office Worker. The enlargement, centralization, and mechanization of the office have served to modify old office roles, to create new ones, and to relate these roles to each other in novel ways. One important development, which began as early as the 1920s, is the increasing importance of the office manager. *Before* that time the management of the office was usually assigned as a part-time duty to an official who held a position in the line. *After* that time office managing became the work of a specialist who knew intimately the work of the office, who knew how to manage, how to route work. In other words, office management emerged as a full-fledged managerial position. By 1929 this movement was already far advanced.[22]

At the same time, the old office role structure began to break down. This structure had been a hierarchy beginning with the relatively lowly typist and ascending through the stenographer who took dictation, to the private secretary who had numerous, often confidential, duties. In the modern office the tendency has been to confine private secretaries

[20] Jean A. Flexner and Anna-Stina Ericson, "White-collar Employment and Income," *Monthly Labor Review*, vol. 79, no. 4, pp. 401–409, 1956; see p. 404.
[21] C. Wright Mills, *White Collar*, Oxford University Press, New York, 1951, p. 195. By permission.
[22] *Ibid.*, p. 205.

to the very highest managerial positions. Even the stenographer has departed. In the place of these specialists have come the dictating machine and a pool of typists to transcribe the recordings. Similarly, the roles of the bookkeeper, the accountant, and even the secretary have been fragmented, rationalized, and mechanized. Many of the tasks connected with these roles have become routinized, specialized operations, performed by relatively unskilled machine operators. Thus, at the same time as office roles have become finely diversified in terms of technical content, the essential differences between them have practically disappeared.

This process is, as we can see, the exact counterpart of what has occurred in the shop. The white-collar worker, often a woman, has become, in effect, a machine operator who performs relatively light work demanding little or no skill. The work is repetitive, and calls for little physical or mental energy. The main differences between light shop work and office work have been the as yet lesser degree of mechanization in the office, and the different aims of the productive process. Where the shopworker deals with inanimate, often inorganic, material, changing this material from one form into another, the office worker is concerned with abstract symbols. Whether this is a significant objective difference or not, it seems to lead to significant subjective differences.

The rationalization and mechanization of the office determine the social relations of the office worker to other members of the office. These social relations tend to approximate those found in the lower reaches of a bureaucratic organization. Thus, the office worker reports to a superior, is judged by this superior, receives orders from him, and so on. The office worker is related socially to fellow workers through the needs of the work flow. In both directions relationships are impersonal and affectively neutral. Furthermore, the office worker is, today, largely judged in terms of universalistic criteria, particularly the norm of efficiency. The rather personal and relatively informal relationships of the prebureaucratic office are largely things of the past.

This, of course, does not mean that nonbureaucratic patterns are absent from the modern office. The influential private secretary is still not completely obsolete. Cliques are formed, broken, and re-formed among office workers as among other personnel. Lines of authority are circumvented in various ways, both for organizational and nonorganizational purposes.

What generalized rewards are attached to the office worker's role? This question has certain puzzling aspects. The relative paltriness of white-collar salaries is well known. Office salaries today are lower than the wages of many skilled workers, and not much higher on the average than the wages of operatives; this is particularly true for men. The median wage in 1954 for male clerks and kindred workers was

$3,735; for craftsmen, foremen, and kindred workers it was $4,246, for operatives and kindred workers it was $3,349. The income of clerks had increased by 62.8 per cent between 1939 and 1954; but the income of skilled workers had increased by 124.4 per cent, and of operatives 132.6 per cent. In 1954, female white-collar workers earned median incomes of $2,468 as compared to a median income of $1,852 for female operatives. But even here the gap between the salaries of white-collar workers and those of operatives was closing; for while female white-collar income was increasing by only 55.5 per cent between 1939 and 1954, the income of female operatives was increasing by 118.2 per cent.[23] This suggests that nonfinancial factors are important in motivating individuals to play the roles of office workers.

Since the office role does not offer superior salary or escape from routinized work as rewards, it would seem that its attractiveness lies in some nonmaterial reward, such as "status." Many observers, in fact, have noted that office workers feel their roles to be strongly superior in this respect to those of shop workers.[24] Office workers believe that their jobs demand high mental power, skill, and education, or at least apprenticeship. Furthermore, office workers seem to feel that their claims to relatively high status are recognized by management in various ways: by permission to wear street clothing at work, by payment in salary rather than in wages, by somewhat different hours of work, by separation from the shop. In general these claims to, and symbols of, higher status seem to be accepted even by many workers, though not by all.

There is further evidence for the hypothesis that status is an exceptionally strong motive for many office workers. In the office there is often an intense concern among office workers with certain symbols of status; with the relative size of desks, with the right of having one's name listed in the company telephone directory, and so on. There is often a rather desperate attempt among them to find reasons for assigning differing measures of status to essentially similar jobs. Very often such assigned status is based on a real or fictitious closeness to management. It is for this reason primarily that the private secretary may be able to command real status among her fellow office workers.

There can be little doubt that the office worker's drive for status has been highly useful to management. It has ensured a continuous supply of cheap labor with strong feelings of loyalty to management. It has resulted in high performance on the job, in resistance to unionization. Some observers have therefore concluded that management has created the status panic, as Mills calls it. But this is too simple a view, by far. Actually, much of the drive for status among office workers is brought

[23] Flexner and Ericson, *op. cit.*, p. 407, table 6.
[24] See, for instance, Gardner, *op. cit.*, pp. 10–12.

into the office from the community. The office worker is typically from a middle-class family which is anxious to attain or retain status. The office role becomes the symbol of the status wishes of this middle-class element. Perhaps it would be asking too much of management not to encourage a feeling so advantageous to managerial aims. At the same time there can be little doubt that the intense concern of the office worker for status has harmed his economic position; e.g., through a failure to unionize, and through a willingness to trade financial gains for the symbols of status.

As might be expected, the white-collar role is exposed to numerous strains. One strain, of course, arises from the relatively low salaries paid office workers, salaries so low that it is difficult to keep up middle-class standards of life. Since wage workers have, in recent years, managed to raise their standards of life, the white-collar worker has been confronted with this dilemma: either to accept his financial status and not to violate his feelings of loyalty to and identification with management, or to unionize and to forfeit these loyalties and status gains. The result of this dilemma can be seen both in the successes and failures of union movements among white-collar workers.

Again, in so far as the modern office takes on the aspect of a factory, the office worker becomes subjected to many of the same strains which beset the worker. For instance, the problem of technological unemployment, previously almost nonexistent for the office worker, becomes a reality with the mechanization and rationalization movements. Furthermore, mechanization and rationalization, leading, as we have seen, to patterns of impersonality and affective neutrality, cut him (or her) off from the possibility of close identification with management. No longer is he in close touch with the business, no longer is he likely to be closely identified with glamorous managerial figures. The office worker today may perform a routinized, repetitive, mechanized task, and the job may be meaningless, dull, monotonous, and boring. At the same time as mechanization and routinization reduce the possibility of human satisfactions on the job, the chance of rising through the office hierarchy is also reduced. All jobs are reduced to the same level; the hierarchy disappears. It is possible, of course, for the office worker to erect artificial job ladders, and this is done (and may even be encouraged by management); but this is taking the shadow for the substance, and, in time, may prove to be thin stuff.

Perhaps the most potent source of strain for the office worker has been the threat to what is most dear to him, his status position. While difficult to measure, it seems safe to say that the white-collar worker's status position has decreased in recent years. Within the office, this reduction in status has been the result of the processes described above;

mechanization, leveling of skills, growing impersonality in the job. Outside the office, the major threat to status seems to arise from the fact that the skills of office work no longer are scarce. The high school diploma, for instance, has become so common as to be almost meaningless as a source of status. The office worker becomes less and less distinguishable from any other type of employee, or at least this seems to him a threatening possibility.

At the same time, the shopworkers have, in many cases, increased their status through unionization, which not only has brought better wages and special privileges, but has seriously cut down the power of management. And, as Mills has pointed out, as management's power decreases, there is less and less prestige to be gained from identification with management.[25]

As is often the case, the office worker has attempted to protect his position in the bureaucracy through the creation of an ideology. The claims of superiority of the office worker over the shopworker must be seen as a portion of this ideology. As it has become less and less possible to justify this claim in terms of salary or the special nature of office work, the office worker has tended to rationalize his status position on other bases. Thus have arisen myths of the superiority of handling abstract symbols as compared to handling materials, myths of the efficacy of education, myths of close identification with management. The office girl's close attention to clothes and style may be considered an expression of this ideology, for in this way she emphasizes her superiority to the common run of workers. Sometimes the identification with management is so strong that the office worker absorbs completely the political or social outlook of management. It should also be noted that white-collar workers have attempted to safeguard and rationalize their status positions by claiming that certain racial or ethnic groups do not have enough intrinsic ability to meet the demands of office work.

There is reason to believe that what has been said above describes the major ideology of office workers. However, this does not mean that all office workers have attempted to compensate for strains by rationalization. A certain proportion of them have turned to collective action through unionization. This group has more or less given up a feeling of identification with management. This movement has, thus far, been less important than adherence to the traditional ideology. But this is no guarantee, of course, that it will be so in the future.

THE ROLE OF THE FOREMAN

Like the office worker, the foreman occupies an ambiguous position in the industrial bureaucracy, one which is not easy to categorize as

[25] Mills, *op. cit.*, p. 249.

"management" or "worker." Theoretically, his status is clear; he is a part of management and a member of the line organization. Actually this theoretical picture has become somewhat clouded; this is especially true of the foreman's position as a part of management. The role of the foreman today is in a state of transition. Like the office worker, he has been the victim of certain underlying forces which have tended to reduce the importance and uniqueness of his role.

Under conditions of relatively small-scale production, the role of foreman was a combination of those of master craftsman, production planner, cost clerk, and personnel director, on the one hand, and of administrator on the other.[26] In his capacity as administrator, his authority and power in the shop were unquestioned. The foreman had the sole right to hire and to fire, to promote or to demote; he held the fate of the workingman in the palm of his hand. Thus even if the "old-fashioned foreman" did not share in profits or make final decisions, there was little doubt of his status in the plant; he was, if not a portion of top management, very close to it indeed. And as far as the individual worker was concerned, the foreman *was* management.

Perhaps no role in the factory has been more decisively changed by modern developments. Increasing size, mechanization, specialization, rationalization, and, perhaps most important, the advent of unionization, have all combined to alter drastically the content of the foreman's role, the relation of the role to managerial roles, the skills needed for the job, and the way in which the foreman must operate in the social structure of the plant. We shall consider each of these points in turn.

Although many of the functions of the foreman's role have been lost (e.g., to specialists such as personnel directors or time-and-motion engineers), from the purely technical point of view the role has lost nothing of its complexity. The reason for this lies in the increased complexity of the productive system. The foreman today may be responsible for an intricate production process, for a long line of complicated machines, for a tightly fitting production schedule. He must be something of a mechanic and must know something of the wage and bonus system, something of the inner working of related departments. It is necessary for him to know how to do every job in his department and to do it well. Above all, he must be able to "get out production" of a specified quality, with the most efficient and least costly use of the men and machines under his jurisdiction.[27]

However, although the technical content of the foreman's role has remained complex, there has been a definite change in his position in

---

[26] *Ibid.*, p. 87.
[27] For a good general account of this aspect of the foreman's role, see Auren Uris, *Improved Foremanship*, The Macmillan Company, New York, 1948.

the social structure of the plant, particularly in his relation to management. Because of the foreman's responsibility for production, it is often claimed that he is the "key man" in management; some industries have instituted courses designed to teach the foreman "the point of view of management." However, an examination of the foreman's role shows that while he is an important part of the line, his claim to managerial status has become rather slim. He does not "manage" in the sense that he makes decisions about, or decides on, strategy concerning industrial operations. Nor does he possess an over-all view of production. Rather it is his function to carry out the orders of management in a carefully defined and delimited area. These developments have come about largely as the result of the increasing size of industry and of its increasing complexity. Furthermore, they have seriously reduced the power of the foreman over his workers. As was mentioned above, many of these powers, such as the right of hiring, firing, promotion, and demotion, have been lost to technical specialists. It is, therefore, more accurate to think of the foreman as an agent of management rather than a portion of management.[28] By way of analogy, although it is not a completely accurate one, we might compare him to the noncommissioned officer in the army. The noncommissioned officer is not a member of the officer corps; rather it is his function to implement the decisions made by officers.

Another change which is taking place in the foreman's role is the development of a need for a new set of skills. It has already been shown that this role demands high technical skill and knowledge. But, in addition, the foreman must be able to wield certain social skills. As industry has increased in size, as bureaucracy has grown, and as specialization has progressed, the interrelationships of his role and other roles have multiplied. The modern foreman interacts not only with his superiors and with the workers, but also with other foremen, specialists, straw bosses, and, of late, representatives of the union, particularly the shop steward.[29] The foreman is faced with the necessity of "getting along" with, of accommodating to, these wide variety of roles.

Furthermore, the foreman must develop new skills in relating to workers and management. Workers, no longer to be browbeaten, must be "handled." Management must still be served, but under conditions of distance and impersonality, without the leavening of personal contact. Under these circumstances, the foreman's role is demanding an increasing amount of skill in human management. He must devote atten-

---

[28] This is also the conclusion of Burleigh B. Gardner and William F. Whyte. See their "The Man in the Middle: Position and Problems of the Foreman," *Applied Anthropology*, vol. 4, no. 2, p. 19, 1945.

[29] Mills, *op. cit.*, p. 88.

tion to understanding personality, his own and that of others. He must learn how to give orders, how to resolve disputes, how to negotiate, how to compromise.[30] As a consequence there is a strong tendency to pick a foreman from the ranks not only on the basis of technical skill, production record, faithfulness to the job, or seniority, but also on the basis of rather intangible qualities of personality, of being able to "get along with people," to "handle the men." It is significant that there is a tendency to select foremen from those who have had special training, either within or without the plant, in both technical and social skills.

Concomitant with these technical and social changes, there has been a drastic reduction in the authority of the foreman. Of course, it is not accurate to say that his role has been rendered completely powerless. By and large, foremen still retain the right to discipline workers by reprimand, by assignment to a less pleasant task, or by complaint to higher management. In addition, the foreman's role still commands a certain status among both workingmen and management. This is especially true where he possesses superior technical competence.

Nevertheless, when all these factors have been taken into account, the fact remains that the foreman does not always have authority commensurate with the task which he must perform. His authority has been sapped by the union and by the technical expert. For instance, he has, in many cases, lost the power of firing a worker without the consent of the union. In other cases, hiring, job assignment, promotion, and demotion have become functions of the personnel department. At the same time as the foreman has lost authority, he has lost status, and this, in turn, has still further reduced his authority.

As a result of this loss of authority, foremen have been forced to rely less on their formal position in the social structure of the plant, and more on certain informal patterns of action and informal social relationships in order to fill their roles successfully. For instance, the foreman may strike up informal patterns of friendship or form patterns of exchange of favor with important specialists. He may agree to accept an innovation desired by a staff member in return for certain favors; e.g., securing needed personnel, or the adoption of certain inspection policies toward the work of his department. The foreman may evolve patterns of relationships of a similar kind with his workers. For instance, he may seek to maintain friendly relationships with certain key workingmen; he may try to bind these workingmen to him through a net of personal obligations and personal loyalties. Thus, the foreman has sought to compensate for the loss of authority and status in his role

[30] See Fritz J. Roethlisberger, "The Foreman: Master and Victim of Double Talk," *Harvard Business Review,* vol. 23, no. 3, p. 286, 1945.

by operating through the informal, nonbureaucratic aspects of the plant organization.

Under these circumstances the rewards or satisfactions which the foreman's role offers have become unclear. For the "old-fashioned" foreman, rewards and satisfactions were not unconsiderable. The role offered increased income, the ability to wield authority. It offered freedom from the routine tasks of the bench, an opportunity to have a wider view of the productive process, and a chance to identify with management. Furthermore, the role provided an outlet for the urge to creativity, the "instinct of workmanship," which, as we shall show in a later chapter, has disappeared from many bench jobs. It may be said that the foreman's role offered perhaps the only channel of mobility for many workers, who could not hope for "success" through education or business.

In contrast, the modern foreman's role cannot guarantee these satisfactions. For one thing, with the rise of unions, his salary is no longer greatly superior to the wage of the workers. During World War II, in fact, the income of some foremen dropped behind those of workingmen. Furthermore, unions and specialists have cut down the power and status of the foreman; he has had fewer chances to gain a wide view of the productive process or to identify closely with management.

All this does not mean, however, that the foreman's job does not still offer compensations. Becoming a foreman still means a gain in status to many workers. It also represents tangible recognition of superior skill and knowledge. Furthermore, the job offers certain economic rewards; usually higher income, and security. Even yet the foreman's role commands authority and prestige in the shop. Nor can there be any doubt of the superior freedom of action of the foreman. Usually he is able to participate more fully and meaningfully in the process of production than can the shopworker. In the community, at least the working-class community, the attainment of a foremanship still means increased status. These rewards are in many, though not all, cases effective in moving individuals to seek this role, and to play it successfully.

Yet it will come as no surprise to learn that the foreman's role is marked by strains which are severe even by the standards of the average industrial bureaucracy. The strain on the foreman received general recognition for the first time during World War II, when the enormous pressure for production, combined with shortages of personnel and sometimes of raw materials, put almost unbearable loads on foremen. However, many of these strains are not the result merely of war conditions but spring from deep-lying conditions and tendencies in industry.

Perhaps the major source of strain arises from the fact that increasingly the foreman is caught between powerful groups which have special interests to pursue and are in conflict with each other. The most important of these groups (as far as the foreman is concerned) are management, specialists, and the union. The foreman, relatively powerless, is truly the "man in the middle" or, as he has been called, "the marginal man of industry."[31]

The foreman feels constant pressure from management to increase production and to cut costs. He is charged with implementing decisions made by management in regard to these matters. Yet he has rarely had any voice in the making of those decisions which he is supposed to enforce. Management is constantly judging him by his productive record. Yet he rarely can communicate directly with management, which is distant and impersonal, about the conditions which he must face. It is not surprising that, under these circumstances, the foreman often feels isolated, ignored by management; that he feels that management looks upon him as a buffer between itself and the workers, and that it is difficult for him to identify with management.

The foreman may also face pressure from specialists and other members of the staff organization. For instance, he may be caught between the drive of the specialists to introduce innovations in the system of production and in the social organization, on the one hand, and a distrust of these innovations by the worker, on the other. Often he is charged with introducing change, such as a new machine, in a situation where the interests of the workers are bound to suffer thereby. It is often the foreman who bears the onus for technological change. Furthermore, he may himself suffer directly from social or technological changes. Thus personnel departments have "stolen" his right to hire and fire, to assign workers to jobs, to promote, to demote, to train new workers. The cost clerk watches over his efficiency record; the time-and-motion engineer, over his production rate. Production engineers may initiate changes in his department without his consent or advice. Exacerbating this situation is the fact that the specialist usually has superior lines of communication to top management and can lay his case before them while the foreman cannot. And, parenthetically, the foreman must expect that management will be informed, through this line of communication, of the way he runs his department and of the mistakes that he makes.

Unionization often greatly worsens the strains in the foreman's role. It has already been noted that unionization results in a drastic reduction in the authority, power, and freedom of action of the foreman. His right to hire, to fire, to reprimand—in fact, to discipline in any way—is usually sharply curtailed. Furthermore, the advent of the union

[31] See Gardner and Whyte, *op. cit.*; see also Donald E. Wray, "Marginal Men of Industry: The Foremen," *American Journal of Sociology,* vol. 54, no. 4, pp. 298–301, 1949.

often means that a new center of power is created in the role of the shop steward, or similar official, who is solidly backed up by the power of the union. The shop steward serves as a spokesman for the workers and transmits their complaints and grievances, some of them directed against the foreman, to higher authorities. This means that the foreman must attempt to carry out the policies of management under the vigilant eye of this union official. If there is conflict between the union and management, the resentment or suspicions of both workers and union officials may be directed at the foreman. In disputes between shop stewards and foremen, the shop steward sometimes has better lines of communication to top management than the foreman, who at any rate may be considered expendable by management in any dispute. Thus, here again the foreman is caught between powerful, conflicting forces. To the workers he may be the symbol of management; to management he is often a minor official, easily replaced.

A second source of strain in the foreman's role arises from a diminution in the generalized rewards which the role can offer. There is a real question in many cases of the extent to which the foreman's job still represents "success" or "rising." Many foremen complain that they get little recognition or reward from management; they feel that management has come to look on them as just another type of worker. Nor is there the old certainty among foremen that their jobs are the "first rung on the ladder." There seems to be an increasing awareness among them that managerial officials are rarely chosen from the ranks; that what seems to count is education, social background, or family relationship. The foreman's job has seemed more and more to be the first step on a ladder which had no more rungs.

Furthermore, the foreman has increasingly had to measure his "success" against the success of unionized workers, and there can be little doubt that the comparison is often unfavorable to him. His wages are not strikingly higher than those of workers, particularly skilled workers. Union workers achieve a measure of job security; the foreman, who does not accumulate seniority, is subject to instant dismissal. Nor is dismissal a remote possibility. Inability to keep up with technological change, a failure to get on with the men, inability to get on with superiors—any of these factors could bring the foreman's career to a sudden end and return him to the ranks.

To sum up, then, just as in the case of the office worker, underlying industrial forces are tending to weaken the foreman's claim to managerial status. It is not so much that the foreman's role is being assimilated to the worker's role, as is the case for the office worker. Rather, the role still retains distinctive features, but it is being reduced in importance; there is less authority, less prestige, less superiority in remuneration attached to it. Less and less, therefore, does it represent a way up, a means of escape from the bottom. The foreman is caught between the conflicting forces of an expanding bureaucracy; he is suspended between management and "managed," between the hierarchy and an increasingly powerful laity.

These conditions and strains of the foreman's role are reflected in the thinking of foremen, in the ideological patterns to which they adhere. One group of foremen seeks to solve the dilemma of their marginal position by reaffirming their allegiance to, and identification with, management. This type of foreman will adopt the social and political viewpoint of management; he may attempt to cut himself off from the workers as much as possible. He may reason that "a foreman is a part of management and ought to act like a manager." To him the union is an excrescence on the industrial body; he may long nostalgically for the good old days, before the Fall, when a foreman's word "really went." Toward the specialist this type of foreman may feel deep suspicion. He considers himself a "practical man," one who "gets things done"; the specialist is a "chair warmer," a "college wonder." The worker is a griper who envies the foreman his superior position—which, incidentally, was achieved solely by hard work and superior merit.

On the other extreme is a type of foreman who, because of social background or personal conviction, identifies with the workers. This type of foreman may consider himself the first line of defense against the demands of management; in fact, he may be completely out of sympathy with management aims. He may be rather strongly union-oriented; he may even have been a union official before he became a foreman. This type of foreman maintains all his social contacts among the workingmen and in the workers' community. He feels no identification with management, which is merely his employer; he considers himself as the holder of a somewhat different type of factory job.

Probably most foremen fall somewhere in between these two extremes in their thinking. Very often there seems to be an ambivalence of feelings; the foreman may be fundamentally nonmanagerial in outlook, yet feel that he is superior to the worker in technical or social skill, and that his job is a recognition of his superiority. This type of foreman may feel that his interests are quite different from those of either management or the workers: "Management and workers are only thinking of themselves, not of the good of the plant." He is likely to accept the presence of a union much as he accepts the presence of management. Both are forces to which adaptations must be made; the question of sympathy or hostility does not arise at all.

It is interesting to note that there has been a history of union organization among foremen. In 1938–1939 large numbers of foremen in the mass-production industries organized themselves into what proved to be a temporary union affiliated with the CIO.[32] In 1941 a group of foremen of the Ford Motor Company founded what was to prove a more stable organization, the Foreman's Association of America. The association has carefully kept free of affiliation with the major labor federations, while attempting to represent the interests of foremen. However, management has been unwilling to deal with this organization, and various labor boards have been uniformly unwilling to extend to the association the privileges granted under law to trade unions.

[32] Herbert R. Northrup, "The Foreman's Association of America," *Harvard Business Review,* vol. 23, no. 2, p. 187, 1945.

CHAPTER 8

The Role of the Worker: Industrial Production and the Worker's Role

The great mass of machine tenders, mechanics, floor sweepers, operators make up the industrial laity, that is, those who are "managed," directed, or led by the industrial hierarchy. In this chapter, all the various jobs which comprise the industrial laity will be considered as one role, the worker's role. This role has formed the basis of some of the most significant social and political movements of our time; it is necessary to consider only the various Marxist parties and their claims to represent "labor," the power of the Labor party of Great Britain, or the trade-union movement in the United States. A role which has been the source of so much strife and change clearly necessitates intensive study in itself. This chapter and the next we shall consider the structure of this role, the demands it makes on workers, and the strains which arise from it.

It is important to note at the outset that in the worker's role, unlike most of the other roles that have been studied, the physical environment is of very great importance in determining the structure and strains of the role. In general, roles differ sharply in the extent to which they are oriented to the actions of other human beings on the one hand or to inanimate objects on the other. The teacher in front of a class is acting in relation to the responses he receives, or expects to receive, from his students; the executive is attempting to control the actions of other human beings. The worker, on the other hand, is usually concerned in his role with inanimate matter, perhaps with changing one form of matter into another form. Furthermore, where the teacher or executive uses social skills, such as communication, negotiation, leadership, the workingman must have at least some technical skills. This chapter will deal with (1) the physical aspect of the worker's role, and (2) strains which arise in this area. In the next chapter we shall deal with the social environment of the worker's role.

TECHNOLOGY AND THE WORKER'S ROLE

The technology of a productive system always has certain definite effects on the role of its workers. It has been shown that in the guild system the role of the worker was shaped by the nature of the productive process, the type of product being manufactured, the raw materials used, a particular type of division of labor, and the tools employed. Similarly, the industrial worker's role is shaped by the nature of industrial production. It has also been shown that the role of the handicraft worker was marked by creativity, control over the process of production, and a knowledge of the "meaning" of the job. Similarly, the role of the industrial worker should be expected to show some characteristics reflecting the nature of industrial production.

Certain aspects of the technology of modern industry seem to be of general importance in shaping the worker's role; these include the division of labor, specialization, mechanization, and standardization. Each of these aspects of the technological process affect the worker's role in various ways. These effects are, as we shall see, in some ways different and in some ways mutually reinforcing.

Division of Labor and the Diversity of Jobs. It has already been shown in Chapter 3 that, while there is some division of labor in all systems of production, labor is more finely divided in the industrial system than in any other. Furthermore, other systems tend to divide production into single, complete jobs; that is, one worker manufactures an entire suit of clothes, another produces an article of furniture, a third a piece of jewelry or a canoe. In the industrial system of production, on the other hand, the single, complete job is divided into smaller parts. The worker in industry may be entirely engaged in manufacturing one minute portion of an automobile or an airplane or a radio. The extent to which labor is divided in this fashion differs from industry to industry and from job to job. In a concrete case a given worker may actually be responsible for several steps in the process of production. However, the trend in industrial production is toward an ever finer division of labor. Certainly, there are many industries in which the division of labor seems to have reached its ultimate limits. In these industries the job may consist of one task—in fact, of one operation. It may be screwing on a bolt, making a mark with a hot iron on a piece of leather, or lifting a block of metal into place.

Labor also tends to divide along another axis in the industrial system. Each year an enormous number of new inventions and new products are thrown on the market. The manufacture of these new products and inventions means even further differentiation of the industrial worker's role.

The great extent of the division of labor, taken in conjunction with the very many different types of goods manufactured by American industry, has resulted in an enormous number of different types of jobs among the industrial "laity." *The Dictionary of Occupational Titles* lists a total of 17,452 distinct types of occupations, most of them clearly industrial in nature. In the petroleum industry alone there are 375 different jobs; in the textile industry the number is 1,850.[1] The *Dictionary* further lists 2,830 different types of skilled jobs, 4,244 types of semi-skilled jobs, and 4,327 types of nonfarm labor or unskilled jobs; this is a total of 11,401 jobs.[2] To grasp the significance of these figures, one should compare the situation in an agricultural society, where there are perhaps no more than half a dozen recognized modes of earning a living.

One result of this enormous diversity is that the technical content of a given worker's role is almost certain to be completely foreign to anyone not directly concerned with a particular industry, perhaps even a very small portion of the industry. For instance, the jobs of creaser or chopper or paster in a leather factory are almost certain to be unknown to anyone who is not familiar with the process of manufacturing leather wallets. Similarly, the meanings of such jobs as puddlers, drill-press operators, tin-plate inspectors are understood only within certain industries or factories. In some cases, even the worker who performs the job is ignorant of its place in the system of production as a whole. For instance, in one case observed by this author, workers had no clear idea as to the use to be made of the rough brass castings on which they were working.[3]

This situation should be compared with that existing in simpler productive systems. For instance, in the guild system, the wheelwright, the tanner, the goldsmith, or the joiner performed tasks whose purpose was known to everyone in the society, although the technique of production may have been a closely guarded secret. It must be assumed, of course, that in the guild system each workingman possessed a clear idea of the meaning of the entire system of production in his guild. It will be shown later in this chapter, that the "meaninglessness" of industrial jobs is responsible for important strains in the worker's role.

The Narrowing of the Worker's Role. Along with the diversification of tasks has gone an increasing narrowing in the content of the worker's

[1] These figures are taken from Wilbert E. Moore, *Industrial Relations and the Social Order*, 1st ed., The Macmillan Company, New York, 1946, pp. 57–58. By permission.
[2] Computed by the author.
[3] The observation was made during World War II, in a small foundry supplying unmachined parts to various industries engaged in war work.

role. The job has been broken down into finer and finer parts, and each (or some) of these parts has come to represent a full-time occupation for a worker. The process is reproduced in the diagram below. Job *A*,

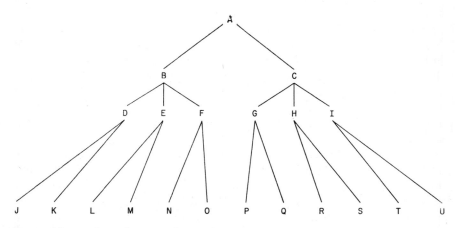

a complete job such as making clothes, has been broken down, first into two distinct jobs *B* and *C*, then into six jobs, then twelve, etc. It can be seen that the job marked *J* must be a minute portion indeed of the total task. The narrowing process reaches its climax, perhaps, in as- sembly-line production; but a great narrowing of tasks is present even in somewhat less specialized industries. The following is the technical content of the job of a pad boy, a job found in the textile industry:[4]

Makes sample pads by hand for use in comparing the color of a batch of rayon, worsted or other textile with standard shades: hands cards fibers freshly removed from dyeing kettle and dries them in an electric oven: weighs dried fibers and mats specified quantity into pads: washes, dries and trims excess fibers from pads; attaches identification tags to finished pads.

Reduction in Skills. A frequent, though *not* inevitable, consequence of diversification and narrowing is a reduction of the skills needed to per- form the worker's role. Although there is certainly room for argument as to whether the number of skilled jobs is increasing or decreasing, there can be little doubt that today a very large proportion of industrial jobs fall within the unskilled, or at the best, semiskilled categories. A glance at Table 1 will show that the categories of "semiskilled workers" and "other laborers" total 8,571 or 75 per cent of the three job categories which seem most nearly to be industrial in nature. The great majority of *types* of industrial jobs seem to call for little or no skill upon the

[4] *Dictionary of Occupational Titles Supplement,* 2d ed. Government Printing Office, 1943, p. 219.

Table 1. Number of Occupational Titles by Socioeconomic Roles

Professional	1,045
Proprietors, managers, and officials, except farmers	2,763
Clerks and kindred workers	1,508
Skilled workers and foremen	2,830
Semiskilled workers	4,244
Farm laborers	274
Other laborers	4,327
Servants	325
Farm owners and tenants	136
Total	17,452

SOURCE: Derived from the *Dictionary of Occupational Titles*, Government Printing Office, 1937.

part of the workingman. In terms of absolute numbers, the numbers of skilled workers increased only from 11.7 per cent of the working force in 1910 to 13.6 per cent of the working force in 1950. The numbers of semiskilled workers rose from 14.7 per cent in 1910 to 22.8 per cent in 1950, while the numbers of nonfarm laborers decreased from 14.7 per cent to 7.6 per cent of the working force in that period. Thus over 30 per cent of the American working force work at jobs requiring little or no skill. If service workers are added to this group, the figure rises to about 38 per cent of the working force.[5]

The skilled worker may need good intelligence, judgment, powers of analysis, considerable mechanical ability, visual acuity, etc. On the other hand, for many jobs in the semiskilled and particularly in the unskilled categories, these skills are either not needed at all or needed only in limited degree. It is to be expected that an intelligent man performing a semiskilled task will learn the task more easily than a less intelligent man. However, it would be difficult to show that persons even with low mental ability are in any way incapable of learning or performing such tasks in an adequate manner.[6] According to some observers, the unintelligent may be actually more suited to certain types of routine jobs, which do not make strong demands on the imagination. Manual dexterity, manipulative ability, physical strength and stamina, are the major capabilities needed for "low-skill" work. Below are reprinted two tests for finger dexterity with some hand and arm coordination, designed to test the suitability of workers for such jobs. These tests illustrate the low level of "skills" needed by many workers in our society.

[5] From a table prepared by the U.S. Bureau of Labor Statistics, "Occupational Trends, 1910–1950."
[6] Joseph Tiffin, *Industrial Psychology,* 3d ed., Prentice-Hall, Inc., Englewood Cliffs, N.J., 1952, p. 109.

Sequence of Trials in Administering the Hayes Pegboard

Trial	Time	Description
1	½ minute	Placing pins from right box in right row with right hand
2	½ minute	Placing pins from left box in left row with left hand
3	½ minute	Simultaneously placing pins from right box in right row with right hand and left row with left hand

SOURCE: Joseph Tiffin, *Industrial Psychology*, 3d ed., Prentice-Hall, Inc., Englewood Cliffs, N.J., 1952, p. 138.

In the Purdue Hand Precision Test—

the applicant punches a stylus into holes that are uncovered by a rotating shutter at the rate of 126 holes per minute. The holes uncovered are .5 inch in diameter and are located on the corners of an equilateral triangle measuring 3.5 inches on a side.

The applicant is shown that his task is to punch the stylus into each hole as it is uncovered without allowing the stylus to touch the side of a hole or be caught by the rotating shutter.[7]

The low level of skills tends to make illusory the great diversity of jobs in the industrial system. A very large percentage of industrial jobs demand about the same types of capacities and skills, however different the industries in which these jobs are found. Later in this chapter some of the consequences of the low level of skills demanded by many industrial jobs will be traced. Here it may be noted that the reduction of skill greatly enhances the specificity and nonextensibility of the worker's role. This, in turn, has had profound effects on the worker's attitude toward his job, on his position within the community, and on the stability of the labor force as a whole.

Mechanization. One of the most important aspects of the physical environment of many worker roles is the machine. Although the machine itself is very old—a primitive steam engine having already existed in ancient Alexandria—only in the industrial system is production based on machinery.[8] In fact, the major instrument of production until well after the establishment of the industrial system, was the tool. The machine entered the process of production as the world market grew larger, as

[7] Joseph Tiffin, *Industrial Psychology*, 3d ed., pp. 139–140. Copyright, 1952, by Prentice-Hall, Inc., Englewood Cliffs, N.J.

[8] For a history of the development of machine technology from the Middle Ages to the decade of the 1930s, see Lewis Mumford, *Technics and Civilization*, Harcourt, Brace and Company, Inc., New York, 1934, chaps. I–V. For a discussion of the development of technology since the 1930s, see J. Frederic Dewhurst and Associates, *America's Needs and Resources*, The Twentieth Century Fund, Inc., New York, 1955, chap. 24, "Technology: Primary Resource."

labor became more divided, and as better sources of power were developed. Once the machine was firmly established in the industrial system, it enabled that system to expand its markets, to increase specialization, and to create new sources of power. This, in turn, has necessitated more machinery.

We may define the machine as a coordinated arrangement of physical units for the accomplishment of some task or types of tasks, power for this process being supplied by some source of energy—human, animal, electrical, chemical, or atomic. The machines of modern industry are of the most diverse sorts; they range in size from simple hand-operated presses to steam hammers, in complexity from machines composed of a few simple parts to "mechanical brains," in power from machines operated by small electric engines to the modern diesel freight locomotive. Some machines are mobile; these include steam shovels, cranes, bulldozers, locomotives.[9] Other machines are so large, or so dependent upon a central source of power, or so neatly fitted into an intricate process of production that they must be firmly anchored, usually within a building. The technical role of each worker depends strongly on the type of machine he is operating; its size, its complexity, its source of power, whether it is mobile or immobile. It is not possible here to describe all the variations in the worker role which may arise from the operation of different types of machines. We shall center our attention, therefore, on the relatively large, complex, automatically powered, immobile machine which is commonly found in our factory system.

In investigating the machine-determined content of the worker's role, two alternative methods may be followed. First, there is the possibility of listing the different types and categories of automatic machines, and the effects of each of these types of machines on workers' roles. Because of the enormous range and diversity of such machines, however, the mere task of classifying them would be beyond the scope of this book. The second method of approach is to analyze certain general effects which automatic machinery has on the worker's role. From this point of view, the most important results of the machine technology seem to be (1) the reduction of the importance of the human element in production, (2) the routinization of the worker's role, and (3) the creation of certain physical conditions of the environment such as spatial separation, noise, and heat. We shall consider each of these effects in turn.

Reduction of the Importance of the Worker. It has frequently been claimed that the machine technology has reduced the role of the worker

[9] Not that this is intended to be a sharp distinction. A potentially mobile machine, such as a crane, may actually remain stationary until a certain piece or course of work is complete. For a discussion of types of machines, see Stuart Chase, *Men and Machines,* The Macmillan Company, New York, 1929, chap. II, "The Anatomy of Machinery."

to that of a mere cog in the process of production.[10] According to this point of view, the automatic machine has made man a mere watcher of the system of production, or relegated him to a minor position in the productive progress. Power is supplied to the machine from a distant source. The speed of the process is controlled automatically, as is the quality of the product. Needed skills are reduced to elementary movements of hands, feeble processes of the brain, simple childlike coordination of arms and legs. The very size and magnificence of modern production strengthens this reductive process. Man is dwarfed beside the vast turbines, the huge presses, the assembly lines, the giant cranes, of modern industry. It is even possible that eventually machines will replace human workers entirely and make them obsolete.

But, this point of view holds, not only has the machine reduced man to insignificance, it has even made man an extension of itself. The machine has fundamentally reversed the nature of the relationships between man and the instruments of production. When tools were the major instruments of production, the worker was the prime mover of the productive process, even if his role in this process was as small as tapping in a nail in a shoe. The tool is merely the extension of the man's hand; the hammer obeys the impulses of the worker, operates by the energy supplied by the worker, responds to his thoughts, habits, skills. But the worker in modern industry is in exactly the opposite relation to the machine; it is the machine which determines the worker's actions, the energies he will expend, the skills he can employ. The machine has no respect for tradition, for habits of work, for individuality; it drives inexorably on, molding the worker's role to its own mode of operation.

That there is some truth in this view no one can deny. In fact, it is precisely in the case of the immobile, automatic machine that the picture presented above approximately reflects reality. The sole duties of the operator of the automatic machine may, in truth, consist of starting the machine in the morning, feeding it raw material (though in many cases this too is an automatic process), watching it for signs of breakdown (usually a skilled mechanic will make whatever repairs are necessary), and stopping it at night. The process of production is carried on almost entirely by the machine itself; it is the machine which spins the cloth, which rolls the steel, which embosses the leather. Man, in this case, is truly reduced to an extension of the machine. In a somewhat different way, the assembly line may accomplish the same thing; the individual worker is made an appendage of the line, conforming to its speed and needs, and performing an insignificant portion of the total task of pro-

[10] See the famous discussion by Thorstein Veblen, *The Instinct of Workmanship*, The Macmillan Company, New York, 1914, pp. 306ff. See also Chase, *op. cit.*, chap. IX, "Skills."

duction. Automation may even more drastically reduce the importance of the worker in the productive process.

However, this point of view needs to be strongly qualified in certain directions. Certainly, the operator of a giant crane, or the skilled lathe worker, or the freight engineer can hardly be described as mere insignificant cogs in the system of production. On the contrary, in each of these cases the judgment, intelligence, and resourcefulness of the worker are crucial if the role is to be played successfully. Indeed, it would seem that certain types of industrial work give fuller reign to man's creativity and individuality than do the tasks in other systems of production. It is only necessary to compare the guild worker using a hammer laboriously to beat out a piece of metal with the operator of a giant steam hammer, or the early American driver of an oxcart with the operator of a modern truck and semitrailer. In both cases, machines greatly extend the power of individuals over nature and demand great proficiency, skill, and resourcefulness.

Furthermore, this point of view does not do full justice to the position of the worker either in modern production or in society as a whole. If the machine molds and controls the worker, it also depends on the worker; if men do not operate the machines, then the machines, no matter how clever, remain idle. Thus, if the worker is a cog in the system of production, it is a cog with certain peculiarities of its own, not shared with other elements in the productive process. The worker is the only element in production which has a purpose, a will, which can consciously withhold labor or increase it. The worker is the least predictable and controllable of the elements which enter into production; his emotions, interests, or needs may determine his capacity for work. Furthermore, as industry as a whole has assumed a larger place in our society, the role of the worker as a whole has acquired more social importance. In no previous system of production has the worker been so relatively numerous. In no previous system has he filled roles so vital to the society as a whole as in our own. Thus, the same system of production which may relegate man to relative insignificance within the plant, may afford him a central position in society as a whole.

The Routinization of the Worker's Role. A further claim often made against the machine is that it has routinized the process of production to an extreme degree. The worker, it is held, has been turned into an automaton, a mere robot performing a task in a never-changing fashion. The machine has not only reduced man to a cog in the system of production and an extension of itself; it has changed man himself into a machine.

There can be little doubt that this point of view correctly describes many industrial roles, but certain qualifications should be made. For one thing, jobs are likely to be excessively routinized only where auto-matic, immobile machinery is used. The operator of a bulldozer may have anything but a routine job. Furthermore, it should be well under-stood that routinization is to be found in every system of production. The farmer performs routinized tasks, even though he is the prime mover in the process of production. Similarly the craftsman may perform the same types of operations over and over again, day after day. Without doubt the bulk of human labor has always been of this routine nature. Routinization seems to be based on the ever-recurring nature of human needs, on the cycle of the seasons, and on the unchanging face of nature. These qualifications should be kept in mind in the following investigation of the sources and nature of routine in the factory system.

Automatic immobile machinery is necessarily marked by a cyclical mode of operation. The cycle of operation begins at a certain point; proceeds through a number of stages, depending upon the complexity of the machine; and at some point begins the process over again. The entire process is almost always completed in the same amount of time. Furthermore, the stages of each cycle are usually separate from each other by definite, often equal, amounts of time. The diagram illustrates the source of routinization in the machine process. The machine process begins at A and again at A' and A'', and so on. This is one source of routinization. Another type of routinization arises from the fact that each cycle is completed by proceeding through points B, B', and B'', etc.; and C, C', C'', etc. The time intervals between these points are always definitely fixed.

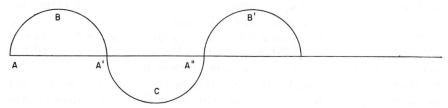

The excessive routinization of automatic machine production ap-parently stems from this double cyclical process. Where mobile ma-chinery is employed, on the other hand, cyclical process may be absent or less marked, though even here it cannot be concluded too hastily that work cycles do not exist. For instance, such work as operating a steam shovel may follow remarkably definite cycles. However, it would seem that the operator of mobile machinery may be able to vary at least some of the intermediate stages of the cycle. In some cases he may be able to vary both cycles.[11]

[11] Some change in the progression of intermediate stages may also be possible where automatic machinery is being employed. Attempts to relieve monotony have been based on this possibility.

This is not the whole story. The routinization of all types of industrial roles has been increased by the movement for the rationalization of production.[12] Proponents of rationalization reason that, since the efficiency of the machine depends on the economy of its movements, the movements of the worker should be arranged in a similar manner. This, in turn, has led to intensive studies of the most efficient methods of employing the worker's time and motions. Time-and-motion studies are, of course, applicable to all types of industrial work, whether mechanized or not. The routinization which results from application of time and motion principles is illustrated by the following rules, offered as guides to efficient industrial work:[13]

1. Successive movements should be so related that one movement passes easily into that which follows, each ending in a position favorable for the beginning of the next movement.
2. The order of movements should be so arranged that little direct attention is needed for passage from one to another . . .
3. . . . An easy rhythm [should] be established in the automatic performances of the various elements of the operation.
4. . . . Continuous movement is preferable to angular movements involving sudden changes in the direction of the movement.
5. The number of movements should be reduced as far as possible within the scope of limitations suggested above. In general, reducing the number of movements will facilitate a rhythmic method of working and automatization as a means of reducing the volitional direction of work.
6. Simultaneous use of both hands should be encouraged.
7. When a forceable stroke is required, the direction of movement and placement of material should be so arranged that, as far as possible, the stroke is delivered when it has reached its greatest momentum.

With the application of such principles, the worker's motions resemble the cyclical, rhythmic, rational motions of the machine.

The Creation of Physical Conditions at Work. Finally, the automatic, immobile machine provides a highly specialized physical environment which affects the worker's role in certain definite ways. This environment differs widely from plant to plant and from job to job; machine operators in the textile industry, for instance, are subjected to differing physical conditions as compared to those in the steel industry, or in an atomic plant, or in a clothing shop. Here we can do no more than suggest some of the more common effects of machinery on the physical conditions of work.

Where the machine is immobile, the worker is, of course, tied to one geographical place. If the machine needs constant attention, or if a

[12] The classic work of this school is by Frederick W. Taylor, *Scientific Management,* Harper & Brothers, New York, 1911.
[13] By permission from Morris S. Viteles, *Industrial Psychology,* W. W. Norton & Company, Inc., New York, 1929, pp. 435–436.

particular posture is required of the worker, spatial mobility is further limited. Variations exist, of course, in the extent of spatial immobility in worker's roles. Some immobile machinery may necessitate or permit a degree of movement. In the case of mobile machinery, on the other hand, the situation may demand an excessive degree of movement; e.g., in the case of train crews. It is important to note that the degree of spatial immobility or mobility in a job may affect the social relationships of the worker. Spatial immobility, for instance, may make communication between workers almost impossible; each worker may be shut during working hours in a little shell whose walls cannot be broken. This, in turn, increases routinization of the worker's role as alternate outlets for expression of human personality are eliminated.

The machine may be responsible for other physical conditions of the worker's environment. For instance, noise is an almost invariable accompaniment of machine production. In some industries, such as steel mills, noise may become an important factor in the causation of fatigue, and as such has occupied the attention of industrial psychologists. It is important to note here the extent to which noise may also be a factor in the isolation of the worker. Communication, other than by facial or arm and hand gestures, is almost impossible under certain conditions. Noise may thus tend to reinforce the routinization of the worker's role by enforcing isolation between workers.

Special types of machinery may create physical conditions of a type which threaten the comfort, or even safety, of the worker. Shock, excessive vibration, exposed moving parts are all examples of physical conditions of this type. Heat, obnoxious gases, dangerous sprays, active chemicals, excessive humidity may be integral parts of certain machine processes. The worker must adapt himself both physically and psychologically to these conditions of work. The safety movement in industry, which stems from the interest of both management and the worker in preventing accidents, has resulted in many special regulations controlling the actions of the workers. Thus safety regulation may decree the wearing of safety masks, the use of double switches on machinery, decontamination processes, etc. The worker's role is still further limited, circumscribed, and isolated in these ways.[14]

Summary. It has been shown that the industrial technology, particularly the division of labor and mechanization, has certain important consequences for the worker's role. Not only does industrial technology determine *what* the worker does, his functions for the plant; but it determines the conditions under which he will perform his functions. The results of industrial technology on the worker's role are (with im-

[14] It is possible that one source of difficulty in getting the worker to comply with safety measures lies in the denial of personal freedom that such measures entail.

portant exceptions) diversification, specialization, reduction of skills, routinization, the reduction of the importance of the role, isolation, and the creation of special physical conditions. In the second half of this chapter, we shall consider certain "strains" which arise in the relationship between the worker and industrial technology. It is not meant to imply, of course, that this relationship is always a stressful one. If we center special attention on the strains of the worker's role, it is because there is good reason to believe that industrial technology may sometimes have certain deleterious effects on the personality of the worker.

STRAINS IN THE WORKER'S ROLE

Industrial technology imposes direct and indirect strains on the worker's role. By the term *direct strains* is meant most notably, fatigue, boredom, monotony, and the loss of a "sense of workmanship." By *indirect strains* we mean technological unemployment, insecurity, and a loss of status in the community. In this chapter, we shall concentrate on the first type of strain, postponing discussion of the second type to those chapters dealing with the psychology of the labor movement and the relation of the worker to the community.

The "direct" strains in the worker's role have received considerable attention from management because they are related to such immediate problems as productivity and morale. However, almost all the massive research in this field has been directly concerned with the solution of the problems involved. Our task, on the other hand, is to show how these unfavorable effects of our technology are related to the personality-role situation of the worker.

Fatigue. One of the most commonly recognized strains in industry is the occurrence of fatigue among workers. One reason for this concern has been that fatigue is apparently related to productivity; in fact, fatigue has been defined as "the sum of the results of activity which show themselves in a diminished capacity for doing work."[15] Interest in the problem of fatigue developed originally in England in connection with the productivity of workers in munition industries in World War I.[16] Industrial engineers have made strenuous attempts to eliminate or control fatigue through time-and-motion studies, control of illumination, control of temperature, control of humidity or ventilation, elimination

[15] H. M. Vernon, *Industrial Fatigue and Efficiency*, Routledge and Kegan Paul, Ltd., London, 1921, p. 1.
[16] For a brief review of the history of research on fatigue in England, see Elton Mayo, *The Human Problems of an Industrial Civilization*, 2d ed., Harvard University, Graduate School of Business Administration, Division of Research, Boston, 1946, chap. I.

or reduction of noise, the use of music, rest pauses, nourishment, and the reduction of hours of work.[17]

Early studies stressed the similarity of certain physiological effects accompanying industrial fatigue on the one hand, and physiological effects associated with excessive physical activity on the other hand. It is known that as a result of physical activity, certain chemical substances are formed in the muscles and waste products enter the blood stream.[18] When these substances cannot be removed with sufficient rapidity through normal bodily processes, movement of the muscles becomes more difficult and may eventually become impossible. Fatigue thus may occur either in individuals who are physically unfit, or as the result of excessive

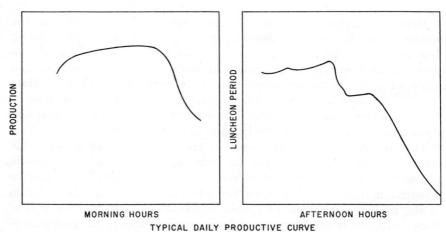

MORNING HOURS   AFTERNOON HOURS
TYPICAL DAILY PRODUCTIVE CURVE

Typical daily productive curve. (*Morris S. Viteles, Industrial Psychology, W. W. Norton & Co., New York, 1929, p. 447. By permission.*)

activity, for either of these conditions will prevent a restoration of normal conditions in the body. Industrial fatigue is considered as a variant of physical fatigue; lethargy, exhaustion, drowsiness, sluggishness at work all represent the result of continued and excessive physical activity. It is held that proof of this process may be seen in the so-called normal production curve, reproduced above. This graph shows that, after an initial period of "warming up" in the early hours of the morning and the afternoon, production climbs to a peak in the forenoon, and to a second, though considerably lower, peak in the afternoon. The closing hours of both morning and afternoon work are marked by sharp decreases in production. This production curve is held to be the reflection of the gradual running down of the human machine. It comes to work refreshed in

[17] For a review of such attempts, see Tiffin, *op. cit.,* chap. 13.
[18] Mayo, *op. cit.,* p. 7.

the morning, and gradually tires; it is somewhat refreshed by the noon pause, and then deteriorates again.

There can be little doubt that some fatigue associated with industrial jobs is the result of excessive activity; e.g., labor in a steel mill or in a coal mine may be of a most demanding kind. However, the number of jobs in industry which are as physically demanding as these is not great and may be decreasing. But it may very well be that, even in the case of "light work," the constant use of one set of muscles, unchanging posture, noise, vibration, and heat may produce physiological fatigue.

This kind of fatigue is the result of the discrepancy between man as a physiological organism and the demands of work. Social factors enter only indirectly into this type of fatigue; e.g., the length of the workday may be determined as part of general relationships between management and labor. In this case, the workingman's fatigue varies with his ability to control the conditions of work.

However, there is considerable doubt as to whether all industrial fatigue can be attributed to the running down of the physical organism as a result of excessive activity. There is good evidence to suggest that, in certain branches of production, work is too light to cause physical fatigue.[19] Yet fatigue is not necessarily absent from such "light work." The typical daily production curve printed above shows a definite falling off of production at certain definite intervals *for all kinds of work*. Furthermore, it can be shown that workers of about equal physical stamina may experience widely varying amounts of fatigue in the same job. It can also be shown that a worker may experience more fatigue on one job than another, although both jobs make about equal physical demands on him. If one takes the rate of production as an index of fatigue, the same lack of a simple correlation between fatigue and the physical demands of work appears.[20] The same worker may have various production rates under the same conditions of work; sometimes production rates may climb under conditions which should be marked by increased physical fatigue. If fatigue *is* the cause of such variations in production, it is safe to conclude that this fatigue is not the type which is caused by excessive physical activity.

There is a widespread reluctance on the part of management—and, for that matter, on the part of other administrators—to take seriously fatigue which is not based on prolonged or violent activity. Accusations of malingering, bitterness toward workers for not showing a managerial type of interest in the job, blaming the worker's environment, heredity, race, or religion are common types of managerial reactions to this

[19] F. Roethlisberger and W. J. Dickson, *Management and the Worker*, Harvard University Press, Cambridge, Mass., 1939, p. 321. See also Mayo, *op. cit.*, pp. 24–25.
[20] Roethlisberger and Dickson, *op. cit.*, pp. 90–97.

situation. But all these reactions miss the point that the fatigue being felt is usually genuine. How can this type of fatigue be understood by students of industry?

A clue to understanding in this case can be found in certain well-established facts concerning the relationship between physical and emotional states. A moment's reflection about ordinary experience will reveal something of the nature of this relationship. It is well known that people who are badly frightened are often capable of making supreme efforts; thus a man pursued by an enemy may be able to attain unusual speed, strength, or agility. In this case, the strength of the physical reaction is directly related to the strength of the emotion; under ordinary emotional conditions the physical reaction would not occur. Another example of the relationship between physical reactions and emotions is provided by the connection between certain illnesses and emotional states. Diarrhea under conditions of anxiety is a well-known phenomenon; types of ulcers, sexual impotence, even certain types of paralysis are also related to emotional states which often lie deeply concealed within the personality. There is a similar relationship between certain types of fatigue and certain emotional states. Chronically tired persons such as the easily fatigued housewife or the overtired student may be the victims of emotions which are deeply rooted in their personalities.

If this theory is correct, it may be possible to explain types of industrial fatigue which are not the result of excessive activity. It has been shown, in the first section of this chapter, that industrial technology has certain effects on the worker's role. Jobs are rendered relatively meaningless. Skills are greatly lowered. The worker is reduced to a cog in production; he is changed into a machinelike being. Noise and heat isolate him from his fellowman. Each of these effects of industrial technology operates to reduce the importance of the worker and the importance of the individual job.

As a result, there is a wide discrepancy between the aspirations of the worker[21] and the technical content of his role. Where the worker aspires to social distinction both on and off the job, his role is specialized to the point of meaninglessness, respect for skill is difficult or impossible to achieve, and he is reduced to an appendage of the machine. Where he aspires to control the condition of work, he is, in actuality, a minute portion of an inexorably moving system of production, tied to a machine which sets the pace of work and which demands of him certain unvarying physical motions or mental processes. Where he wishes to achieve a variety of experience, the machine imposes a strict discipline on him and isolates him from contact with his fellow man.

[21] The aspirations of the worker are considered in more detail in the next chapter.

The result of these discrepancies is that the ordinary industrial job fails to absorb more than a minute portion of the worker's personality. Consequently, he experiences a lack of interest in the job, a sense of meaninglessness and purposelessness in existence (or at least in the portion of the day devoted to work), a sense of unimportance, even of degradation. It is under these circumstances that the worker may exhibit symptoms of fatigue; that is, he may be lethargic, apathetic, easily tired, and manifest a reduced capacity for work. Fatigue is the physical symptom of the underlying stress between personality and role; or, more precisely, it is a physical reaction to an emotional state induced by this stress.

It should be noted that formal alternatives for the expression of personality within the worker's role are rare. The emptiness of the technical content of his role is matched by the emptiness of formal social relationships, which are often equally barren of opportunities for the development and expression of personality. Thus, there seems to be little possibility of reducing industrial fatigue, at least within the formal conditions of factory life. However, as we shall see in the next chapter, relief from emotionally based fatigue may be obtained through informal social relationships of various types.

We have purposely overstated our case in order to point up the nonphysical causes of fatigue. We do not mean to imply here that the industrial system is unique in the amount of fatigue it produces in its workers. Even granting the fact that our technology is of a mechanized, routinized, and specialized sort, the fact remains that it has, in many cases, relieved man of backbreaking toil. Nor do we mean that *all* industrial jobs must necessarily involve a contradiction between personality and role; obviously there are skilled jobs which absorb the attention of the worker completely. Furthermore, even repetitive, unskilled jobs may serve to satisfy certain natures and certain types of intelligence. Finally, it must not be thought that where the personality-role split exists, fatigue will always result. Individual differences, about which very little is known, are important here; one man on a noisy, repetitive job may experience a sense of fatigue which is unknown to a fellow worker equally endowed in respect to qualities of mind and feelings.

Boredom and Monotony. Another commonly noted strain in the worker's role is the boredom or monotony (terms we shall use interchangeably) which often accompanies the worker's role. Boredom has been defined by Elton Mayo as pessimistic revery;[22] that is, Mayo holds, boredom is the name given to the mental state of the worker who defines the situation of work and the future as unfavorable to himself. Another

[22] Elton Mayo, "Revery and Industrial Fatigue," *Journal of Personnel Research,* vol. 3, pp. 273–281, December, 1924.

observer has noted that a mental state of boredom is characterized by "uniformity, changelessness, lack of variety, drabness, absence of stimulation of any kind."[23] Boredom is often marked by a tendency to overestimate the passage of time; the bored worker may often complain about the slow passage of time.[24] It seems to be the general opinion of students of industry that boredom is a widespread phenomenon in industry. One source estimates that in certain industries boredom is present in about 35 per cent of the jobs.[25] Vernon holds that "perhaps a majority" of workers are affected by boredom,[26] and this opinion is concurred in by other students of industry.[27] Some students of industry claim that boredom is reflected in certain variations in productivity, although there is little agreement on this subject. It is held, for instance, that a drop in the rate of work in the middle of a working spell, or increased variability in productivity, are the result of boredom.[28] Thus whatever significance one attaches to boredom, there can be no doubt that it is a characteristic feature of modern industry.[29]

Although fatigue and monotony are closely related in some cases, there is a distinct difference between them. Fatiguing work may be accomplished without a sense of boredom, or work that is not at all fatiguing may generate great amounts of boredom. Even where the two are related, there is this major distinction between them: boredom is an entirely subjective factor, a state of mind, whereas fatigue, whether it is based on excessive physical activity or not, is always accompanied by physical effects such as sleepiness or lethargy. This suggests that the causes of boredom must lie in a somewhat different set of factors from the causes of fatigue. This fact has been generally recognized, and although physiological explanations of boredom have not been lacking, the great majority of students of industry have attempted to understand boredom in psychological terms. These "psychological" explanations have concentrated on several factors, of which perhaps the most important are intelligence and attitudes toward work.

[23] E. P. Cathcart, *The Human Factor in Industry*, Oxford University Press, New York, 1928, p. 20. Quoted by Roethlisberger and Dickson, *op. cit.*
[24] Viteles, *op. cit.*, pp. 528ff.
[25] *Ibid.*, p. 519.
[26] Vernon, *op. cit.*, p. 84.
[27] Mayo, *The Human Problems of an Industrial Civilization*, p. 32.
[28] Viteles, *op. cit.*, p. 521. This opinion is concurred in by Mayo, *The Human Problems of an Industrial Civilization*, p. 31.
[29] Not, of course, that boredom is absent from other systems of production. On the contrary, we must assume that boredom is present in all aspects of human life. What has made boredom so conspicuous in our society is precisely the attention paid to the problem, which in turn is to be traced to such factors as managerial desire to increase efficiency and humanitarian feeling that something ought to be done about an unpleasant mental state. See the discussion by Moore, *op. cit.*, rev. ed., pp. 207–208.

Many observers have held that boredom must be understood as the dissatisfaction of superior intellects with the repetitive, routinized, undemanding nature of industrial work. This school of thought holds that only low-grade intellects can be satisfied with monotonous work, because such work makes no startling intellectual demands on the worker; in fact, monotonous work may offer the inferior individual a feeling of competence and security, since the work can be performed with complete adequacy. A number of studies have been made which seem to indicate this sort of relationship between low intelligence and lack of boredom at repetitive work.[30] Other studies, on the contrary, hold the opposite; one study states that intelligence "plays a minor role in determining susceptibility to monotony, which is an attitude or 'act,' reflecting an emotional 'set' or 'disposition' on the part of the individual toward repetitive work."[31] However, the weight of evidence seems to be on the side of the first theory; the more intelligent worker *does* seem to feel more boredom at repetitive work.

If there is a major objection to this theory, it is that no one is certain whether an intelligence test in fact measures intelligence, or whether there is a single thing called "intelligence" at all. The intelligence test certainly measures the ability of the individual to handle geometric figures, or his literateness, or his mathematical ability. Therefore, all that can be said with certainty is that individuals who are proficient in mathematics and geometry, or who are literate and educated, will be unusually bored with industrial work. From this point of view, it is more accurate to say that individuals with certain interests and backgrounds will become easily bored with industrial work than to say that intelligent people are particularly susceptible to boredom.

This suggests that it is necessary to take into account the entire personality, including "intelligence," values, emotions, attitudes, as well as the relationship of this personality to role if boredom is to be understood properly. Looked at this way, it can be seen that boredom is connected somehow with the failure of the routine industrial role to absorb the personality of the worker on the one hand, or to permit the type of active mental or social life which would serve to counteract boredom on the other. Thus, the most boring types of jobs have been found to be those which are of the semiskilled variety; that is, those which neither demand complete attention nor are so automatic that practically no attention at all is required. It may be suggested that the reason for this is that the highly skilled job absorbs the intelligence, emotions, and perceptions to such a degree that the worker does not feel a slow

---

[30] See Viteles, *op. cit.*, pp. 536–540.

[31] L. A. Thompson, Jr., "Measuring Susceptibility to Monotony," *Personnel Journal*, vol. 8, p. 94, 1929.

passage of time, or engage in pessimistic revery, or feel existence to be colorless and drab. In the case of the purely routine role, the amount of revery engaged in may be great, but it need not be of the pessimistic variety; thus time may pass swiftly for the unskilled worker.

Different personalities vary in their susceptibility to boredom; that is, in their ability to submerge their personalities in work on the one hand or to construct an active mental life for themselves on the other. According to one observer, three types of personalities may be distinguished in relation to susceptibility to boredom at routine jobs. Type A, a "totality type," tends to become absorbed completely in the job. This type is peculiarly susceptible to boredom under monotonous conditions of work. Type B is capable of splitting his attention and is thus not particularly susceptible to boredom on routine jobs. Type C, the least susceptible of all, creates an active mental life of revery and daydreaming.[32]

Boredom must, then, be understood as another symptom of the split between personality systems and the social role that the worker plays. We have already seen that the worker's role is often marked by routinization, specialization, and reduction of the importance of the worker in the productive process. This means that (1) the skills demanded are few in number and are easily acquired, (2) the job is meaningless in many cases not only to the worker but to the society as a whole, (3) the work performed is repetitious to the *n*th degree, with the same motions and mental processes being constantly called into play in a cyclical process. As a result, the industrial job can neither absorb the worker's talents nor give him much to which to look forward. The boredom which results is not merely a matter of low or high intelligence, or of special types of work, or of certain personality types. It is clear that boredom is not something *added* to the personality; it is not something in itself, which can be isolated and controlled like a disease. Rather, boredom is the *absence* of a satisfactory relationship between personality and the environment.

Various proposals have been made to alleviate the monotony and boredom of industrial jobs. We may note several methods which have been tried: (1) rest pauses, (2) changes in method of work, (3) method of payment, and (4) working in compact social groups.

Rest Pauses. One of the commonest devices used in industry to reduce monotony (as well as fatigue) and to increase production is the rest pause. Various combinations of pauses have been used or tested under varying conditions.[33] Stoppages of work have varied in terms of the nature of production, numbers of workers affected, and difficulty or

---

[32] See Morris S. Viteles, *Industrial Psychology*, W. W. Norton & Co., New York, 1929, pp. 542–543. By permission.

[33] Perhaps the most complete research in this connection is reported in Roethlisberger and Dickson, *op. cit.*, chap. III, "Experiment with Rest Pauses."

monotony of work. The effects of rest pauses seem to be uniformly favorable, both for increased production and in terms of reduction of monotony. The rest pause seems to reduce monotony by releasing the worker from the routine of the task; the cyclical process is broken, and the worker has a chance to employ unused physical and mental faculties. The rest pause gives the worker a chance to establish social contacts with other workers, to bring certain social skills into play; to establish or renew friendships, to vary experience by joking or "kidding." Thus the efficacy of the rest pause rests both on the fact that the monotonous task is dropped momentarily, and on the opportunity for the expression of certain portions of personality through the playing of alternative roles.

Changes in Method of Work. Sometimes boredom can be reduced on the job by changing methods of work or by shifting jobs. Of course, it is not always possible to do this; nor would such methods necessarily be welcomed by all workers, especially where more or less complete absorption in revery is possible. Changing methods of work or shifting jobs seems to be most effective in the semiskilled job. The effectiveness of this method lies in the breaking of the routine of work and in the chance it affords the worker to employ somewhat different skills at work.

Method of Payment. It is sometimes held that boredom can be counteracted by adopting a suitable method of payment. Usually this has meant the piecework method of payment or some other sort of financial incentive, such as a bonus plan. The theory behind this method is that the worker will become so absorbed in meeting a certain goal of production that he will come to feel that there is a meaning to the job, and a positive reason for work. Obviously, the effectiveness of this method depends upon the efficacy of financial incentives. In general, if this method is to be effective, it must create certain alternate goals or interests for the worker which will effectively absorb his talents and energies. However, this method has been shown empirically to be limited in value; the goal of financial reward is relatively distant and does not serve to change the nature of the work itself. If work is made more bearable it may be only in the sense that the job takes on a higher instrumental value for the worker.

Working in Compact Social Groups. Perhaps the most interesting proposal of all, from our point of view, is that production be carried out in compact social groups which will permit certain types of social relationships; e.g., the exchange of conversation which does not interfere with production. According to this theory, monotony will be reduced or eliminated as the worker finds alternative expressive outlets. In the next chapter we shall investigate in detail the effect of group life on the worker's personality. Full discussion can be postponed to that point.

Here it is necessary to state only that, at least in certain types of industries, social groups may form which *do* serve the function of relieving monotony. This process seems to operate not only by permitting expression of certain "unused" aspects of personality but by creating new roles which the worker may play. However, it should be pointed out that in some industries, or at certain jobs, the formation of such groups is almost impossible. Furthermore certain informal groups may serve as instruments of additional constriction for the individual worker rather than as outlets for psychological needs. Nor must it be forgotten that social interaction on the job may be secured at the expense of production. For these reasons, one must not jump to the conclusion that the informal social group is the answer for the ills of industry. Nevertheless, with all these qualifications, it remains the most promising weapon against boredom, and perhaps against other types of strain also.

Loss of the "Instinct of Workmanship." Fatigue and boredom are in varying degree observable and even to some degree measurable symptoms of strain in the worker's role. A third strain, of a much more diffuse sort, is the loss of the "instinct of workmanship." The term was given currency in the work of Thorstein Veblen.[34] By an "instinct of workmanship" Veblen meant a basic concern with "practical expedients, ways and means, devices and contrivances of efficiency and economy, proficiency, creative work and technological mastery of facts." Veblen added that "much of the functional content of the instinct of workmanship is a proclivity for taking pains."[35] There are, then, several major aspects of the "instinct of workmanship." First, there is the high positive value attached to high productivity. Second, there is an ideal of doing the job as well as possible. Since these two ideals or values have been found only in certain cultures, it is evident that the term "instinct" is a misnomer. Veblen was really referring to certain values or universally accepted goals which have been relatively prevalent in Western civilization,[36] at certain stages of history.[37] However, there is a third aspect of the "instinct of workmanship" which may reflect a wider human propensity, arising out of certain basic features of personality. This propensity may be described as the urge to create, an urge to stamp something of one's own personality on the environment, whether in the form of a work of art or a piece of work. Investigation of the source of this mysterious

[34] Veblen, *op. cit.*

[35] *Ibid.*, p. 33.

[36] Arthur K. Davis, "Sociological Elements in Veblen's Economic Thought," *The Journal of Political Economy,* vol. 53, no. 2, pp. 132–149, June, 1945.

[37] Not that these values have been the exclusive property of Western civilization or of an industrial technology. On the contrary, they have been highly developed in India, for instance. See Max Weber, *The Hindu Social System,* translated by H. H. Gerth and Don Martindale, University of Minnesota Sociology Club Bulletin 1, Historical Series, vol. I, 1949.

aesthetic impulse does not lie within the scope of this book. But it may be hazarded here that the creative urge is bound up with the integrity and uniqueness of the personality; that it is the "flag" of the individual's disposition. If this theory is valid, then loss in opportunity to express the "instincts of workmanship" might be a serious strain, indeed.

Veblen felt that, in fact, opportunities for fulfilling the instinct of workmanship were rare in an industrial system as compared, for instance, to a guild system of production. The guild system, as we have seen, was marked by (1) a vocational division of labor, in which the process from start to finish was controlled by one worker; and (2) handicraft methods of technology, the use of tools rather than machines. Under this system of production the products of workingmen were never exactly alike; in fact, the individual workingman might never manufacture the same product in exactly the same way. In such a system, there was room for creation; the values of workmanship might assert themselves. The worker, furthermore, could compare his own product with that of his fellows and have a standard by which to judge his own achievements. In the industrial system, on the other hand, the situation is completely different. Little "workmanship" can be expressed in the process of feeding an automatic press. It is the machine which determines the quality and rate of the work, except for that small portion contributed by the dexterity of the workingman. The worker is not creative in our society; he is a cog in the wheel of production, and he turns along with the wheel. So runs Veblen's theory, stated in its sharpest form.

This theory might be extended by pointing out that the value of high productivity is not usually fulfilled in the typical factory. On the contrary, as we shall see in the next chapter, there are certain forces present which in many cases motivate the worker to restrict production. The value of high productivity not only has been obliterated for many workingmen, it has been reversed; the workingman's values are expressed by sabotaging the productive machine. This whole situation is ironical, because while the "instinct of workmanship" becomes progressively weakened, productivity as a whole rises steadily. An examination of Table 2 shows that if 100 equals the amount of productivity per man-hour in 1947, then productivity had increased by 4 per cent since 1939. In 1953 productivity per man-hour was about 23 per cent higher than in 1947. But this increase in production can hardly be attributed to the "instinct of workmanship." On the contrary, since this increase in productivity occurred through division of labor, standardization, routinization, specialization, and mechanization, it depended on obliterating those conditions in which an "instinct of workmanship" might flourish.

Like other theories examined in this chapter, Veblen's seems to need some qualifications. It may be said immediately, though it is no answer

Table 2. Indexes of Physical Output per Man-hour in Manufacturing, 1939,
and Selected Years, 1947–1953

(1947 = 100)

1939	96.0
1947	100.0
1949	108.6
1950	117.7
1951	117.5
1952	119.1
1953	122.7

SOURCE: Leon Greenberg, "Output per Man-hour in Manufacturing, 1939–1947 and 1947–53," *Monthly Labor Review*, vol. 79, no. 1, p. 4, table 3, 1956.

to modern problems, that the amount of "workmanship" present in other systems of production may have been grossly overestimated. It is really not fair to judge the workmanship present in the average guild product by the superb specimens which have survived in museums. It is entirely possible that much guild production was entirely humdrum in nature, allowing only the barest room for individual creativity.

At the same time, it is necessary to point out that "workmanship" survives in certain areas of our industrial system. Undoubtedly, most skilled jobs and perhaps some semiskilled and even unskilled jobs, *do* provide opportunities for the expression of "workmanship"; the skilled lathe worker may be truly stamping his own personality on his work, the semiskilled assembler of radio parts may take pride in efficiency. As Bakke has pointed out,[38] workingmen may attempt to exercise originality even where, to the outside observer, the situation seemed bound to frustrate such attempts. Furthermore, it is not accurate to say that the "instinct of workmanship" has become obsolete in modern industry; rather these values and attitudes have been transferred to specialists, such as designers, production engineers, time-and-motion experts, personnel men, and many other types of specialists. This does not solve the problem for the individual workingman, of course, but it does indicate the necessity for qualifying Veblen's theory.

Yet, when all these qualifications are taken into account, and allowance made for the difficulty of measuring the extent to which a loss of an instinct of workmanship has actually occurred in our industrial system, it would still seem that a large residue of truth remains in Veblen's theory. The fact is that the nature of industrial technology often does destroy the workingman's pride in work and inhibit his creative urges. The overroutinized, overspecialized, unskilled, insignificant modern industrial job is inherently incapable of offering the worker outlets for

[38] E. Wight Bakke, *The Unemployed Worker*, Yale University Press, New Haven, Conn., 1940, p. 13.

expression of the "instinct of workmanship." Proof of this fact may be seen in the fact that the worker's interest is often turned away from the job. The industrial worker often seeks to express his individuality in other directions, perhaps through union organization, perhaps in roles entirely outside industry, or perhaps by the creation of alternative outlets for human ingenuity and inventiveness within the plant.

Many attempts have been made to find "substitutes for workmanship." Shorter hours, "training for leisure," inculcation of pride in the industry as a whole, education in the "meaning of the job"[39]—all have been suggested or tried as ways to re-create in the worker a sense of organic unity with the job, to reawaken his pride in the job and in himself. Veblen thought that the problem could not be solved; he may, however, have overlooked the possibility that the very human creativeness he described so masterfully might be eventually directed at solving the problem of the loss of creativeness. It is difficult at this time to suggest in what direction a solution might be found. It is unlikely that a simple panacea for so complex a problem will be found. Rather, solution will probably entail intensive and long-continued efforts to alter the personality-role situation of the worker as it now exists; this in turn, implies need for long-term changes in the worker's personality, in the worker's role, and in the relations between them.

SUMMARY

This chapter has been concerned with showing how the technology of modern industry shapes the worker's role and with the reaction of the worker to industrial technology. We saw that modern technology tends to make many workers' roles nonextensible, specialized, routinized to reduce their importance, to render them meaningless. We took account of exceptions; e.g., for skilled work. It was then shown that certain discrepancies between personality and the technical content of the role existed. These discrepancies produced strains, notably fatigue, boredom, and a loss of the "instinct of workmanship." Each of these commonly recognized problems of modern industry was shown to be an outcome of the same underlying factors.

Thus far the worker's role has been considered only as it is shaped by the formal demands of industrial technology. Next we shall consider how it is shaped by the social structure of industry.

[39] See Moore, *op. cit.*, rev. ed., pp. 232–236.

CHAPTER 9

The Role of the Worker: Social Relations at Work

In this chapter we shall investigate the other side of the worker's environment—his social relations at work. As we have seen, one side of the worker's role is concerned with and shaped by material objects, particularly machines. But the process of production is not only material, it is also social. Our system of production demands the most intricate forms of social cooperation. The worker in a given industry is related, directly or indirectly, to almost every other person in the plant from top to bottom and from bottom to top. This relationship may be as direct as that involved in two workers lifting the same object, or it may involve obedience to a distant and unknown figure. But in any case the worker is involved in a process of social interaction, whether within a group, along the lines of a hierarchy, or in a process of communication. It is his position in this social system that interests us here.

FORMAL SOCIAL RELATIONSHIPS OF THE WORKER'S ROLE

In general, the worker is part of two networks of social relationships. The first network, which we have called the "formal relations of production," was discussed in Chapter 3. It will be recalled that in the ideal sense, the worker, under our system, is a commodity in the process of production; he is supplying one necessary ingredient for production—his labor. By virtue of this fact, he enters into social relationships of a special type with management. These are the social relationships of the market place; for a certain quantity and quality of labor which the worker provides to management, he receives in return a specified amount of money, which enables him to secure the wherewithal of living. The social relationships between management and the worker are thus bound up with a cash nexus.[1]

This type of relationship of production may be compared with that of the guild system. In the guild system, the apprentice "bound himself

[1] For an excellent discussion of this problem, see Karl Polyani, "Our Obsolete Market Mentality," *Commentary*, February, 1947, pp. 109–117.

over" to the master in a special type of relationship. This relationship was, as we have seen, like the personal, affective relationship between the members of a family. The labor which the guild worker supplied to the master, and the obligations of the master to his workers, were a part of this over-all social relationship. There is thus a striking contrast between the relations of production of industrialism on the one hand and those of the guild system on the other. Where, in the industrial system the relations between management and the worker are wholly "economic," in the guild system these "economic" relations were a relatively small aspect of the total social relationship.[2]

The other network of social relationships in which workers are enmeshed is determined by the nature of industrialism as a system of production and by the nature of industrial bureaucracy. These types of social relationships we have called "the social relations of work." In contrast to the formal relations of production, the social relations of work are primary in character. These primary types of social relationships are independent of the formal relations of production; they will be found in any industrial system, whether the formal relations of production are capitalistic, socialistic, communistic, or fascistic. However, while the formal relations of production are relatively fixed and universally the same for all workingmen in a given culture, primary relationships vary according to the technology of a given process of production and according to particular bureaucratic forms of organization.

Because of the diversity of technology and, to a lesser extent, of bureaucratic forms, it is impossible to do more than indicate certain very general features of the social relations at work. Industrial technology, as we have seen, is marked above all by a fine division of labor and mechanization. In this system of production, the worker is used as a coglike appendage to the industrial process;[3] his work is routinized, specialized, diversified, and simplified in accordance with the needs of efficiency and rationalization. A productive system of this type demands that the worker enter into certain types of social relationships with superiors and with fellow workers. These relationships will necessarily be of a limited type, because they must be confined to those necessary for the productive process. The social contacts of workers may be limited to what is necessary for the circulation of work, or the imparting of necessary information, or supplying raw material.

Of course, as pointed out above, the situation varies in specific cases; technological conditions may require greater or lesser degrees of social contact, depending on circumstances. Thus, intense social cooperation

[2] For a further discussion of the formal relations of management and workers, see Chaps. 13 and 14.

[3] See Chap. 8, "The Worker and the Physical Environment."

is certainly required in a crew working at a blast furnace in a steel mill, or between an engineer and a fireman in a locomotive. But where immobile, automatic machinery is being used in production, these sorts of contacts will be relatively scarce. The workingman, in this case, is tied to a machine, which perhaps demands constant attention (e.g., in the case of a press); he is thus cut off both spatially and socially from his neighbor. Noise may also contribute to his social isolation. Under these circumstances, his social life may be poverty-stricken indeed.

The social relationships at work in which the worker is permitted or required to engage are also directly shaped by the nature of the industrial bureaucracy. The industrial worker, as we have seen, is a part of a laity, ruled or administered by a bureaucratic hierarchy. He is at the bottom of a hierarchy of authority, at the bottom of a prestige ladder, and at the end of a chain of communication and command. He does not occupy an office. It is his function to carry out orders, emanating from above, in a limited sphere.

As a result of his position in the bureaucratic organization, the worker is related socially both to superiors and to fellow workers in certain definite patterns. Ideally, he engages only in those social contacts which are necessary for bureaucratic aims; or at least he should engage in no social contacts which hinder the attainment of those aims. This means that his contacts with superiors are limited to a high degree. He will be obeying the orders of superiors, making requests of them, or imparting necessary information about the job (for instance, as to the need for repairs to his machine). On the side of management, the relationship to the worker ideally is equally cold and impersonal. Furthermore, the only superiors with whom the worker will deal directly are the one or two foremen or straw bosses immediately above him. Contact with the higher levels of management, as far as the worker is concerned, will be limited to impersonal directives or orders handed down through intermediate supervisors. This is the ideal form of the relationships between management and the worker, the type that is usually pictured in managerial charts.

With fellow workers, the bureaucratic organization permits or requires few or no social relationships of any kind. The bureaucracy is essentially an hierarchical organization, in which the major interaction proceeds in a "vertical" direction, that is, between superior and subordinate. Furthermore, whatever "lateral" social relationships are prescribed by a bureaucratic organization are likely to be found at the level of the hierarchy. Thus we have seen that officials of the line organization may be supplied with information or advice by members of the staff. There are relatively few formally prescribed relationships of this type at the level of the laity in industry. The situation, of course, varies from plant to plant. For instance, in some plants the bureaucratic organization may prescribe social interaction between workingmen and inspectors, or between workingmen and staff members.

It seems safe to conclude that the social relations at work of the workingmen are few in number and sharply limited in scope, whether one considers those social relations which are the outcome of technology or those which are bureaucratic in nature. Furthermore, these social relations are limited in intensity. Both technology and bureaucracy demand impersonal, nonextensive, affectively neutral social relationships. Certainly there is little in the prescribed social relations of work which can compensate the workingman for the reduction of importance, the monotony, the fatigue which accompany factory work.

In the remainder of this chapter, we shall study the relationship between the personality of the worker, on the one hand, and the physical and social aspects of the worker's role in industry on the other.

The Structurally Generalized Goals of the Worker's Role. It will be readily apparent that the worker's role contains in itself relatively few possibilities for the gratification of human impulses. This means that the generalized goals of his role are relatively poor in content as compared, say, to those of the executive role. It will be recalled that the executive role held out the promise of power, achievement, independence, and freedom to those who could obtain it. The worker's role, on the other hand, offers few or none of these inducements. It confers little or no power compared with the role of management. The worker's role opens few roads to achievement or creativity; in the face of automatic machinery and the increasing division of labor, skills have been reduced to the vanishing point. The workingman has little opportunity for achieving status or security on the job. His independence and freedom are sharply limited by the inexorable discipline and routine of the industrial process, which, as we have seen, tend to reduce him to a cog in production. These, at least, *would be* the consequences of the worker's role, if there were no other factors to modify the situation.

Under these circumstances, the only important generalized goal offered by the worker's role comes to be the instrumental one. The job becomes the means by which the real goals of life can be obtained—elsewhere, outside the factory. This means that for many workers the job is first and foremost a source of pecuniary return, not something to be enjoyed for its own sake. The difference between the worker's interest in pecuniary return and the manager's drive to maximize profit or to achieve the "top" income illustrates this point. For the executive, financial return is a symbol of success and the recognition of personal worth; for the worker, maximum wages mean that he can begin to play the roles that really matter to him. In addition there are other factors operating to increase the worker's lack of interest in his job other than as a source of income. One factor is the relative abundance of jobs; the retention of one particular job is of much less importance than during the depression years. Another factor is the shortened work week, which means that the worker spends little time on the job in comparison to the time he spends in other roles. Still a third factor is the abundance of life outside the factory; the high standard of living, the possibilities of recreation, vacation, make leisure roles more important than work roles.

The Aspirations of the Worker. Yet, in spite of the poverty of generalized goals in the worker's role, and in spite of the attractions of life outside of the factory, the job undoubtedly still retains a very great importance for the worker. It is the worker's sole means to livelihood. On the job he spends approximately one-half of his waking hours. He inevitably projects on his job certain attitudes, wishes, and values; he seeks to fulfill these deep-lying needs of his personality in his work role. The worker cannot indefinitely compartmentalize his personality like the hold of a battleship; there cannot be one section labeled "work personality" and another labeled "leisure personality." What is important to the worker outside the factory he seeks to achieve inside the factory.

It is for this reason that it is necessary to study the types of attitudes, values, and wishes that the worker holds, a question which has received a good deal of attention, and about which there is some disagreement. Sometimes the acts of workingmen seem mysterious to nonworkers. Why does the worker strike, when it can be so easily demonstrated (apparently) that he will lose economically by striking? Why does he join a union, when management (in its own estimation) has given him no cause for complaint? Why does he restrict production, if it is against his own financial interests to do so? To answer these questions, it is necessary to remember that the worker is acting in terms of certain goals and values which are of great importance from his point of view. In terms of these goals and values he acts as rationally as any other man (but not more so).

Many classifications of the aspirations of workers are possible. In the widest sense, the worker may be regarded as seeking for the satisfaction of basic human wishes; recognition for whatever abilities he may possess, security from want, satisfying emotional response, and a chance to vary or control experience. However, for our purposes it is more useful to break these basic wishes down into somewhat more concrete goals. Four general categories of such goals may be noted here.[4]

1. Community goals. The worker wishes to play certain socially re-

---

[4] This classification is based, by permission, on the sensitive analysis of the worker's goals found in E. Wight Bakke's *The Unemployed Worker,* Yale University Press, New Haven, Conn., 1940, chap. I, "Why Work?"

spected roles in his community, to be an effectively functioning member of the community. For this reason he desires to hold a job which will establish him as a man of substance and importance. In order to get this kind of recognition, he must be acknowledged as holding a good job in a good firm, with a reputation for making superior products, paying good wages and providing good working conditions. To be a member of X firm, to work on diesel locomotives or jet airplanes, to bring home a "fat" pay check, are all means by which he can secure the community response he desires.

Within this general goal, there are certain subsidiary goals that are of importance to the worker. In a society such as ours, which places great importance on economic success, these subsidiary goals are economic in nature. Thus, the worker wishes to be a "buyer," a man with money to spend in the community; he wishes to be known as a "thrifty" man, capable of providing for a "rainy day," a "good provider" giving his family a decent standard of living and perhaps educating his children. Achieving self-respect depends on his ability to integrate himself into the economic life of the community.

2. *Economic security.* A constant and unchanging goal of the worker is economic security. By economic security the worker means wages which are high enough and regular enough to provide for a customary standard of living and yet leave enough over to provide for sickness, accidents, and old age, and to give his children chances superior to his own. What the worker means by economic security is not necessarily what a middle-class man might mean by that term. Thus, for the worker economic security may not mean a house free and clear of a mortgage, but it will certainly mean protection against arbitrary dismissal from his job, a guarantee of his seniority, full employment, or a guaranteed annual wage.

To understand the place which economic security holds in the mind of the worker, it is necessary to recall that at most times in history jobs have been scarce; only rarely have there been more jobs at hand than workers seeking for employment.[5] Usually, the worker has had to strive for this scarce commodity in a market in which he has had many competitors, all driven on by equally strong motives. If he is lucky enough to hold to his job in depression times, he still feels the pressure from the horde of unemployed, all anxious to take his job from him.[6] Even in good times his relation to his job is tenuous; he will be employed for

---

[5] See Selig Perlman, *A Theory of the Labor Movement,* Augustus M. Kelley, New York, 1949 (originally published in 1928), part II. His theory of job-scarcity consciousness is more fully discussed in Chap. 14, "Theories of the Labor Movement."

[6] For a graphic account of the effect of mass unemployment on the psychology of the worker, see Whiting Williams, *What's on the Worker's Mind,* Charles Scribner's Sons, New York, 1926.

only as long as his labor can be profitably used. Even the union cannot guarantee him employment when there is no work to do. Nor should it be forgotten that the impact of technological change and improved production techniques has often been felt most heavily by the worker. It is primarily the worker who has lost his skills to the machine or been displaced by machinery, and as a result has suffered demotion or unemployment. It is no wonder, then, that economic security has always been of first importance for him and that the struggle for security has been a constant factor in the history of labor in the United States.

3. *Good working conditions.* The workers' aspirations for the job itself may be summed up by the phrase "good working conditions," a phrase which is encountered time and again in the literature of and by workingmen in this country. But what the worker means by "good working conditions" is the subject of considerable controversy. One school of thought has always felt that high wages and other cash benefits are the sole aims of the worker on the job. This school of thought views the worker strictly as a commodity in production; since he comes on the job for the purpose of exchanging his labor for cash, his goal is obviously to "take home" as much money as possible. When numerous surveys of the attitudes of the workers themselves revealed that high wages were not the sole, or even most important, goal of the worker on the job, some opinion swung to the opposite pole. This group felt and feels that wages are of little importance and that what the worker wants above all are pleasant physical and social conditions at work; in fact, some observers hold that complaints about wages are essentially symptoms of dissatisfaction with the work situation.

Actually, a balanced view of workers' aspirations on the job needs to be taken; the worker's definition of "good working conditions" has many facets. If one of these facets is stressed while others are ignored, there is serious risk of misunderstanding the worker's motives and actions. While workers' goals may be expected to differ from plant to plant, and in terms of age, sex, personal history, etc., there seem to be certain goals which workers commonly value highly. We reprint in Tables 3 and 4 two lists of workers' aspirations which reveal the common elements in their definition of "good working conditions," as well as the relative importance they assigned to these goals.

It will be noticed that in both these lists "regular work" is put at the top. This may reflect the drive for economic security, the fear of unemployment on the part of a marginal economic group. "High wages," on the other hand, is not mentioned at all in the first list and is placed sixth in the second. This does not mean that wages are of little importance to the worker; rather, a more plausible explanation is that for the worker the necessity of a certain level of wages is bound up with secur-

Table 3. Workers' Definitions of "Good" and "Bad" Jobs

Characteristics of good jobs	*Characteristics of bad jobs*
Regular work	Irregular work
Friendly and reasonable foremen	Driving straw bosses
Opportunity to set pace of work	Pressure (not speed)
Freedom to organize	Union-fighting policy on part of management
Opportunity for pleasant personal relations	Impersonal relations and lack of human contact
Personal knowledge by and interest of management	No apparent interest of management in men
Sanitation and safety precautions	Unsatisfactory sanitary and safety arrangements
Cleanliness	Dirt, dust, and smoke
Comfortable temperature and light	Excessive heating and poor lighting
Working with "high-class" people	Association with "low-class" workers
Opportunity for small distinctions	Little chance to stand out as an individual

SOURCE: E. Wight Bakke, *The Unemployed Worker*, Yale University Press, New Haven, Conn., 1940, p. 12. By permission.

Table 4. Ranking of 10 Items in Order of Importance by 325 Factory Workers

1. Steady work
2. Comfortable working conditions
3. Good working companions
4. Good boss
5. Opportunity for advancement
6. High pay
7. Opportunity to use your ideas
8. Opportunity to learn a job
9. Good hours
10. Easy work

SOURCE: S. Wyatt, J. N. Langdon, and F. G. L. Stock, *Fatigue and Boredom in Repetitive Work*, Industrial Health Research Board Report 77, London, 1937.

ity, and steady work. He cannot secure adequate wages without steady work. The length of the working day, which also has an effect on wages, is apparently of less concern to him than security or the level of wages.

Other items on the lists seem to be concerned mainly with the physical conditions of work, which, as we saw, loom very large in the worker's role. Thus workers express a desire for adequate sanitation, for comfortable temperatures, light, for easy work, etc. The opportunity to express individuality on the job is also valued, as shown by the desire for a chance to use one's ideas on the job, to advance, to achieve small distinctions, and to set the pace of work.

A third group of items is concerned with establishing certain types of social relationships with management and with fellow workers. Both lists stress a desire for friendly and reasonable managers and for some sign of managerial interest in the worker. Similarly, workers wish to establish pleasant social relations with fellow workers; they desire to work with "high-class people," to establish pleasant personal relations, to have "good working companions."

4. *Control of one's affairs.* Another major goal of the worker is some measure of personal freedom, often expressed as a desire to "control one's affairs." This goal must be understood as a reflection of the actual powerlessness of the individual worker, dominated as he is by large economic movements, by vast corporate and labor organizations, and by the inexorable demands of industrial technology. The ability of the working-man to manipulate or control the situation for his own ends has become practically nonexistent. Thus it is not surprising that a desire for personal freedom has loomed so large on the worker's aspirational horizon or has played such a large part in the history of organized American labor. Whether through personal effort or through organized or unorganized social effort, the worker has sought, as best he could, to master the forces which dominate him.

5. *Understanding controlling forces.* In the light of the worker's struggle for personal freedom, it is natural that he should try to achieve some understanding of the world about him. Of course, there are many workers who are so apathetic or uninterested that they never question their environment. Others may be satisfied with personal explanations: "I was laid off because the foreman disliked me." But this does not suffice for all workers.

. . . The number whose horizon is so shortened is limited. One's problem is duplicated by a multitude of associates. One is aware of a community standard of wages about which he has had nothing to say. One pays prices which seem to fluctuate without much rhyme or reason. One reads of labor troubles which seem vastly more sizeable than should result from any causal action by an individual employer. One reads arguments for and against this or that economic policy. . . . [The worker's problem] is a part of a problem much larger than his own, but to which his own is intimately related. His world has become large in spite of him. . . . [7]

When the worker actually tries to discover the forces controlling him, he will find a series of ready-made explanations. Press and radio, political parties, labor and management, radicals and conservatives, compete with each other in getting their versions of events before him. From these sources, as well as from his own personal experience, he tries to fashion a coherent and meaningful picture of the world about him.

The aspirations of the worker, then, are directed toward the fulfillment of certain community goals, toward achieving "good working conditions," toward controlling his own affairs, toward gaining an under-

---

[7] E. Wight Bakke, *The Unemployed Worker*, Yale University Press, New Haven, Conn., 1940, pp. 31–32. By permission.

standing of controlling forces. No one goal, taken by itself, is adequate to explain the worker's motivations except for limited periods of time. The motivations of workers must be considered as some blend of all these aspirations.

Strains in the Worker's Role. What strains arise from the interrelations of the role, generalized goals, and personalities of workingmen? As we have seen, a strain arises when any of these elements fail to "fit in" or "mesh" with other elements. At least five such major strains in the worker's role can be detected: (1) those arising primarily from the physical conditions of his role, (2) those arising from his frustrated desire for status, (3) those arising from his inability to secure satisfying emotional responses from others, (4) those arising from his frustrated desire for independence, and (5) those arising from his sense of insecurity. Some of these strains have already been discussed in other contexts, but we shall include them here for the sake of completeness.

Strains Arising Primarily from Physical Conditions. As we have already seen, the contents of the worker's role in modern industrial production have become extraordinarily diversified at the same time that they have become extremely specialized. Part cause and part effect of this process has been an increasing use of automatic machinery and a rationalization of the use of labor, e.g., in time-and-motion studies. This has led to routinization, the reduction of skills, isolation, and the reduction of the importance of the worker. Strains have risen as a result of the discrepancy between these realities in the worker's situation, on the one hand, and his desire for independence, for pleasant physical conditions at work, for an opportunity to set the pace of work, for a chance to use his own ideas on the job, and for a chance to gain small distinctions, on the other. These strains, in turn, have resulted in monotony, fatigue, and the loss of a "sense of workmanship," or the loss of opportunity for individual creativity.

Frustrated Desire for Status. Another important strain in the worker's role stems from the discrepancy between his desire for personal distinction, to be a "fellow your mates look to,"[8] on the one hand, and the loss of status or the inability to gain status in the role, on the other. The division of labor, the mechanization of work, the loss of skills, the reduction of the worker to a cog in production, his low position in the bureaucratic organization, all combine to frustrate his individuality and creativity. The resulting strains may be detected in feelings of boredom and lack of interest on the job, in a sense of inferiority, in unrest, and in a search for formal or informal means of achieving status. As Bakke says:[9]

[8] *Ibid.*, p. 12.
[9] E. Wight Bakke, *The Unemployed Worker,* Yale University Press, New Haven, Conn., 1940, p. 13. By permission.

To anyone but the worker himself, the abilities upon which for some brief period his superiority rests may seem minor indeed. Mr. Goodwin's ability to use a file two days longer than other workers "because you get a finer finish when the file is partly filled," and Mr. Crane's ability to drive a nail through a saw are examples of such minor distinctions.

It is not likely, however, that such distinctions would get or deserve the attention of management, and thereby increase the status of the workingman.

Inability to Secure Satisfying Emotional Responses from Others. We have already discussed the basis of the human need for emotional responses—the fact that the human personality itself is probably founded to a large extent on the affectional relationships of early childhood. Thus, the failure of a situation to satisfy the desire for response is not a minor strain but, rather, has serious implications for the personality.

The worker is no exception to this rule. As we have seen, he would like to work with people with whom he can have "pleasant personal relations"; he wishes to work with "high-class people," with people who will be "good working companions." He wishes, that is, to work with people with whom he can exchange ideas and emotions with some certainty that he will receive a favorable hearing. Conversely, if he does not find such a situation, he feels isolated and, perhaps, threatened.

Neither the social relations arising from industrial technology nor those formed within bureaucratic organization afford the workingman abundant opportunities for such response. The relationships between supervisors and the workingman are, formally, of a highly impersonal nature. The task of the supervisor is to see that the worker maintains the proper quantity and quality of production; the relation of worker to supervisor is correspondingly cold and impersonal. This situation is reinforced by several other factors, such as the leveling process, which makes it difficult or impossible for the workingman to achieve favorable attention from management. Similarly, the ability of the workingman to obtain satisfactory emotional responses from his fellow workers is limited by the process of production and by bureaucracy. The division of labor, automatic machinery, and the rationalization of labor have all operated to lessen the contacts that he can have with his fellows. Thus, opportunities for emotional responses have also lessened.

Frustrated Desire for Independence. There exists a discrepancy between the limiting and constraining nature of the worker's role, on the one hand, and the worker's aspirations for independence on the other. The worker's desire for independence is expressed in the wish "to control his own affairs," to be free of "driving straw bosses," to "set the pace of work." But these aspirations are inherently opposed to the physical and social demands of the worker's role. The worker is a part of a process of production which more often controls him than is controlled by him; this productive system often sets the pace of work and determines the quality of the product. The worker, as we have seen, is thereby frequently reduced to an appendage of the machine. Furthermore, his power in the factory vis-à-vis management is negligible in the face of management's command of the instruments of discipline and the power of dismissal. Much more than most other roles, the worker's role sharply limits the freedom of the role player.

The strain between role and personality in this case may find expression in various ways: in attitudes of resentment, in servile submissiveness, in organized or unorganized attempts to circumvent the power of management and the demands of production. This is an important theme in the history of American labor, and one to which we shall have occasion to return.

Widespread Feeling of Insecurity. The sources of insecurity are located in both the physical and social sides of the worker's environment.

On the physical side, perhaps the major threat to the worker's security stems from technological change, which, as we have seen,[10] seems to be inherent in the industrial system. The greatest threat to the worker undoubtedly lies in the ever-present possibilities of unemployment; not only single workingmen but whole towns may be displaced by some technological change. The machine is thus a constant threat to the workingman's most basic need—to be the holder of a job. Since, as we have seen, the job is the key to other important goals, the magnitude of the threat from technological change is multiplied many times. Even short of total loss of employment, technological change may threaten the worker with loss of pay, status, or skill, with downgrading, demotion, or transfer. But, even more, the mere possibility of technological change may in itself be sufficient to induce in the worker a feeling of insecurity.

Automation, furthermore, may impose even greater threats to the worker's security in the future. In a fully developed system of automation, the process of production would become almost completely automatic; not only would the machine perform the process of manufacturing, but it would also feed itself and dispose of the completed prod-

[10] For description of the effect of technological change on workingmen, see W. Lloyd Warner and J. O. Low, *The Social System of the Modern Factory,* Yale University Press, New Haven, Conn., 1947, chaps. IV and V; Harriet Laura Herring, *Passing of the Mill Village,* The University of North Carolina Press, Chapel Hill, N.C. 1949. For an historical account of the effects of changing technology on unemployment, see H. Dewey Anderson, *Technology in our Economy,* Temporary National Economic Committee Monograph 22, Government Printing Office, 1941, chap. I. The same monograph deals with the effects of technology on mass unemployment during the twentieth century; see chaps. II and III.

uct. Furthermore, it is possible that, in a system of automation, machines may inspect products, repair themselves, perform intricate calculating operations, and adjust to changing conditions.[11] It can be well understood that the initial effects of this kind of development on employment might well be disastrous. Automation may make the modern assembly-line plant, with its crowds of workers, as obsolete as the water-powered mill. The petroleum-refining industry is already in a relatively advanced state of automation, and one of the most striking characteristics of this industry is the small number of workers it employs relative to the size of its enterprises. Of course, the technological revolutions of the past have, in the long run, created new types of occupations, and the advent of automation also may very well have this long-term effect.[12] But, in the short run, automation can represent only a threat, possibly a serious one, to the worker. The attention which some sections of organized labor are paying to the growth of automation is a sign both that labor recognizes this threat and that it is determined not to permit the workers to bear the cost of this technological revolution as they have borne the costs of others.[13]

On the social side, insecurity arises both from the formal relations of production and from the immediate social relationships at work. Since the worker's job depends on the needs of production and on the demands of the market, his job is always in jeopardy. This is particularly

[11] For discussions of the purely technical aspect of automation, see John Diebold, *Automation: The Advent of the Automatic Factory,* D. Van Nostrand Company, Inc., Princeton, N.J., 1952. The issue of the *Scientific American* for September, 1952, vol. 187, no. 3, has several illuminating articles on the technical aspects of automation: Arnold Tustin, "Feedback," pp. 48–55; Gordon L. Brown and Donald P. Campbell, "Control Systems," pp. 56–64; Eugene Ayres, "An Automatic Chemical Plant," pp. 82–86; William Pease, "An Automatic Machine Tool," pp. 101–115; Louis N. Ridenour, "The Role of the Computer," pp. 116–130; Gilbert W. King, "Information," pp. 132–148. For a general discussion of automation, see J. Frederic Dewhurst and Associates, *America's Needs and Resources,* The Twentieth Century Fund, Inc., New York, 1955, pp. 868–875.

[12] See the article by Wassily Leontief, "Machines and Man," in the issue of the *Scientific American* already cited, vol. 187, no. 3, pp. 150–160, September, 1952. Leontief contends that automation need not mean large-scale layoffs. Support for this point of view may be found in an article, "Adjustments to Automation in Two Firms" (no author given), appearing in the *Monthly Labor Review,* vol. 79, no. 1, pp. 15–19, 1956. In one of the two firms studied, dismissals were confined largely to one class of employees, while in the other firm, all displaced employees were assigned to other jobs.

[13] In October, 1955, hearings were held before the Subcommittee on Economic Stabilization of the Congressional Joint Committee on the general topic of automation and technological change. In these hearings, leaders of business and labor were given a chance to express viewpoints on the nature and implications of automation. See *Automation and Technological Change, Hearings before the Subcommittee on Economic Stabilization of the Congressional Joint Committee on the Economic Report,* 84th Cong., 1st Sess., pursuant to sec. 5(a) of Public Law 304, 79th Cong., 1955.

true in times of depression, but even in times of general prosperity, there may be severe local depression caused by technical conditions, shortages of raw materials, or the situation of a particular industry. Insecurity in the abstract becomes personalized on the job in the shape of the foreman. Where there is no union, the foreman's powers of dismissal over workingmen, his power to promote or demote them, or his power to select them for more or less desirable jobs make him an object of great insecurity to the workingmen.

Summation. Our analysis has thus far been necessarily of a negative nature. Undoubtedly many contrary cases could be shown. It may very well be true that for some workingmen the isolation of the job, the lack of social demands that it makes, the lack of necessity of striving for status, the very loss of freedom, all are attractive aspects of the role. Furthermore, not all work roles contradict the demands of personality. For instance, certain industrial jobs do demand great amounts of social cooperation; thus, consider the sort of cooperation that is necessary between the members of a train crew if the job is to be done satisfactorily. Similarly, many exceptions could be found to our description of the nature of management-worker relationships. Skilled and experienced foremen have succeeded in many cases in maintaining a nice balance between the demands of production and the personalities of workingmen.

Nevertheless, when all these exceptions are taken into account, it can only be concluded that the logics of technology and bureaucratic organization all too often operate against the aspirations of the workingman. The strains which result—monotony, fatigue, a loss of the sense of workmanship, the inability to achieve status or to secure satisfactory emotional responses or to gain independence—all seem to be inherent in the role and personality situation of the worker. Of course, it must not be assumed that the worker simply accepts these unfavorable aspects of his role without some attempt to overcome them. In the remainder of this chapter, one important reaction of the worker to the situation of work will be discussed; that is, the establishment of informal social relationships and informal social groups. In later chapters it will be shown how the worker has reacted to the strains in his role through union organization and in the community.

INFORMAL SOCIAL RELATIONSHIPS AT WORK

Bureaucratic organization and the system of technology determine the *formal* or ideal social relationships of the worker. However, it is only rarely that this ideal situation corresponds with the actual situation. This fact has been universally recognized by all who have had to do with flesh-and-blood workingmen rather than with the lifeless abstractions of the organizational chart.

Informal Social Relations. Deviations from the formal situation such as talking at work, traditional (though unauthorized) breaks in the work at certain times of the day, elaborate patterns of joking, gambling, work exchanges, are all parts of the social life of many factories. These types of deviations are usually called *informal social relationships.* Informal social relationships, as we shall see, do not arise alone from the natural capriciousness of the worker, or from an inherent tendency to disobedience, or from "mob psychology" (as was suggested by one administrator); informal social relationships must be explained in terms of the basic role and personality situation of the worker.

There are two major contexts within which informal social relationships tend to form. First, they tend to form on the basis of the ideal relations; in fact, this process is almost certain to occur in any formal situation. Certain "informal" feelings of attraction, antipathy, hostility, prejudice, identification, projection, etc., are very likely to spring up in any type of social relationships which endure over a period of time (sometimes these feelings may arise even in ephemeral social relations).[14] The relationship, for instance, between foreman and workingman is almost always more than a simple matter of superiority and subordination. Such a relationship always involves intellectual and emotional attitudes on the part of both the worker and the foreman which have nothing to do with the formal situation. If the foreman's attitude toward the worker is impersonal, cold, and harsh, it is not surprising if the worker's attitude toward the foreman is aggressive and hostile. Similarly, two workers who are in contact with one another in the course of work may add to their formal relationships certain informal patterns based on mutual sympathy, admiration, interests, and congeniality. In both cases, the formal relationships at work are being more or less transformed by psychological factors.

Other types of informal social relationships arise in industry which are, in effect, entirely new relationships, having little or no connection with the formal social structure of the plant. These informal relationships may arise, in the first place, when, for whatever reasons, formal relations are meager and limited; for instance, when the formal relationships are too few, or workers are uncongenial, or the turnover of labor is too high. Under these circumstances relationships of friendship or congeniality, "kidding" relationships, or other types of social interaction, may spring up between men who have no direct connections in the formal social system of the plant. In the second place, informal atti-

---

[14] As an example, see William Foote Whyte, *Human Relations in the Restaurant Industry,* McGraw-Hill Book Company, Inc., New York, 1948, chaps. IV–IX.

tudes and sentiments surrounding formal relationships may become so strong as, in effect, to create new types of social relationships. For instance, the members of a work team may enrich and solidify their social relations at work with new meanings, attitudes, and values. In either case, these relationships may sometimes become so entrenched, so surrounded by ritual, so highly structured, that they in effect constitute an informal group. In the next section we shall discuss more fully the informal group as a logical development of the formal and informal social relationships of the plant. Here it may be said that where informal social relationships and groups are given time to mature and develop, they may become strongly entrenched. In fact, these informal relationships and groups may constitute almost an alternative, *sub rosa,* latent social system within the confines of the older formal social system. Even if this does not happen, the informal social system may, as we shall see, still possess great influence and power in the plant and sharply influence the action of both management and labor.

The Informal Group. No development in the field of industrial sociology has attracted more attention than the "discovery" of informal groups among workers. In fact, it's not too much to say that industrial sociology began with the study of the informal group. Sometimes it would almost seem that industrial sociologists have become hypnotized with this topic. But whether interest in informal groups has been exaggerated or not, there can be no doubt of their importance as end products of conditions of work in the modern factory. We shall therefore devote the rest of this chapter to a discussion of the informal group. It will be necessary, first, to define the term "informal group," and to indicate how one may recognize an informal group. Interest will then be centered on (1) examples of informal groups, and (2) the functions of such groups, as well as the reason for their formation and their meaning for various parts of industry.

Definition. Neither in theory nor in actuality can the informal group be understood without special methods of investigation. In commonsense views a group is thought of as having a definite structure, including a leader, bylaws, a purpose, a name, a role structure. The family is obviously a group, since it meets most of these conditions; similarly fraternal clubs are certainly groups. Somewhat less immediately recognizable are groups which possess no definite or known purpose, name, bylaws, or leaders. Examples of such groups include corner gangs,[15] children's play groups, cliques of various sorts, and so on.

Studies of these latter types of groups have shown that they possess

[15] One of the best-known studies of gangs may be found in *Street Corner Society,* by William Foote Whyte, University of Chicago Press, Chicago, 1943. Copyright by the University of Chicago.

definite structures; that is, they may have definite leaders, a set of purposes, and a set of values or rules by which they operate. However, there are two ways by which they differ from the former types. First, no one has knowingly set up the corner gang or the play group; these groups have grown spontaneously out of social and psychological conditions. Secondly, the group is not aware of itself as a group. No one in the group, usually, knows that there is a definite structure to the group, that there is a leader or leaders, that certain values and rules are closely followed, that the group as a whole is striving for certain goals. It is because of these elements of spontaneity and lack of self-awareness that we call this type of group "informal"; it arises directly out of the needs, interests, and feelings of ordinary, daily living.

The informal group, then, is marked by the spontaneous interaction of a number of people (the number usually being small) over a relatively long period of time. The members of an informal group play certain roles tending toward the accomplishment of certain ends, but this action arises and continues without conscious purpose or direction. Obviously, by this definition, there are certain things which an informal group is not; it is not, for instance, a number of people getting on the bus to go to work, or pouring through a factory gate, or rushing toward a cafeteria. Such groups may be called *crowds*. The members of a crowd may act in certain definite ways toward each other; e.g., men may be courteous to women and considerate of children. However, there is nothing permanent in this relationship; the people in a crowd do not act toward each other as members of a stable group. The regularity of this behavior is cultural rather than social; that is, the culture demands certain types of behavior toward certain social objects—e.g., women or children—no matter in what group they may be found. The informal group, on the other hand, is made up—like the formal group—of a relatively stable set of roles, values, and personalities.

The best-known study of the informal group is that reported by Roethlisberger and Dickson.[16] We shall examine this study in greater detail.

Examples of Informal Groups. The informal group was, in a sense, "discovered" during the course of the well-known experiments at the Hawthorne, Illinois, plant of the Western Electric Company which took

[16] Fritz Jules Roethlisberger and William J. Dickson, *Management and the Worker*, Harvard University Press, Cambridge, Mass., 1939, chaps. II–VIII. Copyright by the President and Fellows of Harvard University. For other studies of informal groups, see the following: Nicholas Babchuk and William J. Goode, "Work Incentives in a Self-determined Group," *American Sociological Review*, vol. 16, no. 5, pp. 679–687, 1951; Alexander B. Horsfall and Conrad M. Arensberg, "Teamwork and Productivity in a Shoe Factory," *Human Organization*, vol. 8, no. 1, pp. 13–25, 1949; William J. Goode and Irving Fowler, "Incentive Factors in a Low Morale Plant," *American Sociological Review*, vol. 14, no. 5, pp. 618–624, 1949.

place in the late 1920s. The purpose of the experiments—and it is important to keep this in mind—was to test for correlations between various factors and the output of individual workers. Previous experiments with the effect of variation in the amount of light at work had failed to reveal significant connections between output and physical factors. Consequently it was decided to isolate several workers in a test room where the amount of production could be measured accurately while various conditions were varied. Ingenious arrangements were made to record the rates of production of the individual workers and the variations of the test factors. In addition, a record was kept of daily events, including conversation between the workers and other forms of interaction. A special observer was installed in the test room to take note of what was going on and to keep records.

The results of the experiment were surprising to the experimenters. It was found that apparently none of the factors being tested had much relation to productivity. This conclusion was reached because, no matter which factors were held constant and which varied, production continued to rise until it reached a high plateau, from which it apparently could not be shaken. This held true when improved methods of payment were tried, when rest pauses of various lengths were introduced, and when the length of the working day was shortened. Even after some of these favorable test factors—e.g., rest pauses and shorter hours— were removed and the test conditions were returned to the general conditions of the plant, production continued far above the average rate. The investigators were forced to conclude that some other factor was working to maintain high productivity.

The investigators formulated an ingenious hypothesis to explain the rise in production. They held that[17]—

the experiment they had planned to conduct was quite different from the experiment they had actually performed. They had not studied the relation between output and fatigue, monotony, etc., so much as they had performed a most interesting psychological and sociological experiment. In the process of setting the conditions for the test, they had altered completely the social situation of the operators and their customary attitudes and interpersonal relations.

The x factor in this case, then, was high morale; an intangible feeling of confidence in, and satisfaction with, the work, the test, the supervision, and prospects for the future. High productivity was then considered a natural outcome of this high morale, although the exact nature of the connection remained a matter of debate.

[17] Fritz Jules Roethlisberger and William J. Dickson, *Management and the Worker,* Harvard University Press, Cambridge, Mass., 1939, p. 183. By permission.

Discussion of the connection between productivity and the informal group will be postponed to a later section of this chapter. Here interest will be centered on the new "social situation" which was created by the experiment. There can be little question of the nature of this new social situation; it was undoubtedly an informal group within the meaning given that term in this chapter. This group arose in an industrial situation marked by a minimum of formal social relationships between workers and between workers and management. The girls worked in almost complete formal isolation from one another. Each girl, working alone, assembled 35 parts into a relay. Parts were supplied to the operator, and the finished product was removed by another worker. Furthermore, the job was excessively repetitive and monotonous; in fact, it had been deliberately chosen by the investigators for that reason.

The informal group appeared early in the history of the experiment and became gradually more entrenched, even when individual workers were replaced. Leadership developed gradually. One of the girls established herself in this capacity through superior ability and enterprise. A system of status also emerged, and by the end of the experiment it had become quite hardened. This system of status assigned positions to each of the girls and determined the roles that would be played within them (that is, roles within the informal group). Thus besides the leader's role, there appeared the roles of scapegoat, of jester, of lieutenants to the leader. Even the experimenters, who were very prominent throughout the whole test period, were assigned roles within the group. A system of differential prestige attached to these roles soon appeared. Thus, in time these girls formed a series of social relationships at work which had little to do with bureaucratic relations or with the technology of the job.

The informal group apparently performed two important functions for its members. On the one hand, it offered the workers opportunities for achieving certain personal satisfactions which could not be attained within the regular social structure of the factory. The group, for instance, provided certain sorts of human relations that the formal structure of the plant could not. Within the group the girls could communicate with relative freedom; they could exchange experiences, joke, quarrel. Furthermore, the group assigned definite statuses and roles, positions of power, prestige, and leadership which gave definite satisfactions to those playing the roles. Thus the girl who became the leader of the group was an able person who would have had small chance of showing her ability within the formal social structure of the plant. On the other hand, the group functioned to attain certain group goals which were, apparently, strongly believed in by the girls. The girls felt that they held a favored position in the plant. This position, they believed, could be maintained only by continuing a high level of production. The function of this group, therefore, came to be maintenance of the productive level at all costs. To that purpose girls were chided if they fell behind their quotas, and discipline at work was strictly maintained. In the eyes of the girls, the function of the informal group as a whole was to maintain economic security.

Another type of informal group was discovered at the Hawthorne plant during an experiment undertaken somewhat later than the experiment in the relay-assembly test room.[18] This newer experiment lasted from November, 1931, to May, 1932—a period, it should be remembered, which was marked by constantly increasing layoffs, subsequent insecurity, and depression of living standards. It is also important to remember that this study was made before the large-scale union organizing drives of the 1930s; in fact, this whole period witnessed a considerable decrease in union membership. Nevertheless, there is good reason to believe that the group we are about to describe is typical of many informal groups which exist today in our industrial plant— much more typical, in fact, than the group described above.

The aim of the study was to observe, as closely as possible, a normal work situation. For various reasons of a technical nature, it proved impossible to make these observations in the shop itself. As a consequence it was decided to select a group of workers and move them to a special test room. Great care was taken to select a typical sample of workers from the shop. Fourteen workingmen were finally selected for the test on this basis. No special privileges were given to these workers; neither was the group used as an object of experiments, since it had been decided on the basis of evidence obtained from the previous experiment that factors such as rest pauses and shorter working hours had no direct effect on productivity. The workingmen continued to be responsible to the same foremen under whom they had worked in the shop. An observer was stationed in the test room, but it was made clear to the workers that the observer had no power to secure them privileges or to discipline them. After a short initial period of suspicion, they apparently accepted the situation for what it was.

The 14 workingmen selected for study included nine wiremen, three soldermen, and two inspectors who together were engaged in the task of selector and connector bank wiring. Both tasks involved wiring terminals which were held by the banks; this job was performed by the wireman. The soldermen then soldered the wire to the terminals, where they had been placed by the wiremen; each solderman soldered the work of three wiremen. The finished product was then mechanically

[18] *Ibid.*, part IV.

and visually tested for defects by an inspector; two inspectors served the nine wiremen and three soldermen of the test room. The three kinds of job involved in this test were of a nonmechanized nature; all the workingmen employed tools of a simple kind. The work was routine, but it was not so automatic as many other jobs in industry. For instance, the workingmen could control the pace of the work to some extent. Furthermore, a certain amount of cooperation and communication among the three types of workers was required. However, no very high level of skill was needed at these jobs; this was particularly true of wiremen and soldermen. All the workers were on about the same level of status, prestige, and power in the formal social structure of the plant.

After a short period of time, it became apparent to the observer that, although the formal social relationships between workers and between workers and supervisors were determined directly by the technological process of bank wiring and by the bureaucratic organization, the men had created, in fact, a complex set of informal relations which had little to do with the formal social structure. These informal social relations were coalesced into two informal groups. The situation is diagramed below. The "solid core" of each of these cliques was made up of four

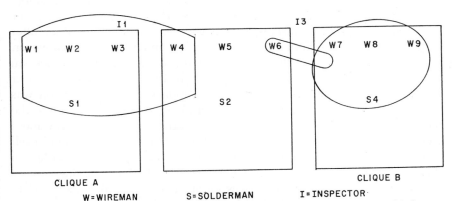

Informal groups in the bank-wiring observation room. (*Fritz Jules Roethlisberger and William J. Dickson, Management and the Worker, Harvard University Press, Cambridge, 1939, p. 509. By permission.*)

workers: in clique A, they were W1, W3, W4, and S1; in clique B, W7, W8, W9, and S4. The positions of W2 and W6 were uncertain; for one reason or another, they did not seem to fit into the informal groups. The attitude of the informal-group members toward S2 was indifferent, but they were definitely hostile toward W5 and 13. The hostility toward 13 was based on his personality and officiousness; W5 was disliked primarily because he refused to live up to the codes of the group, particularly in relation to production. The internal structure of clique A was stronger than that of clique B. Perhaps this was due to W3, who was not only the leader of clique A (clique B seemed to have no definite leader) but the best-liked man in the room.

Many of the informal social relationships in this test room were carried on within these informal groups. The members of clique A (who were mainly connector wiremen) considered themselves above clique B (who were selector wiremen) and tended to exclude clique B members from their activities. For instance, games such as gambling, "binging" (a short hard punch landed without warning on the shoulder), and betting on the horses were conducted within each group. Similarly, job trading, helping at work, friendships, antagonisms, and even quarrels were conducted mainly along lines of the informal-group structure.

The functions of these groups can be divided into two types, as in the case noted before. First, the groups functioned to relieve monotony and boredom, to provide recreation, and as a means of mutual support and aid. Secondly, the groups as a whole functioned to enforce certain codes and practices. Restriction of production was a particularly important aim. Technically, the workers were paid on the basis of an incentive plan. According to this plan, wages were determined by a combination of group and individual production. As a result an individual worker could lower the wages of his fellows, or at least secure an unfair share for himself, by shirking work. The plan was designed to offer maximum incentives both for the individual and the group. However, production was consistently restricted in several ways. For instance, an incorrect total of work would be reported to the foreman at the end of the day. Also, by a sort of unspoken common consent, production was limited to a certain amount of finished products each day, in spite of the fact that several workingmen could have turned out considerably more work than the informal norm. The result was that the production of each worker and of the group as a whole was remarkably uniform, although there were differences in the productivity of individual workingmen.

The restriction of production was enforced by the group in a variety of ways. For those individuals who were members of a group, normal group processes of control operated; that is, each member of the group, in the course of properly filling his role in the informal group, restricted production as one aspect of his role. For outsiders, more direct means, such as ridicule, sarcasm, and ostracism, were used. Of those who were outside of the groups, W5 was the greatest threat to the code of production. W5 was a willing workingman, who would not ordinarily abide by the informal practices. He could not be controlled entirely, but he was rendered fairly harmless by various means: sarcasm, hiding his tools, damaging his completed work, and even threats of physical violence. In all these ways, the informal groups attempted to defend what they considered a desirable standard of production.

In a later section of this chapter, we shall investigate the reasons behind the restriction of production in the test room. Here we may note certain widely held values in which these informal-group members believed and which they tried to enforce:[19]

1. You should not turn out too much work. If you do, you are a "rate-buster."
2. You should not turn out too little work. If you do, you are a "chiseler."
3. You should not tell a supervisor anything that will react to the detriment of an associate. If you do, you are a "squealer."
4. You should not attempt to maintain social distance or act officious. If you are an inspector, for example, you should not act like one.

By attempting to enforce these values, the informal group members were apparently trying both to maintain their organizations and to protect themselves against outside interference.[20]

The Functions of the Informal Group. Many different interpretations of the causes of informal groups and of their significance are possible.[21] Some branches of management have looked at the informal group as the result of the worker's natural laziness, or rebelliousness, or unwillingness to cooperate in the sometimes exacting tasks of industry. Others have seen in the informal group just the opposite—the natural expression of man's friendliness and his needs for cooperation. Organized labor has looked upon the informal group as the natural protective device of a group of unorganized workingmen against the overweening power of management; that is, the informal group has been considered as a sort of preunion. Finally, some have seen the informal group as the answer to the worker's need for an outlet to his sentiments and emotions. The point of view of this book will be that the informal group must be understood in relation to the role-and-personality situation of the worker. However, this point of view is not necessarily opposed to other interpretations; in fact, it should prove possible to incorporate the insights of other schools of thought within a role-personality framework.

There would seem to be a plausible explanation for the formation and nature of informal groups in industry. Their over-all function is to provide alternative outlets for the aspirations of workingmen; that is, they operate to mitigate the effects of strains arising from discrepancies between the worker's role and his aspirations. The informal group is an outgrowth of, and a reaction to, industrial technology and industrial bureaucracy. It is therefore the function of the informal group to afford

[19] Fritz Jules Roethlisberger and William J. Dickson, *Management and the Worker*, Harvard University Press, Cambridge, Mass., 1939, p. 522. By permission.

[20] *Ibid.*, p. 523.

[21] For a discussion of the functions of informal organization from the point of view of management, see Chester I. Barnard, *The Functions of the Executive*, Harvard University Press, Cambridge, Mass., 1945, chap. IX. Copyright by the President and Fellows of Harvard University.

the worker (1) relief from monotony, boredom and fatigue; (2) opportunities for status; (3) an increased flow of emotional responses; (4) opportunities for independence; and (5) increased security.

Relief from Monotony, Boredom, and Fatigue. Clearly, this was the function of the recreational patterns in the bank-wiring test room. It will be recalled that the workingmen engaged in "binging," storytelling, gambling, and other types of horseplay; these practices served at the same time to break up the routine of work and to afford a mode of crude recreation. The informal groups of the bank-wiring test room also protected the worker against fatigue through work exchange and by limiting production. In the case of the relay-assembly test room the informal group functioned to speed up production. But it also provided the girls with alternative outlets for socialization, which undoubtedly relieved the monotony of work. Furthermore, in this experiment the workers were provided with a group goal, which made a real demand on their talents and creativity. Under these circumstances, the gap between worker and role was closed. In general, it may be concluded, from this and other evidence, that an important function of the informal group is to mitigate the harsh routine, discipline, and consequent boredom and fatigue which arise from the nature of industrial production.

Opportunities for Status. The informal group may provide alternative roads to the acquisition of status—in most cases, higher status than could be secured through the formal social structure. Here again the situation must not be presented in too simple terms. The creation of an informal group may mean a *loss* of status for workingmen excluded from the group, or for those defined as inimical to the aims of the group. In the case of the informal groups studied in a small feeder plant, the status assigned to some group members was very low; however, the leaders of the informal groups and their lieutenants enjoyed a gain in status.[22] Perhaps the most balanced statement that can be made is this: the informal group provides opportunities for acquiring and increasing prestige in an informal hierarchy of status.

This function can be seen most clearly, perhaps, in the case of the bank-wiring test room. In clique A, which was an unusually well defined informal group, the assignment of alternative status is very clear. W3 played the role of leader and thereby gained recognition of his undoubtedly high qualities. His capacity for congeniality, his knowledge both of the job and of the men, his ability to get along with and yet circumvent management, the security which he afforded others by his careful regulation of production, his care to settle or stop all dangerous arguments and fights, the grace with which he took the favors offered him—all these qualities established him in the informal group as a

[22] Goode and Fowler, *op. cit.*, pp. 618–624.

"fellow your mates look to." Yet it will be noted that W3 occupied no formal position in the hierarchy of the plant. In fact, it seems doubtful that management recognized his informal position.

Similarly, other members of the informal groups were assigned status, high and low. W6 fulfilled the functions of a clown and comedian, bringing some sort of recreation to his fellow workers and receiving recognition of a kind in return. I1 found recognition within the group, although his formal position separated him from other workers. On the other hand, the informal groups tried very hard to decrease the status of W5, who, ironically, was perhaps entitled to the highest status in the eyes of management. In the same manner, every participant in the bank-wiring test room was assigned informal status.

Thus, the informal group afforded the workingmen (or most of them) opportunities to alter the formal definitions of status in the industrial bureaucracy in their own favor. The informal groups thereby relieved strain in this area.

Increased Flow of Emotional Responses. On the one hand, the informal group brings together workers who are congenial in character and solidifies relationships between those who occupy adjacent places in the productive process or who must work together at a common task. On the other hand, the informal group increases emotional response by increasing the rate of interaction of the workers who are grouped together. The group provides channels for a flow of conversation, the exchange of ideas, the communication of attitudes, and the sharing of values. Thus, it serves to mitigate the affective neutrality and universalism of the worker's role; it provides an alternative outlet to an aspect of the worker's personality for which there is no need or room in an industrial bureaucracy.

Each of the groups described above provides an illustration of the flow of emotional response in informal groups. The friendships, antipathies, and antagonisms of the girls in the relay-assembly test room, for instance, are pertinent examples of an exchange of emotional responses for which there is no provision in the formal social structure. Similarly, in the bank-wiring observation room there was a mutual flow of sentiments and attitudes among the workers in the informal groups, an experience of sharing common values and a heightened sense of solidarity. Even the informal groups of the feeder plant mentioned above permitted the expression of feelings and ideas which would otherwise have remained unexpressed. Thus, in each case, though in varying degree, the informal group provided release to the strain arising from the discrepancy between the needs of personality and the needs of industrial production.

Opportunity for Independence. At least some informal groups provide the workingmen with some opportunity for independence and spontaneity (or the illusion of independence and spontaneity) in the face of the inexorable demands of the industrial process and the power of management. The seemingly meaningless work exchanges of the bank-wiring observation room may have had the function of stressing the worker's independence in the face of the productive process. The restriction of production, whatever other purposes it served, may also have been a symbol of the integrity of the individual caught up in a large impersonal organization. The informal group of the relay-assembly test room, it is true, bound the girls tightly to the productive process, but in so far as this was accomplished through enlisting the voluntary efforts of the girls, their independence was maintained or even heightened. However, no hard and fast rule about this aspect of the functioning of the informal group can be made.

The informal group in many cases operated to increase the worker's freedom and independence of bureaucratic discipline. Examples of this process are to be found in the hatred and control by the informal group of the "squealer"; that is, the worker who reports to management on restriction of production, horseplay, union activities, or other nonsanctioned activities. The persecution of such workers as W5 in the bank wiring observation room should also be considered, at least in part, an attempt to circumvent discipline by controlling a managerially oriented worker.

It is interesting to note that the worker may achieve at least an illusion of independence in other "informal" ways. Perhaps the constant obscenity of many workers, as of soldiers, is an expression of the striving of the "little man" for freedom from the large forces which control him.[23] Such verbal rebellion or expression of lack of interest serve to conceal the real helplessness and weakness of the worker by providing an alternative outlet for feelings which are seemingly violent but actually harmless. Thus, even management-oriented workers may permit themselves verbal expressions of hostility to management, at the same time that they strive to meet management's demands.[24]

It seems doubtful whether the workingman's desire to achieve independence on the job through the use of the informal group is feasible. In practice the informal group, for various reasons, proves to be an imperfect instrument for achieving this end. First, some groups function as an additional means of control over the worker rather than as vehicles of independence. Secondly, although the non-management-oriented group may genuinely seek to curb the power of management or the industrial process, it can do so only in limited ways and degrees. For instance, it

[23] For discussions of the functions of obscenity among workers, see Williams, *op. cit.*, pp. 274–275.
[24] See Goode and Fowler, *op. cit.*, pp. 618–624.

is doubtful if the informal group strengthens by very much the worker's economic bargaining power against management. Nor could such a group exert control over a process of automation. The informal group often furnishes the illusion of independence rather than genuine independence. Thus it would seem that, in relation to the need for independence, the informal group is more important as a symptom of the strivings of the workers than as an answer to those strivings.

Increased Security. Because of the worker's deep-lying concern for the security of his job, we would expect the major function of the informal group to be the attainment of economic security in the face of the double threat arising from technological change and fluctuations in the business cycle. And, in fact, when we examine the evidence presented in this chapter, as well as that available elsewhere, it can be seen that each informal group is much concerned with maintenance of security. The means which these groups use in the attempt are quite diverse. For instance, both the informal group of the relay-assembly test room and those of the feeder plant sought to achieve security by complying with the demands of management. The function of the group, in each case, was to discipline its members into compliance with management's goals. The fact that the mode of operation of the groups differed, that the morale of the first group was high and that of the other group low, does not affect the general similarity in the aims of these groups. In the case of the bank-wiring observation room, on the other hand, the workers defined their position in quite another way. The resultant practices, especially the restriction of production, are so important that they must be discussed in somewhat greater detail.

There are good grounds for assuming that the restriction of production is a widespread, almost universal, practice of American workingmen.[25] In many plants, there seems to be spoken or unspoken agreements among workingmen to maintain the rate of production at some point below what would be possible—in some cases, far below what would be possible. Production is restricted in a number of ways. A common way is to limit the rate of work. If this is not feasible, a daily quota will be established, and work will cease when the day's quota is met. Production may also be limited by misplacing work, passing through defective parts, securing the wrong tools from the supply room, and in many similar ways. Workingmen often become masters at the art of appearing busy without, in fact, being so. It is a prime function of the informal group to enforce the definition of a fair day's work or a fair

[25] See the following: Williams, *op. cit.;* Stanley B. Mathewson, *Restriction of Output among Unorganized Workers,* The Viking Press, Inc., New York, 1931; for a study of the situation in English industry, see F. Zweig, *Productivity and Trade Unions,* Basil Blackwell & Mott, Ltd., Oxford, 1951, part I.

rate of work. The informal-group members regulate production by informing workers when they are producing too slowly or too rapidly, and, if necessary, by helping workers who cannot meet the standard, by coercing workers who exceed the group's standards. Coercion may take the form of explanations of the need for restriction of production, ridicule, ostracism, and, in some cases, the threat or even use of violence. However, such tactics are almost always employed against nonmembers of the group. Membership in an informal group usually ensures compliance with the informal standards.

The importance of these restrictive practices is clear. Although it is impossible to estimate the amount by which the efficiency of our industry is lowered through restriction of production, the total amount of lost production must be very great. This consideration is important to management, since productivity is directly related to costs and thus to profitability. However, the problem is also of concern to our entire society, which not only uses the products of industry but depends upon its productive capacity to maintain its position in the world. As might be expected, considerable controversy has sprung up about the reasons for restrictive practices. Considering the inducements—in the form of bonuses, piece-rate plans, and propaganda—given to the worker to stimulate production, it must be concluded that, if he nevertheless stubbornly refuses to exert himself, there are deep-seated attitudes and values behind his action. Let us review some of the explanations which have been offered for this problem.

One explanation of the restriction of production may be termed the "hedonistic" explanation. This school of thought views the worker as essentially a rational machine which will respond in one direction to financial motivation and in another direction to certain types of discipline. While recognizing the fact that the worker's motives may be complex, this school of thought holds that he will produce efficiently when he has a sufficient incentive in the form of wages or good working conditions, or when he is properly disciplined by management. If production is restricted, it is because of an utilitarian or hedonistic calculus on the part of the workingman; that is, he wishes to give only so much work for so much pay, or has balanced in his mind the costs of additional work against what he can hope to secure in additional wages. This type of thinking leads logically to the piece-rate system or bonus system as a means of increasing productivity.

This explanation has not been satisfactory to what is often termed the "Mayo school" of industrial sociology. This school has noted that incentive programs are by no means universally successful and that in many cases the worker's attitude toward an incentive program is one of deep distrust. The rational explanation of the restriction of production has therefore been rejected.[26] Workers, it is held, frequently act in a nonlogical manner. Nonlogical action, unlike logical action, is based on deep-lying sentiments or feelings, such as a desire for pleasant interpersonal relations, aggressive feeling, or feelings of frustration. The restriction of production, then, is seen as having a double function. In the first place, it reaffirms the worker's sentiments; thus, by restricting production the worker announces his relative independence of management, his stature as a human being, or his affirmation of loyalty to his fellow workers. In the second place, by restricting production, the worker reaffirms the solidarity of the informal group. For work restriction is a truly social practice, shared alike by all informal-group members; a practice which tends to unite workers in a common endeavor to fulfill common values. Thus, according to this school of thought, the restriction of production has certain psychological functions for the individual. At the same time the restriction of production functions for the group in somewhat the same way that a flag functions in a large-scale society, as a symbol of unity and solidarity.[27]

The Mayo school considers that the explanations that workers give for the restriction of production are essentially rationalizations of underlying sentiments. For instance, when the workers in the bank-wiring observation room were asked their reasons for restricting production they replied that "the 'bogey' [the norm of production, set by management, for each job] might be raised, the 'rate' [of payment] might be raised, the 'rate' might be lowered, someone might be laid off, hours might be reduced, or the supervisors might reprimand the slower workers."[28] It is held that these explanations, some of them contradictory, must not be accepted at face value, since the fears they express were justified neither by the experience of the men nor by the policies of management. Rather, the true relationship between motives and actions, according to the Mayo school, should be viewed as pictured in the diagram below. In this

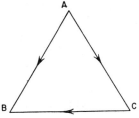

[26] See Roethlisberger and Dickson, *op. cit.*, chap. XXIII, "Formal vs. Informal Organization."

[27] The problem of nonlogical action and the bases of solidarity of social groups are more fully discussed in Chap. 2, "Industry and Sociological Theory."

[28] Fritz Jules Roethlisberger and William J. Dickson, *Management and the Worker*, Harvard University Press, Cambridge, Mass., 1939, p. 532. By permission.

diagram, *A* stands for the sentiments of the group, *B* for the restriction of production, and *C* for the reasons given by the workers for restricting production.[29] According to the workers, *B* was caused by *C*; that is, restrictive practices were caused by the reasons listed above. Actually both restrictive practices and reasons were "caused" by *A*, the underlying sentiments; *C* explained or rationalized *B*—but, of course, incorrectly, according to this school of thought.

A somewhat different theory holds that productivity is directly related to morale; the higher the morale of a worker or group, the higher production will be. Thus Roethlisberger attempts to account for the high productivity of the girls in the relay-assembly test room as follows:[30]

The operators were consulted about the tests to be made . . . they were questioned sympathetically about their reaction to the conditions imposed, and many of these conferences took place in the office of the superintendent. The girls were allowed to talk at work; their "bogey" was eliminated. Their physical health and well-being became matters of great concern. Their opinions, hopes, and fears were eagerly sought . . . the experimenters had completely altered the social situation of the room . . . the customary supervision in the room had been revolutionized. *This accounted for the better attitudes of girls and their improved rate of work.*

And again:[31]

Whether or not a person is going to give his services wholeheartedly to a group depends, in good part, on the way he feels about his job, his fellow workers and supervisors—the meaning for him of what is happening about him.

High productivity is a manifestation of psychological well-being; low productivity is a manifestation of the opposite; psychological dissatisfaction, or low morale. Restriction of production is related to such factors as dissatisfaction with supervisors, the absence of informal groups in which the workingman may express his sentiments, dissatisfaction with the type of work being done, a feeling of a lack of personal interest by management, and so on.

However, while rational and irrational factors are probably universal in situations of work restriction, it is doubtful whether the stated relationship between morale and productivity is generally valid. It has been

[29] Fritz Jules Roethlisberger and William J. Dickson, *Management and the Worker,* Harvard University Press, Cambridge, Mass., 1939, p. 535. By permission.

[30] By permission from Fritz Jules Roethlisberger, *Management and Morale,* Harvard University Press, Cambridge, Mass., 1946, pp. 14–15. Copyright by The President and Fellows of Harvard University. (Italics are the present author's.)

[31] Fritz Jules Roethlisberger, *Management and Morale,* p. 15. By permission.

shown in this chapter that workers and informal groups may be characterized *both* by low morale and high production, as in the case of the feeder plant; or by relatively high morale and restriction of production as in the case of the bank-wiring observation room. This observation is supported by other evidence. For instance, a study of railroad workers revealed a relatively low correspondence between productivity and morale.[32] In this study, the morale of workers was considered as consisting of four separate attitudes:

1. Attitudes toward work groups
2. Intrinsic job satisfaction
3. Satisfaction with the company
4. Financial and job status satisfaction

Some connection between a high valuation of the work group by workingmen and high productivity was found. But there was an inverse connection between satisfaction with the job and productivity; that is, lower-producing workingmen derived more satisfaction from their jobs than higher-producing ones. Little correlation was found between rate of production and satisfaction with the company or with financial and job status.[33] Thus, it would seem that production rates are related to morale only under certain special conditions.

It is not possible at the present time to pass final judgment on the validity of these theories. It is interesting to note that each of these theories of the restriction of production refers to some aspect of the basic personality-role situation of the worker.

Restrictive practices may, in the first place, be understood in relation to the discrepancy between the worker's aspirations for security on the one hand and the realities of his role in the productive process on the other. As we have seen, both the "formal relations of production" and the nature of industrial technology combine to threaten the worker's hold on the job and to induce in him a consciousness of the scarcity of jobs and the tenuousness of his situation. Inevitably, much of his thought and action is concerned with attempts to secure what is for him a vitally important and scarce commodity. The restriction of production flows directly out of this situation; *if the worker restricts production, his motive may be to increase his security on the job.* He knows by experience that his tenure on the job depends upon the flow of orders,

---

[32] Daniel Katz, Nathan Maccoby, Gerald Gurin, and Lucretia G. Floor, *Productivity, Supervision and Morale among Railroad Workers,* Institute for Social Research, Survey Research Center, University of Michigan Press, Ann Arbor, Mich., 1951.

[33] *Ibid.,* chap. III.

material, and manufacturing. Therefore, in order to ensure his tenure, he "stretches out" the work. He reasons, whether mistakenly or not, that working rapidly and efficiently may increase income for a while but may also mean a layoff. Furthermore he believes, perhaps mistakenly, that by restricting production he is warding off technological change or rationalization of production. He feels that these will follow if he earns too much money, that is, if he increases labor costs. One may argue, and with some truth, that the worker's reasoning is fallacious in the long run. But he has only his experience to judge by, and this tells him that if he slows down the pace of work there will be more work; that if he works too fast his job may be "rerated" or abolished entirely by the introduction of a new machine.

Secondly, restrictive practices may also reflect the drive of the worker for independence from the demands of technology and the discipline of the bureaucracy. The worker fights back against the tendency of modern technology to turn him into a cog in production or a machine, by holding the pace of work to what he considers a comfortable level, one which meets the rhythm of his own life. At the same time he gains recognition and response from his fellow workers for adhering to the demands of the group, for refusing to threaten the security and independence of his fellow workers.

Thus it seems possible to account for many restrictive practices without resorting to explanations which reduce the worker to a hedonistically calculating machine, or a nonlogically acting organism, or an unconscious respondent to states of morale. On the contrary, we would hold that the worker is capable of surprisingly logical calculation, given his experience, aspirations, and values on the one hand, and the realities of the role he plays, on the other. If, in fact, his efforts to achieve security by these means are doomed to failure, if his strength is puny compared to the forces which control him, his ignorance or his weakness should be blamed; but one should never make the mistake of denying that the worker has the power of rationality or other attributes of humanity.[34]

Summation. The informal group provides opportunities for the workingman to achieve certain aims and interests which he cannot achieve within the formal social structure of the plant. Without consciousness of rebellion, without consciousness of the social means which he is using, he strives, by social means, to overcome those aspects of the situation which threaten or deprive him. In none of the cases described in this chapter could it be said that leaders consciously formed these groups as devices for circumventing or combating management; rather it is the

---

[34] For a very interesting attempt to define the limits of action of the informal group, see Walter Firey, "Informal Organization and the Theory of Schism," *American Sociological Review*, vol. 13, no. 1, pp. 15–24, 1948.

situation which created the leader, or found the leader, who could give the workingman what he wanted. It may be concluded, therefore, that the informal group represents a basic reaction of the workingman to the social and physical environment of production; it is not a transitory phenomenon which can be abolished by an order of management.

But, on the other hand, the limitations of the informal group should also be stressed. Lacking formal organization, lacking a program or a policy, incapable of uniting with more than a few other groups of like kind, such a group is doomed to puny actions, or to providing illusory benefits to its members. Furthermore, it is relatively susceptible to domination by managerially oriented or self-oriented workers. Thus, under no circumstances should the informal group be considered on the same plane of power or importance as the union for achieving the interests of the workers.

PART THREE

The Social Structure of Trade Unionism

CHAPTER 10

Development of Trade Unionism in the United States

The social and ideological reactions of the worker to his role and to the strains within it form a most important part of the history of our times. To attempt to describe, even briefly, the various types of workers' reactions would demand much more space than there is in this volume. Here it may be said that workers have reacted to the disadvantages of their roles by forming producers' or consumers' cooperatives designed to eliminate management control, by political action aimed either at over-throw of the wage system or at drastic changes of the system, or by forming organizations designed to bring pressure to bear on employers, that is, trade unions. What is of importance to us here is the fact that in the United States the trade union has been the only important mode of worker action.

Early American Trade Unions. The beginnings of the trade-union movement in the United States can be discerned in the latter part of the eighteenth century. In 1786 the first genuine strike occurred—among Philadelphia printers.[1] Between 1792 and 1794 there appeared what were perhaps the first continuous workers' organizations; these also were in Philadelphia, among the shoemakers. Other organizations, already using the strike as their main weapon, soon appeared in other crafts. As-sociations of masters also appeared in opposition to the unions. These associations successfully fought labor through the courts, using the charge of conspiracy.

The nature of these early trade unions reflected the state of the in-dustrial system of the times. Production was in a prefactory stage, carried on in the shop or at home. The first labor organizations were as-sociations of workingmen against shop owners or masters. Just as pro-duction was locally organized, so were the trade unions. In no sense did these early unions constitute an organized labor movement, and, in

[1] John R. Commons et al., *History of Labour in the United States,* The Macmillan Company, New York, 1918, vol. I, p. 25.

207

any case, they soon faded away with the general downturn in business, following the War of 1812.

Unions under Mercantile Capitalism. After the War of 1812 America entered its long period of dominance by mercantile capitalism. Production increased somewhat, and alongside shop and home production there appeared the mill.[2] As the working force grew in numbers and strength, for the first time on American soil a true labor movement appeared. Trade associations or unions were formed or reformed in many crafts, and after 1820 strikes occurred, both in the crafts and in some of the early factories. In 1827 in Philadelphia the first city-wide organization of unions was formed, the Mechanics Union of Trade Associations. This organization set as its aim the attainment of social equality for workingmen.[3] These early union developments were a response to two conditions. On the one hand, under the goading of increased competition, mercantile employers sought to cut costs by holding down wages, lengthening the workday, breaking down the old master-worker relationship, and introducing women and children into industry. On the other hand there was the heady atmosphere supplied by Jacksonian democracy, with its war against the "aristocracy" and its exalting of the common man. Under these circumstances workers organized and raised their voices against "bankers" and other aristocrats. At the same time they demanded an end to social inequality, an end to imprisonment for debt, and an end to child labor in the New England mills. "Equality of opportunity" was their slogan, and the key to opportunity, these workingmen thought, was a system of free education.

It is interesting to note that in the early 1830s American labor moved, for a time, toward politics. Workingmen's parties were formed in various cities; in some cases they operated on state-wide bases. The aim of these parties was not to overthrow the existing society; they aimed, rather, to get labor representatives into the legislatures, in order that labor's goals might be achieved. Within a very short time these political parties had disappeared and labor had merged its political aims with the Jacksonian movement. Thus, even at this early date it can be seen that American workingmen had no aims *as a class;* rather workers wished to better themselves within the framework of capitalism, to share in the benefits of capitalism.[4]

Although labor parties disappeared, the trade-union movement went ahead for a time. Between 1833 and 1837 unions appeared in more and more crafts. In 1834 a National Trades Union met in New York City,

---

[2] For an account of the rise of American industry, see Chap. 3.

[3] Commons et al., *op. cit.*, pp. 189–192.

[4] Foster Rhea Dulles, *Labor in America,* Thomas Y. Crowell Company, New York, 1949, p. 51.

with delegates from various cities. While the union movement as a rule repudiated working-class politics, an attempt was made to influence legislation. The National Trades Union fought for the ten-hour day among government employees, and this was eventually granted, although not until after the National Union had dissolved. Unions also used the strike in the fight for the ten-hour day and other economic demands. Occasionally these strikes were won, although the economic power of the employers as well as the hostility of the courts was usually too much for the workers. In 1842, however, the cause of trade unionism was greatly aided when a decision of the Massachusetts Supreme Judicial Court declared unions nonconspiratorial, a doctrine which was followed for many years.[5]

By this time, however, the trade-union movement was in a serious decline. With the depression of 1837 trade unions began to lose membership, and in many cases disappeared entirely. As has been usually the case in American history, when the trade union sagged, the workers turned to other movements. In the period between 1837 and the Civil War there was considerable interest in the cooperative movement, and in such ventures as the Brook Farm experiment. On the political front labor tended to give strong support to the homestead movement, with its promise of economic independence.

Unions and the Rise of Industrialism. About 1850 began that great explosion of the industrial system, which was to lead to the subordination of the mercantile capitalists and the ruin of the Southern plantation owners. The mechanized factory came into being. Old trades were destroyed; the numbers of skilled workingmen decreased in one industry after another. Manning the new factories were the immigrants, streaming out from Western Europe, first, and then, from Eastern Europe. Strangers to the country, of differing nationalities and religions, it was to be many years before these new immigrants were integrated in the American labor movement. Meanwhile their presence depressed wages and undermined the existing labor organizations.

What unionism there was in the 1850s at the beginning of the period of industrial capitalism was confined to the skilled trades. National unions were formed among the printers, the locomotive engineers, and the hat workers; no attempt was made to enlist the new semiskilled and unskilled factory workers in the union movement. Even in the skilled trades, unions tended to flourish only in prosperous years; they sagged disastrously with every economic downturn. With the Civil War and prosperous conditions in the North, there was an upturn in the labor movement. This upturn reflected not only the increased need for labor,

[5] Selig Perlman, *A History of Trade Unionism in the United States,* The Macmillan Company, New York, 1922, pp. 25–26.

but also an inflation in prices and a lag in wages. Many more national trade unions were formed in the 1860s and in the early 1870s. By the time the depression of 1873 began, the trade unions numbered 300,000 members.

During this time several attempts were made to form associations of trade unions in response to the increasing size and power of industry. Numerous city assemblies of trade unions were formed in the 1860s, and in 1864 there was an abortive attempt at a national association. In 1866 the first national labor organization to have more than an ephemeral existence was formed. This was called the National Labor Union and was composed of national trade unions, city assemblies of trade unions, local trade unions, and reformist movements. The National Labor Union was "political-minded" and began a campaign for an eight-hour day among Federal employees. This was granted in 1868, but, disappointingly, private employers did not follow suit as had been expected. As early as 1866 the National Labor Union had resolved for an independent labor party. In the election of 1872 the National Labor Union constituted itself a political party, came out for Greenbackism, and proceeded to nominate a presidential slate. However, the withdrawal of the candidate for president plus the withdrawal of several national trade unions led to the collapse of the party.

Disappointment with the involvement of the National Labor Union in reformist politics and its failure to influence legislation led to a revival of pure trade unionism in the early 1870s. Several stern battles were waged for the eight-hour day, particularly in New York. However, the severe and long-continuing depression, beginning in 1873, not only put an end to trade-union activity but practically destroyed the labor movement. Of a total of 30 national unions existing in 1873, only 9 were left by 1877.[6] The craft unions had fallen victim to their failure to adapt to new industrial conditions—above all, to enlist the support of the masses of factory labor.

The depression of 1873 marked the beginning of years of hardship for the American worker, as wages fell and jobs disappeared. Lacking an outlet through an organized labor movement, the working class expressed its resentment through a series of bloody encounters with the employers and their agents. By far the greatest labor upheaval of this era—indeed, one of the greatest strikes in American history—occurred in 1877 among the railroad workers. This was the first national strike in America; it signified the national scope which industry was rapidly attaining. The strike was touched off by a reduction in the wages of workers for the Baltimore and Ohio. This reduction followed other pay cuts, which taken together had lowered the pay of even skilled workers to between

[6] Dulles, *op. cit.*, p. 112.

$1.35 and $1.58 for a day of fifteen or eighteen hours.[7] Although there were only a few weak organizations among the workers, strikes broke out and quickly spread to a number of railroads. Militia was called out to keep the trains running. In some places, the militiamen fraternized with the workers; in others, they carried out bloody fights with the strikers. The climax was reached at Pittsburgh when, following the killing of some twenty strikers by the militia, an infuriated crowd drove the militia into a roundhouse, which was then set on fire. The militiamen fought their way out, but the roundhouse and much other property was destroyed by the strikers. Federal troops were now called out, and in a series of bloody fights—most of the blood being spilled by the strikers— succeeded in breaking the strike in one city after another.

Thus ended the great strike of 1877. The total casualties were amazingly high: over a hundred people killed, and several hundred wounded. Millions of dollars of property had been destroyed. The workers had demonstrated their ability to conduct a national strike; the employers, their determination to oppose the strikers. Both parties to the conflict drew several conclusions from it. The employers had been badly frightened. Shaken out of their complacency, they moved to prevent action by workers. The old conspiracy laws were revived, workers were bound by oaths not to join unions, outright intimidation of workers was practiced. As for the workers, they concluded, naturally enough, that above all they needed an organization powerful enough to resist the might of management.

The Knights of Labor. After the failures of the 1870s, only two centers of labor organization remained in the United States: the group known as the Knights of Labor, and a small number of craft unions centering around the International Cigar Makers' Union, headed by men like Adolph Strasser and Samuel Gompers. The Knights of Labor had been founded in 1869 by Uriah S. Stephens, a tailor. It was, at first, a secret organization, surrounded by ritual and composed of skilled workers in the main. In 1878, when it was forced to come out into the open because of public distrust of secret organizations, leadership passed to Terrence V. Powderly, a machinist. Throughout the first years of its existence, the Knights of Labor grew very slowly, and as an organization, it did not play an important role in the 1877 strikes. Its time was to come in the 1880s.

In its stated position, the Knights of Labor was a reformist organization, rather than a revolutionary one. It stood for unionization in order to check the power of capital and for certain types of reformist legislation, for instance, the abolishment of prison labor and of child labor.

[7] Samuel Yellen, *American Labor Struggles,* Harcourt, Brace and Company, Inc., New York, 1936, p. 9.

Perhaps its most radical demand was for government ownership of railways and the telegraph system and for a graduated tax on income. On the economic front, its main demand was for the eight-hour day. But, at least in the thinking of its leader, Powderly, the Knights of Labor was most interested in producers' cooperatives; all other goals were considered subsidiary or merely palliative, as compared to this central purpose. In so far as tactics were concerned, the Knights of Labor officially favored the boycott over the strike as a weapon against employers. In actuality, many of the leaders of the organization deplored the use of the strike and yearned for arbitration to settle disputes, while labor made its way toward its goal—a commonwealth of cooperatives.

The Knights of Labor is usually thought of as an early expression of industrial unionism. This view is accurate in part, but even more the structure of the Knights of Labor organization resembled the structure of the American Federation of Labor, as it developed later. The basic unit of the Knights of Labor was the "assembly," organized in a single craft. Where no effective assembly could be organized on craft lines, workers were admitted indiscriminately to existing assemblies. Such workers were called "sojourners," and their assemblies were called "mixed assemblies." Under this system, miners, steelworkers, railway workers, etc., joined the Knights of Labor. So great was the influx of these mass-production workers that eventually mixed assemblies outnumbered the pure assemblies.[8] Local assemblies of mixed or pure variety were organized either into district assemblies or into trade districts, which were composed of unions of a single craft in a given area. Above these was the General Assembly, with an executive board, which supplied the leadership for the organization. If, then, the Knights of Labor was committed to industrial unionism, it was not primarily in terms of organization, but only in so far as it admitted unskilled workers from different industries to its "mixed assemblies."

In the late 1870s the depression eased off, and the membership of the Knights of Labor began to grow. In 1879 membership totaled 20,151; by 1883 it was 51,914.[9] In the early 1880s the Knights of Labor, in spite of its dislike of strikes, found itself increasingly in the middle of conflicts which were invariably lost by the strikers. When depression returned in 1884 and 1885 the workers, feeling the power of organization, were in a militant mood. General strikes, sympathetic strikes, boycotts, political activity were symptoms of this militancy. With the revival of prosperity in 1885 the strike wave mounted even higher. In that year two major strikes on the railroad system were fought out. The second

[8] Edward Levinson, *Labor on the March,* Harper & Brothers, New York, 1938, p. 29.
[9] Perlman, *op. cit.,* pp. 82–83.

resulted in an astounding victory for the strikers. Although the Knights of Labor was to retreat before this railroad in a few months, nevertheless for the first time an organization of workingmen had taken the measure of a giant corporation.

What happened next was to be paralleled in American labor history only by the growth of the CIO. A great rush began to join the Knights of Labor; skilled and unskilled workers, women, Negroes, even farmers, shopkeepers and small employers flocked in. In the period between July 1, 1885, and June 30, 1886, the number of local assemblies rose from 1,610 to 5,892; the membership rose from around 100,000 to over 700,-000.[10] Nothing like it had ever been seen before; for a time the Knights of Labor had to suspend admissions, so great was the number seeking to join. It is with justice that Professor Perlman has referred to this era as the period of the "great upheaval."

Yet as quickly as the Knights of Labor had flashed up from the horizon, so quickly did it plunge out of sight again. Within two years it lost 200,000 members; by 1893 only 75,000 were left in the organization. What had happened? Many differing answers have been offered. Some of the blame must be assigned to the inept leadership provided by Powderly, with his concern for utopian ideals and his dislike for strikes. Some of the blame must be assigned to the impetuosity of the workers, who joined the organization in order to strike. But the strikes, when they came, all ended disastrously; in the packing industry, on the railroads, in shipping. The workers became discouraged and drifted away. They had overestimated their own power and underestimated the resources and determination of the employers. Nor perhaps was the American working class suitable material at that time for a national, mass labor movement. Of labor's militancy there was no question, but this militancy was confined to a single strike, to a single employer. There was little consciousness among workingmen of the need for labor solidarity. The American working class was split among racial, national, and religious groups, some of which were hostile to each other. It was all too easy for employers to exploit these hostilities. But whatever the reasons, by 1890 mass unionism was dead, and it was not to reappear for almost half a century.

The Haymarket Affair. The year 1886 was also to witness another event destined to have a long and continuing influence on the American labor movement. This was the Haymarket riot in Chicago.[11] The origins of the riot go back to the attempt to bring revolutionary ideas to the American working class. Radicalism made its initial appearance among

[10] Dulles, *op. cit.*, p. 141.
[11] This account is based largely on the work of Henry David, *The History of the Haymarket Affair,* Rinehart & Company, Inc., New York, 1936.

American workers following the Civil War. Various small, revolutionary organizations, often violently disagreeing among themselves as to purposes and methods, appeared at that time. In 1876 the Socialist Labor party was formed, by far the most impressive radical organization to appear up to that time. Even this organization was seriously split internally, and one of the splits centered around the use of force. The group favoring force, composed mostly of German immigrants, eventually formed themselves into several tiny organizations. These organizations, which came to be known popularly as "anarchistic" organizations, were determined to convince the American working class of the necessity for the violent destruction of capitalism. To this end they carried on a campaign of propaganda, both of the "word" and of the "deed."

By 1886 the strongest anarchistic organizations were in Chicago. Anarchists were active there in the labor struggles connected with the "great upheaval." At that time labor was struggling for the eight-hour day in many different industries and crafts. A particularly bitter struggle raged around the McCormick harvester factory. This struggle had begun as a lockout which had turned into a full-fledged strike. In May, 1886, a fight flared between the strikers and the police, which left one striker dead and several strikers and police wounded. The enraged anarchists called for a mass meeting to protest the killings. This meeting was peaceful almost to the end, when for reasons never explained, police suddenly advanced to disperse the crowd. At this point a bomb was thrown—it has never been determined by whom—killing one policeman outright (several more died later) and wounding many others.

Immediately a wave of hysteria of a magnitude never seen before broke over the country. Radicals of all descriptions were rounded up by the police; newspaper headlines screamed out stories of imminent anarchistic revolution. Eventually eight anarchist leaders were arrested and tried in an atmosphere which practically precluded the possibility of a fair trial. Although there was no evidence to prove that any of the anarchists had manufactured or thrown the bomb, all eight were convicted. Seven were sentenced to be hung; one, to fifteen years in prison. Then a reaction set in, and for months a struggle was waged over the anarchists' lives. The Knights of Labor, which had condemned the anarchists in terms as strong as any, split over the issue of clemency. Powderly led the antianarchist faction, but rank-and-file sentiment generally opposed the execution. Prominent liberals rallied behind the anarchists. Gompers made a trip to the Governor of Illinois to plead for clemency. On the other side were ranged almost all the newspapers, most employers, and most of the conservative forces in the country. Eventually the sentences of two of the anarchists were commuted to life imprisonment. However, four others went to the gallows. By this time the protest had grown world-wide, and the executions instantly created four martyrs. Nor was the story to stop there, for in 1893 Governor Altgeld of Illinois pardoned the anarchists and thereby reopened the searing issues of the case.

The Haymarket riot had several consequences, some immediate and some of a long-term nature. It enabled the employers to open an immediate counteroffensive against labor movements in general. This counterattack may very well have played a part in the decline of the Knights of Labor. At the same time, while it is not accurate to say that the Haymarket affair signaled the end of radical unionism in the United States, there can be little doubt that it convinced labor leaders like Gompers of the necessity of staying clear of radicalism. The anti-labor campaign forced labor into political activity, which resulted in several local victories in Chicago and Milwaukee and a relatively large vote for Henry George in his campaign for mayor in New York. In the long run the significance of the Haymarket riot lay perhaps in what it came to symbolize: the possibilities and limitations of radical action by workers on the one hand, and the determination and ability of conservative forces to resist radicalism on the other.

The American Federation of Labor. By the late 1880s both the attempt to organize the great masses of new factory labor and the attempt to turn American labor into a revolutionary path had failed decisively. This left the field clear for the craft union; and, in fact, the craft union was practically to dominate the American labor movement until the middle 1930s.

Oddly enough, the craft-union movement, like the anarchist movement, was an offshoot of labor radicalism. The First International, which was an organization of labor groups dominated by Marxists, had declared for a program of trade unionism, as opposed to a purely political movement.[12] Men like Samuel Gompers and Adolph Strasser were much influenced by this dictum and proceeded to build a strong union among the cigar markers. This union stressed immediate interest in wages and hours, benefits such as unemployment insurance, discipline and organization, and the building up of a central fund as a financial reserve. The union waged several stern battles with employers in its field and, in the end, managed to win through.

In the course of daily struggles with employers and in the course of meeting the problems of organization, discipline, and morale, the thinking of the leaders of the union became transformed. This transformation is typified by the case of Samuel Gompers. Gompers was born in England, and migrated as a boy to the United States.[13] At first attracted

---

[12] Perlman, *op. cit.*, p. 75.
[13] For an account of Gomper's life, his influence on the labor movement, and the development of his thinking, see his autobiography: Samuel Gompers, *Seventy Years of Life and Labor*, E. P. Dutton & Co., Inc., New York, 1925, 2 vols.

by Marxist thought, he soon abandoned interest in revolutionary ideals and utopias, and busied himself, first, with the organization of the workers in his own craft, and later with the growth and federation of craft unions. Although Gompers never formally abandoned interest in the organization of the great masses of unskilled labor, he held firmly to the principles of craft organization, that is, organization in terms of single occupation or skill. His stated hope was to raise all the workers in the United States to the level of "skilled workers."[14] Later his lack of interest in radicalism was transformed into open opposition. He became a firm opponent of socialism, declaring it economically unsound, socially wrong, and industrially impossible.[15] In his opposition to radicalism and to industrial unions, in his emphasis on the politcial neutrality of labor, on the policy of rewarding political friends and punishing enemies, in his concern with immediate goals, Gompers neatly typified conservative trade unionism in the United States.

Although the leaders of craft unionism might eschew the unskilled workers, certain forces were pushing the skilled workers into national federation. These forces included the organization of industry on a national scale, the formation of national employers' associations, and the growing might of management which local craft unions could not match. In addition, craft unionism sought national federation because of fear of the unskilled worker who, with the introduction of machinery, was threatening craft jobs. Consequently, in 1881 was organized the Federation of Organized Trade and Labor Unions of the United States and Canada, a loose alliance of craft unions and dissident groups from within the Knights of Labor. After a struggle, unskilled workers were admitted into the union, but principles of wide-sweeping social reform were rejected in favor of a program of economic reform: child labor laws, immigration control acts, the abolition of prison labor, etc. The model for the constitution of this organization, it is interesting to note, was the British Trade Union Congress.[16]

The Federation was destined to have a short life. The program of economic reforms received short shrift from the major political parties. The craft unions were scarcely interested in the political and economic programs. The immediate spark which was to galvanize them into action to secure a truly workable federation was the threat to craft unionism arising from the Knights of Labor. At first, it seemed that an alliance could be worked out between the two organizations; many of the leaders of the Federation were members of the Knights of Labor, and there was

---

[14] *Ibid.*, vol. I. pp. 147–148.

[15] *Ibid.*, p. 397.

[16] Lewis L. Lorwin, *The American Federation of Labor*, Brookings Institution, Washington, D.C., 1933, pp. 12–13.

a good deal of mutual sympathy between the two organizations. But as the Knights of Labor moved into the "great upheaval" period, a determined drive was opened to capture the craft unions. Craft unions were admitted into the Knights of Labor, expelled members of craft unions were welcomed, and rival unions were encouraged in certain lines, notably among the cigar makers. The result was intense conflict. But while, in one aspect, this was a contest for power and prestige among two rival organizations, basically the question at issue was whether the skilled workers were to be a subordinate part of a mass labor movement, or whether they were to retain their identity, and independence of action. The conflict was, then, between two distinct sections of the working class.[17]

The breaking point between the craft unions and the Knights of Labor was reached in the great strikes for the eight-hour day in 1886, which we have already discussed in connection with the Haymarket riot. The Federation threw itself into the struggle, thereby placing itself at the head of what was essentially an immense grass-roots upsurge. The top leadership of the Knights of Labor bitterly opposed the strike; their motives were fear of a huge industrial conflict and jealousy of the Federation. During the height of the eight-hour movement, five craft-union officials issued a call for a conference. When the conference met it delivered an ultimatum to the Knights of Labor which would have meant in effect the abandoning of industrial unionism and the subordination of the Knights of Labor to the craft unions.[18] The Knights of Labor, then at the height of its power, scornfully rejected this proposal. The craft unions then issued a call for a conference in December, 1886. To this conference came delegates from 25 unions. Resolving that the old Federation was too weak, too diffuse, to carry out labor's program, the delegates decided to create a new organization. Thus was born the American Federation of Labor. Samuel Gompers was elected its first president.

The structure of the new organization was centered on a recognition of the autonomy of each of the constituent unions. The national or international union was to have full power over its members and full power in dealing with employers. The backbone of the Federation was thus the national union, although state federations of labor were also admitted to the organization. The unions were guaranteed certain jurisdictional areas, and machinery was set up for resolving jurisdictional disputes. The executive function of the organization was placed in a council, consisting of a president, two vice presidents, a secretary, and a treasurer. This council had the power to issue charters, to decide

[17] See Perlman, *op. cit.*, pp. 115–116.
[18] Lorwin, *op. cit.*, pp. 20–21.

issues between unions, to draw up legislative programs, to extend financial help to strike- or boycott-bound unions. The whole program was financed by a small per capita tax on members of the Federation. However, the powers of the executive council to tax, to issue orders to unions, to promote legislative programs, were purposely kept weak. Whatever solidarity the AFL was to attain would be based on sentiment, on education, and on moral persuasion.

It should be emphasized that while the AFL, both in its earlier and later periods, backed certain legislative programs, the central purpose of the organization was economic. From the first, the Federation was primarily interested in the issues of wages and hours. It steadfastly refused to endorse a labor party; it contented itself with a policy of "watchful waiting" to see which politicians were friendly or unfriendly to labor. The policy of the AFL may be summed up on the economic side by the slogan "get more" and on the political side by "reward your friends and punish your enemies."

The first years of the Federation's existence were marked by slow growth and by constant struggle with the Knights of Labor. The income of the Federation slowly increased, and by 1892, after five years of existence, the Federation consisted of some 40 unions, of which about 25 or 30 were active. Certainly, the growth of the AFL in those years was very modest. But during those same years the Knights of Labor was fading into insignificance.

In spite of the imposing growth of the Knights of Labor during the "great upheaval," the Federation proved to have superior staying power under American conditions. For one thing, the structure of the AFL, with its provision for union autonomy based on craft principles, suited the non-class-conscious American worker, who was dominated by an individualistic mentality. The skilled worker, often of native stock and with middle-class ambitions, felt precious little identification with foreign-born immigrants, lately removed from peasantry, of differing ethnic and religious background. Furthermore, unlike the Knights of Labor, AFL unions proved that they knew how to organize and win strikes. The similar backgrounds of the union members, the identity of interests of the strikers, the limited objectives and the limited size of Federation strikes made the AFL an effective organization.[19] Furthermore, the Federation quickly took care, under the leadership of Gompers, to dissociate itself from radicals. It thereby escaped the onus of the Haymarket riot, achieving a limited amount of respectability and a degree of acceptance in the country. Yet when all due praise is given to the leaders of the AFL for their knowledge of American life, it must not be forgotten that they achieved their ends at the sacrifice of the great

[19] Perlman, *op. cit.*, pp. 121–122.

masses of factory labor—that they gave up the attempt to secure for labor a powerful voice in national affairs.

The Development of the AFL. By the decade of the 1890s the Knights of Labor was on the decline, the AFL was a small and struggling organization, the left wing was tiny and badly divided. Under the circumstances, the economic and social condition of the American working class was determined by the amount of available labor and the economic cycle. Neither of these factors favored the workers; the mass immigration assured a continual surplus of workers, while the panic of 1893 depressed industrial activity. Wages were universally low, and hours were long. The resultant mass poverty and resentment were to erupt in this decade in bitter labor struggles and, as these failed, in a renewed interest in political programs.

One of the most bitter battles was fought out between the Association of Iron and Steel Workers, an AFL union, and the Carnegie Steel Company, owned by Andrew Carnegie and managed by Henry Clay Frick. This fight centered around the Homestead, Pennsylvania, plant, which had become unionized after a successful strike in 1890. Although relationships between management and the union were never friendly, a contract between the two groups had been worked out. The strength of the contract was seemingly reinforced by the expressed sympathy of Andrew Carnegie for labor unions. Later research has indicated that some of this sympathy may have sprung from Carnegie's scheme to strangle competition by imposing high labor costs on other steel mills.[20] Once competition had been disposed of, Carnegie apparently had no intention of suffering a union in his works. The selection of Frick, who had a long antilabor record, for the post of manager, was thus no accident.

When the time for the renewal of the contract arrived, in 1892, the company demanded that the workers take a wage cut. The workers refused, and the company began a lockout, which, in turn, precipitated a strike. The company determined to break the strike by sending into the plant a force of men recruited by the Pinkerton detective agency. Since it was impossible to bring the Pinkertons through the picket lines which the workers had established around the plant, the company placed the strikebreakers on barges which sailed up the river to the plant. The strikers, however, learned of this maneuver, invaded company property, and offered resistance. A day-long gun fight followed, which resulted in the death of three Pinkertons and seven strikers, besides many wounded. Finally, the Pinkertons surrendered and were marched through the strikers. The company now demanded militia, which was obligingly sent, and relative peace settled over Homestead. The company then moved

[20] See Yellen, *op. cit.*, pp. 75–76.

against the strikers on the legal front. The strike leaders were arrested on charges of murder. Although they were eventually acquitted, the strike was effectively deprived of leadership. Nationally, the company advertised the rightness of its cause, and when Frick was attacked and wounded by an anarchist, the cause of management was greatly aided. Buffeted by militia, by the courts, by public opinion, watching their jobs being taken by others, the strikers weakened and finally broke. The strike ended in November, 1892.

The Homestead strike was a particularly bitter defeat for labor. Again the employers had demonstrated their power. They could use against strikers a whole arsenal of weapons: strikebreakers, scabs, courts, public opinion, militia, Federal troops. Against this the workers could oppose not even an united labor movement, but only their endurance and determination. These were not enough. The steelworkers' union was practically destroyed. Unionism was finished in the whole vast Pittsburgh industrial complex for decades to come.

Labor was soon to get another lesson in the sort of power that employers could command directly or indirectly. This time the test came again on the railroads. Prior to 1893, the only organization among the railroad workers consisted of several "brotherhoods." The brotherhoods had participated in the great 1877 strike, but had thereafter grown increasingly nonmilitant. They had even refused to join the AFL. Dissatisfaction with the conservatism and ineffectiveness of the brotherhoods led to the formation, in 1893, of the American Railway Union, an industrial union. By June, 1894, the union had some 150,000 members. The leader of the railway union was Eugene Victor Debs, formerly secretary-treasurer of the Brotherhood of Locomotive Firemen, and in future years destined to be the standard-bearer of socialism in the United States.

Among the members of the new union were thousands of employees of the Pullman Palace Car Company. By 1894 these workers had accumulated many grievances; unemployment during the depression of 1893 had been very severe, and when employment finally picked up wages were reduced from 25 to 40 per cent. Another source of grievance arose from conditions in the company town of Pullman. Pullman was ostensibly a model town of green lawns, parks, and landscaped gardens. But Pullman was also a company town; the company owned all the houses (for which it charged rather high rents), supplied gas and water, disposed of sewage, ran the bank and the library.[21] Resentment against these conditions finally spilled over into action, and the workers chose a committee to demand the restoration of wage cuts. The answer

[21] *Ibid.*, p. 102.

of the company was to discharge the members of the committee. Immediately, the workers "went out," demanding the reinstatement of the discharged workers, the lowering of rents, and the restoration of the wage cut.

The strike started peacefully. But the company refused to meet officials of the Railway Union. In order to bring pressure to bear on the company, the union decided not to handle Pullman cars on any train in the nation. Railroad management now rallied behind the Pullman Company. The General Manager's Association, representing some 24 railroads, ordered all workers refusing to handle Pullman cars fired. This order immediately resulted in wholesale dismissals, and the strike spread over a good part of the nation's railroad system. The success of the strike was a great surprise to management; the workers were better organized and disciplined than ever before, and through peaceable means they brought to a halt most freight traffic in and out of Chicago. The strikers also stood firm against a newspaper barrage leveled against them. Management now adopted a different tactic. Not trusting Altgeld, the Governor of Illinois, they demanded Federal troops. Cleveland acceded to their wishes, on the grounds that the strikers were interfering with passage of the mail. Although Altgeld protested Cleveland's action, the troops began to move trains. The brotherhoods ordered their men back to work, but the strikers remained firm. The government then sought and obtained an injunction which ordered the Railway Union to refrain from interfering with the mails, with interstate commerce, and from hindering the business of any of the railroad companies. In addition, strikers were forbidden to compel or persuade other workers to go on strike. Picketing thus became a crime, in one case striking was declared a crime. These "crimes" were punishable directly by the judge who issued the injunction. The union refused to abide by these injunctions. The strike leaders were then indicted on grounds of conspiracy to obstruct interstate commerce, to hinder delivery of the mails, and to deprive citizens of their rights under the Constitution. The response of Debs was to attempt to organize a general strike in Chicago, but this failed, at least in part because of the opposition of Gompers. Under the attack of courts and troops, the strike began to weaken. Debs and other strike leaders were sentenced to jail. The strike collapsed.

Thus, in spite of organization, discipline, and peaceful tactics, organized labor had lost another major fight. Once again management demonstrated that it could rely on public opinion, on the mass media, on the government. And, now, for the first time, management demonstrated that it had an ally in the courts. The courts were to prove for many years the strongest of all weapons in the hands of management.

The defeats at Homestead and in the railway strike forced labor on the defensive. Yet even these defeats, taken in conjunction with the hard times of 1893, did not serve to disrupt the American Federation of Labor. Between 1893 and 1896 the membership of the AFL remained stationary at about 275,000. This was the first time that a major labor organization had managed to survive a depression. Elsewhere, labor turned to politics. Socialism grew in strength, under the spur of economic hardship and defeat, and made a determined bid to turn the AFL from an economic organization into a political one. This bid was finally defeated, but not before the AFL was forced to adopt a political program and Gompers was deprived of the presidency for one year, 1895. Other political movements also occupied the workers' attention. Populism attracted some labor support for a while, and the AFL barely resisted being drawn into the campaign to elect Bryan in 1896. But the aspirations of the Middle Western farmers had little intrinsic appeal to the mass of American workers, who knew that, for better or worse, their fate was tied up with industrial-urban civilization.

The Period 1898–1917. This period held different meanings and experience for the American worker. The mass of American factory labor remained unorganized, and for this group the economic and social situation remained unpromising. Real wages actually declined slightly, and working conditions and hours, in spite of some legislation, remained poor. In addition, the constant technological advance and the unceasing waves of migration were continuing threats to the unorganized worker, who was in no position to defend himself.

For the AFL, on the other hand, this was a period of advance, though there were retreats too. After remaining stationary in numbers until 1898 with about 280,000 members, the membership of the AFL began to increase rapidly. By 1904 membership had risen to 1,676,000, a six-fold increase. In 1905 a reaction set in and membership decreased by 200,000. Membership then remained stable until 1910, when growth was resumed. By 1913 the 2 million mark was in sight. But even this figure represented only 7 or 8 per cent of the working force.[22]

During this period the organized, skilled workers made certain gains. The eight-hour day was extended into new fields. Trade agreements were signed in numerous industries. Furthermore, the craft unions successfully resisted wage reductions after the depression of 1907.

Significantly, in the coal strike of 1902 organized labor won at least a partial victory. The strike grew out of numerous grievances: low pay, unfair methods of weighing coal, dangerous conditions at work, long hours. The United Mine Workers, which had been formed in 1897, had succeeded by 1902 in organizing many coal miners; it led the strike in the coal fields. In spite of great propaganda barrages against the

[22] Perlman, *op. cit.*, pp. 163–164.

strikers and the use of militia, the strike continued into the winter months, threatening a coal famine. At the intervention of President Theodore Roosevelt, the strikers agreed to go back to work pending the findings of an arbitration commission. Several concessions were finally granted the miners, but their main aim, the recognition of the union, was denied them. Nevertheless, the miners had demonstrated that they could successfully organize and fight against a large corporation, and even succeed, in some measure, in gaining the support of public opinion.

The employers scarcely viewed these gains with equanimity. A small group of them supported the conciliatory National Civic Federation, of which Gompers was an official. Most of the employers, however, supported the "open-shop" movement. This movement was led by the National Association of Manufacturers. An offshoot of the NAM, the Citizens Industrial Associations, attempted, with some success, to involve nonindustrialists in the fight against labor. Labor was attacked by these groups on two fronts, the political and the judicial. In the crucial Danbury Hatters' Case, the courts declared that the boycott, or any other action designed to hurt the company's business, was illegal and subject to injunction. On the political front, the employers strove mainly to prevent legislatures from interfering with the power of injunction. With the depression of 1907 and the reappearance of mass unemployment, some employers began to void labor contracts. Some unionists replied with violence. This campaign of "dynamite" culminated in 1911 with the bombing of the Los Angeles *Times* building, which resulted in the loss of 20 lives. Tactics of violence succeeded in stemming the employers' counteroffensive in some instances, but it also resulted in alienating public opinion, and labor probably lost more than it gained by these tactics.

As the AFL stagnated or retreated, the stock of radical unionism rose. As early as 1895, the socialist Daniel de Leon, having failed to capture the AFL, had set up a rival organization, the Social Trade and Labor Alliance. This threat to whatever labor unity did exist at that time incurred the bitter enmity not only of the AFL but of other socialists, who were opposed to splitting the trade-union movement. De Leon's maneuver soon failed, but not before a faction of his party had broken away. This dissident faction joined with a group led by Debs to form the Socialist party in 1901. The Socialist party at its first convention affirmed its belief in trade unions and labor solidarity. The Socialists gained considerable support even within the AFL; in the 1912 convention, their candidate for the presidency of the AFL received nearly a third of the votes. On the political scene, the Socialist party, under the leadership of Debs, made good progress; in 1912 it received nearly a million votes in the presidential campaign, the equivalent of four million votes in 1950.

Impatience with AFL also led to the formation, in 1905, of the Industrial Workers of the World. At the core of this organization was the Western Federation of Miners, which had fought many bitter battles with employers, notably in the Cripple Creek section of Colorado, in 1903–1904. In this organization the Western miners joined hands with the radical socialists of the Eastern Cities. The IWW rejected the AFL program of gradual economic betterment and called for the abolition of the wage system. It rejected craft unionism in favor of industrial unionism. Moved by a militant revolutionary fervor, the IWW threw itself into the task of organizing the migratory workers of the West and the immigrant masses of the cities. In the West, members of the IWW engaged in a spectacular series of "free-speech" fights, staging mass invasion of towns in which they felt their rights were being denied. In the East the IWW led several important strikes. Particularly notable was the strike at Lawrence, Massachusetts, in 1912, among Polish immigrant textile workers. This strike began as a spontaneous protest against a reduction in wages; leadership was subsequently supplied by the IWW. After a long fight, marked by some blunders on the part of management, the strike was won. This was perhaps the high-water mark of the IWW.

But the IWW was destined to have a short life. By its very concentration on militant working-class action, it neglected organization. Thus after the victory in the Lawrence strike, no permanent IWW union remained in that city. Furthermore, the victory at Lawrence was not repeated. In 1913 important strikes were lost, notably at Paterson, New Jersey. In addition, the IWW ran into stern opposition, both from the AFL and from employers. An intense propaganda barrage succeeded in convincing many Americans of the foreign and seditious nature of the IWW. The refusal of the IWW to support the war with Germany seemed to many to confirm the treasonable nature of the organization. Propaganda was followed by legislation, by court orders, and by much extralegal violence, lynchings, beatings, tar-and-feather parties. When eventually some 94 members of the IWW, including one of its best-known leaders, William Haywood, were convicted of sedition, the organization was deprived of its effective leadership. By the end of the war, the IWW had practically passed from the picture.

Labor in World War I. The labor movement divided sharply over American entry into World War I. The left wing, including the IWW and those socialists who followed Debs, concluded that the war was among rival imperial powers, and that labor had everything to lose and nothing to gain by supporting the war. Many of the left-wing leaders, including Haywood and Debs, went to jail for their beliefs. Gompers, on the other hand, believed that the contest was between Germanic sub-ordination of individualism on the one hand, and democratic institutions, on the other.[23] Supported in this belief by other AFL leaders, Gompers swung his organization first behind preparations for war and then behind the war effort itself.

However, the AFL, whose membership had grown to 2,371,434 in 1917, demanded certain concessions for its support of the war. Most immediately, it demanded relief from rising prices. Labor also wished representation on the national governmental boards then being formed to manage the war effort. Labor demanded recognition of its right to organize. In response to these demands, Wilson appointed a National War Labor Board to handle all labor disputes which could not be settled by other means. This Board acted on the basis of certain principles for which labor had long striven; the right to organize and bargain col-lectively, the application of the eight-hour day where possible, equal pay for women, etc. In return, labor promised not to strike. Of more uncertain advantage to labor was the provision that all existing agree-ments in respect to union shops or open shops were to be frozen until after the war.[24]

Under the provisions of this agreement, labor made certain advances during the war. Between 1917 and 1919, unions gained more than a million members; by 1919 total union membership was 4,125,000.[25] Real wages advanced considerably, reversing the long downward trend of the early part of the century. And, certainly not least, for the first time labor was given some sort of a voice in national affairs.

Labor in the Decade of the 1920s. The peace between management and labor came to a crashing end with the armistice in 1918. The Labor Board, which had governed labor-management relations during the war, ceased to function. Labor prepared to move for higher wages, to match the soaring postwar prices, and for recognition for many newly formed unions. Management, unhappy over labor's war gains, prepared a grim resistance. Strikes now broke out everywhere; among the shipyard workers of Seattle (this turned into a general strike), among Lawrence textile workers, among miners, among garment workers. Even the actors organized, and then, in an event traumatic to many, the Boston police organized and staged an ill-fated strike.

However, by far the most important strike was staged among the steelworkers. The outcome of this strike was to determine the fate of

[23] Gompers, *op. cit.*, vol. II, p. 350.
[24] Dulles, *op. cit.*, p. 227.
[25] Leo Wolman, *Ebb and Flow in Trade Unionism,* National Bureau of Economic Research, Inc., New York, 1936, p. 16.

organized labor for the next decade and a half. The steelworkers labored under severe conditions. The wages of the skilled workers in the industry were high, but the unskilled and semiskilled workers received wages below the minimum subsistence level in many cases. Hours were long; the twelve-hour day was in force in many mills. Foremen were arbitrary; spies were everywhere.[26] Discontent among steelworkers was so strong that, when an organizing drive was launched by a federation of 24 national and international AFL unions, within a short time 100,000 workers joined up. Impatient for action, the steelworkers practically forced the strike, which began in September, 1919. Under the leadership of William Z. Foster, later to become a prominent Communist, but then a union organizer, some 350,000 men left the mills. A grim struggle began, with the workers pitting their newly formed organization against the might of the United States Steel Corporation. The issue was not long in doubt. The steel company used Negro strike breakers, exploited racial, ethnic, and religious antagonisms, and had the assistance of police and state troopers. In addition, it raised the cry of Bolshevism against the strikers, a weapon all the more effective because of the Red scare through which the nation was going at that time. The employers held that the strike was a part of a Bolshevist plot to turn the United States into a Soviet state. This charge was given wide circulation by the press and received considerable acceptance by the public. Under all these pressures the strike weakened, and by January, 1920, had completely collapsed. The workers had failed to win a single concession from the steel companies.

With strikes lost everywhere, trade unionism beat a universal retreat. The depression of 1921 further added to labor's troubles; five million were thrown out of work, and wages were depressed. This led to further strikes, which management was able to counter through the use of the injunction, notably in the strike of shopmen on the railroads in 1922. Year by year the trade unions lost members; 266,500 were lost in 1921, 733,900 in 1922, and 405,400 in 1923. From its peak of 5,047,800 members in 1920, union membership fell to 3,622,000 by 1923.[27]

With the development of prosperity in the twenties, strike violence and interest in unionism declined. Real wages rose to unprecedented heights. The stopping of immigration removed an important depressant of wages. It was true that perhaps 10 to 13 per cent of the working force was idle at any one time, mostly because of technological change. Nor did all the workers participate equally in prosperity. The outbreak

[26] See the Interchurch World Movement Report, *Report on the Steel Strike of 1919*, Harcourt, Brace and Company, Inc., New York, 1920. For a summary of grievances, see pp. 11–14.

[27] Wolman, *op. cit.*, p. 26.

of bitter strikes in the textile industry, notably at Gastonia and Passaic, attested to depressed conditions in that field. But in general labor had reason to be satisfied with its economic position.

Management, however, did not trust to prosperity alone to check worker interest in unions. A many-sided attack against unionism was launched. Under the attractive title of the "American plan," the NAM and other trade associations led a fight for the open shop as the natural habitat for the free and independent American workingmen. At the same time, unions were castigated as "un-American," "Bolshevistic," corrupt, and exploitative. In nonunion plants, workers were often subjected to "yellow-dog" contracts,[28] labor spies, black lists, armed guards, and the threat of strikebreakers. The courts continued to support management, validating yellow-dog contracts, issuing injunctions more frequently than ever before, and invalidating minimum-wage legislation. On the positive side, management launched a movement which came to be known as "welfare capitalism." This movement aimed to turn the worker from unionism and to increase productivity by bettering the conditions of work. Profit-sharing schemes, stock-owning plans, pensions, insurance programs, shop associations, industrial-relations plans, and perhaps most notably, company unions were the tools with which management hoped to cement the harmony between itself and labor. By 1926 company unions had about half as many members as the AFL.[29]

Under the conditions of prosperity and employer attack, unionism dwindled, something which had never happened before in prosperous times. Between 1923 and 1929, the unions lost membership each year with the exception of 1927. In 1929 union membership totaled 3,442,600, a million and a half less than the peak figure of 1920.[30] These union members were largely skilled workers; the unskilled remained ununionized and ignored.

Under these circumstances the initial reaction of organized labor was to move toward politics. The Progressive party under the leadership of Senator La Follette of Wisconsin had declared for an end to injunctions, recognition of the right to organize, the curbing of monopolies, and other reforms. In the 1924 campaign, the AFL endorsed the candidacy of La Follette; however, it contributed little money to his campaign, and, in fact, several of the most important unions repudiated the action of the AFL entirely. Although La Follette received 5 million votes in the election, he carried only Wisconsin. Discouraged at its failure to deliver the labor vote, the AFL now reasserted its traditional political neutrality.

---

[28] That is, contracts between employers and employees, binding the employees not to join a union during term of employment.

[29] Dulles, *op. cit.*, p. 256.

[30] Wolman, *op. cit.*, p. 16.

The death of Samuel Gompers in 1924 brought William Green to the presidency of the AFL. A supporter of Gompers, he was, like Gompers, a conservative in trade-union policies. He was opposed to government interference in unions and to welfare legislation. He was willing to accept management's attempt to harmonize labor-management relationships, although he drew the line at the company union. Under Green's leadership the AFL offered itself as a bulwark against radical unionism and attempted to persuade management to accept the AFL lest something worse occur. However, AFL attempts to move into Southern industry and into the automobile industry on this basis failed.

The Depression. The crash of 1929 was as much a surprise to labor as to the American nation. By the end of 1930, 7 million people had lost their jobs. By 1932 the figure was 15 million. Before the depression ended, industrial production and national income were to be halved. At first wages held firm, but as the disaster grew, wages began to fall in one industry after another.

Lulled by years of prosperity, the American workers reacted to the depression in an apathetic manner. Strike activity fell to a low point. Riots of the jobless did not break out; no surging mass of workers poured through the streets in search of the perpetrators of their misfortunes. Even the abolition of the much-advertised "welfare capitalism" programs seemingly caused not a ripple. The workers, like other Americans, were waiting helplessly for the return of prosperity.

As jobs and sources of income disappeared, trade-union membership dropped. In 1930 the unions lost 50,000 members, in 1931, 34,000; in 1932, 114,000; and in 1933, another 77,000. In 1933 the total membership stood at 2,973,000—less than in 1917.

AFL leadership was at a loss as to how to deal with this economic catastrophe. Relying on its experience in past depressions, the AFL tried to oppose wage cuts, although unsuccessfully. Only slowly did labor leadership accept the necessity for drastic legislative remedies. It was not until 1932 that the Federation declared for unemployment insurance.

Whatever gains were made for labor during these first bewildering depression years were legislative gains. Although the national adminstration, dominated by conservatives, set its face stonily against remedial laws, various states passed compensation acts, old-age pension laws, and unemployment insurance laws.

Labor gained a great victory with the passage of the Norris–La Guardia Act, which not only declared for labor organization without employer interference but outlawed the yellow-dog contract. Even more important to labor was the prohibition of Federal injunctions except under carefully defined conditions.[31] This marked a radical turning point in the history of American labor.

Labor and the New Deal. When the presidential election of 1932 approached, the AFL stood by its refusal to endorse a presidential candidate, in spite of considerable labor support for Franklin D. Roosevelt. The flood of legislation which the New Deal produced affected labor in various ways. For labor the most important of this early legislation was the National Recovery Act (the NRA), especially its clause *7a*. The NRA was chiefly concerned with the establishment of codes of fair competition in various industries, thereby effectively circumventing the antitrust laws. Clause *7a* was in the nature of compensation to labor for the privileges granted to industry. The clause specified that employees should have the right to organize and bargain collectively with employers, without fear of constraint or reprisal, that no worker should be forced to join a company union, and that employers should agree to minimum wages and maximum hours for workers under codes approved by the President.

The NRA was to collapse even before it could be declared unconstitutional, but not before it set up a great ground swell toward unionism. By October, 1933, 1,500,000 new members had been enrolled in the AFL; total membership rose once again above the 4 million mark. Industrial unions, such as the United Mine Workers and the International Ladies' Garment Workers' Union made particularly striking gains. Progress was made in the mass-production industries; thousands of new members were added to existing unions in the rubber industry, in steel, among the textile workers, and in the automobile industry. In the latter part of 1933 and throughout 1934, bitter strikes for union recognition

---

[31] The use of the injunction as a weapon of management had begun in the 1880s. The courts found legal justification for the use of the injunction on occasion in those clauses of the Interstate Commerce Act and the Sherman Antitrust Act which prohibited "restraint of trade." On other occasions the courts issued injunctions on the grounds that strikes or boycotts injured the use of property without due redress to the owners of the property. Business expectancies being defined as property, the courts found a legal base for their injunctions. In 1897 came the "blanket injunction," which forbade not only specific persons from injuring property, but "all persons"; in this way the injunction was used to halt mass picketing or boycotting. See Perlman, *op. cit.*, pp. 157–160. With the passage of the Clayton Act in 1914, human labor was specifically exempted from operation of the antitrust laws. This, declared Gompers, was the "Magna Charta" of labor. Actually, injunctions were issued even more frequently *after* the passage of the Clayton Act than before. See Felix Frankfurter and Nathan Greene, *The Labor Injunction,* The Macmillan Company, New York, 1930, p. 99. The relevant provisions of the Clayton Act were highly ambiguous. No one was sure whether the act meant to exempt labor unions from the provisions of the antitrust laws or to legalize the existence of trade unions. The courts quickly decided that it was the latter. So the matter stood, until the Norris–La Guardia Act. Even today the issue is far from settled, for the Taft-Hartley Act has again raised the problem of the labor injunction, as we shall see.

were waged in the steel industry, among the automobile workers, long-shoremen, and notably among the textile workers, where hundreds of thousands were involved. It seemed that this time nothing could stop the unions. Yet, as before in American history, the upsurge in the mass-production industries was to prove no more lasting than a flash of light.

Once again the labor movement was hamstrung by labor disunity and by employer resistance. Old-line leaders of the AFL wanted the new union recruits divided among their craft unions. They demanded the dissolution of the "federal unions," into which these recruits had been temporarily herded, pending their division among craft unions. But it was impossible to organize mass-production industries along nonexistent craft lines. Furthermore, some of the old-line leaders were excessively cautious, fearing both the power of management, to which they had to bow so often in the past, and the weight of public opinion, which had been so often against them. In some cases there was grave doubt as to whether old-line leaders really favored an influx of undisciplined, resent-ful, action-demanding, unskilled workers. The recruits disturbed old, safely tried ways, brought in fresh ideas, threatened long-occupied of-fices. Nor was management sitting by idly, waiting for their plants to be organized. Since there was nothing in the provisions of clause 7a to bar the company union, management began to revive this remnant of welfare capitalism. Company-union membership rose in this period by more than a million. Furthermore, management still retained its economic power, it still received a sympathetic press, it retained the sympathy of the middle classes.

By 1935 labor gains began to fade away. The membership of the AFL again fell under the 4 million mark. Most important of all, the gains in the mass-production industry began to melt away. Some 600 federal unions, formed to hold mass-production workers, dissolved. Of the 100,000 workers who had joined the steel workers' union, only 5,300 remained in 1934. Of the 300,000 workers who had belonged to the tex-tile workers' union in 1934, only 79,200 remained in 1935. Of the 60,000 or 70,000 workers who had joined the rubber unions in 1934, perhaps 3,000 remained in 1935.[32] These figures were the measure of labor's defeat.

When the NRA was declared unconstitutional in May, 1935, prolabor legislators, led by Senator Wagner of New York, prepared the bill which came to be known popularly as the Wagner Act. This bill became law in July, 1935, with the support of the administration. The Wagner Act re-created the prolabor provisions of section 7a without concessions to management, and provided means for enforcing its provisions. The Act reaffirmed labor's right to organize. It restrained employers from

[32] Levinson, *op. cit.*, pp. 71–77.

coercing workers not to join unions, from refusing to bargain collectively, from attempting to dominate a union, from discriminating against union members. The union which received the support of a majority of the workers in a plant was to become the sole representative of *all* the employees in the plant. The Wagner Act outlawed company unions.

In order to enforce the Wagner Act, a National Labor Relations Board was set up, a successor to an ineffectual board of the early days of the New Deal. This Board was in no sense a board of arbitration or conciliation; it was not to concern itself with the issues of wages, hours, or working conditions. Its duty consisted of ensuring that management and labor bargained collectively, in good faith. The Board had the power to call plant elections, to hear complaints about "unfair labor practices," and to issue "cease and desist" orders. On the other hand, the Board had no direct power to coerce management or labor. For enforcement of decisions, the Board had to petition the courts.

Thus at one stroke labor gained, at least on paper, all the rights for which it had struggled so long. But would the employers recognize those rights? And, if not, could labor make good the rights which it had been granted? The answer to the first question was not long in coming. Many sections of management were determined to resist the Wagner Act. Many employers and their legal representatives considered the Wagner Act unconstitutional, and they refused to obey its provisions. In some cases employers secured injunctions against the Labor Board. Some employers made more substantial preparations in the form of ammunition, tear gas, machine guns, and other deadly weapons.[33] The size of these preparations was, in some cases, disturbingly large. More tear gas was purchased, over a period of time, by some corporations than by law-enforcement agencies; in fact, one company purchased four times as much as the Ohio National Guard.[34] Extremist employers marshaled their forces of labor spies, strikebreakers, special police. An intense propaganda campaign was begun among the public. Some employers worked out a plan for rallying community forces against labor. This plan included the branding of union organizers as agitators, the use of local police, threats to the community to move the plant, and the organization of back-to-work movements. This came to be called the "Mohawk Valley formula."[35]

Not all employers, of course, were prepared to go to these lengths. But neither was management prepared to sit supinely by and turn its

---

[33] See Report 6, part 3, of the Committee on Education and Labor of the U.S. Senate, *Industrial Munitions*, 1939.

[34] See the Digest of the Report of the Committee on Education and Labor of the U.S. Senate, p. 1.

[35] See Chap. 12.

workers over to the unions, merely because a law had been passed. Labor had two alternatives if it was to make good the benefits of the Wagner Act: court action, or organization. Labor chose the second way.

The Rise of the CIO. The conservatism of the AFL leaders, their refusal to give ground even under the enormous pressures generated by the depression, alienated many of the younger labor leaders. At the 1934 convention of the AFL, this discontent had found powerful voices. The most powerful was that of John L. Lewis, leader of the United Mine Workers, and in many ways one of the most colorful figures ever thrown up by the labor movement in America.

The 1935 convention of the AFL was a fateful one for American labor. Among the militant labor leaders there was anger over the failure of the organizing drives, over jurisdictional disputes, over craft-union raiding. These leaders were determined to force the AFL to recognize the principle of industrial unionism. On the other side was anger at what was regarded as invasions of craft lines, fear of loss of jurisdiction, and a determination to keep the AFL to its old principles. Bitter debates on the issue of industrial unionism ensued, but in a number of ballots it was made clear that a majority of the delegates disapproved of it. The debates were over and the time had come for action, but not before the convention was treated to the sight of Lewis and Hutcheson, head of the carpenters' union, engaged in a bout of fisticuffs. By all accounts Lewis was the victor. It was neither his first nor his last victory.

The dissatisfied delegates, comprised of eight leaders of international unions, proceeded to set up a Committee for Industrial Organization. It was not the purpose of this committee to disrupt the AFL; its first demand, in fact, was for AFL charters in the steel, rubber, automobile, and radio industries. The reply of the executive council of the AFL was to call for the immediate dissolution of the committee on the grounds that it fomented insurrection against the Federation and led to "dual unionism." When the committee refused to dissolve, it was brought to trial before the Executive Council Committee, and 10 unions were ordered suspended. At the 1936 convention of the AFL, the suspensions were confirmed by the delegates, now minus the representatives of the offending unions. Bitter charges of "ingratitude" were hurled against the departing unions by AFL leaders. Attempts to reunite the unions in 1937 failed, although some men on both sides strove sincerely for unity. Finally, the Executive Council of the AFL ordered the CIO unions expelled, with the exception of the Ladies' Garment Workers' Union, which soon returned to the AFL. The rift in American labor had been completed, a rift which was to last for two decades.

The fate of the CIO was not to be decided in the meeting room or before government boards. It was to be decided, as fundamental issues in American labor affairs are always decided, among the workers and on the picket lines. The second "great upheaval" in American labor history began in 1935. The rubber workers of Akron joined the union in a mass rush, went out on strike, and brought the rubber companies to terms. A drive for unionization in the automobile industry then began; this drive soon brought labor the first victories some of it had ever scored in that industry. A most important spur to the labor drive was the overwhelming victory, in 1936, of Roosevelt, who, with labor support, carried all but two of the states.

The CIO now moved to battle with General Motors, the third largest corporation in the United States, and one of the most determinedly antiunion. It was obvious from the first that on the outcome of this battle rested the fate of the CIO and its attempts to unionize the mass-production industries. In duration and scope the strike against General Motors did justice to its historic importance. Strikes broke out at General Motors plants in Atlanta, Kansas City, and Cleveland and then spread to Detroit; plants in many other cities were eventually involved. The union used a new tactic in many of these strikes. Instead of leaving the plant and forming picket lines, the workers simply "sat down"; that is, they occupied the plants, much as an army occupies a city. Every effort was made by the strikers to protect plant property, to maintain discipline; but the fact remained that in essence management was effectively deprived of control over its property. Efforts to end the strike were made by Governor Murphy of Michigan and by the national administration, but in vain. As the strike dragged on, it became apparent that this time labor could not be defeated by the old, tried and true, strike-breaking tactics. The militia was called out, but Governor Murphy would not order it to break the strike. In Flint, Michigan, an attempt of the local police to evict the strikers from a plant ended in an ignominious defeat for the police, "the battle of the running bulls." Injunctions granted against the strikers were simply ignored, and there were none to enforce them. As time went on labor moved on to the offensive and succeeded in occupying additional strategic plants. Management capitulated, in February, 1937. The United Automobile Workers was recognized as the sole bargaining agency in 17 plants. Management agreed not to discriminate against strikers, to end the espionage system, to grant a 5 per cent increase in wages. There had scarcely ever been a labor victory like this in American history, and the rush of automobile workers to join the union foretold victories to follow in other industries.

The victory of the automobile workers led to a wave of sit-down strikes in 1937. In March of that year almost 200,000 workers were engaged in such strikes.[36] Sit-down strikes broke out among store clerks,

---

[36] Levinson, *op. cit.*, p. 169.

miners, farm hands, food packers, to mention just a few fields. The sit-down strike touched off a great legal debate. Conservatives argued that it was, in effect, a seizure of property; labor held that it was merely another labor tactic. Eventually the sit-down strike was declared illegal by the courts, but by that time the major labor battles of the time had been won.

In marked contrast to the bitter struggle in the automobile industry was the campaign to organize the workers of the United States Steel Corporation. United States Steel, the mightiest of all industrial corporations, had successfully repulsed the unions in 1892 and in 1919, and it had been these repulses which had been largely responsible for the preservation of the "open shop" in many other mass-production industries. When it became known that the CIO was planning to organize the steel industry, it seemed that the greatest labor struggle of modern times was in the making. The drive began in June, 1936, rather slowly at first, but picking up as the unions began to work through the existing company unions. Within a few months, the steelworkers' organizing committee had enrolled 125,000 members. At this point Myron C. Taylor, chairman of United States Steel, in a spirit of compromise, entered into negotiations with the union leaders, Lewis and Philip Murray. The result was an astounding labor victory; recognition of the union (though not the closed or union shop), a wage increase, the forty-hour week, and an agreement that all grievances not covered by the contract were to be handled by arbitration. Thus the United States Steel Corporation showed its recognition of changed conditions: the success of the unionization drive, the prolabor attitude of the administration and some state governments, and the change in public opinion.

Not nearly so conciliatory were the "little steel" corporations: the National Steel Corporation, Republic, Bethlehem, Inland Steel, and Youngstown Sheet & Tube. Under the leadership of Tom M. Girdler of Republic Steel, these companies demonstrated what force they were yet able to command. The strike of 70,000 steelworkers that broke out in May and June of 1937 was one of the bloodiest of the decade. Before the strike ended, 18 workers had been killed, 10 of them in the "Memorial Day massacre" before the Republic Steel plant. Strikers were assailed by the police forces of local communities, by "citizens' committees," by "back-to-work" movements, and by an intensive propaganda barrage. Civil liberties were practically suspended in many cities, and hundreds of strikers were arrested.[37] Under this barrage, the strike was called off, although the union was by no means annihilated. Even so,

---

[37] For an account of the little steel strike see *ibid.*, pp. 201–209. See also part IV of the La Follette committee report, *The "Little Steel" Strike and Citizen's Committees,* issued by the Committee on Education and Labor of the U.S. Senate, 1941.

little steel gained only a few years of peace from labor unions. In 1941 the National Labor Relations Board quietly ordered the little steel corporations to recognize the unions and to reinstate workers fired during the strike, and the companies complied.

By the end of 1937, and in spite of the defeat in little steel, the CIO was well on its way toward the organization of the mass-production industries. Starting with less than a million members in December, 1935, by the end of 1937 the CIO numbered 3,718,000 members, a greater number than the AFL possessed. In the years after 1937 one mass-production industry after another was to fall to the CIO, even the individualistic Ford finally capitulating. Most of these successes were due to the efforts of the workers themselves. But at least two other factors greatly aided labor after 1937. One was that in April, 1937, the Supreme Court, much to the surprise of many employers, declared the Wagner Act to be constitutional. Labor, said the Supreme Court, had as much right to organize as management—and more need, because the individual worker was helpless against the power of management. The Labor Board now went ahead with its program of abolishing "yellow-dog" contracts, black-listing, labor spies, antiunion propaganda, and company unions. By 1945 the Labor Board had heard 36,000 cases of unfair labor practices, disestablished 2,000 company unions, ordered the reinstatement of 300,000 employees, and held some 24,000 elections to determine the bargaining agents of 6,000,000 workers.[38] The other factor aiding the workers was the disclosures of the La Follette committee on the use of munitions, spies, and strikebreakers by some employers and their disregard of civil liberties. This report played a considerable part in turning public opinion against the antiunion employer.

In May, 1938, the Committee on Industrial Organization transformed itself into the Congress of Industrial Organizations. In its basic principles and structure it was much more like the AFL than the bitter animosity existing between them at the time would have suggested. No more than the AFL was the CIO prepared to advocate the abolition of capitalism, in spite of the activity of some Communists in the CIO. Like the AFL, the CIO wished to secure certain economic gains, but within the framework of the existing socioeconomic order. No more than the AFL was the CIO prepared to back a labor party, although the CIO was, at first, deeply concerned with politics and existing parties. With the passage of time, the differences between the two labor organizations tended to fade, not to sharpen. By 1955, the two federations were on the way to reunion.

The structure of the CIO was based on the national and international union, as in the AFL. State and city industrial councils, similar to state

[38] Dulles, *op. cit.*, p. 280. By permission.

and city federations of labor, were established. However, the CIO permitted its unions somewhat less autonomy than the AFL.[39] We shall describe these structures more fully in the next chapter.

Labor in the New Deal decade benefited from various types of social laws. In the early days of the depression, unemployed workers received relief benefits; throughout the thirties many workers were on the WPA. The Social Security Act of 1935 was at least a beginning toward protection in old age, and the minimum-wage legislation of 1938 afforded some protection to the unorganized workers of American industry.

Counterbalancing these gains was the split of the trade-union movement. But even this was not without its benefits to labor. The rise of the CIO finally brought the AFL out of its long sleep. In contrast to predictions made at that time, the AFL not only did not disappear, but instead began to move into the mass-production industries.

Labor during World War II. War broke out in 1939, and the Roosevelt administration moved by gradual stages to throw American power behind the Western allies. With the consequent increase in production, unemployment began to dwindle and wages to rise. With the end of the depression conditions, American labor moved into a new phase of development.

This change was symbolized by the resignation of John L. Lewis as president of the CIO in 1940. Lewis resigned because he failed to swing the mass of American workers to the side of the Republican candidate in 1940; even the miners disregarded Lewis's bitter attacks on Roosevelt. Lewis was replaced by Philip Murray, head of the steel union, and a much less flamboyant leader than Lewis. The early crusading days of the CIO were definitely over.

Nevertheless, the year 1941 was an unusually tumultuous one in American labor history. More workers struck than in any year since 1937. Behind the strikes was a story of increased labor power, rising prices, the resurgence from depression conditions, and the intrigue of the Communists, who were at that time, following the Nazi-Soviet pact, opposing the defense program. So bitter were some strikes in war industries that the government seized the plants in order to restore vital production. It was not possible, however, to deal with Lewis in so cavalier a fashion, and after a strike, he forced the coal-mine operators and Roosevelt into what was essentially a capitulation.

The belligerence of labor, the irresponsibility of some labor leaders in the face of near-war conditions, and the unceasing unfriendliness of employers and of many mass media combined to cause a revulsion of feeling against labor. Several antilabor bills were pending at the time of Pearl Harbor.

[39] *Ibid.,* p. 298.

World War II brought many changes to American labor and to the trade-union movement. The depression finally ended, and employment rose to 53 million, while millions of young men were drafted. Organized labor, this time supported by its left wing, threw its support behind the war. Labor representatives agreed to serve on various governmental agencies. A War Labor Board was set up to handle labor disputes and to control wages and hours. Labor yielded the right to strike, and thus, in effect, its right to bargain collectively. Although the Labor Board had no power directly to enforce its decisions, strikes were nevertheless cut down to one-third of the prewar average.

Where strikes did break out they were usually of the wildcat variety. The cause of labor discontent was the rise in prices. By 1943, this discontent had assumed considerable proportions. The Labor Board was usually able to allay this discontent, but in an indirect way. By granting "fringe" benefits, paid vacations, health and insurance plans, the freeze on wages was effectively circumvented. Even these concessions did not prevent serious troubles in the coal fields, with Lewis and Roosevelt again the main protagonists. Although Roosevelt seized the mines on two occasions, the dispute was finally settled on terms favorable to Lewis.

Public indignation over the coal strikes and Lewis's tactics eventuated in Federal antilabor legislation. The Smith-Connally Act gave the President power to seize any plant engaged in war production; the Act also demanded a thirty-day notice of a strike and a strike vote. One provision of the Act forbade labor to contribute money to political campaigns. The bill was passed over Roosevelt's veto. Labor reacted to the bill with increased belief in the necessity of a national administration friendly to labor. As a result labor played an active role in the 1944 campaign and probably contributed significantly to the election of Roosevelt to a fourth term.

In spite of antiunion legislation, the war was a period of great gains for labor. By 1945 more than 14 million workers belonged to unions; some 6.8 millions in the AFL, 6 million in the CIO, and the rest in the mine union and in the railroad brotherhoods. Mass-production industries which had resisted unionization for decades were peaceably organized. Many "open-shop" communities quietly became union towns. Labor contracts were extended until they governed the relationships between employers and millions of workers.

Labor since World War II. With the end of the war, labor moved to secure the wage increases which had been held up by wartime legislation. The year 1946 witnessed the greatest outbreak of strikes in American history; some 2 million workers "went out." There were major strikes in the automobile industry, in steel, in oil, in meat packing. The success of these strikes led to other strikes. Lewis demanded, and won, a royalty of 7 cents on each ton of coal mined, the royalty to be paid into the miners' welfare fund. However, when the railroad workers struck, Truman seized the railroads and ordered the strike ended on the grounds that the economy of the nation was threatened. When the workers refused, Truman asked for the power to draft the strikers, in order to subject them to military discipline. This very radical proposal had already received the support of the House when the strikers capitulated. The Senate then voted down Truman's proposal, largely through the efforts of Senator Taft, later destined to be no hero to labor.

In 1946 Congress refused to renew the power of the administration to control prices, and prices immediately began to spiral upward, quickly outdistancing the wage increases gained earlier. A drive for a "second round" of wage increases began, but even when these increases had been won the lot of the worker was not so good as it had been in the war, so quickly did prices rise again.

Meanwhile the antilabor drive, which had been gaining strength since 1940, continued to grow stronger. Restrictive laws were passed in some 30 states. Nationally, the antilabor forces succeeded in passing the Taft-Hartley Act in June, 1947. We shall discuss this bill in greater detail in a later chapter. Suffice to say that the Taft-Hartley Act aimed to cut down the power of unions in several ways: by prohibiting unions from coercing members, by prohibiting them from engaging in secondary boycotts, by prohibiting jurisdictional strikes, and in other ways. Employers were granted the right to call plant elections and to propagandize among the workers. Closed shops were banned, and union shops closely regulated. Unions were prohibited from making contributions to political campaigns, a renewal of the provisions of the expired Smith-Connally act. Union officials were required to file affidavits swearing that they were not Communists. Elaborate provisions were set up to deal with a strike affecting national health or safety. In this regard, the President was given the power to apply for an injunction to postpone a strike for sixty days. All in all the Taft-Hartley Act seemed capable of imposing severe restrictions on union activity, and it earned the immediate and unrelieved enmity of all sections of organized labor.

However, in spite of the gloomy predictions of the labor leaders, who spoke of a "slave-labor bill," management did not unleash a major offensive against American labor. Employment remained very high through 1947 and 1948; business was extremely profitable. For the workers the main harrassment during this time was the continued rise in prices, which in spite of the efforts of Truman, Congress refused to stem.

Pressure now mounted for a "third round" of wage increases. Strikes broke out in some industries, notably the packing industry and the coal fields. In the latter industry, the government used the Taft-Hartley Act.

Lewis disregarded the government and won the strike, but the union was fined $1,400,000 and Lewis $20,000. Most disputes, however, were settled by arbitration, and in 1948 "third round" increases became general. General Motors signed a contract with the UAW, which adjusted wages to the cost of living, the so-called escalator clause. However, this type of contract did not become generally accepted. The steel industry also granted wage increases, and without a strike. In the fall of 1948 large strikes broke out, most of them over wage increases, but in one case as the result of a ruling under the Taft-Hartley Act that the "hiring hall" of the longshoremen was illegal.

As the election of 1948 approached, both the large labor federations threw their support to the Democrats, endorsed the rearmament program, and called for the repeal of the Taft-Hartley Act. The unexpected reelection of Truman was widely interpreted as a labor victory, but the conservatives in Congress proved strong enough to prevent the repeal or even the modification of the Taft-Hartley Act.

With the beginning of 1949 certain weak spots began to appear in the economy, and unemployment began to mount slowly. In March, 1950, there were 4,684,000 out of work, the highest figure since before the war. Strikes and work stoppages broke out in the coal fields, perhaps because Lewis wished to reduce the amount of mined coal. Strikes also broke out among longshoremen, aircraft workers, and automobile workers. The steelworkers struck briefly for a pension plan. Under the terms of this plan, employees with certain minimum terms of service were granted pensions designed to supplement Federal benefits. The level to which the pension was to bring the income of retired workers was to be figured as a percentage of monthly earnings. It is notable that, in spite of the rising unemployment, wages did not fall during this period of recession.

By 1950 the union movement had run into rougher weather. The AFL, which had spurted far ahead of the CIO in membership, ceased to grow. The membership of the CIO declined somewhat, even disregarding the members lost through the expulsion of Communist-dominated unions. An attempt to unionize the Southern textile mills had little success; only 20 per cent of 600,000 textile workers were organized after three rather intensive years of campaigning. There was no doubt that the Taft-Hartley Act was having a hampering effect on unionization. But perhaps another important factor was simply that the cream had been skimmed by the unions; the mass-production industries had been organized, and what was left, though badly in need of organization, was harder or less profitable to unionize. Thus, while some gains were made among white-collar workers, on the whole these workers remained hesitant about unions. Still another factor in the slowing down of the union drive was the increasing age, conservatism, and quiescence of CIO leadership.[40]

Throughout 1950 business conditions slowly improved. With the outbreak of the Korean War in June and the Chinese Communist intervention in December, a vastly increased armament program was launched. Production began to rise; unemployment dropped off. Of even more importance to labor was a new sharp upturn in prices, an upturn which quickly established new high records. Prices continued to rise throughout 1951. Wages were also raised in many industries, either through the renegotiation of contracts or through "escalator" clauses. Strikes were rare in this period. However, labor felt that the wage increases did not keep pace with the rise in the cost of living.

The government attempted to control wages and prices through two agencies: the Office of Price Stabilization, and the Wage Stabilization Board. A wage and price "freeze" was ordered in January, 1951. Protests from labor brought an order from the WSB permitting 10 per cent "catch-up" increases. This was hardly satisfactory to labor. In protest representatives of labor withdrew from all the defense agencies which had been set up to handle problems created by the Korean War. When the WSB was reconstituted on a basis more friendly to labor, the unions reentered the defense agencies. This development, however, drove management totally out of sympathy with the administration. The steel industry refused to abide by one decision of the WSB. Truman ordered the steel plants seized, but in June, 1952, the Supreme Court invalidated the Presidential order, and Congress refused Truman the necessary power to seize the plants.

The failure of the government agencies to settle economic disputes led to a test of strength between steel management and the union. In May, 1952, began the longest steel strike on record. This strike came to an end on July 25, 1952, with only a moderate wage increase for the workers; management gained the right to raise the price of steel. On the whole these terms represented a victory for management.

As the 1952 election approached, labor again prepared to enter the political struggle. Again the major political aim of labor was the repeal of the Taft-Hartley Act. In addition, labor had grievances against a Congress which had failed to stem the price rise and had seriously weakened the WSB. The executive council of the CIO endorsed the Democratic candidate, Adlai Stevenson. The AFL for the first time in its history, flatly endorsed a presidential candidate, again the Democrat. The election went disastrously against labor; not only was the Republican candidate elected, but two prolabor Senators and ten or twelve prolabor Representatives were defeated.

[40] See *Fortune*, April, 1950, pp. 51–52.

For the first time in twenty years, a Republican administration was in power. It is interesting to speculate on the cause of this reversal. Some importance must be attached to the popularity of Eisenhower; some, to the intensive propaganda campaign of the Republicans, who, as usual, had the support of the press. Some of the blame for the Democrats' defeat undoubtedly attached to labor. Labor unionism was no longer the crusading movement it had been in the thirties. Nor were the workers, lulled by memories of twelve years of full employment, necessarily over-eager to follow the advice of union leaders. But, whatever the reasons, one thing was certain; labor could no longer count on a friendly administration in Washington.

Almost as if symbolizing the new turn in the affairs of labor, both the labor organizations lost their top leaders within a very few days of each other. Philip Murray died in November, 1952, and William Green shortly after. The new president of the CIO was Walter Reuther, and that of the AFL was George Meany.

The year 1953 was a prosperous one for the American workingman and for the unions. Real and gross earnings reached a new peak. Even if Eisenhower's conciliatory gesture in appointing an AFL Democrat to the cabinet proved unsuccessful, nevertheless management failed to unleash a general offensive against labor. AFL membership rose to 9,570,000; the CIO announced that it had gained 450,000 members in a year but did not reveal its total membership. After mid-year 1953, unemployment began to increase, however, and by February, 1954, some 3,700,000 were again unemployed. However, in spite of some misgivings the economy righted itself, and by 1956, employment reached a record high of over 66 million.

By the middle of the 1950s practically all the sharp issues which had divided the CIO and the AFL had faded. The original leaders in that split had passed from the scene, and with them went a reservoir of personal animosity and bitterness. The new leaders, George Meany and Walter Reuther, placed the unity of labor above personal ambition or personal feeling. Furthermore, in both confederations there was a marked desire to eliminate the raiding which had taken the place of the organizing drives of the thirties and forties; amalgamation admirably served this end. On both sides of labor's house there was recognition that the opponents of labor were strengthened by the split; that both in the eyes of the public and in those of the workingman an united labor movement was bound to gain in stature and prestige. In fact, labor hoped to gain politically from amalgamation, and from this point of view the Taft-Hartley Act was a large factor in accomplishing the merger. No doubt many other reasons, such as rivalries between certain labor leaders, played a part in the merger, but the three reasons listed above seem to have been the overriding ones. At any rate a plan of merger was agreed upon early in 1955 and put into operation late in that year. Once again, as in the days before 1935, American labor was dominated by one confederation, but this time a confederation of 15 million, one-quarter of the working force of the United States.[41]

Summary. In a later chapter we shall deal with certain theories of the labor movement designed to interpret the origins and ultimate fate of the American trade-union movement. Here we shall only point up certain conclusions to be drawn directly from the data we have presented.

1. There can be no doubt of the very strong hold of trade unionism over the American workingman. Even at a very early time, he was strongly attracted to trade unionism. Furthermore this attraction has persisted even in the face of determined employer resistance, welfare programs, a hostile press, the dislike of large sections of the general public, and the waves of immigration. The American workingman has shown his readiness to defend his unions by force if necessary; he has been a consistent and loyal striker, picketer, and supporter of his union's struggles. It must be concluded that this attraction must have deep social and psychological roots, a conclusion we shall examine in detail in a later chapter.

2. By and large, the American workingman has shown far more *continuous* interest in trade unionism as a solution to the strains in his role than to any other of the solutions which have been proposed. Thus, at an early time, he showed a decisive lack of interest in consumers' co-operatives. Radicalism, although at times with a following among some American workingmen, has by and large never attracted their loyalties or interest on a large scale. Even "third parties" or "labor parties" have never been able to wean the American workingman from his allegiance to American traditions. Again we are confronted here with a deeply rooted fact, and one whose explanation must concern anyone interested in the American labor movement.

3. The American labor movement, in spite of its long record of defeat and weakness, is now one of the enduring institutions of the nation. Although only one-third of the workers are organized, this third is *strongly* organized. Furthermore, it is the most important industries which are most strongly organized; steel, automobiles, rubber, etc. It is the peripheral and less important groups of workers who remain unorganized. Thus, it seems safe to say that the aspirations, wishes, and dislikes of labor will be a continuing factor in political, social, and military decisions in the nation at large.

[41] We shall discuss the structure of the newly merged labor confederations in the next chapter.

4. The American labor movement is, however, rather definitely limited in its social and political aims. In part this limitation springs from the fact that, in spite of labor's gains, those forces which by interest or prejudice would naturally seek to check the ambitions of labor are still very strong. The power and prestige of management has made a strong recovery from its nadir during the depression. In addition, many middle-class people—those who are generally meant when we speak of the "public"—are, if not hostile to labor, certainly not willing to see it spread its power at the expense of traditional forces or traditional mythologies. In part this limitation is self-imposed; the American labor movement is interested largely in "economic" goals of an immediate sort, not in revolutionizing or even reforming the society as a whole.

Contemporary American Trade Unionism

The American trade-union movement embraces some 16 million workers and is one of the forces shaping our society, although perhaps not the dominant force that some friends and enemies of labor have claimed. In this chapter we shall study the formal internal structure of this vast movement, some major union roles, the relationships of union leadership to rank and file, and some of the major internal strains to which the trade-union movement is exposed.

The Formal Structure of the Trade-union Movement. The structure of the labor movement in the United States represents, largely, an adaptation to the conditions of American life. In the first place, as industrialism has developed in the United States, new occupations have been created, old crafts have been destroyed, and old skills have disappeared. On the other hand, some skilled trades and crafts have been left untouched. As a result American unionism has split among craft unions and industrial unions. A craft union is an organization of workers engaged in a single trade or employing similar skills; an industrial union embraces all the workers in a given industry, whatever their skills or trades. By and large, industrial unionism "fits" mass-production industries, while craft unionism is adapted to such fields as the building industry. But actually the situation is much more complicated than this; as complicated, in fact, as all the infinite variations of industrial processes, changing and interchangeable skills, and evolving technologies can make it. Therefore, in the United States one finds not only craft and industrial unions but also semi-industrial unions enrolling skilled workers, multiple-craft unions made up of separate groupings of skilled workers, and so on.

In the second place, the over-all organization of these unions, the way they are set up internally, the way they are combined into confederations, the means that are used to control the rank and file, and the ideologies of unionism, all reflect what has proved feasible and functional for unionism in the none too favorable American climate.

Trade-union organization in the United States cannot be analyzed with ease in terms of preconceived notions. In some respects trade unions are bureaucracies, some much more highly developed than others; in other respects they are more like democratic states, with their "citizenry" held in line by political parties, promises, and programs.

The AFL-CIO. First we shall examine the over-all structure of the newly merged confederation of labor, the AFL-CIO. Since this federation is still evolving in form after the merger of 1955, it will be well to begin with a description of the preamalgamation organization of labor.

The peculiarly mixed structure of trade unionism was and is reflected in the over-all structure of the great national labor confederations. The old American Federation of Labor was an organization of some 108 separate unions, which were almost completely independent.[1] In fact, the only actual power granted to the Federation was the right to expel a constituent union; the Federation had no power to dissolve a union or discipline its members. In addition, the AFL included some 50 state federations, more than 800 city and county organizations, and over 1,200 locals not affiliated with a national union.

The supreme lawmaking body of the AFL was the national convention, an annual conclave of delegates chosen from the various constituent bodies of the Federation. Delegates from the national unions were allotted on the basis of membership, which, of course, guaranteed control to the large unions. The convention chose a president, a secretary-treasurer, and 13 vice presidents (usually the presidents of national unions), who together made up the Executive Council. The president had relatively little power over the national unions, except in so far as he commanded prestige and influence, but much greater direct power over the other bodies in the federation. The Executive Council carried out the decisions of the convention, watched over government legislation, directed research into labor problems, and supervised organizing drives.

Financial support for Federation activities was secured mainly from a tax of 4 cents per month for each member of the national unions. In addition, the AFL received money from its directly affiliated locals, from state federations and city centrals, and also through special assessments on members. From all these sources the AFL collected annually about 4 million dollars, the largest part of which it spent on organizing drives.

Historically, the AFL espoused craft unionism; in fact, it was partly over this issue that the unions comprising the CIO broke from the AFL in the thirties. Nevertheless the AFL unions found it necessary to combine even across craft lines for certain purposes. Thus in 1907 the AFL

---

[1] Florence Peterson, *American Labor Unions*, Harper & Brothers, New York, 1952, pp. 46ff.

authorized the creation of "departments" of unions with similar interests. Five departments were established; the Building and Construction Trades Department, the Metal Trades Department, the Railway Employes Department, the Union Label and Service Trades Department, and the Maritime Trades Department. The functions of these departments included union organization, the settling of jurisdictional disputes, assisting constituent unions in collective bargaining, and conducting propaganda for the purchase of union-manufactured goods. Another departure from pure craft unionism was the formation of federal unions directly affiliated with the AFL. Theoretically these unions were only stopgaps until craft unions could absorb their membership, but in actuality they were often true industrial unions.

In structural form, the CIO closely resembled its parent body, the AFL, but there were some differences. The supreme lawmaking body of the CIO, like that of the AFL, was the national annual convention, to which delegates were sent from regional groups (such as state or city organizations) and, on a basis proportionate to membership, from the national unions. Like the AFL, then, the CIO was a confederation of independent unions, with the large unions in control. Some 33 national unions made up the CIO, together with 41 state industrial councils; 236 city, county, and industrial councils; and several hundred locals directly affiliated with the CIO.[2] These bodies, assembled in convention, selected a president, 9 vice presidents, and a secretary-treasurer, who together made up an Executive Board. This Board carried on the work of the Congress on a day-to-day basis, functioning very much as did the Executive Council of the AFL.

The differences between the two labor bodies reflected their different histories. Because most CIO national unions were created by the CIO as a whole, the central body exercised considerably more power over its national unions than did the AFL. It was also perhaps true that the CIO was more under the dominance of a few of its large unions than was the AFL; thus the president of the CIO had always been the leader of one of its large unions. On the other hand, the original differences between CIO and AFL in terms of the preponderance of craft and industrial unionism had tended to fade away in recent years.

The structure of the new confederation, the AFL-CIO, differs somewhat from those of both the older organizations. The supreme governing body is still to be the convention, but this convention is to meet every two years, rather than annually. Delegates are to be assigned according to the membership of unions, which assures more than twice as many votes for the old AFL unions as for those which once comprised the

[2] *Ibid.*, p. 59.

CIO. State and local bodies affiliated directly with the confederation, are to be assigned one vote each.[3]

The new organization has two chief executive officers, a president and a secretary-treasurer. Initially, both these officers are to come from the old AFL. Between conventions the organization is to be governed by an Executive Council, consisting of 27 vice presidents and the two executive officers, meeting at least three times a year, at the call of the president. The executive Council is empowered to carry out the decisions of the convention and to take other appropriate action to safeguard the interests of the organization, including the "organization of unorganized industries." Initially 17 of the vice presidents were to be chosen from the old AFL and 10 from the old CIO.[4]

The Executive Council chooses an executive committee made up of six vice presidents; the president and the secretary-treasurer are members of the committee by right of office. This committee is to meet bimonthly, and its duties are to "advise and consult with the executive officers on policy matters."[5] Initially three of these officers were to be chosen from the old AFL and three from the old CIO.

There is also a general board, consisting of the Executive Council and the president (or other principal officer) of each of the national unions. This board is to meet at least once a year and is to decide on "all policy questions referred to it by the executive officers and the Executive Council." Voting on the board is to follow the membership ratios of the unions.

The five "departments" of the old AFL are maintained, but an Industrial Union Department, headed by Walter Reuther, is added. This department, like the others, is autonomous in financial matters and in managing its affairs. The Industrial Union Department initially consisted of some 66 unions, including 35 former AFL unions; however, two-thirds of its membership of 7 million was drawn from former members of the CIO. The aim of the new department is to "promote the interests of industrial unions, assist in collective bargaining, engage in legislative activity with respect to matters of interest to industrial unions, act as a clearinghouse of information, engage in research and related activities, and administer the settlement of organizational disputes."[6] This new department acts almost like a separate organization. Its convention is to meet at least every two years. It is governed by a president,

[3] See "Merger Plans of the Unions and the Leaders' Statements," *The New York Times*, Feb. 10, 1955, p. 21.

[4] Section 3(E) of merger resolution, *ibid.*

[5] Section 3(F) of merger resolution, *ibid.*

[6] Joseph W. Block, "Founding Convention of the A.F.L.-C.I.O.," *Monthly Labor Review*, vol. 79, no. 2, pp. 141–149, 1956; see p. 149.

a secretary-treasurer, and 12 vice presidents; it has an executive council consisting of these officers plus a principal officer from each affiliated union. All the vice presidents chosen initially were from the former CIO, though it was planned that later some posts were to be filled by men from the old AFL.[7]

Various standing committees, responsible to the Executive Council and the convention, deal with matters of interest to labor. Initially standing committees were created on legislation, civil rights, political education, ethical practices, international affairs, education, social security, economic policy, community services, housing, research, public relations, safety and occupational health, and veterans' affairs.

A separate body deals with organization of new union members. The head of this body has the title of Director of Organization, and is selected by the president, with the approval of the Executive Council.

The constitution of the AFL-CIO provides that membership shall be open not only to national and international unions but also to state bodies, to local central bodies, and to local unions affiliated directly with the federation. Mergers between all these organizations on appropriate levels are urged but are not to be imposed by the federation.

The new organization is oriented to several principles, as guides to policy and to action:

1. As noted above, the autonomy of each national or international union, each federal labor union, or each organizing committee, is specifically recognized, though merger is urged where appropriate.

2. Each of the affiliated unions is to recognize the jurisdiction of other unions and agree to cease "raiding" of membership. Existing "no-raiding" agreements are to remain in force. In cases of disputes which are not covered by "no-raiding" agreements, the matter is to be settled by voluntary agreement or merger, in consultation with officials of the federation. If necessary, the Executive Council may arbitrarily arrive at a decision but must submit it to the national convention for approval before acting.

3. The principles of both industrial and craft unionism are recognized as "appropriate, equal, and necessary" for union organization.

4. The federation specifically condemns discrimination in trade unions on the basis of "race, creed, color, or national origin" and provides that machinery is to be set up to end such discrimination.

5. The AFL-CIO denies membership to any Communist-dominated or Communist-affiliated union. Membership is also denied to "racketeer" unions, and the federation intends to proceed sternly against all sorts of corrupt practices in unions.

National Unions. These organizations are, as we have seen, practically

[7] *Ibid.,* p. 149.

autonomous. However, they are dependent upon the central body for aid in crisis, for organizational drives, and for certain specialized tasks. They are independent as regards internal administration and even union policy, so long as that policy does not violate the fundamental principles of the central body. Because of this independence it is difficult to generalize about the national unions. They vary in size from less than a hundred members to hundreds of thousands. They vary in internal organization from almost pure democracies to entirely pure autocracies.[8] Some are politically oriented; some are purely economic-minded. Many differ in other ways.

As a result of the independence of national unions, the limits of jurisdiction are often so vague that clashes occur between unions, even in some cases where the unions belong to the same confederation. The frequency of the jurisdictional dispute has been exaggerated in the public mind; actually only a very small fraction of strikes is over jurisdictional matters. Nevertheless the possibility of such disputes persists, and this possibility is made all the stronger because of the absence of ideological unity in American labor and because of constant technological changes in industry. Furthermore, some national unions possess ambitious presidents bent on aggrandizement.[9] Recent "no-raiding" agreements between the CIO and AFL have perhaps relieved this problem.

The independence of the national union has afforded scope for the development of many different types of union governments, ranging from the purely bureaucratic to the most determinedly democratic. However, even in the democratic unions there has been an increasing tendency to centralize control in the national office and to develop a bureaucratic hierarchy. There is a natural tendency for organizations formed in periods of upheaval to develop routinized and bureaucratized structures; in fact, this development is a virtual necessity if the organization is to survive. Furthermore, the growth in numbers of the unionized workers as well as the need for big, powerful unions to compete with big industry have tended to further this bureaucratic development.

Most national unions possess similar structures; the differences between them lie in the way these structures function. The supreme lawmaking body is the convention, made up of delegates chosen from the locals. Most of these conventions meet once a year or once every two years; some meet much less frequently. Sometimes special conventions are held to consider specific issues. The convention usually selects the president, though in some cases he is selected by referendum. His term

---

[8] For an account of autocratic labor leadership, see Wellington Roe, *Juggernaut*, J. B. Lippincott Company, Philadelphia, 1948, chaps. V–VII.
[9] See Jack Barbash, *Labor Unions in Action*, Harper & Brothers, New York, 1948, pp. 34–39.

in office varies; some presidents must seek reelection each year, while the lucky president of the AFL Longshoremen's Association rules for life. In most unions the president is reelected year after year, for as long as he wishes to be president. Union members rarely dismiss a president either because the rank and file is satisfied with the president, or because they are apathetic, or because the president has built an unbeatable political machine in the union. The convention also usually selects a secretary-treasurer and several vice presidents (often officials of locals), who, together with the president, make up the executive board.

The power of the president and the executive board varies from union to union. Thus John L. Lewis in the United Mine Workers and James Caesar Petrillo in the American Federation of Musicians practically rule their unions as dictators; Lewis appoints officials of the union, while Petrillo has the right to call strikes without consulting the locals and to amend the constitution of his union at will.[10] In other unions the power of the president and the executive board is subject to democratic control. However, even in such democratic unions the power of the union officers is great. The president conducts the day-to-day affairs of the union, sits on all committees, and represents the union to the public. The executive board usually has the power to issue charters to locals and to withdraw them, to repeal locals' rules which violate the union constitution, to repeal the action of national officials, to supervise the union press, and to prepare the report for the convention.

The national union is supported by a combination of initiation fees and dues. Initiation fees and dues were usually higher in the AFL than in the CIO, partly because of greater AFL emphasis on benefits and also, in some cases, because of craft exclusiveness.

Local Unions. The "local," as it is almost always called, is usually the smallest organized unit of the union structure. The locals' jurisdictions are determined either by what has proved convenient for collective action or on the basis of historical accident; e.g., the organization of workers by a craft union rather than by an industrial union. As a result there is a curious diversity in the jurisdiction of various locals. Some locals include all the workers in a given plant, or in a series of plants; some locals are formed on a craft basis, even where the national union is industrial in nature. Sometimes locals are combined into amalgamated locals covering a given geographical area. The same extreme variation may be found in the size of locals; most of the locals have one or two hundred members, but there are some with fewer than a dozen members and two or three with more than a hundred thousand.[11]

[10] Richard A. Lester, *Labor and Industrial Relations,* The Macmillan Company, New York, 1951, pp. 137–138.
[11] Peterson, *op. cit.,* p. 79.

There is also great variation in the relationships of locals to their national unions. Here the situation is often paradoxical. The constitutions of national unions seem to specify rather clear patterns of relationship between the local and the national. The national usually has the right to approve or reject the constitution of the local as well as amendments to the local's constitution. The national also has the right to determine the jurisdiction of the union, qualifications for membership in the local, and methods of disciplining union members. The national usually has the power to suspend locals or to expel them from the union. Balancing this considerable power of the national is the local's right to send delegates to the national convention in proportion to the size of membership.

Actually, the relationship of the local to the national is likely to be determined by several nonconstitutional factors. Industry-wide bargaining, especially in mass-production industries, tends, for instance, to strengthen the hand of the national. Only the national is really in a position to bargain with an entire industry because only the national has staff members to give expert advice on collective bargaining, expert legal counsel, or specialized economic and social data. Aside from these factors, strong, determined, ruthless national leadership can often override the local union and centralize power in the national through manipulation of the bureaucratic structure; this seems to be the case in the United Mine Workers. On the other hand, some locals have managed to retain and even strengthen their independence of the national. This has been the case where bargaining is carried on locally so that a national union effort is not needed, notably in the building trades. Where the local was organized through the spontaneous action of workers, rather than through the aid of national organizers, the local may often retain considerable strength. Finally, locals captured by factions which are dissatisfied with existing leadership may then go their way on many matters, even to the point of seceding from the national.

The structure of the typical local is specified by the national organization. Usually there is a president, a vice president, and a secretary-treasurer, generally elected by the membership. In some unions these are full-time jobs, paid on a scale determined by the membership; in other unions, these jobs are part-time, the official continuing to work at his trade but receiving some extra pay for his union work. Many locals also employ business agents, who are not elected officials but, rather, salaried employees. The functions of the business agent include providing information and specialized services to the officers, and sitting in on conferences with management. The business agent also provides continuity to the policy of the local, since there is often a rapid turnover in local officials. Finally, there is the shop steward, or similar official, who is not, strictly speaking, an officer. The steward is usually chosen by his department on the basis of local intraplant elections. The functions of the steward will be discussed later in this chapter.

The local union usually holds frequent meetings, generally once a month, sometimes oftener. The union meeting is, in a sense, the "actualization" of the union in a given area; it is usually only at the meeting that officers and rank-and-file members congregate, that the union is transformed from an abstraction to a reality. It is through the union meeting that channels of communication between rank and file and the union are established. Here the worker can communicate directly with local officers, perhaps with representatives of the national union as well. Here the worker has the opportunity to learn what his union is doing on both the local and national levels. At the local meeting, furthermore, the worker can obtain specialized economic, social, and industrial information not ordinarily available to him. At the local meeting, the worker can participate directly in union activity by making decisions, by electing officers, by voting on constitutional changes, by deciding on special appropriations.[12]

It is both interesting and significant that in spite of the opportunities for democratic expression afforded by the local meeting—opportunities which are progressively scarcer in American life—the meeting is rarely well attended.[13] Only when there is a great issue to be decided, such as a strike or the acceptance of a union contract, will the rank and file appear as a rule. Many unions attempt to enforce attendance through a system of fines; attempts have also been made to make union meetings more attractive for workers by cutting down the length and technical content of the meetings. Perhaps this rank-and-file apathy reflects the slight amount of ideological involvement in trade unionism on the part of the American worker. What is of significance to the worker is more likely to occur in the grievance-committee meeting than in the local meeting. But, whatever the reasons—and we shall take this up again in a later chapter—the net result of worker apathy has often been to turn over control of the local to "insiders," pressure groups, or organized factions.

Generally speaking, it may be held that union structure is a mixture of bureaucratic and democratic elements. Definite forces are driving the unions toward bureaucracy, especially on the national level. On this level, there often tends to develop a hierarchy of officers pursuing careers, a staff of specialists, and a chain of command culminating in a president who is often only nominally subject to the rigors of reelection. It is true

---

[12] See George Strauss and Leonard R. Sayles, "The Local Union Meeting," *Industrial and Labor Relations Review*, vol. 6, no. 2, pp. 212–219, 1953.

[13] *Ibid.*, pp. 209–210. See also Barbash, *op. cit.*, pp. 66–68.

also at the confederation level, although the power of the hierarchy at that level is always subject to limitation by the national unions. It is even true at the local level to some extent, although here the power of the rank and file can often shatter the power of an entrenched hierarchy, at least in time of crisis.

There are also certain forces within unions which run counter to the development of bureaucracy. Since the power of the union rests, in the last analysis, on the ability of the leadership to gain or retain favorable working conditions for rank and file, the union hierarchy is ncessarily sensitive to pressures emanating from the laity. Furthermore, channels are provided through the local meeting, and through the national and federation conventions, for bringing mass pressure to bear on leadership. In rare cases the bureaucratic organization may be shattered or fundamental changes in policy may be initiated from below. Union structure is a compromise between these two constantly present and conflicting tendencies: toward bureaucracy on the one hand, and toward rank-and-file democracy on the other.

The Role Structure of Trade Unions. We have seen how the aims, technology, and bureaucratic structure of industry create certain roles which determine the actions and outlooks of the men and women who play the roles. Similarly, the aims and organization of the trade union create specific roles, which strongly influence the actions and attitudes of those who play them. In this section we shall briefly consider the trade-union roles of "top" labor leader, union staff member, local leader (including shop steward), and rank and file.

The Labor Leader. The role of the labor leader on the national or confederation level reflects the peculiarly hybrid nature of the trade union, the mixture of bureaucracy and democracy. The labor-leader role is a tissue of paradoxes. It combines the functions and modes of action of the role of leader of a large-scale bureaucracy, on the one hand, and the role of a democratic political leader on the other.[14] As a bureaucratic leader, the labor leader functions in a manner similar to that of other bureaucratic leaders, except that his actions are modified by the nature of the bureaucracy he is heading. Like the corporation executive, the labor leader formulates policy for his organization, attempts to establish proper relationships between his organization and external forces, and administers the internal affairs of his union. But these functions are carried out not in an organization geared to the manufacture of a product for profit but in an organization whose main

[14] See A. J. Muste, "Factional Fights in Trade Unions," in J. B. S. Hardman (ed.) *American Labor Dynamics,* Harcourt, Brace and Company, Inc., New York, 1928, pp. 332–333. Muste, interestingly, views the union as a mixture of an army and a town meeting.

goal is to bring pressure on employers in order to better "working conditions." Thus the union leader must formulate ends for his union which take into account the strength of the employer, the possibility of allies, and the internal state of his own organization. He must seek for alliances which will strengthen him, and attempt to neutralize powers which could, if joined, defeat him. He must try to keep his organization in fighting trim, and to build up reserves to carry it through a crisis. It is perhaps the embattled position of the union leader, his role as a leader of a fighting organization, which accounts in part for the bellicose attitudes, speech, outlook, and reactions of many union leaders.

Unlike the corporation executive, the labor leader cannot rely merely on the prestige and authority of office, on discipline, or economic pressure to control the laity. No corporation executive—or, for that matter, army general or church leader—faces the necessity of persuading workers (or soldiers, or parishioners) to reelect him to his post once a year. But this is precisely what the union leader must do. Furthermore, he is often faced with factions which are aiming to drive him from his job. For these reasons he must be a politician of a very high order. He must know how to build a political machine through a judicious use of rewards and punishments. He must be able to keep factions in line through political maneuver. He must have a knack for political skills; e.g., for settling controversies, soothing ruffled feelings, striking bargains, arranging compromises. Above all, as a political leader he must be able to keep control of his rank and file. This he can do primarily by obtaining benefits for the rank and file, by impressing them with his personality, and, if necessary, by symbolizing and giving expression to what they are thinking and feeling at a given time.

The role of the labor leader offers some genuine rewards to the man who can successfully fill it, although not the rewards which the general public usually thinks of. For instance, contrary to the general impression, the salaries of labor leaders are not particularly high. A survey made in 1944 showed that, of 67 unions investigated, about two-thirds of the presidents received less than $9,500 a year, and two-thirds of other officers received less than $7,500 a year.[15] Undoubtedly these salaries are higher than those usually earned by a factory worker; they are much less, however, than the salaries of people of comparable importance in business. Nor do union roles offer nearly the status and authority in the community which high industrial roles afford.

What makes the union leader's role attractive is not so much what it offers in comparison to other roles in society. Rather its attraction should be measured in comparison to what the labor leader might have ex-

[15] C. Wright Mills, *New Men of Power*, Harcourt, Brace and Company, Inc., New York, 1948, pp. 100–101.

pected had he remained in the factory. From this point of view, his role offers the possibilities of exercising real power and authority, of high status (at least in the working class), of security, of freedom. To understand the ambition of men to be union leaders or officials, it is necessary to understand that the union may offer opportunities for mobility to those whose chances of emerging from the mass would otherwise have been slight indeed.

Furthermore, the role of the union leader or official may offer a type of immaterial reward for which there is no counterpart in industry. The role offers the satisfaction of attaining certain idealistic ends; for instance, raising the living standards and status of labor as a whole or increasing its political power. In some cases union leaders may be motivated by a combination of idealistic ends and some of the "material" goals listed above.

The labor-leader role demands, or breeds, certain personality characteristics in those who attain and hold the role. Ambition, ability, intelligence, hardness to the point of ruthlessness, skill in the manipulation of people, are qualities which one would expect in labor leaders as in leaders of other types of organizations. However, in addition, there are certain special personality characteristics common to labor leaders which are necessitated by the special conditions of trade-union organization. These demands reflect the contradictory nature of the labor leader's role. On the one hand, there is a strong need for a personal, charismatic type of leadership. Holding the rank and file, organizing, leading large-scale conflicts, maintaining the solidarity of the organization in times of crisis—all this demands special qualities such as oratorical ability, aggressiveness, magnetism, courage, decisiveness. It should not be a surprise, therefore, that the labor movement has thrown up some of the most colorful, some of the most richly charismatically endowed figures in American life. On the other hand, the tenuous hold of trade unionism in American life, as well as the entrenched bureaucratic nature of some unions, breeds or calls for exactly opposite types of personalities. The timid, cautious, compromising labor leader is no less indigenous to the American labor movement than the flamboyant leader. It is the juxtaposition of these two personality types which makes for some of the most violent contrasts in the American labor movement.

If the rewards of the labor-leader role are high, its strains are severe. In view of the long tenure of many union presidents, it would seem paradoxical to say the labor leader is often in an impossible position where he must attempt to reconcile the irreconcilable. Yet such is often the case. For instance, he must strike a balance between the demands of administration and the demands of politics. If he neglects his organization and accedes to rank-and-file wishes, he may be endangering the stability of the union. If, on the other hand, he becomes concerned primarily with the bureaucracy, he risks the danger of loss of contact with the rank and file. Similarly the labor leader must attempt to strike a balance between those elements in trade unionism which are excessively cautious and those which are overly militant.[16] He must know how to keep extremists in check at certain times and yet be able to move workingmen to action at another time. The union leader also faces certain "external" strains. His organization exists in an environment containing many powerful enemies, and defeat by these enemies is an ever-present possibility, as the history of the American labor movement richly demonstrates.

Union Staff Roles. A relatively late development has been the appearance of the expert in the union hierarchy. His entrance into the union movement has been the result of several factors. As the union has expanded the services it provides to its members, it has had to acquire specialists in those services. Experts have also been needed to meet, on something like equal terms, the specialists employed by management in collective-bargaining negotiations. Demand for experts has developed also out of the need to present the labor story to the public and to counteract the antilabor propaganda of employers. The expert has also become necessary for dealing with government agencies, which are heavily provided with research experts and legal specialists.

As a result, several types of experts have become regular components of some unions. Perhaps the most important of such experts is the lawyer. The lawyer's functions include contributing advice to the unions in their dealing with the government, advice on the negotiation of collective-bargaining agreements, advice on the legality of internal union affairs. He represents the union in public hearings and on the mass media of communication. The role of the lawyer is becoming increasingly important as open conflict between management and labor has given way to contractual and legal relationships, and new labor laws must be interpreted before a series of judicial and quasi-judicial bodies.[17]

Other types of experts are also employed by unions. Economists may be employed to prepare economic arguments that the union can use in negotiating contracts with employers or in presenting facts to the public. There may be press experts to prepare the union newspapers. Publicity experts strive to present the union in a favorable light to the

[16] See Muste, *op. cit.,* p. 335.
[17] Joseph Kovner, "The Labor Lawyer," in J. B. S. Hardman and Maurice F. Neufeld (eds.), *The House of Labor,* Prentice-Hall, Inc., Englewood Cliffs, N.J., 1951, pp. 397–398.

nation. Teachers, doctors, artists, psychologists, social workers, engineers, recreation directors, legislative experts, political experts, accountants, etc., may be found on the staffs of various unions.

The general rewards connected with a staff role in an union differ somewhat from those found in the industrial staff role. For one thing the financial reward is much greater in industry than in the labor union. Facilities are usually more plentiful in industry than in the union, and the status attached to an industrial job is, at least in the eyes of the public, higher than for a comparable job in the labor world. What the union staff job can offer, however, is the opportunity to do certain types of research which cannot be done in industry; e.g., on labor economics. Another reward of the role may be the opportunity to attain certain idealistic goals, for instance, aiding the union movement and helping to raise the standard of living of the working class. Undoubtedly, as the union movement has become more bureaucratized, many staff members have been added who look on their job non-idealistically. But the idealistic motives are still very real for many men of high ability, who could certainly get higher returns in money and status elsewhere.[18]

The role of the staff member is often a stressful one. With a few notable exceptions, the expert, however necessary to the union, is not generally welcomed or trusted by labor leaders. Distrust of the labor expert seems to arise from three main sources. In the first place, the labor leader and the labor expert rarely come from the same background and rarely talk the same language. The leader usually comes from the working class, the expert from the middle class. Furthermore, the leader has usually come up through the ranks, through many hard and even violent struggles, while the expert has usually entered the union near the top and through his special training. In the second place, the labor leader may have a deep distrust of the universities which have prepared the expert. In part this distrust may be simple anti-intellectualism, but in part it arises from the conviction of some labor leaders that universities are management-controlled and management-oriented. Labor leaders who think this way point to the many "business schools" in the universities, to the large grants provided many universities by business, to the presence of businessmen on boards of trustees. In the third place, the leader may have a deep distrust of the aims which have brought the expert into the labor movement. The labor leader, is probably interested only in immediate problems: wages, hours, organizational details, and political fights. He distrusts the far-sweeping aims of the labor expert,

[18] On the general topic of staff goals and the motivations of union staff members, see *ibid.*, articles by James Carey, pp. 492–493; Mark Starr, pp. 498–500; and Solomon Barking, pp. 500–502.

who seems impractical, without a real knowledge of what the worker wants, thinks, or feels.

The outcome of this distrust is severe strain on the labor intellectual. Some labor leaders make deliberate attempts to keep the position of the expert "cut down to size." The result is that the union movement does not possess nearly the number of experts it needs. Although this situation is due in part to limited union funds, the fact is that many unions are reluctant to hire experts. Many union staffs are undermanned. Often the expert is overworked, and the tasks facing him are too large to be taken seriously. Furthermore, the idealism of the labor expert is likely to receive some rude shocks in the realities of union life. He may find himself a political pawn in some union leader's struggle for power. He will certainly find out quickly that he has little chance to influence policy, except indirectly; that, in essence, he is the servant of a policy which he may consider wrong or shortsighted. Under these circumstances idealism may wane, and the rewards to be found in the "soulless corporation" may seem more promising.

Local Leaders. At the local level two types of roles may be distinguished: official roles such as those of president, secretary, or executive-board member, and the roles of shop stewards, or committeemen, as they are sometimes called.[19] Official roles may be considered true union hierarchy roles, analogous to lower managerial positions, although perhaps less than half of these union roles are filled by full-time paid officers.[20] The roles of shop stewards are analogous to foremen's roles; that is, they are intermediate between the hierarchy and the laity.

In general the functions of the local officials include setting local policy, administering the internal affairs of the union, organizing new members where possible, and, in some matters, representing the workers to management and to the community. The function of the shop steward is to represent the workers on the job, to handle grievances, and, on occasion, to serve as the spokesman for the workers in collective-bargaining negotiations. Both officials and stewards deal directly with the rank and file and with management; local officers, in addition, deal with national union officials.

It is commonly agreed that the local officer's role is a difficult and complex one. Certainly the generalized rewards of the role are not striking, at least at first glance. For instance, the salaries of local officers are only slightly higher than those of benchworkers. Often officers' salaries are tied to going rates in the plant; the officer may be paid at the highest rate paid in the plant or at the foreman's rate. Even where

[19] Philip Taft, "Understanding Union Administration," *Harvard Business Review,* vol. 24, no. 2, p. 246, 1946.

[20] *Ibid.,* p. 254.

the officer receives a flat salary, this is rarely more than what the highly paid worker in the plant could earn.[21] Other generalized rewards, such as prestige, status, and power, may be achieved through these roles. However, these rewards are often recognized only in the community from which the officer comes, that is, the local working-class community. The role of local leader may convey little or even negative prestige in the general public.[22]

What, then, motivates the worker to fill a role with so little intrinsic reward—indeed a role which may incur disapproval of the general public and of management? The importance of this question rests on the fact that, in a very real sense, the union *is* its active members; those willing to do the hard, unrewarding day-by-day tasks of the union. No simple answer is possible. Workers are motivated to play union roles for varying reasons.[23] Unions are different things to different men. Some become active unionists because of certain personal gratifications they may derive from union work. For instance, the role of union officer or shop steward affords an opportunity to talk with management on equal terms; it gives to the unionist a sense of power, which he could never have obtained as a workingman. Some workers find in the union an outlet for their abilities and talents. Some find in union work an opportunity for achievement, for a smoothly running union may be an achievement of a high order. To some unionists the esteem of their fellows is important; for some the lack of esteem accorded unionists in the general public is more than made up in this way. For other workers the union is a sort of social activity in which they can play active parts, a sort of substitute for club life. Some may find in the union a release from a boring job, an unpleasant routine.

It has been noted that the union may serve as a channel of mobility for the ambitious, restless worker, to whom channels of mobility in plant or community are closed. The worker may envision a career

---

[21] *Ibid.*

[22] See, for instance, an article by A. A. Imberman, "Labor Leaders and Society," *Harvard Business Review*, vol. 28, no. 1, pp. 52–60, 1950. Although this article seems to be overdrawn, it is of interest in its revelation of negative status accorded labor leaders by powerful elements in society. It also reveals the degree to which some labor leaders accept and strive for generally recognized standards of status.

[23] See the following studies: Eli Chinoy, "Local Union Leadership," in Alvin W. Gouldner (ed.), *Studies in Leadership*, Harper & Brothers, New York, 1950, pp. 156–173; Joel Seidman, Jack London, and Bernard Karsh, "Leadership in a Local Union," *American Journal of Sociology*, vol. 56, no. 3, pp. 229–237, 1950, copyright by University of Chicago; George Strauss and Leonard R. Sayles, "Occupation and the Selection of Local Leaders," *American Journal of Sociology*, vol. 58, no. 6, pp. 585–591, 1953, copyright by University of Chicago; George Strauss and Leonard R. Sayles, "The Unpaid Local Leader," *Harvard Business Review*, vol. 30, no. 3, pp. 91–104, 1952.

leading to an important position in the national union; or he may, in certain plants, hope to use the union as a steppingstone into the lower reaches of management. On a lesser scale, the union job sometimes, though not often, means an appreciable economic gain and greater seniority and security on the job.

In addition to these self-centered motives, idealistic motives may also spur workers into union activity. Sometimes workers become union officials because they are the best available for the job. These men may feel it a duty to their fellows not to refuse to serve where leadership ability is not too plentiful. Some unionists are motivated by resentment over working conditions or the overweening power of management. There are also workers who are motivated by ideological reasons; a belief in unionism, or adherence to some political creed stressing the importance of the working class.

The popular stereotype of the union leader as a "sorehead," deeply resentful of management and prone to all sorts of irresponsible actions, is more often than not inaccurate. The stereotyped union activist tends to appear during a great organizing campaign, when such talents have a certain value. At other times, the union official is more likely to be a skilled, highly paid worker, with long seniority on the job. He is likely to be popular with the rank and file, coming into contact with many of them in such a way as to impress them. He may be discontented with working conditions, but often he is idealistic and gives his time and energy unselfishly to the union. These are hardly the characteristics of an irresponsible.

The local official's role is, furthermore, subjected to severe strains. The union official is not likely to be esteemed in the predominantly middle-class culture of the nation. Nor is he likely to be approved of by management; in fact, many union leaders are convinced that management is out to "get them." And, although the union leader is generally popular among the workers—he would not be an official otherwise—it may be his unpleasant duty to have to "sell" an unpopular policy to the rank and file.[24] Union work may be so demanding of time, effort, and energy that the family life may suffer. Yet for many workers these strains are more than made up by the satisfactions in union work.

It would appear that a complex social process controls the behavior of union officials. The goals of unionism and the environment in which American unions operate largely determine the hybrid structure of most unions. This structure, in turn, determines the roles that men play in the union. Roles help shape the actions and outlook of the role player. If it has proved difficult to generalize about the specific content of roles, it

[24] An example of this is afforded by the decision of Studebaker workers in South Bend, Ill., to take a large cut in their wages at the urging of union leadership.

is because the union movement has little of the uniformity of industry. Nevertheless, it has been possible to demonstrate several patterns in the functions, rewards, and strains of roles in the union hierarchy. Perhaps the forces driving the union activist are not less powerful and complex than those driving the executive—for whom, incidentally, the goal is clear, stakes are high, and success can be clearly measured.

Rank and File. Union organization in the United States maintains certain definite relationships to the rank and file—the great mass of workers who pay dues, rather infrequently attend union meetings, and go on the picket line when necessary. It is important to note that union hierarchy is not related to rank and file in the same manner as, say, the officer corps of an army to enlisted men, or as management to workers. Unionism has been created for the benefit of the rank and file; improving the lot of the worker is as much the aim of the union as making profit is the aim of business enterprise. This enormously complicates the relationship between hierarchy and laity in the union.

For one thing, the union hierarchy is prevented from pursuing policies which may be necessary to the maintenance of the union organization but which will harm masses of workers over a long period of time. Indeed, the union may not be able to pursue policies which run counter to the short-term interests of workers. The union leader is not in the position of the business executive who, in order to preserve the solvency of his firm, lays off half his working force. Even those powers of coercion over rank and file which unions do possess are rarely used. Expulsions from unions rarely occur, because such expulsions directly contradict the aim and strength of unionism, mass organization of workers.[25] Furthermore, at least in the democratically controlled unions, rank and file has a final veto power over the actions of officers through the union election or through a referendum.[26]

The tenuous and provisional hold of much union leadership over its membership in itself complicates matters for the union hierarchy. However, the situation is further complicated by the fact that unionism needs a strict discipline in rank and file if it is to function effectively as an economic pressure group—or, indeed, if it is to survive in the long run. For instance, the most effective weapon which the union has in its arsenal, the strike, is peculiarly dependent on the discipline of rank and file.[27] Similarly, the ability of the union to live up to the labor contract depends upon restraining the immediate economic aims or resentments

---

[25] Clyde Summers, "Disciplinary Powers of Unions," *Industrial and Labor Relations Review*, vol. 3, no. 4, pp. 487–488, 1950.

[26] See, for instance, Herbert A. Shepard, "Democratic Control in a Labor Union," *American Journal of Sociology*, vol. 54, no. 4, pp. 311–316, 1949, copyright by University of Chicago.

[27] See Chap. 12 for a discussion of the conduct of a strike.

of the worker. Rank-and-file discipline of the firmest kind is necessitated also by the hostility or bare toleration of the union by sections of the employer class, by the mass media of communication, and by conservative forces in the society. Finally, rank-and-file discipline is necessary if the assaults of rival unions are to be warded off and if factionalism within the union is to be curbed.

Under these circumstances, the only way for union leadership effectively to control rank and file, at least in the democratic union, is by gaining and retaining the loyalty of the rank and file to the union. This does not mean that other, less democratic measures may not be used to control rank and file. But, except in those unions dominated by out-and-out underworld forces, in the long run the voluntary allegiance of the rank and file is absolutely necessary for the union and for its leadership.

What has been said thus far raises very important and much-debated questions. On what bases will the American worker give his allegiance to the union movement?[28] How can his loyalty to the union be assured? Does he see the union as strictly an economic weapon? Does he regard it as an insurance policy, to "make sure that nothing will happen"? Does he look at it as an instrument for furthering the aims of the working class? Does he feel that it is essentially a "social" club?

The evidence is by no means clear, nor does it all point in one direction. But the best guess is that the loyalty of the rank and file to union leadership is dependent on the ability of leadership to deal successfully with issues of immediate economic concern. For instance, Rose's study of a large teamsters' local in St. Louis revealed that strict economic goals were considered by most union members to be the proper ends of union activity. Workers also expected unions to fight for "better working conditions," job security, and the protection of seniority.[29] Another study found that the workers were most interested in their unions as protection against arbitrary actions by management, and as agencies for obtaining economic security.[30]

In general, then, it may be said that the rank and file demand of union leadership programs and action in connection with certain immediately important problems or issues arising from economic condi-

[28] This question is discussed in greater detail in Chap. 14, "Theories of the Labor Movement."

[29] See Arnold Rose, *Union Solidarity,* University of Minnesota Press, Minneapolis, 1952, p. 142.

[30] Leonard R. Sayles and George Strauss, "What the Worker Really Thinks of His Union,"*Harvard Business Review,* vol. 31, no. 3, p. 94, 1953. For other studies of the basis of rank-and-file loyalty to union leadership, see Seidman, London, and Karsh, *op. cit.;* Caroline Baer Rose, "Morale in a Trade Union," *American Journal of Sociology,* vol. 56, no. 2, pp. 167–174, 1950, copyright by the University of Chicago.

tions or conditions in the plant. Where management is arbitrary, the rank and file will expect the union to give them protection against management. Where technological change threatens the security of the workers, they will expect union officialdom to be concerned with job security. In times of rising prices, they will be most interested in higher wages. If workers are nearing retirement age, they will look to the union for an adequate pension plan; if they are young, they may be more interested in immediate benefits.

Workers undoubtedly do show some interest in other than immediate or "practical" ends. For instance, some of them evince considerable interest in the free medical care provided by some unions. The rank and file of such "socially minded" unions as the Amalgamated Clothing Workers have a relatively strong interest in long-range welfare programs. But by and large union members do not seem to wish to have their unions engage in political campaigns or undertake large organizing drives. Rank and file do not seem to be particularly interested in having their unions spearhead a working-class movement. Nor do many workers seem to value their unions highly as social clubs or as recreation centers, although unions may serve such functions for a small minority. Finally, allegiance to the union is not, except for a very few, based on a hope of rising through the union structure.

If what has been said above is correct, then allegiance of rank and file to unions depends on the extent to which unions can achieve economic and other "practical" goals dear to the workingman. There is evidence that a large proportion of workingmen feel that unions have benefited them in these ways. For instance, Rose found that three-quarters of the workingmen in the union he investigated thought that the union had benefited them economically, and 30 per cent thought that it had helped them to get job security.[31] About one worker in six thought that the union had helped protect workers from the arbitrary power of the boss. Fewer workers thought that the union was helping to achieve goals not directly connected with the job; e.g., medical or legal advice, adequate recreation, fellowship among workers, and cooperation between management and labor.

Thus it would seem that an overwhelming number of unionized workers are at least mildly behind the leadership of their unions. This support is a tribute to the fact that, by and large, the unions have fulfilled the expectations of the rank and file. The continuing success of the unions in plant elections seem to bear out this view, although, of course, changing economic or technological conditions might upset the present situation.

However, the fact that an overwhelming majority of unionized work-

[31] Arnold Rose, *op. cit.*, p. 63.

ers support their unions does not make them active, enthusiastic rank-and-filers. Union meetings are, as we have seen, often poorly attended. Rank and file often grumble at the dues they must pay, resist assessments, and savagely criticize union leadership. The union press is by no means always read by workers. Few workers seem to be interested in union-sponsored education courses or are willing to attend labor schools. Nor are the rank and file always willing to follow the advice of union leadership on politics, on attitudes toward racial minorities, or on other social issues. Most workers seem to exhibit an ambivalent attitude toward their unions. In times of crisis—for instance, in a strike—they will support the union to the hilt; at other times they feel only a mild interest in it and identification with it.

The reasons for the apathy of rank and file except in times of crisis is a much-debated problem among those interested in the trade-union movement. Several reasons may be advanced here. First, although wages, hours, and other "practical" considerations are of great importance to the worker, they are not "burning issues," except at those isolated times when a wage cut is threatened or negotiations for a new contract are in progress. In the normal course of events, the union barely enters the consciousness of many workers. Not only is the worker innocent of ideological interest in his union, but few unions attempt to do anything to relieve him of ideological innocence.

A second explanation of the peculiar mentality of the worker, "apathy mixed with allegiance," may be found in the fact that many workers apparently feel that they have little or no control over the union, even the local. In the nondemocratically controlled unions, the workers' suspicions are self-explanatory. Even in democratically controlled locals many workers may feel alienated from their unions. That a feeling of alienation may not be entirely unjustified is shown by the fact that in many locals the officers and active members come from a surprisingly narrow portion of the plant. Entire departments may be without representation on the executive board of the local. For instance, one study showed that the leadership of a local tended to be drawn from highly paid skilled workers with outstanding production records.[32] Another study showed that local leaders or influential members of the union came from homogeneous work groups whose members performed similar work, received similar pay, and communicated freely with one another during work. Often such leaders lived close together and had social contacts in the community.[33]

[32] Toimi E. Kyllonen, "Social Characteristics of Active Unionists," *American Journal of Sociology,* vol. 56, no. 6, p. 529, 1951. Copyright by the University of Chicago.
[33] George Strauss and Leonard R. Sayles, "Patterns of Participation in Local Unions," *Industrial and Labor Relations Review,* vol. 6, no. 1, pp. 39–43, 1952.

When a homogeneous group of workers obtains control of a local, its members may be able to prolong their tenure of power by building a political machine. This in itself would be sufficient to increase the apathy of other workers in the plant. But, furthermore, by controlling a local, one group of workers may be in a position to secure advantages for itself at the expense of the other workers. It is not generally realized that the interests of different groups of workers may clash at certain points; e.g., over the question of relative rates of pay for dayworkers as opposed to nightworkers, over the claims of seniority versus the claims of ability or need, over the evaluation of jobs, over the question of laying off workers in slack times versus a policy of "spreading the work."[34] In each of these cases, one group of workers can benefit only if the other groups give something up. The outcome of these conflicts is very often determined by the leadership of the local unions. If workers with special interests in the plant are in control of a local, they can settle these conflicts in their own favor and at the expense of the less powerful workers. For those workers who are not in positions of power in the local, the net result may be a feeling of powerlessness, of resentment, of exploitation, and of apathy to the union.

In the third place, rank-and-file apathy and even hostility to the union arise from the changes which take place within a union once it has passed its early fighting days and has become a stable institution. From an instrument of rebellion the union turns into an instrument of control and coercion over the rank and file. This paradox arises from the fact that as a party to a contract with management the union must keep its rank and file in line. This means that the union must, on occasion, deny worker grievances, demand that the worker keep up a certain level of production, punish him if he goes out on a wildcat strike. Thus the union may become to the worker an alternate source of the onerous discipline to which he is subjected during his working hours. It may seem to the worker that at times the union can hardly be distinguished from management.

Fourth, in some plants lack of interest in the union apparently arises from fear of management retribution, real or imagined. If there is collusion between management and the union, the worker may be intimidated from expressing his resentment against the union. For obvious reasons it is difficult to say to what extent either of these situations exists in industry.

Finally, apathy or hostility to the union may have its source in the general climate of opinion and attitude toward unionism in the nation as a whole. Workers, no less than other Americans, are subject to anti-

---

[34] Leonard R. Sayles and George Strauss, "Conflicts within the Local Union," *Harvard Business Review*, vol. 30, no. 6, pp. 87–88, 1952.

union propaganda, or to the antiunion sentiments of the community in which they live. American workingmen are readers of widely syndicated antilabor columnists, and if these columnists consistently present a distorted and unfriendly view of the labor movement, yet there is enough truth in their writings to strike a note of assent among many workers. Furthermore, many workingmen assent in some degree to the low evaluation which the culture places on the workingman's role. They may feel secret shame and guilt at belonging to so unmistakably a working-class organization as a union, and this shame and guilt may become transformed either into apathy or into hostility toward the union. This general attitude is perhaps most common among unionized white-collar workers, among those who have lately come into the working class, and in general among those who retain hopes of "rising" out of the working class. At the same time this type of union member may nourish secret guilt at attacking so highly valued a figure as a business executive. This guilt may become transformed, through a process of sublimation, into hostility toward the union and a determination to have as little to do with it as possible. It is, of course, difficult to estimate the relative importance of this source of apathy toward unionism, but there is at least some evidence pointing toward the existence of these kinds of attitudes in the minds of some American workers.[35]

Racketeer Labor Unions. Thus far in this chapter we have spoken of the "normal" variety of unionism, that is, unionism whose major organizational aim is to better conditions for the rank and file. From this point of view it has been possible to treat alike craft and industrial unions, AFL unions and CIO unions, democratic and nondemocratic unions.

However, there are some unions whose major organizational aim is not the bettering of working conditions for the rank and file; or, in some cases, this goal is really subordinate to other goals. For instance, the organizational aim of certain "left-wing" unions may be to heighten the worker's political consciousness or to promote revolutionary agitation. In this case, a drive for certain immediate goals such as higher wages or shorter hours may be pursued also, but what is important is the extent to which such a drive may serve the political aims of the organization.

Another sort of deviation from "normal" unionism is the racketeer union. In this case the union is used as an instrument for the enrichment of union officials or as an illegitimate instrument of power. Labor racketeering may occur in "normal" or even idealistically led unions, or entire unions may be given over to racketeering. In the former case, an occasional labor official pursues a racket; or even a normally nonrack-

---

[35] See, for instance, Sayles and Strauss, "What the Worker Really Thinks of His Union," pp. 96–98.

eteering official may use his office for some illegitimate end. In the latter case, the union may be dominated by out-and-out criminals; in fact, it may be scarcely distinguishable from an underworld organization. A continuum might be erected running from the gangster-led and -dominated union on one end, to the union with occasionally dishonest officials on the other end, with some unions falling in between these extremes. This continuum contains, of course, only those unions with any racketeering at all.

In general, the racketeer operates by using the economic power of the union, or by threatening its use. For instance, he may milk union members of fat dues and assessments by threatening them with expulsion from the union and loss of job. He may receive large bribes from employers to call off threatened or existing strikes, or not to organize a given industry. He may join with some employers, for a consideration, to drive competitors out of business, by calling strikes against them. He may undertake to organize an industry with the compliance and financial support of the employer in order to head off the entrance of a militant union of the normal variety. He may, spurred on by a generous bribe, agree to take a lower wage scale for his members. He may become a silent partner in those very firms whose employees he is supposedly representing. He may be tied in with machine politicians, supplying them with money and votes in return for favors, including the overlooking of his crimes.

Since racketeering is necessarily a *sub rosa* activity, it is difficult, almost impossible, to estimate its extent. However, it seems safe to say that, in spite of the alarms raised by some antilabor publicists, large-scale racketeering is confined to a few unions. Racketeering seems to flourish in industries which are divided into small, fiercely competitive units, in industries handling perishable goods, and in businesses which supply local markets.[36] Businesses in competitive fields sometimes use labor racketeers to deal with competition. Businesses handling perishable goods or with local markets are extremely vulnerable to a suddenly called strike or strong-arm tactics. On the other hand, widespread racketeering in industrial unions is much rarer, apparently. It is also quite rare on the national level. Where it does occur, racketeering may be extremely lucrative. Thus Robert P. Brindell, boss of the building-trades unions in New York, amassed a fortune of over a million dollars between 1915 and 1920.

Labor racketeering arises under special social conditions, and it is no accident that it has been more prevalent in the United States than elsewhere. Mills points out that the labor leader who looks on a union in simple business terms, who regards himself as a businessman selling

[36] Mills, *op. cit.*, pp. 128–129.

labor at the highest price, may easily adopt racketeering attitudes and practices.[37] Labor racketeering is the outgrowth of the very lack of ideological motives in American unionism on which many labor leaders pride themselves. The honesty of this or that union official becomes the factor deciding the presence or absence of racketeering in a union. Racketeering also feeds on the lethargy and apathy of rank and file.[38] A vicious circle operates here, because racketeering reinforces the apathy of rank and file.

It is not our intention to gloss over the problem of union racketeering. It is important both in its own right and as a symptom of strains in the American labor movement. However, this drab scene should not be allowed to obscure the larger picture of American unionism, which reveals a unionism dominated by concern with bettering working-class conditions and building the power of the union movement. It is to the functioning of these "normal" unions that we shall now turn our attention.

[37] *Ibid.*, chap. 7.
[38] See Sidney Lens, *Left, Right and Center,* Henry Regnery Company, Chicago, 1949, p. 67.

CHAPTER 12

The Functions of Unionism: Unionism as an
Instrument of Power

Thus far our concern in Part 3 has been with the history and structure of the trade-union movement in the United States. Now we shall turn to the functions of trade unionism in the American industrial system.

At the beginning of such an analysis, we must take cognizance of a basic dichotomy in union functions. On the one hand, the union functions as an instrument for changing certain economic and social conditions in the factory. It fights for higher wages for workers, shorter hours, worker welfare; it also seeks to cut down the power of management and to enhance its own power. We shall postpone discussion of this function to the next chapter, when we take up the topic of collective bargaining. On the other hand, in order to function as an economic and social instrument, the union must operate as an instrument of power; that is, it must function as an army in order to bring its opponents to terms. This is the nature of unionism; it is, in one of its major aspects, a conflict group, and no understanding of unionism is possible without an understanding of this fact.

The Union as a Power Instrument. The inherent militancy of unionism arises, in the first place, from a very real clash of interest between management and labor in several spheres. On the one hand is a cost-conscious management seeking to purchase labor and to use it most economically; on the other hand is labor seeking to maximize wages and other benefits and seeking relief from the discipline of factory life and machine. No amount of talk of "misunderstanding" between capital and labor, or "blocked channels of communication" can serve to gloss over this real area of conflict.

In the second place, the union must function as an instrument of power because it has only recently arrived on the industrial scene in force, because it has not yet become fully institutionalized in our culture, because it is relatively weak on the political scene. Whatever power the union possesses to match the great power of management, it must evolve from its own organization and through its own efforts. It is primarily for these reasons that the union must function as a power instrument and must evolve the necessary structure and attitudes to function effectively as such an instrument.

To say that all unions must function as instruments of power is not to say that all the actions of all unions must be considered as expressions of this underlying function. Generalizations are dangerous in this area and may lead to unwarranted conclusions about the essential hostility of management and labor, or about the inescapable nature of class warfare. Rather, when we speak of the function of power, we mean to describe a basic aspect of unionism, a condition of union survival, not the totality of unionism. Furthermore, to speak of unions as instruments of power is not to say that this power must always be expressed in force; power may function just as effectively when it is held in reserve as when it is converted into force. It should be noted that industrial bureaucracies also dispose of great power, actual or potential, although this function is not their major organizational aim. Thus when we speak of the instruments of power which are in the hands of the union or of management, we do not mean that these instruments are commonly employed, but that in the last emergency they *could* be employed.

It should be understood that unions differ in the extent to which they are willing or able to use their power. A continuum might be erected stretching from those unions which are almost completely somnolent, on the one hand, to those which display the most fiery militancy on the other. (Of course, it does not follow that the most militant unions are necessarily the most powerful.) In general the militancy of a union, its willingness to employ its instruments of power, depends upon such factors as the ideology of the union leaders and members, or the extent of employer opposition. Perhaps the nature of the work also plays a role, hazardous work seeming to produce militant, bold workingmen and unions.[1] Militancy may also be related to the ethnic, racial, and religious backgrounds of the workers. Yet it should be pointed out that even the most apathetic workers may be galvanized into action at times, given the proper combination of resentment and militant leadership.

The union must function as an instrument of power because of a real clash of interest in a number of areas between the workers and management, and because the union has few ways to bring pressure to bear on management other than through its own militancy and strength. However, if we say that one of the functions of trade unionism is to carry out a struggle of power with management, we do not mean that such a

---

[1] See, for instance, Paul Eliel, "Industrial Peace and Conflict: A Study of Two Pacific Coast Industries," *Industrial and Labor Relations Review*, vol. 2, no. 4, pp. 477–501, 1949.

struggle must be carried out to the point of the utter ruin of one of the contending parties. This is a common misconception where there is a struggle between conflicting interest groups. On the contrary, the struggle between management and labor is marked by many long truces; there are many areas in which the struggle may be compromised, in which real cooperation is possible. In fact, the long-range success of a union as an instrument of power can be measured only by its ability to turn a conflict into a period of enduring peace. On the other hand, a permanent condition of cooperation is not natural to the labor-management situation. Where such a condition exists it may be because the power of either management or labor is overwhelming, or because of collusion between the union and management. Nor would a condition of permanent peace between management and labor necessarily be desirable, as we shall see.

The Nature of Power. By *power* we shall mean the ability of an individual, group, or institution to control another individual, group, or institution to its own benefit. On the one hand there is a type of power which involves control of the actions of others through the threat of sanctions of various types. This type of power is what we mean when we speak of *force*. But, on the other hand, force is not the only type of power; power is also the ability to persuade, to mold attitudes, to establish the basic definitions of the situation in terms of which men will feel, think, and finally act. This second type of power we may call *persuasive power* or *propagandistic power*. It is characteristic of this type of power that it is rarely effective when used against opponents unless these opponents are near defeat anyway; it is more effectively used on one's followers, on potential followers, or on the neutral, disinterested, and apathetic.

Power varies not only in type but in degree. It may be unleashed in a single, dramatic, even violent act; e.g., in a strike, or more narrowly in the setting up of a picket line. But it may also be let loose little by little, as when a worker slows down on the job, or when management carefully, systematically, and slowly undermines the militancy of a union, or when the union slowly changes the attitudes of its rank and file or the attitudes of the public at large.

Variation in Types of Power Employed by Unions. The type of power which a union uses differs from situation to situation and at different stages in the development of the union. In general, the type of power employed by the union depends, first, upon the particular situation. One type may be employed during a period of organization, another during a settled period of collective bargaining. The type of power employed also depends upon the attitudes of management; one type must be employed where management is hostile to organized labor, another where management is disposed to compromise. Again, the type of power used by the union depends upon the economic cycle; e.g., coercive measures, such as large-scale strikes, are seldom undertaken in times of rising unemployment and declining wages.[2] The political situation may also strongly influence the types of power used; a large-scale strike may be possible in peace but not in war, or may be possible under one sort of national administration but not under another.

Secondly, the type of power employed by the union differs according to certain internal conditions in the union. For instance, just after a union has been organized, it may be able to count on the enthusiastic support of a certain section of workers. But other groups of workers may be frightened, loyal to management, hostile to the idea of unionism. Often the workers are deeply suspicious of each other because they come from differing ethnic, racial, and religious backgrounds, without traditions of cooperation. In addition, the union may find among its workers bitter memories of lost strikes, of racketeering unions, of "sellouts." All these conditions may pose the need for the use of certain types of power or combinations of types of power. On the other hand, a situation of stable collective bargaining and management-labor compromise may be marked by a disciplined, loyal rank and file, as well as by an effective union organization. Under these conditions, the union may be able to employ quite another type of power. In the former case, coercive power such as violent strikes may be necessary to dramatize the fact of union power and unify the workers; under the conditions of stability, persuasion and tight discipline may be the most effective means of union power.

Types of Union Tactics. We may now turn to a discussion of the tactics which the union employs. By *tactics* we shall mean the specific forms of coercion or persuasion which the union uses in certain situations.

The Organizing Drive. One of the major instruments of force which unions employ is the organizing drive. It is true that the organizing drive is more often thought of as an aim of union organization rather than as a union tactic. But it may also be thought of as a tactic because (1) the mere threat of its use may be enough to bring management to terms, (2) a successful drive may likewise bring management to terms, and (3) an organizing drive may be part of a larger campaign against an entire industry. Furthermore, the organizing drive differs from other types of union tactics in its methods and sequences of action; the organizing drive possesses its own inner dynamic.

The history of the organization of a given plant or an entire industry is always unique;[3] some plants are organized through the spontaneous

---

[2] See K. G. J. C. Knowles, *Strikes: A Study in Industrial Conflict,* Basil Blackwell & Mott, Ltd., Oxford, 1952, p. 144.

[3] For accounts of union organization drives, see Robert R. R. Brooks, *When Labor*

action of the workers, some through the seizure of a company union, and some only through the efforts of outsiders. But it may be safely said that the first stage in every successful organizing drive is always the same: the development of a body of workers who feel either consciously or unconsciously bored, frustrated, resentful, and deprived. Blaming organization on "outside agitators," which was much the fashion at one time, is thus clearly beside the point. The union organizer plays an important part in many organizing drives, but he can operate only on the basis of existing worker dissatisfaction.

The organizer—who may or may not be important in an organizing drive—is usually a paid staff member of the national union. However, the confederation, some state labor bodies, and even some locals also maintain organizers. The organizer is usually a man of wide experience in the field. He is typically tough, resourceful, a good speaker; he has an intimate knowledge of the psychology of American workingmen. Often an organizer is chosen to organize a certain industry or district because of his knowledge of special areas, or because of his racial, ethnic, or religious background. The organizer's ability to speak a foreign language, or to refer to a common ancestry or religion, may be of decisive importance for the success of the organizing drive.

If the organizer has been called in after a spontaneous strike has occurred or an organization has been formed, his job may be merely to help the new local get a charter, to inform the workers of the rudiments of union procedure, and to gain recognition for the local from management. In many cases the organizer arrives before a strike has occurred, or even before a spontaneous organization has been formed. In this case, the organizer will, typically, begin by studying the town and estimating the extent of management influence in the community. He will attempt to uncover possible sympathizers in the community, who may be of use. After this preliminary work is out of the way, the organizer will then seek to discover the actively dissatisfied workers within the plant he wishes to organize. He will try to estimate the influence of these dissidents in the plant; he will also try to estimate the numbers and strength of those workers loyal to management.

If he decides that there is a chance of organizing the plant, he will call a meeting—secretly, if necessary—of the actively dissatisfied. His aim is to get these workers to spread the union message in the plant. A general propaganda campaign is begun to activate more workers, to

Organizes, Yale University Press, New Haven, Conn., 1937, chap. 1; Ruth McKenney, *Industrial Valley*, Harcourt, Brace and Company, Inc., New York, 1939; Eli Ginzberg, *The Labor Leader*, The Macmillan Company, New York, 1948, chap. VIII; Richmond C. Nyman, *Union-Management Cooperation in the Stretchout*, Yale University Press, New Haven, Conn., 1934.

overcome fear, and to isolate and discredit management-oriented workers. This propaganda campaign is carried out by word of mouth, through the distribution of pamphlets, and, at a certain stage, through meetings and speeches by the organizer.

The message of this propaganda campaign is aimed at several attitudes or beliefs commonly found among workers.[4] First is the economic appeal. Workers are promised higher wages, shorter hours; their situation is compared unfavorably with other workers in the same or other industries. Secondly, the propaganda campaign offers explanations to the workers for their poor economic situation; it speaks of "corporate greed," of "high profits and dividends." Workers are charged with apathy, or stupidity, or cowardice for letting this situation continue. In this manner the worker is supplied with arguments and rationalizations which he can use to defend himself and to convince others. Thirdly, the campaign aims to build up the confidence of the workers; it minimizes hazards and stresses the importance and power of the workingman. Brief descriptions of successful labor fights may be circulated; the workingman's fight will be linked to historic movements, such as the fight for democracy or the struggle against totalitarianism.[5] Fourth, the workingman is appealed to on the basis of his desire to be a member of this group, to "go along with the boys." Special appeals may be aimed at the leaders of informal groups; the informal leader may be able to sway his entire group. Finally, the union propagandist will strive, usually through speeches, to tap whatever reservoirs of hostility and aggression against management have accumulated among the workers. The organizer may, for instance, attempt to arouse resentment at the discipline of the plant, at lack of power, or at low status. As we have seen, the conditions of modern factory life offer more than a few opportunities for the worker to become bored, frustrated, resentful, and hostile. The organizer attempts to channel this resentment against the image of the "greedy, tyrannical boss," the "soulless corporation."

At a certain point the union will attempt to achieve a "break-through"; that is, to precipitate a mass rush to join the union. The turning point may be reached during an emotionally charged union meeting. Sometimes the precipitating incident is some act of management, such as a wage cut or the discharge of an employee, acts which might have been overlooked in "normal" times. Once the mass rush has begun, the union organizes a majority of the workers in a plant within a very short space of time, perhaps a matter of days. Sometimes, however, the rush does not begin until after a strike has been actually called.

[4] Benjamin M. Selekman, *Labor Relations and Human Relations*, McGraw-Hill Book Company, Inc., New York, 1947, pp. 14–17.
[5] E. T. Hiller, *The Strike*, University of Chicago Press, Chicago, 1928, pp. 51–52.

Once a majority has been achieved, or nearly achieved, the union approaches management with demands for recognition of the union. Under the Taft-Hartley Act, as under the Wagner Act, elections must be held to determine the right of the union to represent the workers in the plant. But if management contests the validity of the union's claim to a majority, a long and bitter struggle may be necessary before recognition is achieved. Under the Taft-Hartley Act management has the right to call for an election. Management is thus in a position to call an election at a time when it feels it can win, perhaps before the union drive has gained momentum.

The organizing drive, then, is a powerful union weapon. The appeal to economic interests, to class solidarity, to deep-lying resentments may arouse or crystallize antimanagement sentiments which last long after the organization drive itself is over and the union has become a routine part of plant life.

Minor Tactics. Labor has developed several tactics which are rarely used alone, although at one time much was expected of them. One of these tactics is the boycott. There are several types of boycotts. The primary boycott involves a concerted refusal by the employees of a given firm to buy the products they are manufacturing. Obviously this tactic can be effective only when the employees of a given industry consume a sizeable portion of the goods they manufacture. A secondary boycott or general boycott involves not only the employees of a given firm, but other workers, other trade unions, or even the public in general. The "union label" policy of the AFL (the policy of urging union members as well as the general public to buy only goods marked with a union label) is really a form of secondary boycott. A third type of boycott is the refusal of workers to work on goods made in "unfair" shops or where there is a strike; this form of boycott comes close to being a strike in some cases.[6]

In the early years of the AFL a firm attempt was made to apply the weapon of the boycott. But after 1900 the tactic began to fall into disuse, and today its use is rather rare. The decline of this weapon is due, in part, to the difficulty of concerting the action of large numbers of consumers, by no means all of whom are union members or even sympathetic to unionism. In part, the decline of the boycott is due to the many state laws which forbid it and to unfavorable decisions on its use by state and Federal courts. Under the Taft-Hartley Act, injunctions may be granted against boycotts. However, many trade-union members, as well as people sympathetic to labor, carry on a sort of informal boycott against firms with antilabor policies.

[6] S. Howard Patterson, *Social Aspects of Industry*, 3d ed., McGraw-Hill Book Company, Inc., New York, 1943, p. 393.

Another tactic, of which much was expected at one time, is sabotage. Sabotage may involve the deliberate destruction or damaging of machinery or goods. It may also consist of bungling work, turning out improperly made or styled goods. An example of this kind of sabotage would be sewing improperly sized buttonholes on clothing, or cutting a thread of the wrong size on pipes, or mislaying orders. It is difficult to estimate the extent to which sabotage is carried on today; in fact, it is difficult to determine whether sabotage is responsible, in any given case, for damaged or defective goods or machinery. We know that sabotage was used in the past, sometimes as the expression of disgruntled individuals, sometimes in a concerted campaign. Sabotage often accompanied strikes and was used as an auxiliary weapon. Sometimes unionists would take jobs as strikebreakers in order to conduct sabotage. However, sabotage has certain limitations as a tactic. It can rarely be used on a large enough scale to be effective. It cannot serve as a rallying point for the type of collective action which, in the last analysis, wins management-labor disputes. It violates the workers' instincts of workmanship. The public strongly disapproves of sabotage, especially where it poses a danger to public safety.

Another tactic sometimes employed by labor is the slowdown. In the slowdown work proceeds, but at a snail's pace. This tactic is not unlike a sit-down strike in its effects. It is again difficult to estimate the extent or the effectiveness of the slowdown; such tactics do not find their way into statistics. We have seen that even unorganized workingmen are able to practice a partial slowdown through the informal group, and we may hazard a guess that slowdowns are a widespread practice. An interesting form of this tactic, though rarely used in this country, is the practice of strict obedience to rules; for instance, the operation of railroads may be seriously slowed down by strict obedience to the numerous rules governing operations in the field.[7] At any rate, the slowdown is at best a halfway measure and cannot compare in effectiveness to other tactics.

The Strike. By far the most important union tactic is the strike. A strike may be defined as a "concerted and temporary suspension of function, designed to exert pressure upon others within the same social unit. . . . "[8] The reason for the supreme importance of the strike is this: no other tactic can inflict such great damage on management, so quickly. The strike directly suspends production; it cuts out the creation of profit, which as we have seen is the mainspring of our industrial system. The strike, furthermore, cuts off the employer from his market, and there is always danger that the market will be lost while the strike is being fought out. It also cuts off the employer from his sources of raw material

[7] Knowles, *op. cit.*, p. 18.
[8] Hiller, *op. cit.*, p. 12.

—not a small matter in times of prosperity or shortages. In some industries materials may deteriorate during a strike. Fixed charges such as interest, taxes, and salaries for officials must be met during a period when production is suspended.[9] Finally, since a long-continued strike often drastically cuts down the size of dividends, it affects the ability of a firm to raise capital. Strikes may threaten the very existence of a firm.

The use of strikes has fluctuated with changing historical and economic conditions, as Table 5 shows. This table also shows that the strike

Table 5. Percentage of Nonagricultural Workers Involved in Strikes, 1919–1949, Selected Years

	Per Cent
1919–1920	12.9
1921–1922	5.6
1923–1929	1.8
1930–1934	4.4
1935–1939	4.3
1940–1941	5.5
1942–1945	6.2
1946–1949	7.8

SOURCE: Joseph P. Goldberg and Bernard Yabroff, "Analysis of Strikes, 1927–1949," *Monthly Labor Review*, vol. 72, no. 1, p. 6, 1951.

is equally important in times of organization and in times like the present, when organization is largely halted but well-established unions exist. The determining factors in the incidence of strikes seems to be both the state of the economic cycle and the strength of union organization.

Table 5 also shows that the numbers of workers affected by strikes is small as compared to the total number of workers. This, however, does not mean that the strike is unimportant. The strike is a serious matter for workingmen; it is the supreme weapon, brought into play only when other expedients have failed. This evidence should also make us careful of accepting the statement that the strike is being replaced by collective bargaining. Not only does Table 5 show this not to be true, but, as we shall see, the strike or threat of strike plays a major role in collective bargaining.

Although it is possible to define a strike in general terms, actually several different types of strikes may be distinguished.

1. The organizing strike, or the "strike for recognition," may be the most dramatic of all strikes. These strikes are marked, in many cases, by bitter conflict and open violence.[10] In this type of strike a union that is

[9] *Ibid.,* p. 125.
[10] The Pullman strike, the Lawrence strike in 1912, the Ludlow strike of 1913, the Gastonia strike in the mid-twenties, and the bitter strikes of the thirties were organizing strikes. For a detailed analysis of an organizing strike, see W. Lloyd Warner and J. O. Low, *The Social System of the Modern Factory,* Yale University Press, New Haven, Conn., 1947.

as yet untested, with an undetermined hold on its members, is seeking to bring to terms a management which has thus far successfully resisted unionism or has been unmolested by it. In many cases, management can enlist the aid of numerous community forces. These factors would be in themselves sufficient to ensure bitter management opposition to the organizing strike. Furthermore, unionization represents a serious blow to managerial prerogatives and powers and a serious modification in the social structure of the plant. The organizing strike is a sort of minor revolution, pitting class against class in the factory. Before an organizing strike is over it may seriously modify the social structure of the community as well, sharpening the class divisions, rearranging the political structure.

2. The most common strike is the strike for higher wages, shorter hours, and other economic benefits. Sometimes this type of strike aims to secure "better working conditions"; this may mean anything from cleaner lavatories to an end to foreman bullying. The bitterness of this type of strike varies from industry to industry and from time to time. Some "economic" strikes have been as strongly fought out as any organizing strike; the Homestead strike, perhaps, is a famous example, although other issues became important. Under conditions of strong unionization and where there is a firm tradition of collective bargaining, the "economic" strike may be surprisingly peaceful. Some large industrial unions do not find it necessary to maintain more than token picket lines around even large industrial plants during a strike.

3. An even milder form of strike is the demonstration strike. In this case there may be a short work stoppage, designed to impress on management the need for meeting certain labor demands. The demonstration strike may also be a harrying instrument of considerable force, if it is repeated often enough. Of course, behind the demonstration strike stands the threat of the full-scale strike.

4. A rather rare type of strike is the sympathetic strike. In this kind of strike a group of workers stop work in order to demonstrate their sympathy with another strike. If the sympathetic strike is called in an industry directly related to the struck plant, then the maneuver can be very effective. The sympathetic strike is often the reflection of union morality, a feeling of labor solidarity. Sometimes there is an element of logrolling in the sympathetic strike, the trading of favors. This seems to be particularly true in the building industry.[11] Under the Taft-Hartley Act, the sympathetic strike is subject to injunction procedures.

5. The jurisdictional strike has been poorly received in the United States, and like the sympathetic strike it has been outlawed by the Taft-Hartley Act. A jurisdictional strike is a maneuver by which one union

[11] Jack Barbash, *Labor Unions in Action,* Harper & Brothers, New York, 1948.

seeks to oust another union from a given field or area. The jurisdictional strike may be aimed at forcing management to withdraw its support from a rival union, or it may have as its aim the shifting of rank-and-file allegiance. The jurisdictional strike is comparatively rare; only a small percentage of strikes are of this nature.

6. The wildcat strike, or "quickie," is distinguished not so much by any special aim, as by the fact that it occurs without union sanction, in fact sometimes directly against the wishes of the union.[12] The wildcat strike may have certain "economic" goals, but more often it seems to spring from some local dissatisfaction with working conditions; often it may be confined to a single department in a plant. The wildcat strike may indicate dissatisfaction not only with management, but also with the union. The wildcatter feels that the union is failing in some important respect. Thus the wildcat strike represents a threat both to management and union control and is usually roundly condemned by both parties; by management because it represents a breach of contract and an interruption of production, and by the union because it represents a threat to union solidarity and discipline.

The wildcat strike may also pose a serious problem to the union in another way. The union does not wish to appear to the worker as an instrument of discipline for management. Furthermore, worker sentiment is often strongly behind a wildcat strike, which is usually based on a long history of grievances and resentments. Such a strike is always a reminder to union leadership of the possibility of a shift in worker allegiance to leaders more in tune with the workers' needs and aspirations.

7. The rarest of all types of strikes in this country is the general strike. The general strike is a concerted effort by all or large sections of organized labor to bring employers to terms by stopping the essential activities of society. In a complete general strike, factories would cease to operate; streetcars, trains, and busses would halt; firemen would refuse to answer alarms; police would not protect lives and property. There have been hardly more than half a dozen general strikes in this country, and even these have never succeeded in bringing more than a portion of essential activity to a halt. Furthermore, none of these strikes has ever been more than city-wide. The last general strike in the United States occurred in 1934 in San Francisco, and it quickly collapsed.[13]

In Europe, on the other hand, the general strike has been used much more frequently. In the early years of this century the general strike became the aim and myth of a whole section of the working class, par-

[12] For a detailed study of a wildcat strike, see Alvin Ward Gouldner, *Wildcat Strike,* The Antioch Press, Yellow Springs, Ohio, 1954.
[13] See Samuel Yellen, *American Labor Struggles,* Harcourt, Brace and Company, Inc., New York, 1936, chap. X.

ticularly that section which adhered to the doctrines of syndicalism.[14] According to this doctrine, the general strike would overthrow the capitalist system in one fell swoop. Yet one general strike after another, reaching a climax in the English general strike of 1925, failed dismally. The working class proved to be too heterogeneous, too pacific, and too poor to meet the stern demands of a general strike. Furthermore, the general strike alienated the middle class. The employers, with the backing of the state, had little difficulty in crushing these strikes.[15]

A strike is by its nature a test of strength, and if it succeeds in wreaking damage on management, it does so only at the expense of the workers. Furthermore it is a weapon which can easily fail and which has often failed in the past, leaving strikers destitute and without jobs. Strikes are not, therefore, at least in responsible unions, called lightly or without considerable thought about how they are to be fought through to success.

The rules for calling a strike demonstrate the seriousness of taking that step. Most unions require a two-thirds vote of the membership affected by the strike, plus the sanction of the national president or executive board, before a strike can be called; in some unions the required vote is three-fourths of the membership. It is usually only in situations of crisis—for instance, when the existence of the union is threatened—that presidents or executive boards may be empowered to call strikes without vote of the membership.[16]

Unless a union has been pushed into a strike by its membership, the leadership will determine the time, form, and extent of the strike, or whether the strike is to be called at all, in accordance with certain strategic considerations. In the first place, the union attempts to estimate the resources of its opponents: their determination, their financial position, their staying power. In the second place, the union takes into account its own financial power, the determination of its membership, and their morale. A third strategic consideration must be the determination of the time when the employer is most vulnerable to a strike; this is usually at the start of a busy season, or in times of prosperity, or when a large order has been received, or when competition is becoming threatening. Fourth, the union must decide whether more is to be gained by striking an entire industry, or just one or two employers, thereby threatening them with loss of markets. Finally, union leadership must try to gauge the political climate and the temper of public opinion before striking.

[14] For an account of the syndicalist theory of the general strike, see Georges Sorel, *Reflections on Violence*, B. W. Huebsch, New York, 1912, chaps. IV, V.

[15] Hiller, *op. cit.*, pp. 254–265.

[16] Florence Peterson, *American Labor Unions*, Harper & Brothers, New York, 1952, p. 173.

The strike may begin on a publicly announced day, or it may be suddenly "sprung" on management, usually at a time calculated to do the most damage. A strike may begin by all the men quitting work in a body, or production may be stopped gradually, e.g., by the failure of successive shifts to report for work. In organizing strikes, the strike may begin with many dramatic appeals and even violence, but in a condition of settled unionism it is rare that there is even a dramatic walkout from the plant; the day of the strike is announced beforehand, and workers simply do not report on that day.

Once a strike begins, the main aim of the strikers is to keep the plant closed and thereby keep up continuous pressure on management. All the tactics of the strike are directed at this one goal, which now supersedes all others. Where the union is strong, keeping the plant closed may be as simple a matter as issuing an order for the workers not to report; in such cases management makes no attempt to open the plant. Indeed, in some cases of late, management has thoughtfully provided the token pickets with shelters and hot coffee. But, where unionism is not strong and management is determined to resist, keeping the plant closed may be a desperate matter indeed.

Perhaps the most effective device for keeping a plant closed, except for universal unionism, is the sit-down strike. This tactic was used with great effect during the organizing drives of the thirties. In a sit-down strike the workers do not leave the factory; in effect, they occupy the factory. These workers are in a very strong position, "sitting" on costly machinery, in a fine position to repel raiding parties, not subject to the rigors of picketing. Management is wary of using force to oust sit-down strikers, since the battle would be fought inside the plant, with resentful workers in a position to do much damage to plants and machinery. The sit-down strike is almost unknown today, except in the wildcat strike which does not reach the point of an actual walkout. The reasons for the abandonment of this effective tactic are its dubious legality and, perhaps more important, the dislike of the public for a maneuver which smacks of the appropriation of property. An entrenched union, of course, does not need to use the sit-down strike.

The *most commonly used* strike tactic is picketing. Two types of picketing should be distinguished. Token picketing involves only a limited number of workers, whose function it is to advertise the fact that the plant is being struck. Such tactics may be used where unionism is very strong. Where the union is not strong, token picketing is designed to persuade workers not to enter the plant, and customers not to buy the products of the struck plant; it may also be designed to persuade the public of the righteousness of labor's cause. There is rarely any violence connected with token picketing, and its legality is widely recognized.

Mass picketing, on the other hand, may involve thousands of workers who, marching in unison, form a barrier around or in front of the struck plant. The functions of mass picketing differ sharply from those of token picketing. The mass picket line is meant to bar strikebreakers from entering the plant both by moral persuasion (which may include the hurling of epithets such as "scab" and other terms even less polite) and, if necessary, by force. In order to accomplish this, picketers may march in unison, arms locked together. A second function of mass picketing is to discipline the strikers. The picket line, solidly organized under picket captains, with each striker assigned a tour of duty, turns a disorganized, milling mob into an orderly, controlled, and obedient group. A third function of the picket line is to aid the morale of the strikers; the massive picket line acts as a symbol of both the unity and strength of the workers, while the songs, cheering, and gaiety of the picket line, at least in its early stages, may have an heartening effect on the workers.[17] Almost all organizing strikes use the tactic of mass picketing. This tactic is occasionally used in other types of strikes also.

The mass picket line has often been the scene of violence, though it is by no means the only possible area of violence in a strike. Some violence arises from the way the mass picket line functions. The use of moral persuasion often engenders fury in those being morally persuaded or reinforces indignation in the strikers, and violence may easily result. The physical barring of entrance to the plant will almost certainly involve violence. However, there are deeper-lying reasons for violence on the picket lines. The very fact that a mass picket line has been set up is, in a sense, a confession of inherent weakness on the part of the strikers; and violence, as Hiller points out, almost always occurs when one side in a strike is much stronger than the other. Thus where management is strong, and strongly backed by community forces and public opinion, the temptation to break the picket line may be strong. In fact, the job of breaking the line may not be difficult in this case. It is incorrect, therefore, to say that the picket line causes violence; both picketing and violence are the result of the preponderance of force on the side of management.

A strong obstacle in the way of mass picketing has been the numerous state laws, and Federal and state judicial decisions, which have sought to limit picketing or ensure its peaceful character, often in the process destroying its effectiveness.[18] Attempts to enforce local regulations have, in the past, often led to violence, with frequent one-sided contests between police or troops on the one side and strikers on the other. Actually, this type of violence has become much rarer in the North today, though

---

[17] Brooks, *op. cit.*, pp. 106–107.
[18] Patterson, *op. cit.*, p. 392.

it is not unknown. In less heavily industrialized areas, in the South and certain areas of the Far West, attacks on picket lines by law-enforcement officers, including hastily created deputies, is very much a thing of the present. However, the public has increasingly tended to support the picket line as a labor weapon, and many antipicketing laws have become dead letters.

The strike may decide quickly whether management or labor is the stronger party. Even the success or failure of the union in establishing a picket line may indicate clearly which way the strike will go, and an early settlement or abandonment of the strike may result. On the other hand, the strike may turn into a test of strength, a contest of endurance, between the financial resources of the strikers and the financial health of the company. Under these circumstances the morale of the strikers becomes the crucial point; upon their willingness to suffer deprivation while management suffers no personal loss depends the fate of the strike.

In order to keep up morale, the union attempts to do some or all of the following: Strike leadership is formalized, and a strike headquarters is established. The strike headquarters may serve at times as a center of strategy, a barracks, a commissary, a hospital, and an auditorium. If the strike is long, some arrangement must be made for providing relief to the strikers. Sometimes the union provides free food or credit cards good in local stores. The ability of the union to keep its members' heads above water will depend, of course, on its financial reserves. Most unions have strike funds, collected from dues or from special assessments. But a large-scale strike is so costly that often other sources of funds must be found. Sometimes assessments on nonstriking unions are made; sometimes a striking union will appeal to a city labor organization for funds. In crucial strikes rich and powerful unions have made large donations to the striking unions. On rare occasions the public may be appealed to for funds, for food, for clothing, and even for homes for strikers' families.

Strike morale is also maintained in other ways. The very act of striking, of establishing a mass picket line, serves to display the strength of the workers and may offer support to morale. The discipline of the strike may serve to boost spirits and maintain morale. Strikers may be required to report to headquarters, to do a turn on the picket line. Fines may be levied for those who fail in their obligations.

Morale is also maintained by propaganda and exhortation. Frequent mass meetings are called, where workers are assured of the justice of their cause; appeals are made to their pride, their feelings of loyalty to the union and to fellow workers. Mass meetings are supplemented by parades, dances, and picnics. These serve to relieve the tedium of endless picketing and idleness. The union makes special appeals to wives and other relatives and attempts to enlist their support for the strike.

If mass media are available to the union, they will be used to reach and cheer the strikers. If the mass media are hostile, the workers will be reached through pamphlets, strike papers, mimeographed sheets. In this literature strikers are assured of victory, rumors are combated, the villainy of the enemy is stressed, and there is news about the conduct of the strike.

Means for maintaining morale depend on the industry, the age, sex, racial and ethnic background of the workers, their experience with unionization, and the temper of the community. Much depends on the judgment of the strike leadership as to the most effective means of maintaining morale.

In a long-drawn-out strike, and also in some short strikes, the union must try to influence the general public to take the worker's side or, at least, to remain neutral. The general public may become involved in a strike in several ways. Sometimes the public is put to great inconvenience, as in a strike of public transportation workers; sometimes the general public becomes involved because one side seeks to rouse public opinion against the other. The intervention of the public in a strike may be decisive in several ways; for instance, if the public sympathizes with the strikers, management will have a most difficult time in using local police to break the strike or protect nonstrikers. Public opinion may also be forceful enough to make a strike a political issue; e.g., the public may demand that politicians put an end to an harrassing strike.

In any contest to influence public opinion, management is in many ways in a stronger position than labor. Management has large financial resources with which to support advertising campaigns. The mass media of communication are generally sympathetic to its position. Furthermore, the preconceptions of many Americans, especially in the middle class, agree more closely with the individualistic doctrine of management than with the collective doctrine of the unionists. Under these circumstances, labor appeals to the public under great handicaps, but appeal it does nevertheless. The mass media of communication are used where they are available, and where they are not, labor attempts to use the "propaganda of the deed." Thus labor stresses the pathos of the picket line, with its humble men pitted against management's might. If women or children are involved in the strike, a sentimental appeal is made to the public on this basis. Violence against the picket line can be used as a basis for a denunciation of management and its allies in the community. Special appeals are made to various sections of the community. The middle class may be appealed to in terms of the economic benefits to be derived from a wage boost for workers, or in antimonopolistic terms, with labor pictured as carrying on the good fight against the corporation. Professionals may be appealed to in terms of the justice of labor's cause. Politicians may be appealed to in more realistic terms of votes. In this way labor attempts to overcome management's advantages.

The Tactics of Management in Conflicts with Labor. Management, on its side, also has evolved special tactics in its disputes with labor. The tactics which it employs are, like labor tactics, dictated by the strategic end in view. The over-all aim of management is to render collective action by workers ineffective, or at least to limit its effectiveness. Management stands to lose two vital things if it cannot achieve these aims: it stands to lose financially through the necessity of paying higher wages, perhaps for less time spent in production; and it stands to lose control over its workers and the power of disciplining them. These are the general aims of management; the specific aims in a given dispute are adjusted to the realities of the situation, particularly the reality of union strength. Thus, in a conflict with labor, managerial aims may range from crushing the union to defeating it on single issues. In the latter case management may also attempt to lessen the over-all effectiveness and militancy of the union.

First, management seeks to convince the employee that he should identify himself with management. In a small plant this may be as simple a matter as reminding the worker of past friendship, of favors, of a common origin, of a common dislike of "outsiders." Even in unionized plants, the loyalty of many workers to their employers, whether this loyalty is rationally or nonrationally based, is of great importance in curbing the militancy and effectiveness of the union. Again, profit-sharing schemes of various types, e.g., stockownership by employees, are devices which presumably tend to give the worker a stake in the financial well-being of the plant and to make him see things from management's point of view. Retirement and benefit programs, theoretically, operate in the same way, binding the worker to the company through gratitude to management and through economic interest. These tactics supposedly make the worker impervious to the blandishments of unionism.

Machiavellian tactics have been frequently used, particularly in the past, to stop an organizing drive in its tracks. If management was able to discover the union leaders in the plant, they were summarily fired, thereby at one stroke depriving the union drive of its leadership and throwing fear into other employees. Sometimes the employer used spies —"stool pigeons," in the parlance of the workers—to discover the union ringleaders, hiring these spies from detective agencies. These spies often posed as militant unionists, thereby discovering those men disposed to unionization. At times spies worked themselves high up into the union hierarchy, only to betray the union at some vital juncture, or discredit it through the use of violence or by calling premature strikes. By use of "black lists," militant unionists fired from a job were prevented from getting work in other industries. At the same time, management kept up an antiunion barrage.[19] Through personal contacts, through speeches (often on company time), through plant newspapers, or through the mass media of communication the workers were fed a steady diet of antiunion propaganda. They were told that union leaders were "aliens," "racketeers" trying to mulct the workers, that unionism was bound to fail, that it was "un-American." Sometimes agents were hired to spread rumors deleterious to the union, its aims, its prospects, its morals. The workers were told that they had no real grievances; data were provided to show that they were better off than other workers. They were assured that their only choice was between their present jobs or no job at all when the union entered.

These tactics have been used by management most frequently before or during organizing strikes. To win a strike which has been called by an already established union, management uses somewhat different tactics. As we have seen, the aim of the strike is to stop production and to prevent its resumption. Management can react to this maneuver in two ways. It can accept the union challenge and attempt to wait out the strikers, even "locking out" whatever workers are not affected by the strike in order to bring maximum economic pressure on the workers. This type of policy has great advantages for management. Many industries possess financial resources large enough to tide over a long period of nonproduction. Management personnel rarely or never suffer personal privations, in contrast to workers who may quickly become destitute in a strike. Furthermore, the centralization of modern industry makes it possible for employers to communicate with each other, coordinate their activities, and thus lend each other financial and moral support.

Furthermore, just as labor attempts to pick a most favorable time to strike, so does management seek to confine strikes to certain periods. A favorable period for a strike from management's point of view would be when business is sluggish, when there are no large stocks of perishable goods to be lost, or when there are large stocks of completed goods which can be fed into the market. Another favorable time for a strike, from management's point of view, is during a period of unemployment, when workers are most easily replaced. Strikes fought through to a decision in this way are still very common.

The other possible managerial reaction to a strike is to attempt to "break" it and to resume production. Long-drawn-out strikes are costly to management, and lockouts may be even more costly. In the not too distant past, this solution—if it was a solution—to labor troubles was

---

[19] The Wagner Act outlawed many of these tactics, but recent decisions of the National Labor Relations Board under the Taft-Hartley Act have restored many of the employers' rights to propagandize against the union among employees.

very attractive to many employers. Strikebreaking has declined in importance as a weapon of management if for no other reason than that the increased power of the trade unions has made it very difficult to break strikes. However, this tactic has been employed so recently (even today it finds at least limited use in certain areas) that its study is indicated.

There are two types of strikebreaking: (1) replacement of workers by strikebreakers, (2) persuading or forcing the workers to return to work. Strikebreakers are rarely used today. The cessation of immigration has reduced the potential supply of "scabs." The working class as a whole is more thoroughly permeated with certain union values, including the interdiction against "scabbing." Recruiting and training a large number of strikebreakers is often a costly and time-consuming procedure.

The major mode of strikebreaking, then, is through persuading or coercing workers to return to their jobs. In order to do this, management seeks to strike at the sources of striker morale: above all, belief in the success of the strike, a sense of unity among the workers, and confidence in union leadership. Management may, for instance, seek to resume production at all costs. If production can be resumed, even in a limited way, the major tactical aim of the strike has been defeated or dealt a severe blow, and discouragement will quickly spread among the strikers. If the major source of striker morale is the picket line, then this will be the focal point of management's attack. In the past, and even today more than is generally realized, employers have used injunctions to curb picketing. As was pointed out in a previous chapter, an injunction is an order from a court prohibiting a person or group from taking action which will result in harm to another person or group. The court not only issues such an order but determines whether it has been obeyed, hands out punishment for contempt of court if it finds that its injunction has been ignored, and fixes the terms of the penalty. In the past, courts were often inclined to side with management; many injunctions were issued, some of them of a most sweeping character, against picketing as a whole or against specific practices such as insulting strikebreakers. It is true that use of the injunction was drastically limited by the Norris-La Guardia Act, but two things should be noted. First, this Act applied only to Federal courts, and not all states have seen fit to restrain their justices. Second, the Taft-Hartley Act reestablished the use of the injunction in certain cases. Thus the injunction retains considerable importance as a managerial weapon.

Management may seek to harm the morale of the strikers in still other ways. It may seek to break the unity of the workers; e.g., by granting concessions to certain groups of workers on the condition that they return to work immediately, by pitting racial, religious, or ethnic groups against each other, by spreading stories of defections from the strike. Management attempts to destroy the confidence of the strikers in the power of the union and the integrity of its leadership; rumors and propaganda are used to spread stories of the immorality of the union leaders, of their desperation, of their "communistic" connections. Sometimes union leaders have been bribed in such a way that the bribery becomes public; on occasion spies who have worked their way up in the union hierarchy have betrayed the union at a critical moment. The worker is reminded of his economic weakness; he is told that he will lose his job, that he will be black-listed, that the company will leave the community. An attempt is made to question the morality of the strike. The worker is told that striking is "un-American"; it is not the action of a confident American, hopeful of "rising" out of the working class, but of a discouraged "Europeanized" worker.

In the past some extremist branches of management were prepared to crush strikes by use of armed force. As we have seen, Federal or state troops were occasionally used for this purpose. Private police or guard units were maintained by some plants, and as the La Follette committee disclosed, these guards and police were sometimes equipped with tear-gas bombs, machine guns, and other deadly weapons.[20]

Another method of strikebreaking, also commonly used in the past, was the mobilization of certain community forces against the union. This method was most finely developed during a strike at various plants of the Remington Rand Corporation in the 1930s, and has received the title of the "Mohawk Valley formula." According to this formula the following steps were to be taken to combat a strike:

1. Union leaders were to be labeled as "agitators." A forced balloting was to be conducted both in order to ascertain the strength of the union and to establish a claim that the strikers were a small minority of the workers. The issues in the strike were to be confused by accusing the strikers of making arbitrary demands. Threats to move the plant were to be made in order to align the influential members of the community with management. "Citizens' committees" were to be set up composed of prominent businessmen, bankers, real-estate men—those who had the most to lose if the plant should move.

2. Claims were to be made that "law and order" was being violated by the strikers, thereby "causing the community to mass legal and police weapons" against the strikers.

3. Mass meetings of the citizens' committees were to be called in order to bring pressure on local politicians to oppose the strike, and to organize vigilante tactics.

[20] Committee on Education and Labor of the U.S. Senate, *Industrial Munitions,* 1939.

4. Demands were to be raised for the creation of a special police force, composed of local police, state police or troops if possible, and special deputies.

5. "Back-to-work" movements of "loyal employees" were to be secretly organized by the employer. Such a movement was designed to harm the morale of the strikers, persuade the public that the strikers were in a minority, afford an excuse for breaking the picket line, and pave the way for the introduction of strikebreakers.

6. On a publicly announced day, the plant was to be opened with the "back-to-work" movement supplying the workers.

7. The opening was to be accompanied with massed police to intimidate the strikers, with speeches, flag raising, flattery of the local citizens who "have made this all possible."

8. If necessary, the show of force was to be continued and attempts made to have martial law or a state of emergency declared.

9. The publicity barrage was to be closed with a statement that only a small minority of workers were still out.[21]

The "Mohawk Valley formula" was an ideal method for breaking strikes. Modifications of this method, according to local conditions, occurred in each strike.

The Ending of Strikes. Strikes may be fought out on many fronts, with many types of tactics, and sometimes with great bitterness and violence. Yet even the longest strike must come to an end sometime, production must be resumed, the life of the community carried on. How do strikes end?

In general, a strike may end in victory for one side or the other, in compromise, or in postponement.[22] Victory, or a compromise favorable to one party, comes when an employer or a union can no longer bear the cost of a strike—when the employer is threatened by the loss of his business, the striker by destitution. A strike may also end when the climate of opinion turns so decidedly against one party that to continue the strike is obviously futile. It may also end when one side succeeds in demonstrating its superior strength. Postponement often involves a hidden defeat for the strikers, for it usually means going back to work while the issues of the strike are held in abeyance.

Defeat in a strike has different meanings for employers and for labor. Defeat for the employer spells loss of power, financial loss, only rarely annihilation of the plant. Defeat for the union may be more serious. The strike may be called off with the union remaining intact, but with diminished prestige. In some cases the union may disintegrate com-

[21] Adapted from Selden C. Menefee, "Propaganda and Symbol Manipulation," in George W. Hartmann and Theodore Newcomb, (eds.), *Industrial Conflict*, The Dryden Press, Inc., New York, 1939, pp. 483–485. By permission.
[22] Hiller, *op. cit.*, p. 207.

pletely, and the workers may abandon unionism altogether, even in their sympathies.

However, most strikes, even those which may be considered victories for one side or the other, do not actually involve outright capitulation for either management or labor. Such disputes are settled through a process of negotiation. We shall consider this process in more detail.

Settling a strike or other dispute involves all the usual processes of compromise: trading, concessions, "splitting the difference," argument, presentation of data, and so on. In fact, the closer negotiations come to a settlement, the more strongly does it resemble collective bargaining as specific points of difference are taken up and settled. Usually the settlement which the parties finally arrive at represents, in a fairly accurate way, the relative power of the contestants, as established in the strike or threat of strike. This is a point which those who decry force in settling management-labor disputes would do well to remember.

Sometimes, the bitterness between management and labor, the feeling of righteousness on either side, is too great to permit of this type of negotiation, and yet neither side wishes to continue the strike. This has often occurred in organizing strikes, but the situation is fairly common even in "economic" strikes. Under these circumstances, management and labor may turn to outside sources to settle the dispute.

There are three possible ways in which strikes may be settled by outsiders: through conciliation, through mediation, and through arbitration. *Conciliation* is generally taken to mean the process of getting management and labor into contact with each other, so that they may negotiate. It may be necessary in cases where management has steadfastly refused to recognize a union, where bitterness has become too extreme to permit of negotiation, or where personal animosities have arisen between management and labor leaders. After the conciliator arranges the meeting between management and labor, he takes no further part in the negotiations.

The terms "conciliation" and "mediation" are often used interchangeably, but in this book we shall mean by *mediation* that process of settling strikes which involves the mediator directly in the negotiations between management and labor. Whereas the main purpose of the conciliator is to bring management and labor together, the main purpose of the mediator is to get them to agree on some sort of compromise. However, the mediator does not have any more coercive power over management or labor than the conciliator.

A frequently used source of both conciliation and mediation is the Federal Mediation and Conciliation Service. This Service, which has no mandatory powers, was founded in 1913 as a branch of the Department of Labor. The Taft-Hartley Act took the Service from out of the jurisdiction of the Department of Labor and made it independent. Its director was to be appointed by the President, with advice and consent of the Senate. At the same time, the power and scope of the Service was somewhat reduced. The main aims of the Service remain to persuade industrial disputants to choose peace and to gather facts and supply arguments in behalf of peace. Since the director of the Service is politically appointed, the policy of the Service reflects in good part the political complexion of the administration.

On the railroads, disputes are handled by a National Mediation Board, appointed by the President, and by a National Railroad Adjustment Board, composed of equal numbers of representatives from management and labor. Each of these agencies handles different types of disputes. In addition, if a strike threatens on the railroads, the President may appoint a special emergency board to forestall the strike.[23] The existence of these special agencies in this one field reflects the crucial position of the railroads in our economy.

The government mediator represents the public interest in the ending of the dispute, and his chief task is to convince management and labor that it is in their interest to end the dispute. The mediator will, therefore, try to help the disputants to clarify their own objectives, to determine what is really important for them and what can be given up, to understand the objectives, problems, and values of the other side.

In a typical case the mediator will act as follows. Once a dispute has been handed to the mediator, usually by the union, he calls separate meetings of management and labor in order to establish cordial relations with them, to get a preliminary view of the dispute, and to seek out areas of potential agreement. A joint session is then held, at which the mediator presides; here he tries to reduce the differences between management and labor, to guide the session along conciliatory lines, to keep the session on the subject. In the recesses between the joint sessions the mediator holds more separate meetings, attempting further to determine the real issues, to estimate the real determination of each side, to clear up misunderstanding, and to seek for areas of compromise. In this way the mediator tries gradually to create a situation in which compromise is possible. If no compromise seems possible, he will seek the participation of authoritative management and labor figures in the meeting. In rare cases he may himself propose alternative solutions to the dispute. If, finally, there seems to be no way out, he will attempt to postpone further discussion, thereby preventing a complete break in the negotiations.[24]

[23] Peterson, *op. cit.*, pp. 183–184.
[24] See W. Ellison Chalmers, "The Conciliation Process," *Industrial and Labor Relations Review*, vol. 1, no. 3, pp. 347–350, 1948.

Arbitration differs from mediation and conciliation in that the arbitrator hands down a decision on the merits of the case after investigating the data, hearing witnesses, and listening to arguments. Thus arbitration, unlike conciliation and mediation, is a judicial process. Arbitration may be entered into voluntarily or through compulsion; in the United States arbitration is almost always a voluntary matter. Acceptance of the decision of the arbitrator may also be voluntary or compulsory; both types of arrangements are common in the United States. The arbitrator may be specified in a contract between union and management, or may be appointed *ad hoc* for a special dispute.

Arbitration is used only with difficulty in settling fundamental disputes over economic and power questions. The main reason for this is that arbitration is inherently a judicial process and it settles disputes only by reference to the merits of the case. But the merits can be determined in a precise sense only by reference to a body of law or a contract, and it is precisely the absence of such law or contract which marks the types of disputes about which we are speaking in this chapter. Under these circumstances, the arbitrator feels great pressures from either side to act as a mediator, deciding the case not on its merits but in terms of a feasible compromise between management and labor. Arbitration, on the other hand, is much more effective in the collective-bargaining process, as we shall see in the next chapter.[25]

The decision, whether reached in negotiation or through conciliation, mediation, and arbitration, must be approved by the company and by the workers. In the case of management, this assent may be fairly easy to attain; presumably top management has kept in close touch with the negotiations, if indeed it has not participated in such negotiations directly. On the other hand, there have been spectacular cases of management refusal to abide by mediation and arbitration, often with a resulting loss of public good will. On the union side, consent to an agreement must usually be attained through an affirmative vote of the workers affected. In most cases, this must be a majority vote; in some cases an even larger proportion of affirmative votes is necessary. Getting such consent is sometimes a very difficult matter, and the union leader must use all his oratorical and persuasive arts to convince the membership of the necessity for accepting an agreement. The reason for this difficulty seems to lie in the militancy of many strikers. In a compromise settlement, the hopes of some workers are almost bound to be disappointed. In this case, almost inevitably the question arises of whether the strike was worth the few gains achieved. Rejections of agreements at emotionally charged union meetings are by no means rare.

[25] See Harold W. Davey, "Hazards in Labor Arbitration," *Industrial and Labor Relations Review*, vol. 1, no. 3, pp. 385–406, 1948.

Modern Tactics. Many of the tactics discussed in this chapter have been more frequently used in the past than in the present phase of American industrial and labor history. But it would be a mistake to think that the underlying strategic goals of management and labor have changed. These aims remain—in the one case, to decrease the effectiveness of collective action by workers, and, in the other, to increase the solidarity, unity, and discipline of the workers in order to increase the efficacy of collective action. Furthermore, as in the past, this conflict is settled, in the last analysis, on the basis of the respective power of either side; this means, usually, the ability of either side to wage or resist a strike. Both management and labor have changed their tactics to conform with widespread prosperity, full employment, stable unionism, and a public opinion which has accepted a certain amount of union power.

Managerial tactics today rely on the use of economic power, on attempts to win the loyalty of the workers away from the unions, on attempts to decrease the militancy of the unions and of union leadership. Management also tries to control unions through legislation and to convince the public of the necessity of such labor legislation. We shall discuss each of these tactics in somewhat greater detail.

It is clear that all the events of the last twenty years, including the rise of industrial unionism, have left the economic power of management largely intact. Management largely retains its right to hire and fire in spite of certain union restrictions. This power is not only a matter of firing an individual here or there, practices which labor can control; it is a matter of the ability of management to control the economic destiny of its workers. Similarly, management retains its rights to use its productive plant whenever, wherever, and for whatever purposes it sees fit. There is no reason that it could not cease production entirely, though this tactic is rarely adopted. Certainly an employer is entitled to move his plant, or to threaten to move it, and this is no small weapon in the arsenal of management. Similarly, management has the right to introduce technological change, or to threaten its introduction. This can be a powerful weapon in the hands of management, since technological change often involves displacement of labor or the annihilation of skills.

Management may also use its economic power in more dubious ways. We hear hints today of the open bribery of union leaders. There are also rumors of a covert practice in which the union leader agrees to tone down his demands in return for a consideration.[26] This practice may be found among only a small minority of labor leaders, most of these concentrated in certain notoriously racket-dominated unions. But even

[26] See A. A. Imberman, "Labor Leaders and Society," *Harvard Business Review*, vol. 28, no. 1, pp. 52–60, 1950.

if the overwhelming number of union leaders are incorruptible, the existence of such practices and their occasional exposure are enough to sow suspicion of union leaders and of unions in the minds of many workers and among the public at large.

The economic power of management can be used in yet another way to undermine the militancy of unions on the local level. As we have seen, the workers in a plant are often split in terms of interests and also in terms of attitudes toward the union. Management can use its economic power to favor the more satisfied and less militant workers; if there are two or more factions in the union, the least militant can be helped into power or aided to retain power. "Management-oriented" union officials can be encouraged, or created; management may give such officials better jobs, easy work assignment, better rates, desirable days off during the week, and preferred weeks for vacation.[27] This practice is a mild form of bribery, even though it would not seem to violate any laws. Yet the effect on other union members must be somewhat the same as in the case of open bribery: distrust of the union, and a consequent reduction in its effectiveness. Thus this management tactic is doubly efficacious.

A second modern managerial tactic is "competition for the loyalty of employees."[28] The aim of this tactic is to convince the worker that management has his interests at heart and can provide him with much the same benefits as the union. In part this tactic is a revival of the "welfare capitalism" of the twenties. Pension plans, profit-sharing plans, programs of stockownership by workers—all these schemes have been revived, though often in modernized form.

"Competition for the loyalty of employees" also takes the form of a search for the sources of employee dissatisfaction with management and an attempt to eliminate those sources. This tactic has been behind some managerial interest in research in the social relationships of the plant and in research in industrial psychology. Other types of research have sought to uncover the sources of attitude and resentment in the worker, through the use of psychoanalytical technique. Some research has been conducted on the relation of the worker to the community; the community has been studied as a breeding ground for worker dissatisfactions.

Various programs have been proposed or tried in order to eliminate these sources of dissatisfaction. Some employers have encouraged the deliberate formation of informal social groups at work; such groups can,

[27] See Melville Dalton, "Unofficial Union-Management Relations," *American Sociological Review*, vol. 15, no. 5, p. 612, 1950. Dalton regards these practices as examples of "unofficial union-management relations." They undoubtedly are these, but they may also be interpreted as managerial tactics.

[28] See the excellent discussion by Wilbert E. Moore, *Industrial Relations and the Social Order*, The Macmillan Company, New York, 1951, pp. 367–368.

presumably, offer outlets for suppressed or frustrated portions of the worker's personality. Psychotherapy on a large scale has also been tried; interviews with the worker have been designed to give him a chance to recognize and express his resentments, whether these originate in the plant or in the community. Some attempts are being made to overcome insecurity and anxiety by reconstructing plant life on "solidary" bases such as family ties or hierarchical principles, thereby applying certain lessons learned from anthropology and other social sciences. In short management has attempted to avail itself of social scientific knowledge in its contests with labor.[29]

Thirdly, management has moved to reduce the effectiveness of organized labor through legislation aimed at certain labor practices. Organized management long campaigned for a bill like the Taft-Hartley Act, which replaced the Wagner Act in 1947.[30] This complicated act provides, among other things, that employers as well as unions have the right to call elections to determine collective-bargaining units. This provision allows the employer to call for an election when the union position is weak. The Act tends to weaken unions further by forbidding them to coerce employees into joining them. It prohibits the unions from expelling a worker from membership where there is a union-shop agreement, except for failure to pay dues. This weakens the disciplinary power of the union. The Act also weakens the unions' right to picket, since it protects the right of certain classes of employees to cross a picket line. Recent rulings have reestablished the right of employers to spread antiunion propaganda among workers, to question them about their union affiliations, a practice which might frighten some workers off from union activity. The Taft-Hartley Act, further, empowers the National Labor Relations Board to investigate "unfair practices," whether of management or labor, and to hold hearings on these practices. The Board may subpoena witnesses and evidence, issue cease and desist orders, and appeal to the courts for enforcement of its orders.[31] These powers, it will be noted, may be used against either labor or management.

One provision of the Taft-Hartley Act in particular may provide management with a powerful weapon against labor, especially if the

[29] Some social scientists may resent this statement, but no attack on social scientists who work for management is intended. At the same time social scientists should realize that if they are employed by, or subsidized by, management, they must expect management to make use of their findings. See Eugene V. Schneider, "Limitations on Observation in Industrial Sociology," *Social Forces*, vol. 28, no. 3, pp. 279–284, 1950.

[30] It is not meant to imply here that the Taft-Hartley Act is exclusively a management weapon. The Act retains many rights for labor, such as the right to call elections to determine bargaining units. The Taft-Hartley Act is discussed more fully in a later chapter.

[31] Peterson, *op. cit.*, pp. 185–186.

national administration is unfriendly to labor. This is the provision for dealing with "national-emergency" strikes. "National-emergency" strikes are, presumably, strikes in industries which are of strategic importance to the well-being of the American people; obviously the definition of a "national emergency" would, in the nature of things, be flexible. Such a strike cannot be initiated without a sixty-day notice. At that time an injunction may be granted against the strike. The President must then form a board of inquiry, which is to report within sixty days. Fifteen days after this report is issued, an election must be held to determine whether the employees want the strike. Five days after the election, the injunction is voided, and the President is to refer the matter to Congress.[32] It will be immediately apparent that these provisions, which involve a delay of four and a half months, are more than likely to kill any strike. Were a rabidly antilabor administration to come to power, this provision alone might, in effect, outlaw strikes.

In addition to the Taft-Hartley Act, laws have been passed which deny to "Communist-dominated" unions the normal rights granted to labor. It is too early to tell how these provisions will affect the balance of power between management and labor. But it seems safe to say that under a strongly antilabor administration, these bills could become bitter weapons against labor, since any sort of militant union activity might lead to a union's being designated as "Communist-dominated."

Finally, more than ever management seeks to countervail the power of the unions by molding public opinion in a managerial direction. Not that managerial propaganda must be blatantly antiunion; by and large management seems to have recognized the public's acceptance of unionism. Rather this propaganda is more likely to stress the accomplishments of "free enterprise," the high standard of living, productivity, the freedom to choose, in American life. Not much of the credit for these is given to labor. Management propaganda is also likely to stress the need for peace and harmony in management-labor relationships, the eternal desire of management for peace, and the necessity of such peace for America. Managerial propaganda, further, plays on the values of the middle class, which makes up a large portion of the public. This propaganda stresses the possibilities of rising under a system of "free enterprise" and appeals to middle-class biases in favor of "respectability" and "decorum" in national affairs. Only in times of strikes, or when strikes are threatened, will management propagandize directly; e.g., through full-page advertisements in the newspapers or in magazines. It should be remembered that management possesses the large financial resources which are necessary to get access to the mass media of communication. Use of the newspapers, the radio, or the television networks

[32] *Ibid.*, pp. 186–187.

for advertising is extremely expensive. Furthermore, as we have already pointed out, a large part of the mass media, particularly the press, shares the social and economic biases of management.

Unions attempt to counter these managerial tactics in various ways, all of which have the aim of preserving the unity, solidarity, and strength of the unions. To counter the economic power of management, the union tries to build up its financial reserves. It attempts to protect its militant members from being fired or downgraded, perhaps by demanding top seniority for shop stewards or committeemen. It seeks to protect the workers from the worst consequences of technological change; e.g., through the device of the guaranteed annual wage. Yet when viewed in perspective, it is apparent that the union cannot balance the economic weapons of management. The institutional structure of our society, and even our culture, is based in large part on industrialism and the economic power of management.

Lacking management's economic power, the unions attempt to convince the workers of the necessity for loyalty to the union; that is, the union participates in the "competition for the loyalty of employees." It is partly for this reason that unions are adamantly opposed to profit-sharing schemes, to company-backed pension schemes, to stockowner-ship plans. Union propaganda attempts to picture these as mere company maneuvers against the workers.

Some unions try also to combat the "social-science," human-relations programs of management, claiming that such programs are designed to wean employees from the unions and to substitute psychic satisfactions for material gains of all kinds.[33] At the same time the unions have, to a limited extent, attempted to use the findings of friendly social scientists for their own purposes.

Finally, the unions, like management, seek to influence public opinion and to gain favorable legislation. In the former task the unions are apparently at a hopeless disadvantage, except in times of crisis. In so far as the public has swung around to a prolabor point of view, it has been through the pressure of events and against the great weight of management-oriented propaganda. For labor the major legislative aim is the repeal of the Taft-Hartley Act. Labor has become deeply involved in politics in order to accomplish this goal.

[33] See, for instance, "Deep Therapy on the Assembly Line" (no author given), *UAW-CIO Ammunition,* vol. 7, no. 4, pp. 47–51, 1949. The subtitle of this article is: "Moo, moo, moo, say the cow sociologists but they don't even give skimmed milk."

CHAPTER 13

The Functions of Unionism: Collective Bargaining

As we have seen, the first, and in many ways primary, function of the trade union is to create and wield power which, within the legal processes of the country, can be used to bring management to terms. Its second major function is to bargain collectively with management about these terms.

Although we have separated these two major functions of unionism for purposes of analysis, it would be a mistake to think that collective bargaining is the opposite of the use of power; that collective bargaining is equal to industrial peace while the clash of the rival powers is equivalent to industrial war. The relationship between collective bargaining and power is much more complicated than that. For one thing, collective bargaining is brought about by the application of power or by the threat of its use, and often it is maintained by the threat of the use of power. For another thing, collective bargaining is itself a technique or tactic in labor's contests with management. It might be said that collective bargaining is the continuation of the power struggle by other means.

For these reasons it is not possible to accept those views which hold collective bargaining to be merely the higgling of a market relationship or which see collective bargaining essentially as a social process between individuals with varying and often antagonistic sentiments, beliefs, and attitudes. Collective bargaining undoubtedly contains both these elements, but it is more than either. It involves negotiating, administering, and enforcing a treaty between two organizations, some of whose interests are similar, some of whose interests are antagonistic, on the basis of the power which either side disposes of.[1] Perhaps the best statement of the nature of collective bargaining was made by Perlman, who said:[2]

[1] See Frederick H. Harbison and John R. Coleman, *Goals and Strategy in Collective Bargaining*, Harper & Brothers, New York, 1951, pp. 5–6.
[2] By permission from Selig Perlman, "The Principle of Collective Bargaining," *The Annals of the American Academy of Political and Social Science*, vol. 84, pp. 154–160, 1936.

Collective bargaining is not just a means of raising wages and improving conditions of employment. Nor is it merely democratic government in industry. It is above all a technique whereby an inferior social class or group carries on a never slackening pressure for a bigger share in the social sovereignty as well as for more welfare, security, and liberty for its individual members. As such it is not confined to a single arena, the industrial one, where employers and labor unions meet directly, but manifests itself equally in politics, legislation, court litigation, government administration, religion, education and propaganda. . . . Collective bargaining as a technique of the rise of a new class is quite different from the class struggle of the Marxians. . . . It derives its emotional impetus not from the desire to displace or "abolish" the "old ruling class" but from the wish to bring one's own class abreast of the superior class; to gain equal rights as a class and equal consideration for the members of the class with the members of that other class; to acquire an exclusive jurisdiction in that sphere where the most immediate interests, both material and spiritual, are determined, and a shared jurisdiction with the older class or classes in all other spheres.

However, although collective bargaining may be a "technique" of applying a "never slackening social pressure," it emphatically does not follow that the collective-bargaining relationship is in all cases marked by hostility, opposition, or recrimination. On the contrary, the overwhelming majority of collective-bargaining relationships are peaceful.[3] If this were not so, then the wheels of our industry would quickly grind to a stop. Unions and management find many areas of identical interests, where real cooperation is possible through collective bargaining. In those areas in which cooperation is not possible, where there is a real clash of interest, compromise or "antagonistic cooperation" is almost always possible.[4]

Compromise, cooperation, or "antagonistic cooperation" can be based only on the relative power of each side and is subject to any shift in the power of labor or management. Even peaceful collective-bargaining relationships, even those marked by friendliness and a spirit of give-and-take, are the outer shell underneath which a constant testing and matching of rival powers is going on. In this case, however, the clash of power between management and labor does not take the tactical form of strike, sabotage, or lockout, but rather negotiation, compromise, argument, and arbitration.

There can be little doubt that from the point of view of the general public, as well as from that of management and labor on most occasions, the tactics of collective bargaining are to be preferred to the tactics

[3] Many case studies might be cited. See Frederick H. Harbison and King Carr, *Causes of Industrial Peace under Collective Bargaining*, National Planning Association, Washington, 1948.

[4] E. Wight Bakke, *Mutual Survival*, Harper & Brothers, New York, 1946, p. 81.

of force or propaganda in the settlement of industrial disputes. This fact has received general recognition in legislation; thus both the Wagner Act and the Taft-Hartley Act declare the encouragement of collective bargaining to be public policy. In spite of many antilabor provisions, the Taft-Hartley Act makes it an unfair labor practice for either labor or management to refuse to bargain collectively, once a union has been certified as a bargaining agency. Under this act, labor and management are required to meet at "reasonable times" and to bargain "in good faith" about "wages, hours, and other terms and conditions of employment, or the negotiation of an agreement, or any question arising thereunder" and to incorporate their agreement in a written contract, if either side desires it. Furthermore, the government has extended to the collective-bargaining contract the protection of the courts; the collective-bargaining contract is enforceable in the same manner as any other contract.

With the rise of unions in the last two decades and the official encouragement given to collective bargaining, large numbers of workers have come to be covered by collective-bargaining agreements. At the present perhaps 50 per cent of all privately employed persons are subject to a collective-bargaining agreement of some kind; the figure is 70 per cent for manufacturing workers. More than 90 per cent of workers are covered by agreements in the following fields: aluminum fabrication, automobiles, aircrafts, clothing, nonferrous smelting and refining, shipbuilding, basic steel, mining, maritime industry, commercial construction, railroads, local transit, airlines, trucking, and telegraph. On the other hand, less than 10 per cent of our clerical force is working under contracts. It should be noted that unionism has extended collective-bargaining coverage to many workers who are not union members. At the same time, some unions, such as those existing among government employees, do not seek to negotiate contracts. It is for this reason that the figures for those covered by collective-bargaining contracts and those in unions are not identical.[5]

The Content of Collective-bargaining Agreements. The content and form of collective-bargaining agreements vary from plant to plant, from industry to industry, and from one geographical area to another. Some contracts, negotiated between giant unions and giant corporations, are "generating" agreements, which set patterns for satellite or related industries; some contracts are negotiated for a given industry or even a given plant.[6] Some contracts, especially those signed after the recog-

[5] Florence Peterson, *American Labor Unions,* Harper & Brothers, New York, 1952, pp. 164–165.
[6] Frederick H. Harbison, Robert K. Burns, and Robert Dubin, "Toward a Theory of Labor Management Relations," in Richards A. Lester and Joseph Shister (ed.), *Insights into Labor Issues,* The Macmillan Company, New York, 1948, pp. 21–24.

nition of a union, are short and concerned with a few fundamental procedures; some are long and contain a large amount of detail. But, whatever the form or content of the contract, both management and labor are trying to attain certain fundamental goals. For the union, three goals are most important: to make the union secure in the plant, to gain certain "practical ends" for the workingmen, and to establish a procedure for handling grievances arising under the contract. We shall discuss each of these aims in greater detail.

Union Security. Much more than in other countries, American unions are, and must be, concerned with union security. One underlying reason for this concern is the long record of employer opposition to unions. Suspicion of employers is still strong among unionists. Another reason for the concern with security is the apathy of many workers toward their unions. Few unions feel that they can depend solely on the loyalty and morale of the workers to guarantee the union's existence. A minor motive is the fear of raids by rival unions.[7]

To attain security, the union seeks through collective bargaining to ensure its hold over the workers, mainly by making membership in the union and financial support for the union compulsory for workingmen. But to attain these ends the unions must come to some sort of understanding with management. Management controls the right to hire and fire and thus the economic fate of union and nonunion workingmen. If the union is to achieve security, it must somehow persuade or force management to use its economic power to enforce union goals.

The maximum security for the union is the *closed shop,* which, however, since 1947 has been outlawed by the Taft-Hartley Act. In the closed shop all workers must be members of the union, and all new workers must be members of the union or hired through the union. The *preferential* shop is closely related to the closed shop, and, for this reason, is of dubious legality. In this arrangement, union members are given preference in hiring, firing, promotions, transfers, layoffs. In hiring new employees, the union man is given preference over a nonunion man of equal qualifications. However, once hired, the nonunion man does not have to join the union.

Under the *maintenance-of-membership* arrangement, new workers have the option of joining or not joining the union. But once the union is joined, membership must be maintained during the life of the agreement, or to the end of the contract. Under the Taft-Hartley Act, a maintenance-of-membership arrangement can be used only when a majority of workers agree to it in a secret ballot.

[7] Carroll R. Daugherty and John B. Parrish, *The Labor Problems of American Society,* Houghton Mifflin Company, Boston, 1952, pp. 337–338.

Perhaps the most common union security arrangement is the *union shop*. Where there is a union shop, all permanent employees are members of the union. The employer has complete freedom in hiring new workers, but within a stipulated time, usually thirty days, the new worker must join the union. The Taft-Hartley Act affected the union shop also, since it provided that a union shop could be installed in a plant only after a majority of workers had voted for it in a secret ballot. Apparently the authors of the Taft-Hartley Act hoped to prevent workers from being coerced into union shops; but of the thousands of elections held since the Act was passed in 1947, the union shop triumphed in more than 90 per cent.

A large number of workers are members of union shops or work under some of the other arrangements noted above. By 1946 some 11½ million workers were covered by union security arrangements. These arrangements applied to more than three-fourths of all the workers in the manufacturing industries.

Many unions not only insist on union security arrangements, duly acceded to by management, but also seek to have management aid in collecting union dues, fines, initiation fees, and special assessments from the workers. The ideal here for the union is the "automatic checkoff," that is, the deduction of union dues from the pay check of the worker. The automatic checkoff was outlawed by the Taft-Hartley Act, and today the checkoff can be used only with authorization of the workers. Such authorizations can be made for not more than a year's duration. Where the checkoff is not used, management, in some cases, grants the unions the right to collect dues within the plant or to set up a dues booth on company premises on payday.

The checkoff, or some other arrangement, is a necessity to the union because of the apathy of many workingmen toward their unions. Nevertheless voluntary authorizations for the checkoff are fairly common today. One study, made in 1949, of over two thousand contracts, found that 65 per cent contained checkoff arrangements. In the CIO unions, where comparative youth, lack of union tradition, and heterogeneous membership make the problem of union security especially pressing, about 90 per cent of the agreements with management contained some provision for a voluntary checkoff.

The "Practical" Ends of Collective Bargaining. From the point of view of the rank and file, the most important function of the union is not the attainment of security for the union, but certain "practical" or "economic" ends. The American workingman expects his union to secure for him (1) above all, better wages; (2) more favorable hours; (3) job tenure; and (4) congenial work rules and conditions of work. We shall discuss each of these "practical" ends.

WAGES. There has been a tendency of late to deny the overriding importance of wages as a goal of workingmen. Yet wage levels continue to be by far the most frequent issue in management-labor disputes in this country. It is probably true that wages symbolize many irrational motives and attitudes. But the fact remains that the urban-industrial workingman is completely dependent on his wages for existence and for the comfort of his family. He is also dependent on wages as a means of attaining nonmaterial goals, such as status in the community. The workingman's drive for financial return is a part of the "ageless story of the people at the bottom of the economic ladder seeking more of the finer things of life."[8]

Since wage levels are of such great importance to the worker, they must be of importance to the union also. It is not too much to say that the survival of the union or its leadership depends in good part on the extent to which the workers are satisfied economically. It is mainly for this reason that union leaders strive to secure wage raises and that they look with fright on wage cuts, even if justified economically.

Theoretically, the union is seeking to maximize wages, but in actuality the specific wage level at which the union is aiming is determined by several other factors. The most important of such factors is without doubt the bargaining power of either side; that is, the relative ability of either side to apply force in a final showdown. Several other factors, however, help to determine the wage level in a specific case; whether an entire industry is unionized or merely a part of it, the state of the business cycle, the attitudes and determination of management, the degree of competition in the industry, the numbers of unemployed workers, the friendliness of political bodies to either side. Any of these factors may determine the wage level at which the union aims or which management will be disposed to grant. For instance, the employer may point to competition from nonunionized competitors as a reason for not granting a raise, or the mere presence of large numbers of unemployed workers may stay the unions' demands for higher wages. Other reasons for a specific wage level, reasons which are often cited by either side in wage disputes, seem to be largely rationalizations. These reasons include "comparable" wage rates (what other workers in the same or allied fields are getting), worker productivity, the cost-of-living index, the ability of the employer to pay, and so on. When these reasons are cited the aim is oftener to influence public opinion than the other side.[9]

---

[8] Clinton S. Golden and Harold J. Ruttenberg, *The Dynamics of Industrial Democracy*, Harper & Brothers, New York, 1942, p. 151.

[9] Actually these "reasons" are largely inapplicable as criteria for determining wage rates, at least in any precise sense. See John T. Dunlop, *Collective Bargaining*, Richard D. Irwin, Inc., Homewood, Ill., 1949, chap. V.

The union is concerned not only with the level of wages but also with the structure of wages. Of the two general types of wage systems used in this country—hourly rate systems, and incentive systems—most unions favor the hourly rate system. In fact some unions such as the UAW are bitterly opposed to incentive systems. The UAW holds that incentive systems lead inevitably to a speed-up of the work, a serious matter on an assembly line. On the other hand, incentive systems are in force in about 30 per cent of the industries where they would be at all feasible; they are especially common in metal and mining industries. Whatever the system of wages, the union is interested above all in maximizing the worker's earnings, in achieving equity and justice in wages, and in eliminating discrimination. Thus the unions have consistently opposed wage differentials related to sex, race, regions, or management favoritism. Unions have insisted on impartial evaluation of jobs, or minimum (or minimum or maximum) rates for jobs, and on regular advancement from one job to another or from one rate to another. They have insisted on the application of standards of ability and/or seniority in all these matters. Where incentive systems are used, the unions have insisted on a base or guaranteed rate, thereby eliminating some of the pressure on the worker.

In addition to straight wage demands, unions seek to obtain certain "fringe" benefits, which do not figure as part of the wage rate but which are, nevertheless, economic in nature. Such benefits may include paid holidays and vacations, sick pay, portal-to-portal pay (pay for time spent traveling on company property), travel pay, "cleanup" pay (a considerable item in such "dirty" industries as the packing industry). Many of these benefits effectively increase the average hourly rate. Another type of fringe benefit is the pension, which has become of increasing importance of late. In 1950 about 5,100,000 workers were covered by collectively bargained private pension systems; about 55 per cent of these workers in the CIO, 25 per cent in the AFL, and 20 per cent in non-affiliated unions. About 75 per cent of these pensions were supported entirely by the employers; the rest, by a combination of workers' and employers' contributions. These pensions paid from $100 to $125 a month, after a period of service ranging between fifteen and thirty-five years.[10]

The unions consider changes in wage rates as a matter of union concern and collective bargaining. This, of course, is especially true for downward movements in wage rates; very few unions can afford not to oppose a wage cut. If a wage cut is agreed to by a union, it will be only after long study and copious explanations to the workers for the reasons

[10] Daugherty and Parrish, *op. cit.*, pp. 531–532.

for the cut. But the main concern of the union is with raising wages, since the loyalty of the workers may be at stake. Many unions follow the lead of certain strong unions, such as the steelworkers' union or the UMW; if these unions receive wage boosts, other unions will try to get comparable wage raises. The desire of the union to secure credit for wage increases is so strong that the union may oppose unilateral wage increases; that is, wage increases about which the union has not been consulted. Some unions, for instance the UAW, have sought to make wage increases automatic by tying the wage rate to a cost-of-living index; this is known as the "escalator" clause. From the union point of view this has worked well in times of rising prices, but of course wages may also fall under this system; an escalator may run down as well as up.

HOURS. The great bulk of collective-bargaining agreements specify a forty-hour week, composed of five eight-hour days. On the other hand, union contracts rarely specify a *total* number of hours to be worked. Rather the contract is likely to specify extra pay for work over the basic forty, or for work outside regularly scheduled hours even if the total does not exceed forty. Much higher rates, often double the normal rate, are usually specified for Saturday or Sunday work. Where the hours worked are unfavorable, e.g., nightwork, many contracts specify increases of 5 to 10 per cent in the hourly rates. The historic goal of unionism has been, of course, to shorten the workday with no decrease in the wage, which amounts to an increase in the rate of pay. Even the forty-hour week seems too long to many unionists, and such unions as the ILGWU and the UMW specify a thirty-five-hour week in their contracts as a normal work week.

JOB TENURE. Scarcely of less importance to the worker than wages and hours is the matter of job security; in fact, in many cases, especially in depressions, security on the job is the first aim of the workers. Threats to security arise, as we have seen, from the fact that labor is a commodity which can be used and compensated only during production, and from the constant technological changes to which industry is subject. The union seeks to protect the worker from both these threats in various ways through the collective-bargaining process. We shall discuss, first, the ways in which the union seeks to protect the worker in the labor market.

First, most unions support a policy of *seniority*, that is, a policy of favoring the worker employed the longer in a given plant in matters of layoffs, rehiring, promotions. Labor's insistence on seniority is a mysterious matter to laymen, but it should not be. Seniority means to the workingman above all an antidote to insecurity, a guarantee that his job is safe while there is work to do. It means an end to fear of displeasing the foreman, of discrimination, of arbitrary dismissal, of nepotism. It means a fair chance at promotions.[11] In short, seniority means for the workingman a limited, but nevertheless real, property interest in the job. The job, in a sense, "belongs" to the worker; it is a scarce and valued commodity, to the use of which he has received certain limited rights. In the next chapter we shall comment on the extent to which the principle of seniority has modified the traditional role of the worker in the factory.

Most union contracts specify that the principle of seniority applies to layoffs, rehiring, promotions, demotions, and transfers. The contract also usually specifies the length of time for which seniority may be retained while the worker is absent from the shop. One year is the most usual period, but in some contracts the period is indefinite.

It will be apparent that the structure of seniority is of supreme importance to the worker; in fact, setting the rules of seniority is a most difficult matter for both the union and management. For the worker, seniority rules may mean the difference between employment and no job, especially during periods of layoffs. It may mean a promotion for one worker and not for another. It may mean a pleasant job or an unpleasant job, a "dirty" job. For these reasons most unions and many managers prefer to have the workers formulate their own seniority rules.

Under the best of circumstances, however, seniority inevitably hurts the interests of management and of many workers. For management, the principle of seniority represents a serious inroad on the rights of hiring and firing, promotion and demotion. For this reason, many contracts specify that both seniority and ability will be considered in promotions, demotions, etc.; that is, where seniority is about equal, the decision will be made on the basis of ability. Worker opposition to seniority comes largely from younger men who may be "bumped" out of their jobs in slack times and whose chances of promotion are blocked by older workers.

However, not all unions stress seniority in all circumstances. For instance, some unions prefer to share the work during slack seasons. A contract may specify sharing the work until a week of thirty-two or thirty hours is reached; only then will layoffs begin. Seniority is not particularly important in industries with a high turnover of labor; e.g., where large masses of women are employed for short periods of time. In skilled trades, the principle of seniority is generally self-applying and so is not stressed in the contract.

Second, the unions seek to protect the worker against arbitrary loss of job or pay. All unions concede to management the right to dismiss or otherwise punish workers for specified cause, e.g., drunkenness, insub-

[11] For an excellent statement of the need for seniority from the worker's point of view, see Golden and Ruttenberg, *op. cit.*, chap. V.

ordination, and fighting on the job. But many unions insist that management notify the worker of intended punishment, that the worker be given the chance to appeal through the grievance machinery, and that, in case the layoff or punishment is adjudged unjustified, the worker be given back pay.

Third, although the trade unions in the United States must accept the right of the employer to lay off or dismiss his workers when there is no work to do, they make certain attempts to circumvent or prevent layoffs where possible, or at least to mitigate their severity. One device for mitigating the severity of the layoff is the *guaranteed annual wage*, that is, the guarantee of a certain minimum yearly income to the worker. The guaranteed annual wage has been pushed strongly in those industries, such as the automobile industry, where there are frequent and lengthy layoffs. However, the guaranteed annual wage has been strongly opposed by management, and where it has been granted it amounts to little more than supplements to unemployment insurance.

The unions adopt other devices for combating unemployment; some of these devices, interestingly enough, are a continuation of the practices of the informal group. For instance, the union may set certain limits on production, or curtail the use of machinery, or specify what tools can be used on the job. Some unions demand the employment of unnecessary workers; a prime and often cited example is the "fireman" on the coal-less diesel locomotive. Where unneeded workers are employed, there has often been a history of technological change and worker displacement. Finally, most unions demand "make work" in order to tide the workers over a period of unemployment. For reasons that we have already discussed, these devices are of limited importance and usefulness to the worker. The fight against unemployment must be carried out largely through political maneuvering.

Fourth, some unions try to limit the number of workers in a given industry. Limitation is supposed to prevent workers from competing with each other for jobs. Limitation is imposed through the use of high initiation fees, qualification tests, or outright refusal to admit newcomers to membership.

The union, in addition to protecting the worker in the labor market, tries to protect him against technological change. Where it can, the union may simply forbid the introduction of a new machine, but such a policy is almost always only temporarily successful. Sometimes the union may attempt to ward off the threat of a technological change by accepting a wage cut, or by demanding that the new machinery be operated only on the basis of high wage rates. Where the machine can be neither prohibited nor warded off, the union may attempt to limit the pace at which the machinery is introduced; it may demand that men displaced by the machine be given first chance at the newly created jobs, through a process of retraining. Finally, if the dismissal of workers cannot be prevented by any of these means, the union may demand a lump sum for each worker, as dismissal pay.

Similarly, the union attempts to guard the workers against changes in production methods. For many years the unions were suspicious of the time-and-motion study, opposing it where possible and sabotaging it where not. Much of this suspicion remains, but if the time-and-motion study cannot be halted, many unions will reserve the right to challenge any of the rates. In some instances, the unions will demand the right to cooperate in the time-and-motion study, even to the point of furnishing the engineers for the study.[12]

CONDITIONS OF WORK. The unions have also been traditionally concerned with working conditions. What constitute good working conditions vary, of course, from plant to plant. In hazardous industries the union may insist on certain safety provisions or on the formation of safety committees. Clean lavatories, proper light and ventilation, shower rooms, lockers, dressing rooms may be all specified in the union contract. The contract may also specify what constitutes a proper work load, how many assistants and apprentices each worker is to have, what sorts of jobs are to be given to older workers, etc. The variety of provisions is almost infinite.

Grievance Procedure. The third major aim which the union seeks to gain through collective bargaining is efficient and validly functioning procedures for handling and settling grievances. The explicit function of the grievance system is to interpret the contract in the light of the continuing but changing daily relationship between management and labor and to settle whatever disputes may arise in the course of this relationship. But the grievance procedure has a somewhat different significance to the worker, to the union, and to management. For the worker, the presence of grievance machinery means a considerable enhancement of power in the plant, a lessening of vulnerability to plant discipline. For the worker, the grievance procedure represents industrial democracy; it provides a channel of communication to higher authority. For both the union and management, the grievance procedure is a means by which the collective-bargaining agreement can be made to work. It is also a means for locating the sources of dissatisfaction both among the workers and in the lower reaches of the management hierarchy.[13] Thus, providing the grievance machinery is used in good faith—and it sometimes is not—it fulfills functions of considerable and novel importance within the plant.

[12] Daugherty and Parrish, *op. cit.*, pp. 352–357.
[13] Dunlop, *op. cit.*, pp. 78–82.

The structure of grievance machinery differs from plant to plant, but a typical case might look like this. The contract specifies a set of officials, designated by both sides, for handling grievances. On the company side grievances are handled first by the foreman, then perhaps by a department superintendent, next by a division superintendent, and finally by the plant manager. On the union side, grievances are handled first by the shop chairman or steward, and then, if necessary, by local officials, and even by national officials. In general, in smaller companies, there are three or four steps in the grievance procedure; in larger companies, four or five. However, it should be noted that under the Taft-Hartley Act a dispute between a worker and a minor official may be taken directly to management, which has the power to settle the dispute. The union has the right to send a representative to such "privately" conducted negotiations, and, in any event, management cannot settle the dispute in a way which would be inconsistent with the terms of the contract.

The collective-bargaining agreement may also specify other details of the grievance procedure: at what stage a grievance is to be put into writing, the maximum time to be spent on judging a grievance at each step, whether management has the right to file grievances, the ratio of stewards to workers or to foremen, whether stewards are to be paid for time spent adjusting grievances, what penalties are to be fixed for failure to use or abide by decisions of the grievance procedure, etc.[14]

The contract often defines with care what is to be considered a grievance. Depending on this definition, the union has more or less freedom in challenging or modifying management control in a plant; management will agree to talk with and negotiate with the union on more or fewer issues.

Four general types of grievances may be distinguished (the specific variety may be practically endless), though not all these grievances may be recognized in a labor contract. Grievances may arise as a result of a conflict between sections of the agreement, or as a result of a conflict which is not covered by the agreement but is within its scope, or as the result of the application of a general rule to a particular case. Sometimes miscellaneous grievances may arise from conflicts which are outside the scope of the contract.[15] The contract may provide that *any* conflict or grievance is to be handled through the grievance machinery, or it may specify precisely what types of grievances are to be handled. The union, of course, favors the former type of contract as a rule, management the latter type. But even where the definition of a grievance is

---

[14] Harold W. Davey, *Contemporary Collective Bargaining*, Prentice-Hall, Inc., Englewood Cliffs, New Jersey, 1951, pp. 275–278.
[15] See Dunlop, *op. cit.*, p. 82.

carefully specified, disputes frequently arise as to whether a given complaint is a legitimate grievance.

At rare intervals grievances may go even to the highest authority without being settled. What is to be done then, short of the use of force? Most contracts specify some sort of arbitration procedure to settle disputes of this type. Contracts differ in this respect. Sometimes the contract directs the disputants to take their problem to the state or Federal mediation agency. Some contracts specify a particular arbitrator, who has the confidence of both sides, to handle unresolved disputes. A closely allied method specifies a panel of arbitrators, from which one individual will be chosen for a particular case. Sometimes the arbitrator acts as a chairman of a board composed of equal numbers of management and labor representatives; in this case, the arbitrator may or may not have a vote. Finally, some contracts specify that unresolved disputes be settled by an arbitrator especially chosen for the occasion, that is, an *ad hoc* arbitrator.

The duties of the arbitrator are to hold hearings, to take testimony, to conduct independent investigations, and to render a decision on the merits of the case (though often other considerations enter, as we shall see). In this connection, the permanent arbitrator has these advantages over the *ad hoc* arbitrator: the permanent arbitrator knows the industry, its problems, the structure of management and labor and their problems, the personalities involved. On the other hand, he is at a disadvantage as compared to the *ad hoc* arbitrator in that, precisely because he is immersed in the industry, he may have offended one side or another; the professional life of an arbitrator is notoriously short.

No matter how the arbitrator is chosen, his decision is binding on both parties and may be enforced by court action.

Factors in the Collective-bargaining Relationship. It is important to note that collective bargaining, although itself a peaceful relationship, is based ultimately on the underlying power of management and labor to apply force, particularly economic force, to each other. Collective bargaining may proceed on the basis of a completed test of the power of both sides, e.g., after a strike; or it may proceed on the basis of mutual estimates of the power of either side to inflict damage on the other. But the principle is the same: underlying the bargaining tactics of either labor or management is the ability of one side to do a maximum of damage to the other side, with a minimum of loss to itself.

It is this possibility of resort to force, spoken or unspoken, which forms the penumbra of all collective-bargaining relationships. This, however, most emphatically does not mean that either side is necessarily eager to use force; on the contrary, both sides may feel equally that the use of force should be avoided. Different types of collective-bargaining relationships may be distinguished in terms of the readiness of one side or the other to use force.[16]

One type of relationship between management and labor is hardly more than an armed truce, during which both management and labor seek to build up their power, and each seeks to weaken the power of the other.[17] In such relationships, which are by no means uncommon in America, especially in the mass-production industries, the threat of force is always present and the use of force is frequent.

In other types of relationships there may be a real accommodation in certain areas, but these areas are strictly delimited. In the area of accommodation, the threat or use of force may have subsided into the background, to be brought out only in times of crisis. However, in this type of relationship either side is quite willing to use force outside the area of accommodation. For instance, if the union attempts to encroach on areas of traditional management prerogatives, management may resist violently.

Finally, there are true cooperative relationships between management and labor. In these cases labor may almost fill the role of a junior partner; it may cooperate with management to eliminate waste, increase efficiency, introduce technological advances, and guarantee the solvency of the firm.[18] In this case force is almost never used, or its use lies far in the past. However, it should be noted that true cooperative relationships are rather rare in the United States. Furthermore, such relationships almost always occur where the power of the union is overwhelming, a rather rare situation in this country. In a case of this kind, the use of force is pointless; the union has already achieved as much as it can through the use of force. To advance further, the union must cooperate in building up the industry as a whole.

Thus, it will be noted that all types of collective-bargaining relationships (except possibly those which are collusive) are based ultimately on power, in much the same way that international relationships reflect the power of nations. It is of the greatest importance not to lose sight of this power basis in looking at collective bargaining, precisely because this base is often hidden. At the same time, it must not be assumed that the underlying power relationships between management and labor are

[16] It is still too early to tell what effect the merger of the AFL and CIO will have on collective bargaining. In an address to the initial convention of the united labor movement, the Secretary of Labor expressed the hope that the merger would "make for greater labor-management peace" and for "improvements in union management relationships." Since the merger may have the effect of more nearly equalizing the power of management and labor in this country, this may very well be the case.

[17] Harbison and Coleman, *op. cit.*, p. 20.

[18] Benjamin M. Selekman, Sylvia K. Selekman, and Stephen H. Fuller, *Problems in Labor Relations*, McGraw-Hill Book Company, Inc., New York, 1950, pp. 8–9.

fixed and unchanging. Nor must it be assumed that power relationships are the sole important elements in the collective-bargaining relationship. On the contrary, there are other elements which help to shape collective-bargaining relationships, elements which cause collective bargaining to deviate from the form it would take if issues were settled solely on the basis of relative power.

We shall discuss first certain conditions which tend to affect the collective-bargaining power of management and labor either temporarily or permanently. For instance, in industries which use a large amount of skilled labor, the bargaining power of the union is generally higher than in industries which employ masses of unskilled or semiskilled workers. As compared to unskilled workers, skilled workers are often difficult to replace, have high morale, and long traditions of organization. Furthermore, a preponderance of skilled workers is often found in small-scale industries, where the power of management is not great to begin with. It is for these and other reasons that some of the most powerful unions and best working conditions are found in the building trade.

Bargaining power may also be affected by the capital and competitive situation of an industry. For instance, where competition between firms is keen, the bargaining power of the union is increased, since a stoppage in one plant may greatly benefit a competitor. However, in the case of a monopoly, a work stoppage may hold little terror for management, since its market will not be lost, and in the long run its sales will not be affected. On the other hand, even a monopoly has reason to fear the power of the union under certain circumstances. If capital costs are high relative to labor costs, the power of the union is increased, since a work stoppage means a loss on a large capital investment. Furthermore some monopolies produce perishable commodities, which quickly deteriorate or lose their value if operations cease. Such monopolies or near monopolies may be found in communications, in the field of entertainment, and in public utilities. The bargaining power of labor in such industries may be very great. Finally, even monopolies may need a continuous flow of capital, and a long costly stoppage in production may easily lead to the drying up of the sources of capital supply.

The state of the business cycle also affects bargaining power. During times of prosperity, when labor is in short supply, the power of the union is obviously increased, and of course the reverse holds during an economic downswing. On the other hand, a downswing may increase the militancy of the rank and file and thus heighten the bargaining power of the union.

Bargaining power also reflects the political situation in the nation. The Taft-Hartley Act's prohibition of the closed shop, its regulation of union shops and maintenance-of-membership clauses, have served to weaken the power of labor to bargain collectively.[19] As a result, managerial bargaining power has been heightened, especially where there are "armed truce" relationships or accommodative relationships, though not where there are cooperative relationships.[20] At the same time, the political climate of the nation, or of a community, serves to hearten or dishearten one side or the other as the case may be. It may be, however, that labor, with its great heterogeneous masses, is more sensitive to this kind of pressure.

Certain other factors may also influence collective bargaining, though not necessarily by increasing the power of one side or the other. For instance, the historically determined attitudes of management and labor toward each other are certainly of great importance in determining the willingness of either side to bargain in good faith. Where management and labor have fought each other bitterly and even violently, where each side is suspicious of the motives of the other, where the union is looked on as an interloper and management as greedy and power-mad, it is hardly to be expected that bargaining relationships will be of a cooperative kind. It is in a situation of this kind that much can be done to improve bargaining relationships through the application of social-science techniques, or simply through a process of "learning to live with each other." But, of course, the application of social-science techniques in collective bargaining cannot be substituted for the underlying power relationship. "Learning to live with each other" means learning to recognize and respect the power of the other side.

The collective-bargaining relationship may be affected by other factors. If a given contract will set a pattern for other firms or industries to follow, bargaining may be sharp and prolonged; threats of force may be easily used, and every last element of power exploited. However, if a contract merely follows a pattern already set in other firms or industries, the bargaining may be perfunctory. Trouble may arise in bargaining if the union seeks at all costs to equal the gains set by a "generating pattern," as it may do if it is threatened by a rival union or internal factionalism. In this case, the union may attempt to exceed its power, in order to protect itself against competition, and management may feel called upon to resist.

The collective-bargaining relationship, finally, is influenced by the skill of management and labor in the tactics of negotiation. The limits of these tactics are set by the power of management and labor, by the political situation, and by other factors we have mentioned; but within these limits there is still room to maneuver. Consequently both manage-

---

[19] Samuel Harris Cohen, "Labor, Taft-Hartley and the Proposed Amendments," *Labor Law Journal*, vol. 5, no. 6, p. 418, 1954.

[20] Harbison and Coleman, *op. cit.*, pp., 129–131.

ment and labor have evolved special collective-bargaining tactics. These tactics differ quite sharply from most of the "classical" tactics which were discussed in the previous chapter. There is room for trading, argument, persuasion, and rebuttal. We shall discuss these tactics.

Individual Bargaining and Multiple Bargaining. As in any contest, each side attempts to ensure a favorable base from which to conduct its campaign. In labor-management relationships this means primarily that each side seeks to regulate the number of firms and local unions involved in the negotiations, in accordance with certain tactical considerations. For purposes of simplicity, we shall speak here only of two cases: where one firm or one plant deals with the union (either the local or the national), and where a union or unions deals with more than one employer. Of course, there are many variations possible; for instance, a union may deal with an entire industry or with a portion of it, a group of unions may deal with employers drawn from a certain geographical area (often a city), or one employer may deal with a group of unions. Our choice is dictated by our interest in those general factors which drive management and labor to seek individual bargaining, on the one hand, or multiple bargaining, on the other.

It is often assumed that unions favor multiemployer bargaining—in fact, industry-wide bargaining, if possible—while management is naturally opposed to this type of bargaining. However, the situation is much more complicated than that. Whether management or the union favors individual or multiple bargaining in any single case may depend on one or several factors.

The unions generally have favored multiple bargaining because wage differentials have historically proved dangerous to the existence of unions. Multiple bargaining is the best way to wipe out wage differentials. Where wage differentials exist, management has a powerful weapon to hold over the union; management can move its plants, or bring in lower-priced labor, or depress wages in the entire industry.

But there are other motives driving unions to seek ever-widening bargaining units. In highly competitive industries, where labor forms a high proportion of the total product cost, there is strong pressure on wages, a pressure which cannot be met by dealing with this or that employer but only by dealing with the entire industry. In industries, such as the maritime industry, where workers are constantly shifting from one employer to another, multiple bargaining is necessary if the union is not to lose its hold on the workers. In all cases, multiple bargaining is less costly to the union than individual bargaining; there is only one set of negotiations and negotiators, one set of experts, involved. Furthermore, in multiemployer bargaining the union can sometimes count on the employers themselves to enforce adherence to the contract. Finally, multiple bargaining builds up the security of the union; it protects the national from jealousies between locals, and it protects the entire union from raids by other unions.[21]

It is interesting to note that multiple-employer bargaining may be attained, for all practical purposes, even where management and labor bargain individually. For instance, where numerous small firms in an industry or related industries sign contracts negotiated on the model of some large-scale collective-bargaining agreement, multiple bargaining exists in effect. Practically the same results may be achieved by a provision in the union constitution demanding national approval of local contracts, or by national requirements for local contracts; in fact, some nationals supply standard contracts to the local. *De facto* multiple bargaining may also be obtained through the union-label or union-shop-card methods; that is, by supplying these tokens of union approval only to employers who have met the national's standards.[22]

However, management also, under certain circumstances, may find multiple bargaining useful, or even necessary. Often it is favored by management as a defense against union power. This situation is likely to arise in industries marked by many small firms, any one of which would be powerless against the union. By combining, management can prevent the union from picking off one firm at a time. Also, in such industries, unionized firms may fear the competition of nonunion firms and thus positively demand even industry-wide bargaining. Industries in the same geographical area may favor multiple bargaining in order to equalize wage rates, and to avoid cutthroat competition for labor. Management may also hope for fewer strikes, fewer jurisdictional disputes, and less costly negotiations through multiple bargaining.

However, it is more common to find management opposed to multiple bargaining. This opposition arises from the enhanced power which the union derives from it; a firm which is powerful enough to cope with a local union may be overwhelmed by a national union. In general, firms which enjoy national markets and relatively little competition and which have large, mobile capital units will oppose multiple bargaining.[23]

Employer opposition to it may also arise from certain economic factors. Employers may oppose it because they oppose the equalization of wages. For instance, they may feel that wage differentials are due to certain conditions for which they are not responsible; e.g., the amount and skill of local labor, the differences in local or regional wage levels, the size and type of industry, the rate of return on capital, the practice

[21] Daugherty and Parrish, *op. cit.*, pp. 383–384.
[22] Peterson, *op. cit.*, p. 155.
[23] Frank C. Pierson, "Prospects for Industry-wide Bargaining," *Industrial and Labor Relations Review*, vol. 3, no. 3, p. 358, 1950.

of calling quite different jobs by the same name. Furthermore, employers have often felt that in multiple bargaining the union invariably attempts to bring working conditions up to the level of the most advanced firms. This practice threatens the existence or profitability of less efficient firms. On the other hand, the more efficient firms may oppose multiple bargaining because they wish to use their ability to pay higher wages to lure skilled workers to their plants.

Employers may also oppose multiple bargaining because they consider it an encroachment on their power in the plant. It not only forces management to accept wage and hour rates determined in other places, but it inevitably decreases the respect of the workers for the power of management and enhances the prestige of the union. Thus, for the employers, multiple bargaining may conceal a vicious circle; unions seek it

Table 6. Types of Bargaining Units, 1950

Types of contract	*Per cent of workers covered*	
Single-employer..................	67	
Single-plant.....................		28
Multiplant......................		39
Multiple-employer...............	33	
National.......................		4
Regional.......................		6
Local..........................		23

SOURCE: Carroll R. Daugherty and John B. Parrish, *The Labor Problems of American Society*, Houghton Mifflin Company, Boston, 1952, p. 512. By permission.

in order to increase bargaining power, but in the process the strength of the union as a whole is increased.

Under certain circumstances the union also may find individual bargaining to its advantage. If a given industry contains a few prosperous firms and numerous less prosperous ones, the unions will seek to bargain individually with the prosperous firms in order to set a pattern. Furthermore, multiple-employer bargaining has the undesirable result, from the point of view of the union, of causing management to band together. A union may be much more powerful than a single firm; it may be much less powerful than an entire industry.

The outlooks of management and labor on this question may also differ in relation to the business cycle. During an upswing in business, management tends to favor multiple bargaining in order to eliminate competitive bidding for labor. During a downswing, the union favors multiple bargaining in order to prevent employers from cutting wages.

In spite of the diversity of interests pictured above, there are certain definite patterns in bargaining arrangements. Most bargaining today occurs between single units, or between unions and single employers, as Table 6 shows. However, there does seem to be a definite trend toward wider bargaining. Much of this trend seems to be the result of pressure from the unions, not the employers. Yet the authors of the Taft-Hartley Act, who were set to outlaw industry-wide bargaining, found that many employers favored it. Experience during World War II, when government policy dictated uniform working conditions in order to eliminate labor turnover, seems to have convinced wide sections of management of the advantages of multiple bargaining.

Negotiations. If the determination of the bargaining unit is analogous to the jockeying for position prior to a contest, the collective-bargaining negotiations are the contest itself. It is true that the outcome of the contest has been predetermined, to a large extent, by the power which each side has been able to build up; but this does not mean that skill in bargaining does not have a role to play in the outcome of the negotiations.

Each side attempts to build up the most effective team possible for the negotiations. On the union side, local bargaining is conducted either by the officers of the local union or by a joint board chosen from several locals, or by a committee chosen by the rank and file, or by some combination of these. Ideally, rank-and-file committees should represent the major divisions of interests among the workers in a plant. If there is a business agent, he is usually present at the negotiations. Sometimes national officers sit in on the negotiations. There are a number of reasons for their presence; negotiations require special skills which interim negotiators cannot supply, settlement often depends on national trends which are not always known to local officials or committees, and, of course, a national representative is immune to company pressure in the plant.[24] Multiple bargaining is usually conducted by national officials and the national's staff.

For the management of a small plant, negotiations may be carried on directly by the owner, perhaps with the assistance of a lawyer. Where there is multiple bargaining between a union and a number of small employers, the negotiations may be carried on by an employers' association. In the case of large plants or industries, management negotiators reflect the structure of the firm. In some instances, negotiations are carried on by a plant manager; in others, by the central office. In a few cases, the chief negotiator for management is the president of the firm. Sometimes it is a line officer; sometimes, an industrial-relations officer, that is, a staff man. Occasionally negotiations are carried on by legal counsel. Other management negotiators may be chosen from the departments which will be affected by the collective-bargaining agreement.

In addition to the negotiators, various types of experts may sit in on the negotiations, a practice which is becoming more common. The most

[24] Sidney Garfield and William F. Whyte, "The Collective Bargaining Process: A Human Relations Analysis, IV," *Human Organization*, vol. 10, no. 1, p. 31, 1951.

frequently used expert is the lawyer; this practice reflects the importance of political and legal factors in labor-management relations.

The meetings themselves are usually held in neutral territory, perhaps a hotel. A chairman is sometimes engaged to conduct the meetings; sometimes chairmen are selected on alternate days from either side. Usually there is a recording secretary. An agenda may be agreed upon, but this is by no means a universal practice, for reasons which will appear below.

During negotiations, management seems to have one considerable tactical advantage over the union, which arises from the differences in structure between the industrial firm and the union. Because industry is nonpolitical in structure, management can adopt a flexible policy in the negotiations, shaping its demands to the situation. Furthermore, management can decide on its policy in secrecy and maintain this secrecy throughout the meetings. The union, on the other hand, is a political organization, which must live up to certain promises made to the rank and file. It therefore has less room for maneuver than management. Furthermore, the demands to be made on the employer are usually submitted to the rank and file for ratification, and the final agreement must be ratified again; even in large-scale bargaining the local usually submits a list of demands to the conference. Thus, not only is the union bound by a set of instructions from the rank and file, but all possibility of secrecy is lost. Management knows what its opponents want, and even how determined they are in their demands; the union can never have comparable knowledge of management.

Certain tactics used during the negotiations are common to all negotiations; others are unique to labor-management relations. It is not peculiar to collective bargaining that each side commonly sets forth a maximum set of demands and reserves a minimum set, past which it will not go. Any settlement above the minimum may then be counted a clear gain. Each side of course attempts to size up the other side, to determine how sincere it is in its demands, how strong it is, whether it is bluffing about force or is really prepared to "go the limit." Skillful negotiators will try to avoid pushing the opposition past its limit, where it would risk loss of face, or into a corner, where it could do nothing but fight. Concession is needed as well as stubbornness, and yet the concessions must be made in such a way as not to seem confessions of weakness and, in the case of the union, in such a way that the rank and file does not become disheartened. Tactics, successful tactics, must be flexible, and it is for this reason that each side will attempt to have different types of personalities on its team: aggressive fighters for hard fighting, soft-spoken personalities to smooth over rough spots, stubborn personalities to resist through long wearying hours, quick-witted personalities who can pick a flaw in an opponent's argument and improvise a defense.[25]

Certain tactics are unique to labor-management relationships. For instance, the fact that the union is a reaction to industrial conditions—an outgrowth of, and an answer to, strains felt in certain industrial roles—means that the union must be inherently on the offensive. Whatever gains a union makes are at the expense of the freedom and power of management. Consequently, in the collective-bargaining conference the union is usually attempting to extend the scope of its power or maintain gains which have only recently been acquired by offensive maneuver. Thus the union will attempt to broaden the scope of the contract. It will oppose management attempts strictly to delimit the areas of collective bargaining; it will argue for flexibility in the type of problems to be taken up in collective bargaining.

More specifically, the union will challenge management's right to make unilateral changes in technology, to change wage rates, to promote or demote without consulting the union, and so on through a host of issues. The union will attempt to get management to recognize the status of union stewards and officials, to secure them from management reprisal, to guard them against loss of income.[26] To consolidate its position, the union tries to achieve maximum union security. In all these cases, it is the union which is demanding something of management; it is the union which is attacking an entrenched management.

To buttress its arguments, the union will come to the conference with data which it has amassed not so much to convince management as to rationalize the union position, to convince both rank and file and the community of the rightness of its cause. The union will emphasize those statistics which seem favorable to its cause; e.g., financial records of the company, economic data on the industry as a whole, comparable wage and working conditions in other industries, prices and cost of living. Amassing this data cannot be the work of amateurs; the unions often employ trained economists and research staffs for this purpose.

For management the tactics of collective bargaining are essentially defensive; it is management which is usually the vested interest, strongly supported by the values and institutions of the society. This in itself is of considerable value to the company, for it can plead tradition and precedent for its arguments and can enlist on its side all the conservative forces in the community. Management will resist wage demands and other demands for changed working conditions, though without alienat-

---

[25] Daugherty and Parrish, *op. cit.*, p. 538.

[26] See Harbison and Coleman, *op. cit.*, chap. II. The authors state that these are the tactics of management under "armed truce." It would seem more accurate to say that in an "armed truce" relationship these tactics are more sharply defined but that they are present in all collective-bargaining relationships.

ing its workers, if possible. Management will resist, even more strongly in many cases, union attempts to widen the scope of collective bargaining. Management seeks to stake out certain limited areas in which it *will* bargain collectively, e.g., in relation to wages and hours; but it will resist union attempts to control, or interfere in, financing of the business, the sale of products, production standards, the selection, promotion, or demotion of employees, supervision of the working force. Management seeks, further, not only to constrain the union but to discipline it. Thus management will argue for the right to discipline union members, including union officials, for violation of contract; it may oppose union security for the same reason. Finally, whatever specific tactics it adopts, management seeks to avoid building the prestige of the union; it may oppose wage demands primarily for this reason. Management will attempt to maneuver in such a way that it will seem that the union is unreasonable, unfair, noncooperative; for instance, if there must be a strike, management will attempt to have the strike fought over seemingly trivial or obscure issues.

The threat of force may also serve a tactical purpose. The union may get an authorization for a strike before or during the negotiations, as a reminder to management of what might happen. Sometimes workers refuse to work overtime during the negotiations, or slow down the work, or institute a large number of grievances. These tactics are designed to bring pressure on management during the period of negotiations. Union leaders may attempt to arouse the rank and file during the negotiations. Meetings are held and speeches made, designed to build up morale and to provide outlets for resentment against management.

Management for its part also tries to apply force during negotiations, but in other ways. It may, for instance, raise wages before or during the negotiations and adopt other measures aimed at meeting employee grievances. Direct appeals may be made to the workers, through letters, through the plant newspaper, or through speeches—practices which have become again permissible under the Taft-Hartley Act. Management may remind the worker of those community forces which it can bring to its aid and of the extreme hardship that a strike may bring to the workers.

It is by tactics such as these, by the whittling away of demands on either side, by trading, by bluffing, by threats, that an agreement can usually be reached. However, if settlement cannot be attained, there is one more step that may be taken before the issue is resigned to force. This is placing the dispute before an outside agency, that is, either an arbitrator or a mediator. In the event of arbitration, the case is presumably settled on its merits, with each side presenting the strongest possible arguments. That is, the dispute now proceeds on a quasi-juridical level.

It must be understood, furthermore, that when negotiations go into mediation, this does not alter fundamentally the nature of the collective-bargaining relationship, nor does it mean that either side drops its basic aims. In fact, it is the function of the mediator to point out to each side the realities of the power situation and the point at which a compromise might be reached which would reflect fairly the balance of power. This does not mean that the mediator does not have some room for maneuver. One mediator has said:[27]

The solution [depends] ultimately on the way in which one party [reacts] to the pressure generated by the other, [but] it is occasionally possible for the mediator to modify or control the level of pressure. His efforts often exert a direct effect on the bargaining positions of the parties and on their willingness to compromise.

A mediator may operate in the following manner. He informs the contestants about industrial precedents and procedures; he collects data about prevailing wages, ability to pay, productivity, the national interest. He may reveal or conceal this information on either side as he thinks it may effect or retard a settlement. The mediator is constantly in consultation with either side, persuading or cajoling them. He constantly offers summations of progress, of points of agreement; he attempts to keep the conference on the subject, to stress its progressive and hopeful sides. He may engage in "logrolling," attempting to get one side to trade off a point for a concession on another point.

Contracts and Grievance Procedures. Barring a final breakdown in negotiations the contract is eventually signed—sometimes casually, sometimes with considerable ceremony—and a ratification secured from the rank and file. Usually the contract runs for a definite period of time, often for a year. Some contracts are of indefinite length; some are subject to renegotiation on the demand of either party. The Taft-Hartley Act specifies that either party desiring to end a contract must give the other side sixty days' notice, during which time negotiations must be carried on. But, at any rate, once the contract is signed and ratified, labor-management relations enter a new phase, in which each side must attempt to live with, and accommodate to, the other within the provisions of the contract.

"Living within the provisions of the contract," however, may prove to be a complex matter indeed. The contract is, necessarily, abstract and generalized, but it must be applied to concrete situations, and very few concrete situations ever exactly fit the terms of the contract. The contract must be interpreted and implemented in daily relationships be-

[27] By permission from Hugh G. Lovell, "The Pressure Lever in Mediation," *Industrial and Labor Relations Review*, vol. 6, no. 1, p. 27, 1952.

tween foremen and workers, between union and management, in new situations and in old; it must be applied to varying personalities, values, attitudes, and interests.

Under these circumstances, it is not surprising that disputes about the contract may break out, disputes which may rival in virulence those arising prior to a strike or during collective bargaining. The meaning of the terms of the contract may be disputed. The proper application of the contract to a particular situation may be disputed. New situations, not foreseen in the contract, inevitably arise and must somehow be adjudicated.[28]

Management and labor may take certain steps to forestall disputes or to handle them if they arise. An attempt may be made, in the first instance, to avoid misunderstandings by explaining the contract to those who must enforce its provisions; foremen, shop stewards, personnel experts, as well as the workers themselves. When disputes nevertheless break out they may be handled in one of two ways: by a special conference of labor and management officials, or through the grievance machinery. The function of the grievance machinery is, in this case, juridical, at least in theory; it is to handle disputes which arise as to the nature and scope of the contract. This is a crucial function; the prospects of industrial peace rest quite as much on the success of this function as on successful collective bargaining.

However, the adjudication of disputes of this kind is a complex affair. Reduction of the daily relationships between management and labor to grievance procedures does not, as if by some magic spell, suddenly transform the basic nature of those relationships. Management and labor remain in conflict or competition in all the traditional areas. The operation of grievance machinery does, however, transform the manner in which these conflicts of interest are fought out and resolved. It places the conflicts, and their possible solutions, within the framework of rule and precedent. Thus, just as collective bargaining is a continuation of power tactics by other methods, so grievance procedure is a continuation of collective bargaining by somewhat different tactics.

This parallel can be seen if the aims of labor in grievance procedures are compared to labor's aims in collective bargaining, and if the tactics of collective bargaining and grievance procedure are contrasted. Labor seeks to use grievance procedure to further certain of its historic objectives. Thus, while wage rates are presumably set by the contract, there is still plenty of room for labor to maneuver in an attempt to raise wages or to preserve existing rates. For instance, a legitimate dispute may arise, for the grievance machinery to settle, as to when premium rates

[28] Neil W. Chamberlain, *Collective Bargaining*, McGraw-Hill Book Company, Inc., New York, 1951, p. 96.

are to be paid. Are they, for example, to be paid on all Sundays and holidays, even when a total of forty hours in the work week has not been exceeded? Furthermore, disputes may arise over wage rates to be paid on new jobs, or on old jobs altered by technological change, or on jobs marked by old, inefficient machinery. Questions may arise about inequities in rates on various jobs or about wage differentials between departments. Another question that may arise is this: Is the company to pay wages when "conditions beyond the control" of management bring work to a halt? And when do such conditions exist? Or, in case the contract calls for renegotiation of wage issues in certain situations, when does a situation of this kind exist?[29]

Disputes may also arise over the issue of hours. Management naturally desires a work schedule arranged to maximize efficiency and to reduce costs; labor desires a schedule of hours which suits the tastes of the worker. Conflict, therefore, may arise as to the necessity for irregular hours. A clash may also occur over the question of who shall work undesirable hours, with management wishing to settle the question on the basis of efficiency, and the union perhaps on the basis of seniority, or through a plan of rotation.

Similarly, although a union contract contains specific clauses about the allocation of jobs, promotions, demotion, layoffs, etc., there are many dubious or borderline cases which are not clearly covered by the rules of seniority. If a case involves a matter of principle, there is almost certain to be a conflict between management and labor which may have to be carried to the grievance machinery. A clash may occur over such questions as whether a given act is a transfer, involving loss of seniority, or a layoff. Or, questions may arise as to whether a layoff is temporary or permanent, for if it is permanent, seniority may be lost. Disputes often arise as to when seniority begins to accumulate, what constitutes a promotion, how much better qualified one worker must be than another if seniority principles are to be set aside. Another type of question which strikes directly at the heart of management power concerns management's right to transfer workers against their will, if such transfer involves loss of seniority. What is at stake in all these problems is management's right to run the plant according to its values, as opposed to labor's right to safeguard the economic and social well-being of the workers.

Closely related to disputes over security are those disputes which arise in connection with management's right to discipline its workers. The contract, it is true, may specify quite closely what rights of discipline management retains; but this does not prevent all sorts of disagreements

[29] See Part 2 of Dunlop, *op. cit.*, for various cases illustrating the grievances mentioned in this chapter.

from occurring in borderline cases. In such cases the question is often not so much whether this or that worker has been unjustly treated; it is a question of the relative power which management and labor can wield in the plant. Thus a dispute over the firing of an employee for activity outside the plant involves the question of where management's authority over its workers ends. Similarly, if a worker is fired for disobeying a rule which is customarily disobeyed, the underlying question may be management's right to use unusual means to punish the worker; or the question may be whether management is not seeking an excuse to punish the worker for other, not stated, reasons. In the case of a wildcat strike, the right of management or of the union to punish the strikers may involve questions of power which far transcend in importance the strike itself.

The signing of a contract does not necessarily end the struggle between management and labor over union security and the status of union representatives in the plant. For instance, bitter disputes may arise over a question of whether management is bound to fire certain employees in a union shop for failure to join the union. Can the union discipline such workers in other ways? Can it discipline workers who have been expelled from the union? Where there is a checkoff, does the union have the right to raise dues? Can the union punish workers who refuse to disobey company rules, e.g., workers who exceed the going rate of work? To what extent should union stewards be free from plant discipline? To what extent are they entitled to the protection of seniority? When is a steward being disciplined for legitimate reasons, and when is he being persecuted for his union activity? Here again are real clashes of interest which may be resolved through grievance procedures.

The tactics used by management and labor in the grievance procedure are similar in many ways to those used in collective bargaining—so much so, in fact, that many observers and participants in industry consider the resolution of grievances a form of collective bargaining. On the labor side, just as in collective bargaining, the union will attempt to combat "legalism," the strict interpretation of the contract. The union strives for general terms, "set forth in general language, lending themselves to flexible administration and day-to-day interpretation according to changing conditions."[30] Union tactics in grievance procedure include the familiar parliamentary ones: the amassing of data to support the case, "logrolling," argument and debate, rationalization. Behind the scenes, and in spite of the contract, the union may marshal force to back up its complaints; e.g., strike threats, slowdowns. At the same time it may demand that the company fire officials hostile to the union or those who might sabotage a union victory.

[30] Golden and Ruttenberg, *op. cit.*, p. 105.

Actually the tactics of the union in grievance procedure are dictated by certain long-range aims. As we have seen, the union may be prepared to fight a grievance bitterly, if a matter of basic principle is involved. Grievances may also be pushed vigorously as a means of expressing worker resentment against management. Or the union may seek, through the grievance machinery, to raise issues to be settled at the next collective-bargaining negotiations.

On management's side, tactics may also be divided into the short-range and long-range. Management's immediate aims are to win at least certain important grievance cases and to protect itself against the encroachment of the union. Therefore, management also seeks to employ "negotiating skills" to win its cases; it comes prepared to buttress its arguments with data, argument, and interpretation. It argues for a strict, "legalistic" interpretation of the contract. It seeks to place the union on the defensive, to throw the burden of proving the legitimacy of a grievance on the union. As in collective bargaining, management has the advantage of arguing from a securely established, institutionally supported position.

Management may also back up its verbal arguments with more substantive arguments, the arguments of force. Thus militant stewards may be fired or intimidated; workers who press grievances may be disciplined indirectly. Management may counter the threat of strike or slowdown by reminding the union of those clauses in the Taft-Hartley Act which forbid such stoppages and which grant to management the right to sue for restitution of damages. Or management may seek to discredit the grievance procedure entirely, e.g., by resolutely and lengthily combating each grievance, by settling workers' complaints outside the grievance machinery.

Management may, furthermore, attempt to manipulate the grievance machinery in such a way as to achieve other long-range aims not directly connected with the matter of grievances. Thus, management like the union may fight grievances or institute grievances in order to build up a bargaining position for the renegotiation of the contract. Or management may use the grievance machinery as a channel of communications with the workers; e.g., in order to determine worker sentiment, or in order to make management's position on various matters unmistakably clear to the workers. For instance, management may use the grievance procedure to impress on the workers the need for more production, the poor competitive situation of the company, the possibility of technological changes if efficiency is not increased.[31]

[31] See, for instance, Frederick H. Harbison and King Carr, *The Libby-Owens-Ford Glass Company and the Federation of Glass, Ceramic and Silica Sand Workers of America,* National Planning Association, Washington, 1948, pp. 34–36.

As we have seen, disputes which cannot be resolved through the grievance machinery are usually arbitrated, either by a regular arbitrator specified in the contract, or by an *ad hoc* arbitrator. We have already discussed the tactics of disputants and arbitrators. Suffice to say that, in theory, the role of the arbitrator in grievance procedures is a judicial one; the arbitrator supposedly decides grievances on the merits of the case. In actuality, many arbitrators settle cases on other bases. Sometimes a certain proportion of cases is settled in favor of management and a certain portion in favor of labor. In fact, both management and the union may press a maximum number of grievances on the theory that they are bound to win a certain percentage of them. Sometimes grievances may be pressed to arbitration (usually by labor), in the hope that they will be lost; not only may a union official be able thereby to shift the blame from himself to the arbitrator, but he is in a position to demand a favorable settlement in a more important case.

Sometimes arbitrators frankly seek to settle disputes on the basis of the balance of power between management and labor. Such arbitrators conceive of their function as first determining what the balance of power is and then getting management and labor to recognize and act on it. It is an open question whether this form of arbitration is not, in the last analysis, the only effective one.

CHAPTER 14

Theories of the Labor Movement

This chapter will examine three theories of the labor movement which have had wide acceptance among students of the labor movement and in some cases have influenced the movement itself. The major purpose of this examination is to determine to what extent these theories accord with the role-and-personality framework of this book. We shall also be interested in extracting what seem like valid insights from these theories and incorporating them within the role-and-personality framework. Of course, the serious student of industry and labor should be acquainted with these theories.

An examination of existing theories, as well as an empirical study of trade unionism, shows that trade-union phenomena are too complex to be placed under the rubric of one theory without serious distortion or oversimplification. Actually the labor theorist must deal with various *aspects* of the labor movement. There are perhaps two major and many minor aspects of the trade-union movement which are sufficiently distinct from each other to deserve separate theoretical treatment.

One major aspect concerns the internal development of the trade union. Under this heading alone one finds many important theoretical problems. One such problem concerns the question: Why do workers form, join, and support unions? Another is: In what forms and in what sequences have trade unions appeared? Still a third problem is posed by the aims of the trade-union movement within the factory: Do the trade unions aim at displacing management entirely, at sharing control with management, or merely at assuring job control to the worker?

The second major aspect of the trade-union movement is the relationship of trade unions to the environment in which they exist. Here also are found many important theoretical problems. One concerns the environmental factors, political, economic, social, and intellectual, which help to determine the nature and development of trade unionism. Another problem concerns the degree to which labor can use community forces, such as the state, to attain its aims. And, finally, there is the problem of the ultimate effects of the trade-union movement on society as a whole.

THEORIES OF THE INTERNAL DEVELOPMENT OF TRADE UNIONS

The first theory that we shall consider is that put forward by Professor Selig Perlman.

The Theory of Selig Perlman. We shall not consider this theory *in toto* but, rather, only those sections which deal with the reasons for the emergence of trade unionism and the ultimate aims of the trade union within the factory. Other sections of this important theory, particularly those which deal with environmental forces acting on and shaping the American trade-union movement, will be dealt with in a later chapter.[1]

Perlman makes a basic distinction between "organic" labor, that is, labor *as it actually exists* in the factory, and the various conceptions of what it should be or will inevitably be—conceptions which are the products of intellectuals (who in most cases, says Perlman, have not originated in the working class). Perlman seeks to show that the "mature" trade-union movement is dominated not by the intellectuals' conceptions, but by a "homegrown philosophy" or ideology, which arises out of the needs and aspirations of "organic labor." In order to understand unionism it is necessary to examine "organic labor," its needs and its aspirations.

What Perlman seeks to discover about "organic labor" is those elements in its collective psychology which lead to the adoption of unionism. His method of analysis is to examine the working rules,[2] "customs and practices," with which unionized workingmen have surrounded their jobs. Investigating the working rules of the oldest trade union in the United States, the International Typographical Union, Perlman finds that the rules are concerned mainly with worker control of jobs: with hiring and firing, discipline on the job, layoffs, sharing of jobs, hours of work, establishment of a closed shop, apprenticeship, limitations on admissions to the trade, and the introduction of new machinery. In each of these cases the specified rules are designed to safeguard the interests of the workers in their jobs.

Perlman next attempts to deduce from these rules the basic psychology of the workingman. The clear purpose of the rules described above is to control the numbers of workers admitted to the job, to control the number of hours worked, to divide up work when it is scarce, and to protect the job against annihilation by technological change. These rules

---

[1] This theory is most succinctly and fully stated in Selig Perlman, *A Theory of the Labor Movement*, Augustus M. Kelley, New York, 1949 (originally published in 1928).

[2] *Ibid.*, p. 237.

can only reflect *a consciousness of scarcity on the part of the working-man*—a feeling that job opportunities are a limited and scarce commodity which must be protected at all costs. The source of this consciousness of scarcity Perlman finds in two areas, one lying outside the workingman, one lying inside him.[3] On the one hand, the worker feels inadequate to take advantage of the many economic opportunities which lie outside the field of labor; he is neither a "born taker of risks nor . . . the possessor of a sufficiently agile mind ever to feel at home . . . in the uncertain game of competitive business."[4] On the other hand, the fact is that jobs *are* scarce, that economic opportunities for the workingmen are limited, and no matter how the workingman explains this fact, he must recognize it, react to it, and protect himself if possible.

A consciousness of scarcity leads almost inevitably to the development of trade unionism and, Perlman thinks, only to trade unionism—not, for instance, to political action. Why is this so? Essentially because a consciousness of scarcity breeds a desire in the worker to "own" the precious, scarce commodity, the job. It is only through "ownership" of the totality of job opportunities that the workers—[5]

having determined who are entitled to claim a share in that opportunity [can undertake] to parcel it out fairly. . . . Free competition becomes a sin against one's fellows, antisocial, like a self-indulgent consumption of the stores of a beleaguered city, and obviously detrimental to the individual as well.

Therefore, if the individual worker is to make good his desire for control of the job, he must act in unison with his fellow workers; that is, he must organize. In the process he may have to give up much that he prizes, even immediate benefits such as higher wages or shorter hours, at least for a time. But the consciousness of scarcity is so strong that it can ride right over personal ambition. In this respect, says Perlman, " . . . unionism is . . . not unlike patriotism, which may and does demand of the citizen the supreme sacrifice, when the integrity of the national territory is at stake."[6]

Of course, the worker also desires the largest possible return for his labor; that is, he desires higher wages, shorter hours, "better working conditions." But this desire merely reinforces the drive to job control. By "owning the job" the worker is in a position to check competition for jobs, which is, of course, one of the strongest weapons in the hands of

[3] *Ibid.,* pp. 239–240.
[4] Selig Perlman, *A Theory of the Labor Movement,* Augustus M. Kelley, New York, 1949 (originally published in 1928), p. 239. By permission.
[5] Selig Perlman, *A Theory of the Labor Movement,* p. 242. By permission.
[6] Selig Perlman, *A Theory of the Labor Movement,* Augustus M. Kelley, New York, 1949 (originally published in 1928), p. 273. By permission.

management. The workers can, through the medium of job control, create a solid front against the employers for bargaining purposes. And since, as we have seen, job control can be achieved best, or perhaps solely, through union action, there is another powerful motivation for the worker to embrace unionism as his salvation in the factory.

For Perlman, the ultimate aims of the labor movement are defined and limited largely by the basic consciousness of scarcity. Above all, ultimately the trade-union movement seeks for a maximum of control over the job and for a maximum number of jobs. A secondary, though very important, aim is the bettering of economic and "working conditions," step by step. Thus the trade-union movement is basically "job-conscious." Perlman sees no evidence that the trade-union movement, when it is validly expressing the psychology of the workingman, is interested in displacing management, in shouldering the risks of management, or in uniting the working class to achieve these aims. This, however, does not mean that the union movement is incapable of uniting the working class for certain limited aims; e.g., to remove legislation which hampers job control or to influence public opinion in behalf of labor. Nor does Perlman mean to imply that, under certain circumstances, the union would not be willing to take over certain managerial functions; but this would be only when such intervention by the union would increase job opportunities or protect existing jobs. The point is that whatever policy labor adopts, be it a political program or intervention in managerial affairs, its ultimate aims are limited to the control and ownership of the job, within the framework of the existing social order.

The Theory of Frank Tannenbaum. Perlman sees the worker, lashed by a consciousness of scarcity, as striving toward ownership of the job. Tannenbaum, on the other hand, sees the worker as driven by a sense of alienation from both job and society, striving to create or recreate a collectivity in which he will be related by the solid ties of status to employer, to fellow worker, and to job. For Tannenbaum, the trade union is the major means of achieving these goals.

The starting point of Tannenbaum's analysis is a description of the social situation of the worker under the guild system of production. The salient fact about the guild, according to Tannenbaum, was that it included the worker within a tightly knit social group, a group in which the worker was assured a secure status, a secure income, protection against the accidents of life, and a chance of identification with his job and with his fellow workers. The guild offered the worker a chance to gain distinction in his work, but at the same time it made him responsible for the quality of his work. As tightly knit social groups the guilds acquired, in their own right, political power and judicial authority with which to discipline and punish members. The guild was also an integral part of the larger society; it had a role to play in the religious life of its times, it contributed to pageants, it was an element of power in the political structure of feudalism. Similarly, the manor provided a tightly knit, predictable, secure, social life for the mass of rural populations.

Under the impact of the machine and industrialism, guild and manor dissolved, leaving the city artisans and the peasants bereft of their communities, of the very tools or land by which they lived. The mill towns which now set their squat factory buildings and towering chimneys against the skies were not communities at all; they offered the worker no coherent social groups, no set of values (except the cold doctrine of individualism and the "survival of the fittest"), no secure and respected roles to play. Instead, industrialism brought long hours, low wages, terrible economic insecurity; it brought, as a substitute for the power and authority of the guild, only the tyranny of the mill owner. Furthermore, the physical environment of the mill town was scarcely fit for humans: slums, narrow streets, an absence of greenery, disease. Under the circumstances, it is not surprising if man himself became less than human—that families dissolved or weakened, that drunkenness became common, that lewdness and obscenity flourished.

But for man this situation was intolerable. On the purely economic side the worker wished to maximize his pecuniary income, as everyone else was doing; he wanted shorter hours of work, more security. He wanted an end to the intolerable conditions of mill life and mill communities. But these aims were merely a part of his larger aim: to re-create a community, to play a significant part in the "drama" of life, to live within a common framework of shared values.

At the same time that the worker was driven to attempt to re-create the community in his working life, the very conditions of factory life were creating the basis for the achievement of his aspirations. For in the factory the workers had—[7]

in common . . . their employer, the industry they worked in, the hours they labored, the bench or the machine they worked at, the wage rate they received, the foreman who ruled over them . . . In addition they had each other in common. They worked together at the same bench, inside the same mill or mine . . . were dependent on one another's cooperation.

Factory life inevitably drew men together, men who shared a common helplessness, a potentiality of collective strength, mutual association, a common craft.

The trade union is both the expression and extension of the basic sociability created by men's psychological needs and by factory condi-

[7] By permission from Frank Tannenbaum, *A Philosophy of Labor,* Alfred A. Knopf, Inc., New York, 1951, p. 59.

tions. The trade union "reflects the moral identity and psychological unity men always discover when working together";[8] but the union does not create worker sociability, it rests upon it. At the same time, the formal trade-union organization greatly multiplies the power and effectiveness of the naïve, informal groupings of workers. This accounts in part for constant union growth; another cause for the growth lies in the workers' desires to increase the boundaries of their new-found communities.

Thus, for Tannenbaum, men join and support the union primarily because the union returns to them what the Industrial Revolution took from them: the sense and actuality of "community." As Tannenbaum puts it, "the union returns to the worker his 'society.' It gives him a fellowship, a part in a drama that he can understand, and life takes on meaning once again because he shares a value system common to others."[9] Thus, like Perlman, though for other reasons, Tannenbaum considers the narrow "economic" aims as subsidiary to certain underlying psychological drives in accounting for the development of unionism.

What, in Tannenbaum's view, are the ultimate aims of the trade-union movement? Like Perlman, he rejects the notion that the historically defined task of labor is to overthrow capitalism and to introduce socialism. Again, like Perlman, Tannenbaum denies that labor has any ultimate aims at all. On the other hand, Tannenbaum feels that, in the course of achieving its immediate goals, labor cannot but fundamentally change the nature of our society. Above all, labor is aiming, though unconsciously, to re-create, or to return to, an older order of things, in which men would be related not by contract or by an impersonal cash nexus but by status, by mutual obligation and duty—an order in which men could achieve economic, psychological, and social security. For Tannenbaum, the future holds a society divided into "estates," each with strictly delimited rights and duties, and with strictly defined interrelationships between them. Evidence for this is seen in the collective-bargaining process, with its strict control over both worker and management; it is seen in the union's drive to gain ever greater power over ever larger numbers of workers. In the course of this process, the union will inevitably attempt to gain control over management also for a number of reasons: because such control will be necessary to achieve the aims of labor, because labor must at times intervene with management in order to preserve the factory or the corporation. But Tannenbaum does not believe that labor will ever displace management entirely; its aims can be achieved far short of that eventuality.

The future, then, belongs to the past. The future will witness a re-

[8] *Ibid.,* p. 60.
[9] *Ibid.,* p. 10.

creation, under modern industrial conditions, of the status societies associated with medievalism. The trade-union movement, says Tannenbaum, is counterrevolutionary.[10]

The Theory of Sidney and Beatrice Webb. In contrast to both Perlman and Tannenbaum, Sidney and Beatrice Webb regard the worker as most directly concerned with immediate economic "working conditions": "wages, hours, health, safety, comfort."[11] The worker is also concerned with his powerless position in relation to the employer, since he may find himself at the mercy of the autocratic employer. As an individual, the worker can do nothing to improve or safeguard his economic and "working conditions." His power against the organized employer, who is secured by vast financial resources, amounts to nothing. Furthermore, the worker must compete for jobs with his fellow workers, all equally anxious for work; the result can only be the deterioration of the conditions of work or its stabilization at a low level. Under these circumstances, the worker turns to collective action; he combines with his fellows, both in order to be able to confront the employer on something like equal terms and also in order to reduce the evil consequences of competition for jobs. The most effective instrument of collective action for the worker is the trade union.

The immediate aim of the labor movement is "the deliberate regulation of the conditions of employment in such a way as to ward off from the manual-working producers the evil effects of industrial competition."[12] In order to regulate the "conditions of employment" to the advantage of labor, the trade union seeks to achieve two goals. First, trade unions strive for the adoption of common rules to govern wages, to ensure a standard number of hours in the working day, and to enforce common regulations for safety and sanitation. They hope, thereby, to eliminate competition among workingmen and to deprive employers of the opportunity and pretense for lowering wages. They also work for a common policy in the adoption of new processes and techniques and for an equal opportunity to share in what employment opportunities exist. It should be noted that almost as important as the actual working conditions achieved, if not more important, is the stipulation that these conditions be shared equally by all workers.

The second goal which the trade union seeks, in order to regulate the conditions of employment to its advantage, is the restriction of the numbers of workers in a given field. By this method labor again hopes to reduce competition among the workers in a given field. It is for this reason that trade unions attempt to limit the numbers of workers who may enter a trade or that they try to determine (and limit) those who have the right to participate in a trade or industry. However, the Webbs consider the method of restriction inapplicable to the conditions of modern industry; they do not, therefore, consider restrictive practices an important method for trade unionism.[13]

Labor adopts three methods in its drive for common rules. First, there is the method of mutual insurance; that is, insurance of the worker against loss of pay through strikes or unemployment. The aim of this insurance is not primarily a humanitarian one; it is, rather, to ensure that no worker will be compelled to break the common rule through economic pressure. Similarly, for the Webbs the second and third methods, collective bargaining and legislation, are directed primarily at achieving the common rules which labor needs if it is not to be defeated in detail. Collective bargaining makes possible the establishment of common rules, through equalization of the power of labor and management. Legislation, such as minimum-wage laws, is even more effective in establishing the common rule, for it can bring to bear on management all the force of the government; it is universal in its application. The effectiveness of each of these methods varies according to shifting conditions. For instance, when industry becomes very large and concentrated, the method of legislative enactment is the most effective. The method of mutual insurance becomes unnecessary where the government enforces a widespread system of social security.

The Webbs are not so much interested in predicting the ultimate aims of the trade-union movement as in advocating particular aims. But, with careful analysis of these, it seems possible to deduce what the Webbs regard as the ultimate aims of labor itself. One basic belief of the Webbs is that labor is not united on any goal other than a maximum solidarity and organization of the industrial workers into trade unionism and a maximum application of the doctrine of the common rule to employer-employee relations. But, within the boundaries set by these aims, there are the widest divergences in labor's outlook for the future. Some branches of labor are essentially conservative and wish to stabilize the *status quo;* these branches are against any sort of social or industrial change. Another branch of labor is *individualistic,* and its major aim is to secure maximum benefits from employers. But, like the conservatives, the individualists wish to act within the framework of the present social system. Finally, there are the collectivists, who wish to reorganize society: its systems of production, of service, and of apportionment of income.[14]

[13] *Ibid.*, p. 561. Compare Perlman on this point.
[14] *Ibid.*, pp. 597–599.

The Webbs deny that the trade unions favor the "abolition of the wage system" or that labor even wishes to tamper with that system. On the contrary, trade unionism is founded on the wage-earning system; it is composed precisely of people who earn wages. It is for this reason that it opposes all schemes designed to change the worker from a wage earner into a non–wage earner; thus trade unionism opposes alike profit-sharing schemes and communism, both of which propose to change the status of the worker as an earner of wages.

Nevertheless, the Webbs believe, trade unionism has definite and far-reaching goals both within industry and in society at large. In the case of industry, the aim of the trade union is to further "democracy," which, in this case, means an equalization of power with management. But because the trade unionist speaks of "democracy" as equalization of power, this does not mean that he wishes to divide industry into two homogeneous classes, a working class and a managerial class, facing each other warily. On the contrary, labor seeks for an industry in which separate statuses and even standards of life are granted those who do special work demanding or lacking skill, as the case may be. In an industry organized in this fashion there would be opportunity for workers to rise through a social ladder to gain distinction and power. These opportunities would not be monopolized by the managerial class.

The ultimate goals of the working class, then, are confined to the classical area of trade-unionist interest: "economic" interests, and the "conditions of work." Thus the Webbs deny that the trade unions are seeking, or should seek, or would be successful if they did seek, control over other areas of the system of production; for instance, the area of decision as to what should be produced and in what quantity, or the area of the managerial and technological process of production. The question of deciding what and how much should be manufactured is the function of the market; the managerial and technological processes of industry are the functions of management. In neither of these two fields does labor have special competence.

The Webbs note that labor's goals might be achieved within a number of different forms of government; however, a government which guaranteed political democracy and helped labor achieve its "democratic" goals in industry would afford labor its most favorable opportunities for achieving its aims. Nevertheless, the attitude of labor toward all governments, even a democratic government, is necessarily ambiguous. It is true that the trade union wishes government intervention for certain purposes, such as minimum-wage legislation; but it wishes to be entirely free of government control in organizing and in directing the internal affairs of its organizations. Similarly, while it might seem that the trade unionist would welcome government ownership of industry, at the same time he cannot but see that in the state the union would be confronted with an overwhelmingly powerful employer, who could not be bankrupted and whose officials could not be subjected to economic pressure. Furthermore, against the state, the trade-union methods of insurance and collective bargaining would have no force at all. Even if the union could be ensured of complete control of the state machinery, not all workers would benefit equally. In fact, certain groups of workers, occupying special positions of privilege, might have much to lose thereby; for a democratically run state would necessarily be most concerned with the desires of the largest groupings of workers. In a modern industrial society, the largest grouping would inevitably be the unskilled workers of the mass-production industries. Thus, whatever path labor chooses to tread, the goal is always the same: moderate demands for the democratization of industry within the framework of the present social system.

LABOR THEORY AND SOCIOLOGICAL THEORY

It is not our intention to criticize these theories in a systematic way. However, before discussing the relationship between labor theory and sociological theory, one major point should be made about the theories of Perlman, Tannenbaum, and the Webbs. Each of these writers conceived of his theory of the causes and development of unionism as a general one, intended to apply to all stages of unionism and types of unionists. Perhaps the tenaciousness of unionism, its almost universal hold on working-class mentality in all countries, has led these writers to seek for just one universal factor, or a few universal factors, which could explain all the diverse types and phenomena of unionism. This raises the possibility that each of these theories is too general and abstract to apply to the entire labor movement, however much it may illuminate this or that aspect of unionism. Unionism, although itself a stable phenomenon, is being constantly re-created, by workingmen (and others) who are themselves constantly exposed to differing social and physical conditions and whose motives may be constantly changing. Furthermore, it seems doubtful whether single- or few-factor theories can adequately explain the actions of all the diverse groups which make up the labor movement.

For a theory of labor to be valid for today it must, first, take account of the social, political, economic, and technological conditions existing in the present period; that is, a period of relative prosperity, relative peace, relatively low though steady unemployment, rapid advances in technology, and relatively strong unionization. Such a theory should, then, distinguish between various classes of individuals involved in unionism: the rank and file, the activist, and the careerist. The existing social, political, technological, and economic conditions should be analyzed as they affect the motives, roles, and strains of each type of unionist and the development of the labor movement as a whole. The roles, motives, and strains among just these three types of unionists seems to be so different in each case that it is doubtful whether any single- or few-factor theory can adequately interpret them. On the other hand, we believe that role-and-personality theory offers a framework within which a more inclusive approach to unionism is possible. The remainder of this chapter will be devoted to the presentation of a preliminary analysis of unionism within this framework.

An analysis of unionism within the role-and-personality framework may well start with a consideration of the relation of the rank and file to unionism. We have seen evidence of the relatively low involvement of the worker in the affairs of the union. We have investigated the apathy of the worker, except in times of decision or crisis, toward the local meeting, the area in which the worker comes most directly into contact with his union. There has already been considerable discussion of the reasons for this apathy; suffice to say here that this apathy seems to be the result of such factors as antiunion propaganda, a feeling of guilt at joining unions, and a lack of interest in the job as compared to the attractions of nonfactory life.[15] More evidence for this apathy may be found in the failure of rank and file to evince interest in those issues which exercise the activists and careerists, issues such as the repeal of the Taft-Hartley Act, political campaigns, race relations, or foreign policy.

It seems safe to say that the rank-and-file unionist in the United States is not attracted to his union for ideological reasons. Furthermore, it must also be concluded from this evidence that he is not attracted to it for the social benefits which he might attain; e.g., a feeling of participation in an ongoing organization, a sense of status, the use of power, or an opportunity for expression. Of course this statement must be modified in "more or less" terms; some unionist rank-and-filers may belong to unions or give loyalty to them for precisely these reasons. But, for the mass of workers in the United States, *at the present time* (and note this qualification), the attraction of unionism can probably not be found in these areas.

If this is the case, if the adherence of the rank and file to unionism in the United States is confined to a vague sort of allegiance but does not include emotional or ideological involvement, then we are faced with two questions: On what bases *does* the loyalty of the American worker to unionism rest? And how strong is this loyalty? We shall attempt to

[15] See Chap. 11.

answer the former question first, for the strength of rank-and-file loyalty to unionism rests on the sorts of loyalties among the workers that unionism can command.

From the evidence presented in this book, it seems possible to trace the allegiance of rank and file to trade unionism to certain stresses and strains in the worker's role *on the job* which are incapable of alleviation except through trade unionism. We shall briefly review these stresses and strains.

One set of stresses arises from the formal relations of production. As we have seen, these relationships are of such a nature as to make of the worker a commodity whose employment depends on the state of the economy as a whole. Furthermore, even given good business conditions, the worker's employment may be threatened at any time by technological change. Thus there arises this major pressure on the worker; the role on which he depends may be, at any time, abruptly and arbitrarily annihilated. It should be noted that there are relatively few roles of comparative importance, in this or any society, which can be destroyed so arbitrarily and so one-sidedly. Certainly, in no primitive society of which the author has knowledge would it be possible thus to destroy the major economic role of a mature adult, or his means of access to livelihood.

Furthermore, not only is the worker thus threatened in his essential being by a loss of the job, but, as Perlman has pointed out, there are almost always fewer desirable jobs to go around than there are workingmen to fill them. Only briefly, and then in times of crisis, is the situation reversed. Under these circumstances, it is not surprising if the workingman does indeed become conscious of a "scarcity of jobs" or that workers consistently list job security as one of their most important goals. A consciousness of scarcity is, thus, the reflection in the worker's mind of a major discrepancy between his individual needs and the formal relations of production.

The function of the union for the rank and file in this connection is to modify the formal relations of production in such a fashion as to assure security to the worker. That is, one major function of unions is to close an important gap between the personality of the worker and the role he must fill. But, note that this aim is directed *at the job;* the union is not the important source of satisfaction in itself. The worker is job-conscious, and his loyalty to his union is based on the ability of the union to help him achieve his goals in relation to his role. It would seem, therefore, to be in this sense that a consciousness of scarcity is one major motivation for the rank and file in supporting the trade unions. In so far as the worker is in danger of losing his job, whether this danger is remote or near, he strives for the retention—if possible, the ownership —of the job. If this goal is lost, all else is lost; without job security, then the goals of higher wages or "better working conditions" have no meaning to the worker.

But, while the theory of "consciousness of scarcity" correctly explains one relation of rank and file to unionism, it does not explain the phenomenon of unionism as a whole. In the first place, Perlman's theory does not explain the motivations of activists or careerists. In the second place, it does not take account of other strains in the worker's role—strains which also drive the rank and file toward unionism and which may, under certain circumstances, assume great importance. A "consciousness of scarcity" is only one strand, though an exceedingly important one, of the rope which binds the average workingman to his union.

Another set of strains, for instance, in the worker's role arises also from the formal relations of production. These strains center around the "economic" conditions of the job; wages, hours, fringe benefits (which are really, in one respect, a matter of wages and hours). Management considers wages paid to workingmen one of its costs of production and, in many industries, a major cost of production. Therefore, it is to management's advantage to keep the costs of labor low, either through minimizing wages, maximizing hours, reducing the number of employed workingmen, or making their labor more efficient through the use of machinery. This means that there is a constant downward pressure on the remuneration attached to the worker's role as a structurally generalized goal.

However, where management regards worker remuneration as an item to be figured in the cost of production, to the workingman the amount of remuneration has other meanings. In the first place it is through remuneration secured on the job that it becomes possible for the worker to play roles of vital importance to him in the community and to buy a certain standard of living. In the second place, there is a general absence of other attractions in the worker's role; prestige, status, or opportunities for creativity and interesting work.

Thus, the workingman is motivated to play his roles in purely expedient terms, as a means for achieving other ends. Yet this role is deficient in the only respect for which it is important to the workingman, and managerial pressure is constantly tending to worsen this deficiency. There is, consequently, a gap between the rewards of the role and the psychology of the worker. It is a gap which the worker tries to fill through unionism.

Still another strain which arises primarily from the formal relations of production and which motivates the worker to unionism is the powerlessness of the worker's role. As we have seen, the formal relations of production place the workingman in a position of subordination to management. Theoretically, management may hire or fire the workingman at its pleasure and discipline him in the interests of production and efficiency. Against this power the individual workingman can oppose only his relatively feeble power to withdraw his labor.

The worker's role is not unique in its weakness; the child is similarly weak in relation to its parents, the patient in a certain sense is under the power of his doctor. However, in the case of the workingman the absence of power is not compensated by certain service: by protection, by love, or by similar benefits.[16] Furthermore, it is the absence of power in the worker's role which underlies his inability to attain security or good working conditions on the job. And, finally, the worker is denied whatever intrinsic satisfactions the enjoyment and use of power might afford. Thus there is a great gap between this aspect of the worker's role and the worker's needs and aspirations.

Unionism bridges this gap. In the first place, the union, by uniting workingmen into a militant organization, by providing financial and human reserves, and by providing knowledge of techniques of combat, vastly increases the sum total of power of the workingmen. In the second place, the union, by creating a new institutional arrangement within the factory for the handling of worker grievances, provides the workingman with an instrument for bringing this power to bear on management.

The loyalty of the rank and file to unionism is based on the fact that the unions provide means by which the formal relations of production may be modified in certain directions of importance and advantage to workingmen. It is not primarily the union which is the focus of worker attention but the industrial role, or more precisely, the ways in which this role may be modified to fit the workingman's aspirations.

However, not all the strains in the worker's role rise from the formal relations of production. Numerous strains arise also, as we have seen, from the relations of the worker to the physical aspects of his job and from the social relations at work. The worker in many areas of modern industry suffers a considerable diminution of personal importance in an environment of large-scale mechanization and large-scale bureaucracy. Skills are lost, the work is excessively routine and boring, the job is specialized to the point of meaninglessness, the ability to create independently has disappeared. Social relationships are reduced to those consonant with the productive process; thus social relationships become cold, perfunctory, hierarchical, and impersonal.

It is difficult to determine to what extent these strains are *directly* important in motivating the rank and file to unionism. The union, it is true, may, by increasing the power of the workingman, greatly reduce the amount of discipline to which the worker is subjected. More informal socialization may also be possible in an unionized plant, although as

---

[16] This may not be true under a paternalistic industrial system.

far as this author is aware, this has not been demonstrated. Nor should it be forgotten that the union may serve as an added lever of discipline over the worker on the job.

However, it would seem that these strains may have several important *indirect* effects on motivating the rank and file to support unionism. For instance, the worker may be compensating for the diminution of personality within the physical conditions of the factory and the social relationships of production by becoming a member of a collectivity. When the union enters, he thinks, the boss may be "told off." The union will show that workers too can "throw some weight around," that their likes and dislikes must be taken into account.

It may be possible to discover similar indirect motives for rank-and-file motivation by psychoanalytical investigation. For instance, it may be that in joining unions, the worker is seeking to release very considerable reservoirs of frustration which have been built up inside of him as a result of the frustration of his job. Perhaps such a point of view might prove valuable in explaining the militancy of organization drives, the occurrence of physical violence in strikes, the belligerence of workingman speech, etc. But in a condition of stable unionism, where joining the union is, for most workers, an automatic act, the explanatory value of such concepts seems limited. This does not mean, however, that this free-floating aggression or mass frustration might not be tapped, especially in times of crisis, by leaders seeking to incite action.

We may say that the American rank and file is bound to unionism because the trade union can modify certain aspects of the worker's role. That is, the American workingman is primarily job-conscious; he regards the union as a powerful weapon for securing the job, establishing rules of seniority, increasing the remuneration attached to the role, decreasing hours, heightening the power which the role affords, and perhaps modifying some aspects of the physical and social environment of the role. The American workingman seems to have little interest in the union itself; it is considered more as a form of insurance against the hazards of the industrial role. There is little interest in unionism as a cause or as an ideology. And there is no indication that more than a tiny minority of American workingmen support unionism for idealistic reasons.

This does not mean, however, that the American workingman is not capable of a militant defense of his union, if it is attacked, and of great loyalty to it in times of crisis. The history of American labor abundantly demonstrates that he is.[17]

We have seen that, at the present time, involvement in union affairs, except in times of crisis, seems to be confined to small energetic groups, "activists," who occupy the local union offices, attend local meetings,

[17] See Chap. 10.

and, in general, take an active part in the life of the union. From the intensity alone with which these activists engage in union affairs, it would seem that their motivation and attitudes toward unionism differ quite markedly from those found among the rank and file. The nature of this activist group cannot be understood in terms of the same theoretical concepts with which we analyzed the rank and file.

The salient fact about the activist group, as compared to the apathetic rank and file, is that, while the latter is oriented to the job and is interested in unionism in so far as unionism can secure modifications in the worker role, the activist group is interested primarily in the union itself and in the roles which it provides. Of course, this is an "ideal" statement; a local leader may not necessarily be without direct concern for role modification. But the statement, extreme though it may be, serves to point up the *essential* difference between rank and file and activists.

It will be recalled that we discussed certain reasons which lead workingmen to take an active part in the union. We saw that one set of reasons for union activism includes a desire for prestige, for status, for power, for the opportunity to talk to management on equal terms, for the esteem of one's fellows. A second drive to activism is based on a desire to use the union as an alternate area of social activity, in the narrow sense of that term; e.g., for recreation, for engaging in a sort of "club activity." Another motive for activism is the sense of achievement which a successful career in a local union, or successful participation in a union campaign or even in a union meeting, can provide. Again, some unionists hope to use the local union as a springboard to a career in the union hierarchy or in management. Certain "rational" motives may play a part in activating workers toward union activity; e.g., the slightly higher salaries connected with some local union posts, the greater seniority which can be achieved in some cases. Finally, there may be ideological motivation: resentment over working conditions, a sense of loyalty and responsibility to one's fellows, or political and social convictions. Thus, as compared to rank and file, the aspirations of the activist are varied and often complex.

However, the activist resembles the rank-and-filer in this: the motivation to unionism in both cases seems to stem from the basic split between role and personality which the workingman in our society typically experiences. However, it may be said here, though with due caution, that while the major strains for the rank-and-filer arise from the formal relations of production, in the case of the activist the strains arise primarily from the technical content of the worker's role and the social relations at work. Thus, the activist seeks to compensate for the low status of the worker's role through playing a role which *does* confer prestige and distinction, at least within his own world. Similarly, the powerlessness of the role, its endless subordination, is replaced, for the activist, by the power and freedom of the role of the union official or shop steward, a role in which management may be met on something like equal terms. Further, in playing a union role, or even in attending a union meeting, the worker may be able to attain a sense of individual achievement, no matter how intangible, in a way which he never could on the job. Thus for the activist, the union may represent release from a boring, dull, repetitious, meaningless routine. Still further, the union may open up vistas of a career, of a progression up a job ladder through merit and effort, whereas in the factory such a dream would be palpable nonsense. Again, the union may be offering the worker, trapped on an isolated, repetitious, mechanical job, an opportunity to meet his fellows and to achieve some of the psychic rewards of social life among a group of peers. Thus, for the activist the union represents a device for creating new roles as substitutes for unsatisfactory work roles. In this the activist differs from the rank-and-filer, who attacks his unsatisfactory role situation by seeking to modify the role itself.

Ideological motives toward activism probably also spring from the basic role-and-personality situation of the industrial worker, though not in so direct a manner. In one aspect, ideological motivation may be considered as reaction to the role-personality situation in factory jobs. Ideological reaction differs from other reactions in that it aims at a more general solution or a more radical solution of the strains in the worker's roles. Such solutions might include abolition of the wage system entirely or, on a more moderate basis, a sharing of power through some device like joint labor-management councils or the establishment of producers' cooperatives. Such solutions are not popular in this country, but this does not mean that their importance in other countries should be minimized or that their potential importance in this country be overlooked. Nevertheless, it seems safe to say that such idealized reactions to the strains of the worker's role are not now playing an important part in the American labor movement, and therefore it is not necessary to consider this area.[17a]

Finally, we should note that there is a great difference between the motivations and attitudes toward unionism of rank and file and activists, on the one hand, and those of union careerists, on the other. It seems safe to say that neither "consciousness of scarcity" nor desire to escape the unrewarding routines of the factory nor even desire to increase the economic benefits to the worker can by itself serve to explain the nature

---

[17a] The theory of Tannenbaum seems to be most applicable to the activist. It is for the activist, primarily, that the union represents a new "society," with solid ties of status and an opportunity to participate in closely knit social groups and to share common values.

of union leadership in the United States. Of course, the union leader must consider these motives of rank and file and activists if he wishes to keep his organization in an healthy and functioning state. But this is not the same thing as saying that union leaders are themselves driven by these motives, even where these careerists have originated in the working class.

In attempting to picture the motivation of the union careerist we must, then, go beyond the role-personality scheme which we have employed thus far. It is true that unionism is built on the basic split between personality and role which arises from the formal relations of production, the nature of mechanical work, and the social relations at work. If it were not for these strains, it is probable that unionism would not exist. However, just as the reactions to these strains may be guided in one of several directions, of which unionism is one, so the directions of unionism may be themselves varied, as long as at least the major underlying needs of rank and file and activists are being met. For this reason, it is dangerous in the extreme to picture the direction of unionism as a whole as a projection of the underlying psychological needs of workers.[17b]

Thus, when we turn to the motivations of union leaders and the reflection of this motivation in union policy, we find considerable diversity. One type of union leader is ideologically motivated. We do not have reference here to those few Communist or Communist-dominated leaders who are left in the union movement. Rather by ideological motivation we mean here motivation toward bettering the economic, political, and social position of the working class as a whole in the United States. Such a union leader not only will emphasize the underlying goals of rank and file and activist but will be concerned also with increasing the political power of unionism. He may also be concerned with increasing the solidarity of the working class, perhaps through combating racial prejudice. A union leader of this type may concern himself with group insurance, rest homes, theaters, education, housing. The careerists in such a union are really the leaders of a social movement which seeks a fundamental solution to the strains of the worker's role.

At the other pole is that type of union leader who has been called a "business unionist."[18] This type of leader views the union primarily as an organization which sells a sort of service to its members. In honestly

---

[17b] We believe that Perlman makes this mistake. He considers the union movement as a whole, and the political course it will take, a reflection of underlying "consciousness of scarcity." But even granting that the worker is dominated by scarcity consciousness, this need might be met in many ways. The fact that, in the United States, the union movement has happened, because of historical circumstances, to take one direction does not mean that other directions are not possible.

[18] For a discussion of business unionism, see Robert Franklin Hoxie, *Trade Unionism in the United States,* Appleton-Century-Crofts, Inc., 1928, pp. 45–46.

run business unions, the aim of the leaders will be to attain maximum economic benefits for the union members. If such unionists turn to politics, it is with no ideological goal in mind, but simply as a means for increasing the power of the union and its ability to supply services. Unions dominated by these motives may tend to become "corporations for supplying labor" at the highest possible price, and they may be surprisingly like the corporations to which they sell labor. The size and growth of a "business union" depends in good part on the skill and sagacity of its leader, and in this too business unionism resembles business.

In between these two polar types, there are no doubt all sorts of mixed types. A union may be led by men driven both by ideological motives and by a shrewd sense of business. But there seems little reason to doubt that, in the peculiar environment furnished by American culture and society, business unionism, though not unchallenged by ideologically dominate unionism, has predominated. Put in other words, this is to say that most of the leadership of American unionism is dominated by motives of a "businesslike" sort, including a desire to maximize size, income, stability, and efficiency. Here again it is necessary to insert a word of caution. The fact that this is the present state of affairs in American unionism does not mean that American unionism must necessarily be of this type or that the unionism of countries like Great Britain is somehow unnatural.

SUMMARY

In this chapter we have attempted to sketch out an outline within which a theory or theories of the labor movement might be formulated. We have been able to show why a labor theory must take into account the various sections of the labor movement, and the great possible diversity of directions in which the union movement might develop in this country. It must take into account the real difference in the aims and outlooks and interests of rank and file, activists, and careerists. It must show how these aims, outlooks, and interests are related to the social position of each group. Finally, an adequate theory of the labor movement must interpret the development of unionism in terms of the changing social positions of each of these groups and in terms of the constantly changing relationships between them. Part 4 will, among other things, treat the labor movement in its relation to American culture and society.

PART FOUR

Industry and Society

CHAPTER 15

Industry and Community

Thus far we have dealt with industry as a phenomenon isolated from all other social organizations and institutions. We have looked on it as an independent little society, complete with its own culture, roles, personalities, strains, and stresses. We have purposely limited ourselves in this way in order to investigate the influence of *industrial* conditions on the roles that men play and on their characters. However, industry does not exist in isolation. On the contrary, our industries are embedded in a social matrix of community and nation, and both industry on the one hand and community and nation on the other are constantly influencing each other in many diverse ways.

Unfortunately, it is all too easy to overlook this interdependence of industry and society, to concentrate on one area to the exclusion of the other. Yet industry is manned by masses of people—workers, engineers, managers, bookkeepers, stenographers, salesmen—who bring into industry already formed personalities, with preconceptions, attitudes, prejudices. And industry feeds back into the community people whose personalities reflect their experience at work. In addition, through its influence on the character of men and women, industry is fundamentally affecting the institutions, organizations, and groups of the community: the family, social classes, neighborhoods, recreational groups, churches. It is in ways such as these that industry and the community mutually influence each other.

Furthermore, industry and society influence each other in more direct ways. Industry must to some extent reflect the character of the community in which it is located: its means of transportation, its location on a river or a railroad or a lake, its attitudes toward work, toward management, toward labor. The community, on the other hand, and many or all of its institutions feel directly the effect of what is happening in industry. Thus, a technological change in a factory which necessitates nightwork may affect, in surprisingly fundamental ways, the potentialities of family life, including relationships between husband and wife or between parents and children. Similarly, other technological or organizational changes in industry may rearrange the social classes of a community or transform the basic nature of its population. In some cases, such change may annihilate an entire community, or move it a hundred miles away, or transform it from a sleepy little town to a roaring boom city.

There are also conscious and purposive attempts by industry to affect society, or by society to affect industry. Both management and labor may seek to decide a dispute in the community; e.g., by influencing public opinion or by influencing politicians and legislation. Analogously, the state in our times has more and more moved to control industry—to regulate its internal organization, the relationship between management and labor, and even the terms under which products may be sold and the prices at which they may be sold. As we shall see, industry is imperfectly integrated with society, and in some ways, the lack of integration has resulted in a conflict in which each side has attempted to control the other to its own advantage.

Types of Industrial Communities. One of the most important results of the rise of industrialism has been the construction of new communities, or the rapid growth and change of already existing ones. It is true that some industry, both past and present, has been located outside existing towns and near to sources of power or raw materials. However, even such industries have rapidly built up communities around them.[1] We may say that the existence of industry is almost inconceivable without some sort of community in the neighborhood.[2]

The almost invariable coexistence of an industry and a local community arises from various causes.[3] One of the sources of this coexistence, and one whose influence was felt at the earliest times, was the need of

[1] See Margaret Terrel Parker, *Lowell: A Study of Industrial Development,* The Macmillan Company, New York, 1940; Vera Shlakman, "Economic History of a Factory Town," *Smith College Studies in History,* vol. 20, nos. 1–4, 1934–1935. Both these studies trace the development of communities about industries which were originally located near sources of water power. For a general account of the rise of American cities, see Arthur Meier Schlesinger, *The Rise of the City,* The Macmillan Company, New York, 1933, chaps. I–III.

[2] The "neighborhood" has of course expanded with the development of means of mass transportation, such as rapid transit systems, or with the rise of the privately owned automobile.

[3] Our discussion of the location of industries is confined to the sociological aspects of the problem. But, of course, the location of industry is affected by a great variety of factors. A wide literature has grown up in this field. See Alfred Weber, *Theory of the Location of Industries,* translated by Carl Friedrich, University of Chicago Press, Chicago, 1929, Copyright by the University of Chicago; Edgar M. Hoover, *The Location of Economic Activity,* McGraw-Hill Book Company, Inc., New York, 1948, particularly parts I and II; Carter Goodrich et al., *Migration and Economic Opportunity,* University of Pennsylvania Press, Philadelphia, 1936, chap. VII.

industry for a labor supply. An industrial system demands labor which can be depended on to report to work each day and on time, which can be quickly called back to work after a period of layoff, and which will have no other source of livelihood than the industry. In order to create or to find such a supply of labor, industry had either to enter already existing communities, where a labor force existed, or to create communities into which the labor force could be attracted. It is for the latter reason that early New England industrialists built rows of tenements for their workers or dormitories for the unmarried female operatives. Such tenements or dormitories tended, at first, to cluster around the mills and were built practically in their shadows. But today, with better, more easily available, and individually owned means of transportation, the workers' houses may extend for a distance of some miles from the industry. Nevertheless, as in the early days of industry, modern industry must, of necessity, locate within an area of a permanently settled working force, within a community.

A second reason for the connection of at least some industries and communities is the great market for industrial products which exists in the community. By locating in proximity to an urban market, industry can cut transportation costs, particularly where a major portion of the market of an industry is located within a large metropolitan center. In addition, industry may find it necessary to locate in a community because the urban center controls changes in fashion, with which industry must keep pace.

Thirdly, industrialism needs a community as a source of special services. One such service may be transportation; a given community may be a center of rail lines, of roads and trucking routes, suitable for bringing in raw materials and exporting finished products. The community may also be able to supply machinery, or parts of machinery, as well as skilled mechanics such as toolmakers, tool repairers, plumbers, and carpenters. Industry also may share other benefits of community life; protection from fire, police protection, education of the working force in industrial skills, a water supply, and other services. Finally, the community as a whole may provide those sorts of attractions—higher standard of living, recreation, good education, closeness to fashion—necessary to attract and hold a working force at all levels of industry.

However, although industries must seek out, or create, local communities, there is a very great variety in *types* of communities in which industry may locate. These variations, in turn, have important effects on the social life within each community. We shall consider these possible variations in greater detail.

Variations in Origin. The community may have originated as an industrial community or in some other form. Urban communities are not, of course, found *only* in industrial society; in America, for instance, fairly sizeable cities existed prior to the industrial era. With the onset of industrialism on a large scale, after 1850, many cities which in origin had been trading cities, or port cities, or centers of communications, were converted in part or whole into industrial cities. On the other hand, as we have already seen, the establishment of new industries close to sources of power or raw materials led to the development of brand-new communities; this process is by no means finished even today. Depending on the origin of the city, we may expect to find concomitant variations in certain features of the community. For instance, the physical layout of a city, the nature of housing, the proportion of industrial establishments as compared to mercantile establishments, the nature and traditions of the social classes in town, and, perhaps, the psychology of the people of the urban community may all differ in significant ways, depending on the origin of the community.[4]

Variations in Size. Although industry seems necessarily to imply some sort of a community, there is a great variation in the size of industrial communities. On the one extreme is the great metropolis, which may serve as the social matrix for scores of different industries, as well as numerous single industrial plants. On the other extreme is the mining camp, consisting often of a score or so of tenements, a store, and a few private homes. In between are communities of various size, ranging from those which would not even be classified as urban communities under our census, to the near metropolis.

Mere size, it should be noted, is an important sociological variable in community life. In the case of industrial phenomena, size may affect some of the following: the state of unionization, the attitudes of the population toward work, attitudes toward management and toward the industry, the feeling of solidarity between the worker and management, solidarity between workers, the freedom of action of management, and so on. Size may also affect the level and quality of education, the numbers of alternative opportunities, the origins of the industrial worker, the level of wages, and other phenomena.[5]

---

[4] See, for instance, the *Yankee City Series* by W. Lloyd Warner and his associates (Yale University Press, New Haven, Conn.) for a description of a city, now largely industrial, but formerly based largely on the whaling trade. It will be noted that social stratification assumes a peculiar form in a city of this type. See vol. I, *The Social Life of a Modern Community,* by W. Lloyd Warner and Paul S. Lunt, 1941; vol. II, *The Status System of a Modern Community,* by W. Lloyd Warner and Paul S. Lunt, 1942; vol. III, *The Social Systems of American Ethnic Groups,* by W. Lloyd Warner and Lee Srole, 1945; vol. IV, *The Social System of the Modern Factory,* by W. Lloyd Warner and J. O. Low, 1947.

[5] Studies of communities of less than metropolitan size are listed in the following pages. For studies of the metropolis, the student is referred to such basic works as R. D. McKenzie, *The Metropolitan Community,* McGraw-Hill Book Company, Inc.,

Variations in the Independence of the Community. Industrial communities may vary in terms of the degree of their independence of other communities. This distinction is, of course, relative, for it would be difficult indeed to find an industrial community which is not dependent on one or more other communities as markets, for raw or semifinished materials, and for services. What we have in mind here is the distinction between the industrial center and the industrial suburb. In the industrial center are found usually the major industries, the largest and densest population, the most desirable shopping center, the locus of recreation, and so on. In contrast, the industrial suburb lacks some of the features of a community life; e.g., the industrial center may be the shopping and recreation center for the industrial suburb, the source of various services for the industry, the location of the local press, radio and television stations. The industrial suburb may often follow the lead of the industrial center in such matters as unionization, technological changes, and community improvements.[6]

Variations in Types of Industry. While some communities in the United States may possess numerous different types of industries, no community can hope to avoid some sort of industrial specialization. This is true even of a metropolis like New York City. Variations in the types of industries featured in an industrial community may be the result of the location of some natural resource such as cotton or iron ore. Such variations may also reflect the existence of certain types of transportation or the presence of large amounts of empty land suitable for industrial development. In some cases, the location of types of industry in a given community is accidental; thus the inventor of an industrial process may found a plant in his home community, and this, in turn, may attract other industries of a similar nature or of a related kind. In one or more of these ways a city like Pittsburgh became a steel center, Akron became a rubber center, and Detroit an automobile manufacturing center.

The particular type of industry in a community may have important effects on the social life of that community. For instance, the seasonal nature of some industries or the cycles of production may subject some

---

New York, 1933; Don J. Bogue, *The Structure of the Metropolitan Community,* University of Michigan, Horace H. Rackham School of Graduate Studies, Ann Arbor, 1949; Noel P. Gist and L. A. Halbert, *Urban Society,* Thomas Y. Crowell Company, New York, 1941, part II; Wilbur C. Hallenbeck, *American Urban Communities,* Harper & Brothers, New York, 1951, chap. 13. See also *A Social Profile of Detroit: 1955,* A Report of the Detroit Area Study of the University of Michigan, Institute for Social Research, Survey Research Center, 1956.

[6] For a general discussion of industrial suburbs as compared with other types of suburbs, see Harlan Paul Douglass, *The Suburban Trend,* Appleton-Century-Crofts, Inc., New York, 1925, chaps. III and IV.

communities to periodic layoffs of thousands of workers. In other communities the factories may operate steadily for years, only to close down suddenly to meet a shift in fashion or the demand for a new product. Thus, the economic life of the community, its periods of prosperity and depression, reflects the rhythm of its industries.[7] Furthermore, the particular type of technological processes used in industries often has certain definite effects on the social life of the community. For instance, where a technological process involves the use of female labor, the relationships between husbands and wives, between parents and children, the relative economic independence of unmarried girls, will almost certainly be affected in some degree. Or where a technological process demands continual operation, social life may reflect the fact that a portion of the working force will be employed at night. The varying effects of technological processes on social life are almost infinite in number.

Single-industry Towns Versus Towns with Diversified Industries. Closely related to the distinction made above is the distinction between towns which are based on single industries or factories and those which possess diversified industries. A single-industry town may result when an industry locates near a body of raw materials. Company towns, in which all the property in the community is company-owned, are frequently single-industry towns. Small communities may be built around one industry or a very few.[8] Diversification of industries within a community, on the other hand, is often related to a numerous population, to the presence of a large working force in the community or nearby, to the presence of facilities attractive to a wide range of industries, or to accidental factors. Sometimes a community makes a purposeful attempt to attract a wide range of industries.

The relative diversification or lack of diversification of industry may have important consequences for the community. One-industry towns are, of course, peculiarly susceptible to the economic situation of that industry; thus, towns based on textile mills have, in late years, felt the effects of severe competition and depressed economic conditions. Such communities have suffered chronic or intermittently heavy unemployment. Even a metropolis like Detroit, where a large portion of the working force is employed by the automobile industry, may suffer from inter-

[7] For a recent example, see "Bayonne Sapped by Work Decline," *The New York Times,* Feb. 28, 1955, pp. 21 and 33.

[8] For descriptions of one-industry or one-factory towns, see the following: Lois Macdonald, *Southern Mill Hills,* Alex L. Hillman, New York, 1928, chaps. II–V; Herbert J. Lahne, *The Cotton Mill Worker,* Rinehart & Company, Inc., New York, 1944, chaps. III–V; Lois Macdonald, *Labor Problems and the American Scene,* Harper & Brothers, 1938, chaps. V and VI. For an account of decline in this type of community, see Harriet Laura Herring, *Passing of the Mill Village,* The University of North Carolina Press, Chapel Hill, N.C., 1949.

mittent unemployment due to slowdowns or stoppage of production in that one industry. Communities with diversified industries, on the other hand, are more secure against such "spotty" economic reversals, barring a general depression. Furthermore, one-industry towns are much more susceptible to technological change than communities with a range of industries. In certain cases, a technological change is capable of almost entirely wiping out a one-industry town.[9] Communities which are industrially diversified are relatively protected against such catastrophes.

Other social effects flow from the diversification, or lack thereof, of industry. A one-industry town would seem to be more susceptible to control by a single individual or a family. In an industrially diversified community, the patterns of power and control will usually assume less centralized forms. The working class in a diversified community may be more heterogeneous socially than that in a one-industry town. Patterns of stratification may vary from community to community.

Variations in the Nature of Power Structure. Although it is true that industrial management is almost always a factor of considerable importance in the power structure of an industrial community, there may be considerable variation in both the amount and type of power which management wields in different communities. On the one extreme is the completely managerially dominated or company-dominated town. In the company town, management may own the land on which the community is built; it may own and rent all the houses, run the general store, own the church and pay the preacher, own the school and hire the teacher. Formerly common in the New England textile industry, the company town is now found most frequently in the South (although it is beginning to decline there) and also in mining areas. In the company town the power of management, is, of course, very great. Not only does the worker in such a town depend economically upon the company mill, factory, or mine, but he can usually trade only at the company store and must pay whatever prices are charged there. In practice, this often means that the worker is continually in debt to the store, a debt which is deducted from his wages. Furthermore, the worker may be evicted from his house at any time. Studies have shown that in company towns the employer is able to stamp his point of view on the lessons taught in the classroom and on the sermons preached in church.[10]

For these reasons the social life of company towns is remarkably

[9] See W. F. Cottrell, "Death by Dieselization," *American Sociological Review,* vol. 16, no. 3, pp. 358–365, 1951.

[10] For a discussion of the relations between management and the church in what is, to be sure, not a company town, but one in which many features of the company town exist, see Liston Pope, *Millhands and Preachers,* Yale University Press, New Haven, Conn., 1942. For an account of a company town based on mining, see Lauren Gilfillan, *I Went to Pit College,* The Viking Press, Inc., New York, 1934.

limited; it is marked by a monolithic power structure, an absence of unionization or other movements opposed to management, the virtual nonexistence of a middle class, except for a small group of professionals tightly controlled by management.

Shading off from the company towns is a variety of communities more or less dominated by management until a type is reached in which management, though not without power, must share that power with various other organizations, groups, or institutions. For instance, management may share power with a powerful union organization, with an entrenched middle class, with a local "aristocracy" whose wealth is not based on industry.[11] Furthermore, in some communities managerial power may be so effectively split among various industries, sometimes competing with each other, that management as a class wields relatively little power. The possible variations here too are very numerous.[12]

Ghost Towns and Boom Towns. Another axis of variation is marked on the one extreme by the annihilation of communities and on the other extreme by the mushrooming community, commonly called "boom town" in the United States. In between these extremes are those communities in which both constructive and destructive forces are at work simultaneously and in varying proportions.

The annihilated city, the so-called "ghost city," or the rapidly declining town or industrial section is the result of the disappearance of industry, whether sudden or gradual, and the failure to replace it. Industry may disappear from a community for a variety of reasons. Sometimes a natural resource, such as a body of ore, on which local industry is based, may suddenly disappear or peter out. Sometimes, as we have seen, a technological change may remove the *raison d'être* of industry or, at least, greatly reduce the need for a working force. Sometimes an industry may leave a community in search of cheaper labor elsewhere.

When an industrial community is suddenly bereft of its industry or a major portion of it, social effects are profound. New ways of making

---

[11] For an account of such a community, see C. W. M. Hart, "Industrial Relations Research and Social Theory," *The Canadian Journal of Economics and Political Science,* vol. 15, no. 1, pp. 53–73, 1949. For accounts of other types of industrial communities which reveal various configurations of power structures, see the following: Alfred Winslow Jones, *Life, Liberty and Property,* J. B. Lippincott Company, Philadelphia, 1941; Robert S. Lynd and Helen M. Lynd, *Middletown in Transition,* Harcourt, Brace and Company, Inc., New York, 1937; Everett Cherrington Hughes, *French Canada in Transition,* University of Chicago Press, Chicago, 1943, copyright by the University of Chicago; Alvin W. Gouldner, *Patterns of Industrial Bureaucracy,* Free Press, Glencoe, Ill., 1954.

[12] Investigations in the field of the power structure of communities are now getting under way. For a recent study of the power structure of a community, see Floyd Hunter, *Community Power Structure: A Study of Decision Makers,* The University of North Carolina Press, Chapel Hill, N.C., 1953.

a living must be found. The community must provide new services, such as relief or public employment. Buildings are allowed to decay; no new housing is constructed. Declining communities have a characteristically "mean," drab, or slummy appearance. The middle class in such a community is shorn of the basis of its support. A vast apathy hangs over a declining town; the young people move away, and the older people who remain often seem to be without energy or hope. Usually the outflow stops short of complete abandonment of the community, but not before the total population declines in greater or lesser measure.

Boom towns, on the other hand, are, in the cases in which we are interested, the result of a sudden influx of industry. A sudden influx of this kind may result from various factors: the discovery of a natural resource, a decision to locate an industry in a previously nonindustrialized area (e.g., certain government-sponsored atomic-energy plants), the sudden needs engendered by war or preparations for war, or a search for cheap labor. The social effects of an influx of industry are hardly less startling than those which result from the sudden disappearance of industry. A mass of people suddenly descends on what may have been heretofore a small agricultural town. Often these people are drawn from different regions, races, ethnic backgrounds, or religions. Unless there has been a degree of planning which is rather unusual in this country, there is usually not nearly enough housing for these workers. As a result, cheap housing is hastily thrown up or barrackslike buildings are constructed; sometimes vast auto-trailer parks appear. Typically, community facilities are lacking for these people: schools are inadequate, stores are small, drainage systems are inadequate or nonexistent. Everything must be constructed quickly, and there is usually an air of impermanence about the boom town which inhibits building. Family life is disrupted in such a community. With the indiscriminate mixture of all kinds of people, old class lines or status distinctions rapidly become meaningless or ignored.[13] Since wages in a boom community are usually high and work plentiful, there is plenty of money to spend, though few places to spend it. As a result a series of shady businesses or recreations may arrive in town. The boom community is notoriously a "wide-open" town.

In between these extremes are found a great many communities which are variously affected by those forces which are producing ghost towns or boom towns. Industries may leave or enter an established community on a scale large enough to affect sections or neighborhoods of the community, though the nature of the community as a whole may not be significantly changed. For instance, the sudden departure or closing of

---

[19] See, for instance, Robert J. Havighurst and H. Gerthon, *The Social History of a War Boom Community*, Longmans, Green & Co., Inc., New York, 1952.

an industry may throw out of work large numbers of the workers of a single neighborhood. In this neighborhood the phenomena of the declining town may appear: reliance on public support, the exodus of the young, the formation of grimy slums. Of course, since the neighborhood is a portion of a larger community, where other work opportunities presumably exist, the displaced workers may find new employment. However, it is not, as we know, an easy matter for workers, particularly older ones, to change jobs, learn new skills, and adjust to new social situations. Analogously, a stable or declining industrial town may be suddenly revivified by the appearance of new industry, and many of the boom-town characteristics may appear in such communities. In one community, observed by this author, the influx of airplane factories into what was previously a declining textile industry town has radically changed the appearance of the town, the type of worker, and the morale of the entire community.

The Individual and the Community. There is a second sense in which the sociologist uses the term *community*. In this second sense, by a "community" is meant a tightly knit social group, in which individuals are united by common values, habits, and definitions, in which they fill definite statuses and roles and have a feeling of solidarity with the group, a feeling of belonging and membership. These sentiments do not exist in a vacuum; they solidly support, and are supported by, identical or complementary economic interests. In fact, one of the marks of a community is a finely developed division of labor, in which each man is dependent on the labor of other men. It is this combination of common interests and common sentiments which gives to the community a sense of purpose and ensures its continuity. And it is these common sentiments and interests which come to be expressed in the external symbols of the community—its houses, streets, and monuments—and in its myths and beliefs.[14]

For the individual, the fully developed community is one of the most important of social groups. The individual is dependent on the community economically; there he must find employment, there he can secure the necessary specialized services he needs. He depends on the community also for protection against calamity: fire, theft, or disease. Furthermore, he is dependent on the community for psychic satisfactions, for it is within the community that he can acquire the security to be found in identification with other men. It is there that he can gain recognition, response, affection, a sense of purpose to life. The com-

---

[14] For various definitions of the community, see R. M. MacIver, *Society: A Textbook of Sociology,* Rinehart & Company, Inc., New York, 1937, pp. 151–153. See also Robert A. Nisbet, *The Quest for Community,* Oxford University Press, New York, 1953, pp. 71–73; and Lewis Mumford, *The Culture of Cities,* Harcourt, Brace and Company, Inc., New York, 1938, chap. VII.

munity provides an arena within which he can develop and realize whatever potentialities he may possess. In fact, where the community has been highly developed it has provided physical and psychic satisfaction second only to the family in importance.

It follows that if the individual is removed from the community, or if for some reason the community itself disintegrates, then the individual will suffer physical or psychic loss to a greater or less degree. For instance, if a community ceases to provide economic opportunities the individual may not only suffer material loss; he may also suffer from a sense of insecurity. He may feel threatened and anxious when he is cut off from the solid social ties of community life, when he can find no outlet for the expression and satisfaction of deep-lying psychological needs. Under these circumstances he is thrown back on his own resources; he can no longer count on invoking those responses in other men which are necessary to his existence. He must seek his own salvation, even at the expense of others. But this, in turn, can only increase the insecurity and anxiety of others and thus worsen his own situation in the long run; inevitably, he will be exploited by others in a position similar to his own. Where community is absent, when men are no longer parts of a whole, they are reduced to a "disordered dust of individuals"; they must to some degree engage in a war of "all against all."

The description of a functioning community offered above is an ideal one. However, this ideal condition has been approximated at certain times and places. The medieval manor, with its sharply defined statuses, its rigid hierarchy, its religious unity, and its self-sufficiency was rather close to what we have designated as a "community." Similarly, some primitive tribes seem to reveal signs of sharply defined community life. Of more direct pertinence to this book is the example provided by the guilds, which as Tannenbaum has pointed out, provided workingmen with exceptionally well defined and cohesive community life.[15]

In all these communities men were guaranteed an equal right, according to their status, in whatever economic opportunities the community could provide. Thus they were not threatened by economic destitution, or at least they were threatened only when the community as a whole was threatened; if one was destitute, all were destitute. The closely knit community also provided men with certain psychic satisfactions. Thus, it has been claimed (though the evidence on this point is not clear) that

[15] The ideal community may also be approximated in isolated rural communities in the United States. See for instance, Kenneth MacLeish and Kimball Young, *Culture of a Contemporary Rural Community*, U.S. Department of Agriculture, Bureau of Agricultural Economics, Rural Life Studies, no. 3, April, 1942; and Walter M. Kollmorgen, *Culture of a Contemporary Rural Community: The Old Order Amish of Lancaster County, Pennsylvania*, U.S. Department of Agriculture, Bureau of Agricultural Economics, Rural Life Studies, no. 4, September, 1942.

where men are united in communities, they are less subject to neuroses, psychoses, or psychosomatic disorders. In stable communities there are fewer political upheavals or other signs of social unrest.

The Effects of Industrialization on the Community. As industrialism began to develop, much of the more or less closely knit fabric of the medieval guild or town community began to melt away. This process was sudden in some places, more gradual in others. The early New England industrial community, for instance, seemed to maintain many aspects of a closely knit community for a relatively long time. This was due, in part, to the smallness of these early industrial communities; in part it was due to the similarity in the ethnic and religious background of their members.[16] In those communities there was a common value system, centering around the religion and shared by all members of the community; there was a well-recognized hierarchy of statuses and a strong feeling of identification between worker and employer, between individual and community. However, these communities must have been exceptional even in the early days of industrialism. Certainly, no later than the early nineteenth century, there were beginning to emerge large and small urban agglomerations, which were hardly communities as we have used the term. These new communities have been modified by time but are not essentially changed to this day.

These new urban or industrial communities were the products of an early stage of rapidly developing industry; they tend to appear today under the same conditions, particularly where industry proceeds at a forced pace. This suggests that the early industrial community is no less suited to a certain stage of industrialism than the medieval community was to the medieval economy of manor, town, and guild. To point this out is not to deny the salubrious features of the medieval communities. Nor should we overlook the many evil features, physical, social, and psychological, of the industrial community. However, the industrial community cannot be understood by denouncing its evils or by speculating about other types of urban communities which might have been erected had men been more rational or humane. Like any other social fact, the urban community must be understood as the part purposive, part accidental creation of groups of men working toward certain ends and creating the means to achieve those ends in light of the conditions facing them.

What factors operate to overthrow the traditional community and to create the specific form of the urban-industrial community? The first, and in many ways most important, is the nature of the working force

---

[16] Certain economic conditions in the textile industry also contributed to the maintenance of these communities. See Shlakman, *op. cit.,* p. 240; and Warner and Low, *op. cit.,* chaps. VIII and IX.

which industrialism demands. As we have seen in Chapter 3, a fully developed industrial system of production would be virtually inconceivable without a mobile working force, that is, a working force tied neither to place nor to person. An industrial working force must be mobile for various reasons. Industry must be ready to move at any time to take advantage of new resources, new sources of power, and new markets. Industrialism, furthermore, demands a tight discipline, which might be impossible to achieve without a working force which had no resources, no ties, no rights, other than those conferred by the factory system. The very antithesis of the conditions needed by industrialism is supplied by the tightly knit community, for such a community *does* provide alternative economic opportunities and *does* interfere, through its rigid social ties, with the mobility of labor. It seems highly unlikely that the existence of industrialism, at least in the phase of rapid growth, is at all compatible with the existence of community in the traditional sense.

The traditional community would seem to be incompatible with the fulfillment of the profit motive. We have seen that an inherent aspect of a rapidly developing industrialism (and perhaps of stable industrialism) is a striving toward maximum profits. This is not merely a matter of the motivation of this or that individual (motives other than profit seeking might conceivably move men to build industry) but rather a functional necessity if industry is to grow where it has no outside means of support or subsidy. If the goal of maximum profitability is to be achieved, then many important community ties must necessarily be discarded. In a rapidly developing industry, labor must be treated as a commodity. But the use of labor as a commodity, to be bought at the lowest possible figure and only when needed, implies social relationships which are the very antithesis of those found in a traditional community. The relationships between management and labor must be impersonal (if not anonymous), transitory, expedient, and often ruthlessly oriented to self-interest. It is no wonder, then, that industrialism has shattered the traditional community. It is no accident that precisely where the struggle for profits has been at its most fierce—for instance, in highly competitive industrial fields—the ties of community have been most thoroughly shattered.

There is a second factor which has led to the disintegration of traditional communities. Industrialism creates great disparities in wealth, security, standard of living, and way of life. Industrial owners, industrial management, and skilled and unskilled workingmen tend to develop separate cultures, separate standards of living, and separate, if not opposed, interests. It is true that great social and economic disparities existed in the medieval community also, but these disparities were justified by long traditions. Industrialism, on the other hand, is much too recent a development to have evolved such traditions; perhaps industrialism is inimical to the development of such traditions. The result is not only a situation of social and economic inequalities, but a sense of inequality which is often accompanied by a sense of injustice. It is this combination which tends to destroy the unity and cohesion of the industrial community.[17]

Industrialism very often has still a third shattering effect on the traditional community. Once industrialism develops past a certain point, it quickly uses up the supply of labor existing in the community. In order to man the factories, a working force must be recruited from outside the community. In practice this very frequently means that men and women of the most diverse ethnic, religious, and racial backgrounds are thrown together, helter-skelter. This has been particularly true of the United States, whose working force has been recruited from many different nations and cultures, but, to a greater or lesser extent, this process occurs in almost all industrial communities. The juxtaposition of these diverse cultures quickly shatters the consensus and unity of the old community. Wide divergences may exist in values, habits, traditions, even in language. The relationships between these groups may be dominated by misunderstanding and by mutual suspicion.

The Urban-Industrial Community. Such a community possesses a characteristic structure and functions in characteristic ways, but this structure and function are not always easy to detect. As compared to traditional communities, urban-industrial communities are marked by great diversity and range. Furthermore, where the social structure of the traditional community is relatively simple, the urban community is made up of differing groups, classes, nationalities, races, religions, neighborhoods, sections, and associations, all jammed together side by side, or sometimes on top of each other. Where the traditional community was marked by a few well-defined roles, in the urban-industrial community there is a veritable plethora of roles.

Still further differentiating the two types of communities is the fact that in the modern community roles are often sharply separated from each other. Men have contact with each other only as they play these roles; social relationships are of a segmental nature and do not involve the entire personality as they do in traditional communities. Social contacts in the modern community often proceed on the basis of expediency, rather than on the basis of status; men interact for purely selfish ends, and often such interaction involves exploitation. Others are judged not as

---

[17] MacIver notes (*op. cit.*, p. 361) that economic disparity, where accompanied by a sense of injustice, is one of the major factors in the disintegration of any community.

specific personalities but in their capacities as players of roles; it is not who the person is, but what he does, and how well, and for what considerations, that is of importance in modern urban life.

Again in sharpest contrast to the traditional community, urban life to-day possesses few shared values and definitions. What is common may be quite superficial: a fad, a taste, a fashion. As a matter of fact, in modern urban life tolerance of deviations and innovations is a necessity, if people are to live together at all. Since social life cannot be based on shared values, other sources of social control and order must be found. The symbols of urban order are the policeman, the court, and the law— not custom, traditions, folkways, or mores. People do not obey social codes because they believe in the code, necessarily, but because it is expedient to do so.[18]

Because roles are segmented in the modern community and a common value system is lacking, the unity or cohesion of the modern community is weak. This lack of unity in urban-industrial communities contrasts sharply to the situation which exists in the traditional community. Civic spirit, a pride in the community, loyalty to it, a sense of responsibility for its well-being, are all greatly weakened in modern urban communities.[19] The individual may feel loyalty to his family, to his trade union, to his business association, or to his nationality group. But it is rare that his horizon extends beyond these relatively restricted groups; the city is too vast, too complex, too abstract, and the individual knows too little of it.

The lack of unity and the lack of community feeling find expression in the physical form of the modern city. The industrial city is usually a vast sprawl of buildings radiating outward from a central shopping center, through slums, through neat middle-class districts, through far and distant suburbs, until it merges gradually with the countryside. Within this complex can be found the greatest sorts of diversities and paradoxes. District crowds upon district. Factories are interspersed among residential districts; often the factories occupy what would normally be the most favorable residential sites. Railroads radiate in all directions. Automobiles crowd onto the too narrow streets, disputing the right of way with trolley cars and busses. In the suburbs are found neat little houses, standing at attention like soldiers, down the side

[18] This discussion has been based on the excellent summary of aspects of city life contained in a publication of the National Resources Committee, *Our Cities: Their Role in the National Economy*, Government Printing Office, 1937, p. 52. See also the well-known article by Louis Wirth, "Urbanism as a Way of Life," *American Journal of Sociology*, vol. 44, no. 1, pp. 1–24, July, 1938. Copyright by the University of Chicago Press.

[19] For an account of the absence of civic spirit and the consequences thereof in early urban communities, see J. L. Hammond and Barbara Hammond, *The Town Labourer*, Longmans, Green & Co., Inc., New York, 1917, chap. III.

streets. In other districts, grimy slums spread over miles of blocks, marching to an horizon dominated by gas tanks and towering factory chimneys. The architecture of the city also reflects this lack of inner unity and cohesion; a Grecian temple (housing a postoffice or railroad terminal) stands cheek by jowl with a sixteenth-century French chateau.[20] This is the face of the urban-industrial community; grimy, diverse, disordered. But this very disorder and lack of unity are adapted to the industrialism which gave birth to them.

It seems clear that urban-industrial communities are not communities at all in the traditional or technical sense of that word. The urban community lacks a common value system; it lacks a sense of identification between the individual and his fellow man, between the individual and itself; it lacks, that is, unity, cohesiveness, purpose. Urban-industrial communities are, to some extent, in what Durkheim called states of *anomy;* that is, they are composed of isolated individuals or isolated groups. Under these circumstances we might predict that modern urban communities would evince signs of disorganization. There should be myriads of frustrated, insecure, anxious, despairing, purposeless, and rootless individuals; there should be high rates of crime, racketeering, prostitution.

Are these rather gloomy predictions borne out by the evidence? There is a general tendency among social scientists to characterize the personalities of modern man in precisely the terms used above. Thus Horney speaks of a neurotic personality which is characteristic of our times,[21] beset by anxieties and insecurities. Fromm pictures man as attempting to flee from modern life into the arms of demagogues and dictators.[22] Mumford speaks of the inhumanity of the modern city, of its unfitness for human needs, physical or psychological, and of the consequences on human personality.[23] Nisbet says that the key words of our times are "disorganization, disintegration, decline, insecurity, breakdown, instability, frustration, anxiety.[23a] These quotations might be extended almost indefinitely; all observers seem to agree on the existence of harsh stresses and strains besetting the individual in urban-industrial communities.

There is much evidence of a more concrete nature to support the thesis which holds modern communities to be productive of social disorganization and breakdown. Crime rates are universally high in cities, particularly in certain districts. Predatory crime, organized racketeer-

[20] See Mumford, *op. cit.*, chaps. III and IV.
[21] Karen Horney, *The Neurotic Personality of Our Times,* W. W. Norton & Company, Inc., New York, 1937.
[22] Erich Fromm, *Escape from Freedom,* Rinehart & Company, Inc., New York, 1941.
[23] Mumford, *op. cit.*
[23a] Nisbet, *op. cit.*, p. 7.

ing, juvenile delinquency, and white-collar crime are common urban phenomena. If one looks at the suicide rates in modern cities, one finds that these rates are 50 per cent higher in cities of 10,000 or more people than in rural areas. The isolation of modern man is demonstrated by his failure to join organizations; this situation is particularly true of working-class individuals.[24] Rates of insanity in urban areas are very high; though it is not certain that they are higher than for traditional communities, there is a strong supposition that this is true. Furthermore, a direct connection can be shown between specific types of mental disease and certain sections of the city.[25] It is harder to gather statistics on the rates of neurosis in urban-industrial communities, but there is no reason to assume that these rates too are not high.

There is, however, another side to this picture; it is possible that it has been painted in too dark a color. For one thing there seems to be no reason to accept the argument of those who hold that urban life is in itself necessarily abnormal, that cities are abnormal and deviate from some ideal standard of human social life. We know that man can constitute successful social life under the most widely varying conditions. Since this is the case, it is at least possible that urban-industrial communities may hold certain satisfactions for city dwellers. Furthermore, some of those very aspects of urban life which are most strongly denounced may be functionally necessary for the existence of an industrial society.

For instance, it seems reasonable to suppose that, since industrialism rests on a division of labor which sharply separates men on the basis of technology, power, and ownership, it could not exist in a community adhering to one common value system. If this is true, then it follows that it is precisely the community in which men *are* separated from the community that is adapted to industrialism. Industrialism can flourish only in a community in which roles *are* segmental and social relationships impersonal. Similarly, the very frustration, anxiety, and insecurity which so many social scientists deplore may play an important part in motivating men and women to perform the exacting tasks of an industrial society. If we reverse the terms used above we can see this more clearly. Substitute "unfulfilled ambition" for "frustration," "concern for the future" for "anxiety," and "absence of apathy" for "insecurity," and we have three compellingly important motives for playing the most diverse and difficult roles within industrial society. Thus, unless one can demonstrate some transcendental standard of human

[24] See Mirra Komarovsky, "The Voluntary Associations of Urban Dwellers," *American Sociological Review*, vol. 11, no. 6, pp. 686–698, 1946.

[25] See Robert E. L. Faris, and H. Warren Dunham, *Mental Disorders in Urban Areas*, University of Chicago Press, Chicago, 1939. Copyright by the University of Chicago.

social conduct which is violated by urban life, this life cannot be called abnormal.

Let us examine the argument that, although urban social life is functional for the industrial system, it nevertheless violates basic and inherent needs of human nature and that, in this sense, urban-industrial communities are abnormal. There is, of course, some justification for this argument. There can be no doubt, for instance, that slum conditions violate some of the basic physical needs of human beings. However, we would deny that this argument is applicable to urban life as a whole or that it correctly represents the essential nature of urban life. For one thing, although rates of crime, suicide, or insanity are high in urban communities (though not much higher than rates in rural areas, as commonly supposed) nevertheless the vast majority of city dwellers do make some sort of adjustment to urban life. There are certain satisfactions which can be attained within city life. Certainly, the many attractions of urban life—the centers of amusement, the many cultural advantages, the very color and noise of the ever-changing crowds—compensate in good measure for the lost benefits of the traditional community. Indeed, many rural dwellers seem to find these and other attractions a continuing lure.

Furthermore, it may be that many individuals do find satisfaction and fulfillment precisely in the anonymous, segmental, ever-changing nature of urban social life. In the city there is an absence of onerous social control over personal habits and hedonistic practices. There seems no reason to suppose that man is incapable of being socialized into wanting those social experiences which city life provides; nor is there any reason to doubt that man can evolve a system of values which can be fulfilled within the city. In all probability this is exactly what happens; myriads of city dwellers are truly urbanized in their values, habits, and attitudes. They would suffer great psychological loss if they were suddenly deprived of their urban environment.

Of course, it may be argued that the fact remains that many cases of individual disorganization exist in our cities. But these cases may very well be the external symbols not of the abnormality of city life or even of the inherent stress and strain of city life alone. They may reflect the fact that many individuals are not yet integrated into urban society and culture. The flow of rural dwellers into our cities continues, bringing in masses of people reared in traditional communities. These people cannot easily integrate themselves into urban life, except on the shallowest level. Furthermore, the urban community is highly dynamic, and in the course of the constant changes attendant on city life some individuals are certain to be uprooted socially and disorganized personally. One example, chosen from among many, is the continual influx of Negroes into our Northern cities, with a consequent disorganization of relatively stable sections and neighborhoods. But mass migrations to the city cannot continue forever. Perhaps we are even now reaching a period of slowing down of this process, and in the course of time at least this source of disorganization will be removed.

But, whether or not we like the urban community and its culture, it seems entirely probable that the present form of urban-industrial community is transitory and is in a state of rapid evolution toward other forms. Prediction of the nature of these new forms is a risky business, but let us say that it seems highly unlikely that the industrial-urban community can or will turn back the clock and become again, in structure and function, traditional communities. This, however, does not preclude the possibility that certain modified trends in that direction may develop.

Perhaps something of the outline of the future urban-industrial community can be detected in trends which are visible today. The movement toward the suburbs continues, creating in the process new communities which differ both physically and socially from the old urban centers. The physical form of the city itself is changing; these changes are due in part to the demands of new transportation routes, in part to a new conception of city planning, in part to certain economic forces. In turn, certain social changes accompany these physical changes. Industries are increasingly being located away from the centers of cities—in some cases, ten or twenty miles outside city limits. New communities have sprung up around these industries. This is only one example of change. Of course, at any time economic changes, technological developments, the threat of atomic warfare, or war itself may radically alter or reverse or even abolish these trends.

Predicting the future social structure of industrial-urban communities would seem to be impossible in our present stage of knowledge. However, we may venture one guess, based on at least one important trend. As cities in the United States reach something like their ultimate proportional size, and as more and more of their inhabitants are socialized into urban life, the urban community should be able to achieve some of the stability of traditional communities, at least on a local scale. Something of this trend may be discerned in the attempt to create unified neighborhoods based sometimes on slum-clearance projects, sometimes on suburban developments, sometimes on plans of development of entire cities. Within such areas it may prove possible eventually to recreate a modified form of stable community life, based on the relative homogeneity and common interests of the neighborhood. The creation of self-contained settlements outside city limits may provide even better opportunities for stable community life; in such communities a sense of identification between the individual and the community and at least some elements of a common value system may have a chance to appear. Nor must we overlook the attempts of both industry and labor unions to foster community ties among certain sections of the population. Thus, Hart's study of Windsor showed that the UAW locals there had, in effect, constituted themselves a center of community life for many members of the working class and were gradually taking over many of the functions usually performed by the community.[26]

Summary. The industrial system destroys traditional communities and substitutes for them noncohesive, segmented, and highly dynamic urban agglomerations. In the process individuals are cut off from the psychological satisfactions provided by the traditional community. Some individuals disintegrate under this pressure, but the great mass of them absorb urban values and make a relatively satisfactory adjustment to urban life. The dynamic nature of the industrial community is constantly threatening this adjustment. However, the urbanite can take such changes in stride, because change is a portion of his experience and his personality is attuned to a rapid tempo of change.

[26] Hart, *op. cit.*, pp. 63–73.

CHAPTER 16

Industry and Social Stratification

We shall now turn to a study of the way in which industry, including trade unionism, affects or is influenced by separate parts or areas of society. These separate parts or areas with which we shall be dealing are both local and national in scope. This chapter will concentrate on the relationship of industry to the system of stratification prevalent in the United States today. In the subsequent chapters we shall study the relationship of industry to minority groups, to the family, and to politics.

Social Stratification. One of the most important aspects of the social structure of both community and nation is the prevalent system of social stratification. By stratification is meant the division of the social group into levels or strata, which are united by some common attribute or characteristic. But, since such a definition might apply equally well to a family or to an Indian tribe, we must add that this "striking attribute" or "characteristic" cannot be taken to be membership in a racial group, an ethnic group, in some institution (e.g., in a given religion), or in a group or organization such as the army. Thus we cannot speak of a "class of Catholics," a "military class" (though one does hear the term used), or a "class of New Yorkers" or "class of Chicagoans." It is characteristic of a system of stratification that, actually or potentially, it cuts across institutions, organizations, ethnic groups, racial groups, communities, or geographical divisions. Thus a given stratum may include Negroes, Catholics, soldiers, members of the American Legion, and workingmen.

Even with the limitations noted above, there remains a vast number of criteria which might be used to stratify a community or society. Thus, it has been pointed out that a community might be stratified on the basis of hair color; one could speak of a "class of blondes." However, if a system of stratification is to possess any meaning, it must be based on criteria which have some significance either for the society as a whole, or for the individuals in the strata, or for both.

From this point of view, two criteria of stratification have come to be generally recognized as of paramount importance. On the one hand, a society or even a community may be stratified in terms of the differential interests, differential life chances, or different relations to the market, of its members.[1] From this point of view, individuals are united into a stratum because they have similar economic interests. They are alike in that they own property or that they own the same kinds of property, or they are alike in owning no property. They may also be alike in that they buy and sell the same kinds of products, under similar conditions, in the market. Whenever we find a group of individuals who possess in common the "striking attribute" of a common economic interest, we shall call that group a *class*. It will be noted that this is a purely objective definition; what is important is not what the individual feels, or thinks, or states, but to what group he actually belongs by virtue of his economic interest, his life chances, his ability to buy and sell.

On the other hand, a society or a community may be stratified on the basis of the differential prestige, esteem, or social honor accorded its members. Individuals may, for instance, possess in common membership in a high-ranking profession, or they may belong to high-ranking families, or they may have uncommon talent, or they may maintain a favored and envied style of life. When we find a group of individuals who possess about equal amounts of social honor on the basis of one or more of these criteria, or on the basis of some other criterion not named here, we shall speak of a "status group."[2] In contrast to a class, a status group is based on subjective definitions; it is the very essence of a system of status that it involves ranking by the members of the society. This occupation is considered honorable, that one dishonorable; this style of life is considered reputable, that one disreputable.

But the fact that status is based on subjective definitions does not thereby make status any the less "real" than class. Men may act as determinedly and as stubbornly on the basis of status distinctions as on the basis of class interests. In fact, in certain situations a status group may unite individuals of different class positions, and there are no abstract criteria by which we may say that one is more real or important than the other.

[1] Max Weber, *From Max Weber: Essays in Sociology*, edited by H. H. Gerth and C. Wright Mills, Oxford University Press, New York, 1946, pp. 181–183. See also Talcott Parsons, "An Analytical Approach to the Theory of Social Stratification," *American Journal of Sociology*, vol. 45, no. 6, pp. 841–862, 1940, copyright by the University of Chicago; Wilbert E. Moore and Kingsley Davis, "Some Principles of Stratification," *American Sociological Review*, vol. 10, no. 2, pp. 242–249, 1945. See the attack on the Moore and Davis hypothesis by Melvin Tumin, "Some Principles of Stratification: A Critical Analysis," *American Sociological Review*, vol. 18, no. 4, pp. 387–394, 1953; and the rejoinders by Davis, pp. 394–397, and by Moore, p. 397.

[2] Weber, *op. cit.*, pp. 186–187.

It should also be noted that status and class often coincide. Thus workingmen not only tend to form a distinct class in this society, but they also fill occupational roles which tend to confer on them about the same amounts of prestige. Similarly, those who hold great amounts of property not only form a distinct class but also often form a sharply defined status group. This type of coincidence has led to confusion and a tendency on the part of some to reduce class differences to status differences, or status differences to class differences. But the two systems of stratification, although coinciding here and there, are fundamentally distinct. Thus members of a class which is based on property ownership may nevertheless belong to different status groups on the basis of membership in differentially ranked families. And, even where class and status coincide, as in the case of the workingmen noted above, nevertheless the meaning and significance of these two principles of stratification, their psychological and ideological results, remain quite distinct.

Industry and the Class System. According to the definition of classes offered here it is possible to distinguish a number of classes in the United States. For instance, there are various agricultural classes: a propertied agricultural class, an agricultural class made up of tenants and sharecroppers, and an agricultural class of hired workers. Similarly, there is a class of industrial entrepreneurs, a class of owners of stocks and bonds, a managerial class, a class of small businessmen, a white-collar class, and a working class—all distinguished from each other by the types of products that they are trying to buy or sell, or by whether they are buying or selling, or by other economic interests. Furthermore, each of these classes may be still further subdivided. For instance, the industrial entrepreneurial class is split at least along these axes: large-scale business versus small-scale business, production for external markets versus production for internal markets, extractive industries versus productive or service industries, industries depending on government orders versus those whose market is found almost entirely among the general public. Similarly, the working class is split among the skilled and the nonskilled. However, it is not the purpose of this chapter to attempt to picture this vast, complex class structure. Rather we are interested in determining what effects industry and the class structure are having on each other. First we shall try to determine which aspects of the class system are based on industry and in what measure.

One way of picturing the influence of industry on the class system of the United States as a whole is to examine the composition of the labor force. By the *labor force* we mean that portion of the population which is engaged in economic activity. In April, 1950, this force measured over 62 million persons (in July, 1955, it was over 64 million). About 90 per cent of all families had one or more of its members in the labor force.[3] Thus the labor force directly or indirectly affects the vast majority of people in the United States, and the composition of the labor force may be taken as a fairly reliable guide to the composition of the nation's class system.

In 1950, 12.3 per cent of the labor force was employed in agriculture and thus need not be considered here. We shall consider the remaining 87.7 per cent of the laboring force first in terms of the types of formal social relationships of work which governed their employment; that is, we shall ask how many individuals worked for others, and how many worked for themselves. Table 7 is of interest to us in that it shows

Table 7. Numbers and Percentage of Individuals Working for Others or Self-employed in Nonagricultural Pursuits

Occupation	Number (in thousands)		Per cent	
Total employed in nonagricultural industries.....	51,473		100	
Wage or salary workers........................	45,032		88	
Private workers.............................		38,877		76
Government workers.................		6,155		12
Self-employed workers........................	6,050		12	
Unpaid family workers........................	391		1	

SOURCE: A. J. Jaffee and Charles D. Stewart, *Manpower Resources and Utilization*, John Wiley & Sons, Inc., New York, 1951, abstracted from Table 7, p. 143. The percentages, which have been rounded off, have been computed by the present author.

that, of the total number of individuals in the working force (engaged in nonagricultural industries), 76 per cent or more than three-fourths were wage or salary workers in the sphere of private industry. This is the category which includes the workers, hired managers, foremen, and professionals of industry. Only 12 per cent of the working force (nonagricultural) is self-employed.

Table 8 contains a detailed breakdown of the major occupational categories in the labor force. This table enables us to derive a rough picture of the class structure of the United States (in so far as it is based on occupation) and of the industrial contribution to that structure.

In Table 9 we have arbitrarily grouped together several occupational categories in three wide class divisions.[4] In the middle class we have

[3] A. J. Jaffee and Charles D. Stewart, *Manpower Resources and Utilization*, John Wiley & Sons, Inc., New York, 1951, p. 136, table 5.

[4] It is difficult to estimate the numbers of "upper classes." Corey estimated the large-propertied class to number, in 1940, 0.5 of 1 per cent of the total working force. If that rate were applied to the figures for 1950, the upper classes in the labor force would number approximately 290,000. See Lewis Corey, "The Middle Class," *The Antioch Review*, 1945, table 1, col. 1.

Table 8. Numbers and Percentage of Individuals in Major Occupational Groups in the United States, April 1950

Major occupational group	Number (in thousands)	Per cent
Total employed...............................	58,128	100
Professionals and semiprofessionals....................	4,457	7.6
Farmers and farm managers.........................	4,596	7.8
Proprietors, managers, and officials, except farm........	6,379	10.9
Clerical and kindred workers........................	7,657	13.1
Salesmen and saleswomen...........................	3,887	6.6
Craftsmen, foremen, and kindred workers..............	7,500	12.8
Operatives and kindred workers......................	11,390	20.3
Domestic service workers...........................	1,923	3.3
Service workers, except domestic.....................	4,773	8.1
Farm laborers and foremen..........................	2,424	4.1
Laborers, except farm and mine......................	3,142	5.4

SOURCE: A. J. Jaffee and Charles D. Stewart, *Manpower Resources and Utilization*, John Wiley & Sons, Inc., New York, 1951, abstracted from Table 8, p. 146.

Table 9. Approximate Class Structure of the United States in Terms of Occupations, 1950

Class	Number (in thousands)	Per cent
Total..................	58,668	100
Middle class............	22,380	38.1
Working class..........	29,268	49.9
Agriculture............	7,020	12.0

included "professionals and semiprofessionals," "proprietors, managers, and officials, except farm," "clerical and kindred workers," and "salesmen and saleswomen." In the working class we have included "craftsmen, foremen, and kindred workers," "operatives and kindred workers," "domestic service workers," "service workers, except domestic," and "laborers, except farm and mine." Our criterion of classification has roughly followed the division between occupations dealing with nonorganic material, occupations dealing primarily with ideas or other people, and occupations dealing with the production of organic materials. From this point of view, the working class constitutes about half the laboring force and, with dependents, at least half the population as a whole. The middle class, with dependents, numbers about a third or more of the population, while the agricultural classes are much less significant numerically.

The industrial contribution to this class structure can be roughly estimated. In Table 10 we have abstracted from Table 8 those occupational categories which seem roughly to correspond with the industrial worker's role. When this figure is compared with the total number estimated to be in the working class, it can be seen that two-thirds or so of the working class is made up of industrial workers. It is much more difficult to estimate the industrial contribution to the middle class, since the occupational categories include both industrial and non-industrial pursuits. However, it may be noted that in 1940 the salaried

Table 10. Numbers and Percentage of Industrial Workers in the Working Class

Occupational category	Numbers	Per cent of total in working class
Total in the working class....................	29,268,000	100
Industrial workers:		
Operatives and kindred workers.............	11,390,000	39
Craftsmen, foremen, and kindred workers....	7,500,000	26
Total industrial workers.....................	18,890,000	65

middle class made up approximately three-fourths of the middle class. Those categories likely to include industrial roles, such as technical-managerial roles and clerical roles, constituted more than a third of the middle class.[5] The industrial contribution is less than this figure, but there is no doubt that it is a sizable one.

If we examine the relationship between industry and class on the community level, additional evidence may be found to support the picture of the relationships between industry and class which has been drawn here. For instance, McKee found that in Lorain, Ohio, just one steel mill supplied about half of all local jobs, almost all of them falling in the general category of "working-class" roles as we have defined that term.[6] Similarly, the Lynds, in their classical study of the city they called Middletown, also found a working class based largely on the industry in town. They also found a small element of industrial entrepreneurs and

[5] *Ibid.*, table 1. Incidentally, we can form a very rough idea of the industrial contribution to the upper class. Corey estimated (*ibid.*, table 2) that in 1940 there were 145,000 entrepreneurs in the manufacturing industries. However, this figure includes manufacturing industries of all sizes.

[6] James B. McKee, "Status and Power in the Industrial Community: A Comment on Drucker's Thesis," *American Journal of Sociology*, vol. 58, no. 4, p. 366, 1953. Copyright by the University of Chicago.

industrial managers, who belonged generally to the upper rungs of the stratificational ladder.[7]

Industry and the Status System. The status system of the United States comprises a vast congeries of differing groups arranged along diverse axes of ranking. Our concern in this book is, of course, with the relationship between industry and this status system. Perhaps the most important influence of industry on the status system arises from the fact that occupational role is one of the major bases of status in this nation; thus, the occupations which individuals hold in industry tend to confer certain amounts of status in the community.

Various studies have tended to show that various occupations are consistently ranked in the community in terms of social honors or prestige. In Table 11, groups of occupations are arranged according to

Table 11. Ranking of Occupations

Occupation	Number of occupations	Average score
Government officials	8	90.8
Professional and semiprofessional workers	30	80.6
Proprietors, managers, and officials, except farm	11	74.9
Clerical, sales, and kindred workers	6	68.2
Craftsmen, foremen, and kindred workers	7	68.0
Farmers and farm managers	3	61.3
Protective service workers	3	58.0
Operatives and kindred workers	8	52.8
Farm laborers	1	50.0
Service workers, except domestic and protective	7	46.7
Laborers, except farm workers	6	45.8

SOURCE: Cecil C. North and Paul K. Hatt, "Jobs and Occupations: A Popular Evaluation," *Opinion News*, Sept. 1, 1947, pp. 3–13.

the prestige accorded them by a national sample. In this table the highest possible score would be 100, the lowest 20. The relative prestige of industrial occupational roles in the community may be derived from this table. Thus the category of nonagricultural "proprietors, managers, and officials" is ranked third on the scale. Skilled workers and foremen are ranked fifth. The category "operatives and kindred workers" is ranked fourth from the bottom.

In a rough way a role acquires prestige according to the amount of income it brings and the amount of specialized training it requires. (There are, of course, other bases of prestige.) In Table 12 is shown the median money incomes and median training in years of various

[7] Robert S. Lynd and Helen Merrell Lynd, *Middletown in Transition,* Harcourt, Brace and Company, Inc., New York, 1937, pp. 25–34 and 74–101.

classes of occupations. What is of interest here is not the figures themselves, which are somewhat dated, but the relative rank order of the occupations. We see that, except for government officials, who are not listed in the table, professionals, proprietors, managers, officials, clerks, sales personnel, craftsmen, and foremen are listed in the same order as in Table 11. However, in Table 11 the industrial worker is ranked over farmers, farm managers, and protective workers.

The contribution of industry to status systems in the United States may now be assessed. In general, the industrial "owners" possess the highest status, but managers and some technicians may also occupy high

Table 12. Median Money Income and Educational Level of Occupational Groups (Males)

Occupational group	Median money income, 1947	Median years of school completed, 1940
Professional and semiprofessional................	$3,500	Over 16
Proprietors, managers, and officials, except farm ...	3,400	10.9
Clerical, sales, and kindred workers..............	2,700	12.1
Craftsmen, foremen, and kindred workers.........	2,700	8.6
Operatives and kindred workers..................	2,400	8.5
Service workers:		
Protective....................................	......	8.9
Domestic.....................................	......	7.3
Other..	2,100	8.3
Laborers, except farm and mine..................	1,700	7.7
Farmers and farm managers.....................	1,500	7.6
Farm laborers and foremen.....................	800	7.5

SOURCE: Based on table 56, p. 389, in A. J. Jaffee and Charles D. Stewart, *Manpower Resources and Utilization*, John Wiley & Sons, Inc., New York, 1951.

status positions. Most technicians, white-collar workers, foremen, and at least some skilled workers occupy middle status position. The mass of semiskilled and unskilled workers occupy rather low status positions in the community. Thus, to some degree, the class positions of owners and managers on the one hand, and of workers on the other tend to accord with their positions on the status scale. Confirmation, in a general way, for this statement is offered by a study of the upper strata of Philadelphia. This study showed that 45 per cent of the engineers and 42 per cent of the businessmen who were successful enough to be listed in *Who's Who* were also listed in the *Social Register,* that is, were members of the highest status group in Philadelphia.[8]

[8] E. Digby Baltzell, "'Who's Who in America' and 'The Social Register': Elite and Upper Class Indexes in Metropolitan America," in Reinhard Bendix and Sey-

However, the coincidence of status and class position in certain industrial roles should not blind us to the very different consequences of status and class. Thus, one workingman may react primarily to his low status position; he may be concerned with educating his children. Another workingman may act primarily in relation to class position, perhaps by taking political or economic action. Similarly one must be careful to distinguish the action and ideology of the industrial owner or engineer on the one hand, and the ideology and action of the high-status individual, on the other, even though one is dealing with the same person.

The influence of industry on status systems may also be detected on the local or community level. In a study of a small Middle-Western community, Hollingshead found that the owners of the local industries formed a part of the upper status group, while those who tended the machines of the industries were found almost exclusively in the three lowest strata.[9] While there is much variation and many local peculiarities in communities, it seems safe to say that the status systems of local communities regularly reveal five or six major strata.[10] On the top is an upper-upper stratum, which includes industrial entrepreneurs, occasionally managers, and other high-ranking officials. Next is a lower-upper stratum which is generally based on the unattached professionals in town and the local successful businessmen; however, this group may also include individuals from modest industry in the community. Below this is a level based on small business, but including skilled workers; this stratum may be dependent on industry indirectly. Still lower on the status scale are the sales personnel, white-collar workers, and clerks, some of whom are attached to industry. On the bottom are several strata of skilled, semiskilled, and unskilled workers, mostly finding their livings in the community's industries.

Thus, on both the national and community level the industrial occupational system and the status system are interrelated. Industry, being

mour Martin Lipset (eds.), *Class, Status and Power*, Free Press, Glencoe, Ill., 1953, p. 184, table 3.

[9] August B. Hollingshead, *Elmtown's Youth*, John Wiley & Sons, Inc., New York, 1949, pp. 84–120.

[10] See, for instance, C. Wright Mills, "The Middle Classes in Middle-sized American Cities," *American Sociological Review*, vol. 11, no. 5, pp. 520–529, 1946; W. Lloyd Warner and Paul S. Lunt, *The Status System of a Modern Community*, Yale University Press, New Haven, Conn., 1942, chap. V. For accounts of local peculiarities and departure from the type pictured here, see Gregory P. Stone and William H. Form, "Instabilities in Status: The Problem of Hierarchy in the Community Study of Status Arrangements," *American Sociological Review*, vol. 18, no. 2, pp. 149–162, 1953; Thomas E. Lasswell, "A Study of Social Stratification Using an Area Sample of Raters," *American Sociological Review*, vol. 19, no. 3, pp. 310–313, 1954.

one of the prime sources of occupations, is at the same time one of the prime, if indirect, sources of status in the community. However, it must not be thought that occupation is the only basis of status in the community; a given group of workingmen may be ranked not only on the basis of their occupation but also on the basis of ethnic origin, racial background, religious affiliation, and so on.[11] These latter components of status not only are separate from occupation but may even react on and seriously modify the prestige of occupations. For instance, certain jobs in industry may acquire low prestige because they are manned by a low-ranking racial group, or certain jobs may be ranked high because they have been preempted by workingmen coming from a high-ranking ethnic stock.

Industry and the Life Chances of the Various Strata. The occupational structure of industry, as we have seen, influences the stratificational system of community and nation. Owners, managers, and technicians are found on the upper status and class levels. In the middle levels are found many technicians, white-collar workers, and foremen, and in the lower levels of society the great mass of factory workers. Now, these various strata differ from each other in many significant ways; perhaps the most significant is in terms of the life chances which the individuals in each of these strata will face. By *life chances* we mean the opportunity to acquire the desirable things of life, including health, a high standard of living, education, power, and so on. Life chances are strongly influenced by the amount of economic power which each strata possesses; but they are also strongly influenced by the culture of each level, by its prevailing values, attitudes, and aspirations. Finally, life chances are influenced by the status position of an individual and by the opportunities, or lack of them, which the status position opens. In this section we shall indicate briefly some of the major differences in life chances and culture between the various strata and the relationship of these differences to industry.

Life chances are affected, in the first place, by the amount of remuneration which each stratum in society can command. Lynd has put it as follows: "Who one is, whom one knows, how one lives, what one aspires to be—these and many other urgent realities of living are patterned for one by what one does to get a living and the amount of living this allows one to buy."[12] It has already been shown in Chapter 6 that there is a great difference in the amount of remuneration attached to industrial roles. The difference between the income of the top executive and that of the unskilled worker in the factory may be five hundred

[11] See C. Wendell King, "Social Cleavage in a New England Community," *Social Forces*, vol. 24, no. 3, pp. 322–327, 1946.

[12] Lynd and Lynd, *op. cit.*, p. 7.

or a thousand times. This is an extreme, but as Table 11 shows, there are consistent differences between the various occupational strata in terms of income.

The relative position of industrial incomes as compared to incomes in the United States as a whole may be derived by reference to Table 13, which depicts family incomes and the percentage of families falling in various income brackets for 1950. In that year average weekly wages in the durable goods industries were $63.32, or about $3,300 a year; in the nondurable industries wages averaged $54.71 a week, or about $2,840 a year (assuming a full year worked in both cases). In the construction industry, which employs large numbers of skilled workers, wages aver-

Table 13. Distribution of Income in the United States, by Families, 1950
(All figures rounded out)

Family income	Per cent of families in each group	Cumulative per cent
Under $1,000	11.5	11.5
$1,000–$1,999	13.2	24.7
2,000–2,999	17.8	42.5
3,000–3,999	20.7	63.2
4,000–4,999	13.6	76.8
5,000–5,999	9.0	85.8
6,000–6,999	5.2	91.0
7,000–9,999	5.8	96.8
$10,000 and over	3.3	100.1

SOURCE: U.S. Bureau of the Census, ser. P-60, no. 9, Mar. 25, 1952.

aged $73.73 a week, or more than $3,800 a year, again assuming a full year's work.[13] Thus the skilled, semiskilled, and unskilled workers of industry fell into income categories toward the lower end of the income scale (third and fourth items from the top in Table 13). But they were by no means the lowest-paid workers. Office workers and kindred white collar workers were in about the same income categories. Technicians, managers, and officials of various kinds were in higher income brackets as a rule, while the executives of large firms received some of the most princely incomes in American life.

The amount of income received not only determines standard of living but is closely correlated with other chances or opportunities which the individual will have in life. We shall consider, by way of illustration, two aspects of life chances: the chances for health and long life, and

[13] *Economic Indicators, June 1955,* Government Printing Office, 1955, p. 11. The figures are not strictly comparable, since Table 13 refers to the income of entire families, while the figures for earnings of workers refer to individuals.

the chances for education. Table 14 shows the differences in expectation of life at birth between the lowest and highest economic groups in Chicago, between the period 1920 and 1940. It has been necessary in this table to separate whites and nonwhites (largely Negroes), because of the great differences in life expectancies between these two races. It will be noticed that an individual from the lowest economic class could expect, in 1940, to live five years less than the average person, and ten years less than a person from the highest economic group. This difference has been decreasing but is still marked. The greatest difference in the table is

Table 14. Expectancies of Life at Birth by Economic Class and Race

Year and economic class	Total population	White	Nonwhite
Total:			
1920................	56.1	56.7	42.3
1930................	58.4	59.7	44.5
1940................	63.7	64.9	53.6
Lowest economic class:			
1920................	....	51.8	....
1930................	51.9	53.7	40.0
1940................	58.7	60.2	49.9
Highest economic class:			
1920................	....	61.8	....
1930................	65.0	63.0	45.4
1940................	67.8	67.8	55.9

SOURCE: Albert J. Mayer and Philip Hauser, "Class Differentials in Expectation of Life at Birth," *La Revue de l'institut de statistique*, vol. 18, pp. 197–200, 1950; reprinted by permission from Reinhard Bendix and Seymour Martin Lipset (eds.), *Class, Status and Power*, Free Press, Glencoe, Ill., 1953, abstracted from table III, p. 283.

the eighteen years' difference in life expectancy between the nonwhite lower-class individual and the white upper-class individual.

A close correlation can also be found between occupation and education. It has already been shown in Table 12 that "operatives" had only about half the education of professionals. Confirmation of this finding is offered in Table 14. Here it can be seen that, in general, the boy of average or slightly better than average intelligence who came from a home where the father occupied a high-ranking occupational role had a better chance of completing high school, and a much better chance of going to college, than an equally intelligent boy from a lower-ranking family. This was also true for boys of superior intelligence, a situation which might well cause some misgivings.

Thus, it seems safe to say that chances for life and health and chances for education are directly correlated with position in the stratificational structure. The Lynds are indeed justified in saying that occupation determines how much of a living an individual can buy.

Position in the stratificational structure has a still more subtle influence on life chances. To some extent each class or status position is a closed subculture, with indigenous values, ideologies, myths, and pat-

Table 15. Amount of Schooling Completed, by Intelligence Quotient and Occupation of Father

Occupation of father	Intelligence quotient 100–111	Intelligence quotient 124 and over
Percentage completing 9 or more grades		
Class I	90	82
Class II	92	100
Class III	93	97
Class IV	95	100
Class V	96	100
Percentage completing 12 or more grades		
Class I	63	65
Class II	63	87
Class III	67	79
Class IV	72	85
Class V	74	87
Percentage completing 13 or more grades		
Class I	2	0
Class II	2	10
Class III	4	5
Class IV	14	18
Class V	26	37

Class I: Representative occupations include hoboes, day laborers.
Class II: Miners, policemen, bakers, etc.
Class III: Metal workers, carpenters, salesmen in stores, etc.
Class IV: Highly skilled craftsmen, clerks, etc.
Class V: Executives and professional workers.

SOURCE: Elbridge Sibley, "Some Demographic Clues to Stratification," *American Sociological Review*, vol. 7, no. 3, pp. 322–330, 1942. By permission.

terns for action and thinking. The individual who is born into these subcultures is influenced to think and act, to dream and aspire, to feel and to react, in certain set ways. Thus individuals are rendered more or less fit to cope with the exigencies of our culture, more or less fit to acquire the good things of life, by virtue of their belonging to a given class or status group.

In the matter of education, for instance, the boy from the lower classes or lower status groups is handicapped not only by a lack of financial resources, but also by certain negative attitudes toward education. In Table 16 is stated the opinions of a large sample of individuals as to the necessity for a college education. As can be seen, while more than two-thirds of the prosperous class recommended a college education, only 39 per cent of the lower class feel the same way. In terms of occupations the figures range from the 74 per cent in the professional group who approve of college to the 35 per cent among the nonfarm laborers. Those occupational categories which include industrial roles are in the middle ranges in their attitude to education.

Table 16. How Different Classes and Occupational Groups Feel about the Necessity of College Education

	Per cent recommending college education
Class background:	
Wealthy and prosperous	68
Middle class	52
Lower class	39
Occupation:	
Professional	74
Businessmen and proprietors	62
White-collar workers	65
Skilled labor	63
Semiskilled labor	49
Domestic and personal service workers	42
Farmers	47
Nonfarm laborers	35

SOURCE: Herbert H. Hyman, "The Value Systems of Different Classes: A Social Psychological Contribution to the Analysis of Stratification," by permission from Reinhard Bendix and Seymour Martin Lipset (eds.), *Class, Status and Power*, Free Press, Glencoe, Ill., 1953, p. 430, abstracted from table 1.

There are other elements in the culture of lower classes and lower status groups which operate in similar fashion to handicap or inhibit the individual in life's competition. The lower-class or lower-status individual inherits a culture which places a low value on abstract things or abstract ideas, such as mathematics or science, or reading, any of which may be necessary for success in many occupational roles. The lower-level individual may inherit a culture which is suspicious of the new, the strange, the untried; he may feel that any change will not be to his benefit. Yet, at the same time, the lower-level man may be naïve and credulous; he may be easily influenced by propaganda, even when this propaganda is directed against his interests. Very often the lower-level man has inherited (culturally) or acquired a deep-seated feeling of inferiority, which makes for habits of submission and acquiescence to the powerful in the world around him. From this world he may expect very little; his horizon may be limited, and the level of his aspirations low.

Perhaps since he hopes for little, he wishes for little. Thus the life chances of the lower-class man are basically handicapped by his attitudes toward the world around him and by the habits he forms in response to those attitudes.[14]

The lower-class individual is also handicapped because he participates very sparingly, if at all, in the organized life of the community. Many observers have noted that typically he joins fewer formal associations than individuals from any other level in the community. Thus Komarovsky found the following: 6 per cent of a sample of unskilled male workers belonged to two or more formal organizations, 8.4 per cent of a sample of skilled workers, 10.5 per cent of a sample of white-collar workers, 19 per cent of a sample of businessmen, and 16 per cent

Table 17. Reading Habits of Occupational Prestige Groups and Income Groups
(Percentages)

Reading habits	Occupational prestige groups			Income groups		
	High	Low	Difference	High	Low	Difference
Books (two or more read in a three-month period)........	50.8	35.7	15.1	50.8	36.7	14.1
Magazines (four or more read regularly)................	67.7	39.3	28.4	72.1	36.7	35.4

SOURCE: Leonard Reissman, "Class, Leisure and Social Participation," *American Sociological Review*, vol. 19, no. 1, abstracted from table 1, p. 80, 1954. By permission.

of a sample of professionals.[15] The lower-level individual typically confines his acquaintanceship to his close relatives; he knows relatively few people in the community and is known by few.[16] Not only does he not participate in formal associations, but he rarely takes part in, or has much knowledge of, politics in community or nation; lower-level individuals typically form the largest segment of nonvoters during elections.

Finally, the life chances of the lower-level individual remain low because of his ignorance of the world about him—of its economic process, its political maneuvering, its occupational opportunities, its demands in manners, morals, customs, and fashions. Typically the lower-level individual reads few books or magazines. Table 17 describes the reading

[14] See Genevieve Knupfer, "Portrait of the Underdog," *Public Opinion Quarterly*, vol. 11, no. 1, pp. 103–114, 1947.

[15] Mirra Komarovsky, "The Voluntary Associations of Urban Dwellers," *American Sociological Review*, vol. 11, no. 6, table 1, 1946. See also W. Lloyd Warner and Paul S. Lunt, *The Social Life of a Modern Community*, Yale University Press, New Haven, Conn., 1941, chap. XVI.

[16] Floyd Dotson, "Patterns of Voluntary Association among Urban Working-class Families," *American Sociological Review*, vol. 16, no. 5, pp. 687–693, 1951.

habits of a sample of individuals from different income and occupational prestige levels in Evanston, Illinois. In this sample, 72.1 per cent of high income groups read four or more magazines regularly, but little more than a third of lower income groups had the same reading habits. Furthermore, the lower-level individual rarely reads books which will inform him of the conditions of his life or help him to acquire necessary social and technical skills; his reading is more likely to be in the fields of fantasy, adventure, sports, and romance.[17] Thus the lower levels are self-inhibited from acquiring the general knowledge and specific information which would be of great help in increasing life chances.

Does trade-union membership increase life chances for the working-class man? As we have seen, some trade unions conduct educational

Table 18. Relationship between Union Membership and Membership in Voluntary Organizations

Membership in organizations	Nonunionists, per cent	Active unionists, per cent	Inactive unionists, per cent
None...............	34	35	45
One...............	29	35	26
Two or more........	36	31	29

SOURCE: Seymour Martin Lipset and Joan Gordon, "Mobility and Trade Union Membership," by permission from Reinhard Bendix and Seymour Martin Lipset, (eds.), *Class, Status and Power*, Free Press, Glencoe, Ill., 1953, abstracted from table 13, p. 498.

programs; some sponsor information programs designed to bring to workingmen knowledge of pertinent economic and social facts. Some unions have sponsored cultural programs, e.g., serious music or drama. Unions have tried to increase the self-confidence of the working class, to build up favorable self-images among workingmen, in part by claiming equality with the upper levels, in part by denying the values and way of life of upper-class groups. Estimating the success of this program is difficult. Undoubtedly, in so far as unionism has increased the wages of workingmen, shortened hours, improved sanitary conditions within the factories, and sponsored health, welfare and recreational programs, the chances of the workingman for life and health have been increased. But it must remain an open question as to how much unions have increased the capacity of the workingman to move successfully through the culture. Thus Table 18 seems to indicate that even active unionists belong

[17] See Warner and Lunt, *op. cit.*, chap. XIX, for a full discussion of the reading habits of various classes in Yankee City.

to no more community organizations than inactive unionists; it is true, however, that nonunionists belong to the fewest groups of all. Besides, as we have seen, the hold of unions on the daily life, thoughts, attitudes, and feelings of the mass of workers is slight; other, nonunion voices and influences largely affect and mold the worker's personality in our society.

Industry and Social Mobility. Another important problem in connection with stratification is the extent to which movement is occurring between the various strata. Are individuals moving from level to level, and if so, in what directions and in what numbers? Are changes occurring in the stratificational structure itself; that is, are occupational categories acquiring or losing status or economic power? Here again our concern will be with those strata which are closely related to industrial occupations.

First we shall consider social mobility within the top leadership of industry. To what extent is the top leadership in our industries drawn from upper-class and upper-status groups, and to what extent is this leadership drawn from the lower levels of the social scale?

Although evidence in regard to the social origins of top leadership in industry is not conclusive, there are some indications that a rather large proportion of this leadership has originated in the upper levels of society. The classic study of Taussig and Joslyn showed that only about 10 per cent of top leadership in all types of business came from families in which the father was a workingman, skilled, semiskilled or unskilled.[18] About 57 per cent of the fathers of business leaders were major or minor executives or owned large and small businesses. About 45 per cent of the leaders occupied positions in the same firms as their fathers, in a sense "inheriting" their occupations; this, however, was less true in large firms.[19] About 40 per cent of the leaders had had influential connections or private financial aid to help them in their careers. Thus, although a sizable percentage of top leadership was "self-made" to some extent, yet a very sizable and perhaps increasing proportion was not.[20]

Various other pieces of evidence may be put together in an attempt to form a picture of the extent of mobility into the ranks of top leadership. A study of Marion County, Indiana, showed that about 2½ times as many sons of managers, proprietors (of all sizes of establishments), and officials were in the occupational level of their fathers as might be expected statistically. Also heavily represented in this high occupational level were the sons of professionals, clerks, and sales personnel. Below

[18] F. W. Taussig and C. S. Joslyn, *American Business Leaders,* The Macmillan Company, New York, 1952, p. 78, table 17.

[19] *Ibid.,* p. 110, table 45.

[20] These findings have, in a broad way, been confirmed by the study of W. Lloyd Warner and James C. Abeggeln, *Occupational Mobility in American Business and Industry,* University of Minnesota Press, Minneapolis, 1955, chap. II.

"normal" contributions were made by sons of skilled, semiskilled, and unskilled fathers.[21] Centers found that the fathers of large business owners and managers came from the following occupational strata: 18 per cent from large business, 13 per cent from the professions, 30 per cent from small business, 13 per cent from white-collar occupations, 24 per cent from skilled occupations, 1 per cent from semiskilled occupations, and none from unskilled occupations.[22] A study in Massachusetts and in Ohio showed that movement into the level containing industrial leadership was becoming progressively easier, and that this was a long-term trend which has been interrupted only during the depression decade, 1930–1940.[23] North and Hatt found that businessmen came from families where fathers followed these occupations: 31 per cent were businessmen, 18 per cent were skilled workers, 9 per cent were white-collar workers, 8 per cent semiskilled workers, 4 per cent professionals, 3 per cent service workers, 25 per cent farmers, and 2 per cent nonfarm laborers.[24] Davidson and Anderson found in a study of San Jose, California, that 73.1 per cent of proprietors (of all sizes of establishments) had fathers who were likewise proprietors. In 11.5 per cent of the cases the fathers were skilled workers, in 1.4 per cent of the cases semiskilled workers, and 7.2 per cent of the cases unskilled workers.[25] Over 50 per cent of the proprietors began in that occupation; 17 per cent began as professionals, 11.1 per cent as semiskilled workers, 8.9 per cent as clerks, 6.7 per cent as unskilled workers, and 4.4 per cent as skilled workers.[26]

It is difficult to draw definitive conclusions about the extent of mobility into the top levels of industrial leadership. Nevertheless, the following opinions may be tentatively suggested:

1. All studies show that proprietors of all sizes of establishments tend to be drawn heavily from the same or closely related occupational strata. These proportions do not seem to vary significantly whether all proprietors are being considered or big businessmen and industrial executives alone.

2. A sizable proportion of business leadership at all levels is drawn from the working class. In the studies quoted here, business leadership

[21] Natalie Rogoff, *Recent Trends in Occupational Mobility*, Free Press, Glencoe, Ill., 1953, p. 48, table 4.

[22] Richard Centers, "Occupational Mobility of Urban Occupational Strata," *American Sociological Review*, vol. 13, no. 2, p. 203, table 5, 1948.

[23] Stuart Adams, "Trends in Occupational Origins of Business Leaders," *American Sociological Review*, vol. 19, no. 5, pp. 546–547, 1954.

[24] Cecil C. North and Paul K. Hatt, "Jobs and Occupations: A Popular Evaluation," *Opinion News*, Sept. 1, 1947, p. 473.

[25] Percy E. Davidson and H. Dewey Anderson, *Occupational Mobility in an American Community*, Stanford University Press, Stanford, California, 1937, p. 20, table 5.

[26] *Ibid.*, p. 95, table 50.

came from the working class in 10 to 26 per cent of the cases. (In Centers' sample of big businessmen, the figure was 25 per cent.)

3. One must balance the positive versus the negative factors in considering the possibility of entrance into the business class from the lower levels of society. On the one hand, a large number of business and industrial leaders are drawn from that level. On the other hand, there is a small but significant proportion of top-leadership positions open to the ambitious sons of the working class.

At least an equally tentative answer must be given if the question is asked: How much mobility is there into and out of the working class? One type of evidence is furnished by studies of the changing numbers and percentage of individuals in the working class, decade by decade. It can be seen in Table 19 that the ratio of manual workers to the total

Table 19. Distribution of Percentage of Labor Force in Working Class, 1910–1950

Occupational category	1950	1940	1930	1920	1910
Total manual workers.............	49.9	51.5	49.1	49.6	47.9
Skilled workers and foremen........	12.8	11.7	12.9	13.5	11.7
Semiskilled workers...............	*	21.0	16.4	16.1	14.7
Unskilled workers.................	*	18.8	19.8	20.0	21.5

* Figures not available.

SOURCE: A. J. Jaffee and Charles D. Stewart, *Manpower Resources and Utilization*, John Wiley & Sons, Inc., New York, 1951, p. 190, adapted from Table 22.

labor force has not changed significantly since 1910. Skilled workingmen and foremen also were about as numerous proportionately in 1950 as in 1910. However, there has been an interchange between semiskilled and unskilled workers. Where unskilled workers were more numerous than the semiskilled in 1910, the reverse is true today. In terms of total numbers of individuals, there has been little movement out of the working class in the last forty years; this, of course, does not mean that *individuals* have not moved out of this class. There has been, however, a change within the working class in an upward direction.

If this problem is looked at from the point of view of the entire class, rather than of individuals within the class, certain contradictions in facts and trends appear. Centers found, in a national example, that 50 per cent of the skilled workers, 45 per cent of the semiskilled, and 28 per cent of the unskilled workers were in the same occupational level as their fathers. On the other hand, he also found both upward and downward mobility. Thus 31 per cent of semiskilled workers came from families where

the father was a skilled worker, and 47 per cent of the fathers of unskilled workers were skilled or semiskilled workers. On the other side
were these facts: 25 per cent of large business owners and managers
came from working-class homes, 28 per cent of small business owners
and managers, and fully 40 per cent of white-collar workers.[27]

Studies on the local level also reveal various trends in the social mobility of the working class, depending in part on the community studied
and when it was studied. For instance, a study of four Pennsylvania mining towns showed that "inheritance" of mining as an occupation was
common but becoming less so. Where 64.5 per cent of the older of two
generations had followed the same paths as their fathers, only 34.2 per
cent of the younger generation would go into the mines.[28] A study in
Oakland, California, revealed that almost half the workers investigated
had at one time held non-working-class jobs, and over 60 per cent of the
nonmanual workers had at some time held working-class jobs.[29] Forty-
four per cent of skilled workers, 30 per cent of the semiskilled, and 42
per cent of the unskilled had tried at some time to own their own businesses.[30] However, when *all* job shifts were considered, it was found that
these shifts tended to occur *within* the same class, not between classes.
Thus 84.3 per cent of all shifts into skilled jobs had been preceded by
occupancy of other working-class roles; the figures for semiskilled and
unskilled workers were 78.6 per cent and 75.1 per cent respectively.[31]
The study by Davidson and Anderson of San Jose, California, showed a
considerable "inheritance" of jobs in the case of skilled and unskilled
workers (38.8 per cent and 39.5 per cent respectively), but a lower proportion of inheritance in the case of the semiskilled (9.6 per cent).[32]
The skilled workers tended to be more upwardly mobile than the semiskilled and unskilled workers.[33] Finally, the Lynds' study of Middletown
seemed to show that "rising" out of the working class was becoming an
almost impossible task.[34]

[27] Centers, *op. cit.*, p. 203, table 5.
[28] William Wance and Richard Butler, "Industrial Changes and Occupational 'Inheritance' in Four Pennsylvania Communities," *Social Forces,* vol. 27, no. 2, p. 162,
1948.
[29] Seymour M. Lipset and Reinhard Bendix, "Social Mobility and Occupational
Career Patterns. I. Stability of Jobholding," *American Journal of Sociology,* vol. 57,
no. 4, p. 374, 1952. Copyright by the University of Chicago.
[30] Seymour M. Lipset and Reinhard Bendix, "Social Mobility and Occupational
Career Patterns. II. Social Mobility," *ibid.*, no. 5, p. 503, table 23. Copyright by the
University of Chicago.
[31] *Ibid.*, p. 496, table 16.
[32] Percy E. Davidson and H. Dewey Anderson, *Occupational Mobility in an American Community,* Stanford University Press, Stanford, California, 1937, p. 20, table
5. By permission.
[33] *Ibid.*, p. 91, table 47.
[34] Lynd and Lynd, *op. cit.*, p. 71.

The evidence presented here about working-class mobility leads to the following conclusions:

1. The proportional size of the working class is not changing significantly. Its total number is, of course, increasing, but no more rapidly than the population as a whole.

2. The internal structure of the working class has changed significantly. More workers are now in semiskilled jobs than before; fewer are in unskilled jobs. The proportion of skilled workers has remained about the same.

3. From the point of view of individual mobility, the evidence is contradictory or, at least, open to interpretation. This is true both on the national and community levels. A considerable proportion of the working class is not mobile; it tends to remain and work within the class of its origin. However, a sizable proportion *does* move out of the working class, particularly into the white-collar class and into the small-proprietor class.

4. Finally, there is considerable intraclass mobility, on both the local and national levels.

It may be concluded that the American working class is stable in its structural relations to the class system as a whole but that internally its structure is changing. Individuals move freely out of and into this class or between the various levels within the class.

Has unionization tended to change the position of the working class as a whole, or of individuals within the working class? Evidence is not too plentiful here. However, it seems doubtful whether unionism has played a significant part in altering the structure of the working class as a whole.[35] On the other hand, unionism has undoubtedly succeeded to some extent in bettering the position of the working class as a whole; it has improved the generalized rewards of the worker's role and significantly changed the relationships of the working class to the employer in favor of the working class. In so far as unionism has increased the remuneration of the worker, it has increased his ability to buy those symbols which confer prestige in the United States. Thus it may be hazarded that unionism has tended to raise the working class toward a middle-class position.

The unions seem to have had contradictory effects on the mobility of the individual worker. To some extent, they have prevented intraclass mobility by the practice of excluding outsiders from certain jobs. The seniority system has also decreased the mobility of workers, particularly young workers. Perhaps also the fact that the job has been made more

[35] George H. Hildebrand, "American Unionism, Social Stratification, and Power," *American Journal of Sociology*, vol. 58, no. 4, p. 385, 1953. Copyright by the University of Chicago.

attractive by the union has lessened the worker's desire to "rise" out of his class; as his stake has increased in the job, he has tended to postpone his dreams of mobility or abandon them or transfer them to his children. However, the picture should be balanced by noting that the hierarchy of the union has served as a channel of mobility for a small number of workers, who have become union leaders or officials of some sort.

In contrast to the working class, the white-collar class—by which we mean here specifically clerks, office workers, and kindred workers—has been steadily increasing both absolutely and proportionately. Thus whereas white-collar workers numbered about 10 per cent of the labor force in 1910, by 1950 they had increased to almost 20 per cent.[36] This increase in the size of the white-collar class has had this effect on the system of stratification; it has opened up numerous jobs of relatively high rank. And, as we have seen in Chapter 7, a sizable proportion of this increase in white-collar jobs resulted from industry's increasing demand for office help of all kinds.

Rising into the white-collar class is the stated object of many working-class people, either for themselves or for their children. It is, therefore, important to attempt to discover the extent to which this dream approaches reality. Specifically, our problem is to discover how many white-collar workers have originated in the working class. Centers' study showed that 40 per cent of the white-collar workers came from homes with working-class fathers; 26 per cent of the fathers were skilled workers, 11 per cent were semiskilled, and 3 per cent were unskilled.[37] According to Davidson and Anderson, in their study of San Jose, California, 37 per cent of the clerks originated in the working class; 20 per cent were from homes with skilled fathers, 2.7 per cent from homes with unskilled fathers, and in 15 per cent of the cases the fathers were unskilled workingmen.[38] According to Rogoff's study of Marion County, Ohio, the white-collar class was one of the easiest of all classes to enter, though it was true that entrance had been somewhat easier in 1910 than in 1940. Furthermore, this level was open to all comers, with relatively little discrimination shown against individuals in terms of their class backgrounds.[39] The study of Oakland, California, undertaken by Lipset and Bendix, showed that 50 per cent of a sample of white-collar workers and sales personnel had started their careers as manual workers.[40] Finally, Mills found in a study of middle-sized cities that the lower white-collar

---

[36] Jaffee and Stewart, *op. cit.*, p. 190, table 22.

[37] Centers, *op. cit.*, p. 203, table 5.

[38] Davidson and Anderson, *op. cit.*, p. 20, table 5.

[39] Rogoff, *op. cit.*, p. 53, table 8, and p. 54, table 9.

[40] Lipset and Bendix, "Social Mobility and Occupational Career Patterns. II. Social Mobility," p. 498, table 18.

class was tied by marriage, by job history, and by origin both to the working class and to the higher levels of the middle class.[41]

The evidence thus seems to be clear that the white-collar group serves as a channel of mobility to the working class. The white-collar stratum is steadily increasing in numbers, opening up opportunities for the sons and daughters of the working class and for ambitious workers. The studies examined here show that the working class is, by and large, making good on these opportunities. About 40 per cent of the white-collar workers originated in the working class; a sizable proportion of white-collar workers began as manual workers. Thus industry has, by helping to swell the numbers of white-collar jobs, changed the class-structure and social-mobility patterns of American society.

But we must be clear about the sense in which it can be said that movement from the working class to the white-collar class constitutes "rising." As we have seen, the white-collar workers and the manual workers are subject to exactly the same formal relations of production; both groups sell their labor to management, both are subjected to the discipline of the productive process. From this point of view, it is a mistake to think that the worker has risen in the class structure by moving from a working-class job to a white-collar job. On the other hand, it has been shown in Chapter 7 that the white-collar worker is subject to physical conditions and to social relations at work which differ from those of the factory workers. It is by virtue of these differences that the white-collar worker may be said to have risen in the *status structure*. By holding a white-collar job the individual achieves the right to claims of prestige or social honor, to the deference of others, and to the symbols of this deference and honor. Thus the factory girl who becomes a clerk may gain in status among her fellows and may adopt a new mode of dress and address. Since the gain in status is defined as real by both the white-collar worker and the factory worker, then it is real in its consequences, particularly in its psychological consequences.

Whether the relatively high prestige of white-collar jobs will prove to be permanent under modern conditions is another question. We have seen that the factory office is coming to resemble, in its technology and in its organization, the factory itself. We have also seen that trade unionism has served to narrow or close the gap between factory jobs and white-collar jobs in income, in security, and perhaps in prestige also. It is significant that white-collar workers have become an object of union organization. In 1948, over 16 per cent of white-collar workers were in unions, where in 1900 the corresponding figure was $2\frac{1}{2}$ per cent.[42]

[41] Mills, "The Middle Classes in Middle-sized Cities."
[42] C. Wright Mills, *White Collar*, Oxford University Press, New York, 1951, p. 302.

Class and Status Consciousness. Up to this point the class and status systems have been considered objectively, as if they were as visible and tangible as the streets and buildings of a city. But actually we have not determined to what extent the men and women who move within and make up the system of stratification are aware that there is such a system. Do individuals identify with the class or status group to which they have been assigned in this study? Do they feel that they have a chance of rising through the stratificational system? Do they view other strata in society with hostility, with friendliness, or with indifference?

Many students of American life have been intrigued by evidence pointing to the fact that Americans in all walks of life seem to be singularly non-class-conscious. The famous *Fortune* polls seemed to show that, in fact, most Americans considered themselves middle-class.[43] Thus when a sample of individuals was asked whether they were upper-class, middle-class, or lower-class, 7.6 per cent replied upper-class and 79.2 per cent replied middle-class, while 5.3 per cent could not place themselves. Table 20 states the relationship between identification with class and the

Table 20. Relationship between Social and Economic Position of Respondents and Their Identification with Class

Answered that they were	People Who Actually Were				
	Prosperous, per cent	Upper middle, per cent	Lower middle, per cent	Poor, per cent	Negro, per cent
Upper class.........	23.6	7.9	4.6	4.5	16.1
Middle class.........	74.7	89.0	89.4	70.3	35.7
Lower class.........	0.3	0.6	3.1	19.1	26.2
Don't know.........	1.4	2.5	2.9	6.1	22.0

"actual" position in the social structure. From this table we find that 74.7 per cent of the prosperous and 70.3 per cent of the poor considered themselves to be of the middle class.

Numerous other studies have shown that the *Fortune* poll is accurate, at least when the same type of question is used. In a study of Minneapolis, 76 per cent of a sample identified with the middle class, 5 per cent with the upper class, 10 per cent with the lower; the rest of the sample failed to identify with a class.[44] When, in the same study, respondents were asked to name their class without being given alterna-

---

[43] See *Fortune*, February, 1940, pp. 14 and 20, for the figures quoted in this paragraph.
[44] Neal Gross, "Social Class Identification in the Urban Community," *American Sociological Review*, vol. 18, no. 4, p. 401, table 2, 1953.

tives to choose from, there was a surprising vagueness and indecision: 1 per cent said they were upper-class, 31 per cent middle-class, 11 per cent working-class, 3 per cent lower-class, and 54 per cent failed to identify themselves with a class.[45] This same vagueness was uncovered in a study of textile workers in Paterson, New Jersey.[46] Of a sample of 95 workers, only 4 spontaneously identified themselves with classes or referred to classes. This is all the more surprising because Paterson has a long history of industrial strife and union organization.

However, it must not be concluded too quickly that Americans are "middle-class" or free of identification with classes. After all, the terms "middle class," "lower class," and "upper class" may mean many different things to different people. Or people may use other terms when they speak of classes. It would, in fact, be surprising indeed if the great mass of workingmen in the United States, product of the world's greatest industry, were not to some degree cognizant of their position in the social structure.

As a matter of fact, when a national sample was asked to choose between identification with upper class, middle class, lower class, and *working* class, the results were quite revealing. In Table 21 it can be

Table 21. Class Identifications

Class of identification	Per cent saying
Upper class.................	3
Middle class................	43
Working class...............	51
Don't know.................	1
"Don't believe in classes".....	1

SOURCE: By permission from Richard Centers, *The Psychology of Social Classes,* Princeton University Press, Princeton, N.J., 1949, p. 77, table 18.

seen that a majority of the sample identified with the working class. In terms of occupations, 78 per cent of large business leaders identified with the middle class, as did 70 per cent of the white-collar workers. However, one-fourth of the white-collar workers identified with the working class. Significantly, among manual workers more than three-quarters identified with the working class.[47] Centers' findings have been corroborated by other studies.

[45] *Ibid.,* p. 402, table 4.
[46] Jerome G. Manis and Bernard N. Meltzer, "Attitudes of Textile Workers to Class Structure," *American Journal of Sociology,* vol. 60, no. 1, pp. 30–35, 1954. Copyright by the University of Chicago.
[47] Richard Centers, *The Psychology of Social Classes,* Princeton University Press, Princeton, N.J., 1949, p. 85, table 20.

How are these somewhat contradictory findings to be interpreted? It would seem inadmissible to say that this is a "middle-class" country or that there is no class consciousness in the United States. Perhaps the most plausible interpretation of the *Fortune* polls and similar studies is that the choice of terminology could lead only to biased results; not many people can, with equanimity, admit to being of the "lower class." Centers' study shows that Americans are not unconscious of class or unconscious of themselves as members of classes. American workers may not be revolutionary in outlook, but neither are they blind to the differences between themselves and other groups in society; they recognize differences between themselves and others in economic interest, in styles of life, and in culture.

As significant as identification with class is the extent to which the various strata feel that they can *rise* through the social ladder. Since the upper class has "arrived," and in a sense the middle class also, we shall concentrate here on the working class. We have noted that the working class is conscious of the system of stratification as a whole and of their place in it. But does the working-class individual feel that he is "trapped" in his class, or does he feel that the class and status system is a channel for movement upward?

Research on this question reveals seemingly contradictory trends in the workers' thinking. There is very little desire on the part of many American workingmen to attempt to change the class and status system, that is, to revolutionize society. Their thinking proceeds within the framework of the present order of society. Within this order some of them desire to rise, while others are content to remain where they are. Thus, one study of production workers showed that over 43 per cent of the workers in a factory wished to remain where they were, 36 per cent desired nonproduction work, 6.9 per cent supervisory work, and 3.5 per cent clerical work.[48] The ambitions of most workingmen are modest. They do not dream of "rising to the top"; where they dream at all, it is of bettering themselves within their own class. The author of another study has said:[49]

With few exceptions [the workingmen] see little chance of ever rising into salaried positions in the large corporation in which they work. . . . They are clearly aware that engineering and management have become so highly

[48] Robert H. Guest, "Work Careers and Aspirations of Automobile Workers," *American Sociological Review*, vol. 19, no. 2, pp. 155–163, 1954. The other 9.9 per cent of the workers desired jobs in other factories or gave indeterminate answers.

[49] By permission from Ely Chinoy, "The Tradition of Opportunity and the Aspirations of Automobile Workers," *American Journal of Sociology*, vol. 57, no. 5, p. 455, 1952. Copyright by the University of Chicago. Chinoy's study is reported in greater detail in his book, *Automobile Workers and the American Dream*, Doubleday & Company, Inc., New York, 1955.

selective as to exclude them almost completely. . . . Only foremanship, which itself rarely leads to better managerial posts, remains as an obvious escape hatch from wage labor on the factory floor.

And even this seemed to hold little promise for most of the workers who were interviewed.

Yet American workers are Americans; they too may have the American dream of success, of "rising." But this dream has become transformed in the minds of many workers. Perhaps some workers dream of rising to the top through some "lucky break," in the manner copiously pictured by Hollywood. Certainly a very large percentage of workingmen think that their children have as "good a chance or better" to rise in the world as anyone else's children.[50] Many workingmen hope for small advantages within their own class—a better job, better pay, more interesting work.

But probably most workingmen have reconciled themselves to their present job and class position. Thus Centers found that 79 per cent of the workers in his sample were satisfied with their jobs,[51] and 73 per cent replied affirmatively when asked, "Do you think you have as good a chance to enjoy life as you should have?"[52] Perhaps the American workingman feels that his ability to participate in the American way of life— to enjoy a relatively high standard of living, to own an automobile, to take vacations, to buy a television set, to educate his children—are sufficient compensations for his inability to better his class or status positions.

A third important aspect of class consciousness concerns the question of how social classes view each other. Even where there is considerable consciousness of class, there is still room for a wide range in the attitude of classes toward each other. Classes and status groups may regard each other as sworn enemies or as partners in a paternalistic framework, or they may be barely aware of each other's existence.

In America, there is a wide range of differences in interclass feeling, but certain patterns may be detected nevertheless. One clue to these patterns may be found in the attitudes of different strata to the power of other strata. Centers studied the attitude of various classes to the power of the working class. "Do you feel," he asked in effect, "that the working class should have more power than it now does, or no more power?" Almost 75 per cent of the leaders of large enterprises in the sample were not willing to see an increase in working-class power. The white-collar workers were about equally divided on the question. But over 60 per cent of the urban working class favored more power for themselves.[53]

Another clue is provided by the attitudes of various classes to private

[50] Centers, *The Psychology of Social Classes*, p. 148, table 60.
[51] *Ibid.*, p. 149, table 61.
[52] *Ibid.*, p. 150, table 64.
[53] *Ibid.*, p. 60, table 9.

property, particularly to corporate property. Presumably, such attitudes reveal satisfaction or dissatisfaction with the upper class, which has large investments in corporate property and whose power rests on that property. In a study made during the depression years in Akron, Ohio, it was found that industrial executives and business leaders strongly upheld their rights in property and denied the right of other classes to assail their property, no matter what the justification. On the other hand, the working class was much less favorably disposed to the rights of property, though they showed no such unanimity as the upper class. The middle class tended to diverge in their attitudes toward private property; most were moderate, but there was a tendency for many individuals to be drawn toward the position of the upper class or the working class.[54]

This evidence, plus what we know of the bitter strife in American labor history, indicates that there is a certain amount of suspicion and even hostility between the upper class and the working class. However, this suspicion and hostility do not carry, except in a few extreme cases, to the point of revolution. The working class has not gone over to Marxism, with its program for the expropriation of private property; nor has the upper class supported a Fascistlike movement with a program for crushing labor organization. Furthermore, along with this suspicion and hostility between classes, there exist many other attitudes: indifference, ignorance, snobbishness, jealousy, a desire for partnership, or a desire for paternalistic relationships.[55] American workingmen and industrial executives may react to their class positions in terms of identification with and loyalty to their class, they may feel suspicious and resentful of each other, they may even fight each other; but apparently it is not part of their thinking to wish to change the basic framework within which all this happens.

[54] Alfred Winslow Jones, *Life, Liberty and Property*, J. B. Lippincott Company, Philadelphia, 1941, pp. 318–324.
[55] Manis and Meltzer, *op. cit.*, p. 33. All these attitudes were found to exist among the sample of textile workers studied.

CHAPTER 17

Industry and Minority Groups

Thus far we have dealt with the relations between industry and communities as a whole and between industry and social stratification. Now we shall turn to the relations between industry and minority groups, which constitute an important element in the social life of the United States.

Three types of minority groups are usually recognized: racial, ethnic (e.g., nationality background), and religious. In this chapter we shall not deal with religious minorities as such, unless Jews are considered a religious minority. Our concern will be mainly with the relationships of industry, on the one hand, to racial and ethnic minorities on the other. Of these racial and ethnic groups, the main focus of concentration will be on the Negro. This choice is dictated both by limitations of space and by the fact that the Negro is probably the most distinctive minority group in industry today and in many ways constitutes the most vexatious social problem. The integration of the Negro into industry bids fair to be one of the major concerns of our society in the near future. However, we shall make some references, especially when these may be used for comparative purposes, to the position of other racial and ethnic groups in industry.

Immigration and American Industry. Industry in the United States has, historically, drawn its labor supply in good part from various minorities. At an early time Irish immigrants were the machine tenders, laborers, and skilled and semiskilled craftsmen of industry; at later times these roles were shared by Germans, Jews, Poles, Scandinavians, Italians, etc. Wave after wave of these ethnic groups came to the United States, found work in one or more types of industries, usually as unskilled labor, only to be followed by another wave. These waves of immigrants left residues in our cities, which formed the basis of distinct ethnic areas and ethnic subcultures: the Little Italies, the ghettos, Hunkyvilles, and so on.[1] Much

---

[1] The literature on immigration is a very large one. The books mentioned below are a few outstanding examples of work in this field. See the classic work of W. I.

of our industry was founded and grew great on the labor of these ethnic groups; the Irish in the textile industries of New England, the Jews in the garment industry of New York, the Slavs in the mines of Pennsylvania, provided the labor with which America overtook and surpassed all other industrial nations.

In the 1920s this source of labor was finally dammed up by the passage of legislation which strictly limited immigration. But, oddly enough, this limitation has not stopped the successive invasion of industry by one minority group after another. French-Canadians have continued to move into the industry of New England. Mexicans have spread up and down the Mississippi Valley. The Indians of Oklahoma have left their reservations to seek work in the booming industries of the Southwest. "Hillbillies" from Kentucky and Tennessee, and many other Southerners, have poured into the automobile factories of Detroit. Puerto Ricans have moved into the light industries of New York City. And up from the farms, villages, and cities of the South has poured a flood of Negroes, drawn from a minority which numbers no less than one-tenth of the entire population.

Thus, there has always been a close historical relationship between industry and minority peoples in the United States. The reasons for this are manifold. For one thing, immigrant labor, having been most frequently drawn from areas of low standard of living and from economically depressed peoples, has always been cheap labor. Being able to use this labor, American industry was not hampered by the high wage scale which would naturally have resulted from the relative scarcity of labor in a new and underpopulated country and from the presence of an open frontier. Furthermore, immigrant labor has been typically docile and easily disciplined. Immigrants have usually come from authoritarian societies, where the word of those in authority was not to be questioned. This docility was transferred to the factory. Added to this have been the ignorance and low cultural level of many immigrants, which have made them typically impervious, at first, to the propaganda of the union or other movements designed to make them dissatisfied with their lot. Many an American union and many a strike have, in the past, foundered in a sea of recently arrived Slavs or Negroes.

Thomas and F. Znaniecki, *The Polish Peasant in Europe and America,* vols. I–V. The first two volumes were published in 1918, by the University of Chicago Press, Chicago, copyright by the University of Chicago. Volume III was published by the same press in 1919. Volumes IV and V were published by Richard G. Badger, The Gorham Press, Boston, 1920. See also R. E. Park and H. A. Miller, *Old World Traits Transplanted,* Harper & Brothers, New York, 1921; Oscar Handlin, *Boston's Immigrants,* Harvard University Press, Cambridge, Mass., 1941; Oscar Handlin, *The Uprooted,* Little, Brown & Company, 1951.

But perhaps there is a larger reason for the wedding of industry and minority groups in our society. As we have seen in Chapter 4, America never had a native peasantry which could be first displaced from its land and then forced by economic necessity into the factories. Lacking such a potentially mobile peasantry, American industry has perforce turned to whatever sources of labor supply were available. As long as industry continued to expand, new sources of labor had to be found, for technological improvements could not completely fill the gap between production and total demand; this is true even today where industry is expanding rapidly. Thus industry, with a fine disregard for cultural differences, religious hostility, or status claims, has drawn on many different areas of the world for its labor supply, whether this supply has consisted of Russian peasants, Negro sharecroppers, or Mexican peons.

Minority Groups in the Labor Force. It is, unfortunately, impossible to state with accuracy the proportion of minority groups in American industry either in the past or today. A major reason for this difficulty is that our census does not attempt to record the nationality backgrounds of those it counts, except for the foreign-born. However, the census does distinguish between whites and nonwhites, between native-born and foreign born, between native-born of foreign parentage, and native-born of native parentage; thus certain clues are provided to the distribution of minority groups in our industry. Since practically all those listed as nonwhite are, in fact, Negroes, figures on this minority should be reasonably accurate. At the same time, since almost all Negroes are native-born of native parentage, they do not overlap in the census with the "foreign-born" and related categories; thus, we should have a reasonably good picture of the distribution of first- and second-generation immigrants in our industry.

The Position of Negroes in the Labor Force. In 1950 there were over 15 million Negroes in the United States in a total population of about 150 million; that is, Negroes constituted about 10 per cent of the population. Other races—American Indians, Japanese, Chinese—numbered only about 700,000 individuals.[2] Over 82 per cent of the population consisted of native-born whites, and 6.7 per cent of the population was foreign-born. About 67 per cent of the population was of native parentage, 9.8 per cent was of foreign parentage, and 5.8 per cent was of mixed parentage.[3] Assuming that the foreign-born and the native-born of foreign or mixed parentage constitute the backbone of our ethnic groups, then we can estimate that 22 per cent of the American people—about 33 million—are members of ethnic groups of varying distinctiveness.

[2] U.S. Bureau of the Census, *Statistical Abstract of the United States: 1954*, p. 26, table 16, and p. 37, table 26.

[3] *Ibid.*, p. 40, table 31.

Turning now to the place of minority groups in the labor force, we find that in 1950 the Negroes constituted about 10 per cent of the labor force, 6 million colored workers out of a total of 60 million.[4] This represented an increase of about 31 per cent in the proportion of Negroes in the labor force as compared to 1940. These Negro workers were unequally distributed over the country; for instance, in the heavily industrialized Northeast there were about 900,000 Negroes in a labor force of over 16,000,000, while in the South roughly one-fifth of the labor force was composed of Negroes. It is more difficult to estimate the proportion of ethnic-group members, but we may note that in 1940 there were over 11 million foreign-born workers in the labor force,[5] while by 1950 the *total* of foreign-born in the population was only 10 million.[6] Another clue may be found in the fact that the numbers of foreign-born in our cities decreased by about 7 per cent between 1940 and 1950.[7] These decreases must be attributed to the slow attrition by retirement and death of the foreign-born workers. Perhaps there is a foreshadowing here of the eventual disappearance of clear-cut ethnic groups from our industrial system.

Turning now to a closer look at the distribution of Negroes in the occupations, we find that, according to Table 22, of the occupations which include industrial roles, 2 per cent of Negro workers are managers, officials, and proprietors of very small establishments; 4½ per cent are clerks; 5 per cent are skilled workers or foremen; 19 per cent are operatives; and 16 per cent are common laborers. As compared to the distribution of white workers in the labor force, in the urban North and West there are fewer Negro professionals, proprietors, managers, officials, clerical workers, craftsmen (except among college graduates), and operatives (except among Negroes who have completed high school or college). On the other hand, there are proportionately more Negroes who are laborers and service workers than there are white workers in the same fields.[8] It should be noted that Negro workers in industry are almost exclusively operatives. Negro industrial enterprisers are extremely rare. The white-collar jobs which Negroes hold are found almost entirely in the government. Industry employs very few Negro specialists.

[4] *Ibid.*, p. 197, table 221.
[5] Donald J. Bogue, "Urbanism in the United States, 1950," *American Journal of Sociology*, vol. 60, no. 5, p. 483, table 6, 1955.
[6] Frederick B. Parker, "The Status of the Foreign Stock in the Southeast: A Region-Nation Comparison," *Social Forces*, vol. 27, no. 2, p. 141, table 6, 1948. Copyright by the University of Chicago.
[7] U.S. Bureau of the Census, *Census of Population: 1950*, vol. II, *Characteristics of the Population*, part I, United States Summary, 1953, pp. 1–122, table 71.
[8] Ralph H. Turner, "Occupational Patterns of Inequality," *American Journal of Sociology*, vol. 59, no. 5, p. 440, table 3, 1954. Copyright by the University of Chicago.

Table 22. Numbers and Percentage of Negro Labor Force in Certain Occupational Classes, 1950

Major occupational group	Number of Negro workers	Per cent of Negro workers
Total employed, 14 years and over...................	5,376,917	100
Professional, technical, and kindred workers...........	179,188	3
Farmers and farm managers........................	502,088	9
Managers, officials, and proprietors, except farm.......	94,966	2
Clerical, sales, and kindred workers..................	250,606	4½
Craftsmen, foremen, and kindred workers.............	282,427	5
Operatives and kindred workers.....................	1,009,849	19
Private household workers..........................	821,623	16
Service workers, except private household.............	820,699	16
Farm laborers....................................	498,046	9
Laborers, except farm and mine.....................	844,163	16

SOURCE: U.S. Bureau of the Census, *Statistical Abstract of the United States: 1954*, p. 41, table 32. The rough percentage figures have been computed by the present author.

Table 23. Percentage of Negro Workers in Occupational Classes, 1940 and 1950

Occupational class	Percentage distribution		Difference
	1940	1950	
Professionals...........................	2.6	3.0	+0.4
Proprietors, managers, officials...........	16.1	11.0	−5.1
Clerks and kindred workers..............	2.2	4.5	+2.3
Skilled workers and foremen..............	2.9	5.0	+2.1
Semiskilled and unskilled workers.........	76.2	76.0	−0.2

SOURCE: The figures for 1940 are taken, by permission, from *Negroes in American Society*, by Maurice R. Davie, McGraw-Hill Book Company, Inc., New York, 1949, p. 112. The figures for 1950 are derived from table 22.

To what extent are Negroes moving up and down the occupational ladder? By looking at Table 23 it will be seen that between 1940 and 1950 there was almost no change in the percentage of unskilled and semi-skilled Negro workers. This does not mean that there was no change in the types of jobs held by Negroes; as we shall see directly below, there was a considerable shift of Negroes into industry during this period. There were sizable percentage increases among Negro craftsmen, fore-men, clerks, and kindred workers. The decrease in the numbers of proprietors, managers, and officials is probably to be attributed to the Negro exodus from farming. Negro professionals increased only slightly during the decade. Thus it can be concluded that, in relation to classes of occupations (not to individuals), the great mass of Negro workers experienced little mobility between 1940 and 1950, unless the shift into industry is itself to be considered evidence of mobility in a vertical direction.

To what extent are Negroes individually mobile? The very narrowness of numbers in Negro occupational classes above the level of semiskilled and unskilled indicates that there could be little upward mobility for the mass of Negroes. This is born out in Rogoff's study of Marion County, Ohio. Rogoff found that the sons of Negro skilled workers, professionals, and clerks were more likely to enter unskilled work or service work than to follow their father's occupations. For the sons of unskilled workers, the chances were 13 to 1 that they would "inherit" their father's occupation.[9] It is interesting to compare this situation with that of the sons of foreign-born whites. In 1910, the second generation was, perhaps, at a slight disadvantage as compared to the sons of native Americans in the same classes. But in 1940 the second generation was, if anything, more mobile in an upward direction than "native Americans" in the same occupational classes. This indicates, perhaps, that by 1940 ethnicity had ceased to be much of a handicap in the race for mobility; the situation is in sharpest contrast to that of the Negro.

Further evidence for the comparative lack of mobility of the Negro in our occupational structure may be found in a comparison of the extent to which the two races can use education as a channel of upward mobility. It will be noted from Table 24 that, as education increases, there is a greater movement of whites into "higher" occupations than of Negroes. To take an example, among whites who finish high school there is a decrease of over 16 per cent in the numbers of operatives as compared to white elementary school graduates; among Negroes the corresponding decrease is only 3.2 per cent. Furthermore, there are indications here of differing definitions of mobility as among Negroes and whites. College graduation meant for whites a decrease of about 10 per cent in clerical occupations as compared to white high school graduates. Among Negro college graduates there was an increase of almost 4 per cent in clerical jobs. Perhaps Negroes do not raise their sights as high as do whites, even when, educationally speaking, they have a right to do so.

We may say, then, that minority groups form an important part of our labor force and that the Negro in particular forms an important part of

[9] Natalie Rogoff, *Recent Trends in Occupational Mobility*, Free Press, Glencoe, Ill., 1953, p. 72, table 20. For whites the chances were between 3 and 4 to 1 that the sons of unskilled workers would become, in turn, unskilled workers.

Table 24. Percentage Differences of Changes in the Occupational Levels of Negroes and Whites as Education Increases, 1940, Urban North and West

Occupational category	Per cent increase of those having 7–8 years of grade school over those having 5 years or less		Per cent increase of high school graduates over elementary school graduates		Per cent increase of college graduates over high school graduates	
	Native white	Negro	Native white	Negro	Native white	Negro
Professional..............	−.2	.5	4.5	2.9	48.6	44.1
Proprietors and farmers...	.8	−.1	8.3	.3	.4	3.4
Clerical workers..........	4.8	2.4	20.0	7.6	−9.9	3.8
Craftsmen...............	5.5	1.0	−7.5	2.5	−13.6	−7.0
Operatives...............	−1.1	−1.0	−16.1	−3.2	−16.2	−14.7
Labor and services........	−10.9	−2.9	−9.2	−9.0	−10.0	−30.0

SOURCE: Derived, by permission, from Ralph H. Turner, "Occupational Patterns of Inequality," *American Journal of Sociology*, vol. 59, no. 5, p. 439, table 1.

that force. Well over 20 per cent of the Negro labor force is employed in industry. As compared to the white workers, Negroes occupy the lower occupational levels and have considerably less chance for rising.

Negroes in American Society. Since Negroes form a large and growing portion of our labor force, it is important to study their position in the community as a whole.[10] In the South, the Negro's position in the community has, in the past, and to some extent in the present, resembled that of a caste. That is, the Negro has been forbidden to intermarry with whites, to eat with whites, or in any other way to associate with whites on a plane of equality. A rigid etiquette has surrounded the relations of the races; modes of address, gestures of deference, patterns of commingling in public places—all have been rigidly prescribed by the dominant group. It is true that in some ways the Negro's position is uncastelike; he is not confined to a single occupation as in India, nor is his position in

[10] Unfortunately we do not have time to go into the intricate questions and debates which surround the problem of the Negro's position in society. It is expected that the reader will have some knowledge of these debates. For a defense of the caste hypothesis, see the following: Allison Davis, Burleigh Gardner, and Mary Gardner, *Deep South*, University of Chicago Press, Chicago, 1941, copyright by the University of Chicago (see the introduction by W. L. Warner); Gunnar Myrdal, *An American Dilemma*, Harper & Brothers, New York, 1944; John Dollard, *Caste, and Class in a Southern Town*, Yale University Press (for the Institute of Human Relations), New Haven, Conn., 1937. For a general attack on the caste hypothesis, see Oliver Cromwell Cox, *Caste, Class and Race*, Doubleday & Company, Inc., New York, 1948.

society sanctioned by religion. But, on the balance, it seems useful to employ the term "caste" when describing the position of the Negro in the South, although this position is rapidly changing.[11]

In the North, on the other hand, the use of the term "caste" can only serve to obscure and distort the general picture. Negroes are not, in the North, bound by a caste etiquette; for instance, they are not, and cannot be, compelled to sit in the back of busses or to use separate washrooms. Intermarriage with whites and other social familiarities are, it is true, rare, but not as a result of caste restraints. Rather, the position of the Negroes in the North resembles more that of a recently arrived ethnic group, which is suffering the disadvantages of humble background, poverty, lack of education, and general dislike by better-entrenched earlier arrivals. That is, in the North, the position of the Negroes is that of a discriminated-against minority but one which, like other such minorities, has political power and social and economic ambitions. In the North, the Negro, in spite of his high physical visibility, tends to merge into the ethnic mosaic which makes up our urban civilization.

The position of the Negro in society—his castelike position in the South and the discrimination to which he is subjected in the North—has certain definite effects on his life chances. We have already seen that the Negro tends to fill the lowest occupational roles, both within and without industry. His occupational position is directly and indirectly the result of his position in society. In the South, the caste system relegates the Negro to the hardest, dirtiest, and worst-paid occupations and effectively prevents him from rising. In the North, the Negro has arrived too recently to have had a chance as yet to follow other ethnic groups up the occupational ladder. Besides, even in the North, discrimination against the Negro is strong—stronger perhaps than the discrimination which other minority groups have faced and partially overcome.

As might be expected from the distribution of Negroes in occupational roles, their income is considerably lower on the average than that of whites. Table 25 shows that, in 1950, 28 per cent of Negro families were getting under $1,000 a year, as compared to 10 per cent of white families; 77 per cent of Negro families had incomes of less than $3,000 a year, but this was true of only 40 per cent of white families. The median income of white families was not far from twice as high as the median income of Negro families.

[11] For a very readable account of this change, see Alan Paton, "The Negro in America Today," *Colliers*, Oct. 15, 1954, pp. 52–56, 60, 62, 64, 66. The decision of the Supreme Court on May 17, 1955, that state laws providing for the segregation of Negro and white children in separate schools are unconstitutional is bound to have drastic effects on the position of the Negro, particularly in the South, although the first reaction of many Deep Southern states was to seek ways and means to circumvent the Court's decision.

Table 25. Comparison of Percentage of Negro and White Families Having
Specified Incomes, 1950

Family income	Cumulative per cent of white families	Cumulative per cent of Negro families
Under $1,000............	10	28
$1,000–$1,999............	22	53
2,000– 2,999............	39.5	77
3,000– 3,999............	61	90
4,000– 4,999............	75	95
5,000– 5,999............	85	97
6,000– 6,999............	90	98
7,000– 9,999............	96.4	99.8
$10,000 and over.........	99.9	100
Median income..........	$3,445	$1,869

SOURCE: U.S. Bureau of the Census, ser. P-60, no. 9, Mar. 25, 1952.

Furthermore, Negroes were much more prone to unemployment and layoff than were whites. They suffered more intensively from unemployment during the depression of the 1930s than did the white workers. Even in March, 1950, when the American economy was recovering from the mild recession, over 13 per cent of Negro males and 11 per cent of Negro women were out of work, as compared with 7.4 per cent of male white workers and 6.5 per cent of white female workers.[12]

The low standard of living of the Negro people is a reflection of the social and economic realities of Negro life. Notoriously poor Negro housing, which is one of the grimmest problems facing many American cities, is the combined result of segregation, overcrowding, low cultural level, and low income. Most Negroes must live in slums or near slums, and Negro children are exposed to all the normal hazards of slum life.

Other indexes of low Negro life chances are found in infant-mortality rates, in life-expectancy rates, and in educational achievement. Life expectancy for a Negro male baby born in 1950 was over seven years less than for a white male baby; for a Negro girl baby, expectancy of life, though higher than for Negro males, was over nine years less than for a white girl baby.[13] In 1950 infant-mortality rates among Negroes were almost twice as high as for white babies.[14] In general, the greater the con-

---

[12] These figures are taken from Morris Fine and Jacob Sloan (eds.) *The American Jewish Year Book, 1951,* The American Jewish Committee and the Jewish Publication Society of America, New York, 1951, p. 29.

[13] U.S. Bureau of the Census, *Statistical Abstract of the United States, 1954,* p. 76, table 71.

[14] *Ibid.,* p. 74, table 75.

centration of Negroes in an area in which a Negro baby was born, the less was the chance of his surviving the first year of life.[15]

Although an equivalent amount of education provides whites with better chances for rising than Negroes, nevertheless, education remains one of the few channels through which Negroes may rise in society. The amount of education received is both a reflection of the life chances of Negroes and an important determinant of those chances. Table 26 shows that, in 1950, over 40 per cent of Negroes 25 years or older had had less than 5 years of education as compared with about 11 per cent of whites having that little education. Only 4.4 per cent of Negroes had finished high school, as compared with 15 per cent of whites. The disadvantaged position of the Negro in respect to life chances may be found in each of the categories described in the table. Thus the chances of most Negroes for using education as a road to higher status in society were quite poor.

Table 26. Comparison of Percentage of Negroes and Whites, 25 and over, Receiving Specified Amounts of Education, 1950

Race	Grammar school education			High school education		College education	
	Less than 5 years	5–7 years	8 years	1–3 years	4 years	1–3 years	4 years
White......	10.8	17.2	29.4	15.6	15.1	5.8	4.9
Nonwhite...	41.1	29.4	11.7	8.5	4.4	1.9	1.3

SOURCE: U.S. Bureau of the Census, *Statistical Abstract of the United States, 1954*, p. 121, table 135.

To sum up, the Negro in American society is a strongly discriminated-against minority at the best, and a member of a lower caste at the worst. His social position determines his relatively poor life chances. He is relegated to the poorest jobs and provided with relatively low income. His chances for survival, for long life, and for education are adversely affected by his social and economic position.

The Negro in Industry in the Past. The position of the Negro in industry is strongly influenced by certain peculiarities of Negro history. The great mass of Negroes has always lived in the Southern states, as a residue of the slavery system; even today three-fourths of all Negroes are found there. Negroes have worked in Southern industry since the Civil War, though in undesirable jobs. As the South has been industrialized, the numbers of Negroes in industry have gradually increased; however,

[15] Alfred Yankauer, Jr., "The Relationship of Fetal and Infant Mortality to Residential Segregation," *American Sociological Review*, vol. 15, no. 5, p. 645, table 1, 1950.

this increase has not been nearly at the same rate as the increase in the rate of white workers in industry. By 1940, Negroes were fairly heavily represented in such Southern industries as the chemical industry, the logging industry, and the railroad industry. However, almost all Negro jobs are unskilled or semiskilled; for instance, in the railroad industry, Negroes were largely maintenance men.

In the North, there were relatively few Negroes at all, prior to about 1910. The great expansion of American industry in the latter half of the nineteenth century had been built on the labor of North Europeans (Irish, German, and British) and later on the labor of Southern and Eastern Europeans (Italians, Poles, Russians, Jews, and so on). The Negro, for reasons which are not entirely clear as yet, did not participate in this movement into industry, in spite of his dire economic necessity and the increasing social discrimination which were his lot in the South.[16] But in 1910 a great migration of Negroes to Northern cities began. Between 1910 and 1920 the Negro population of New York, Chicago, Philadelphia, and Detroit increased by more than three-fourths of a million.[17] Perhaps the major lure that the North held for these Negroes was the possibility of securing jobs in war-swollen industries, even if these jobs were not always desirable by white standards. Another factor in this early Negro migration was the desire of some Northern employers to use the Negro to break unions or strikes. The Negro was well suited to the role of strike-breaker. Often he felt that his natural enemy was the white worker who tried to exclude him from jobs. Furthermore, he was willing to work for low wages, and his docility was assured. By 1930 there were sizable numbers of Negroes working in Northern blast furnaces, steel-rolling mills, coal mines, and automobile factories, in the clothing industry, and in the meat-packing industry.[18] As in the South, almost all these jobs were unskilled or, at the best, semiskilled.

The depression which began in 1929 struck a hard blow at the Negro worker, South and North. It is a measure of the strength of this blow that, in the North, the number of employed Negroes remained almost stationary throughout the decade of the 1930s while the *total* Negro population in the North increased by 23 per cent. For the country as a whole, in 1940 about 12½ per cent of the white labor force was unemployed, but over 19 per cent of the Negro working force was unemployed.[19] Even preparations for World War II, and then the war itself, which opened a host of jobs for white workers, offered few opportunities

---

[16] Myrdal, *op. cit.*, pp. 195–198.
[17] E. Franklin Frazier, *The Negro in the United States*, The Macmillan Company, New York, 1949, p. 191.
[18] Myrdal, *op. cit.*, p. 294.
[19] *Ibid.*, p. 298, table 5.

to the Negroes at first. It was only through the demand for war goods and after great pressure had been applied by the Negroes and their supporters that Negroes were admitted into industry. However, once this process began they made significant gains in industry, entering many fields and jobs from which they had been barred previously. For instance, in the field of electrical equipment, where practically no Negroes were working in 1942, they constituted almost 5 per cent of the working force by January, 1945. For war industries as a whole, Negro workers increased from 5.8 per cent of the total in July, 1942, to 8.2 per cent of the working force in January, 1945.[20] The number of Negroes employed as skilled workers and as semiskilled workers doubled during the war period.[21]

To what extent did the Negro retain his gains in industry after the war ended? His situation immediately after the war was not favorable; jobs in war industries were, of course, lost, while the end of the FEPC (discussed below) removed the shield of government protection from the Negro's job. However, the relatively full employment which the country has enjoyed since World War II has favored the Negro's attempt to maintain his foothold in industry. Unskilled and semiskilled jobs have remained relatively numerous; there are proportionately as many Negro "operatives" in the labor force as there are "operatives" in the labor force as a whole.[22] Skilled Negro workers and foremen have increased in numbers since 1940.[23] Thus it seems safe to say that, barring a catastrophic depression, the Negro is today firmly established in industry. His position seems fairly secure even in those fields which he has entered only recently and which are not traditionally "Negro" fields.

The Integration of Minority Groups in American Industry. There are certain similarities in the histories of ethnic groups in American industry. First, a demand is created for labor, either by the location of a factory within the living area of a minority group[24] or by the creation or expansion of industry in another place. Secondly, the members of the minority group are attracted to the industry, either because of the higher wages which can be earned there, or because of the excitement of working in the city, or because of economic need. Thirdly, the minority group members enter the factory at the bottom level, filling the unskilled roles,

[20] Robert C. Weaver, *Negro Labor*, Harcourt, Brace and Company, Inc., New York, 1946, p. 80, table 1.
[21] Davie, *op. cit.*, p. 96.
[22] Thus 20.3 per cent of the working force as a whole was composed of "operatives and kindred workers"; the figure for the Negro working force was 19 per cent. See Chap. 16, Table 7, and in this chapter, Table 22.
[23] See Table 22.
[24] For an account of a case of this sort, see Everett Cherrington Hughes, *French Canada in Transition*, University of Chicago Press, Chicago, 1943. Copyright by the University of Chicago. Cases of this sort are rare in American history.

performing the hard, "mean," dirty jobs. Their entrance is bitterly opposed by the earlier arrivals. Fourth, a struggle develops between earlier arrivals who hold the better positions in the factory—who are skilled workers and foremen—and the new arrivals who quickly begin to strive for the better things they see about them. This struggle sometimes involves physical violence. More often it is fought out by discriminating against the new arrivals. The ranks of the entrenched groups are closed to the new arrivals. Mythologies are created respecting the superiority of the entrenched group and the natural ineptitude of the new group. Derogatory names are applied to the out-group. Fifth, the new minority breaks through the walls erected by the entrenched older workers, perhaps in a crisis such as might be brought on by a war, perhaps through superior energy. The newly successful group then consolidates the ground it has won; it sees to it that only compatriots are hired or promoted. It reserves the best jobs for itself. Sixth, the cycle begins over again with the arrival of a new group.

This, in brief, has been the oft-repeated story of ethnic groups in our industry. We have suggested that Negroes constitute an ethniclike minority in the North, albeit heavily discriminated against. If this hypothesis is correct, then the Negro should be, at the present time, launched on the preliminary stages of this cycle.

In our examination of the position of the Negro in the industrial labor force, we found that he is either excluded from certain industries or is concentrated in the unskilled and semiskilled jobs in other industries. Here and there he has made certain important break-throughs into skilled work, largely as the result of the wars. It is only in isolated instances that Negroes are as yet permitted even as high as minor supervisory positions.[25] Thus, by and large, the Negro is now in the second and third phases of the cycle described above and is heading directly into the fourth and fifth phases of this cycle. Evidences of physical violence between Negroes and whites are, fortunately, rare, but there can be little doubt that Negroes are meeting social and verbal opposition from white workers in many industries. Several studies have shown that the lower socioeconomic groupings are at least as prejudiced against Negroes as other groupings; in fact, perhaps more prejudiced.[26] The continued existence of discrimination in some trade unions, which is discussed later in this chapter, is further proof of the resistance of some white workers to the industrial advancement of Negroes. However, the

[25] See Frank F. Lee, "The Relations Pattern by Areas of Behavior in a Small New England Town," *American Sociological Review,* vol. 19, no. 2, p. 141, 1954.
[26] See Frank R. Westie, "Negro-White Status Differentials and Social Distance," *American Sociological Review,* vol. 17, no. 5, p. 554, table 2, 1952; Eugene L. Horowitz, " 'Race' Attitudes," in Otto Klineberg (ed.), *Characteristics of the American Negro,* Harper & Brothers, New York, 1944, part IV; Myrdal, *op. cit.,* pp. 388–390.

opposition which the Negro is meeting in industry, though it borrows from the language of caste, is not a continuation of caste into industry; it is the "normal" result of the ethnic cycle we have described, though the situation is exacerbated, no doubt, by the tradition of race prejudice and discrimination in this country.

Any minority group faces a hard fight in attempting to break through the "unskilled" phase of the ethnic cycle. This problem has two aspects. On the one hand, the minority group must master the industrial technology. But these minority groups are handicapped by their background, culture, and training. Negroes, who are, in effect, first-generation immigrants, share the handicaps of these ethnic minorities. Like these latter, Negroes have been hampered by lack of education, or by lack of the proper type of education.[27] Like other first-generation immigrants, the newly industrialized Negro has had to acquire new skills, aptitudes, and habits, knowledge of machine techniques, habits of promptness, an ability to yield to discpline. Furthermore, even where he has mastered skilled trades, the Negro, like other first-generation immigrants, has been exposed to the hazards of demotion to unskilled work, as a result of technological changes. Rationalization plans and the introduction of new machines and processes are often carried on at the expense of semi-skilled or skilled jobs, thereby often destroying whatever foothold the Negro may have gained in those roles.[28]

On the other hand, the minority group must somehow integrate itself into the social system of the factory. Here the problem is to establish successful social relationships with fellow workers and with management. For the Negro, these are specially difficult problems. When he enters the factory, he finds himself in the midst of an impersonal, neutral bureacracy, in which he is supposedly being evaluated by universalistic criteria: e.g., efficiency, dependability, skill, etc. But, as we have seen, he also finds a complex system of informal groups, cliques, friendships, and alliances functioning to safeguard the interests of the members of various sections of the plant. Many of these informal groups and relationships are organized on ethnic bases. For instance, one student of industry found that in a factory in which he worked, the informal association functioned to preempt certain jobs and privileges for certain minority members and to exclude other minority members.[29] Similarly, it was found in a shoe factory in New England that the members of one high-ranking ethnic group dominated a desir-

---

[27] Weaver, *op. cit.*, pp. 41–60.

[28] *Ibid.*, pp. 97–108.

[29] Orvis Collins, "Ethnic Behavior in Industry: Sponsorship and Rejection in a New England Factory," *American Journal of Sociology*, vol. 51, no. 4, pp. 293–298, 1946. Copyright by the University of Chicago.

able department, received a superior wage, and excluded all others.[30] Still a third study found that the informal groups of a plant posed a formidable barrier to the advancement of Negroes; they were excluded from practically all informal activities which were necessary for successful maneuvering through the social structure of the factory.[31] These examples might be multiplied, but they all point to the same general conclusion: the Negro must somehow leap over the barrier posed by informal organization if he is to become firmly established in the more desirable roles of industry.

How can the Negro succeed in piercing the walls which the white worker erects against him in industry? On occasion he has broken his way through the white barriers by grim force: by acting as a strikebreaker, or by underbidding white labor. On other occasions economic necessity, shared alike by whites and Negroes, has broken down the walls of discrimination and exclusion, at least in certain areas. In industries like the packing industry and the automobile industry, a common need has drawn whites and Negroes together, at least for certain aims; e.g., in strikes and during organizing drives. Sometimes the union has led the fight against white exclusionism, although at other times it has abetted it. On rare occasions Negroes have succeeded in entering informal white groups on an individual basis and gaining status there, but such Negroes are exceptions and are usually extraordinarily adept at getting along with whites.[32] Finally, Negroes may achieve toleration by whites through a process of mass education. But such a program usually requires the cooperation of management, union, and the community and has been tried only during wartime, and then on a limited scale.

The relation of management to the Negro in industry cannot be described simply. In the past, and to a lesser extent in the present, management has sometimes welcomed the Negro as a source of cheap, if inefficient, labor, or as a strikebreaker. More often, however, management has not been anxious to take Negroes into its plants or to upgrade them if they already are in the plant. Some managers share the general attitudes toward Negroes; these managers feel that Negroes are lazy, or childlike, or undependable, or, at any rate, that they are unsuited to machine work. Since Negroes are seldom given the opportunity to acquire mechanical skills, the prejudice of these managers is reinforced. But probably, in most cases, management decides on the exclusion or

---

[30] W. Lloyd Warner and J. O. Low, *The Social System of the Modern Factory,* Yale University Press, New Haven, Conn., 1947, pp. 92–95.

[31] Everett Cherrington Hughes, "The Knitting of Racial Groups in Industry," *American Sociological Review,* vol. 11, no. 5, pp. 512–519, 1946.

[32] Everett Cherrington Hughes, "Race Relations in Industry," in William Foote Whyte (ed), *Industry and Society,* McGraw-Hill Book Company, Inc., New York, 1946, p. 115.

inclusion of Negroes on bases other than its own prejudices.[33] Most often management excludes Negroes because it feels that the introduction of Negroes would disrupt the social structure of the factory, that it would arouse discontent and apprehension among workers who would fear that Negroes might underbid their labor. Management argues that old prejudices and hatreds will be revived; for instance, whites will object to Negro men and white women working side by side. It is held that under these circumstances reduction in efficiency, labor turnover, even wildcat strikes are distinct possibilities. Management may also fear the increased expense involved in separate facilities for Negroes and whites: washrooms, cafeterias, etc.[34] Since management is in business for profit, not social reform, the wisest course (according to this point of view) is to exclude Negroes, or to admit them only to the most menial tasks and to deny them promotion, or to tolerate them only in times of great manpower shortages.

However, there is good evidence to indicate that the fears of management may be exaggerated. If management is determined to follow a policy of equality in its plants, and if it follows certain techniques in hiring, introducing, and upgrading Negroes, white workers will usually learn to accept the Negroes as fellow workers, though perhaps not as social equals. The success of a plan of integration depends, first, on the strength of management's determination to back the plan. When the hiring or upgrading of Negroes is announced, there will always be a certain amount of verbal opposition. Some of this is the result of prejudice; some arises from the natural dislike and fear of many working-men for any new *type* of worker.[35] Experience has shown that if management announces, firmly, that it will accept the resignations of whites who cannot tolerate Negroes, relatively few whites will quit their jobs.

Secondly, the success of a program of integration depends on the skill with which the program is conducted. Education of the white workers, especially if this is undertaken with the backing of the union, may be valuable. An attempt to allay the natural fears of the white workers as to wage cuts and job security should probably be made, again with union help if possible. Some plants have adopted the policy of introducing Negroes gradually or upgrading them one at a time; the mass introduction or upgrading of Negroes seems to be especially frightening

[33] This is indicated by a study by Henry Allen Bullock, "Racial Attitudes and the Employment of Negroes," *American Journal of Sociology*, vol. 56, no. 5, p. 453, 1951. Copyright by the University of Chicago.

[34] Clara A. Hardin, *The Negroes of Philadelphia* (privately printed), Bryn Mawr, Pa., 1945, p. 54.

[35] See Chap. 14, "Theories of the Labor Movement," for a discussion of the psychology of the workingman. Note how Perlman's concept of "scarcity consciousness" may be used to explain the discrimination practiced by white workers against Negroes.

to many white workers. It should be emphasized that the aim of a program such as this is not social equality; the aim is to get the white workers to accept and tolerate the Negro in the factory, just as he is accepted and tolerated (in the North) in schools, busses, or baseball parks.

Experience gained during World War II and since then shows that this type of program can be successful, though, of course, failures may occur also. One example of a successful program is supplied by the experience of a large aviation plant during World War II. Although 48 per cent of the employees of this plant objected to the use of Negroes, most employees had come to accept and tolerate Negroes within about two years after the policy of hiring them was begun. A very small group of white workers resigned rather than work next to Negroes. A much larger group came to tolerate Negroes but remained aloof from them in all matters not connected with work. A sizable group developed some in-plant friendships with Negroes, but there was little socializing outside of the plant. Management used three tactics in its successful program: first, since it was wartime, a patriotic appeal was made to the white workers to accept the Negroes; second a humanitarian appeal was made; and third, workers were reminded of the possibility of dismissal if they tried to thwart management's policy, which was then government policy also.[36] Similarly, another study showed that in the North, even in a plant which employed a sizable proportion of "hillbillies," race relations could remain harmonious if management were determined to have it so.[37] Finally, still another study showed that even in the South, a determined and enlightened policy on Negro integration was perfectly feasible.[38]

It may be reiterated that the Negro is following a well-marked path in industry, the path beaten out by other minority groups. It is true that the Negro's position is worse than that of other minority groups because (1) he is highly visible; (2) in one large section of the country he is caught within a net of caste; and (3) in all sections of the country there is a long tradition of prejudices and discrimination against him. However, these disadvantages may be overcome. In order to do so, Negroes will have to make an all-out effort, but the success of this effort can be made fairly certain with the help of management and the unions.

[36] Bernice Anita Reed, "Accommodation between Negro and White Employees in a West Coast Aircraft Industry, 1942–1944," *Social Forces,* vol. 26, no. 1, pp. 76–84, 1947.
[37] Lewis M. Killian, "The Effects of Southern White Workers on Race Relations in Northern Plants," *American Sociological Review,* vol. 17, no. 3, pp. 327–331, 1952.
[38] John Hope II, *Selected Studies of Negro Employment in the South,* case study 1, *Negro Employment in Three Southern Plants of International Harvester Co.,* National Planning Association, Washington, 1953.

Negroes and Trade Unions. The relations between Negroes and trade unions both in the past and today have been ambiguous to a high degree. Some of the earlier unions, including the National Labor Union and the Knights of Labor, were willing to admit the Negro, recognizing in him an important part of the working class as well as a potential threat to white labor.[39] Left-wing unions have also made more or less determined efforts to enroll the Negro worker in union ranks. Throughout the course of American labor history, isolated examples can be found of Negro-white solidarity in both unions and strikes.

However, until the advent of the CIO, the relationships between the Negro and the union was often one of hostility. When the AFL rose to power following the demise of the Knights of Labor, it established a policy of exclusionism or discrimination against the Negro. In attempting to understand this policy, one should not make the mistake of thinking that the AFL aimed at upholding the caste system. As we have seen, the AFL was composed of independent craft unions, enrolling the elite of the American workers: carpenters, plumbers, skilled machinists, etc. This elite felt itself threatened from several directions. For one thing, the waves of immigrants who were pouring into America in the latter half of the nineteenth century posed a grave threat to the skilled native worker; one of the major early aims of the AFL was to eliminate the threat from the immigrant. The Negro also represented a potential or actual threat to the native white's monopoly of skilled jobs. In some ways the Negro was even more threatening than the immigrant. The Negro, unlike the immigrant, was a product of the American culture, familiar with the language and values of the country. Furthermore, he had inherited from slavery a reservoir of skills; during slavery, and for a long time thereafter in the South, Negroes were skilled carpenters, plumbers, masons, etc. Thus the policy of craft unions toward the Negro was a harsh one. He was to be kept out of skilled jobs at all costs; he was to be relegated to inferior jobs, kept out of unions, or segregated in separate locals. Purely as a policy, the AFL program was a success; the skilled jobs became purely white jobs and have remained so largely to this day.

The Negro had no choice but to accept the situation imposed upon him by the craft unions. As a result, he came to recognize in the union a natural barrier to his progress—in fact, a determined enemy. It was partly for this reason that he was willing to act as a strikebreaker; the union which excluded him could hardly appeal to him in terms of working-class solidarity. One segment of Negroes came to look upon

[39] Sterling D. Spero and Abram L. Harris, *The Black Worker*, Columbia University Press, New York, 1931, pp. 23–40.

strikes as golden opportunities; in fact, entrance into a number of industries was gained in just this way.[40] Excluded by the unions, the Negro gave his support to the white employer. In doing this he was following the slave tradition of seeking the protection and benevolence of a powerful white man; but at the same time he was expressing his own fundamental distrust of the white worker. Thus there has been a long history in the United States of bitter hostility between unions and Negroes, exacerbated no doubt by caste and discrimination, but not essentially different from the traditional struggle between the skilled and the unskilled worker, between the native and the immigrant.

The unionization of Negroes, except in isolated industries, did not begin until the rise of the CIO. The CIO unions attempted to sign up *all* workers—skilled, semiskilled, unskilled. This was not only an idealistic aim for the leaders of the CIO; it was an important element of strategy. Relying on the solidarity of the workers to counter the power of management, the CIO could not afford to risk divisions in its ranks by excluding any group from its organization.[41] Thus for both idealistic and practical reasons the CIO appealed to all workers, even those who came from the most prejudiced backgrounds, to lay aside the bitter memories of strikebreaking, discrimination, and prejudice. The victories of the CIO in the 1930s were in no small part due to the success of its racial policy.

Negro membership in trade unions increased substantially during World War II. In 1940 about 600,000 Negroes belonged to unions; by 1945 this figure had doubled. There were, in 1945, 500,000 Negroes in the CIO, 650,000 in the AFL and 100,000 in independent unions.[42] In 16 industries in which Negroes were numerous, collective-bargaining agreements covered between 80 and 100 per cent of the workers. However, by 1947 Negro trade-union membership was receding; there were then 380,000 Negroes in the AFL and 356,000 in the CIO.[43]

At the present time, union policy toward Negroes varies from direct exclusion, enshrined in the union constitution, on the one hand, to complete acceptance on the other. In between can be found a jumble of policies, many of them in a state of flux. In some unions Negroes are segregated in separate locals; sometimes entire unions are made up only of Negroes. Within the confines of a single union may be found segregated and nonsegregated locals. In other cases, unions ostensibly

[40] For accounts of the Negro as strikebreakers, see Hardin, *op. cit.*, pp. 60–63; Spero and Harris, *op. cit.*, pp. 128–146.

[41] Herbert R. Northrup, *Organized Labor and the Negro*, Harper & Brothers, New York, 1944, pp. 14–16.

[42] Davie, *op. cit.*, p. 128.

[43] Florence Murray (ed.), *The Negro Handbook 1949*, The Macmillan Company, New York, 1949, p. 162, table 2.

accept Negroes on an equal plane, but actually discriminate against them; e.g., in job referrals, or in backing them up in the plant.[44] Unions also vary in the extent to which they admit Negroes to positions of leadership. On the one extreme (barring pure white unions) is the union in which the Negro is a rank-and-filer but never an officer. On the other extreme may be found unions in which leadership is shared by whites and Negroes in something like their proportions in the union membership. In between are cases in which one or two Negroes are admitted to the union or local hierarchy, as a sop to Negro membership or as liaison between trade-union leaders and Negro rank and file. Sometimes Negroes are made leaders when there is a situation of conflict; e.g., when a protracted struggle with management is at hand, or when there is a threat to leadership from another faction within the union. In the all-Negro union, of course, there is all-Negro leadership and staff.[45]

The most prejudiced segment of organized labor is still to be found in the AFL. Negroes are excluded by AFL unions in several ways. One union excludes them through a provision in its rituals. Several exclude them through a provision in their constitutions. Some AFL unions exclude them by a tacit understanding, while others offer them only auxiliary status. In addition certain independent unions, particularly railroad unions, exclude Negroes through constitutional provision.[46]

However, there is some indication of change favorable to the Negro. Some unions have dropped those provisions in their constitutions which bar Negroes from membership. In other unions, segregated locals have been abolished. Even in the South, unions have pressed, though cautiously, for unsegregated locals and have been successful in certain areas in spite of the strong caste tradition. This process of liberalization stems from several sources. The unions have been feeling some pressure from public opinion, which has been turning against exclusionist policies in general. Furthermore, the growing strength, organization, and technical proficiency of the urbanized Negro people are making it difficult or dangerous for the unions to follow a practice of exclusion; the Negro today forms too important a part of the industrial-urban working force. Competition among unions also benefits the Negro; in the struggle to increase or maintain membership, he is courted by various unions. All these factors and others beside seem to ensure the eventual integration of the Negro in the trade-union movement.

Some unions not only have admitted Negroes to their membership on absolutely equal terms but have conducted vigorous campaigns to com-

[44] Weaver, *op. cit.*, p. 219.
[45] William Kornhauser, "The Negro Union Official; A Study of Sponsorship and Control," *The American Journal of Sociology*, vol. 57, no. 5, pp. 443–452, 1952. Copyright by the University of Chicago.
[46] Northrup, *op. cit.*, pp. 3–5.

bat prejudice and discrimination. The motives behind such campaigns seem to be a mixture again of the idealistic and the practical. Unions such as the United Automobile Workers are dedicated to certain social aims, including racial equality; but at the same time the UAW must deal with a rank and file which contains large numbers of Negroes and large numbers of recently arrived Southern workers. The bitter riots between Negroes and whites in Detroit during World War II are still a recent memory,[47] and a warning of the bitter gulf which divides these groups. Under these circumstances, the UAW has been seriously concerned with race prejudice and has made a strong effort to convince Negroes and whites of the necessity of setting aside traditional hostilities. Other CIO unions have made similar efforts to stamp out prejudice among white and Negro workers.[48]

With the merger of the two confederations of labor in 1955, the labor movement adopted an open antidiscriminatory policy. According to the merger resolution of February, 1955, the labor movement agreed to recognize the "right of all workers, without regard to race, creed, color, or national orgin to share in the full benefits of trade union organization in the merged federation."[49] The AFL-CIO further decided to "establish appropriate internal machinery to bring about at the earliest possible date, the effective implementation of the principle of nondiscrimination."[50] It would seem fairly certain that the merger of the AFL and CIO will hasten the incorporation of Negro workers into trade-union organizations.

Governmental Legislation. The integration of minority groups in industry has been affected not only by social and economic factors but also by governmental legislation designed to end discriminatory practices in industry. The history of this legislation dates back to the early years of World War II. At that time, in spite of a growing shortage of manpower and a consequent lag in war production, Negroes were being systematically excluded from most war industries. The threat posed by this situation, plus the added threat of concerted action by Negroes, induced President F. D. Roosevelt in 1941 to issue an executive order prohibiting discrimination in war industries and in government and setting up a Fair Employment Practices Commission.[51] This Commission hung on precari-

---

[47] See Alfred McClung Lee and Norman Daymond Humphrey, *Race Riot*, The Dryden Press, Inc., New York, 1943.

[48] See, for instance, "Democracy Means Fair Employment Practices," *Economic Outlook*, vol. 12, no. 10, Congress of Industrial Organizations, Department of Education and Research, pp. 73–80, October, 1951.

[49] "Merger Plans of the Unions and the Leaders' Statements," *The New York Times*, Feb. 10, 1955, p. 21.

[50] *Ibid.*

[51] Malcolm Ross, *All Manner of Men*, Reynal & Hitchcock, Inc., New York, 1948, pp. 19–21.

ously against stern congressional opposition until 1946, when it was finally abolished by Congress. During its five-year life, the FEPC (as it was popularly known) aroused about as much condemnation and praise as have been accorded any piece of domestic legislation in recent years.

The functions of the FEPC were limited, and its power was small. It served as a repository for complaints from those who felt they were being discriminated against in industry. It had the power to investigate such complaints, to decide on their validity, and, after 1943, to make recommendations as to the elimination of discrimination. Actually, its main power consisted of its ability to bring down on the head of an offending employer or labor union leader a great deal of unpleasant publicity.

Between 1941 and 1945, the FEPC handled about 8,000 complaints. If the year 1943–1944, during which the FEPC was active, is taken as an example, it will be found that complaints originated from various sources. Over 80 per cent of complaints were from Negroes. About 8 per cent of the complaints were about discrimination due to religion; most of these complaints came from Jews. Six per cent of the complaints concerned discriminations due to national origins, and 4.3 per cent were from those who felt they were being discriminated against because they were aliens. Almost 70 per cent of these complaints were against business, about 25 per cent were against government, and 6 per cent were against unions.[52] That the FEPC handled these cases effectively, for all its lack of power, may be seen from the following statistics. Between July, 1943, and December, 1944, 64 per cent of complaints were dismissed, while 36 per cent were satisfactorily adjusted. During its most active period the FEPC was handling 250 cases a month and settling 100 by negotiation.[53]

Some states have followed the lead of the Federal government and have set up state programs to combat discrimination in the economic field. Eight states (New York, Massachusetts, Connecticut, New Jersey, New Mexico, Oregon, Rhode Island, and Washington) passed laws forbidding discrimination and set up commissions to enforce the laws. In three other states laws have been passed, but with inadequate or no provision for enforcement. These state laws are modeled on the original Federal legislation.[54] They specifically prohibit discrimination and define what is meant by discrimination; they set up agencies with the power to hear and investigate complaints of discrimination, to render a decision as to the merits of the case, and to enforce their decisions. However, the state FEPC has not proved particularly effective; for instance, in New York, the law has been freely violated, and the commission has

[52] *To Secure These Rights*, The Report of the President's Committee on Civil Rights, Simon and Schuster, Inc., New York, 1947, p. 54.

[53] Louis Ruchames, *Race, Jobs and Politics*, Columbia University Press, New York, 1953, p. 149.

[54] *Ibid.*, p. 165.

not enforced the law with vigor.[55] Perhaps the absence of a governmental commission accounts for the ineffectiveness of the state programs.

Since the abolition of the Federal FEPC, a debate has been raging as to the necessity for reenacting similar legislation. Opponents of the measure argue that the FEPC is an unwarranted invasion of the rights of individual employers; it tells the employer whom he may hire or fire, whom he may upgrade or demote. The FEPC is considered by this group as another invasion of the sphere of private industry by government— and a particularly pernicious invasion at that, because it interferes in the internal administration of the plant, precisely where management has most jealously guarded its power. It is argued, furthermore, that legislation of this type will not work. It is said that it is not possible to legislate away the prejudices of an entire population. Laws do not create the mores; either they express the mores, or they are unenforceable, as witness the case of prohibition. According to this point of view, industry did not create these mores and prejudices, and it is unfair to demand of industry that it bear the cost of stamping them out.

Proponents of the FEPC laws argue that the best refutation of most of these arguments is that the FEPC *did* work. It *did succeed* in getting Negroes and other minority group members into the factories, and with a minimum of coercion or friction. Furthermore, the FEPC worked without invading the rights of private enterprise and without undue intervention in the affairs of management. All that the FEPC asked of management was that it not consider color or religion or ethnic background in hiring, firing, etc.; it never denied management's rights to make its decisions on the basis of efficiency or the needs of the organization.

As for the argument that laws cannot change mores, values, and prejudices, defenders of the FEPC would argue as follows. In the first place, they would point out, the immediate aim of the legislation was *not* to eradicate such beliefs and attitudes; the immediate aim was to prevent certain overt acts of discrimination, and this it did. But, in the long run, the argument would continue, law does have a profound effect on mores. Laws are instrumental in determining the standards of right and wrong, of the proper and the improper. When a law against prejudice is passed, then prejudice becomes illegal, and in time prejudice may become if not immoral at least shameful. At least a law may act this way for those who do not have particularly strong convictions about the matter of legislation, which is probably the case for the majority of the American people in regard to the Negro question.[56] Secondly, those who support antidiscriminatory legislation argue that while an FEPC might violate the

[55] *Ibid.,* pp. 171–175.
[56] John P. Roche and Milton M. Gordon, "Can Morality Be Legislated?" *The New York Times Magazine,* May 22, 1955, p. 4.

mores of some members of the community, it would accord exactly with the interests and mores of another large segment of the community. Any FEPC law would not wither away for lack of mass support or interest, as did prohibition. Finally, it is pointed out that antidiscrimination laws like the FEPC result in mixing together diverse peoples in unfamiliar situations; in housing projects, on the job, in schools. When such commingling occurs, old prejudices and misconceptions break down under the weight of experience.[57] In all these ways, it is maintained, laws have a profound effect on the mores.

Thus the debate goes on. In the meantime, opponents of the FEPC retain a firm grip on Congress, effectively blocking the oft-repeated pledges of both parties for legislation of this type. Interest in antidiscriminatory legislations has shifted to housing and schooling, but it seems safe to predict that the question of antidiscriminatory legislation in the occupational field is bound to be raised again, and with new firmness and urgency.

[57] *Ibid.,* p. 6.

CHAPTER 18

Industry and the Family

In this chapter we shall consider the way in which industry and the family are related in our society. For reasons that have already been discussed in Chapter 2, the family must be considered the oldest and probably most important of human groups. It is within the family that man has his most significant educational, emotional, affectional, and sexual experiences. The family is the most vulnerable and most easily modified of all institutions, and at the same time one of the toughest. It bows before all the passing winds of fortune; it is easily crushed by physiological, social, and economic changes. And, yet, in one form or another, it always survives, weathering crises, adapting to changes in the environment, ever re-creating itself.

Industrialism and the Traditional Family. When industrialism knocked on the door of Western civilization, it found a tightly knit feudal society composed of rigidly defined social classes bound to each other by a complicated set of rights and duties, the whole sanctified by a powerful church.[1] It also found mankind organized into a series of cohesive families, closely tied to the soil or to some location. This institution also was strongly supported by the church. Within this feudal family, there was a patriarchal father who ruled his household in a thoroughly feudal manner; that is, he owed to his family certain rights and exacted from them certain duties, including the duty to obey him. The wife in this family was subordinate to her husband, but in her own domain, whether farmstead or a house in the town, she was a person of prestige and of great influence over her children. The children were minor parts of the family. There were many of them in each family, except where disease carried them off, and no matter how great the affection of the parents for them en masse, they were relatively unimportant as individuals. Therefore childhood was not considered a time for play, but, rather, a time of

---

[1] For a description of the medieval family, see George Caspar Homans, *English Villagers of the Thirteenth Century,* Harvard University Press, Cambridge, Mass., 1941, part II.

preparation for life, a time for learning tasks and moving to new tasks when strength and agility would permit. Finally, to round out the complement of the family, there were the aged, who could no longer work but who were respected and perhaps a little feared.

This family was enmeshed in a large network of kinship ties. Close relationships were maintained with families related by marriage or by blood. Since families were stable and migration limited, all relatives were likely to be well known to each other. A whole neighborhood or even a village[2] might be made up of a few extended families. The extended family not only was the product of a stable society, it helped guarantee this stability. The extended family lent support to the smaller families within it; it enforced traditional standards and values.

Marriage in the traditional family was rarely a matter of choice. Marriages were arranged, and they were arranged not in terms of romantic attraction but in terms of socioeconomic realities. In a peasant village, the son of a peasant married the daughter of a peasant of equal status and wealth.[3] The daughter of a nobleman was married to a nobleman whose rank would not disgrace her family. The traditional family, supported by the extended kin group, could be counted on to enforce first acceptance of the chosen mates, and then, to a certain degree, harmony within the home.

It is this type of family, or some version of it, which lies in the immediate background of most Americans. Either they are descended from peasant families of the traditional type, or they come from rural areas where a modified form of the traditional family is still in existence. Even urban families of a few generations ago were not unlike the traditional family described above. Nor is this type of family extinct today. It continues to exist wherever industrialism has not penetrated, for instance, in India, or China, or sections of Latin America.

Industrialism quickly and permanently shattered this family form, and it continues to do so wherever it enters a region or a nation.[4] It does so first, because it must break the ties of the family to land or location in order to fill cities with propertyless workers, dependent solely on the factories for their livings. Industrialism cannot even tolerate a deeply rooted urban family, for it requires a mobile population, mobile in both the social and geographical senses.

[2] This has been true even in the United States in the past. See James West, *Plainville, U.S.A.,* Columbia University Press, New York, 1945, pp. 57–69.

[3] Oscar Handlin (lecture notes), Harvard University, fall, 1946. Compare the situation which exists today in rural French Canada. See Everett Cherrington Hughes, *French Canada in Transition,* University of Chicago Press, Chicago, 1943, pp. 4–9. Copyright by the University of Chicago.

[4] For a general account of the relationship between industrialism and the family in the past, see Arthur W. Calhoun, *A Social History of the American Family,* Arthur H. Clark Company, Glendale, Calif., 1919, vol. III, chap. IV.

Secondly, industrialism is incompatible with traditional family relationships. It must use the labor of father, mother, adolescents, and even children on an equal plane; it has no affinity for the fine distinctions of status and authority in the traditional family. Industrialism separates the place of work from the place of family life, and in doing so it pulls parents away from children, husbands away from wives. It breaks up the continuity of the traditional family; in industrial society the family no longer can function as a face-to-face group except at comparatively rare times. Industrialism leads the individual to chafe at the bonds of the traditional family; children who can earn almost as much as their fathers, and who know as much, will not readily accept his authority. Nor will such children readily consent to marry those whom their parents have selected for them. Since the traditional family is not able to control marriages, its homogeneity and unity may be shattered with the introduction of spouses of differing nationalities, perhaps even of different religions.

Thirdly, industrialism has shattering effects on the extended family. The extended family is often scattered; the component parts of the extended family may live in different sections of the city, in different cities, sometimes even in different nations. Ties between relatives become looser and, in many cases, disappear entirely. In turn, the weakening of the extended family still further weakens the smaller families.

Fourthly, industrialism radically changes the physical environment of the family and, as a result, induces certain changes in the family structure. The home is transferred from the country to the city or town, where living space is scarce. In the city homes often become crowded and unattractive and may positively repel family members. Outside the home are all the attractions of urban life; places of recreation, clubs, corner gangs, etc. The family tends to drift apart; the home becomes a place for meals and for sleeping, but other activities transpire outside the home.

Thus, in these and other ways, industrialism dissolves the hard lines of relationships in the traditional family. Does this mean that the family is doomed to disappear, as some have warned? From what we now know, nothing seems less likely. All the deep-lying psychological needs of men and women for family existence remain. What has changed is the *way* these needs can be filled in industrial society; what has changed is the form of the family—its structure and its inner relationships.

The General Form of the Industrial-Urban Family. There are two ways of looking at the form of the industrial-urban family. One may consider the general form of the industrial-urban family, that is, those elements which are common to *all* families of this type. Or one may consider the various subtypes of this general urban-industrial family. Here we shall do both; first we shall consider the general form of the family, and then we shall consider certain subtypes as *deviations* from this general form. Our choice of subtypes will be dictated by the interest of this book.

In general, various aspects of the industrial-urban family have been shaped by the needs of industrialism in various ways.[5] One striking peculiarity of the industrial-urban family is its isolation from other areas of society. As has been shown, the industrial-urban family is not embedded in a matrix of extended kin relationships. Relatively few urban families maintain close relationships with more than a handful of relatives not in the immediate family. This isolation of the family is reflected in our kinship terminology, which fails to distinguish between near or remote cousins, between paternal or maternal aunts, uncles, or grandparents.[6] For the industrial-urban family, most relatives outside the immediate family are alike.

Another characteristic of urban-industrial families is that, to a degree unheard of in other cultures, the family is based on the conjugal relationship. Since the family no longer rests on ties to property, to location, to land, or to extended family, the stability of the family, its success or failure, depends on the compatibility of husband and wife. It is the ability of the husband and wife to adjust to each other, to compromise their difficulties, which is crucial in our family system. Since so much hinges on the conjugal relationship, mates must be chosen in terms of personal preference; e.g., in terms of romantic attraction, sexual compatibility, and personality affinity. Even if there were no reason of an ideological nature, it is doubtful whether a system of arranged marriages could work in our society.

Within this isolated, conjugal family, certain types of roles appear. Caution must be exercised here, because it is precisely in the area of roles and role playing that the greatest variations exist in our families. However, certain generalizations about these roles may be made.

In general, the modern family is marked by a relatively great degree of equality in its roles.[7] For instance, the father is less of an authoritarian figure than in the patriarchal family; he cannot command the obedience of his wife or children to nearly the same degree that the patriarch could.

[5] Other forces also have helped shape our family, for instance, the democratic ideology and the Judaeo-Christian tradition.

[6] Talcott Parsons, "The Social Structure of the Family," in Ruth Nanda Anshen, (ed.), *The Family: Its Function and Destiny,* Harper & Brothers, New York, 1949, p. 175.

[7] See the following for discussions of family roles: Margaret Park Redfield, "The American Family: Consensus and Freedom," *American Journal of Sociology,* vol. 52, no. 3, pp. 175–183, 1946, copyright by the University of Chicago; Arnold W. Green, "The Middle Class Male Child and Neurosis," *American Sociological Review,* vol. 11, no. 1, pp. 31–44, 1946; Talcott Parsons, *op. cit.;* Robin M. Williams, Jr., *Modern American Society,* Alfred A. Knopf, Inc., New York, 1951, chap. 4; Kingsley Davis, *Human Society,* The Macmillan Company, New York, 1949, chap. 15.

The father of the industrial-urban family must adjust his personality to the emotional needs of his wife; he must, in a sense, cultivate the good will of his children. By the same token, the wife enjoys a relatively high status in our family system. Though her duties in the home remain largely traditional, these duties have been lightened by her relationship with her husband, by the easing of household drudgery through technological applications, and by the possibility of taking employment on the outside. Furthermore, to a greater degree than ever, the wife is close to and can influence her children.

The role of the child has been drastically altered. Still speaking generally, we may say that the child is less of an economic asset, and in some instances may be a burden. This fact, coupled with the spread of contraceptive knowledge, has resulted in the reduction of number of children per family. The child thus has a better chance for survival and for health. At the same time, the child also has the opportunity to emerge as an individual in the family—if not an individual of equal status to the adults, at least one with definite rights. Childhood today involves not a dreary preparation for adult life but a separate culture of school and of recreation. Furthermore, the very fact of the relative scarcity of children in our families increases the emotional involvement of parents in their children; the child in our society is the object of a great deal of parental affection and concern.

Another important facet of the role structure of our families is the separation of place of work and the home. Unlike the peasant, who worked perhaps within sight of his home, the modern man goes to work; that is, he leaves his family for eight hours or more a day. Furthermore, what he does in his place of work is usually incomprehensible to his family or of little interest to them. Thus the child or the adolescent or the wife is cut off from the occupational world almost entirely. One consequence is that the father can no longer serve as a model for his son, or, at least, it is more difficult for him to do so; the result is that relatively few sons in our society consciously desire to emulate their fathers. Another consequence is that children are thrown upon their mother; it is she who must give them affection, care for them, and discipline them.

The functions of the family are also drastically altered under modern conditions. The family is no longer the main economic unit of society. Its productive functions have almost entirely disappeared. In the economic sphere, the family functions chiefly as a consuming unit and to motivate economic activity. Religious functions, recreational functions, even educational functions are appropriated by other institutions under modern conditions of urban life. On the other hand, the affectional function of the family gains new importance. In contrast to the impersonality, anonymity, and harshness of modern society, and not least in its industrial sector, are the warmth, tenderness, and intense personal qualities of family life. The fact that many marriages end in divorce because of the failure of the affectional function points up the importance of this function in the modern family.

Industry, then, affects the form of the modern family in many ways. The isolation of the family may be traced to the overriding demand of industry for mobility. The stress on the conjugal relationship is in turn related to the isolation of the family. The equality of roles is related to the employment opportunities opened by industry, as well as to the equalitarian ideology which is partly the result of industrialism. The functional nature of the family represents a compromise between the needs of industrialism and the emotional needs of humanity.

Industrially Influenced Families and Aspects of Family Living. The general features of the family described above are well-nigh universal in our society; they exist among families which are entirely outside the industrial sphere as well as among those which have direct connections with industry. The family form which we describe has become a part of our culture, which is itself in part a product of industrialism. But, in addition to this general influence on our family system, industry is directly influencing those families whose members are connected with industry.

In general, the direct influence of industry on the family is bound up with the occupational structure of industry. This works in two ways. On the one hand, the particular occupation which an individual follows in industry determines many immediate aspects of family living. For instance, the occupation determines the amount of income which the family will live on, the amount of "living" which it can buy. Furthermore, occupation determines the amount of time which the job holder will spend in the home, whether that time will be in the night or in the day. Occupations create tensions and strains, as we have seen, which may be transferred to family life. Certain attitudes and values are created by occupational experience, and these may infiltrate family relationships in many subtle ways.

On the other hand, in so far as occupation determines class and status position, many indirect influences on family life are being felt. Class and status groups are, as we have seen, really subcultures in our society, with indigenous habits, values, attitudes, speech, definitions of the situation, and so on. The fact that a given family belongs to a particular class or status group determines many structural and functional features of that family: the number of children in the family, the role of the father, the position of the mother, the role of the aged, the vulnerability of the family to crisis.

In the discussion that follows we shall concentrate on the influence of industry on certain aspects of family life: the formation of families, family structure, family roles, and family disorganization. As we shall see, sometimes this influence is of the direct or "occupational" variety, sometimes it is indirect, mediated through class and status.

Families in the Labor Force. How many families are directly connected with industry by virtue of having one or more members working in industry? Unfortunately a precise estimate is not possible. It is known, however, that there are over 40 million families in the United States.[8] Over 31 million of these reside in urban areas; the rest, in rural nonfarm or rural farm areas. Of the total number of families, about 10 per cent have no member in the working force. About 56 per cent of the families have one person in the labor force, about 25½ per cent have two, 6½ per cent have three, and 2.2 per cent have four or more.[9] Thus a total of about 36 million families were connected with the labor force.

Using these figures, and from what we know of the composition of the working force, it may be estimated that about two-thirds of families have one or more members earning a wage or salary in a nonagricultural industry. In absolute figures, about 24 million families are connected with industry. Though the figures presented here are not precise, it can be clearly seen that a large proportion of American families have one or more members connected with industry.

The Formation of Families. We have seen that families in our society are formed through the "free choice" of men and women. This does not mean, however, that the formation of marriages in our society is purely a matter of chance physical attraction. On the contrary, it is strongly influenced by social and economic conditions. These conditions set limits within which "free choice" operates in the selection of marriage mates.

Directly or indirectly, industry helps form the socioeconomic environment within which marriages are formed. In the first place, industry may have a *direct* effect on the formation of marriages, by the simple fact of bringing together large numbers of men and women where propinquity may exert its force. Unfortunately, studies of this topic are lacking.[10] It can be shown with more concreteness that there is a high mar-

[8] U.S. Bureau of the Census, *Statistical Abstract of the United States: 1954*, p. 54, table 50.

[9] A. J. Jaffee and Charles D. Stewart, *Manpower Resources and Utilization*, John Wiley & Sons, Inc., New York, 1951, p. 136, table 5.

[10] The only existing evidence of which this writer has knowledge are such studies as those conducted by Popenoe in 1932. Popenoe found that of a group of educated married couples, 13 per cent had originally met through business contacts. Quoted by Willard Walter Waller in his *The Family: A Dynamic Interpretation*, revised by Reuben Hill, The Dryden Press, Inc., New York, 1951, p. 206. The present author certainly had the opportunity to observe numerous marriages between factory employees during his experience of two years as an industrial worker.

riage rate between men and women in the same occupation or between men and women who come from the same occupational levels. Thus Sundal and McCormick in a study of marriage in Madison, Wisconsin, found that over 45 per cent of unskilled or semiskilled male workers married women who were operatives or domestic workers.[11] Centers found that 33 per cent of a national sample of business executives married women whose fathers were also businessmen; 26 per cent of the white-collar workers, 52 per cent of skilled workers, 48 per cent of the semi-skilled, and 25 per cent of the unskilled likewise married women whose fathers were in the same occupational classes as themselves.[12] It is impossible to state to what extent these intraoccupational marriages are the result of direct contacts at work, and to what extent they reflect similar class and status backgrounds of the spouses. Probably both factors are at work here.

In the second place, industry affects the formation of marriages indirectly, through the medium of class and status. It has been shown in Chapter 16 that class and status are intimately linked to the occupational structure of industry. Therefore, if there is evidence of the influence of social stratification on marriage, there is, at the same time, evidence for the influence of industrialism on marriage. Such evidence exists. For instance, several studies have shown that a large number of marriages occur between men and women who live within a relatively short distance of each other. The pioneer study of Bossard showed that over 50 per cent of 5,000 applications for marriage made in Philadelphia in the early 1930s were between parties who lived within 20 blocks or less of each other; in fact, in over 12 per cent of the cases, the applicants gave the same address. Since people who live in the same neighborhood are likely to come from the same economic class and, though less certainly, from the same status group, there is evidence that these marriages took place between people with the same socioeconomic backgrounds.[13]

[11] A. Philip Sundal and Thomas C. McCormick, "Age at Marriage and Mate Selection: Madison, Wisconsin, 1937–1943," *American Sociological Review*, vol. 16, no. 1, p. 43, table 5, 1951.

[12] Richard Centers, "Marital Selection and Occupational Strata," *The American Journal of Sociology*, vol. 54, no. 6, p. 535, table 9, 1949, copyright by the University of Chicago. A study of marriages occurring in Norwood, Mass., between 1923 and 1927 offers additional evidence for the prevalence of intraoccupational marriages. See Thomas C. Hunt, "Occupational Status and Marriage Selection," *American Sociological Review*, vol. 5, no. 4, p. 502, table 3, 1940.

[13] James H. S. Bossard, "Residential Propinquity as a Factor in Marriage Selection," *The American Journal of Sociology*, vol. 38, no. 2, p. 221, table 2, 1932. Copyright by the University of Chicago. For corroboration of Bossard's study, see the following: August B. Hollingshead, "Cultural Factors in the Selection of Marriage Mates," *American Sociological Review*, vol. 15, no. 5, pp. 619–627, 1950; Alfred C.

Further evidence of the prevalence of intraclass marriages may be found in the similarity of the financial situations of the parties to the marriage. Homogamy in financial background is, of course, implied in the similarity of occupational background, which has been described above. Scattered studies tend to support this deduction. For instance, a study of 1,000 engaged couples, largely middle-class, in Chicago showed a "moderate" degree of correlation between the financial standings of the parents of the couples.[14] Sundal's and McCormick's study of Madison, Wisconsin, showed similarity in the assessed evaluations of the homes from which married couples came.[15]

Finally, similarity in the amount and type of education of married couples supports the thesis of the similarity of the socioeconomic backgrounds of many spouses.[16] It was shown in Chapter 16 that education is a particularly sensitive index of socioeconomic position, because education is both the product of life chances and, at the same time, a major determinant of those chances.

From the evidence at hand, it may be concluded, therefore, that marriages in our society do not occur randomly. Marriages occur between people who are thrown together at work or who are brought together by their positions in the social structure. In both ways, though to an undetermined degree, industrialism affects the formation of marriages in our society.

Status-Class Position and Family Structure. The influence of industrialism on families is not confined merely to their formation; in numerous direct and indirect ways industrialism helps to shape various *subtypes* of the American family. Subtypes of families occur in relation to regions, religions, ethnic groups, races, and other factors. The subtypes which are of interest to us deviate from the "ideal" American family in terms of

---

Clarke, "An Examination of the Operation of Residential Propinquity as a Factor in Mate Selection," *American Sociological Review,* vol. 17, no. 1, pp. 17–22, 1952; Joseph P. Marches and Gus Turbeville, "The Effect of Residential Propinquity on Marriage Selection," *The American Journal of Sociology,* vol. 58, no. 6, pp. 592–595, 1953, copyright by the University of Chicago; Maurice R. Davie and Ruby Jo Reeves, "Propinquity of Residence before Marriage," *The American Journal of Sociology,* vol. 44, no. 4, pp. 510–517, 1939, copyright by the University of Chicago; Ray H. Abrams "Residential Propinquity as a Factor in Marriage Selection: Fifty Year Trends in Philadelphia," *American Sociological Review,* vol. 8, no. 3, pp. 288–294, 1943.

[14] Ernest W. Burgess and Paul Wallin, "Homogamy in Social Characteristics," *The American Journal of Sociology,* vol. 49, no. 2, p. 113, table 1, 1943. Copyright by the University of Chicago.

[15] Sundal and McCormick, *op. cit.,* p. 46, table 8.

[16] In a study of the married in New Haven, Conn., it was found that the men had in fact married women of equal or lower educational attainment. See Hollingshead, *op. cit.,* pp. 625–627, tables 4, 5, 6.

their position in the class and status system, which in turn is, as we have seen, linked to industrialism.[17]

Demographic Deviations. Certain demographic characteristics of American families vary in relation to position in the status-class system. This is true, for instance, of the *size* of families. Numerous studies have demonstrated an *inverse* relationship between status-class position, on the one hand, and fertility, on the other; that is, the "lower" classes have more children than the "upper" classes. From an inspection of Table 27, it

Table 27. Number of Children Ever Born to Women of 45 and Over, by Occupation and Income of Husband

	Number of children per 1,000 women
Income:	
Under $1,000	3,551
$1,000–$1,999	2,854
2,000– 2,999	2,683
3,000– 3,999	2,417
4,000– 4,999	2,178
5,000– 6,999	2,208
7,000 and over	2,095
Occupation:	
Professional, technical, and kindred workers	1,780
Managers, proprietors, and officials, except farm	2,104
Clerical and kindred workers	2,013
Sales workers	1,831
Craftsmen, foremen, and kindred workers	2,575
Operatives and kindred workers	2,828

SOURCE: U.S. Bureau of the Census, *Statistical Abstract of the United States: 1954*, p. 50, table 43.

can be seen that families are largest among "operatives and kindred workers"; families are smallest among professional and technical workers and among sales personnel. Similarly, an inverse relationship can be demonstrated between education and fertility, between rental paid for homes and fertility, and between fertility and other socioeconomic indices.[18] However, there is now some indication that the difference in size of families by socioeconomic status is beginning to decrease; indeed, for certain high-level occupations, the relationship has become a direct one, higher

[17] See Don Martindale, "The Variety of the Human Family," and Manford Hinshaw Kuhn, "American Families Today: Development and Differentiation of Types," in Howard Becker and Reuben Hill (eds.), *Family, Marriage and Parenthood,* D. C. Heath and Company, Boston, 1948, pp. 50–83 and 131–168; and Clifford Kirkpatrick, *The Family as Process and Institution,* The Ronald Press Company, New York, 1955, chap. 4.

[18] Everett S. Lee and Anne S. Lee, "The Differential Fertility of the American Negro," *American Sociological Review,* vol. 17, no. 4, p. 445, table 5, 1952; Clyde V. Kiser, "Fertility Trends and Differentials in the United States," *Journal of the American Statistical Association,* vol. 47, no. 257, p. 43, fig. 5, 1952.

occupational levels tending to show larger families than somewhat lower occupational levels.[19]

American families of differing socioeconomic status also show variations in the ages at which the spouses marry. However, here the relationship is a direct one; the higher the occupational position and the greater the money income, the later the age of marriage. Men of higher occupational levels tend to marry women nearer their own ages, while members of lower-ranking occupations tend to marry women further from their own age.[20] Thus there is a median difference of 2.4 years in the ages of husbands and wives on the level of clerical workers, and a difference of 2.7 years in the ages of spouses on the "operative" level.[21]

Differences in the Extended Family by Status-Class Levels. It has been shown that industrialism tends to lessen the importance of the extended family. Actually, the extended kin-group does retain some functional importance in our society, but its significance varies in the various class and status levels. On the upper-class and upper-status levels, the kin-group may be both of great extent and functional significance. A great deal of importance may be attached to the family name, to the family estates, to ancestry, to genealogies and degrees of relationship.[22] Furthermore, the extended upper-class family has important functions. The extended kin-group functions to exclude outsiders who might threaten the class and status privileges of its members. Strangers are carefully rated in terms of their suitability for entrance into the upper levels of society, and their ancestry and accomplishments are thoroughly reviewed. Above all, the extended kin-group seeks to control choice of marriage mates. It is typical of an upper-class or upper-status level that marriage mates are chosen from the same level of society. Since the number of marriageable individuals is limited, there is inevitably a great deal of intermarriage, even between quite close relatives. As a result, the upper strata are dominated by a relatively few large extended families.[23]

[19] See Charles F. Westoff, "Differential Fertility in the United States: 1900 to 1952," *American Sociological Review,* vol. 19, no. 5, pp. 559–561, 1954; Kiser, *op. cit.,* pp. 46–48; Evelyn M. Kitagawa, "Differential Fertility in Chicago, 1920–40," *The American Journal of Sociology,* vol. 58, no. 5, p. 485, table 1, 1953. Copyright by the University of Chicago.

[20] Paul C. Glick and Emmanuel Landau, "Age as a Factor in Marriage," *American Sociological Review,* vol. 15, no. 4, p. 529, table 4, 1950.

[21] *Ibid.*

[22] See Allison Davis, Burleigh B. Gardner, and Mary R. Gardner, *Deep South,* University of Chicago Press, Chicago, 1941, pp. 84–87. Copyright by the University of Chicago.

[23] For accounts of the great extent of intermarriage among extended upper-class families, see the following: Ferdinand Lundberg, *America's 60 Families,* Vanguard Press, Inc., New York, 1937; Cleveland Amory, *The Last Resorts,* Harper & Brothers, New York, 1952.

The extended upper-class family may also have important economic functions. The amalgamation or the splitting of fortunes may closely follow the lines of marriage and family connections. Business maneuvering, corporation alliances, business mergers, the exchange of vital information—all may follow the lines of relationship of the extended family. The tentativeness of our statements here reflects the lack of research in this field; entirely too little is known of this vital area.

Extended families on the working-class level may also possess important functional attributes, though little importance is attached on this level of society to family name or ancestry. The extended family may act as an employment agency; individual family members may be placed in those factories where the family has influence. In fact, a large number of workers in a given plant may belong to a relatively small number of extended families.[24] The extended family may also seek to safeguard its members against the hazards of industrial employment: layoffs, technological change, for instance. During times of depression, the extended family may serve as a cushion for the less fortunate family members; food, living quarters, even income may be shared with relatives during hard times.[25] The extended family also functions to ameliorate the normal crises of life; children are boarded during times of sickness, female members of the family act as nurses or housekeepers.

The middle-class family tends to approximate the "ideal" type, described at the beginning of this chapter. That is, in the middle classes the extended family has relatively little functional importance. Indeed, for the middle-class family which is socially mobile, it may be necessary to break with sections of the family on "lower" levels of society.[26]

Industry and the Role Structure of Families. The influence of industrialism penetrates the inner structure of family life. Industrialism, directly or indirectly, helps to shape the roles which are played within the family, as well as the relationships between these roles. The roles of husbands, wives, children, of adolescents, and of the aged, all are responding in some degree to the forces emanating from our productive system. But, the specific nature of this response reflects the specific relationship between the family and industry—above all, the relationship between family and occupation.

Family Roles of Adult Men. The role of the husband in the family is, perhaps, most directly influenced by industry. Both direct economic ne-

---

[24] This pattern was observed in operation by the author in a plant employing about two hundred workers.

[25] See Allison Davis, "The Motivation of the Underprivileged Worker," in William Foote Whyte (ed.), *Industry and Society*, McGraw-Hill Book Company, Inc., New York, 1946, p. 91.

[26] James H. S. Bossard, *The Sociology of Child Development*, Harper & Brothers, New York, 1954, p. 335.

cessity and the values of our society make it mandatory for men to have an occupation; in an industrial society, many of these occupations will be in industry. This means that men at all levels of society concentrate daily at a central place of production, leaving their homes for a world of different values and traditions. In all levels of society, therefore, the husband is a part-time member of the family, who must seek somehow to integrate the work he does with the demands of family life. He may fail to achieve integration, or he may succeed, but even if he does succeed it is at the cost of the compartmentalization of his personality, that is, by dividing himself into a "work" self and a "family" self.

The nature of the integration of these selves differs by occupational levels. At the upper levels of society, the role of the man in the family may have little relationship to his role at work. The man's occupational attainments may be impressive, but there may be little carry-over of the prestige and authority gained at work into family life. Often, the status of the wife's family equals or surpasses the status that the husband has attained at work; the wife, furthermore, may possess large financial reserves, and she may have influential connections in her extended kin-group. Besides, the pressure of life at high occupational levels is such as to minimize the amount of time and energy which the man can devote to his family. Family life may thus become a subordinate part of the man's life, not nearly equaling in importance or satisfaction work life.

In the middle-class world of white-collar workers, technicians, and professionals, the position of the man in the family is somewhat different. The earning power of the middle-class man is usually superior to that of his wife, who, at any rate, rarely possesses financial resources of her own. Thus both the financial standing of the family and the status of the family is dependent on the occupation that the husband follows and on his success within it. For these reasons, the middle-class husband and father is necessarily a personage of considerable importance to the family. However, his importance and authority *to* the family is rarely matched by his importance and authority *within* the family. For one thing, he usually follows a technically complicated occupation, which is incomprehensible to other members of the family. Under these circumstances, he cannot serve as a role model for his children, nor can his wife often identify strongly with his work. He can rarely transfer to his family the enthusiasms, the strains, the victories of his occupational life.

The husband in the middle class must, then, usually try to construct a family role for himself, which has little or nothing to do with his work role. In the nature of things, this must be a subordinate role, for the *essential* relationships in the family cluster around the mother and her children. The man is then reduced to playing the role of stern disciplinarian, or jovial good companion, to his children according to the ideology of the family—more often the latter than the former in our middle-class families. Toward his wife, the middle-class husband must often adopt a peculiarly dependent role. Since he can neither call upon tradition to command her nor transfer to his relationship with her the prestige of his occupation, he must necessarily "adjust" to her personality, her needs, her aspirations;[27] it is her home, and if he wishes to make a success of his marriage, he must recognize this fact.

Furthermore, the husband is dependent on his wife in another way. His occupational success will depend, in part, on the style of life which she maintains; her ability to entertain, to cajole the proper superiors, to maintain an up-to-date home (often with limited financial resources) may be decisive for his career. On another plane, his wife's success in raising children by middle-class standards, and inculcating in them the "proper" attitudes and motives, may be crucial for the ability of the family to maintain middle-class status.

The position of the working-class husband in the family also has direct relationship to his position in the occupational world. As compared to the middle-class man, the workingman's occupation commands neither superior financial returns nor high status; the wife, and even the children, may obtain and hold jobs not greatly inferior in either of these respects. Indeed, in times of depression women and adolescents may have an advantage in securing employment. For these reasons, the authority of the father and husband in the working-class family is constantly threatened. In fact, a tendency for the emergence of matriarchal families in the lower reaches of society has been noted.

If, nevertheless, the authoritarian father and husband is probably more common in the working-class family than in other types of families, it is for these reasons. In spite of what has been said about the potential earning power of women and adolescents, the father and husband remains the sole source of income in a myriad of working-class families; this is especially true where there are small children and the wife cannot work. The financial weakness of the average working-class family increases the importance of the income of the husband. Furthermore, the very weakness of the father's position in the occupational world may drive him to play an authoritarian role in the family, either as compensation for the disadvantages of his occupational life or to make secure his shaky authority and prestige in the family. Finally, it should be remembered that large sections of the working class have only recently sprung

[27] For a discussion of the position of the man in the family, see Ernest Rutherford Groves and William Fielding Ogburn, *American Marriage and Family Relationships,* Henry Holt and Company, Inc., New York, 1928, chap. III.

from areas in which the traditional family is strong or adhere to religions which sanctify the traditional family.

Thus occupation and family life are intertwined in many diverse ways, each status-class position engendering a pattern peculiar to itself and determining, in part, the roles that men play in the family.

Industry and the Role of Married Women. Industrialism has two major effects on the role of women. On the one hand, industry directly employs a large mass of married women. On the other hand, industry has certain effects on the position of women in the family. We shall consider both aspects of the question.

In 1953 over 37 million women were married and living with their spouses; an additional 11 million women were married, or had been married, but were not living with their spouses. Of the married women who were living with their spouses, 25 per cent were in the labor force; about 20 per cent of married women between the ages of 14 and 19 were working, about 33 per cent of those 35 to 44, but only 5.5 per cent of those 65 and over. Of the married women who were not living with their spouses, about 38 per cent were in the labor force; over 65 per cent of these women in the age category 35 to 64 were working.[28] These figures contrast sharply with the 4.8 per cent of married women who were in the labor force in 1890, and with the 32 per cent of the widowed and divorced who were in the labor force in that year.[29]

The employment of married women seems to be related to two factors: the number and age of children in the family, and the socioeconomic status of the husband. In 1949, when 22.5 per cent of all married women living with their spouses were in the labor force, only 10 per cent who had children under 6 years of age were working. This figure goes steadily up as the age of children increases; over 31 per cent of the women whose children were between 12 and 17 years old were working.[30] In relation to the socioeconomic status of husbands, it appears that the lower the status of the husband, the higher the percentage of wives who are working. One study made in the 1930s showed that in the lowest income brackets, between 30 and 35 per cent of all women with no children were working, and over 15 per cent of women with children under 10; in the highest income brackets about 7 per cent of women with no children under 10 were working, and only about 3 per cent with children under 10.[31]

[28] U.S. Bureau of the Census, *Statistical Abstract of the United States: 1954*, p. 204, table 230.
[29] Jaffee and Stewart, *op. cit.*, p. 172, table 18.
[30] *Ibid.*, p. 133, table 4.
[31] Ruth Shonle Cavan, *The American Family*, Thomas Y. Crowell Company, New York, 1953, p. 105, fig. 17.

While direct data on the type of occupations filled by *married* women is lacking, we do know the types of occupations filled by the urban female working force as a whole. Table 28 shows that about 27 per cent of women in the labor force are clerical workers. About 20 per cent are operatives. Sizable proportions of the female labor force are either domestic workers or else technicians and professionals. As compared to men, women are proportionately more numerous in the professional, technical, clerical, and sales-worker categories; they greatly outnumber men in the clerical fields. Proportionately, about as many women in the

Table 28. Numbers and Percentages of Men and Women in Various Occupations Compared, 1950

Occupation	Numbers (rounded off)		Per cent of total labor force		No. of women expressed as a percentage of men
	Men	Women	Men	Women	
Professional and technical.....	2,970,000	1,939,000	7.3	12.3	65
Managers, officials, and proprietors, except farm........	4,340,000	677,000	10.7	4.3	16
Clerical and kindred workers...	2,602,000	4,292,000	6.4	27.3	165
Sales workers.................	2,596,000	1,329,000	6.4	8.5	51
Craftsmen, foremen, and kindred workers..............	7,546,000	236,000	18.6	1.5	3
Operatives and kindred workers	8,120,000	3,019,000	20.0	19.2	37

SOURCE: U.S. Bureau of the Census, *Census of Population: 1950*, part I, United States Summary, 1953, p. 102, table 54. The column headed "Per Cent of Total Labor Force" does not add up to 100 per cent, since not all occupational categories have been listed.

labor force are employed as operatives as are men. On the other hand, there are relatively few female managers, officials, proprietors, craftsmen, or foremen. The relative importance of women in "operative" roles may also be seen by the fact that by 1944 women constituted a sizable proportion of the total union membership.[32]

The income of female workers is, on the whole, inferior to that of men. For instance, in 1952 only 14 per cent of men earned less than $1,000 a year, but over 40 per cent of working women earned less than that amount. Again, about 55 per cent of men earned $3,000 and over, but only 13 per cent of working women earned that much.[33] It can be seen, from an examination of Table 29 that in the occupations which

[32] Gladys Dickason, "Women in Labor Unions," *The Annals of the American Academy of Political and Social Science*, vol. 251, p. 70, table 1, 1947.
[33] U.S. Bureau of the Census, *Statistical Abstract of the United States: 1954*, p. 318, table 354.

contain large numbers of industrial workers, women's salaries were between 30 and 66 per cent that of men. The differential in the salary of men and women is also found in the same type of occupational roles *within* industries.[34]

Obviously, where the wife is working there must be important effects on the role she plays in the family; her separation from the home alone would be enough to ensure this result. But the specific type of effect which results from her holding a job will depend in good part on her motives for working. Motives for working differ among women individ-

Table 29. Median Salary of Men and Women in Certain Occupations Compared, 1952

Occupation	Median salary		Salary of women expressed as a percentage of that of men
	Men	Women	
Professional and technical....................	$4,691	$2,695	57
Managers, officials, proprietors, except farm...	4,696	2,705	58
Clerical and kindred workers................	3,421	2,270	66
Sales workers.............................	3,576	1,075	30
Craftsmen, foremen, and kindred workers.....	3,756	2,075	55
Operatives and kindred workers.............	3,216	1,908	59

SOURCE: U.S. Bureau of the Census, *Statistical Abstract of the United States: 1954*, p. 318, table 355.

ually and from class to class. In the upper and upper-middle classes, the wife may work to relieve boredom, to fulfill a creative urge, or to continue an interest, perhaps first acquired at college. Since the values of this section of society are generally against the employment of married women, the woman must choose her occupation with care; e.g., she may, with propriety, become the owner of an expensive female clothing store, but not a school teacher or a factory operative. She undoubtedly gains a certain independence of her family role by working; she is no longer tied to the home and its chores, or to her children. However, the income which she gains from her job is rarely of significance to the financial standing of the family; actually most or all of it may go to pay for domestic help or education. Nor is the status of the family likely to be affected by the occupation which the woman pursues. It is doubtful, therefore, that she gains authority or prestige within the family by holding a job outside of it.

On the lower levels of society, motives for working may include

[34] Dorothy S. Brady, "Equal Pay for Women Workers," *The Annals of the American Academy of Political and Social Science*, vol. 251, p. 58, table 1, 1947.

a tradition of working where there are no children, a desire to maintain a certain standard of living, or direct economic necessity. In any case, the woman may be making a substantial contribution to the finances of her home. This is all the more true because her income is rarely spent on domestic help or education; she usually shoulders the burden of housekeeping, along with her occupational duties. Since the motives of the woman in filling a job are not peripheral or ephemeral, her position in the family may be enhanced; she is a personage of real importance to the financial well-being of the family.

There can be no doubt, of course, that the removal of the woman from the home implies new modes of adjustment to husband, children, and to the home. However, these new modes of adjustment, although difficult to achieve, often eventuate in satisfactory adjustments between husbands and wives.[35] It is, perhaps, more difficult for the working mother to achieve a satisfactory adjustment to her children, a point to which we shall return later.

However, the great majority of married women in all classes—even in the working class—are entirely employed as housekeepers, wives, and mothers. The traditional family role is strongly supported by the values of our society, which hold that married women, especially if there are children, should devote their full time to family roles. This does not mean, however, that industrialism has not had strong indirect effects on the role of the woman within the family.

In general, industrialism seems to increase the power and freedom of women within the family. The very fact that the talents and energy of the husband are drawn off into the occupational world, away from the family, means that the importance of the wife in the family is increased. The home becomes the almost exclusive preserve of the wife. How the home is run, how the children are socialized, what moral and cultural tone the home attains—all depend primarily on her aptitude and energy.

More specifically, the position of the woman in the family also varies in terms of the social and economic status of the family. On the upper levels, she may enjoy a position of high status within the family. This status often rests, as we have seen, on the financial resources and family background of the wife; in fact, the status of the family as a whole may depend on the status of her family. In addition, since the upper-class wife can afford domestic help, mechanical gadgets, and education of the children away from home, she is consequently freed from the routine, commonplace tasks of family life. The upper-class wife may be a person of considerable leisure.

[35] Harry J. Locke and Muriel Mackeprang, "Marital Adjustment and the Employed Wife," *The American Journal of Sociology*, vol. 54, no. 6, pp. 536–538, 1949. Copyright by the University of Chicago.

The middle-class wife, by contrast, often finds herself faced with a difficult and complex role. On the one hand, since her financial resources are usually limited, she must bear the full burden of housework and the work connected with rearing the children. Her task may be lightened by mechanical gadgets and prepared foods, but it is rare that she can afford domestic help or can send her children to boarding schools. She may also be faced by the necessity of helping her husband in his career; e.g., by maintaining a certain style of life, by entertaining peers or superiors, by making a "good impression" at parties, and so on.[36] To a surprising extent, the husband may be judged by the over-all effect produced by his wife on peers and superiors.

The working-class wife may be just as burdened as her middle-class sister by housework, and usually she has more children to raise, but it seems safe to say that as a rule there is less tension in her role. She does not have to maintain her house as a showpiece; nor must her children be raised in such a way as to enhance the middle-class status of the family. The working-class wife is not a part of her husband's career; indeed, he has no career in the technical sense of the term, and the wife does not have to impress his superiors or peers. Coupled with this freedom from tension is the general freedom which the working-class wife shares with other women in an industrial society: the freedom to manage and direct her home. On the other hand, the working-class wife rarely has the same independence of her husband as the upper-class wife, or the position of equality with her husband that the middle-class wife possesses. Often the working-class wife must adjust to a husband who has authoritarian attitudes toward family life. But she is not without power even in the face of the most rigidly authoritarian husband. Her values do not prevent her from taking work which would be considered menial at other levels of society. And, if it should be necessary to dissolve the marriage, she often has an extended kin-group on which she can rely for support.[37]

Childhood and Industry. The relationship between industrialism and the role of children is, today, almost entirely an indirect one; whatever impulses from industry affect children are transmitted through the structure of the family. In an earlier day, industry had a more direct— and grim!—influence on large numbers of children. In 1870, when the development of industry in the United States had begun, almost 1 out of every 5 boys between the ages of 10 and 15 was working, and about 1 out of every 14 girls of the same age was employed. The

---

[36] For a very readable account of the problems faced by the wives of young corporation officials see the two articles by William H. Whyte, Jr., "The Wives of Management," *Fortune*, October, 1951, pp. 86ff., and "The Corporation and the Wife," *Fortune*, November, 1951, pp. 109ff.

[37] Davis, Gardner, and Gardner, *op. cit.*, pp. 118–121.

year 1900 was the peak year in the employment of children; about 1 in 4 of boys between 10 and 15 was working, and about 1 in 10 of the girls.[38] By 1950 only 7.8 per cent of boys between 10 and 15 were in the working force, and less than 3 per cent of the girls. This decrease in the employment of children has been due largely to state and Federal legislation. In 23 states, the legal minimum working age is 16; in 22 states it is 15 years; while one state does not specify a minimum, but controls child labor through school attendance laws.[39] The Federal government also controls child labor through various provisions in the Wagner Act and its successor, the Taft-Hartley Act.[40]

Although industrialism is no longer a direct influence on children, the role of the child is nevertheless influenced by industry at all levels of society. The influence of the father's occupation is, in the first place, transmitted to the child in many subtle ways. All occupations breed certain types of tensions and strains in the individuals who fill the roles; conversely occupations afford certain degrees of status, authority, and prestige. These tensions, strains, prestige, and power (or the absence of any of these) are carried over to the family and become part of the environment in which the child's mind and personality are molded.[41]

In the second place, the status-class position of the family has important influences on the socialization of the child. The crucial role for the child in this connection is that of the mother, for in the absence of the father at work, it is she who for all practical purposes transmits the impulses arising from the status and class group to her children. The values, morals, prejudices, definitions, tastes, and aversions which she has learned during her life in a particular section of society inevitably influence the personality development of the child. The finished personality inevitably reflects, then, certain major socioeconomic divisions in society, which, as we have seen, are closely related to industrialism.

It follows, then, that each level of society produces a specific type or pattern of role for children. At upper class and status levels, the child occupies an important role in the family, even though the father is occupied elsewhere, the mother may be pursuing an outside interest, and the care and raising of the child is left in the hands of governesses

---

[38] Jaffee and Stewart, *op. cit.*, p. 168, table 16.

[39] See Russell H. Kurtz (ed.), *Social Work Year Book 1954*, American Association of Social Workers, New York, 1954, p. 310.

[40] *Ibid.*, pp. 310–311.

[41] For a general discussion of the relationship between occupation and the personality of *disturbed* children, see Bruno Bettelheim and Emmy Sylvester, "Notes on the Impact of Parental Occupations; Some Cultural Determinants of Symptom Choice in Emotionally Disturbed Children," *American Journal of Orthopsychiatry*, vol. 20, pp. 785–787, 1950.

and nurses. The child is the heir of the family name; the boy may someday inherit his father's high occupational position, the girl will someday make a "suitable" marriage. The socialization of the child is directed at transmitting to him the values and morals of upper classes; upper-class standards of taste, criteria for picking of friends and associates, modes of dress and of speech, and so on. The child may be under considerable tension to live up to family traditions, but he is compensated for this by exceptional personal, social, and economic security.

In the middle class, children and parents are much more directly concerned with each other. One of the reasons for this is that the child may directly affect the ability of the family to maintain a middle-class position. The child may, for instance, be a considerable economic burden to the family. Furthermore, the status of the family is determined in part by the behavior of the child; the child is, so to speak, a part of the "front" which the middle-class family shows to the world. Consequently one major direction of socialization in the middle class is along the lines of teaching the child how to act "properly"; to dress properly, speak properly, eat properly. Another major direction of socialization is along the lines of inculcating in the child a desire to "rise," to "succeed." Children are taught to excel other children in school and on the playground; they are taught the value of higher education and pointed toward some occupation with prestige. The success or failure of the child in these endeavors confers prestige on, or subtracts it from, the family.

The burden of socializing the child in the middle classes almost always falls on the mother; it is up to her to inculcate the proper attitudes and aspirations in the child. But here the middle-class mother is faced with a dilemma. The child must be made to "want" to excel in school, to dress, eat, and talk properly. He cannot be coerced with any great degree of success; in fact, coercion may backfire disastrously. Consequently, as Margaret Mead has pointed out, the middle-class mother tries to control her children by giving or withdrawing love; in effect she says to them "either act properly or I will not love you."[42] Since the middle-class child is strongly attached to the mother, this threat can be efficacious. Or, the middle-class mother may attempt to control her children by granting them or denying them access to the rich childhood culture of toys, television sets, and movies which are made symbols of the love of parents for their children in this class.

The position of the working-class child differs from that of children in other classes. The working-class child is important neither for the

[42] Margaret Mead, *And Keep Your Powder Dry*, William Morrow & Company, Inc., New York, 1943, chap. VI.

career of his father nor for the position of the family in society;
nor is there much interest in the family name. Consequently, the working-class child is rarely driven to "succeed" or to live up to what
are considered higher-class standards of propriety and decorum.[43] This
does not mean that the child is not supposed to behave according to certain values, but they are the values of his class. The child must not
disobey his parent, he must not get into trouble at school or with the
police. The boy must be masculine, ready and able to fight; the girl is
often expected to perform certain chores in the home, perhaps minding
a younger child. Obedience is exacted from the child at the pain of
corporal punishment or other rigorous sanctions. Love may be given
freely in the working-class family, but it is rarely used as a means of
control.

Adding to the rigor of the working-class child's position is the poor
financial position of the family, the relative lack of security, the lack of
family status. If the child goes to a school where there are children
from other classes, he may be severely handicapped, perhaps most of all
by his failure to share with his middle-class schoolmates the value of
"success."

However, in spite of the physical rigors to which the working-
class child may be exposed, from another point of view he enjoys a
peculiar degree of freedom in various directions. He is not expected
to devote his time to preparing for a career; he is not constantly being
compared with other children, nor is he expected to live up to
the standards of some neighborhood paragon. He may have a great
deal of physical freedom; he may spend a good deal of time on the
streets, or with the neighborhood gang. He is usually subjected to fewer
taboos concerning cleanliness or sexual experimentation. This is not
meant to be an idyllic picture; the "freedom" pictured above may imply
a hard, dangerous, unhealthy existence. But it is meant to show that
children in the working class undergo experiences quite different from
those faced by children in other classes.

Adolescent Roles and Industrialism. Adolescents play diverse roles in
our society. One large group enters the labor force, in many cases
becoming connected with industry. An examination of Table 30 reveals
that more and more adolescents enter the labor force as their age increases. By the time the age level 18 to 19 is reached, over 71 per cent
of the men and over 45 per cent of the women are in the labor force.
On the other hand, another large portion of adolescents is not in the

---

[43] See Allison Davis, "American Status Systems and the Socialization of the Child,"
American Sociological Review, vol. 6, no. 3, pp. 345–354, 1941; Robert J. Havighurst
and Allison Davis, "A Comparison of the Chicago and Harvard Studies of Social
Class Differences in Child Rearing," *American Sociological Review,* vol. 20, no. 4,
pp. 438–442, 1955.

labor force at all; they are supported by parents, usually while going through high school and college.

The paths that adolescents follow, whether into the labor force or into higher education, are strongly correlated with the status-class position of the families from which they come. Lower-class or working-

Table 30. Numbers and Percentage of Adolescents, 14–19, in the Labor Force, by Sex, 1950

Age	Numbers		Percentage of population in labor force	
	Male	Female	Male	Female
14–15	528,000	181,000	24.4	8.6
16–17	901,000	513,000	44.0	25.2
18–19	1,366,000	983,000	71.1	45.6

SOURCE: Abstracted from A. J. Jaffee and Charles D. Stewart, *Manpower Resources and Utilization*, John Wiley & Sons, Inc., New York, 1951, p. 123, table 1.

Table 31. Numbers and Percentage of Adolescents, 14–19, in Various Occupations, by Sex, 1950

Occupation	Numbers		Per cent of total employed in given occupation	
	Males	Females	Males	Females
Professional, technical, and kindred workers	26,363	64,624	0.9	3.0
Managers, officials, and proprietors, except farm..............................	17,876	5,939	0.5	0.7
Clerical and kindred workers..............	136,842	446,644	5.0	14.0
Sales workers...........................	210,663	172,848	8.0	13.0
Craftsmen, foremen, and kindred workers..	112,137	8,078	1.0	4.0
Operatives and kindred workers...........	399,823	171,980	5.0	6.0

SOURCE: U.S. Bureau of the Census, *Census of Population: 1950*, vol. II, *Characteristics of the Population*, part I, United States Summary, pp. 273–276, table 127.

class adolescents tend to drop out of school at an early age, often the minimum age allowable, sometimes earlier.[44] These adolescents enter the working force, often filling the most poorly paid, low-status, unskilled occupational roles. In Table 31, it can be seen that the largest number of male adolescents become operatives and the largest number of female adolescents become clerks or hold kindred jobs. In terms

[44] See August B. Hollingshead, *Elmtown's Youth*, John Wiley & Sons, Inc., New York, 1949, p. 330.

of both absolute figures and percentage of the total employed, adolescents have the poorest chances of becoming professionals, technicians, managers, officials, or proprietors.

The culture of upper class and status groups decrees that adolescents enter private secondary school and afterward go on to college, often one traditionally chosen. But the upper-class adolescent does not always finish school; going to college is a sort of obeisance to family tradition and status-class expectation. The upper-class adolescent may enter the occupational world at a rather early age, usually at a high level, often in his father's or some relative's firm.

In the middle class the major adolescent roles are concerned with education; for instance, more upper-middle-class adolescents are in college than the adolescents of any other class. The reason for this is probably bound up with the middle-class drive to success and high status; going to the proper college and, to a lesser extent, succeeding academically, socially, or athletically may be of vital importance to the adolescent's future career or marriage. As professional and technical education becomes more complex and as educational requirements for entrance into professional and technical roles increases, there is a growing hiatus between physical and occupational maturity; the adolescent may not enter an occupation until his early or mid-twenties or even later. It is this hiatus which, as Parsons has pointed out, leads to a frivolous "youth culture" with its bizarre modes of speech and dress and its strange values.[45]

In sum, the "lower"-ranking occupations of industry are the first to be entered by adolescents, and these occupations are filled by working-class youth. The more desirable jobs are filled later, by and large from youth from other classes. Explanations of this pattern in terms of voluntary choice have been put forward, but such explanations hardly seem to fit the facts, at least at the lower levels of society. In fact, according to one study, only a very small proportion of adolescents engaged in semiskilled or unskilled work are satisfied with their jobs; it is only in the case of professionals and technicians that young people evince great satisfaction with their occupational roles.[46] The explanation for the distribution of adolescents in our working force must be sought in the differing life chances provided by families: the financial resources available to the adolescent, his chances for education, the contacts he will be provided in the industrial world. The explanation must also be sought in the class and status culture which has been transmitted to each

[45] Talcott Parsons, *Essays in Sociological Theory, Pure and Applied*, Free Press, Glencoe, Ill., 1949, chap. X, "Age and Sex in the Social Structure."

[46] Howard M. Bell, *Youth Tell Their Story*, American Council on Education, Washington, 1938, p. 135.

adolescent, for it is this culture which will determine, in good part, his attitudes toward success, achievement, work, education, his dress, speech, and style of life.

The Role of the Aged in Industrial Society. The position of the elderly and the aged in our society has, of recent years, become the focus of increasing concern. The immediate reason for this concern is the increase in the number of aged people in our population. In 1890 only 3.9 per cent of the population was 65 years and over; in 1950, 8.2 per cent were 65 and over. In absolute figures, over 12 million people were 65 or over in 1950.[47]

Turning to the position of the aged in the labor force, we find that in 1950 about 23½ per cent of the population 65 and over were working; 41 per cent of the men and 7.8 per cent of the women were in the labor force.[48] Conversely over 76 per cent of people 65 and over were not working; 59 per cent of the men and over 92 per cent of the women were not productive workers. As age increases, more and more people drop out of the working force; only 4 men out of every thousand drop out of the working force between the ages of 30 and 34, but over 312 men out of every thousand drop out of the labor force between the ages of 65 and 69.[49] On the average, the white male worker will hold a job for 41.1 years, and spend 15.9 years in retirement; fifty years ago he would have spent as long a time in the working force, but only 9.5 years in retirement. For white women the corresponding figures would be 12.2 years spent in the labor force today with 48.7 years not in the labor force, while fifty years ago women worked for an average of 7.6 years and spent 44.6 years out of the working force.[50]

The trend in the participation of elderly males in the labor force has been steadily downward since 1900. In that year almost two-thirds of the men who survived to 65 or more were working, as compared to the 40 per cent of modern times. If the rate of decrease continues at the same pace in the future, hardly more than a third of elderly males will be in the labor force in 1975. The rate of female participation in the labor force after the age of 65 has been remarkably steady.[51]

Elderly people are unevenly distributed in various occupations. From Table 32 it can be seen that about 6½ per cent of all male managers, officials, and nonfarm proprietors are 65 and over, but only 2.7 per cent of

[47] U.S. Bureau of the Census, *Census of Population: 1950*, vol. II, *Characteristics of the Population*, part I, United States Summary, p. 176, tables 99 and 100.
[48] *Ibid.*, p. 247, table 118.
[49] Jaffee and Stewart, *op. cit.*, p. 223, table 32.
[50] *Ibid.*, p. 317, table 50.
[51] Philip M. Hauser, "Changes in the Labor-force Participation of the Older Worker," *The American Journal of Sociology*, vol. 59, no. 4, p. 315, table 2, 1954. Copyright by the University of Chicago.

male operatives are of that age level. These lower rates of retirement in
the "higher"-ranking occupations may reflect the greater life expectancy
of men in those occupations. More likely, however, they reflect the ability of higher-status men to control the age of their retirement. Operatives
and clerical workers may have little chance of continuing past the normal
age of "retirement."

The problems which beset elderly people in our society are both directly and indirectly related to industry. Undoubtedly, industry most

Table 32. Numbers and Percentage of Men and Women, 65 and over,
in Various Occupations, 1950

Occupation	Per cent that individuals 65 and over of either sex constitute of total working force in a given occupation	
	Male	Female
Professional, technical, and kindred workers.........	4.9	3.0
Managers, officials, and proprietors, except farm.....	6.5	5.6
Clerical and kindred workers......................	4.0	1.0
Sales workers...................................	5.0	2.6
Craftsmen, foremen, and kindred workers...........	4.4	3.0
Operatives and kindred workers...................	2.7	2.2

SOURCE: U.S. Bureau of the Census, *Census of Population: 1950*, vol. II, *Characteristics of the Population*, part I, United States Summary, pp. 273–275, table 127.

directly affects the elderly in a negative way—by refusing them employment. Industrialism is becoming increasingly the province of the young
worker. The reason lies not so much in the greater speed and agility of
the young worker as in the constant technological revolution in our industry. New technologies destroy the usefulness of old skills, habits, attitudes, work routines; they render obsolescent the older worker.[52] Ad-
mitting no ties of sentiment or other affectual relationships, industry
seeks to rid itself of the encumbrance of the obsolete worker, to replace
him with the young, adaptable man, who is not committed to a routine
of work.

Separation from occupation, "retirement," has several effects on the
worker, most of them adverse, though perhaps they need not all be so.
In the first place, it almost always means a drastic loss of status. As we
have seen, status is peculiarly bound up with holding a job in our society; conversely, a failure to have a job means loss of prestige and
power. By assigning our elderly people to the status of "retired," we are

[52] Ewan Clague, "Employment Problems of the Older Worker," *Monthly Labor
Review*, vol. 65, no. 6, pp. 662–663, 1947.

undermining the basis of their self-respect and depriving them of the respect of others.

In the second place, retirement means a drastic reduction in income for most elderly people. The median incomes of persons 65 and over—those who have incomes—is only about $874 a year; $1,247 for men and $654 for women.[53] For family units in which the head is 65 or over, median income is about $1,900 a year.[54] Since an elderly couple may live comfortably on about $1,700 to $1,800 a year,[55] it can be seen that about half our elderly families are adequately provided for but the other half are below the level of comfort. Even if income is adequate, the elderly may be still suffering a drastic reduction in their standard of living; the median income of families whose heads are between 55 and 64 is over $3,200 a year, while the median income of families whose heads are 65 and over is only $1,900 a year, a drop of 40 per cent. Along with this reduction in income and standard of living goes a drop in status, since in our society money income and material possessions are apt to be the most immediate indices of status.

What are the sources of income for those over 65 who are not in the labor force, or married to someone in the labor force, a total of more than two-thirds of our elderly population? Perhaps two-thirds of those not in the labor force are receiving some sort of pension; either old-age and survivors insurance, or pensions from the civil service, from the Veterans Administration, from the railroads, or from private pension plans.[56] The rest are living from savings, or are receiving public assistance, or are supported by their children, or are in institutions.

Of the pension programs, by far the most important is the old-age and survivors insurance, originally provided for in the Social Security Act of 1935. Over 25 per cent of our elderly people are receiving benefits under this program.[57] Industry-provided pension plans are becoming increasingly important sources of income for industrial employees. Perhaps three-fourths of industrial firms provide pension plans for wage employees, and about 88 per cent provided pensions for executives and salaried employees.[58] Some of these pension plans are specified in the union con-

[53] U.S. Bureau of the Census, *Statistical Abstract of the United States: 1954*, p. 263, table 287. These figures are for those not in institutions.

[54] Clark Tibbitts, "Retirement Problems in American Society," *The American Journal of Sociology*, vol. 59, no. 4, p. 304, 1954. Copyright by the University of Chicago.

[55] Robert K. Burns, "Economic Aspects of Aging and Retirement," *The American Journal of Sociology*, vol. 59, no. 4, p. 386, 1954. Copyright by the University of Chicago.

[56] Tibbitts, *op. cit.*, p. 304.

[57] Burns, *op. cit.*, p. 387.

[58] Laurence J. Ackerman and Walter C. McKain, Jr., "Retirement Programs for Industrial Workers," *Harvard Business Review*, vol. 30, no. 4, p. 100, 1952.

tract; some are wholly management-sponsored. In general, the larger the firm, the more likely is there to be a pension plan.[59] With the increased interest of both management and organized labor in benefits for elderly and retired workers and employees, the industrial pension is apt to be an increasingly important source of income for the aged.

Industrialism also has certain indirect effects on the position of the aged in our society, effects which are often of an adverse kind. Perhaps the most important indirect industrial influences are transmitted through the family system. In this connection, perhaps the most important point to stress is that the elderly in our society are cut off from participation in the isolated, conjugal, child-bearing and -rearing families which make up the core of our family system. Of the population 60 years and over, only 1 man in 9, and 1 woman in 4, live with their children or other relatives; 78 per cent of the men and 67.5 per cent of the women live in their own homes.[60]

There are several reasons for this separation of the aged from the nucleus of the family system in our society. For one thing, the industrial-urban family typically occupies cramped living quarters, barely adequate for parents and children. The mere presence of the elderly may impose almost untolerable physical burdens on the family. Another point to consider is the real financial burden that the elderly, with their special medical and nursing needs, may impose on the family, particularly the socially mobile family. The elderly may also be a burden on the physically mobile family. The migrating family tends to "travel light"; very few families can afford to add to the burdens of migration by bringing along their old. Nor can the modern family, which is typically a consuming, not a producing unit, provide useful economic roles for the elderly to fill.

Separated from significant family life, the elderly in our society are often exposed to numerous tensions and strains. There is the problem of finding adequate housing, housing which is suitable to the limited income of the elderly and to their physical needs. Another strain arises from the lack of affection and other emotional responses in the lives of many elderly people who are separated from their children; even the traditional satisfaction of vicariously experiencing and helping in the rearing of grandchildren is often denied them. Since women tend to survive their husbands, the emotional problems of old age strike them with particular severity. Another type of strain arises from the inability of the elderly to play ritualistic roles which might confer status on them, for instance, roles in a family ritual or in religiously oriented rituals. This

[59] *Ibid.*, p. 102.
[60] Ruth Shonle Cavan, "Family Life and Family Substitutes in Old Age," *American Sociological Review*, vol. 14, no. 1, p. 71, table 1, 1949.

situation may be compared with that existing in other societies, where the elderly may play vital roles at feasts, at weddings, and in family-centered religious rituals.

The position of the aged in our society differs from class to class, although certain problems connected with physical deterioration and disease do not spare anyone, no matter what the class. The aged of the upper class are, of course, relatively secure financially. Furthermore, they are in a more fortunate position in regard to status than the aged in other classes. For the elderly upper-class person, "retirement" may mean very little or no status loss; financial resources and the family name remain as solid bases for status. In some upper-class families the elderly person may assume increased status, since he symbolizes the family lineage; through his or her person pass the bonds of kinship among various cousins and other relatives. He is often the final authority on family history and family values,[61] the final arbiter of manners.

It is among the elderly in the other classes of society that tensions and strains are largely felt. It is here that financial problems arise—that strains result from loss of occupation, diminution of status, lack of affection, the cutting of family ties. These are the common problems of almost all our elderly people in these classes. There is little evidence to show that, short of the top level of society, status-class position plays an important part in determining what problems the elderly will face or whether the adjustment they make to their position will be good or poor.[62]

The problems of the aged have arisen in a society which only yesterday was concerned with child labor; these problems are too new, too little understood, and too little recognized to have aroused, as yet, a determined and concentrated effort to solve them. But preliminary studies indicate the directions in which solutions may be found. For instance, it may be possible to educate management and the public as to the desirability of allowing elderly people in certain types of occupations to retain their jobs past the age of retirement. Conversely it may be possible to educate the old as to the desirability of retirement and the possibility of living useful lives in the postoccupation years. Certainly more study should be devoted to finding substitute roles for the elderly, even if these are leisure roles or community roles, or roles in a community of the elderly.[63] Migration of the old to less climatically rigorous sections of the

[61] Davis, Gardner, and Gardner, *op. cit.*, p. 89.

[62] John Frank Schmidt, "Patterns of Poor Adjustment in Old Age," *The American Journal of Sociology,* vol. 57, no. 1, p. 42, 1951. Copyright by the University of Chicago.

[63] For a general statement on this problem see Robert J. Havighurst, "Flexibility and the Social Roles of the Retired," *The American Journal of Sociology,* vol. 59, no. 4, pp. 309–311, 1954. Copyright by the University of Chicago.

country might be combined with migration toward areas in which satisfactory social conditions for the old exist. Medical research might be directed at the physical and mental problems connected with aging. At all events, an industrial society which, by raising standards of living and health, has created a great mass of elderly people, and which by increasing productivity has deprived them of usefulness, must make some move to solve the problems it has created.[64]

Industry and Family Disorganization. If industry has had certain direct and indirect effects on the structure and function of family life, it has also had direct and indirect effects on the disorganization and dissolution of families. Certainly, it is easy to show that the rate of divorce has increased in the United States with the rise of industrialism. Between 1867 and 1929, a period coinciding with the great growth period of American industry, the divorce rate increased about five times as fast as the population.[65] It is more difficult, however, to discover the nature of the relationship between the rise of industrialism and family disorganization.

Perhaps one clue to this relationship is provided by statistics on the relationship of divorce and desertion to occupation. A number of studies have shown that both desertion and divorce are most frequent among holders of lower-ranking occupational roles. Among the varied occupations, divorce rates are highest among the semiskilled; next among craftsmen and foremen; then among clerical and sales people; followed by proprietors, managers, and officials; and least frequent among professionals.[66] Rates of desertion show the same tendency to follow the occupational scale from lower- to higher-ranking occupations, although the *total* of desertions among all higher-ranking job holders is not much less than among *all* holders of lower-ranking jobs.[67]

The inverse relationship between desertion and divorce and occupational rank suggests the possibility that industry is having some influence

---

[64] Increased concern with problems of the old is reflected in an increasing amount of activity in this area. See T. Lynn Smith (ed.), *Living in the Later Years*, a report on the Second Annual Southern Conference on Gerontology held at the University of Florida, Jan. 28–29, 1952, University of Florida Press, Gainesville, Fla., 1952; and Irving L. Webber (ed.), *Aging and Retirement*, a report on the Fifth Annual Southern Conference on Gerontology, held at the University of Florida, December 28–30, 1954, University of Florida Press, Gainesville, Fla., 1955.

[65] Alfred Cahen, *Statistical Analysis of American Divorce*, Columbia University Press, New York, 1932, p. 21.

[66] See the following studies: William M. Kephart, "Occupational Level and Marital Disruption," *American Sociological Review*, vol. 20, no. 4, p. 459, table 1, 1955; William J. Goode, "Economic Factors and Marital Stability," *American Sociological Review*, vol. 16, no. 6, p. 805, 1951; H. Ashley Weeks, "Differential Divorce Rates by Occupations," *Social Forces*, vol. 21, no. 3, p. 336, table 1, 1943; William J. Goode, *After Divorce*, Free Press, Glencoe, Ill., 1956, chaps. IV–VI.

[67] Kephart, *op. cit.*, p. 461, table 3.

on family disorganization, at least where the spouse or spouses fill low-ranking occupational roles. Unfortunately, research in this area is almost totally lacking. We shall speculate briefly here on the relationship between family disorganization and industry, confining these speculations to working-class families.

It is possible that industry is *directly* contributing to the disorganization of some working-class families by imposing certain deleterious physical conditions on those families. The absence of the father from the home, work on the night shift, or, as in the case of truck drivers and railroad workers, entire days spent away from home, may tear at the basic fabric of the family, separating husband and wife, parents and children.

It seems more likely, however, that industry influences family disorganization in the working class by creating certain economic and social conditions which, when taken in conjunction with certain psychological and cultural factors peculiar to the working class, may lead to family disorganization. For one thing, the fact that some working-class families have incomes which are below the level of adequacy as defined in this country must impose severe strains on the self-respect of the husband and the patience of the wife. Under the influence of the constant nagging of economic uncertainty, the conjugal relationship may begin to dissolve.

Another indirect influence of industry on family stability is the opportunity which industry offers the woman for financial independence. The working-class woman need not be tied to a spouse through economic need, or through a feeling of inadequacy for the occupational world. Nor is she committed to her husband because she is dependent on him for her status position. Consequently in a family crisis she may seek a way out by going to work, or she may even choose dissolution of the marriage with the knowledge of the possibility of taking work.

In times of depression, or even in normal times during a period of layoff, the woman may have to go to work to supplement income or even to support the family. Under these circumstances, if there is little sympathy between spouses, the wife may see no reason to support an idle husband, or a husband may refuse to submit to the "humiliation" of being supported by his wife. Since the man cannot play the role in the family that is his by tradition and that others expect of him, the structure of the family begins to crack. Actually, divorces drop off during periods of severe depression, frequently because of the expense involved, but apparently the groundwork for later divorces is laid then.[68]

A still more remote industrial influence on family disorganization may be found in certain social and economic conditions. It is relatively rare for the working-class family to possess a large property stake; rarely

[68] See Robert S. Lynd and Helen Merrell Lynd, *Middletown in Transition*, Harcourt, Brace and Company, Inc., New York, 1937, pp. 152–162.

are there bonds or stocks, a house, expensive furniture. A family so constituted can be dissolved with a minimum of trouble. Furthermore, since the working-class family is not mobile socially, there is not a pressing need to preserve the unity of the home as a symbol of social-class status. Divorce may or may not confer disgrace on a working-class spouse, but it certainly interferes very little with the "career" of the husband or the social position of the wife.

Certain aspects of working-class culture—a subtype of industrial culture—would seem also to lead to family disorganization in certain cases. For instance, there may be surprisingly little emotional stake in the family, at least on the part of the father. Lower-class and working-class culture does not taboo extramarital sexual experience for the husband to nearly the same extent as in the middle class.[69] Nor does the father have the same emotional stake in his children as the middle-class father; he may think of the children as belonging primarily to the mother.[70] Not only may these acts and attitudes be in themselves causes of family instability, but they may also indicate a readiness on the part of the man for the dissolution of the marriage.

The tendency of some working-class fathers to define their family roles in authoritarian terms may lead to family crises. This is all the more true because the husband's authoritarian attitude is backed up neither by his financial power, nor by his high occupational status, nor by the general culture. Thus there is little reason for the wife or for the children to accept the tyranny or brutality of the husband and father.

Finally, if the marriage actually dissolves, the wife is not without support in her extended kin-group, which may care for her children while she goes to work. Furthermore, the frequent remarriage of divorced people in the working class may reflect an attitude which makes for a certain equanimity in accepting divorce.

In short, industrialism strikes at the working-class marriage mainly by failing to provide economic and social ground in which the family might take root. Without ties to property, without a sizable financial income, without claims to status, the stability of the working-class family must rest largely on the congeniality of the spouses, or on extraneous factors such as religious convictions. Apparently these are not enough; where there are temperamental differences, personality incompatibilities, where there is constant bickering, the structure of the family tends to give way.

[69] Alfred C. Kinsey, Wardell B. Pomeroy, and Clyde E. Martin, *Sexual Behavior in the Human Male*, W. B. Saunders Company, Philadelphia, 1948, p. 592.
[70] Goode, *op. cit.*, p. 809.

CHAPTER 19

Industrialism and Government

We have investigated the interrelationships of industry and several diverse areas of social life: the community, social class and status groups, minorities, and the family. The processes of interaction between industry and these areas of social life have had this in common—they have not been the result of a consciously directed social process. No one planned to change the shape of the community, or to transform the patriarchal family into an isolated, conjugal family; these and other changes both in industry and society have been the unintended result of myriad attempts by men and women to adapt their lives to the realities of an industrial civilization. However, in the case of the institution we wish to consider now—government—the opposite has often been true. Here the various elements of industry have aimed consciously at control, either for purposes of achieving their interests, or in order to mold the institution in the shape of some ideal image. At the same time government has tried consciously to control and shape industry.

In order to understand why, in this one area, social interaction has been purposive, it is necessary to understand some of the essential functions of government in society.[1] Above all, government is that institution by which men everywhere seek to order society, that is, to control the structure and functioning of society. As an instrument for ordering society, government has this unique advantage: it possesses a monopoly of

---

[1] Precisely because of the purposive nature of government, there has been wide disagreement as to what are or ought to be these functions. The definition of the functions of government offered here is couched in terms of the interests of this book. The student will undoubtedly be familiar with the great classical works in this field, such as Thomas Hobbes, *Leviathan*, Oxford University Press, New York, edition of 1909, chaps. XIII–XXIII; John Stuart Mill, *Utilitarianism, Liberty, and Representative Government*, E. P. Dutton & Co., Inc., New York, edition of 1910, especially the essay "On Liberty"; V. I. Lenin, *State and Revolution*, International Publishers Co., Inc., New York, 1932, chap. I. For a review of several theories of the functions of the state, see Harold D. Lasswell and Abraham Kaplan, *Power and Society*, Yale University Press, New Haven, Conn., 1950, chap. VIII.

many of the major instruments of force in a given area.[2] Armies, navies, police forces, investigative committees, courts, information and propaganda bureaus—all are at the disposal of government and of those who control the government. The force which a modern government commands overshadows the power of all other organizations in modern society, even the power of industrial bureaucracies. It is no wonder, then, that any group which wishes to control the order of society must first aim at influencing, controlling, or even capturing the governmental institutions.

It is the essence of democratic government that it provides means by which the major groups in society may peaceably struggle to attain control of the government and to impose a certain order on society. It is also an essential part of a democratic government that it provide opportunities for social groups to compromise their various versions of correct societal order. But democratic government is not in itself a guarantee against a condition where just one or a very few powerful organized groups dominate government.

Both the managerial and labor components of industrialism try, of course, to influence or, if possible, control governmental institutions. Industrialism can exist only within a framework of values, laws, and social relationships of certain definite types. In order to construct and maintain such a social structure, industrialism everywhere has had to use the power of government; e.g., to root out feudal social relationships, to destroy parasitic social classes, and to guarantee the sanctity of contracts.

Historical Review of Relationships between Government and Industry. In the past, the relationship between industrialism and government was obscured by the doctrine of *laissez faire* and by the underlying conditions which gave rise to that doctrine. The doctrine of *laissez faire* held that each man naturally and logically seeks to better his economic interests. The sum total of individual efforts is an efficiently functioning society with an expanding industry, lively trade, and prosperity for all, capitalist and worker alike, although perhaps individual capitalists and workers who cannot stand the competitive pace may go under. Thus each man, in working for himself, is at the same time furthering the interests of all. According to Adam Smith, it is as if an "unseen hand" is guiding the destiny of men. But there is one necessary condition if the "unseen hand" is to operate effectively: there must be no interference from government in the natural laws which directed men to their individual pursuits and thus to the betterment of all society.

There is grave doubt as to whether this doctrine gave an accurate picture of the relationship between industry and government, even in the

---

[2] Max Weber, *From Max Weber: Essays in Sociology*, translated and edited by H. H. Gerth and C. Wright Mills, Oxford University Press, New York, 1946, p. 78.

early days of industrialism. The laissez-faire doctrine ignored the fact that industrialism had always operated in an economy whose orderliness was guaranteed by the government. An aura of sanctity may have surrounded the contract, but in the last analysis, it was only the state which could enforce the contract.[3] Similarly the entrepreneur may have considered his property as belonging to him by virture of divine right, or as a reward for his virtue, or as the outcome of a natural economic law, but it was only the government which could guarantee him continued possession and use of his property. Furthermore, even in the early days of industrialism, the entrepreneur looked to government for, and received from government, many special favors. Tariffs protected him from foreign competition. His labor supply was ensured by the destruction, through governmental acts, of feudal ties between men and land, between peasants and noblemen. Later the judicial machinery of government would protect him against the "conspiratorial" efforts of his workingmen to form unions. Franchises, grants of land, outright subsidies—all these special privileges and many others besides attested to the existence of a strong relationship between industry and government.

Furthermore, the doctrine of *laissez faire* presupposed an economy of small, intensely competing firms, with unlimited opportunities for new entrepreneurs. A condition something like this may have existed in the early days of industrialism, though it is easy to exaggerate the prevalence of this condition. At any rate, it was only in such a society that the intervention of government in industry could be held to externals such as those enumerated above. As industries grew and then combined into still larger industries, the relationship between industry and government became more direct and inclusive. Thus, in the United States, the Civil War ushered in an entirely new set of relationships between government and industry—relationships which differed as much from those of the laissez-faire period as the relationships of the laissez-faire period differed from those of mercantilism.

From the Civil War to 1900. Whatever the causes and aims of the Civil War may have been, one of its effects was the ousting of the old planter aristocracy, together with its sympathizers and allies, from the Federal government. In their place came new men, representing among other things the new, rapidly expanding, aggressive industrialism of the North. It was the historical task of these men first to overthrow the old

[3] That the highly developed classical economic theory was based on an image of a certain kind of society, and was applicable only to that type of society, has come to be generally recognized in this century. See Thorstein Veblen, *The Place of Science in Modern Civilization and Other Essays*, The Viking Press, Inc., New York, 1919, pp. 56–81 and 161–179; O. H. Taylor, "Economics and the Idea of Natural Laws," *Quarterly Journal of Economics*, vol. 44, pp. 205–241, 1929; O. H. Taylor, "Economics and the Idea of the *jus naturale*," *ibid.*, pp. 1–39, 1930.

social order of the South and then to erect a new social and economic order in the nation as a whole. How this latter task was accomplished has already been told in Chapter 4: tariff walls were erected to protect domestic industries, large grants of land were given to railroads, other types of communications were improved, corporations were placed under the protection of a constitutional amendment, and labor was subjected especially to judicial restrictions. By the end of the nineteenth century the design of the new social order was complete. The social order of the small independent farmer, the mercantilist, and the planter was gone; in its place was a social order suited to giant industry and centralized finance.

In the course of accomplishing this transformation in the social order, new relationships between government and industry were established. Industrialism, particularly industrial management, became a dominant influence in the Federal government and in many state governments. The "gilded age" was also the age of the bribed legislator, the corporation lawyer sitting on the bench, the controlled political convention. But it is neither fair nor accurate to say that industrial ownership established its influence over government against the wishes of the mass of the American people. On the contrary, the American electorate demonstrated on more than one occasion its enthusiasm for the new social arrangements and the new order in government.

Along with the transformation in the relationship between industry and government, the nature of government was radically changed. In place of the small, relatively weak, relatively decentralized government of the pre–Civil War period, there grew a large bureaucratized government with an efficient Navy, a growing civil service, and an expanding budget.[4] As compared to modern government, the government of the "gilded age" may seem insignificant, but this is not a valid comparison; the correct comparison is between the rapidly developing bureaucracy of the period, on the one hand, and the type of government which existed in laissez-faire society on the other.

From 1900 to World War I. At the beginning of this century, a reaction against managerial influence over government began. Goaded by unrest among farmers, among city workers, and in the middle classes, the governmental bureaucracy began, as it were, a counterattack on industrial institutions.[5] Under Presidents Theodore Roosevelt and Wil-

---

[4] The change in the structure and function of the Federal government may be found described in any of the standard American histories. For a detailed account of this development, see Lloyd Milton Short, "The Development of National Administrative Organization in the United States," thesis, The Institute for Government Research, Urbana, Ill., 1923, chaps. XI–XX.

[5] For literature on this period the student is again referred to the standard works on American history (see bibliography for this chapter at the end of the book).

son, the government moved against the large industrial corporation in some areas. Some industrial practices were regulated, some were prohibited; in a few cases, large corporations were dissolved. Government also intervened in the internal affairs of industry at least to the extent that it undertook to control the quality of some industrial products. The government also tried to establish control over the working conditions of women and children. Finally, the government made what proved to be an abortive attempt at freeing unions from the control of the courts.

However, the governmental campaign to control industry was successful only to a very limited degree. Whatever attempts were made to limit the size of corporations or to dissolve them—and the attempts were not numerous—were largely unavailing. The courts made short shrift of the labor laws; laws prohibiting the employment of children, or regulating the conditions of work for women, were held to be undue violations of the freedom of individuals. The provisions of the Clayton Act which were designed to protect labor from the courts did not curtail the issuance of antilabor injunctions by the courts. Indeed, practically all that remained of this first large-scale governmental incursion against industry were the letter of the antitrust laws, the pure food and drug acts, and the memory of a time when the industrial bureaucracy had had to bow, however slightly, to government.

From World War I to the New Deal. The third phase of governmental-industrial relationships began with the end of World War I. Under the lulling sun of prosperity, the American people dropped their interest in governmental reforms of industry and turned the government over to men who were sympathetic with industrialism, particularly industrial management.[6] Tariff rates were raised above any other level in American history. Taxes on industry and profits were minimized; regulation of financial procedure was practically abolished. The government still undertook to safeguard the quality of certain products, but otherwise it remained strictly out of the internal affairs of industry. It is true that government upheld the right of management to form company unions, to black-list union men, to conduct propaganda against unions; but since industry had always had these rights, this hardly appeared as governmental intervention in industry, at least not to industrial management. Parenthetically, it is interesting to note that in a period when big industry (along with big business and finance) had established virtual

Works dealing with this period in greater detail include Harold Underwood Faulkner, *The Quest for Social Justice*, The Macmillan Company, New York, 1931, chap. V; Harold U. Faulkner, *The Decline of Laissez-faire*, Rinehart & Company, Inc., New York, 1951, chap. XV; Louis Filler, *Crusaders for American Liberalism*, Harcourt, Brace and Company, Inc., New York, 1930.

[6] See George Soule, *Prosperity Decade*, Rinehart & Company, Inc., New York, 1947, pp. 131–138 and, of somewhat more general interest, chap. VIII.

hegemony over the government, industrialists and politicians alike still talked in the language of *laissez faire*.[7]

The New Deal. The first, second, and third phases in the relationships between government and industry had passed into each other in imperceptible stages; the fourth phase was heralded by the sound of crashing stocks and failing businesses, the closing of doors and the shuffling feet of the unemployed.[8] The New Deal, which began as a series of emergency measures, supported by all sections of the population including industrial management, resulted in a fundamental transformation in the relationship between industry and government.[9] These events are still so recent, still so painful or glorious to many, that it is difficult to discuss them in terms which will seem objective. But it should be remembered that the New Deal had deep roots in American history and that, if the period of the 1920s was an attempt to revive the careless freedom of the "gilded age," then the New Deal in part strove to extend and magnify a movement which had been begun in the early days of the century.

In order to understand the nature of the New Deal transformation of government-industry relationships it is necessary to understand something of its inner nature. It is probably a mistake to think of the New Deal as possessing a coherent economic philosophy, or as moving along a determined path to a known goal; certainly it is a grievous error to think of it as some sort of conspiracy. But it may be said that what the New Deal was aiming at, in an almost incoherent way, was to bring industry into line with the demands of a large-scale modern society. It was a cardinal tenet of the New Deal that industry had grown so large, so complex, so productive, had such great effects on

[7] A general survey of governmental functions during the decade of the 1920s may be found in an article by Carroll H. Wooddy, "The Growth of Governmental Function," in *Recent Social Trends in the United States,* McGraw-Hill Book Company, Inc., New York, 1933, vol. II, chap. XXV.

[8] The story of the great crash has been told and retold. An extremely well written account is provided by Frederick Louis Allen, *Only Yesterday,* Harper & Brothers, New York, 1931, chaps. 12–14. A more recent account may be found in *The Great Crash* by John Kenneth Galbraith, Houghton Mifflin Company, Boston, 1955.

[9] The student who is interested in the New Deal will find a voluminous literature on the subject. A few works may be offered here as a guide to further study. See Broadus Mitchell, *Depression Decade,* Rinehart & Company, Inc., New York, 1947; Basil Rauch, *The History of the New Deal 1933–1938,* Farrar, Straus and Cudahy, Inc., 1944; Dixon Wecter, *The Age of the Great Depression,* The Macmillan Company, New York, 1948. It is also of considerable value to look at accounts of insiders; see Harold L. Ickes, *The Secret Diary of Harold L. Ickes,* vol. I, *The First Thousand Days,* Simon and Schuster, Inc., New York, 1953, and vol. II, *The Inside Struggle,* Simon and Schuster, Inc., New York, 1954; and Raymond Moley, *After Seven Years,* Harper & Brothers, New York, 1939. Probably the most definitive biography of Franklin Delano Roosevelt to date is by Frank Freidel, *Franklin D. Roosevelt,* vol. I, *The Apprenticeship,* Little, Brown & Company, Boston, 1952; *Franklin D. Roosevelt,* vol. II, *The Ordeal,* Little, Brown & Company, Boston, 1954.

lives of millions that the nation could no longer afford to permit this vast industry to operate in a haphazard way. The New Deal believed that large-scale planning and central direction were necessary to bring production into line with the demands of society as a whole and with other institutions. It was in order to accomplish this social change that the New Deal undertook to reform the relationships between industry and government. The major changes took place in four major areas and in numerous minor ones.

In the first place, the New Deal established the right of government to intervene in the national economy as a whole—in which, of course, industry occupied the most important place. Operating according to Keynsian principles, the New Deal tried to stimulate production by increasing the consumer's purchasing power. It believed that, by increasing demand, industrial activity would be stimulated; that this would lead to increased employment and capital investment, which would, in turn, increase demand; and so on. This policy, which led to various governmental spending programs, represented, of course, a wide-sweeping change in the traditional relationships between government and industry.[10]

In the second place, the New Deal intervened in the internal affairs of industry, sometimes in new and unheard-of ways. It sought to regulate corporate organization, for instance, by forbidding holding companies. It imposed new types of controls on the financial practices of industrial firms, e.g., it demanded the publication of certain types of information on securities. It moved with renewed vigor against monopolies and trusts, even though, paradoxically, emergency legislation such as the National Recovery Act fostered the monopoly.[11]

In the third place, the New Deal intervened in the relationships between industrial management and organized labor. It announced that the furthering of collective bargaining was government policy. It established the positive *right* of labor to organize, and it cut down the power of the courts to issue injunctions against labor practices. Even more, it specifically forbade management to oppose labor organization; it declared that management had no right to fire employees for union activity, or to form company unions, to propagandize against unions, and so on. It provided machinery—not compulsory machinery, it is true—for settling management-labor disputes. For an industry which had been accustomed to use government as a weapon against labor, this was a reversal indeed.[12]

---

[10] See Mitchell, *op. cit.*, chap. XI.

[11] For an account of the National Recovery Act see *ibid.*, chap. VII.

[12] The relation between labor and the New Deal has already been discussed in Chap. 10. Here we may note that this topic is covered in brief by Wecter, *op. cit.*, chap. VI; Rauch, *op. cit.*, pp. 184–190. Additional bibliography will be found for Chap. 10 at the end of this book.

In the fourth place, the New Deal assumed direct responsibility for the welfare and security of a myriad of individuals, including many industrial employees. Legislation was passed to regulate the labor of women and children, and this time the courts found no constitutional grounds on which to veto the legislation. A "floor" was put under wages, and a "roof" was erected over hours, while organized labor was permitted to make the best bargains it could within these limits. Perhaps not least important for the industrial worker, the New Deal established the right of elderly people, their dependents or survivors, to some sort of income, partly at their own expense, partly at the expense of the state, partly at the expense of industry. Thus it moved directly to close the gap between the needs of the workers and the generalized goals of their industrial roles.

These were the major areas of governmental intervention in industry under the New Deal. A more complete account is not possible here. Suffice it to say that the New Deal intervened in industry in many small, though significant ways, by such laws as those which tightened the food and drug acts, and by such executive directives as those which established fair employment practices in war industry.

But where did the impulse for these wide-ranging changes in the social order and in government-industry relations originate? How, in the midst of a powerful industrial society and against the determined and vocal opposition of management and a good share of the press, were these changes made? It is necessary to answer these questions if one is to grasp the essential nature of government-industry relationships, of the balance of power of these two great forces.

One major impulse for the New Deal was undoubtedly the mass revulsion against those industrial practices which led to the depression. Perhaps it is more accurate to say that the American people had little idea about which industrial practices were at fault, but they wished to see somebody punished, and the New Deal seemed to be a promising instrument for belaboring somebody. From this point of view, the fact that the New Deal chose industrial management, among other groups, to belabor is somewhat accidental. Certainly, just as the New Deal possessed little coherent social philosophy, so did the American people as a whole lack an image of some sort of social order toward which they wished to move. Therefore, the impulses toward the new order in society and toward the new relationships between industry and government were not the product of a mass movement, though undoubtedly the New Deal needed the support of the masses for its own program.

Nor can the New Deal be satisfactorily explained as the brain child of narrow pressure groups which took advantage of the confusion resulting from the depression to change the face of American society.

Undoubtedly organized labor, certain agricultural groups, and groups of unemployed or WPA workers were able to throw considerable support behind the New Deal. But it would be a mistake to think that they created the New Deal; if anything, it was the other way around. It was the New Deal, for instance, which created the conditions in which organized labor could undertake its campaign against the mass industries.

This suggests that the major impulse toward the New Deal changes must be sought in other areas. To this author it seems that this somewhat mysterious source must be found within the New Deal itself. As we have seen, the foundations of modern large-scale government in this country were laid three-quarters of a century ago; but it was the historic work of the New Deal to blow up government into an immense bureaucracy, with greatly increased scope and power. No doubt, this expansion was initially the result of attempts to ward off the worst results of the depression and to bring industry into line with the demands of modern society. But once the impulse to governmental expansion was given, government bureaucracy continued to expand under its power. Just as industrial bureaucracy possesses an inherent dynamic tendency to grow in size and power, gobbling up smaller organizations in the process, so the governmental bureaucracy tends constantly to enlarge its sphere of power and control at the expense of whatever other centers of power and control exist in the society. One of the first victims of expanding governmental bureaucracy are the smaller and less powerful governmental units: state, county, and municipal governments. And it is a foregone conclusion that at some point the vast expanding bureaucratic systems of industry and government will come into conflict—will try, that is, to grow at the expense of each other.

By the time the last major New Deal legislation was passed in 1937, the size and power of government bureaucracy had expanded enormously. World War II further increased the size and power of the governmental bureaucracy, and the Korean War and the demands of the "cold war" have maintained them. In the meantime, it is true, there has been a swing back to managerial influence in government. But by the time this happened, the changes in government had been institutionalized. Today, there is no longer any doubt that governmental bureaucracy cannot be diminished greatly; it stands powerful, unshakable, potent. An administration friendly to industrial management may try to reduce the influence of government in certain areas of industry. Thus far, except perhaps in the field of labor relationships, it has not been conspicuously successful. Government control over industry remains unchallenged at numerous important points.

The Present Structure of Government-Industry Relationships. The relationships which prevail in the United States today between government and industry form an intricate network of mutual influence and control. As compared to the 1930s, government-industry relationships have achieved something like stability; that is, neither institution is at the present time gaining much ground at the expense of the other. A description of present government-industry relationships can, therefore, be safely confined to the *structure* of those relationships without much attempt to describe the underlying forces which might eventually change them.

The Influence of Government on Industry. As one looks at the myriad laws, agencies, executive and judicial decisions through which government attempts to control industry, the first impression is of an enormous jumble without order or purpose. However, if one keeps in mind the picture of government and industry as two vast, competitive bureaucratic systems, it will be seen that the relationships between them fall into certain patterns. Governmental action in relation to industry must be seen as a part of the wider bureaucratic competition. Thus, it will be found that one great class of governmental legislation is concerned with regulating the economy as a whole. In the process, industry is made, directly or indirectly, dependent on government. A second type of governmental action is concerned with the regulation of the internal structure of industry. A third type is concerned with protecting the weak and disadvantaged within the industrial system. The result of such action is, usually, to bind these industrial masses to government, to weaken their allegiance to industry. A fourth type of governmental action is concerned with safeguarding the public as buyers of industrial products. Still a fifth type tends toward the establishment of control over the relationships between industrial management and labor. And, finally, government intervenes in the internal affairs of labor unions. We shall discuss these various phases of governmental action in relation to industry in greater detail.

Legislation Regulating Economic Practices. It has been shown that, even in the heart of the laissez-faire age, government had already intervened in the economy of industrial society. Today, of course, governmental intervention in this sphere is even more intricate, more vital to the functioning of the economy as a whole. As in the past, American industry is protected by tariff walls against foreign industries with cheap labor supply, superior access to certain raw materials, or superior techniques. In a sense, the government guarantees industry a lion's share of the American market. It is true that lately there has been a tendency to remove some of this protection, to make the American market more accessible to the industry of other countries. But this movement has gone only a short distance; America is still far from possessing a free-trade economy. Government-sponsored tariff walls remain a key part of our national economy and undoubtedly save numerous American industries from competition, perhaps even extinction.[13]

Furthermore, American governmental institutions, taking this now to mean state and Federal governments, directly regulate or control the economic practices of industrial firms. For instance, fair-trade laws regulate the relationships between manufacturers and wholesalers or retailers. Other types of laws are designed to prevent ruinous competition between industries. These types of laws may have been originally passed, with industrial backing, to further the interests of industry; their net effect is to increase the power of government over industry.

Perhaps of even greater importance to our industry and economy than the foregoing legislation are the vast government spending programs. The defense program alone calls for the expenditure of tens of billions of dollars, a large proportion of which finds its way into industry. This program has specially important effects on heavy industry, as well as on industries engaged in the direct manufacture of armaments. It is true that defense orders represent only a small proportion of the total amount of business done by American industry. However, it is a crucial proportion. Defense orders act as a vast sponge, absorbing excess industrial production, which could probably not be disposed of here or abroad. Were it not for defense spending, a certain proportion of men and machines would be idled, and disturbing reverberations might be set up in the economy as wages and profits dropped.

Inevitably, government spending on this scale greatly increases government's power over industry. The fate of certain industrial firms is entirely in the hands of government. Not only is this true of armaments industries, such as airplane plants, but it may be true also of industries which manufacture mainly for the general market but whose profitability depends on extra production for the government. To industries in this situation, the government is in a position to dictate terms; thus in various cases government has specified internal working conditions, hours, and wages, demanded the abolition of discrimination in hiring and firing, and intervened in union-management relations.

Furthermore, in an armament-supported economy, the stability of the entire country depends on government spending. Most generally, this is true because the purchasing and investment power gained by workers or investors in armaments industries or the armaments program directly or indirectly infiltrates the other sections of the economy and quickens its pace. In certain specific cases, government can determine the pros-

---

[13] It is not a question here of whether the reduction or abolition of tariff rates would benefit the American economy as a whole in the long run. The point is that if tariff rates were reduced there would be an immediate adverse effect on many industries.

perity or decline of the industry of a region or a city; for instance, the government has prevented serious local depressions by placing armaments orders in a given area, or by locating new plants there. Even industries which are not directly engaged in the armaments program are, therefore, dependent on government spending. As a result, the power of government to dictate certain terms to industry, to regulate it internally, to control its economic practices, is greatly enhanced.

Regulation of the Internal Structure of Industry. One of the earliest forms of governmental intervention in industry was the attempt to regulate the structure of industrial corporations. As we have seen, within a generation after the formation of large-scale industry, legislation was enacted which was designed to prevent the undue growth of industrial (and other) monopolies through combination and to break up existing monopolies. This legislation was strengthened in the early part of this century, and the New Deal struck at certain new monopolistic practices which had evolved in the meantime. All this legislation stands today; none of it has been repealed. It is still the declared policy and the stated aim of our government to break up industrial organizations which are in "restraint of trade."

It is true that for certain historical reasons this legislation has not prevented the growth of great industrial concentrations. The claim has been made that the reason for this failure is that government is inherently unable to stop the growth of industrial concentration. Considering the demands of modern technology and of large-scale production, there is undoubtedly much truth in this claim. However, it would be a mistake to think that government is entirely powerless to control the internal organization of corporations. For one thing, some of its failures in the past were due to the fact that government itself was firmly in the hands of monopolists, their friends or allies, who could hardly be expected to move enthusiastically against monopolies. And, for another thing, the government demonstrated in several important instances that it *did* have the power to break up industrial concentrations, at least under certain conditions.

At any rate, the important point is that government has the *potential* power to control the structure of industrial corporations, and there seem to be few inherent factors which could prevent it from using this power, if it so desired. If the encroachment of government on industry were to be resumed at some future date, antimonopoly legislation might prove to be an important weapon for the governmental bureaucracy. Nor is there any way of knowing now where such a movement would stop; conceivably it could proceed to a point where the structure of industry would be radically altered.

Legislation Protecting Weak or Disadvantaged Groups in Industry. Industrialism, particularly in its early phases, creates many weak and disadvantaged groups who lack the power to protect themselves against exploitation and who are almost helpless in the face of the hazards of the industrial system. Before the advent of unionism, the unskilled and semi-skilled workers constituted such a group; that is, at most times the socio-economic power of these workers is negligible in the face of the power of management and the hazards of industrialism. Special groups of workers, such as women and children, constitute particularly impotent and exploitable groups in industrial society. Sometimes the workers of an entire region are, because of low cultural level or the absence of or-ganization, extremely vulnerable to the hazards of industry. Minority groups such as the Negroes or the Mexican-Americans rarely have the power to protect themselves from discrimination in industry. Even unionized workers are vulnerable to unemployment, layoff, sickness, dis-ability, and old age.

Under these circumstances, government has moved to erect certain safeguards around the weak and disadvantaged. In the process it has encroached on the domain of industrialism in such a way as to limit the freedom of management. Not less significant is the fact that government greatly increases its power and prestige by binding to itself great masses of people who have no other resource in an industrial society.

It should be noted that although protective legislation has a long his-tory in the United States, it was under the New Deal that this legisla-tion was first introduced on a large scale. Today there are a number of major types of protective legislation, dealing with (1) conditions of work; (2) children, youth, and women; (3) wages and hours; (4) pay-ment of workers; (5) industrial homework; (6) minorities; (7) accident insurance; (8) vocational rehabilitation; (9) unemployment insurance; and (10) old-age insurance.

CONDITIONS OF WORK. Various laws are designed to meet certain types of industrial hazards. Thus many states have enacted laws which specify certain precautions against fires, as well as certain conditions of ventila-tion and sanitation. Many laws provide safeguards against injury from machinery or other technological processes. Hazardous industries, such as mining, are subject to especially rigid laws, though the continuation of fatal accidents in this and other hazardous industries suggests the probability of even more stringent laws and enforcement.

CHILDREN, YOUTH, AND WOMEN. Children and youth working in indus-try are protected by both state and Federal legislation. Various state laws protect the young person against a too early termination of educa-tion, set limits to the number of daily and weekly hours spent at work, prohibit nightwork and work in hazardous occupations. The Federal government, operating mainly through the Federal Fair Labor Stand-ards Act of 1938, sets a general sixteen-year minimum age for all types of employment, and an eighteen-year minimum age for hazardous employ-

ment, in all industries engaged in foreign or interstate commerce. According to the Public Contracts Act, a manufacturer supplying $10,000
or more worth of goods or services to the government must agree not to
employ boys under sixteen or girls under eighteen.

Women in industry are also protected in various ways, mostly through
state laws. In certain states there are minimum-wage and maximum-hour
laws, which apply only to women; other states specify that women must
receive the same pay as men for equal work. Various states prohibit
women from working for certain specific periods before and after childbirth; in one instance, women are entitled to cash benefits both before
and after childbirth. Other laws prevent women from working at night
and exclude them from certain hazardous occupations or from heavy jobs
which require great physical effort. In some cases the law states that
women working in industry must be provided with rest pauses and given
seats for their work.

WAGES AND HOURS. These are the subject of special laws in 26 states
and in several territories, and of various pieces of Federal legislation.
State and territorial laws specify minimum wages ranging from 40 to 75
cents an hour, and various minimum work weeks, past which overtime
must be paid. The basic Federal legislation in this field is the Fair Labor
Standards Act of 1938. In 1950 this law was amended to provide a minimum wage of 75 cents an hour and time and one-half for all work over
forty hours in one week. In addition, the Federal government controls
wages and hours through the Public Contracts Act of 1936 and the Prevailing Wage Law of 1931, both of which provide minimum wages and
maximum hours in work done for the government.

Why is legislation of this type needed, when the 75 cents an hour
provided by law amounts to only $30 for a forty-hour week—far below
the hourly rates in organized industries, or even in many unorganized
industries? The laws are necessitated by the presence in industry of
many weak and exploitable groups who are not organized and are not
likely to be organized. For instance, the South has been traditionally an
area of low wages, primarily because of a large surplus rural population
and the absence of unionization. Members of discriminated-against minority groups may also suffer from depressed wages and excessive hours
because of low cultural level, weak economic position, exclusion from
unions, or as a part of the general pattern of discrimination against them.
This is particularly true of Negroes in industry. Children and women
likewise are usually poorly equipped to defend themselves against exploitation. Old people, defective individuals, and the physically handicapped often have difficulty securing employment and may be forced to
take employment at low wages and long hours.

There can be no doubt that wages-and-hours legislation represents a formidable encroachment on managerial prerogatives. The right of management to determine hours and wages through bargaining either with individual workingmen or with their representatives is basic to our form of industrialism. It is true that thus far the government has not tried to set specific wages or hours, except in time of war; it has merely set wide limits within which wages could be determined in the traditional way. However, government has firmly established its *right* to control hours and wages; this is a right which could be employed in surprising ways under certain conditions.

PAYMENT OF WORKERS. Various state laws establish the right of the worker to be paid regularly, to be paid in full, and to be paid in cash. Some laws specify that a worker who is discharged or quits his job must be paid promptly and in full. In a number of states the labor commissioner or some other officer has the power to collect back pay for workers without cost to the workers.

"INDUSTRIAL HOMEWORK." The practice of performing industrial work in the home is regulated by various special state and Federal laws. The reasons for this are that industrial homework is frequently performed for very low wages and at excessively long hours and that it gives to certain manufacturers an unfair competitive advantage. Some states prohibit this type of work entirely; in other states, old or disabled people are allowed to perform industrial jobs at home, but under carefully controlled conditions. Federal legislation in one instance prohibits homework entirely in work done for the government, and in another makes it subject to the provisions of the Fair Labor Standards Act, establishing minimum wages and maximum hours for this type of work.

MINORITIES. Special state and, in the recent past, Federal legislation is designed to safeguard the rights of minorities in industry. Legislation against discrimination in industry has already been discussed in Chapter 17. Suffice it to say here, that 12 states forbid employers from discriminating against minority groups in hiring, firing, upgrading, etc. However, in four states the laws call for only voluntary compliance, and even where laws are mandatory, the main means of enforcement are education and persuasion. Federal legislation, originally enacted during the war, was allowed to lapse shortly after the war ended.

It can be seen that antidiscriminatory legislation has not progressed very far in the United States. However, what is most significant about this legislation is not what has been actually enacted, but rather the *potential* control which government is afforded over industry. Antidiscriminatory legislation penetrates one of the most sacred managerial prerogatives: the right of hiring, firing, demotion, and promotion. It demands that management treat its workers according to certain values, e.g., that management hire workers solely on the basis of competence. Furthermore, such legislation inevitably binds great masses of minority peoples to government. thereby substantially increasing the power of government. Here, too, the power is not so much actual as potential; the potentiality, however, in a society such as ours, is very great, and it is entirely possible that in the future minority groups will come to depend more and more on government, so that the power of government will be correspondingly enhanced.

ACCIDENT INSURANCE. Another type of state and Federal legislation is designed to compensate the worker for accidents on the job.[14] The possibility of injury or death to industrial workers is a very real one in a machine technology, more so in some industries than in others. In the past there was little recognition of hazard as a normal part of the industrial process; an employer could not be held responsible for injury to a worker, unless neglect on the employer's part could be shown. Today all states have laws designed to provide compensation to injured workers, or to their survivors in case of death, regardless of who is at fault.

Compensation to injured workers is figured as a percentage (usually between one-half and two-thirds) of the wages the injured worker was earning, with a maximum weekly income centering around $25 to $35.[15] In case of a permanently disabling injury, about half the states specify compensation for a varying period of time; the other states, as well as the Federal government, specify compensation for life. In case of death, most states specify compensation to the survivors for a certain length of time; a few specify compensation for life, or until a widow remarries or children reach a certain age. In all states, the laws specify medical aid to the injured workingmen, though in varying amounts.

In all except four states, the employer bears the entire cost of the compensation program; in the four exceptional states, the employee pays a small percentage of the costs. The universal practice of employers is to take out insurance against injury or death of their workingmen. In most cases this insurance is carried with private concerns, but some seven states require employees to use special state insurance, and in eleven other states the employer may choose between state and private insurance.

VOCATIONAL REHABILITATION. The Federal government has, since 1920, recognized the right of disabled workers to vocational rehabilitation. In that year, Congress passed the Vocational Rehabilitation Act; this act was expanded during the New Deal and again during World War II. For the most part, the Federal government provides the states with funds

[14] For a brief statement on the history and present nature of workmen's compensation laws see Max D. Kossoris, "Workmen's Compensations in the United States," *Monthly Labor Review*, vol. 76, no. 4, pp. 359–366, 1953.

[15] Russell H. Kurtz (ed.), *Social Work Year Book 1954,* American Association of Social Workers, New York, 1954, p. 488.

for carrying out various rehabilitation services; the percentage of cost carried by the Federal government varies according to the type of service. Disabled workers are given special training to enable them to overcome their handicaps or to fit them for new jobs, or they may be provided with medical care, surgery, psychiatric treatment, special equipment. The handicapped are also provided with special counseling service until the time that they become fully retrained and adapted to a new job.

UNEMPLOYMENT INSURANCE. One of the most important acts of the New Deal was the enactment of legislation to mitigate the hazards of unemployment and layoff.[16] This legislation was passed during a period of very high unemployment; but layoff or loss of job is a hazard to which all industrial workers are potentially subject, and one which a surprisingly large percentage actually meet, even in times of prosperity. Unemployment-insurance legislation thus establishes the right of workers to be protected against one of the traditional hazards of industrialism. This legislation also establishes the duty of employers to share the costs of unemployment; it denies the classical principle that, once the worker is discharged, the responsibility of the employer comes to an end.

The unemployment-insurance program is a complicated system whereby the Federal government gives support to state programs which meet certain standards. Among these standards are provisions that workers can be denied unemployment insurance only for certain reasons; e.g., for leaving a job without cause, discharge from a job for misconduct, for refusal to take a suitable job. Workers cannot be refused unemployment insurance for refusing to take a job during a strike, or for refusing a job at poorer wages than is usually paid in a given area, or for refusing to take a job where it is necessary to join a company union or to resign from a labor union.

Most unemployment-insurance programs are designed to provide the worker with about 50 to 60 per cent of his normal weekly wage for a certain period of time. Actually, since maximum benefits are prescribed in these laws, and since wage rates have risen, perhaps only about one-third of wage loss due to unemployment is recovered under this program.

The significance of unemployment-insurance programs resides, first, in the fact that it establishes the *right* of the Federal government to force industry to bear the costs of one of the economic hazards of industrialism; industry can no longer shift the costs of unemployment entirely onto the worker. Thus the freedom of management to lay off workers as it sees fit is limited. These limitations are, it is true, relatively slight; but

---

[16] For a description of the prevailing system of unemployment insurance, see Eveline M. Burns, *The American Social Security System,* Houghton Mifflin Company, Boston, 1951, chaps. VI and VII.

here again it is the potential power to control industry which is significant. Furthermore a program of unemployment insurance serves to enhance the dependence of masses of industrial workers and white-collar workers on government, thereby further increasing the power and prestige of government.

OLD-AGE INSURANCE. In the industrial system, old age has been a traditional hazard. In the classical formulation, people saved a certain proportion of their income during their productive years in order to tide them over their nonproductive years, which, in any case, were likely to be short. If a person entered old age without savings, it was up to his family to support him; failing that, he would have to throw himself on the poor laws of city or county. In the United States, widespread recognition of the right of elderly people or their survivors to support in old age at public expense was achieved only a generation ago. In 1935, the Social Security Act inaugurated a program of Federal old-age and survivors insurance (OASI). This act was amended in 1939 and again in 1950 to bring more people under its jurisdiction and to increase benefits.[17]

In 1953 about 5,500,000 persons were drawing monthly benefits under OASI provisions of the Social Security Act.[18] Benefits were paid to retired workers over sixty-five years of age, their wives, dependent husbands of working wives if the husbands were sixty-five or over, children under eighteen years of age, widows, dependent widowers, orphans, and dependent parents of retired workers. The average payment to a retired worker was $50 a month; for a retired worker with a wife sixty-five or over, the average payment was about $80 a month. A widow with two dependent children received about $100 a month.

In 1952 a total of 2 billion dollars was paid out in old-age and survivors benefits. Yet even this sum of money is inadequate to care for our elderly people and their survivors or dependents. There are over 2½ million people receiving old-age assistance, that is, relief. For every 100 people who are receiving old-age and survivors insurance, 68 are receiving some form of old-age assistance. In fact, one of every six persons receiving benefits under OASI is also receiving old-age relief. These figures suggest the probability of increased government action in this sphere.

The cost of OASI is borne equally by employers and employees. Their contributions are made in the form of a tax on a certain amount of wages; for instance, in 1953 both employer and worker paid a tax of 1½ per cent on the first $3,600 of yearly income. Old-age assistance is supported by general taxation.

The significance of old-age and survivors insurance, as far as it relates

---

[17] *Ibid.,* chaps. IV and V. There is a large literature on this subject, and the student is referred to the bibliography for this chapter at the end of the book.

[18] Kurtz, *op. cit.,* p. 494.

to the connections between industry and government, is threefold. First, the cost of old age is thrown, in part, onto the employer; the traditional laissez-faire principle that the employer's obligation to his employee is ended when the latter leaves the factory gates is contravened. There is here a radical denial that the factory work is a "hand" to be used when it can produce efficiently and to be discarded when it can no longer do so. Second, OASI represents another area of encroachment by government on the power and freedom of industrial management. Under this legislation, management is "directed" to bear the costs of old age and is taxed to do so. Third, great masses of industrial workers are rendered dependent on the government for support through their old age—a period which, on the average, is becoming longer. Here, again, then, government has created a basis for mass support.

Laws Designed to Safeguard the Public. Various types of law are aimed at safeguarding the public interest from certain industrial practices. The necessity of such legislation springs both from certain consequences of the operation of the profit motive and from the complexity of modern production. Where the mainspring of industrial action and expansion is profit, the possibility always exists that investors may be defrauded, that the quality of goods may be adulterated, that products may be misrepresented. And, since the industrial process is technologically complex, there is little chance for the average consumer to have much knowledge about the product he is buying or the stock in which he is investing. Thus the necessity for public protection seems to be inherent in our industrial system; it is the price we pay for its efficiency and dynamism.

Since the early days of the New Deal, Federal legislation has protected the investor against certain types of financial practices. It is the function of the Securities and Exchange Commission, set up in 1934, to furnish information to investors on stocks offered for sale in interstate commerce and to guard against fraud and misrepresentation. According to this legislation, furthermore, the prospective investor must be furnished with information about the issuer of the stock.

The government also intervenes to protect the public against the adulteration of products and their misrepresentation in advertising.[19] It is the function of the Food and Drug Administration to test the quality of products and to compare their quality with claims made for them. The Administration has the power to inspect plants and to impound adulterated products; it may petition the courts for injunctions to restrain violations of the law. However, the only potent weapon which the Ad-

---

[19] The original government program in this area dates to 1908, but the New Deal strengthened the program. See Ford P. Hall, *Government and Business*, 3d ed., McGraw-Hill Book Company, Inc., New York, 1949, chap. XIX.

ministration wields is publicity. The Food and Drug Administration is authorized to publish court proceedings against violators of the law and to disseminate information about food, drugs, devices, or cosmetics which might threaten the public health. This publicity might be even more effective were it not for the refusal of most newspapers and other media of communication which depend upon advertising to publish the findings of the Food and Drug Administration.

Nevertheless, the various state and Federal food and drug acts represent a significant limitation on the power of industry. Perhaps the potential limitation is even more significant than the actual limitation. Through these acts the government intervenes in industry in several crucial areas, e.g., the productive process and the sales process. Furthermore, the prestige of government with the public is probably enhanced through these acts.

Laws Regulating Labor-Management Relationships. In a sense, government has intervened in labor-management relationships since the start of industrialism. However, in the laissez-faire epoch society was so arranged that this intervention was practically invisible. Thus, at an early time the courts declared unions conspiracies and outlawed them, basing their decisions on the common law.[20] Later the courts upheld the legality of the "yellow-dog" contract, and regularly issued injunctions against strikes, boycotts, picketing, and other union tactics, on the ground that they violated the rights of individuals. These governmental actions were considered not as antilabor moves but as decisions based on natural law and natural right.

This "negative" intervention of government in labor-management relationships gave way to "positive" intervention under the New Deal. The Wagner Act, passed in 1935, and its later modification, the Taft-Hartley Act, stated that government had a positive interest in the relations between management and labor, particularly in promoting collective bargaining between them. Thus, these acts established the *right* of government to intervene in what had been previously an area governed only by the balance of power between management and labor—a balance which, in the nature of things, was favorable to management.

The provisions of the Wagner Act and the Taft-Hartley Act have already been discussed in Chapters 12 and 13.[21] It will only be necessary here to mention certain provisions of the acts in order to indicate the extent of government intervention in this field. The original National Labor Relations Act (Wagner Act) not only stated that the promotion

[20] For a fuller account of the history of the relations between government and labor, see Chap. 10.

[21] See the bibliography for these chapters at the end of the book. In addition the student may consult the bibliography for this chapter.

of collective bargaining was governmental policy but guaranteed the right of employees to organize. Employers were forbidden to discriminate against workers on account of union membership, to propagandize against unions during work hours, to use spies, to form company unions, etc. Provisions were made for calling secret elections to determine whether the workers wanted to be represented by a union; if the union received a majority, it was recognized as the sole bargaining unit for all the workers in the plant.

Under the Labor Management Relations Act of 1947 (Taft-Hartley Act) the balance of power in industry was shifted to management, but the intervention of government in labor-management relationships did not thereby cease or even greatly diminish. While it is true that the Taft-Hartley Act gives to management more freedom in opposing unions, it does not return to management its pre–New Deal prerogatives; actually the Taft-Hartley Act reenacts many of the provisions of the Wagner Act which prohibit management from interfering in union organizing. On the other hand, the Taft-Hartley Act forbids the closed shop, prohibits picketing or striking under certain conditions, outlaws boycotts, and allows the use of injunctions against unions under certain conditions.

Numerous state laws also control management-union relationships, often in a manner favorable to management.[22] Four states have labor laws based on the Wagner Act and thus favorable to labor. In nine states there are labor laws based on the Taft-Hartley Act. In addition about one-third of the states specifically prohibit certain union practices; e.g., picketing by nonemployees, picketing where there is no strike in progress, secondary boycotts. Most drastically antiunion are the "right-to-work" laws which have been enacted in 12 states. According to these controversial laws, all types of union security agreements, even the union shop, are, in effect, unlawful.

Thus government, no matter what its bias, is solidly entrenched in the field of labor-management relationships. The fact of this intervention is, in the long run, more significant than the particular bias of a specific law or board. The rightward shift in American politics after World War II increased the influence of management in government; a subsequent shift, however, may throw government over to the labor side. The most significant fact about governmental intervention in management-labor relations is that no one seriously questions government's *right* to intervene and to force labor and management to certain courses of action.

[22] For reviews of state labor legislation, see Charles C. Killingsworth, *State Labor Relations Acts*, University of Chicago Press, Chicago, 1948; and "Terms of State Labor Relations Acts" (no author given), *Monthly Labor Review*, vol. 71, no. 2, pp. 214–218, 1950.

Governmental Intervention in the Internal Affairs of Labor Unions.
Just as government controls certain internal affairs of the industrial corporation, so it intervenes in the internal affairs of labor unions. As might
be expected, this tendency increases in importance with the general
movement in government toward a managerial point of view. Examples
of this tendency may be found in the various laws, or sections of laws,
which prohibit unions from contributing to a political campaign or which
require non-Communist affidavits from labor officials who wish to use the
facilities of the National Labor Relations Board. Demands for even more
stringent controls of the internal affairs of labor unions are heard from
time to time.

Present Trends. Three other points about the influence of government
on industry may be made. First, there is today an uneasy balance between
government and industry, an unstable equilibrium. This can be seen from
the fact that the encroachment of government on industry has, in many
areas, reached no logical stopping point; for instance, there is no *logical*
reason to confine government inspection of food, drugs, etc., to its present
limits. If anything, there are logical reasons for supposing that government would control the quality of a much wider range of products than
it does now and that the controls would be more severe. In this and
other areas, the point which government encroachment has reached has
been determined by a temporary balance of power among industry (and
other businesses), the government, and the public.

Second, in the last quarter of a century, industrial bureaucracy has
steadily lost power and initiative to the government. This movement has
been now fast, now slow. It was greatly accelerated under the New Deal
and during World War II. It has been slowed down since World War
II, particularly under the Eisenhower administration. But this author can
find no inherent reason to suppose that the movement has been permanently stopped or that there will be a radical shift in its direction. There
is no reason to think that the inherent dynamic tendencies within government bureaucracy have been halted, much less stifled, or that governmental bureaucracy will cease its movement toward the regulation and
control of all centers of power outside itself, including industry.

The third point is that, even at this point of development, the relationships between industry and government are intricate and extensive. The
previous review of specific areas of relationship between government and
industry will serve to demonstrate this point. It may be added that the
growth of governmental control of industry is a movement which can be
observed in other societies of the most diverse kind: Communist, Fascist,
democratic, and semidemocratic. As compared with these countries,
American industry has resisted governmental encroachment with relative
success. However, if the situation in this country today is compared with

that which existed, say, in the 1920s, a more accurate measure will be afforded of how far we have moved from an era of corporate *laissez faire*.

The Influence of Industry on Government. Thus far we have considered government as if it were an entirely independent entity, operating according to its own interests and needs and impervious to outside influences. But this is hardly a complete picture of the way in which government does in fact function. Actually, numerous outside forces are constantly trying to shape governmental policy in one direction or another. If, as we have claimed, governmental bureaucracy is developing according to its own inner needs, it does so in spite of outside influences. Actually its direction of movement is not like that of an arrow flying directly to one definite point, but rather that of a river, which flows between wide banks, meandering along a course which is susceptible to change, though the ultimate destiny remains the sea. Similarly, the development of governmental bureaucracy may be retarded, accelerated, shunted now in this direction, now in another, though in the long run its cumulative forward movement cannot be halted and the direction of its movement remains the same.

The power to direct the pace and temporary shifts which the governmental bureaucracy will follow lies in the hands of the men who occupy its executive positions, that is, the "administration." It is these men, for instance, who will determine whether government will seek further encroachment on the industrial domain, whether government will intervene on the side of labor or management, the extent to which government will seek to regulate the internal affairs of unions or corporations, the burden of taxation to be imposed on industry, whether food and drug acts will be rigidly or laxly enforced, and so on.

This list of alternatives, though far from complete, suggests why the ability to control or influence the administration of government is of such vital moment to labor and to management. Depending on the bias of a particular administration, the power of government can be used to advance the interests of one group or the other. For instance, a promanagement administration could adopt a fiscal policy relieving industry of a heavy tax burden, put promanagement individuals on labor boards, fail to prosecute firms for violations of the antimonopoly laws, fail to provide sufficient funds for the enforcement of the food and drug acts, or grant important concessions to industry in the use of raw materials or power sources. A prolabor administration might place prolabor men in key spots to deal with labor-management relationships, curtail the financial power of management through heavy taxation, protect labor from the power of the courts, refuse to prosecute unions for violations of the labor laws. Since there is so much at stake for both sides, it should not come as a surprise, except to the very naïve, to find that both management and labor are heavily engaged in "politics," that is, in the selection of an administration to control the governmental bureaucracy.

The Political Tactics of Management. In the struggle to control or influence national and state governments, industrial management has many advantages.[23] First and foremost, perhaps, is the great socioeconomic power of management. Management still retains great social prestige among masses of industrial workers and employees, technicians, white-collar workers, and benchworkers. It also retains great economic power over these groups. It would be a mistake to think that management's position of leadership within industry cannot be transferred in some measure to a position of leadership within politics. On the contrary, there are undoubtedly great numbers of people who, through fear, apathy, admiration, or identification with management, follow the political leads indicated by management.

Management's vast social and economic power can also be used to influence politics and politicians directly. The use of open bribery, while not unknown even today, seems to be, happily, declining. However, the need of politicians for financial resources has not declined; on the contrary, it has greatly increased. Political campaigns, particularly campaigns for Federal government posts, have become very costly; radio and television time must be bought, advertisements must be taken in newspapers, money must be found for a retinue of speech writers, research men, local politicians. Modern politics demands access to large financial resources, and management possesses such resources. Irrespective of the personal sympathies of politicians, they often tend to become mortgaged to managerial groups. While such mortgaging does not guarantee managerial influence in administration—independent politicians are not unknown, though rare—there can be no doubt that it greatly increases the politician's willingness to listen to managerial arguments.

In some cases the prestige and manifest ability of individual managers is so great that they are called directly into high government posts.[24] In wartime, industrial managers have received high-ranking commissions in the armed services because of their specialized knowledge in such fields as transportation or procurement. Even with the best will in the world, industrial managers in this position cannot help transferring to government their own biases and values.

Managerial political action is greatly aided by the sympathy of the

[23] For a somewhat old, but still timely, study of the power and tactics of management in its attempt to control government, see Donald C. Blaisdell, *Economic Power and Political Pressures*, Temporary National Economic Committee Monograph 26, Government Printing Office, 1941, chaps. I–X.

[24] For a study of the interrelations of business men and politicians, see C. Wright Mills, *The Power Elite*, Oxford University Press, New York, 1956, chap. X, "The Political Directorate."

mass media of communication, particularly the press.[25] There are several reasons for this sympathy. Perhaps a relatively minor reason, though an important one, is that industrial management is one of the largest sources of advertising revenue in the country. But perhaps a more important reason is that there is a certain basic similarity of interests and outlook on many issues between industrial management and the leaders of the various mass media. Mass communications is itself a big industry, with many of the same problems of production, selling, and labor relations. The leaders of the mass media can be expected, therefore, to understand and sympathize with the point of view of industrial management in each of these areas. However, irrespective of the socioeconomic outlook of the mass media, it is management which possesses the financial resources to purchase the often exorbitantly expensive facilities of the mass media.

Access to the mass media is a crucial element in political power in the modern, complex society. Technological advances in the field of newspaper printing, publishing, motion pictures, and television have made it possible to reach great masses of people. A political message, whether open or concealed, can now be counted on to reach a large portion of the electorate within a very short period of time. Furthermore, the mass diffusion of political messages has been made possible at a time when millions of people, bewildered by the complexity of large-scale society, are searching for personal guidance, even if this often conceals a definite socioeconomic point of view as well.

Another great political advantage of industrial management springs from the fact that it is firmly entrenched in the social structure and culture of our society; in fact, it is, in many ways, the foundation of that structure and culture. This means that all those who support the structure of our society, whether through interest or tradition or sentiment, are the natural allies of management. The significance of this fact needs underlining. It means that management can count on the natural allegiance of those who accept the dominant values of our society: competition, success, material betterment. It means that management can count on at least the tacit support of those institutions and groups which are naturally conservative, e.g., the churches, patriotic organizations, veterans' groups. It means that, in a certain sense, the very concept of "Americanism" becomes identified with the continued existence of management and with management's values, outlooks, and biases. This is an overwhelming political advantage.

Political advantage cannot, by itself, guarantee political success. Organization for political action is also needed. To some extent this or-

[25] A very interesting, though highly critical, analysis of the influence of business on the mass media of communication will be found in Harold J. Laski, *The American Democracy*, The Viking Press, Inc., New York, 1948, chap. XIII.

ganization is provided within the framework of the existing political parties. Traditionally, industrial management has been most influential in the Republican party, although at least a small section of management has consistently supported the Democratic party. However, managerial control of the existing political parties has never been complete. Even in the Republican party, management has had to share power with agricultural groups, with mercantile and financial interests, with certain regional and ethnic groupings; in the Democratic party, especially since the time of Roosevelt, the influence of industrial management has been much less.

Management has, therefore, organized itself into associations charged directly or indirectly with the furthering of managerial political action.[26] The numerous trade associations function, in part, as political organizations. By far the most important political organization of management is the National Association of Manufacturers. In general this association serves as focal point for gathering and expressing managerial opinion. It conducts extensive research, designed to support the economic and social views of management. It also issues numerous pamphlets, books, and other printed matter in support of the managerial position. The NAM seeks to lay the case of management before the teachers of America and others who are in a position to influence public opinion. During political campaigns the association throws its considerable weight behind managerially oriented candidates. Between campaigns, the NAM and other trade associations are influential in lobbying for managerial interests.

The Political Tactics of Organized Labor. Many of the advantages which management possesses are denied to labor. Thus the financial resources of management far surpass those of organized labor. This means that labor cannot influence political campaigns financially to nearly the degree that management can; labor can make only moderate contributions to political coffers. Labor can neither afford to buy the facilities of the mass media on a large scale nor count on the natural sympathy of the directors and owners of the mass media. The relative absence of prolabor columnists, radio, or television commentators is sufficient proof of this point.

Furthermore, unlike management, labor cannot rely on the support of the very powerful conservative forces in American society. On the contrary, since labor must necessarily attack the prerogatives of management, it has seemed to these conservative forces that labor was attacking the basic fabric of American society. Consequently, these conservative forces have often looked on labor unions as "subversive" or at least

[26] For an analysis of business organization, see Robert A. Brady, *Business as a System of Power*, Columbia University Press, New York, 1943, chap. VI.

somewhat un-American. Adding to antilabor sentiment in the United States has been the fear among certain status groups, classes, and ethnic and religious groups that the changes labor wished to institute would somehow reduce their status and economic power. For instance, certain sections of the middle class seem to fear and resent the economic gains of organized workers, because they believe that their own position in society is diminished thereby.

In other industrial societies, the power of conservatism is counterbalanced by a class-conscious working force. However, in the United States class consciousness among workers does not seem to have passed a very rudimentary stage.[27] Organized labor, therefore, cannot count on a reservoir of class consciousness or a tradition of working-class solidarity to further its political ends. As a matter of fact, it seems probable that the majority of American workers accept the dominant values of American society, including the high social position assigned to management.

The disadvantages under which organized labor operates in the United States make a labor party on the English model an impossibility at this time.[28] Organized labor has, therefore, had to work through the existing political parties, where it can. In the past, under the doctrine of Gompers, labor did not seek to support any party as such, but it did support individuals within either party who would act in labor's interest. At the present time organized labor has become strongly identified with the Democratic party, although a small minority of labor leaders in the skilled trades continue to support the Republicans.

It would be a mistake, however, to think of the Democratic party as in any sense a "labor party." Any party which unites Southern millowners, Minnesota farmers, and Detroit automobile workers could hardly be labeled in that fashion. The Democratic party, rather, is a loose coalition of often diverse or even inimical groups which include, besides labor, agricultural groups, regional groups, ethnic and racial groups. It is true that organized labor is a powerful force within the Democratic party; but it is certainly not the directing force. It is significant that even Democratic-controlled Congresses have refused to repeal the Taft-Hartley Act.

Labor's inability to dominate the Democratic party reflects its limited political power. The main strength of labor is not, as we have seen, its financial power; its main strength lies in whatever ability it possesses to control the vote of the industrial workers, plus whatever groups in society vote along with the industrial workers. When the influence of the unions on the worker's vote is strong, labor has a strong voice in party councils; when the reverse is true, labor has little political influence. In

[27] See Chap. 16.
[28] But Laski (*op. cit.*, pp. 214–263) argues strongly on the other side.

general, depressed economic conditions seem to favor labor's political strength, while prosperous times weaken it.

Since labor can rarely use the mass media, it must rely on other means to reach the industrial worker. But here labor is not without certain resources: there are several channels of communication available to it. For instance, the local officials or the shop stewards may impress on the worker certain political lessons. The local meetings may also be used as media of political propaganda. Labor newspapers, pamphlets, labor schools, all offer outlets for the political point of view of organized labor.

During various political campaigns labor has formed special "political action" committees, which apparently have operated with considerable effect at various times.[29] These committees and similar organizations have served as a rallying point around which both labor and other forces have gathered. At the same time, they have performed the hard, unremitting work which is necessary for a successful campaign. It is by the use of these means that labor has been able to overcome to some extent the great advantages of industrial management.

With the merger of the AFL and CIO, labor also united its political action programs; in fact, one of the motives for the merger may very well have been a desire to increase the political effectiveness of labor. It is still too early to tell whether this merger will actually operate to increase the political power of labor. But certainly the success of the merger will be judged in good part by whether the political power of labor does increase; the election of a Democratic administration and Congress and the repeal of the Taft-Hartley Act would certainly be construed as proof of such an increase in the effectiveness of labor's political program.

[29] For descriptions of how these committees actually operate, see Fay Calkin, *The CIO and the Democratic Party*, University of Chicago Press, Chicago, 1952.

CHAPTER 20

Industrialism and Social Change

The picture that has been sketched thus far of the structure of relations of industry and society has been essentially static. Indeed, structure
is, by definition, stable and unchanging. In reality, however, whatever
appearances may be, American society is highly dynamic; it is constantly
changing in response to extremely powerful, underlying forces. If the
picture of American society offered here has more than a momentary
validity, like a snapshot, it is only because change in American society
has been relatively slow since World War II. It is significant that this
picture would hardly "fit" the structure of American society as it existed,
say, in the 1920s. The extent to which the image of the 1920s would be
distorted is a measure of the social change which has taken place in the
course of just a few years.

All societies change, some slowly, some more rapidly. On occasion this
change is initiated by some outside force: an earthquake, an invasion, or
the importation of a new idea. *All* societies are undergoing some process
of internal evolution. New ideas are formed, new customs arise, novel
social groups are born, and old ones die. But not all the parts of a society change at an equal rate, and not all parts of a society are equally
productive of change. In each society there seems to be some area in
which the activity and thought of men is concentrated, which is constantly developing, and from which emanate impulses which change
other parts of the society. That is, there is an active principle in society
and there is a passive principle; the active principle initiates those
changes which the passive receives. The passive is not without influence
on the active, but it is a reactive influence, an environmental influence
which limits what the active area may achieve.[1]

The active principle differs from society to society. In some societies the activity and thought of men have been concentrated on religion;

[1] This idea of "active" and "passive" principles in society is related, the author believes, to the theory of cultural focus put forth by Melville J. Herskovits in his *Man
and His Works*, Alfred A. Knopf, Inc., New York, 1949, chap. 32.

in such societies religious thought and religious ritual have had an enormous development. From religion have flowed those forces which have stamped the rest of society into a certain mold. In other societies the shape of social life has taken its stamp from the ideas and activities of a class, perhaps an aristocracy or a dominant economic group, or from one occupational group.

In the United States, one of the most important active principles, perhaps the most important, is industrialism. Just as in other societies men and women have concentrated their energy on religion, so in our society this energy has been concentrated on the productive system. As a consequence, the industrial institutions have changed with extreme rapidity relative to other areas of society. In the process of change, industrialism has, at the same time, changed practically every other area of American life. It is true that there has been a certain countereffect on industry, particularly from the governmental institutions, which is the other major active principle in American society; but the major direction of influence has been from industry outward to the rest of society.

This suggests that in order to understand the course of development of American society, it is necessary to understand certain internal changes in industry and how these changes affect nonindustrial areas. It will be the task of this chapter to investigate the dynamics of industrialism and to suggest several possible alternatives of development in the society as a whole.

The Dynamics of Industrialism. The investigation of industry followed in this book would seem to indicate that there are three major sources, internal to industry, which have changed and are changing our productive system and which have had, directly or indirectly, major effects on the rest of society.

The Role of Management. There can be little doubt that the role of management in industry has been an extremely important factor in the development of American society. In order to understand why this is so, it is necessary to understand the peculiar nature of the managerial role. This role is so constructed that, in order to play it successfully, it is necessary to transcend it; in a sense, the manager who is successful is so by virtue of the fact that he destroys his initial role and substitutes for it one with greater power, scope, and freedom. This contrasts sharply with other roles in society; for instance, the successful father is one who stays within the limits of his role. There is a dynamic principle "built into" the manager's role.

Furthermore, there is a readily available means for measuring the extent to which a manager has played his role successfully. This measure is the profit record. If the profit record is one of decline, the failure of the manager is immediately apparent. Even the maintenance of profit at a certain level may spell out inadequacy, if in other industries profits are increasing. Indeed, there can be no doubt that the maximally successful manager is one who outdistances his rivals in the production of profit. Thus the record of the manager is spread out for all to see; success, failure, mediocrity, in their exact proportions, are all written in the profit record.

In the process of achieving the ends of the manager's role, as measured by profit, society is being constantly transformed in certain areas. For instance, the constant growth of our urban agglomerations, with all the myriad social changes attendant on that growth, is, in part, the result of the constant drive of management to expand industry in order to maintain or increase the rate of profit. Expanding industry requires a growing labor force, technical supplies, intricate communications, all of which can be supplied only within the urban environment. In turn, the urban-industrial environment is constantly transforming the nature of our family system, our religious institutions, our educational system. Further, man's basic definitions, values, and outlooks change as the urban environment in which he lives develops and alters.

Not only does the managerial drive to profit result in the transformation of existing urban areas, but it also results in the invasion of new areas. Management is ever seeking new, possibly cheaper, sources of labor supply, undeveloped sources of raw materials, new markets. Under the compulsion of this drive, American industry has spread from its original area of development in the Northeast into the South, into the Middle West, and into the Far West; it has even invaded less developed countries. As industry invades an hitherto nonindustrialized area, it sets in motion a vast train of social changes: cities are built; rural populations are urbanized; families, customs, and traditions are wrenched out of their accustomed molds. This process will be undoubtedly repeated many times in the future as more and more regions and countries pass into an industrial phase.

Furthermore, managers, or would-be managers, seeking ever new sources of profit, are constantly pushing the industrial system into ever new areas of production. Within the very recent past, industrialism has invaded various fields of agriculture; it has been shown in Chapter 7 how the industrial system has invaded the field of office work. It seems reasonable to suppose that in the future the system will invade areas which have hitherto resisted it; e.g., housebuilding, agriculture. As industrialism moves into these areas, it triggers certain social changes. Workers are displaced, new workers are brought in; old habits and rhythms of life are disturbed. For instance, the intrusion of the industrial system into the field of agriculture has meant the destruction of the old rural mode of life, with its stress on inherited property and close family ties. As another example, industries may transform typical rural, market communities into small industrial cities, with consequent social changes in other areas of life.

Social changes may also result from the many strains attendant on the managerial role. It will be recalled that the role of management was described in Chapter 6 as extraordinarily stressful. The major reason for this strain was found to arise from the great pressure for success in this role and, at the same time, the ever-present possibility of failure. In an attempt to relieve this stress, management has attempted, and does attempt, to control and change certain significant parts of the environment. For instance, as we have seen, management has played a major role in changing governmental institutions in such a way as to serve as an instrument of industrial expansion. Management is also concerned with changing our political party system, legal interpretations, and the court system in certain definite ways. Of late it has taken steps, largely through the subsidization of education, to prevent the closure of our class system, a situation which management rightly interprets as dangerous to itself. These are scattered examples of management's attempt to control the environment, but they serve to indicate how social change may arise out of the stress and strain contained within the managerial role.

Technology. Another source of social change is the constantly developing technologies of industry. One of the most marked features of the industrial system, and one which places it in sharp contrast with other productive systems, is the constant invention of new machines, new physical or chemical processes, new organizational principles. No doubt, one of the impulses for this amazing development stems from the managerial drive for profit. But technology also seems to develop through an internal process; one invention leads to another invention, a new organizational principle suggests another, the introduction of a new chemical process may suggest a new product. Furthermore, although industrial technology has been developing rapidly in the United States for the last eighty-five years, at least, there is no indication that the rate of development is slowing down. On the contrary, we are probably about to witness fantastic new developments in the field of atomic energy, in automation, in electronics, in plastics, and in many other fields besides. The development of technology is tied inexorably to the development of science, and to the development of science there seem to be no limits at all.

Practically every area of social life, and the life of almost every individual, has been in some sense changed by the development of technology. Two major modes of technological influence on social life may be detected.

On the one hand is that type of social change which results directly from a change in a technological process. Thus an invention may destroy the economic basis of a city, displace thousands of workers; yet the same invention may result in the creation of a new city somewhere else and create even more jobs than it originally destroyed. Technological changes of this sort create a constant turmoil in society, with socially uprooted, mobile populations drifting about in search of new centers of employment. Sometimes this drifting may result in new geographical distributions of population; an example is provided by the constant drift of population into atomic-energy centers.

Technological change not only uproots populations but directly changes the patterns of their social life. For instance, the family, that sensitive recorder of all types of change, alters with technological development. An invention may open new employment opportunities to women, radically change hours spent at work and in the family, increase available leisure time, open jobs to youth, and deny them to middle-aged or old workers. Technological developments may basically change the stratificational system of a community. Skilled jobs, carrying great prestige, may be destroyed. Jobs may be opened to members of discriminated-against and low-ranking or racial groups. Sometimes an invention, or a series of inventions, destroys the basis for the existence of a class or status group; e.g., the mechanization of office work negates one important claim of white-collar workers to superior status. At the same time, technological development may increase or decrease the homogeneity of the working class, depending on whether the development tends to equalize or differentiate jobs.

It is difficult to discern a definite pattern in that type of social change which results directly from technological development. But, *in general,* technological change seems to have the effect of *smoothing out* social differences. For instance, under the influence of a developing industrial technology, the differences between the sexes within the family tend to decrease. Similarly, the differences between parents and children tend to be ironed out; indeed, the young may have a definite advantage in modern society, since they adapt easily to technological change. In like manner, the *general tendency* of technological development has been to wipe out status differences. Undoubtedly, opposite cases could be shown, but in general the status homogeneity of the working class, for instance, owes as much to technological development, perhaps, as it owes to similar economic position.

On the other hand, there is social change which results from the *products* of a developing technology. As our technology has conquered the problems of mass production, great quantities of commodities that were formerly rare, expensive, or unobtainable have become available to the general population. Another striking feature of our technology is the extent to which it is constantly lifting from men the burden of heavy labor or routine drudgery. Technological developments are also constantly improving communications, and the inventions resulting in the mass media of communication are daily improving the possibilities of instantaneous communication. Perhaps even more important for mankind are the ever more efficient instruments of war which our technology is producing, culminating in such technological and scientific triumphs, if that is the word, as the atom and hydrogen bombs. All these changes have effects on our social life, trivial or fundamental, lasting or temporary, as the case may be.

So numerous are these social changes that it is almost impossible to enumerate them. Confining ourselves to certain areas of social life, it may be shown that new products are constantly changing the shape of some of our major institutions. For instance, our courting and dating systems have been fundamentally revised by the invention of the automobile. The role of the mother in the family has been drastically altered by the washing machine, the range, the refrigerator, canned foods, prepared bread, and a host of other products. The shape of our cities has been transformed by the automobile and now is responding to the airplane. Our system of stratification has felt the effects of cheap, mass-produced clothes, cars, and home accessories, all styled to resemble expensive products. At the same time improved communications make possible the organization and solidification of parties. Politics has been transformed, and will be further changed in the future, by the mass media of communication. The reader is without doubt familiar with all these examples, and could add many more.

As to the future, it would be hazardous in the extreme to predict the cumulative effect on the pattern of social life. Judging by the past and present, we might guess that family life will continue to be based less on traditional roles, and more on personal ties, as new products and services replace traditional ones. But whether this development will make for a more stable or less stable family life is an open question. Similarly, it would seem that the mass media of communication provide the necessary conditions for the establishment of totalitarian states. But the mass media might also be used to widen and strengthen the participation of peoples in government. Technological development poses a great number of alternatives for social development; the way in which a technological development will be allowed to influence social life cannot be predicted from the nature of that development alone.

The Organized Labor Movements. The development of industry brings into being everywhere one of the greatest of social changes recorded in history: the development of a working force with no ties to land, to family, or to lord, a force essentially cut off from every access to a means of making a living except through employment in industry. As industry develops, as it expands in size, enters new areas, or displaces older systems of production, the ranks of this working force inevitably increase.

This great social change is itself the *result* of changes which emanate from the dynamics of industrial and technological development; in itself the working force is, at first, one of the passive principles in society. What changes this working force into an active principle, itself productive of social change, is its relationship to industrial management. This relationship is essentially, as we have tried to show in Chapters 12 and 13, one of conflict, or antagonistic cooperation. Management can fulfill its role only by curbing, to some extent, the workingman's chance for achieving satisfaction in *his* role; the same thing is true of the workingman in relationship to management. In the course of this conflict, the working force solidifies into a class and then evolves forms of organization, dedicated to bringing about social change.

The working class may try to bring about several types of social change. For instance, in an early stage of industrialism, the working class may engage in violent riots aimed at destruction of machinery or in vast disordered strikes. However much destruction of property, or disruption of individual lives may result from such violent conflict, it is doubtful whether permanent social change eventuates from it.

Permanent social change begins only when labor organizes into permanent associations and begins to conduct its disputes with management in a systematic fashion. To begin with, labor organization is in itself a great and permanent social change. It fundamentally alters the balance of power between management and labor, curtailing the power and freedom of management and vastly increasing labor's power and prestige in society. Labor organization changes the working force from an inchoate mass of individuals who perceive their common interests only dimly into a more or less self-conscious class, ready to pursue its own interests.

Furthermore, labor organization sets off certain reactions which induce social change in the society at large. Labor unions tend to expand according to their own "laws of movement." As they do so, they tend to appropriate to themselves certain social functions which were formerly performed by other institutions and associations. In effect, labor unions serve as an alternative focus for community organization and provide such services as legal advice, recreation, counseling, and political protection. These developments in turn alter the traditional form of the community, depriving classes of their accustomed power and status groups of their prestige. In such communities middle-class groups may, perforce, switch their allegiance to labor. Change in class alignments may also result from the greater income and prestige of the organized worker in the community. It is a reasonable supposition that the social structure of all communities with highly organized industries is under-going more or less rapid alteration.

Labor organization also induces changes in the form of political in-stitutions. As labor has grown in numbers and in power of organization, it has tended to intervene progressively in the sphere of politics and gov-ernment. For certain historical reasons, which have already been dis-cussed in Chapter 10, this intervention has not taken the form of a labor party; nor has labor aimed directly at forming an administration. But labor does form an important part of the Democratic party and has succeeded in changing that party into at least a somewhat labor-oriented party. Further increases in the power of organized labor may mean still greater influence in the Democratic party, although whether labor can reach the goal of transforming the Democratic party into a labor party must remain an open question. It is significant of the changes in politics brought about by labor that a major issue of each national election is that of the rights and position of organized labor.

Organized labor also is changing the structure and function of gov-ernment, to some extent. Special departments devoted to the problems of labor have become firmly established in the government. Other changes in government have resulted directly from the fundamental management-labor split. We have reference here to the governmental machinery for accrediting unions, preventing unfair practices by labor and management, and adjudicating labor-management disputes. Both types of governmental changes have, in turn, necessitated fundamental changes in legal interpretations; a whole body of "labor law" has grown up to handle the relationships of government, management, and labor. It seems safe to say that this tendency of change in governmental insti-tutions is in its initial stages; further changes are almost a certainty in the future.

The influence of organized labor on other areas of society is less tangible, though it undoubtedly exists. Thus it is not hard to suppose that the families of organized workingmen are feeling the effects of in-creasing security and financial income. On the other hand, it is difficult to see much labor influence as yet on religious or educational institutions. Nor has organized labor succeeded in breaching the virtual monopoly by conservative forces on our mass media of communication; it is sig-nificant that labor does not as yet possess a single daily national news-paper. Whatever influence labor has had over these mass media, it has been able to wield as a sort of pressure group made up of consumers whose good will is of importance to press, radio, and television.

There is little reason to suppose that labor has, thus far, been as pro-ductive of change in our society as management or technology. But nevertheless, labor-induced changes there are. Furthermore it is only necessary to look at the influence of labor in other countries to recognize the enormous potential for change which is represented in American labor organizations.

Industrialism and the Future. Industrial institutions have been instrumental in forming our society, and there is little reason to doubt that they will strongly influence the future form of American society. But there is a great deal of doubt as to what this future form will be. The future is always the result of a delicate balance of forces in the present. This balance is extremely difficult to measure because of the difficulty of estimating the relative weight of the present forces. Furthermore, calculations may always be upset by the introduction of totally new and unforeseen forces. Thus war, depression, or some form of national calamity such as droughts may totally upset the present balance of forces.

However, it is possible to speak of certain alternatives of future development, without attempting to estimate the chances of one alternative prevailing. We shall present four such alternatives, three of them of an extreme variety, one based on the continuation of present trends.

The Managerially Dominated Society. In one sense a managerially dominated society would be a return to certain past epochs when managerial power was almost unchallenged. In another sense, however, it would be reasonable to suppose that a managerially dominated state would resemble a modern totalitarian society, perhaps Fascist rather than Communist totalitarianism.[2] In a completely managerially dominated state, labor unions would, presumably, be dissolved or made a part of industrial organization. Governmental institutions would become an instrument of managerial policy. The guarantee of monopoly would become governmental policy; indeed, the giant monopoly might be made an official organ of the state. The maximization of profit would become the supreme value of the society.

Actually, under modern conditions, it seems unlikely that a completely managerially dominated society of this kind could exist. Managers form a numerically insignificant portion of our society. Nor does it seem likely that a program aimed at realizing the maximum program of management could achieve a mass appeal in a society where the masses are made up of industrial workers and the middle class. Yet it is clear that the road to effective political action in the modern state lies directly through the ability to appeal to masses and to hold mass support. For this reason, wherever management has attempted to enact its maximum program it has done so in alliance with a party which had mass support.

[2] The managerially dominated society has been forecast by James Burnham in *The Managerial Revolution*, The John Day Company, Inc., New York, 1941. In some of his work, Thorstein Veblen also seemed to be forecasting a managerial or technician-dominated society; see his *The Engineers and the Price System*, The Viking Press, Inc., New York, 1933.

But, invariably, once power has been attained, the party of alliance turns to its own programs, sometimes at the expense of industrial management.

What is a more real possibility, at least for the United States, is a society in which industrial management thoroughly dominates all existing institutions. That this is a real possibility can be deduced from the reality of managerial power and influence today. Management in the United States has enormous prestige, especially with the middle classes. Management has control of, or access to, the vital mass media of communication. Management possesses enormous financial resources, with which to influence political parties and campaigns.

It is possible, therefore, to envision a future in which management would possess the only effective voice. Labor unions could be corrupted into impotence, or their influence with workingmen could be sapped through welfare programs or long-continued prosperity. Government could be dominated, perhaps through the use of "window-dressing" candidates or parties. The public at large could be thoroughly controlled and confused by a mass propaganda barrage. Educational institutions and religious institutions could be manipulated through a combination of force, propaganda, and the judicious use of financial power.

The Labor-dominated Society. As in the case of the managerially dominated society, we may envision two types of labor-dominated societies: a society in which labor is in absolute control, and a society in which it dominates existing institutions. In the former case, society would be again totalitarian, though it is not clear whether such a society would resemble modern communism. At any rate, in a completely labor-dominated society, governmental institutions would become an extension of organized labor; in fact, councils of organized labor might replace government entirely. Other foci of power, such as the mass media, would, of course, become dominated by organized labor. Within industry, the managerial class would be entirely eliminated as a class. Production would be carried on by local labor associations; perhaps managers might be hired for special tasks. The middle classes as we know them now would disappear. White-collar workers would lose any claim to distinction and would become a part of the organized mass. Professionals, storekeepers, and technicians would assume the status of skilled workingmen. The supreme values of society would become the values of organized labor: collective action, equalization of income, equalization of working conditions, equalization of status.[3]

[3] This, of course, is the famous socialist state, forecast (though not described) by Karl Marx and Friedrich Engels. See *The Communist Manifesto*, translated by M. Lawrence, M. Lawrence, Ltd., London, 1930; and *Capital*, translated by Samuel Moore & Edward Aveling, International Publishers Co., Inc., New York, edition of

This is, of course, a fanciful program which has not been approached in any society, though this fact is not in itself a guarantee of what could or could not happen in the future. In actuality, even if we assumed conditions maximally favoring the power of organized labor in this country, it is difficult to conceive of more than a situation in which labor dominated existing institutions. For instance, it is conceivable that, at some future time, labor might come thoroughly to dominate one of the political parties. Using its vast membership and its influence over that membership, labor might then succeed in establishing an almost unshakable grip on the government; it might, conceivably, never lose an election. In this type of situation, other classes would not be eliminated, but their power would be drastically reduced. Management, for instance, would be thoroughly hedged around by antimonopoly laws, by heavy taxes, by laws regulating working conditions and the quality of products. The mass media of communication might be controlled by labor-sponsored legislation, or labor might succeed in establishing its own network of communications. The middle class would be permitted to exist, but only on the basis of loyal support for labor.

It is reasonable to suppose that such a society would carry out an immense welfare program. Strong legislation would safeguard working conditions. Unemployment insurance and social security would become one of the major concerns of society. Vigorous steps would be taken to combat unemployment; for instance, the doctrine of Keynes might become official policy. Probably, in this type of society, mass education would be encouraged, and it might become available to the able of all classes irrespective of economic background. The costs of such an immense welfare program would be thrown largely on the wealthy, and it is doubtful whether large fortunes or incomes would continue to exist.

Unlike the first, fanciful program, certain approaches have been made to this second program. The reader will recognize, of course, that what has been described above is a sort of super New Deal. Furthermore, the Labor party administrations in England actually have made large strides in the direction of such a society. For better or worse, this program outlined above is far from being mere fantasy.

A Society Dominated by Technicians. In the recent past, a considerable amount of attention has been given to the possibility of a society dominated by technicians and scientists. Those who hold this point of view

---

1939, vol. I. Perhaps the best American Marxist analysis of American society is by Paul M. Sweezy, *The Theory of Capitalist Development,* Oxford University Press, New York, 1942. However, Sweezy's book is largely an analysis of present American society, not a forecast of what a future socialist America might be like. The prospects of socialism are discussed from a non-Marxist point of view by Joseph A. Schumpeter in *Capitalism, Socialism, and Democracy,* Harper & Brothers, New York, 1942.

maintain that modern society is based on its technology, which, in turn, is closely allied to science. Management can pursue its goals only by virtue of an advancing technology. Labor is inexorably tied to the overwhelming industrial technique. As for the public at large, its way of life and its customary standard of living—indeed, its survival—are entirely dependent on the skills of technical and scientific specialists. Thus, the technician and the scientist are the key men of our civilization. However (this theory goes on to state), the values of the specialist, which are above all efficiency and rationality, are impossible to achieve either in a society dominated by a profit-oriented management, or in one dominated by a welfare-oriented labor organization. Eventually, the technicians and scientists will want to rid themselves of the restrictions imposed by management and labor. A "revolution of the technicians" will be assured of success because of the strategic power of the technician in industrial society. Indeed the technicians might come to power bloodlessly, e.g., through the threat of a strike, which would be fatal to industrial society if prolonged. Or power might drop into the laps of the technicians, like ripe fruit, through the sheer inability of any other group to handle a complex industrial society.

It is interesting to speculate on what a technician-dominated society would look like. The supreme values of such a society would be productivity, rationality, and efficiency. Nothing that stood in the way of these values would be tolerated. Thus management would become a purely technical job; the manager would be another type of technician. Labor would be regarded as one factor in the process of production. It would be deprived of its rights to organize or to strike; it would be shunted about from one plant to another as needed. The control of both management and labor would make possible planning on a national, perhaps a world, scale. All production would proceed according to a master plan, from which no deviations would be permitted.

Since large-scale industry is more efficient than small-scale industry, the economy would be organized around a series of giant monopolies. Industry, indeed the whole society, would be thoroughly bureaucratized. There would be no room for the small producer, the retailer, the unattached professional. Consequently there would be no place for the middle classes as we know them now.

Other institutions in society would be reconstructed, or perhaps eliminated. For instance, the family might well prove an anachronism in such a society. Family loyalties might well interfere with efficiency and rationality. The procreative functions could be carried on through artificial insemination, and according to the laws of eugenics. Education could be made a purely pragmatic institution, devoted to the technical and scientific disciplines. Similarly, religion could be eliminated, or if it proved necessary in order to control the people, a scientific or state religion could be created.

Does this Orwellian society[4] represent a real possibility for the future? There is no gainsaying the fact that there are certain tendencies in modern society and in modern man pushing toward some form of technocratic society of this type. But it seems to this writer that a completely technician-dominated society is a much more remote possibility than a managerial or labor-dominated society. For one thing, it is difficult to see where the technicians could obtain mass support, the *sine qua non* of modern political power. The numbers of technicians and scientists are very small. Nor does it seem likely that the sort of grim program outlined above would ever have much appeal to masses of people, except perhaps in a completely war-devastated world. It is significant that there is as yet little sign of independent political action among technicians and scientists. Even the protest among scientists against the use of the atom bomb in war has been, thus far, of little effect in removing this weapon from the arsenals of the world. Nor do the social conditions of the technician or scientist seem to favor the growth of class consciousness among them and the development of independent political action.

A Society Based on the Continuation of Present Trends. The fourth possibility that we wish to consider is that at least the immediate future will witness a continued development of the present trends in society.[5] Considering the relative stability of American society in the last decade or two, this seems the likeliest by far of all the alternatives presented here. But social trends and conditions can change with startling rapidity. Consider the difference between the United States of 1929 and the United States of 1933; or, on a less startling scale, the difference between

---

[4] George Orwell presents a frightening picture of a society of this type. See *Nineteen Eighty-four*, Harcourt, Brace and Company, Inc., New York, 1949.

[5] But even among those who adhere to the present institutional order of society, there is wide disagreement, first, as to what those trends are, and second, as to what they ought to be. Among the conservatives there is much concern with preserving what is mislabeled the "free-enterprise system" from what are seen as unjustified attacks by misguided (or worse) persons. See The Economic Principles Commission of the National Association of Manufacturers, *The American Individual Enterprise System*, McGraw-Hill Book Company, Inc., New York, 1946, vols. I and II. Other observers see American industry as evolving within and along with the rest of society. See Adolf A. Berle, Jr., *The 20th Century Capitalist Revolution*, Harcourt, Brace and Company, New York, 1954; and John Kenneth Galbraith, *American Capitalism; The Concept of Countervailing Power*, Houghton Mifflin Company, Boston, 1952. The possibility of preserving the essential features of our society, but at the same time planning both for change and for the future, is discussed from various points of view by Barbara Wootton, *Freedom under Planning*, The University of North Carolina Press, Chapel Hill, 1945; Albert Lauterbach, *Economic Security and Individual Freedom*, Cornell University Press, Ithaca, 1948; and Karl Mannheim, *Man and Society in an Age of Reconstruction*, translated by Edward Shils, Harcourt, Brace and Company, 1941.

the United States just prior to World War II and the United States of 1950. Predicting social change by projecting social trends is the riskiest of businesses.

Barring these unforeseen changes, we may expect the following future developments. The present extremely powerful position of management will in all likelihood be maintained. Solidly based on economic power, access to the mass media, and vast prestige, the power of management seems unshakable, at least as long as it can continue to deliver prosperity, full employment, and a rising standard of living.

The power of labor will, in all probability, continue to grow slowly. In the future it can be expected that a larger percentage of the working force will be organized. Organization may spread to the South and into agriculture; it will also become more important among white-collar workers. On the political scene there seems to be little likelihood of a labor party, unless labor despairs of achieving its aims through the Democratic party. In this conception of the future, then, labor will continue to play a role subordinate to that of management.

It is also reasonable to suppose that the power of government over both management and labor will continue to increase, though perhaps much more slowly than in the 1930s. Continued and even strengthened attempts by government to smooth out the economic cycle will be almost certainly made. Government control over labor-management disputes will be extended. More and more will government regulate the internal affairs of both labor and managerial organizations; finances, the quality of products, perhaps even the choice of officers will fall within the purview of government. There seems to be little reason to suppose that the vast armaments program will be dropped in the foreseeable future, and it must be expected that the power over industry and labor which this gives to government will be maintained. It is also reasonable to suppose that the "protective" functions of government will increase; unemployment laws will be strengthened, social security will be extended to more and more American workers and middle-class people.

Finally, there is no reason to suppose that the technological development will be slowed up or stopped. On the contrary, most signs seem to point to even vaster changes in this area. Certainly, the productivity of American industry, both absolutely and in terms of individual output, will continue to increase. Shorter hours, with consequent greater leisure, seem a real possibility. The use of atomic energy in some areas and perhaps the eventual displacement of other sources of power also seem indicated. Continued improvements in communications and in the mass media seem almost a certainty.

If this conception of the future is correct, then most social change will be the outcome not of change in the role of management, labor, or even government but of technological change. But along what lines technologically induced social change may move is impossible to foresee. At any time, some new technological development—as an example, the discovery of an infinitely inexpensive source of atomic power—may virtually overturn present social trends. It is possible to be certain only that technological change will continue and that, as it does, the lives of all Americans will be changed in almost numberless small and great ways.

Bibliography

CHAPTER 1. INTRODUCTION

Bibliographies

Hauser, Philip M.: "The Labor Force as a Field of Interest for the Sociologist," *American Sociological Review*, vol. 16, no. 4, pp. 530–538, 1951.

Smigel, Erwin O.: "Trends in Occupational Sociology in the United States: A Survey of Post-war Research," *American Sociological Review*, vol. 19, no. 4, pp. 398–404, 1954.

Tagliacozzo, Daisy L.: "Trade Union Government, Its Nature and Its Problems: A Bibliographical Review, 1945–55," *The American Journal of Sociology*, vol. 61, no. 6, pp. 554–581, 1956.

Wilensky, Harold L.: *Syllabus of Industrial Relations: A Guide to Reading and Research*, University of Chicago Press, Chicago, 1954.

General

Caplow, Theodore: *The Sociology of Work*, University of Minnesota Press, Minneapolis, 1954.

Dubin, Robert: *Human Relations in Administration*, Prentice-Hall, Inc., Englewood Cliffs, N.J., 1951.

Knox, John B.: *The Sociology of Industrial Relations*, Random House, Inc., New York, 1956.

Meadows, Paul: *The Culture of Industrial Man*, University of Nebraska Press, Lincoln, Nebr., 1950.

Miller, Delbert C., and William H. Form: *Industrial Sociology: An Introduction to the Sociology of Work Relations*, Harper & Brothers, New York, 1951.

Moore, Wilbert E.: *Industrial Relations and the Social Order*, The Macmillan Company, New York, 1951.

Criticism and Comment on Industrial Sociology

Bell, Daniel: "Adjusting Men to Machines," *Commentary*, vol. 3, no. 1, pp. 79–88, 1947.

Bendix, Reinhard, and Lloyd H. Fisher: "The Perspectives of Elton Mayo," *Review of Economics and Statistics*, vol. 31, no. 4, pp. 312–319, 1949.

Bladen, Vincent W.: "Economics and Human Relations," *The Canadian Journal of Economics and Political Science*, vol. 54, pp. 310–311, August, 1948.

Blumer, Herbert: "Sociological Theory in Industrial Relations," *American Sociological Review*, vol. 12, no. 3, pp. 271–278, 1947.

Eby, Kermit: "Research in Labor Unions," *The American Journal of Sociology*, vol. 56, no. 3, pp. 222–228, 1950.

Elmer, Glaister A.: "Maintaining Rapport Necessary for Reliability in Industrial Research," *American Sociological Review*, vol. 16, no. 1, pp. 91–93, 1951.

Friedmann, Georges: "Philosophy Underlying the Hawthorne Investigations," translated by William J. Goode and Harold L. Sheppard, *Social Forces*, vol. 28, no. 2, pp. 204–209, 1949.

Hart, C. W. M.: "Industrial Relations Research and Social Theory," *The Canadian Journal of Economics and Political Science*, vol. 15, pp. 53–73, February, 1949.

Homans, George C.: "The Strategy of Industrial Sociology," *The American Journal of Sociology*, vol. 54, no. 4, pp. 330–337, 1949.

Koivisto, W. A.: "Value, Theory, and Fact in Industrial Sociology," *The American Journal of Sociology*, vol. 57, no. 6, pp. 564–572, 1953.

Mills, C. Wright: "The Contributions of Sociology to Studies of Industrial Relations," *Proceedings of the First Annual Meeting, Industrial Relations Research Association, Cleveland, Ohio, December 29–30, 1948*, pp. 199–222.

Moore, Wilbert E.: "Current Issues in Industrial Sociology," *American Sociological Review*, vol. 12, no. 6, pp. 651–657, 1947.

———— with discussion by Robert Dubin, Delbert C. Miller, Paul Meadows, and Alvin W. Gouldner: "Industrial Sociology: Status and Prospects," *American Sociological Review*, vol. 13, no. 4, pp. 382–400, 1948.

Schneider, Eugene V.: "Limitations on Observation in Industrial Sociology," *Social Forces*, vol. 28, no. 3, pp. 279–284, 1950.

Sheppard, Harold L.: "The Treatment of Unionism in 'Managerial Sociology,'" *American Sociological Review*, vol. 14, no. 2, pp. 310–313, 1949.

Van Kleeck, Mary: "Towards an Industrial Sociology," *American Sociological Review*, vol. 11, no. 5, pp. 501–505, 1946.

Sociology and the Social Sciences

Parsons, Talcott: *The Social System*, Free Press, Glencoe, Ill., 1951, chap. XII.

Sorokin, Pitirim A.: *Society, Culture, and Personality*, Harper & Brothers, New York, 1947, pp. 6–18.

CHAPTER 2. INDUSTRY AND SOCIOLOGICAL THEORY

NOTE: The bibliography for this chapter is in no sense meant to be inclusive of the field, but, rather, to list some of the sources for the theory put forth in this chapter.

Aberle, D. F., A. K. Cohen, A. K. Davis, M. J. Levy, Jr., and F. X. Sutton: "The Functional Prerequisites of a Society," *Ethics*, vol. 60, no. 2, pp. 100–111, 1950.

Benedict, Ruth: *Patterns of Culture*, Penguin Books, Inc., Baltimore, 1934.

Cohen, Albert K.: *Delinquent Boys: The Culture of the Gang*, Free Press, Glencoe, Ill., 1955.

Cooley, Charles H.: *Social Organization*, Charles Scribner's Sons, New York, 1924.

Davis, Kingsley: *Human Society*, The Macmillan Company, New York, 1949.

Durkheim, Emile: *The Division of Labor in Society*, translated by George Simpson, The Macmillan Company, New York, 1933.

———: *The Elementary Forms of the Religious Life*, Free Press, Glencoe, Ill., 1947.

———: *Suicide: A Study in Sociology*, translated by John A. Spaulding and George Simpson, Free Press, Glencoe, Ill., 1951.

Herskovits, Melville, J.: *Man and His Works*, Alfred A. Knopf, Inc., New York, 1949.

Kluckhohn, Clyde: *Mirror for Man*, McGraw-Hill Book Company, Inc., New York, 1949.

Levy, Marion J.: *The Structure of Society*, Princeton University Press, Princeton, N.J., 1952.

Linton, Ralph: *The Study of Man*, Appleton-Century-Crofts, Inc., New York, 1936.

MacIver, R. M.: *Society: A Textbook of Sociology*, Rinehart & Company, Inc., New York, 1937.

Mannheim, Karl: *Ideology and Utopia: An Introduction to the Sociology of Knowledge*, Harcourt, Brace and Company, Inc., New York, 1946.

Marx, Karl: *Capital, The Communist Manifesto, and Other Writings*, edited by Max Eastman, Modern Library, Inc., New York, 1932.

Mead, George H.: *Mind, Self and Society*, University of Chicago Press, Chicago, 1934.

Mead, Margaret: *Coming of Age in Samoa*, The New American Library, New York, 1928.

Merton, Robert K.: *Social Theory and Social Structure*, Free Press, Glencoe, Ill., 1949.

Parsons, Talcott: *Essays in Sociological Theory: Pure and Applied*, rev. ed., Free Press, Glencoe, Ill., 1954.

———: *The Social System*, Free Press, Glencoe, Ill., 1951.

Selznick, Philip: "The Foundations of the Theory of Organization," *American Sociological Review*, vol. 13, no. 1, pp. 25–35, 1948.

Thomas, W. I.: *The Unadjusted Girl*, Little, Brown & Company, Boston, 1923.

Weber, Max: *From Max Weber: Essays in Sociology*, edited and translated by H. H. Gerth and C. Wright Mills, Oxford University Press, New York, 1946.

———: *The Theory of Social and Economic Organization*, translated by A. M. Henderson and Talcott Parsons, Oxford University Press, New York, 1947.

Williams, Robin M., Jr.: *Modern American Society*, Alfred A. Knopf, Inc., New York, 1951.

CHAPTER 3. TYPES OF PRODUCTIVE SYSTEMS

Ashley, William James: *An Introduction to English Economic History and Theory*, 2 vols., Longmans, Green & Co., Ltd., London, 1923.

Bücher, Carl: *Industrial Evolution*, Henry Holt and Company, Inc., New York, 1901.

Cole, G. D. H.: "Industrialism," in *Encyclopedia of the Social Sciences*, The Macmillan Company, New York, 1932, vol. 8, pp. 18–26.

Corey, Lewis: "Machines and Tools: Modern," in *Encyclopedia of the Social Sciences,* The Macmillan Company, New York, 1933, vol. 10, pp. 21–26.

Cunningham, William: *The Growth of English Industry and Commerce,* Cambridge University Press, London, 1890.

Dietz, Frederick C.: *An Economic History of England,* Henry Holt and Company, Inc., New York, 1942, chaps. 11, 12, 19.

Durkheim, Emile: *The Division of Labor in Society,* translated by George Simpson, Free Press, Glencoe, Ill., 1947.

Gay, Edwin F.: "Putting Out System," in *Encyclopedia of the Social Sciences,* The Macmillan Company, New York, 1934, vol. 13, pp. 7–11.

Gras, N. S. B.: *Industrial Evolution,* Harvard University Press, Cambridge, Mass., 1930.

————: *An Introduction to Economic History,* Harper & Brothers, New York, 1922.

Hamilton, Walton H., and Irene Till: "Property," in *Encyclopedia of the Social Sciences,* The Macmillan Company, New York, 1934, vol. 12, pp. 528–538.

Hammond, John Lawrence: "Factory System," in *Encyclopedia of the Social Sciences,* The Macmillan Company, New York, 1931, vol. 6, pp. 51–54.

———— and Barbara Hammond: *The Rise of Modern Industry,* Methuen & Co., Ltd., London, 1925, chaps. IV–VII.

Hauser, Henri: "Journeymen's Societies," in *Encyclopedia of the Social Sciences,* The Macmillan Company, New York, 1932, vol. 8, pp. 424–447.

Heaton, Herbert: "Industrial Revolution," in *Encyclopedia of the Social Sciences,* The Macmillan Company, New York, 1932, vol. 7, pp. 255–260.

Knight, Melvin Moses: *Economic History of Europe,* Houghton Mifflin Company, Boston, 1926.

————: "Handicraft," in *Encyclopedia of the Social Sciences,* The Macmillan Company, New York, 1932, vol. 7, pp. 255–260.

Lipson, E.: *The Economic History of England,* The Macmillan Company, New York, 1929, chaps. VII, VIII.

Mantoux, Paul: *The Industrial Revolution in the Eighteenth Century,* Harcourt, Brace and Company, Inc., New York, no date.

Marshall, Leon Carroll: *Readings in Industrial Society,* University of Chicago Press, Chicago, 1918, pp. 79–91.

Marx, Karl: *Capital,* translated by Samuel Moore and Edward Aveling, International Publishers Co., Inc., New York, edition of 1939, vol. 1, chap. XIV.

Moffit, Louis W.: *England on the Eve of the Industrial Revolution,* P. S. King & Staples, Ltd., London, 1925.

Moore, Wilbert E.: *Industrialization and Labor,* Cornell University Press, (published for the Institute of World Affairs, New School for Social Research), Ithaca, N.Y., 1951.

Mumford, Lewis: *Technics and Civilization,* Harcourt, Brace and Company, Inc., New York, 1934.

Pirenne, Henri: "Guilds, European," in *Encyclopedia of the Social Sciences,* The Macmillan Company, New York, 1932, vol. 7, pp. 208–214.

Polyani, Karl: *The Great Transformation,* Rinehart & Company, Inc., New York, 1944.

Smith, Adam: *The Wealth of Nations,* Modern Library, Inc., New York, 1937, book I, chaps. I–III.

Sombart, Werner: "Capitalism," in *Encyclopedia of the Social Sciences,* The Macmillan Company, New York, 1930, vol. 3, pp. 195–208.

————: *The Quintessence of Capitalism,* E. P. Dutton & Co., Inc., New York, 1915.

Sweezy, Paul M.: *The Theory of Capitalist Development,* Oxford University Press, New York, 1942.

Tawney, Richard Henry: *The Acquisitive Society,* Harcourt, Brace and Company, Inc., New York, 1920.

————: *Religion and the Rise of Capitalism,* Harcourt, Brace and Company, New York, 1926.

Taylor, R. Whately Cooke: *An Introduction to a History of the Factory System,* Richard Bentley & Son, London, 1886.

Usher, Abbott Payson: *An Introduction to the Industrial History of England,* Houghton Mifflin Company, Boston, 1920.

Veblen, Thorstein: *Absentee Ownership and Business Enterprise,* B. W. Huebsch, New York, 1923.

————: *Imperial Germany and the Industrial Revolution,* The Viking Press, Inc., New York, 1939.

Weber, Max: *General Economic History,* translated by Frank H. Knight, Free Press, Glencoe, Ill., 1950.

————: *The Protestant Ethic and the Spirit of Capitalism,* translated by Talcott Parsons, George Allen & Unwin, Ltd., London, 1930.

————: *The Theory of Social and Economic Organization,* translated by A. M. Henderson and Talcott Parsons, Oxford University Press, New York, 1947.

CHAPTER 4. THE DEVELOPMENT OF INDUSTRY IN THE UNITED STATES

Adelman, M. A.: "The Measurement of Industrial Concentration," *The Review of Economics and Statistics,* vol. 23, no. 4, pp. 269–296, 1951.

Allen, Frederick Lewis: *The Lords of Creation,* Harper & Brothers, New York, 1935.

————: *Only Yesterday,* Harper & Brothers, New York, 1931.

Arnold, Thurman: *The Folklore of Capitalism,* Yale University Press, New Haven, Conn., 1937.

Beard, Charles A.: *An Economic Interpretation of the Constitution of the United States,* The Macmillan Company, New York, 1923.

———— and Mary R. Beard: *The Rise of American Civilization,* 2 vols., The Macmillan Company, New York, 1927 (vol. I) and 1928 (vol. II).

Berle, Adolph A., Jr.: *The Twentieth Century Capitalist Revolution,* Harcourt, Brace and Company, Inc., New York, 1954.

———— and Gardiner C. Means: *The Modern Corporation and Private Property,* The Macmillan Company, New York, 1933.

Brady, Robert A.: *Business as a System of Power,* Columbia University Press, New York, 1943.

Clark, Victor S.: *History of Manufactures in the United States,* 3 vols., Carnegie Institution of Washington, Washington, 1929.

Cochran, Thomas C., and William Miller: *The Age of Enterprise,* The Macmillan Company, New York, 1942.

Commons, John R., et al.: *A Documentary History of American Industrial Society,* Arthur H. Clark Company, Glendale, Calif., 1910.

Diamond, Sigmund: *The Reputation of the American Business Man,* Harvard University Press, Cambridge, Mass., 1955.

Dorfman, Joseph: *The Economic Mind in American Civilization,* vol. III, The Viking Press, Inc., New York, 1949.

Galbraith, John Kenneth: *American Capitalism: The Concept of Countervailing Power,* Houghton Mifflin Company, Boston, 1952.

———: *The Great Crash,* Houghton Mifflin Company, Boston, 1955.

Hacker, Louis M.: *The Triumph of American Capitalism,* Simon and Schuster, Inc., New York, 1940.

Josephson, Matthew: *The Robber Barons,* Harcourt, Brace and Company, Inc., New York, 1934.

Laski, Harold J.: *The American Democracy,* The Viking Press, Inc., New York, 1949, chaps. 1, 2, 5.

Lynch, David: *The Concentration of Economic Power,* Columbia University Press, New York, 1946.

Magdoff, Harry, Irvin H. Siegel, and Milton B. Davis: *Production, Employment and Productivity in Fifty-nine Manufacturing Industries, 1919–1936,* Works Project Administration, National Research Project on Reemployment Opportunities and Recent Changes in Industrial Techniques, Studies of the Labor Supply, Productivity and Production, Report S-1, Philadelphia, 1934.

Miller, William (ed.): *Men in Business: Essays in the History of Entrepreneurship,* Harvard University Press, Cambridge, Mass., 1952.

Myers, Gustavus: *History of the Great American Fortunes,* Modern Library, Inc., New York, first published in 1907.

National Resources Committee, *The Structure of the American Economy,* Government Printing Office, 1939–1940.

Nevins, Allan: *John D. Rockefeller,* 2 vols., Charles Scribner's Sons, New York, 1940.

Schlesinger, Arthur Meier: *Political and Social History of the United States, 1829–1925,* The Macmillan Company, New York, 1925.

Shannon, Fred Albert: *America's Economic Growth,* The Macmillan Company, New York, 1940.

Smaller War Plants Corporation, *Economic Concentration and World War II,* Government Printing Office, 1946.

Stafford, Alfred B.: "Is the Rate of Invention Declining?" *The American Journal of Sociology,* vol. 57, no. 6, pp. 539–545, 1952.

Stocking, George W., and Myron W. Watkins: *Monopoly and Free Enterprise,* The Twentieth Century Fund, Inc., New York, 1951.

Sward, Keith: *The Legend of Henry Ford,* Rinehart & Company, Inc., New York, 1948.

Temporary National Economic Committee: *The Distribution of Ownership in the Two Hundred Largest Non-financial Corporations,* Monograph no. 29, Government Printing Office, 1940.

Temporary National Economic Committee: *Final Report and Recommendations,* Government Printing Office, 1941.

Turner, Frederick Jackson: *The Frontier in American History,* Henry Holt and Company, Inc., New York, 1920.

Warner, W. Lloyd, and J. O. Low: *The Social System of the Modern Factory,* Yankee City Series, vol. IV, Yale University Press, New Haven, Conn., 1947.

CHAPTER 5. THE INDUSTRIAL BUREAUCRACY

Bakke, Wight E.: *Bonds of Organisation: An Appraisal of Corporate Human Relations,* Harper & Brothers, New York, 1950.

Barnard, Chester I.: *The Functions of the Executive,* Harvard University Press, Cambridge, Mass., 1945.

————: "Functions and Pathology of Status Systems in Formal Organizations," in William E. Whyte (ed.), *Industry and Society,* McGraw-Hill Book Company, Inc., New York, 1946.

————: *Organization and Management,* Harvard University Press, Cambridge, Mass., 1949.

Bendix, Reinhard: "Bureaucracy: The Problem and Its Setting," *The American Sociological Review,* vol. 12, no. 5, pp. 493–507, October, 1947.

Blau, Peter M.: *The Dynamics of Bureaucracy,* University of Chicago Press, Chicago, 1955.

Boulding, Kenneth E.: *The Organizational Revolution: A Study of the Ethics of Economic Organization,* Harper & Brothers, New York, 1953.

Dimock, Marshall E.: *Bureaucracy and Trusteeship in Large Corporations,* Temporary National Economic Committee, Monograph no. 11, Government Printing Office, 1940.

Drucker, Peter F.: *Concept of the Corporation,* The John Day Company, Inc., New York, 1946.

Dubin, Robert: *Human Relations in Administration,* Prentice-Hall, Inc., Englewood Cliffs, N.J., 1951.

Ellsworth, John S., Jr.: *Factory Folkways: A Study of Institutional Structure,* Yale University Press, New Haven, Conn., 1953.

Florence, P. Sargant: *The Logic of Industrial Organization,* Routledge and Kegan Paul, Ltd., London, 1933.

Friedrich, Carl J.: *Constitutional Government and Politics,* Harper & Brothers, New York, 1937.

Gardner, Burleigh B.: *Human Relations in Industry,* Richard D. Irwin, Inc., Homewood, Ill., 1945.

Gouldner, Alvin W.: *Patterns of Industrial Bureaucracy,* Free Press, Glencoe, Ill., 1954.

Henry, William E.: "The Business Executive: Dynamics of a Social Role." *The American Journal of Sociology,* vol. 54, pp. 286–291, January, 1949.

Jaques, Elliott: *The Changing Culture of a Factory,* The Dryden Press, Inc., New York, 1952.

Laski, Harold J.: "Bureaucracy," in *Encyclopedia of the Social Sciences,* The Macmillan Company, New York, 1933, vol. 3, pp. 70–73.

Lepawsky, Albert: *Administration: The Art and Science of Organization and Management,* Alfred A. Knopf, Inc., New York, 1952.

Merton, Robert K., Ailsa P. Gray, Barbara Hockey, and Hanan C. Selvin: *Reader in Bureaucracy,* Free Press, Glencoe, Ill., 1952.

Roethlisberger, Fritz Jules: *Management and Morale,* Harvard University Press, Cambridge, Mass., 1946.

Selznick, Philip: "Foundations of the Theory of Organization," *American Sociological Review,* vol. 13, no. 1, pp. 25–35, February, 1948.

————: *The Organizational Weapon: A Study of Bolshevik Strategy and Tactics,* McGraw-Hill Book Company, Inc., New York, 1952.

————: *TVA and the Grass Roots: A Study in the Sociology of Formal Organization,* University of California Press, Berkeley, Calif., 1949.

Simon, Herbert A.: "Decision-making and Administrative Organization," *Public Administration Review,* vol. 4, no. 1, pp. 16–25, winter, 1944.

Taylor, Frederick Winslow: *The Principles of Scientific Management,* Harper & Brothers, New York, 1911.

Weber, Max: *From Max Weber: Essays in Sociology,* translated by H. H. Gerth and C. Wright Mills, Oxford University Press, New York, 1946, part II.

————: *The Theory of Social and Economic Organization,* translated by A. M. Henderson and Talcott Parsons, Oxford University Press, New York, 1947, part III.

CHAPTER 6. THE EXECUTIVE IN THE INDUSTRIAL BUREAUCRACY

Argyris, Chri: *Executive Leadership: An Appraisal of a Manager in Action,* Harper & Brothers, New York, 1953.

Bakke, E. Wight, and Clark Kerr (eds.): *Unions, Management and the Public,* Harcourt, Brace and Company, Inc., New York, 1948.

Barnard, Chester I.: *The Functions of the Executive,* Harvard University Press, Cambridge, Mass., 1945.

————: "Functions and Pathology of Status Systems in Formal Organizations," in William F. Whyte (ed.), *Industry and Society,* McGraw-Hill Book Company, Inc., New York, 1946, pp. 46–83.

Berle, Adolf A., Jr., and Gardiner C. Means: *The Modern Corporation and Private Property,* The Macmillan Company, New York, 1933.

Burnham, James: *The Managerial Revolution,* The John Day Company, Inc., New York, 1941.

Chamberlin, Neil W.: *Management in Motion,* Labor and Management Center, Yale University, New Haven, Conn., 1950.

Chapple, E. D.: "Organization Problems in Industry," *Applied Anthropology,* vol. 1, no. 1, pp. 2–9, 1941.

Copeland, Melvin T.: *The Executive at Work,* Harvard University Press, Cambridge, Mass., 1952.

Dalton, Melville: "Conflicts between Staff and Line Officers," *American Sociological Review,* vol. 15, no. 3, pp. 342–351, 1950.

Dimock, Marshall Edward: *The Executive in Action,* Harper & Brothers, New York, 1945.

Drucker, Peter F.: "The Employee Society," *The American Journal of Sociology,* vol. 58, no. 4, pp. 358–363, 1953.

————: "The Function of Profits," *Fortune,* March, 1949.

Fernstrom, Karl D., and Robert F. Elder: *Organization and Management of a Business Enterprise,* Harper & Brothers, New York, 1935.

Fisher, Burton R., and Stephen B. Withey: *Big Business as the People See It,* Michigan University Research Center, University of Michigan Press, Ann Arbor, Mich., 1952.

Fortune, "The 30,000 Managers," vol. 21, no. 2, February, 1940.

————, "What Makes the Boss Work?" vol. 37, no. 4, April, 1948.

Harbison, Frederick H., and Eugene W. Burgess: "Modern Management in Western Europe," *The American Journal of Sociology,* vol. 60, no. 1, pp. 15–23, 1954.

Janney, J. Elliott: "Company Presidents Look at Themselves," *Harvard Business Review,* vol. 30, no. 3, pp. 59–70, 1952.

Katz, Daniel, Nathan Maccoby, Gerald Gurin, and Lucretia G. Floor: *Productivity, Supervision and Morale among Railroad Workers*, Survey Research Center, Institute for Social Research, University of Michigan Press, Ann Arbor, Mich., 1952.

——, ——, and Nancy C. Morse: *Productivity, Supervision and Morale in an Office Situation*, Michigan University Research Center, University of Michigan Press, Ann Arbor, Mich., 1951.

Kimball, Dexter S., and Dexter S. Kimball, Jr.: *Principles of Industrial Organization*, 6th ed., McGraw-Hill Book Company, Inc., New York, 1947.

Knowles, Asa S., and Robert D. Thompson: *Management of Manpower*, The Macmillan Company, New York, 1943.

Lane, Robert E.: "Government Regulation and the Business Mind," *American Sociological Review*, vol. 16, no. 2, pp. 163–173, 1951.

Lauterbach, Albert: *Men, Motives, and Money: Psychological Frontiers of Economics*, Cornell University Press, Ithaca, N.Y., 1954.

Learned, Edmund P., David N. Ulrich, and Donald R. Booz: *Executive Action*, Harvard University Graduate School of Business Administration, Cambridge, Mass., 1951.

Lepawsky, Albert: *Administration: The Art and Science of Organization and Management*, Alfred A. Knopf, Inc., New York, 1952.

Maier, Norman R. F.: *Principles of Human Relations: Applications to Management*, John Wiley & Sons, Inc., New York, 1952.

Metcalf, H. C.: *Business Management as a Profession*, McGraw-Hill Book Company, Inc., New York, 1927.

Mills, C. Wright: "The American Business Elite: A Collective Portrait," *The Journal of Economic History*, vol. 5, supplement V, pp. 20–44, 1945.

Person, H. S. (ed.): *The Taylor Society, Scientific Management in American Industry*, Harper & Brothers, New York, 1929.

Redfield, Charles E.: *Communication in Management: A Guide to Administrative Communication*, University of Chicago Press, Chicago, 1953.

Roethlisberger, Fritz Jules, and William J. Dickson: *Management and the Worker*, Harvard University Press, Cambridge, Mass., 1939.

Scott, Jerome F., and R. P. Lynton: *Three Studies in Management*, Routledge and Kegan Paul, Ltd., London, 1952.

Selekman, Benjamin M.: *Labor Relations and Human Relations*, McGraw-Hill Book Company, Inc., New York, 1947.

Sutherland, Edwin H.: *White Collar Crime*, The Dryden Press, Inc., New York, 1949.

Taussig, F. W., and C. S. Joslyn: *American Business Leaders*, The Macmillan Company, New York, 1932.

Taylor, Frederick W.: *Scientific Management*, Harper & Brothers, New York, 1947.

Warner, W. Lloyd, and James C. Abeggeln: *Occupational Mobility*, University of Minnesota Press, Minneapolis, Minn., 1955.

Whitehead, T. N.: *Leadership in a Free Society*, Harvard University Press, Cambridge, Mass., 1936.

Whyte, William F., et al.: *Money and Motivation: An Analysis of Incentives in Industry*, Harper & Brothers, New York, 1955.

Whyte, William H., Jr.: "The Corporation and the Wife," *Fortune*, November, 1951.

——: "The Wives of Management," *Fortune*, October, 1951.

CHAPTER 7. "MINOR" ROLES: THE SPECIALIST, THE OFFICE
WORKER, THE FOREMAN

Anonymous: "The Scientists," *Fortune*, October, 1948.

Barber, Bernard: *Science and the Social Order*, Free Press, Glencoe, Ill., 1952.

Barnard, Chester I.: *The Functions of the Executive*, Harvard University Press, Cambridge, Mass., 1945.

Becker, Howard S., and James W. Carper: "The Development of Identification with an Occupation," *The American Journal of Sociology*, vol. 61, no. 4, pp. 289–298, 1956.

Corey, Lewis: *The Crisis of the Middle Class*, Covici, Friede, Inc., New York, 1935.

Dalton, Melville: "Conflicts between Staff and Line Officers," *American Sociological Review*, vol. 15, no. 3, pp. 342–351, 1950.

Drucker, Peter F.: "Management and the Professional Employee," *Harvard Business Review*, vol. 30, no. 3, pp. 84–90, 1952.

Flexner, Jean A., and Anna-Stina Ericson: "White Collar Employment and Income," *Monthly Labor Review*, vol. 79, no. 4, pp. 401–409, 1956.

Gardner, Burleigh B.: *Human Relations in Industry*, Richard D. Irwin, Inc., Homewood, Ill., 1945.

Gardner, B. B., and W. F. Whyte: "The Man in the Middle: Position and Problems of the Foreman," *Applied Anthropology*, vol. 4, no. 2, pp. 1–28, 1945.

Homans, George C.: "The Cash Posters: A Study of a Group of Working Girls," *American Sociological Review*, vol. 19, no. 6, pp. 724–733, 1954.

Katz, Daniel, et al.: *Productivity, Supervision and Morale among Railroad Workers*, Survey Research Center, Institute for Social Research, University of Michigan, Ann Arbor, Mich., 1951.

Merton, Robert K.: *Social Theory and Social Structure*, Free Press, Glencoe, Ill., 1949.

Mills, C. Wright: *White Collar*, Oxford University Press, New York, 1951.

Moore, Wilbert E.: *Industrial Relations and the Social Order*, The Macmillan Company, New York, 1951, chap. VI.

Morse, Nancy: *Satisfactions in the White Collar Job*, Institute of Social Research Publications, University of Michigan Press, Ann Arbor, Mich., 1954.

National Institute of Industrial Psychology, *The Foreman: A Study of Supervision in British Industry*, Staples Press, Ltd., London, 1951.

Northrup, Herbert R.: "The Foreman's Association of America," *Harvard Business Review*, vol. 23, no. 2, pp. 187–202, 1945.

Parsons, Talcott: "The Professions and Social Structure," *Social Forces*, vol. 17, no. 4, pp. 457–467, 1939.

Reiss, Albert J.: "Occupational Mobility of Professional Workers," *American Sociological Review*, vol. 20, no. 6, pp. 693–700, 1955.

Riesman, David: "Toward an Anthropological Science of Law and the Legal Profession," *The American Journal of Sociology*, vol. 57, no. 2, pp. 121–135, 1951.

Roethlisberger, Fritz J.: "The Foreman: Master and Victim of Double Talk," *Harvard Business Review*, vol. 23, no. 3, pp. 283–298, 1945.

—— and William J. Dickson: *Management and the Worker*, Harvard University Press, Cambridge, Mass., 1939.

Ulrich, David N., Donald R. Booz, and Paul R. Lawrence: *Management Behavior and Foreman Attitude: A Case Study,* Harvard University Graduate School of Business Administration, Cambridge, Mass., 1950.

Uris, Auren: *Improved Foremanship,* The Macmillan Company, New York, 1948.

Veblen, Thorstein: *The Engineers and the Price System,* The Viking Press, Inc., New York, 1933.

Wray, Donald E.: "Marginal Men of Industry: The Foremen," *The American Journal of Sociology,* vol. 54, no. 4, pp. 298–301, 1949.

Zaleznik, A.: *Foreman Training in a Growing Enterprise,* Harvard University Graduate School of Business Administration, Boston, 1951.

CHAPTER 8. THE ROLE OF THE WORKER: INDUSTRIAL PRODUCTION AND THE WORKER'S ROLE

Ayres, Eugene: "An Automatic Chemical Plant," *Scientific American,* vol. 187, no. 3, pp. 82–96, 1952.

Bakke, E. Wight: *Citizens without Work,* Institute of Human Relations, Yale University Press, New Haven, Conn., 1940.

———: *The Unemployed Worker,* Yale University Press, New Haven, Conn., 1940.

Brown, Gordon L., and Donald P. Campbell: "Control Systems," *Scientific American,* vol. 187, no. 3, pp. 56–64, 1952.

Chase, Stuart: *Men and Machines,* The Macmillan Company, New York, 1929.

Davis, Arthur K.: "Sociological Elements in Veblen's Economic Thought," *Journal of Political Economy,* vol. 53, no. 2, pp. 132–149, 1945.

Dewhurst, Frederic J., and Associates: *America's Needs and Resources,* The Twentieth Century Fund, Inc., New York, 1955.

Dictionary of Occupational Titles, Government Printing Office, 1937.

Dictionary of Occupational Titles Supplement, ed. II, Government Printing Office, 1943.

Florence, P. Sargant: *Economics of Fatigue and Unrest and the Efficiency of Labour in English and American Industry,* Henry Holt and Company, Inc., New York, 1924.

Friedmann, Eugene A., and Robert J. Havighurst: *The Meaning of Work and Retirement,* University of Chicago Press, Chicago, 1954.

Friedmann, Georges: *Industrial Society: The Emergence of the Human Problems of Automation,* Free Press, Glencoe, Ill., 1955.

Gardner, Burleigh B.: "The Factory as a Social System," in William F. Whyte (ed.), *Industry and Society,* McGraw-Hill Book Company, Inc., New York, 1946.

Greenberg, Leon: "Output per Man-hour in Manufacturing, 1939–1947 and 1947–1953," *Monthly Labor Review,* vol. 79, no. 1, pp. 1–6, 1956.

King, Gilbert W.: "Information," *Scientific American,* vol. 187, no. 3, pp. 132–148, 1952.

Leontief, Wassily: "Machines and Man," *Scientific American,* vol. 187, no. 3, pp. 50–160, 1952.

Marx, Walter John: *Mechanization and Culture,* B. Herder Book Company, St. Louis, 1941.

Mayo, Elton: *The Human Problems of an Industrial Civilization,* Harvard University Graduate School of Business Administration, Division of Research, Boston, 1946.

————: "Revery and Industrial Fatigue," *Journal of Personnel Research,* vol. 3, pp. 273–281, December, 1924.

————: *The Social Problems of an Industrial Civilization,* Harvard University Graduate School of Business Administration, Division of Research, Boston, 1945.

Meadows, Paul: *The Culture of Industrial Man,* University of Nebraska Press, Lincoln, Nebr., 1950.

Mumford, Lewis: *Technics and Civilization,* Harcourt, Brace and Company, Inc., 1934.

Nagel, Ernest: "Automation Control," *Scientific American,* vol. 187, no. 3, pp. 44–47, 1952.

Patterson, S. Howard: *Social Aspects of Industry,* 3d ed., McGraw-Hill Book Company, Inc., New York, 1943.

Pease, William: "An Automatic Machine Tool," *Scientific American,* vol. 187, no. 3, pp. 101–115, 1952.

Report of the Joint Committee on the Economic Report, *Automation and Technological Change,* Government Printing Office, 1956.

Ridenour, Louis N.: "The Role of the Computer," *Scientific American,* vol. 187, no. 3, pp. 116–130, 1952.

Roethlisberger, Fritz Jules, and William J. Dickson: *Management and the Worker,* Harvard University Press, Cambridge, Mass., 1934.

Subcommittee on Economic Stabilization of the Joint Committee on the Economic Report, *Automation and Technological Change,* Government Printing Office, 1955.

Taylor, Frederick W.: *Scientific Management,* Harper & Brothers, New York, 1947.

Tiffin, Joseph: *Industrial Psychology,* Prentice-Hall, Inc., Englewood Cliffs, N.J., New York, 1952.

Tripp, L. Reed (ed.): *Industrial Productivity,* Industrial Relations Research Association, Madison, Wis., 1951.

Tustin, Arnold: "Feedback," *Scientific American,* vol. 187, no. 3, pp. 48–55, 1952.

Veblen, Thorstein: *The Instinct of Workmanship,* The Macmillan Company, New York, 1914.

Vernon, H. M.: *The Health and Efficiency of Munitions Workers,* Oxford University Press, New York, 1940.

————: *Industrial Fatigue and Efficiency,* Routledge & Kegan Paul, Ltd., London, 1921.

Viteles, Morris S.: *Industrial Psychology,* W. W. Norton & Company, Inc., New York, 1929.

————: *The Science of Work,* W. W. Norton & Company, Inc., New York, 1934.

Walker, Charles R., and Robert H. Guest: *The Man on the Assembly Line,* Harvard University Press, Cambridge, Mass., 1952.

CHAPTER 9. THE ROLE OF THE WORKER: SOCIAL RELATIONS AT WORK

Anderson, H. Dewey: *Technology in Our Economy,* Temporary National Economic Committee, Monograph no. 22, Government Printing Office, 1941.

Anonymous: "Adjustments to Automation in Two Firms," *Monthly Labor Review,* vol. 79, no. 1, pp. 15–19, 1956.

Babchuk, Nicholas, and William J. Goode: "Work Incentives in a Self-determined Group," *American Sociological Review,* vol. 16, no. 5, pp. 679–687, 1951.

Bakke, E. Wight: *The Unemployed Worker,* Yale University Press, New Haven, Conn., 1940.

Barnard, Chester I.: *The Functions of the Executive,* Harvard University Press, Cambridge, Mass., 1945, chap. 9.

Blum, Fred H.: *Toward a Democratic Work Process: The Hormel-Packinghouse Workers' Experiment,* Harper & Brothers, New York, 1953.

Chinoy, Ely: *Automobile Workers and the American Dream,* Doubleday & Company, Inc., New York, 1955.

Collins, Orvis: "Ethnic Behavior in Industry: Sponsorship and Rejection in a New England Factory," *The American Journal of Sociology,* vol. 51, no. 4, pp. 293–298, 1946.

Cottrell, William Frederick: *The Railroader,* Stanford University Press, Stanford, Calif., 1940.

Diebold, John: *Automation: The Advent of the Automatic Factory,* D. Van Nostrand Company, Inc., Princeton, N.J., 1952.

Firey, Walter: "Informal Organization and the Theory of Schism," *American Sociological Review,* vol. 13, no. 1, pp. 15–24, 1948.

Goode, William J., and Irving Fowler: "Incentive Factors in a Low Morale Plant," *American Sociological Review,* vol. 14, no. 5, pp. 618–624, 1949.

Gross, Edward: "Some Functional Consequences of Primary Controls in Formal Work Organizations," *American Sociological Review,* vol. 18, no. 4, pp. 368–373, 1953.

Guest, Robert H.: "Work Careers and Aspirations of Automobile Workers," *American Sociological Review,* vol. 19, no. 2, pp. 155–163, 1954.

Herring, Harriet Laura: *Passing of the Mill Village,* The University of North Carolina Press, Chapel Hill, N.C., 1949.

Horsfall, Alexander B., and Conrad M. Arensberg: "Teamwork and Productivity in a Shoe Factory," *Human Organization,* vol. 8, no. 1, pp. 13–25, 1949.

Hughes, Everett C.: "The Knitting of Racial Groups in Industry," *American Sociological Review,* vol. 11, no. 5, pp. 512–519, 1946.

Katz, Daniel, Nathan Macoby, Gerald Gurin, and Lucretia G. Floor: *Productivity, Supervision and Morale among Railroad Workers,* Institute for Social Research, University of Michigan, Ann Arbor, Mich., 1951.

——, ——, and Nancy C. Morse: *Productivity, Supervision and Morale in an Office Situation,* Institute for Social Research, University of Michigan, Ann Arbor, Mich., 1951.

Lyman, Elizabeth L.: "Occupational Differences in the Value Attached to Work," *The American Journal of Sociology,* vol. 61, no. 2, pp. 138–144, 1955.

Magistretti, Franca: "Sociological Factors in the Structuring of Industrial Workers' Teams," *The American Journal of Sociology,* vol. 60, no. 6, pp. 536–540, 1955.

Mathewson, Stanley B.: *Restriction of Output among Unorganized Workers,* The Viking Press, Inc., New York, 1931.

Mayo, Elton, George F. F. Lombard: *Teamwork and Labor Turnover in the Aircraft Industry of Southern California*, Harvard University Graduate School of Business Administration, Bureau of Business Research, Cambridge, Mass., 1944.

Miernyk, William H., with the assistance of Nadine P. Rodwin: *Inter-industry Labor Mobility: The Case of the Displaced Textile Worker*, Bureau of Business and Economic Research, Northeastern University, Boston, 1955.

Morse, Nancy C., and Robert S. Weiss: "The Function and Meaning of Work and the Job," *American Sociological Review*, vol. 20, no. 2, pp. 191–198, 1955.

Perlman, Selig: *A Theory of the Labor Movement*, Augustus M. Kelley, New York, 1949 (originally published in 1928).

Polanyi, Karl: "Our Obsolete Market Mentality," *Commentary*, vol. 3, pp. 109–117, 1947.

Roethlisberger, Fritz Jules: *Management and Morale*, Harvard University Press, Cambridge, Mass., 1946.

———— and William J. Dickson: *Management and the Worker*, Harvard University Press, Cambridge, Mass., 1939.

Roy, Donald: "Efficiency and the 'Fix': Informal Intergroup Relations in a Piecework Machine Shop," *The American Journal of Sociology*, vol. 60, no. 3, pp. 255–256, 1954.

————: "Quota Restriction and Goldbricking in a Machine Shop," *The American Journal of Sociology*, vol. 57, no. 5, pp. 427–442, 1952.

————: "Work Satisfaction and Social Reward in Quota Achievement: An Analysis of Piecework Incentive," *American Sociological Review*, vol. 18, no. 5, pp. 507–514, 1953.

Seashore, Stanley: *Group Cohesiveness in the Industrial Work Group*, Institute of Social Research Publications, University of Michigan Press, Ann Arbor, Mich., 1955.

Subcommittee on Economic Stabilization of the Congressional Joint Committee on the Economic Report, *Automation and Technological Change*, Government Printing Office, 1955.

Viteles, Morris S.: *Motivation and Morale in Industry*, W. W. Norton & Company, Inc., New York, 1953.

Walker, Charles R., and Robert H. Guest: *The Man on the Assembly Line*, Harvard University Press, Cambridge, Mass., 1952.

Warner, W. Lloyd, and J. O. Low: *The Social System of the Modern Factory*, Yale University Press, New Haven, Conn., 1947.

Whyte, William F.: *Human Relations in the Restaurant Industry*, McGraw-Hill Book Company, Inc., New York, 1948.

————: *Street Corner Society: The Social Structure of an Italian Slum*, University of Chicago Press, Chicago, 1943.

————, et al.: *Money and Motivation: An Analysis of Incentives in Industry*, Harper & Brothers, New York, 1955.

Williams, Whiting: *What's on the Worker's Mind?* Charles Scribner's Sons, New York, 1926.

Worthy, James C.: "Organizational Structure and Employe Morale," *American Sociological Review*, vol. 15, no. 2, pp. 169–179, 1950.

Zweig, F.: *Productivity and Trade Unions*, Basil Blackwell, & Mott, Ltd., Oxford, 1951.

CHAPTER 10. DEVELOPMENT OF TRADE-UNIONISM IN THE UNITED STATES

Adamic, Louis: *Dynamite,* The Viking Press, Inc., New York, 1931.

Commons, John R., et al.: *History of Labour in the United States,* 2 vols., The Macmillan Company, New York, 1918.

David, Henry: *The History of the Haymarket Affair,* Rinehart & Company, Inc., New York, 1936.

Dulles, Foster Rhea: *Labor in America,* Thomas Y. Crowell Company, New York, 1949.

Faulkner, Harold U., and Mark Starr: *Labor in America,* Harper & Brothers, New York, 1944.

Foster, William Z.: *Misleaders of Labor,* Trade Union Educational League, 1927.

Frankfurter, Felix, and Nathan Greene: *The Labor Injunction,* The Macmillan Company, New York, 1930.

Ginger, Ray: *The Bending Cross,* Rutgers University Press, New Brunswick. N.J., 1949.

Gompers, Samuel: *Seventy Years of Life and Labor,* 2 vols., E. P. Dutton & Co., Inc., New York, 1925.

Hoxie, Robert Franklin: *Trade Unionism in the United States,* Appleton-Century-Crofts, Inc., New York, 1928.

Interchurch World Movement, *Report on the Steel Strike of 1919,* Harcourt, Brace and Company, Inc., New York, 1920.

Levinson, Edward: *Labor on the March,* Harper & Brothers, New York, 1938.

Lorwin, Lewis L.: *The American Federation of Labor,* The Brookings Institution, Washington, 1933.

McKenney, Ruth: *Industrial Valley,* Harcourt, Brace and Company, Inc., New York, 1939.

Millis, Harry A., and Emily Clark Brown: *From the Wagner Act to Taft-Hartley: A Study of National Policy and Labor Relations,* University of Chicago Press, Chicago, 1950.

O'Connor, Harvey: *The History of the Oil Workers' International Union (C.I.O.),* Oil Workers International Union (CIO), Denver, Colo., 1950.

Perlman, Selig: *A History of Trade Unionism in the United States,* The Macmillan Company, New York, 1922.

—— and Philip Taft: *History of Labor in the United States, 1896–1932,* vol. IV, *Labor Movements,* The Macmillan Company, New York, 1935.

Saposs, David J.: *Left Wing Unionism,* International Publishers Co., Inc., New York, 1926.

Seidman, Joel: *American Labor from Defense to Reconversion,* University of Chicago Press, Chicago, 1953.

Shultz, George P., and John R. Coleman: *Labor Problems: Cases and Readings,* McGraw-Hill Book Company, Inc., New York, 1953.

United States Senate Committee on Education and Labor (La Follette committee): *Industrial Munitions,* report 6, part 3, Government Printing Office, 1939.

——: *Digest of Report of Committee on Education and Labor: Industrial Munitions,* Government Printing Office, 1939.

——: *Labor Policies of Employers' Associations, part IV: The "Little Steel" Strike and Citizens' Committees,* Government Printing Office, 1941.

Wolman, Leo: *Ebb and Flow in Trade Unionism,* National Bureau of Economic Research, New York, 1936.

Yellen, Samuel: *American Labor Struggles,* Harcourt, Brace and Company, Inc., New York, 1936.

CHAPTER 11. CONTEMPORARY AMERICAN TRADE UNIONISM

Barbash, Jack: *Labor Unions in Action,* Harper & Brothers, New York, 1948.

Chinoy, Ely: "Local Union Leadership," in Alvin W. Gouldner (ed.), *Studies in Leadership,* Harper & Brothers, New York, 1950.

Coleman, John R.: "The Compulsive Pressures of Democracy in Unionism," *The American Journal of Sociology,* vol. 61, no. 6, pp. 519–526, 1956.

Eby, Kermit: "The Expert in the Labor Movement," *The American Journal of Sociology,* vol. 57, no. 1, pp. 27–32, 1951.

Goldstein, Bernard: "Some Aspects of the Nature of Unionism among Salaried Professionals in Industry," *American Sociological Review,* vol. 20, no. 2, pp. 199–205, 1955.

Gullahorn, John T.: "Measuring Role Conflict," *The American Journal of Sociology,* vol. 61, no. 4, pp. 299–303, 1956.

Hardman, J. B. S. (ed.): *American Labor Dynamics,* Harcourt, Brace and Company, Inc., New York, 1928.

—— and Maurice F. Neufeld (eds.): *The House of Labor,* Prentice-Hall, Inc., Englewood Cliffs, N.J., 1951.

Herberg, Will: "Bureaucracy and Democracy in Labor Unions," *Antioch Review,* vol. 3, pp. 405–417, fall, 1943.

Imberman, A. A.: "Labor Leaders and Society," *Harvard Business Review,* vol. 28, no. 1, pp. 52–60, 1950.

Karsh, Bernard, Joel Seidman, and Daisy M. Lilienthal: "The Union Organizer and His Tactics: A Case Study," *The American Journal of Sociology,* vol. 59, no. 2, pp. 113–122, 1953.

Kyllonen, Toimi B.: "Social Characteristics of Active Unionists," *The American Journal of Sociology,* vol. 61, no. 6, pp. 528–533, 1951.

Lens, Sidney: *Left, Right and Center,* Henry Regnery Company, Chicago, 1949.

Lester, Richard A.: *Labor and Industrial Relations,* The Macmillan Company, New York, 1951.

Lipset, S. M., Martin Trow, and James Coleman: *Union Democracy: The Inside Politics of the International Typographical Union,* Free Press, Glencoe, Ill., 1956.

Mills, C. Wright: *The New Men of Power,* Harcourt, Brace and Company, New York, 1948.

Peterson, Florence: *American Labor Unions,* Harper & Brothers, New York, 1952.

Purcell, Theodore V.: *The Worker Speaks His Mind: On Company and Union,* Harvard University Press, Cambridge, Mass., 1954.

Roe, Wellington: *Juggernaut,* J. B. Lippincott Company, Philadelphia, 1948.

Rose, Arnold M.: *Union Solidarity,* University of Minnesota Press, Minneapolis, Minn., 1952.

Rose, Caroline Baer: "Morale in a Trade Union," *The American Journal of Sociology,* vol. 56, no. 2, pp. 164–174, 1950.

Rosen, Hjalmar, and Hudson R. A. Rosen: *The Union Member Speaks,* Prentice-Hall, Inc., Englewood Cliffs, N.J., 1955.

Sayles, Leonard R., and George Strauss: "Conflicts within Local Unions," *Harvard Business Review*, vol. 30, no. 6, pp. 84–92, 1952.

——— and ———: *The Local Union: Its Place in the Industrial Plant*, Harper & Brothers, New York, 1953.

——— and ———: "What the Worker Really Thinks of His Union," *Harvard Business Review*, vol. 31, no. 3, pp. 94–102, 1953.

Seidman, Joel, Jack London, and Bernard Karsh: "Leadership in a Local Union," *The American Journal of Sociology*, vol. 61, no. 3, pp. 229–237, 1950.

Shepard, Herbert A.: "Democratic Control in a Labor Union," *The American Journal of Sociology*, vol. 54, no. 4, pp. 311–316, 1949.

Starr, Mark: "Role of Union Organization," in William F. Whyte (ed.), *Industry and Society*, McGraw-Hill Book Company, Inc., New York, 1946.

Strauss, George: "Control by Membership in Building Trade Unions," *The American Journal of Sociology*, vol. 61, no. 6, pp. 527–535, 1956.

——— and Leonard R. Sayles: "The Local Union Meeting," *Industrial and Labor Relations Review*, vol. 6, no. 2, pp. 212–219, 1953.

——— and ———: "Occupation and the Selection of Local Union Officers," *The American Journal of Sociology*, vol. 58, no. 6, pp. 585–591, 1953.

——— and ———: "Patterns of Participation in Local Unions," *Industrial and Labor Relations Review*, vol. 6, no. 1, pp. 31–43, 1952.

——— and ———: "The Unpaid Local Leader," *Harvard Business Review*, vol. 30, no. 3, pp. 91–104, 1952.

Summers, Clyde: "Disciplinary Powers of Unions," *Industrial and Labor Relations Review*, vol. 3, no. 4, pp. 483–513, 1950.

Taft, Philip: *The Structure and Government of Labor Unions*, Harvard University Press, Cambridge, Mass., 1954.

———: "Understanding Union Administration," *Harvard Business Review*, vol. 28, no. 2, pp. 245–257, 1946.

Tagliacozzo, Daisy L., and Joel Seidman: "A Typology of Rank-and-file Union Members," *The American Journal of Sociology*, vol. 61, no. 6, pp. 546–553, 1956.

Tannenbaum, Arnold S.: "Control Structure and Union Functions," *The American Journal of Sociology*, vol. 61, no. 6, pp. 536–545, 1956.

Ulriksson, Vidkunn: *The Telegraphers: Their Craft and Their Unions*, Public Affairs Press, Washington, 1953.

CHAPTER 12. THE FUNCTIONS OF UNIONISM: UNIONISM AS AN INSTRUMENT OF POWER

Adamic, Louis: *Dynamite*, The Viking Press, Inc., New York, 1931.

Barbash, Jack: *Labor Unions in Action*, Harper & Brothers, New York, 1948.

Brooks, Robert R. R.: *When Labor Organizes*, Yale University Press, New Haven, Conn., 1937.

Chalmers, W. Ellison: "The Conciliation Process," *Industrial and Labor Relations Review*, vol. 1, no. 3, pp. 347–350, 1948.

Chamberlain, Neil W., and Jane Metzger Schilling: *The Impact of Strikes: Their Social and Economic Costs*, Harper & Brothers, New York, 1954.

Dalton, Melville: "Unofficial Union-Management Relations," *American Sociological Review*, vol. 15, no. 5, pp. 611–619, 1950.

Davey, Harold W.: "Hazards in Labor Arbitration," *Industrial and Labor Relations Review*, vol. 1, no. 3, pp. 385–406, 1948.

Eliel, Paul: "Industrial Peace and Conflict: A Study of Two Pacific Coast Industries," *Industrial and Labor Relations Review,* vol. 2, no. 4, pp. 477–501, 1949.

Ginzberg, Eli: *The Labor Leader,* The Macmillan Company, New York, 1948.

Goldberg, Joseph P., and Bernard Yabroff: "Analysis of Strikes, 1927–1949," *Monthly Labor Review,* vol. 72, no. 1, pp. 1–7, 1951.

Gouldner, Alvin W.: *Wildcat Strike,* The Antioch Press, Yellow Springs, Ohio, 1954.

Hartmann, George W., and Theodore Newcomb (eds.): *Industrial Conflict,* The Cordon Company, Inc., New York, 1939.

Hiller, E. T.: *The Strike,* University of Chicago Press, Chicago, 1928.

Kerr, Clark: "Industrial Conflict and Its Mediation," *The American Journal of Sociology,* vol. 60, no. 3, pp. 230–245, 1954.

Knowles, K. G. J. C.: " 'Strike Proneness' and Its Determinants," *The American Journal of Sociology,* vol. 60, no. 3, pp. 213–229, 1954.

———: *Strikes: A Study in Industrial Conflict,* Basil Blackwell & Mott, Ltd., Oxford, 1952.

Kornhauser, Arthur, Robert Dubin, and Arthur M. Ross: *Industrial Conflict,* McGraw-Hill Book Company, Inc., New York, 1954.

Lorwin, Lewis L.: *The American Federation of Labor,* Brookings Institution, Washington, 1933.

McKenny, Ruth: *Industrial Valley,* Harcourt, Brace and Company, Inc., New York, 1939.

Nyman, Richmond C.: *Union-Management Cooperation in the "Stretch Out,"* Yale University Press, New Haven, Conn., 1934.

Patterson, S. Howard: *Social Aspects of Industry,* 3d ed., McGraw-Hill Book Company, Inc., New York, 1943.

Peterson, Florence: *American Labor Unions,* Harper & Brothers, New York, 1952.

Selekman, Benjamin M.: *Labor Relations and Human Relations,* McGraw-Hill Book Company, Inc., New York, 1947.

United States Senate Committee on Education and Labor (La Follette committee): *Industrial Munitions,* report 6, part 3, Government Printing Office, 1939.

———: *Labor Policies of Employers' Associations, Part IV: The "Little Steel" Strike and Citizens' Committees,* Government Printing Office, 1941.

Warner, Lloyd, and J. O. Low: *The Social System of the Modern Factory,* Yale University Press, New Haven, Conn., 1947.

CHAPTER 13. THE FUNCTIONS OF UNIONISM: COLLECTIVE BARGAINING

Anonymous: "Factors Relied on by Arbitrators in Determining Wage Rates," *Columbia Law Review,* vol. 47, no. 6, pp. 1026–1041, 1947.

Backman, Jules: *Economic Data Utilized in Wage Arbitration,* University of Pennsylvania Press, Philadelphia, 1952.

Bakke, E. Wight: *Mutual Survival: The Goal of Unions and Management,* Harper & Brothers, New York, 1946.

Barbash, Jack: *Labor Unions in Action,* Harper & Brothers, New York, 1948.

Chalmers, Ellison, Margaret K. Chandler, Louis L. McQuitty, Rose Stagner, Donald E. Wray, and Milton Derber: *Labor-Management Relations in Illini City,* vol. 1, *The Case Studies,* vol. 2, *Explorations in Comparative*

Analysis, University of Illinois, Institute of Labor and Industrial Relations, Champaign, Ill., 1953–54.

Chamberlain, Neil W.: *Collective Bargaining,* McGraw-Hill Book Company, Inc., New York, 1951.

Cohen, Samuel Harris: "Labor, Taft-Hartley and the Proposed Amendments," *Labor Law Journal,* vol. 5, no. 6, pp. 391–438, 1954.

Ernest, Dale: *Greater Productivity through Labor-Management Cooperation: Analysis of Company and Union Experience,* American Management Association, New York, 1950.

Daugherty, Carroll R., and John B. Parrish: *The Labor Problems of American Society,* Houghton Mifflin Company, Boston, 1952.

Davey, Harold W.: *Contemporary Collective Bargaining,* Prentice-Hall, Inc., Englewood Cliffs, N.J., 1951.

Dubin, Robert: "Decision-making by Management in Industrial Relations," *The American Journal of Sociology,* vol. 54, no. 4, pp. 292–297, 1949.

———: "Union-Management Cooperation and Productivity," *Industrial and Labor Relations Review,* vol. 2, no. 2, pp. 195–209, 1949.

Dunlop, John T.: *Collective Bargaining,* Richard D. Irwin, Inc., Homewood, Ill., 1949.

Garfield, Sidney, and William F. Whyte: "The Collective Bargaining Process: A Human Relations Analysis," *Human Organization,* vol. 9, no. 2, pp. 5–10, 1950; no. 3, pp. 10–16, 1950; no. 4, pp. 25–29, 1950; and vol. 10, no. 1, pp. 28–32, 1951.

Golden, Clinton S., and Harold J. Ruttenberg: *The Dynamics of Industrial Democracy,* Harper & Brothers, New York, 1942.

Harbison, Frederick H.: "Some Reflections on a Theory of Labor-Management Relations," *The Journal of Political Economy,* vol. 54, no. 1, pp. 1–16, 1946.

Harbison, Frederick H., and King Carr: *Causes of Peace under Collective Bargaining,* National Planning Association, Washington, 1948.

——— and ———: *The Libby-Owen-Ford Glass Company and the Federation of Glass, Ceramic and Silica Sand Workers of America,* National Planning Association, Washington, 1948.

——— and John R. Coleman: *Goals and Strategy in Collective Bargaining,* Harper & Brothers, New York, 1951.

——— and Robert Dubin: *Patterns of Union-Management Relations,* Science Research Association, Chicago, 1947.

Heron, Alexander R.: *Beyond Collective Bargaining,* Stanford University Press, Stanford, Calif., 1948.

Knight, Charlotte (ed.): *The Economics of Collective Bargaining,* Institute of Industrial Relations, Berkeley, Calif., 1950.

Landsberger, Henry A.: "Interaction Process Analysis of Professional Behavior: A Study of Labor Mediators in Twelve Labor-Management Disputes," *American Sociological Review,* vol. 20, no. 5, pp. 566–575, 1955.

Leiserson, William M., William Smith, Harry Shulman, and Solomon Barkin: "Symposium on Arbitration Issues in Labor-Industry Disputes," *Labor and Nation,* vol. 4, no. 4, pp. 14–24, 1948.

Lester, Richard A.: *Labor and Industrial Relations,* The Macmillan Company, New York, 1951.

——— and Joseph Shister: *Insight into Labor Issues,* The Macmillan Company, New York, 1948.

Lovell, Hugh G.: "The Pressure Lever in Mediation," *Industrial and Labor Relations Review*, vol. 6, no. 1, pp. 20–30, 1952.
Perlman, Selig: "The Principle of Collective Bargaining," *The Annals of the American Academy of Political and Social Science*, vol. 84, pp. 154–160, March, 1936.
Peterson, Florence: *American Labor Unions*, Harper & Brothers, New York, 1952.
Pierson, Frank C.: *Collective Bargaining Systems*, American Council on Public Affairs, Washington, 1942.
———: "Prospects for Industry-wide Bargaining," *Industrial and Labor Relations Review*, vol. 3, no. 3, pp. 341–361, 1950.
Scott, W. H.: *Industrial Leadership and Joint Consultation: A Study of Human Relations in Three Merseyside Firms*, University Press of Liverpool, Liverpool, 1952.
———: *Joint Consultation in a Liverpool Manufacturing Firm: A Case Study in Human Relations in Industry*, University Press of Liverpool, Liverpool, 1950.
Selekman, Benjamin M.: *Labor Relations and Human Relations*, McGraw-Hill Book Company, Inc., New York, 1947.
———: "When the Union Enters," *Harvard Business Review*, vol. 23, no. 2, pp. 129–143, 1944.
———, Sylvia K. Selekman, and Stephen H. Fuller: *Problems in Labor Relations*, McGraw-Hill Book Company, Inc., New York, 1950.
Thompson, Kenneth: "Human Relations in Collective Bargaining," *Harvard Business Review*, vol. 31, no. 2, pp. 116–126, 1953.
Whyte, William F.: *Pattern for Industrial Peace*, Harper & Brothers, New York, 1951.
Wolf, Richard B.: "Collective Bargaining in Small-scale Industry—A Case Study," *Harvard Business Review*, vol. 27, no. 6, pp. 706–714, 1949.
Wolman, Leo: *Industry-wide Bargaining*, The Foundation for Economic Education, Irvington-on-Hudson, N.Y., 1948.

CHAPTER 14. THEORIES OF THE LABOR MOVEMENT

Anonymous: "Perlman's Theory of the Labor Movement," *Monthly Labor Review*, vol. 72, no. 2, pp. 121–126, 1951.
Brooks, George W., Milton Derber, David A. McCabe, and Philip Taft (eds.): *Interpreting the Labor Movement*, Industrial Relations Research Association, Madison, Wis., 1952.
Gulick, Charles A., Roy A. Ockert, and Raymond J. Wallace: *History and Theories of Working-class Movements: A Select Bibliography*, University of California Press, Berkeley, Calif., 1955.
Hoxie, Robert Franklin: *Trade Unionism in the United States*, Appleton-Century-Crofts, Inc., New York, 1928.
Muste, A. J.: "Factional Fights in Trade Unions," in Jacob B. S. Hardman (ed.), *American Labor Dynamics*, Harcourt, Brace and Company, Inc., New York, 1928.
Perlman, Selig: *A Theory of the Labor Movement*, Augustus M. Kelley, New York, 1949 (originally published in 1928).
Sturmthal, Adolf: *Unity and Diversity in European Labor: An Introduction to Contemporary Labor Movements*, Free Press, Glencoe, Ill., 1953.

Tannenbaum, Frank: *A Philosophy of Labor,* Alfred A. Knopf, Inc., New York, 1951.

Webb, Sidney, and Beatrice Webb: *Industrial Democracy,* Longmans, Green & Co., Inc., New York, 1926.

CHAPTER 15. INDUSTRY AND COMMUNITY

Arensberg, Conrad M.: "Industry and the Community," *The American Journal of Sociology,* vol. 48, no. 1, pp. 1–12, 1942.

Bakke, E. Wight, et al.: *Labor Mobility and Economic Opportunity,* John Wiley & Sons, Inc., and the Technology Press of Massachusetts Institute of Technology, New York, 1954.

Bogue, Don J.: *The Structure of the Metropolitan Community,* University of Michigan, Horace H. Rackham School of Graduate Studies, Ann Arbor, Mich., 1949.

Carr, Lowell Juillard, and James Edson Sterner: *Willow Run: A Study of Industrialization and Cultural Inadequacy,* Harper & Brothers, New York, 1952.

Cottrell, W. F.: "Death by Dieselization," *American Sociological Review,* vol. 16, no. 3, pp. 358–365, 1951.

Cuzzort, Raymond P.: *Suburbanization of Service Industries within Standard Metropolitan Areas,* Scripps Foundation, Oxford, Ohio, 1955.

Douglass, Harlan Paul: *The Suburban Trend,* Appleton-Century-Crofts, Inc., New York, 1925.

Faris, Robert E. L., and H. Warren Dunham: *Mental Disorders in Urban Areas,* University of Chicago Press, Chicago, 1939.

Fisher, Burton R., and Stephen B. Withey: *Big Business as the People See It,* Survey Research Center, Institute for Social Research, University of Michigan Press, Ann Arbor, Mich., 1951.

Fromm, Erich: *Escape from Freedom,* Rinehart & Company, Inc., New York, 1941.

Gilfillan, Lauren: *I Went to Pit College,* The Viking Press, Inc., New York, 1934.

Gist, Noel P., and L. A. Halbert: *Urban Society,* Thomas Y. Crowell Company, New York, 1941.

Goodrich, Carter, et al.: *Migration and Economic Opportunity,* University of Pennsylvania Press, Philadelphia, 1936.

Gouldner, Alvin W.: *Patterns of Industrial Bureaucracy,* Free Press, Glencoe, Ill., 1954.

Gras, N. S. B.: *An Introduction to Economic History,* Harper & Brothers, New York, 1922.

Hallenbeck, Wilbur C.: *American Urban Communities,* Harper & Brothers, New York, 1951.

Hammond, J. L., and Barbara Hammond: *The Town Labourer,* Longmans, Green & Co., Inc., New York, 1917.

Hart, C. W. M.: "Industrial Relations Research and Social Theory," *The Canadian Journal of Economics and Political Science,* vol. 15, pp. 53–73, 1949.

Havighurst, Robert J., and Gerthon H. Morgan: *The Social History of a War Boom Community,* Longmans, Green & Co., Inc., New York, 1952.

Hawley, Amos H.: *The Changing Shape of Metropolitan America*, Free Press, Glencoe, Ill., 1955.

Herring, Harriet Laura: *Passing of the Mill Village*, The University of North Carolina Press, Chapel Hill, 1949.

Hoover, Edgar M., Jr.: *The Location of Economic Activity*, McGraw-Hill Book Company, Inc., New York, 1948.

———: *Location Theory and the Shoe and Leather Industries*, Harvard University Press, Cambridge, Mass., 1937.

Horney, Karen: *The Neurotic Personality of Our Times*, W. W. Norton & Company, Inc., New York, 1937.

Hughes, Everett Cherrington: *French Canada in Transition*, University of Chicago Press, Chicago, 1943.

Hunter, Floyd: *Community Power Structure: A Study of Decision Makers*, The University of North Carolina Press, Chapel Hill, N.C., 1953.

Jones, Alfred Winslow: *Life, Liberty and Property*, J. B. Lippincott Company, Philadelphia, 1941.

Kitawaga, Evelyn M., and Donald J. Bogue: *Suburbanization of Manufacturing Activity within Metropolitan Areas*, Scripps Foundation, Oxford, Ohio, 1955.

Komarovsky, Mirra: "The Voluntary Associations of Urban Dwellers," *American Sociological Review*, vol. 11, no. 6, pp. 686–698, 1946.

Lanne, Herbert J.: *The Cotton Mill Worker*, Rinehart & Company, Inc., New York, 1944.

Lösch, August: *The Economics of Location*, translated by William H. Woglom and Wolfgang F. Stopler, Yale University Press, New Haven, Conn., 1954.

Lumpkin, Katharine Du Pre, and Mable V. Combs: "Shutdowns in the Connecticut Valley," *Smith College Studies in History*, vol. 19, nos. 3–4, April, 1934–July, 1934.

Lynd, Robert S., and Helen M. Lynd: *Middletown in Transition*, Harcourt, Brace and Company, Inc., New York, 1937.

Macdonald, Lois: *Labor Problems and the American Scene*, Harper & Brothers, New York, 1938.

———: *Southern Mill Hills*, Alex L. Hillman, New York, 1928.

MacIver, Robert M.: *Community: A Sociological Study*, St. Martin's Press, Inc., New York, 1929.

———: *Society: A Textbook of Sociology*, Rinehart & Company, Inc., New York, 1937.

McKenzie, R. D.: *The Metropolitan Community*, McGraw-Hill Book Company, Inc., New York, 1933.

Michigan University, Detroit Area Study: *A Social Profile of Detroit: 1953*, University of Michigan Press, Ann Arbor, Mich., 1953.

———: *A Social Profile of Detroit: 1954*, Institute of Social Research Publications, University of Michigan Press, Ann Arbor, Mich., 1955.

Mumford, Lewis: *The Culture of Cities*, Harcourt, Brace and Company, Inc., New York, 1938.

National Resources Committee, *Our Cities: Their Role in the National Economy*, Government Printing Office, 1937.

Nisbet, Robert A.: *The Quest for Community: A Study in the Ethics of Freedom and Order*, Oxford University Press, New York, 1953.

Palmer, Gladys L., with the assistance of Carol P. Brainerd: *Labor Mobility in Six Cities*, Social Science Research Council, New York, 1954.

Park, Robert Ezra: *Human Communities: The City and Human Ecology,* Free Press, Glencoe, Ill., 1952.

Parker, Margaret Terrell: *Lowell: A Study of Industrial Development,* The Macmillan Company, New York, 1940.

Pellegrin, Roland J., and Charles H. Coates: "Absentee-owned Corporations and Community Power Structure," *The American Journal of Sociology,* vol. 61, no. 5, pp. 413–419, 1956.

Pope, Liston: *Millhands and Preachers,* Yale University Press, New Haven, Conn., 1942.

Schlesinger, Arthur Meier: *The Rise of the City,* The Macmillan Company, New York, 1933.

Shlakman, Vera: "Economic History of a Factory Town," *Smith College Studies in History,* vol. 20, nos. 1–4, October, 1934, to July, 1935.

Walker, Charles R.: *Steeltown: An Industrial Case History of the Conflict between Progress and Security,* Harper & Brothers, New York, 1950.

Warner, W. Lloyd, and J. O. Low: *The Social System of the Modern Factory,* Yale University Press, New Haven, Conn., 1947.

———— and Paul S. Lunt: *The Social Life of a Modern Community,* Yale University Press, New Haven, Conn., 1941.

Weber, Alfred: *Theory of the Location of Industries,* University of Chicago Press, Chicago, 1929, translated by Carl Friedrich.

Whitehead, T. N.: *Leadership in a Free Society,* Harvard University Press, Cambridge, Mass., 1936.

Wirth, Louis: "Urbanism as a Way of Life," *The American Journal of Sociology,* vol. 44, no. 1, pp. 1–24, 1938.

CHAPTER 16. INDUSTRY AND SOCIAL STRATIFICATION

Adams, Stuart: "Regional Differences in Vertical Mobility," *American Sociological Review,* vol. 15, no. 2, pp. 228–235, 1950.

————: "Trends in Occupational Origins of Business Leaders," *American Sociological Review,* vol. 19, no. 5, pp. 541–548, 1954.

Anderson, H. Dewey, and Percy E. Davidson: *Ballots and the Democratic Class Struggle,* Stanford University Press, Stanford, Calif., 1943.

———— and ————: *Occupational Trends,* Stanford University Press, Stanford, Calif., 1940.

Bakke, E. Wight, et al.: *Labor Mobility and Economic Opportunity,* John Wiley & Sons, Inc., New York, 1954.

Baltzell, E. Digby: " 'Who's Who in America' and the 'Social Register': Elite and Upper Class Indexes in Metropolitan America," in Reinhard Bendix and Seymour Martin Lipset (eds.), *Class, Status and Power,* Free Press, Glencoe, Ill., 1953, pp. 172–185.

Breifs, Goetz A.: *The Proletariat: A Challenge to Western Civilization,* McGraw-Hill Book Company, Inc., New York, 1937.

Centers, Richard: "Occupational Mobility of Urban Occupational Strata," *American Sociological Review,* vol. 13, no. 2, pp. 197–203, 1948.

————: *The Psychology of Social Classes,* Princeton University Press, Princeton, N.J., 1949.

————: "Social Class, Occupation, and Imputed Belief," *The American Journal of Sociology,* vol. 58, no. 6, pp. 543–555, 1953.

Chinoy, Ely: *Automobile Workers and the American Dream,* Doubleday & Company, Inc., New York, 1955.

————: "The Tradition of Opportunity and the Aspirations of Automobile Workers," *The American Journal of Sociology,* vol. 57, no. 5, pp. 453–459, 1952.

Clark, Robert E.: "Psychoses, Income, and Occupational Prestige," *The American Journal of Sociology,* vol. 54, no. 5, pp. 433–440, 1949.

Davidson, Percy E., and H. Dewey Anderson: *Occupational Mobility in an American Community,* Stanford University Press, Stanford, Calif., 1937.

Davis, Beverly: "Eminence and Level of Social Origin," *The American Journal of Sociology,* vol. 59, no. 6, pp. 11–18, 1954.

Dotson, Floyd: "Patterns of Voluntary Associations among Urban Working-class Families," *American Sociological Review,* vol. 16, no. 5, pp. 687–693, 1951.

Duncan, Otis Dudley, and Beverly Duncan: "Residential Distribution and Occupational Stratification," *The American Journal of Sociology,* vol. 60, no. 5, pp. 493–503, 1955.

Edwards, Alba M.: *Comparative Occupation Statistics for the United States 1876–1940,* Government Printing Office, 1943.

Foote, Nelson N.: "The Professionalization of Labor in Detroit," *The American Journal of Sociology,* vol. 58, no. 4, pp. 371–380, 1953.

Gross, Neal: "Social Class Identification in the Urban Community," *American Sociological Review,* vol. 18, no. 4, pp. 398–404, 1953.

Guest, Robert H.: "Work Careers and Aspirations of Automobile Workers," *American Sociological Review,* vol. 19, no. 2, pp. 155–163, 1954.

Hatt, Paul K.: "Occupation and Social Stratification," *The American Journal of Sociology,* vol. 55, no. 6, pp. 533–543, 1950.

Hildebrand, George H.: "American Unionism, Social Stratification, and Power," *The American Journal of Sociology,* vol. 58, no. 4, pp. 381–390, 1953.

Hollingshead, August B.: *Elmtown's Youth: The Impact of Social Classes on Adolescence,* John Wiley & Sons, Inc., New York, 1949.

————: "Trends in Social Stratification: A Case Study," *American Sociological Review,* vol. 17, no. 6, pp. 679–686, 1952.

Hunter, Floyd: *Community Power Structure: A Study of Decision Makers,* The University of North Carolina Press, Chapel Hill, N.C., 1953.

Hyman, Herbert H.: "The Value Systems of Different Classes: A Social Psychological Contribution to the Analysis of Stratification," in Reinhard Bendix and Seymour Martin Lipset (eds.), *Class, Status and Power,* Free Press, Glencoe, Ill., 1953, pp. 426–442.

Jaffee, A. J., and Charles D. Stewart: *Manpower Resources and Utilization,* John Wiley & Sons, Inc., New York, 1951.

Jones, Alfred Winslow: *Life, Liberty and Property,* J. B. Lippincott Company, Philadelphia, 1941.

King, C. Wendell: "Social Cleavage in a New England Community," *Social Forces,* vol. 24, no. 3, pp. 322–327, 1946.

Knupfer, Genevieve: "Portrait of the Underdog," *Public Opinion Quarterly,* vol. 11, no. 1, pp. 103–114, 1947.

Komarovsky, Mirra: "The Voluntary Associations of Urban Dwellers," *American Sociological Review,* vol. 11, no. 6, pp. 686–698, 1946.

Kuznets, Simon, and Raymond Goldsmith: *Income and Wealth of the United States: Trends and Structure,* Bowes & Bowes, Cambridge, Mass., 1952.

Lasswell, Thomas E.: "A Study of Social Stratification Using an Area Sample of Raters," *American Sociological Review,* vol. 19, no. 3, pp. 310–313, 1954.

Lipset, Seymour M., and Reinhard Bendix: "Social Mobility and Occupational Career Patterns. I. Stability of Jobholding," *The American Journal of Sociology,* vol. 57, no. 4, pp. 366–374, 1952; "II. Social Mobility," no. 5, pp. 494–504, 1952.

———— and Joan Gordon: "Mobility and Trade Union Membership," in Reinhard Bendix and Seymour Martin Lipset (eds.), *Class, Status and Power,* Free Press, Glencoe, Ill., 1953, pp. 491–500.

Lundberg, Ferdinand: *America's 60 Families,* Vanguard Press, Inc., New York, 1937.

Lynd, Robert S., and Helen M. Lynd: *Middletown in Transition,* Harcourt, Brace and Company, Inc., New York, 1937.

Manis, Jerome G., and Bernard N. Meltzer: "Attitudes of Textile Workers to Class Structure," *The American Journal of Sociology,* vol. 60, no. 1, pp. 30–35, 1954.

Mayer, Albert J., and Philip Hauser: "Class Differentials in Expectation of Life at Birth," reprinted from *La Revue de l'institut international de statistique,* in Reinhard Bendix and Seymour Martin Lipset (eds.), *Class, Status and Power,* Free Press, Glencoe, Ill., 1953, pp. 281–284.

McGuire, Carson: "Social Stratification and Mobility Patterns," *American Sociological Review,* vol. 15, no. 2, pp. 195–204, 1950.

McKee, James B.: "Status and Power in the Industrial Community: A Comment on Drucker's Thesis," *The American Journal of Sociology,* vol. 58, no. 4, pp. 364–370, 1953.

Miller, Herman P.: *Income of the American People,* John Wiley & Sons, Inc., New York, 1955.

Miller, William: "The Recruitment of the American Business Elite," *Quarterly Journal of Economics,* vol. 64, no. 2, pp. 242–253, 1950.

Mills, C. Wright: "The American Business Elite," *Journal of Economic History,* vol. 5, supplement V, pp. 20–44, 1945.

————: "The Middle Classes in Middle-sized American Cities," *American Sociological Review,* vol. 11, no. 5, pp. 520–529, 1946.

————: *White Collar,* Oxford University Press, New York, 1951.

Moore, Wilbert E., and Kingsley Davis: "Some Principles of Stratification," *American Sociological Review,* vol. 10, no. 2, pp. 242–249, 1945.

North, Cecil C., and Paul K. Hatt: "Jobs and Occupations: A Popular Evaluation," reprinted from *Opinion News,* in Logan Wilson and William L. Kolb (eds.), *Sociological Analysis,* Harcourt, Brace and Company, Inc., New York, 1949, pp. 464–474.

Ogburn, William Fielding: "Technology and the Standard of Living in the United States," *The American Journal of Sociology,* vol. 60, no. 4, pp. 380–386, 1955.

Parsons, Talcott: "An Analytical Approach to the Theory of Social Stratification," *The American Journal of Sociology,* vol. 65, no. 6, pp. 841–862, 1940.

Pfautz, Harold W.: "The Current Literature on Social Stratification: Critique and Bibliography," *The American Journal of Sociology,* vol. 58, no. 4, pp. 391–418, 1953.

Reissman, Leonard: "Class, Leisure and Social Participation," *American Sociological Review,* vol. 19, no. 1, pp. 76–84, 1954.

Rogoff, Natalie: *Recent Trends in Occupational Mobility*, Free Press, Glencoe, Ill., 1953.

Sibley, Eldridge: "Some Demographic Clues to Stratification," *American Sociological Review*, vol. 7, no. 3, pp. 322–330, 1942.

Sjoberg, Gideon: "Are Social Classes in America Becoming More Rigid?" *American Sociological Review*, vol. 16, no. 6, pp. 775–783, 1951.

Sorokin, Pitirim: *Social Mobility*, Harper & Brothers, New York, 1927.

Spengler, Joseph J.: "Changes in Income Distribution and Social Stratification: A Note," *The American Journal of Sociology*, vol. 59, no. 3, pp. 247–259, 1953.

Stone, Gregory P., and William H. Form: "Instabilities in Status: The Problem of Hierarchy in the Community Study of Status Arrangements," *American Sociological Review*, vol. 18, no. 2, pp. 149–162, 1953.

Stone, Robert C.: "Factory Organization and Vertical Mobility," *American Sociological Review*, vol. 18, no. 1, pp. 28–35, 1953.

Taussig, F. W., and C. S. Joslyn: *American Business Leaders*, The Macmillan Company, New York, 1932.

Veblen, Thorstein: *The Theory of the Leisure Class*, The Viking Press, Inc., New York, 1945.

Wance, William, and Richard Butler: "Industrial Changes and Occupational 'Inheritance' in Four Pennsylvania Communities," *Social Forces*, vol. 27, no. 2, pp. 158–162, 1948.

Warner, W. Lloyd, and James C. Abeggeln: *Occupational Mobility*, University of Minnesota Press, Minneapolis, Minn., 1955.

——— and Paul S. Lunt: *The Social Life of a Modern Community*, Yale University Press, New Haven, Conn., 1941.

——— and ———: *The Status System of a Modern Community*, Yale University Press, New Haven, Conn., 1942.

Weber, Max: *From Max Weber: Essays in Sociology*, edited by H. H. Gerth and C. Wright Mills, Oxford University Press, New York, 1946, chap. VII.

CHAPTER 17. INDUSTRY AND MINORITY GROUPS

Benyon, Erdmann D.: "The Southern White Laborer Migrates to Michigan," *American Sociological Review*, vol. 3, no. 3, pp. 333–343, 1938.

Berger, Morroe: *Equality by Statute*, Columbia University Press, New York, 1952.

Bogue, Donald J.: "Urbanism in the United States, 1950," *The American Journal of Sociology*, vol. 60, no. 5, pp. 471–486, 1955.

Brown, Morgan C.: "The Status of Jobs and Occupations as Evaluated by an Urban Negro Sample," *American Sociological Review*, vol. 20, no. 5, pp. 561–566, 1955.

Bullock, Henry Allen: "Racial Attitudes and the Employment of Negroes," *The American Journal of Sociology*, vol. 56, no. 5, pp. 448–457, 1951.

Burma, John H.: "Race Relations and Antidiscriminatory Legislation," *The American Journal of Sociology*, vol. 56, no. 5, pp. 416–423, 1951.

Collins, Orvis: "Ethnic Behavior in Industry: Sponsorship and Rejection in a New England Factory," *The American Journal of Sociology*, vol. 51, no. 4, pp. 293–298, 1946.

Cox, Oliver Cromwell: *Caste, Class and Race*, Doubleday & Company, Inc., New York, 1948.

Davie, Maurice R.: *Negroes in American Society*, McGraw-Hill Book Company, Inc., New York, 1949.

Davis, Allison, Burleigh B. Gardner, and Mary R. Gardner: *Deep South,* University of Chicago Press, Chicago, 1941.

Dollard, John: *Caste and Class in a Southern Town,* Yale University Press (published for the Institute of Human Relations), New Haven, Conn., 1937.

Drake, St. Clair, and Horace R. Cayton: *Black Metropolis: A Study of Negro Life in a Northern City,* Harcourt, Brace and Company, Inc., New York, 1945.

Feldman, Herman: *Racial Factors in American Industry,* Harper & Brothers, New York, 1931.

Frazier, Franklin E.: *The Negro in the United States,* The Macmillan Company, New York, 1949.

Handlin, Oscar: *Boston's Immigrants,* Harvard University Press, Cambridge, Mass., 1941.

————: *The Uprooted,* Little, Brown & Company, Boston, 1951.

Hardin, Clara A.: *The Negroes of Philadelphia,* privately printed, Bryn Mawr, Pa., 1945.

Hatt, Paul: "Class and Ethnic Attitudes," *American Sociological Review,* vol. 13, no. 1, pp. 36–43, 1948.

Hope, John, II: *Selected Studies of Negro Employment in the South,* Case Study 1, *Negro Employment in Three Southern Plants of International Harvester Co.,* National Planning Association, Washington, 1953.

Horowitz, Eugene L.: "'Race' Attitudes," in Otto Klineberg (ed.), *Characteristics of the American Negro,* Harper & Brothers, New York, 1944.

Hughes, Everett Cherrington: *French Canada in Transition,* University of Chicago Press, Chicago, 1943.

————: "The Knitting of Racial Groups in Industry," *American Sociological Review,* vol. 11, no. 5, pp. 512–519, 1946.

————: "Queries Concerning Industry and Society Growing out of Study of Ethnic Relations in Industry," *American Sociological Review,* vol. 14, no. 2, pp. 211–220, 1949.

————: "Race Relations in Industry," in William F. Whyte (ed.), *Industry and Society,* McGraw-Hill Book Company, Inc., New York, 1946, pp. 107–122.

———— and Helen M. Hughes: *Where People Meet: Ethnic and Racial Frontiers,* Free Press, Glencoe, Ill., 1952.

Killian, Lewis M.: "The Effects of Southern White Workers on Race Relations in Northern Plants," *American Sociological Review,* vol. 17, no. 3, pp. 327–331, 1952.

Klineberg, Otto, editor: *Characteristics of the American Negro,* Harper & Brothers, New York, 1944.

Kornhauser, William: "The Negro Union Official: A Study of Sponsorship and Control," *The American Journal of Sociology,* vol. 57, no. 5, pp. 443–452, 1952.

Lee, Alfred McClung, and Norman Daymond Humphrey: *Race Riot,* The Dryden Press, Inc., New York, 1943.

Lee, Frank F.: "The Relations Pattern by Areas of Behavior in a Small New England Town," *American Sociological Review,* vol. 19, no. 2, pp. 138–143, 1954.

Myrdal, Gunnar: *An American Dilemma,* Harper & Brothers, New York, 1944

Noland, William E., and E. Wight Bakke: *Workers Wanted: A Study of Employers' Hiring Policies, Preferences and Practices,* Harper & Brothers, New York, 1949.

Northrup, Herbert R.: *Organized Labor and the Negro*, Harper & Brothers, New York, 1944.

Park, Robert E., and H. A. Miller: *Old World Traits Transplanted*, Harper & Brothers, New York, 1921.

Parker, Frederick B.: "The Status of the Foreign Stock in the Southeast: A Region-Nation Comparison," *Social Forces*, vol. 27, no. 2, pp. 136–143, 1948.

Reed, Bernice Anita: "Accommodation between Negro and White Employees in a West Coast Aircraft Industry, 1942–1944," *Social Forces*, vol. 26, no. 1, pp. 76–87, 1947.

Roche, John P., and Milton M. Gordon: "Can Morality Be Legislated?" *New York Times Magazine*, May 22, 1955.

Rogoff, Natalie: *Recent Trends in Occupational Mobility*, Free Press, Glencoe, Ill., 1953.

Ross, Malcolm: *All Manner of Men*, Reynal & Hitchcock, Inc., New York, 1948.

Ruchames, Louis: *Race, Jobs, and Politics*, Columbia University Press, New York, 1953.

Smith, Stanley Hugh: *Freedom to Work*, Vantage Press, Inc., New York, 1955.

Southall, Sara E.: *Industry's Unfinished Business: Achieving Sound Industrial Relations and Fair Employment*, Harper & Brothers, New York, 1950.

Spero, Sterling D., and Abram L. Harris: *The Black Worker*, Columbia University Press, New York, 1931.

Thomas, W. I., and F. Znaniecki: *The Polish Peasant in Europe and America*, vols. I, II, III published by the University of Chicago Press, Chicago, 1918–1919; vols. IV and V published by Richard G. Badger, The Gorham Press, Boston, 1920.

To Secure These Rights, The Report of the President's Committee on Civil Rights, Simon and Schuster, Inc., New York, 1947.

Turner, Ralph H.: "Foci of Discrimination in the Employment of Nonwhites," *The American Journal of Sociology*, vol. 58, no. 3, pp. 247–256, 1952.

————: "Occupational Patterns of Inequality," *The American Journal of Sociology*, vol. 59, no. 5, pp. 437–447, 1954.

————: "The Relative Position of the Negro Male in the Labor Force of Large American Cities," *American Sociological Review*, vol. 16, no. 4, pp. 524–529, 1951.

Warner, Robert Austin: *New Haven Negroes*, Yale University Press, (published for the Institute of Human Relations), New Haven, Conn., 1940.

Warner, W. Lloyd, and J. O. Low: *The Social System of the Modern Factory*, Yale University Press, New Haven, Conn., 1947.

———— and Leon Srole: *The Social System of American Ethnic Groups*, Yale University Press, New Haven, Conn., 1945.

Weaver, Robert C.: *The Negro Ghetto*, Harcourt, Brace and Company, Inc., New York, 1948.

————: *Negro Labor*, Harcourt, Brace and Company, Inc., New York, 1946.

Westie, Frank R.: "Negro-White Status Differentials and Social Distance," *American Sociological Review*, vol. 17, no. 5, pp. 550–558, 1952.

———— and David H. Howard: "Social Status Differentials and the Race Attitudes of Negroes," *American Sociological Review*, vol. 19, no. 5, pp. 584–591, 1954.

Yankauer, Alfred, Jr.: "The Relationship of Fetal and Infant Mortality to Residential Segregation," *American Sociological Review*, vol. 15, no. 5, pp. 644–648, 1950.

CHAPTER 18. INDUSTRY AND THE FAMILY

Aberle, David F., and Kaspar D. Naegele: "Middle-class Fathers' Occupational Role and Attitude toward Children," *American Journal of Orthopsychiatry*, vol. 22, pp. 366–378, April, 1952.

Abrams, Ray H.: "Residential Propinquity as a Factor in Marriage Selection: Fifty Year Trends in Philadelphia," *American Sociological Review*, vol. 8, no. 3, pp. 288–294, 1943.

Ackerman, Laurence J., and Walter C. McKain, Jr.: "Retirement Programs for Industrial Workers," *Harvard Business Review*, vol. 30, no. 4, pp. 97–108, 1952.

Anshen, Ruth Nanda (ed.): *The Family: Its Function and Destiny*, Harper & Brothers, New York, 1949.

Becker, Howard, and Reuben Hill (eds.): *Family, Marriage and Parenthood*, D. C. Heath and Company, Boston, 1948.

Bell, Howard M.: *Youth Tell Their Story*, American Council on Education, Washington, D.C., 1938.

Bettelheim, Bruno, and Emmy Sylvester: "Notes on Some Impact of Parental Occupations: Some Cultural Determinants of Symptom Choice in Emotionally Disturbed Children," *American Journal of Orthopsychiatry*, vol. 20, pp. 785–795, October, 1950.

Bossard, James H. S.: "Ecological Areas and Marriage Rates," *The American Journal of Sociology*, vol. 44, no. 1, pp. 70–85, 1938.

———: "Residential Propinquity as a Factor in Marriage Selection," *The American Journal of Sociology*, vol. 38, no. 2, pp. 219–224, 1932.

———: *The Sociology of Child Development*, Harper & Brothers, New York, 1954.

Brady, Dorothy S.: "Equal Pay for Women Workers," *The Annals of the American Academy of Political and Social Science*, vol. 251, pp. 53–60, 1947.

Breckenridge, Elizabeth Llewellyn: *Effective Use of Older Workers*, Wilcox & Follet Co., Chicago, 1953.

Burgess, Ernest W., and Paul Wallin: "Homogamy in Social Characteristics," *The American Journal of Sociology*, vol. 49, no. 2, pp. 109–124, 1943.

Burns, Robert K.: "Economic Aspects of Aging and Retirement," *The American Journal of Sociology*, vol. 59, no. 4, pp. 384–390, 1954.

Cahen, Alfred: *Statistical Analysis of American Divorce*, Columbia University Press, New York, 1932.

Calhoun, Arthur W.: *A Social History of the American Family*, Arthur H. Clark Company, Glendale, Calif., 1919, Vol. III.

Cavan, Ruth Shonle: *The American Family*, Thomas Y. Crowell Company, New York, 1953.

———: "Family Life and Family Substitutes in Old Age," *American Sociological Review*, vol. 14, no. 1, pp. 71–83, 1949.

Centers, Richard: "Marital Selection and Occupational Strata," *The American Journal of Sociology*, vol. 54, no. 6, pp. 530–535, 1949.

Clague, Ewan: "Employment Problems of the Older Worker," *Monthly Labor Review*, vol. 65, no. 6, pp. 661–663, 1947.

Clarke, Alfred C.: "An Examination of the Operation of Residential Propinquity as a Factor in Mate Selection," *American Sociological Review*, vol. 17, no. 1, pp. 17–22, 1952.

Davie, Maurice R., and Ruby Jo Reeves: "Propinquity of Residence before Marriage," *The American Journal of Sociology,* vol. 44, no. 4, pp. 510–517, 1939.

Davis, Allison: "American Status Systems and the Socialization of the Child," *American Sociological Review,* vol. 6, no. 3, pp. 345–354, 1941.

———: "The Motivation of Underprivileged Workers," in William F. Whyte (ed.), *Industry and Society,* McGraw-Hill Book Company, Inc., New York, 1946.

———, Burleigh B. Gardner, and Mary R. Gardner: *Deep South,* University of Chicago Press, Chicago, 1941.

Davis, Kingsley: *Human Society,* The Macmillan Company, New York, 1949.

———: "The Sociology of Parent-Youth Conflict," *American Sociological Review,* vol. 5, no. 4, pp. 523–535, 1940.

Dickason, Gladys: "Women in Labor Unions," *The Annals of the American Academy of Political and Social Science,* vol. 251, pp. 70–78, May, 1947.

Dinkel, Robert M.: "Occupation and Fertility in the United States," *American Sociological Review,* vol. 17, no. 2, pp. 178–183, 1952.

Donahue, Wilma, James Rae, Jr., and Roger B. Berry: *Rehabilitation of Older Workers,* University of Michigan Press, Ann Arbor, Mich., 1953.

Friedmann, Eugene A., and Robert J. Havighurst: *The Meaning of Work and Retirement,* University of Chicago Press, Chicago, 1954.

Glick, Paul C.: "The Life Cycle of the Family," *Marriage and Family Living,* vol. 17, no. 1, pp. 3–9, 1955.

——— and Emmanuel Landau: "Age as a Factor in Marriage," *American Sociological Review,* vol. 15, no. 4, pp. 517–529, 1950.

Goode, William J.: *After Divorce,* Free Press, Glencoe, Ill., 1956.

———: "Economic Factors and Marital Stability," *American Sociological Review,* vol. 16, no. 6, pp. 802–812, 1951.

Green, Arnold W.: "The Middle Class Male Child and Neurosis," *American Sociological Review,* vol. 11, no. 1, pp. 31–44, 1946.

Groves, Ernest Rutherford, and William Fielding Ogburn: *American Marriage and Family Relationships,* Henry Holt and Company, Inc., New York, 1928.

Hajnal, John: "Differential Changes in Marriage Patterns," *American Sociological Review,* vol. 19, no. 2, pp. 148–154, 1954.

Hauser, Philip M.: "Changes in the Labor-force Participation of the Older Worker," *The American Journal of Sociology,* vol. 59, no. 4, pp. 312–323, 1954.

Havighurst, Robert J.: "Flexibility and the Social Roles of the Retired," *The American Journal of Sociology,* vol. 59, no. 4, pp. 309–311, 1954.

——— and Allison Davis: "A Comparison of the Chicago and Harvard Studies of Social Class Differences in Child Rearing," *American Sociological Review,* vol. 20, no. 4, pp. 438–442, 1955.

Hollingshead, August B.: "Class Differences in Family Stability," *The Annals of the American Academy of Political and Social Science,* vol. 272, pp. 39–46, November, 1950.

———: "Class and Kinship in a Middle Western Community," *American Sociological Review,* vol. 14, no. 4, pp. 469–475, 1949.

———: "Cultural Factors in the Selection of Marriage Mates," *American Sociological Review,* vol. 15, no. 5, pp. 619–627, 1950.

———: *Elmtown's Youth: The Impact of Social Classes on Adolescence,* John Wiley & Sons, Inc., New York, 1949.

Homans, George Caspar: *English Villagers of the Thirteenth Century,* Harvard University Press, Cambridge, Mass., 1941.

Hughes, Everett Cherrington: *French Canada in Transition,* University of Chicago Press, Chicago, 1943.

Hunt, Thomas C.: "Occupational Status and Marriage Selection," *American Sociological Review,* vol. 5, no. 4, pp. 495–504, 1940.

Jaco, E. Gartley, and Ivan Belknap: "Is a New Family Form Emerging in the Urban Fringe?" *American Sociological Review,* vol. 18, no. 5, pp. 551–557, 1953.

Kephart, William M.: "Occupational Level and Marital Disruption," *American Sociological Review,* vol. 20, no. 4, pp. 456–465, 1955.

Kinsey, Alfred C., Wardell B. Pomeroy, and Clyde E. Martin: *Sexual Behavior in the Human Male,* W. B. Saunders Company, Philadelphia, 1948.

Kirkpatrick, Clifford: *The Family as Process and Institution,* The Ronald Press Company, New York, 1955.

Kiser, Clyde V.: "Fertility Trends and Differentials in the United States," *Journal of the American Statistical Association,* vol. 47, no. 257, pp. 25–48, 1952.

Kitagawa, Evelyn M.: "Differential Fertility in Chicago, 1920–40," *The American Journal of Sociology,* vol. 58, no. 5, pp. 481–492, 1953.

Kyrk, Hazel: *The Family in the American Economy,* University of Chicago Press, Chicago, 1953.

Lee, Everett S., and Anne S. Lee: "The Differential Fertility of the American Negro," *American Sociological Review,* vol. 17, no. 4, pp. 437–447, 1952.

Locke, Harvey J., and Muriel Mackeprang: "Marital Adjustment and the Employed Wife," *The American Journal of Sociology,* vol. 54, no. 6, pp. 536–538, 1949.

Lynd, Robert S., and Helen M. Lynd: *Middletown in Transition,* Harcourt, Brace and Company, Inc., New York, 1937, Ch. V.

Macdonald, Margherita, Carson McGuire, and Robert J. Havighurst: "Leisure Activities and the Socioeconomic Status of Children," *The American Journal of Sociology,* vol. 54, no. 6, pp. 505–519, 1949.

Manley, Charles R., Jr.: "The Migration of Older People," *The American Journal of Sociology,* vol. 59, no. 4, pp. 324–331, 1954.

Marches, Joseph R., and Gus Turbeville: "The Effect of Residential Propinquity on Marriage Selection," *The American Journal of Sociology,* vol. 58, no. 6, pp. 592–595, 1953.

Mead, Margaret: *And Keep Your Powder Dry,* William Morrow & Company, Inc., New York, 1943.

Nye, Ivan: "Adolescent-Parent Adjustment: Socio-economic Level as a Variable," *American Sociological Review,* vol. 16, no. 3, pp. 341–349, 1951.

Ogburn, William Fielding, and M. F. Nimkoff: *Technology and the Changing Family,* Houghton Mifflin Company, Boston, 1955.

Parsons, Talcott: "Age and Sex in the Social Structure," *Essays in Sociological Theory: Pure and Applied,* Free Press, Glencoe, Ill., 1949.

———: "The Social Structure of the Family," in Ruth Nanda Anshen (ed.), *The Family: Its Function and Destiny,* Harper & Brothers, New York, 1949.

Redfield, Margaret Park: "The American Family: Consensus and Freedom," *The American Journal of Sociology,* vol. 52, no. 3, pp. 175–183, 1946.

Schmidt, John Frank: "Patterns of Poor Adjustment in Old Age," *The American Journal of Sociology,* vol. 57, no. 1, pp. 33–42, 1951.

Schnore, Leo F.: *The Separation of Home and Work in Flint, Michigan*, University of Michigan Institute for Human Adjustment, Ann Arbor, Mich., 1954.

Seidman, Jerome M.: *The Adolescent*, The Dryden Press, Inc., New York, 1953.

Smith, T. Lynn (ed.): "Living in the Later Years," *A Report on the Second Annual Southern Conference on Gerontology, Held at the University of Florida, January 28–29, 1952*, University of Florida Press, Gainesville, Fla., 1952.

Sundal, Philip A., and Thomas C. McCormick: "Age at Marriage and Mate Selection: Madison, Wisconsin, 1937–1943," *American Sociological Review*, vol. 16, no. 1, pp. 37–48, 1951.

Sussman, Marvin B.: "The Help Pattern in the Middle Class Family," *American Sociological Review*, vol. 18, no. 1, pp. 22–28, 1953.

Tibbitts, Clark: "Retirement Problems in American Society," *The American Journal of Sociology*, vol. 59, no. 4, pp. 301–308, 1954.

Tuckman, Jacob, and Irving Lorge: *Retirement and the Industrial Worker: Prospect and Reality*, Bureau of Publications, Teachers College, Columbia University, New York, 1953.

Waller, Willard: *The Family: A Dynamic Interpretation*, The Dryden Press, Inc., New York, 1935.

Webber, Irving L. (ed.): *"Ageing and Retirement,"* A Report on the Fifth Annual Southern Conference on Gerontology, University of Florida Press, Gainesville, Fla., 1955.

Weeks, H. Ashley: "Differential Divorce Rates by Occupations," *Social Forces*, vol. 21, no. 3, pp. 334–337, 1943.

West, James: *Plainville, U.S.A.*, Columbia University Press, New York, 1945.

Westoff, Charles F.: "Differential Fertility in the United States: 1900 to 1952," *American Sociological Review*, vol. 19, no. 5, pp. 549–561, 1954.

Whyte, William H., Jr.: "The Corporation and the Wife," *Fortune*, November, 1951.

——: "The Wives of Management," *Fortune*, October, 1951.

CHAPTER 19. INDUSTRY AND GOVERNMENT

Allen, Frederick Lewis: *Only Yesterday*, Harper & Brothers, New York, 1931.

Andrews, John Bertram: *Labor Laws in Action*, Harper & Brothers, New York, 1938.

Anonymous: "Terms of State Labor Relations Acts," *Monthly Labor Review*, vol. 71, no. 2, pp. 214–218, 1950.

Arnold, Thurman: *The Folklore of Capitalism*, Yale University Press, New Haven, Conn., 1937.

Blaisdell, Donald C.: *Economic Power and Political Pressures*, Monograph no. 26, Temporary National Economic Committee, Government Printing Office, 1941.

Brady, Robert A.: *Business as a System of Power*, Columbia University Press, New York, 1943.

Burns, Eveline M.: *The American Social Security System*, Houghton Mifflin Company, Boston, 1951.

Calkin, Fay: *The C.I.O. and the Democratic Party*, University of Chicago Press, Chicago, 1952.

Commons, John R.: *Legal Foundations of Capitalism,* The Macmillan Company, New York, 1924.

Dahl, Robert A., and Charles E. Lindblom: *Politics, Economics, and Welfare,* Harper & Brothers, New York, 1953.

Faulkner, Harold U.: *The Decline of Laissez-faire,* Rinehart & Company, Inc., New York, 1951.

————: *The Quest for Social Justice,* The Macmillan Company, New York, 1931.

Filler, Louis: *Crusaders for American Liberalism,* Harcourt, Brace and Company, Inc., New York, 1930.

Freidel, Frank: *Franklin D. Roosevelt,* vol. I, *The Apprenticeship,* Little, Brown & Company, Boston, 1952; vol. II, *The Ordeal,* 1954; vol. III, *The Triumph,* 1956.

Galbraith, John Kenneth: *The Great Crash,* Houghton Mifflin Company, Boston, 1955.

Hall, Ford P.: *Government and Business,* 3d ed., McGraw-Hill Book Company, Inc., New York, 1949.

Hobbes, Thomas: *Leviathan,* Oxford University Press, New York, edition of 1909.

Ickes, Harold L.: *The Secret Diary of Harold L. Ickes,* vol. I, *The First Thousand Days,* Simon and Schuster, Inc., New York, 1953; vol. II, *The Inside Struggle,* 1954.

Killingsworth, Charles C.: *State Labor Relations Acts,* University of Chicago Press, Chicago, 1948.

Kossoris, May D.: "Workmen's Compensations in the United States," *Monthly Labor Review,* vol. 76, no. 4, pp. 359–366, 1953.

Lane, Robert E.: *The Regulation of Businessmen: Social Conditions of Government Economic Control,* Yale University Press, New Haven, Conn., 1954.

Laski, Harold J.: *The American Democracy,* The Viking Press, Inc., New York, 1948.

Lasswell, Harold D., and Abraham Kaplan: *Power and Society,* Yale University Press, New Haven, Conn., 1950.

Lauterbach, Albert: *Economic Security and Individual Freedom,* Cornell University Press, Ithaca, N.Y., 1948.

Lenin, N. V.: *The State and Revolution,* International Publishers Co., Inc., New York, 1932.

MacDonald, Lois: *Labor Problems and the American Scene,* Harper & Brothers, New York, 1938.

Mannheim, Karl: *Man and Society in an Age of Reconstruction,* translated by E. Shils, Harcourt, Brace and Company, Inc., New York, 1941.

Mill, John Stuart: *Utilitarianism, Liberty, and Representative Government,* E. P. Dutton & Co., Inc., New York, edition of 1910.

Mills, C. Wright: *The Power Elite,* Oxford University Press, New York, 1956.

Mitchell, Broadus: *Depression Decade,* Rinehart & Company, Inc., New York, 1947.

Moley, Raymond: *After Seven Years,* Harper & Brothers, New York, 1939.

Moore, Wilbert E.: "The Emergence of New Property Conceptions in America," *Journal of Legal and Political Sociology,* vol. 3, nos. 3 and 4, pp. 34–58, 1943.

National Association of Manufacturers, Economic Principles Commission, *The American Individual Enterprise System,* 2 vols., McGraw-Hill Book Company, Inc., New York, 1946.

Ogburn, William F.: *Recent Social Trends in the United States,* McGraw-Hill Book Company, Inc., New York, 1933, vol. II.

Patterson, S. Howard: *Social Aspects of Industry,* McGraw-Hill Book Company, Inc., New York, 1943.

Rauch, Basil: *The History of the New Deal,* Creative Age Press, Inc., 1944.

Raushenbush, Carl, and Emmanuel Stein (eds.): *Labor Cases and Materials,* Appleton-Century-Crofts, Inc., New York, 1941.

Schumpeter, Joseph A.: *Capitalism, Socialism and Democracy,* Harper & Brothers, New York, 1942.

Short, Lloyd Milton: *The Development of National Administrative Organization in the United States* (thesis), The Institute for Government Research, Urbana, Ill., 1923.

Soule, George: *Prosperity Decade,* Rinehart & Company, Inc., New York, 1947.

Taylor, O. H.: "Economics and the Idea of Jus Naturale," *The Quarterly Journal of Economics,* vol. 44, pp. 1–39, 1930.

———: "Economics and the Idea of Natural Laws," *The Quarterly Journal of Economics,* vol. 44, pp. 205–241, 1929.

Veblen, Thorstein: *The Place of Science in Modern Civilization and other Essays,* The Viking Press, Inc., New York, 1919.

Weber, Max: *From Max Weber: Essays in Sociology,* translated by H. H. Gerth and C. Wright Mills, Oxford University Press, New York, 1946, part II.

Wecter, Dixon: *The Age of the Great Depression,* The Macmillan Company, New York, 1948.

Wells, Henry A.: *Monopoly and Social Control,* Public Affairs Press, Washington, 1952.

Wooton, Barbara: *Freedom under Planning,* The University of North Carolina Press, Chapel Hill, N.C., 1945.

CHAPTER 20. INDUSTRIALISM AND SOCIAL CHANGE

Berger, Morroe, Theodore Able, and Charles H. Page: *Freedom and Control in Modern Society,* D. Van Nostrand Company, Inc., Princeton, N.J., 1954.

Berle, Adolf A., Jr.: *The 20th Century Capitalist Revolution,* Harcourt, Brace and Company, Inc., New York, 1954.

Burnham, James: *The Managerial Revolution,* The John Day Company, Inc., New York, 1941.

Childs, Marquis W., and Douglass Cater: *Ethics in a Business Society,* Harper & Brothers, New York, 1954.

Galbraith, John Kenneth: *American Capitalism: The Concept of Countervailing Power,* Houghton Mifflin Company, Boston, 1952.

Lauterbach, Albert: *Economic Security and Individual Freedom,* Cornell University Press, Ithaca, N.Y., 1948.

Mannheim, Karl: *Freedom, Power, and Democratic Planning,* Oxford University Press, New York, 1950.

———: *Man and Society in an Age of Reconstruction,* translated by E. Shils, Harcourt, Brace and Company, Inc., New York, 1941.

Marx, Karl: *Capital,* translated by Samuel Moore and Edward Aveling, International Publishers Co., Inc., New York, edition of 1939, vol. I.

——— and Friedrich Engels: *The Communist Manifesto,* edited by D. Ryzanoff, translated by M. Lawrence, M. Lawrence, Ltd., London, 1930.

National Association of Manufacturers, Economic Principles Commission, *The American Individual Enterprise System,* 2 vols., McGraw-Hill Book Company, Inc., New York, 1946.

Orwell, George: *Nineteen Eighty-four,* Harcourt, Brace and Company, Inc., New York, 1949.

Schumpeter, Joseph A.: *Capitalism, Socialism and Democracy,* Harper & Brothers, New York, 1942.

Sweezy, Paul M.: *The Theory of Capitalist Development,* Oxford University Press, New York, 1942.

Veblen, Thorstein: *The Engineers and the Price System,* The Viking Press, Inc., New York, 1933.

Wootton, Barbara: *Freedom under Planning,* The University of North Carolina Press, Chapel Hill, N.C., 1945.

Name Index

Abeggeln, James C., 110, 389, 509, 526
Abel, Theodore, 534
Aberle, D. F., 21, 502, 529
Abrams, Ray H., 433, 529
Ackerman, Laurence J., 451, 529
Adamic, Louis, 515, 517
Adams, Stuart, 390, 523
Adelman, M. A., 72, 505
Allen, Frederick L., 462, 505, 532
Altgeld, John P., 215, 221
Amory, Cleveland, 435
Anderson, H. Dewey, 182, 390, 392,
    394, 512, 523, 524
Andrews, John B., 532
Anshen, Ruth N., 428, 529
Arensberg, Conrad M., 187, 513, 521
Argyris, Chri, 508
Arnold, Thurman, 505, 532
Ashley, William J., 31, 32, 37, 503
Ayres, Eugene, 183, 511

Babchuk, Nicholas, 187, 513
Backman, Jules, 518
Bakke, E. Wight, 168, 175, 178–180,
    302, 507, 508, 511, 513, 518, 521,
    523, 527
Baltzell, E. Digby, 380, 386, 523
Barbash, Jack, 250, 253, 280, 516–518
Barber, Bernard, 510
Barkin, Solomon, 258, 519
Barnard, Chester I., 22, 85–87, 89, 97,
    101, 107–109, 112, 193, 507, 508,
    513
Beard, Charles A., 54, 56, 57, 505
Beard, Mary R., 56, 57, 505
Becker, Howard, 434
Becker, Howard S., 510, 529
Belknap, Ivan, 531
Bell, Daniel, 501
Bell, Howard M., 448, 529
Bendix, Reinhard, 380, 381, 384, 388,
    392, 394, 501, 507, 523–525
Benedict, Ruth, 15, 502
Benyon, Erdmann D., 526

Berger, Morroe, 526, 534
Berle, Adolf A., Jr., 61, 66, 68, 69, **97,**
    99, 497, 505, 508, 534
Berry, Roger B., 530
Bettelheim, Bruno, 444, 529
Bladen, Vincent W., 501
Blaisdell, Donald C., 480, 532
Blau, Peter M., 507
Bloch, Joseph W., 248, 249
Blum, Fred H., 513
Blumer, Herbert, 502
Bogue, Don. J., 357, 404, 521, 522, **526**
Booz, Donald R., 509, 511
Bossard, James H. S., 436, 529
Boulding, Kenneth E., 507
Brady, Dorothy S., 441, 529
Brady, Robert A., 67, 482, 532
Brainerd, Carol P., 522
Breckenridge, Elizabeth L., 529
Breifs, Goetz A., 529
Brooks, George W., 520
Brooks, Robert R. R., 274, 284, **517**
Brown, Emily Clark, 515
Brown, Gordon L., 183, 511
Brown, Morgan C., 526
Bücher, Carl, 45, 503
Bullock, Henry A., 416, 526
Burgess, Ernest W., 433, 529
Burgess, Eugene W., 508
Burma, John H., 526
Burnham, James M., 99, 493, 508, **534**
Burns, Eveline M., 473, 532
Burns, Robert K., 303, 451, 529
Butler, Richard, 392, 526

Cahen, Alfred, 65, 529
Calhoun, Arthur W., 426, 529
Calkin, Fay, 484, 532
Campbell, Donald P., 183, **511**
Caplow, Theodore, 501
Carey, James, 258
Carnegie, Andrew, 219
Carper, James W., 510
Carr, King, 302, 328, **519**

537

Subject Index